Consumer Behaviour
Third Edition

Peter M. Chisnall

McGRAW-HILL BOOK COMPANY

London · New York · St Louis · San Francisco · Auckland
Bogotá · Caracas · Lisbon · Madrid · Mexico
Milan · Montreal · New Delhi · Panama · Paris · San Juan
São Paulo · Singapore · Sidney · Tokyo · Toronto

87187

Published by
McGRAW-HILL Book Company Europe
Shoppenhangers Road, Maidenhead, Berkshire, SL6 2QL, England
Telephone 01628 23432
Fax 01628 770224

British Library Cataloguing in Publication Data

Chisnall, Peter M.
   Consumer Behaviour – 3Rev.ed
   I. Title
   658.8342

ISBN 0–07–707616–8

Library of Congress Cataloging-in-Publication Data

Chisnall, Peter M.
   Consumer Behaviour / Peter M. Chisnall, – 3rd ed.
      p.   cm.
   Rev. ed. of Marketing, 2nd ed. c1985.
   Includes bibliographical references and index.
   ISBN 0–07–707616–8
   1. Motivation research (Marketing)   2. Marketing.   3. Consumer behavior.
   I. Chisnall, Peter M. Marketing. II. Title.
HF5415.3.C45   1994
658.8′342–dc20
                                                                          94–31098
                                                                              CIP

Reprinted 1997
Typeset by Computape (Pickering) Ltd, North Yorkshire,
and printed and bound in Great Britain at the University Press, Cambridge
Printed on permanent paper in compliance with ISO Standard 9706

CONTENTS

page

PREFACE TO THE THIRD EDITION   xi

PART ONE   INTRODUCTION   1

CHAPTER 1   THE MARKETING CONCEPT: A REVIEW   3
       1.1   Development of the marketing function   4
       1.2   Characteristics of marketing   7
       1.3   Service economy   8
       1.4   Marketing is a team effort   9
       1.5   Twin responsibilities of marketing management   9
       1.6   Marketing in a dynamic environment   10
       1.7   Behavioural studies related to marketing   11
       1.8   Research into behavioural influences   15
       1.9   Systematic approach to the study of behavioural influences in marketing   16
       1.10   Summary   17
            References   18
            Review and discussion questions   19

PART TWO   PERSONAL ASPECTS OF BEHAVIOUR   21

CHAPTER 2   COGNITIONS, PERCEPTIONS, AND LEARNING PROCESSES   23
       2.1   Introduction   23
       2.2   Definition of cognition   23
       2.3   Cognitive map   23
       2.4   Fundamentals of perception   24
       2.5   Factors affecting perception   24
       2.6   Subliminal perception   27
       2.7   Characteristics influencing cognitive change   27
       2.8   Cognitive dissonance   28
       2.9   Critical review of cognitive dissonance theory   29
       2.10   A dissonance study: *When Prophecy Fails*   30
       2.11   Learning processes   30
       2.12   Definitions of learning   31
       2.13   Learning theories   32
       2.14   Cognitive theories   34
       2.15   Bridging the gap   36
       2.16   Stochastic learning models   36

2.17   Summary   37

        References   37

        Review and discussion questions   38

CHAPTER 3   MOTIVATION   40

3.1   Introduction   40

3.2   The nature of needs   41

3.3   Hierarchy of needs   43

3.4   Maslow's 'smaller hierarchy of needs'   48

3.5   Wants do not exist in isolation   50

3.6   Motivation: an overview   50

3.7   The question of motivation   52

3.8   Theories of motivation   52

3.9   Nature of motives   54

3.10   Aspirations affect motivation   55

3.11   Summary   56

        References   56

        Review and discussion questions   57

CHAPTER 4   PERSONALITY   59

4.1   Introduction   59

4.2   Definition of personality   59

4.3   Theories of personality   60

4.4   Trait theories   60

4.5   Psychoanalytic theories   65

4.6   Social learning theories   66

4.7   Self-concept theories   68

4.8   Self-concept and self-gifts   71

4.9   Stereotypes   71

4.10   Marketing studies related to personality   73

4.11   Consumer involvement theories   74

4.12   Summary   75

        References   76

        Review and discussion questions   78

CHAPTER 5   ATTITUDES   79

5.1   Introduction   79

5.2   Definitions of attitudes   79

5.3   Attitudes and marketing strategy   80

5.4   Components of attitudes   81

5.5   Characteristics of attitude components   81

5.6   Attitude clusters   82

5.7   Attitude constellation   82

5.8   Importance of interrelationships between attitudes   82

5.9   Formation of attitudes   83

5.10   Sources of attitudes   84

5.11   Change in attitudes   87

5.12   Attitudes and behaviour   92

5.13   Moods, attitudes, and behaviour   97

5.14   Summary   98

References   98
Review and discussion questions   100

PART THREE GROUP ASPECTS OF BEHAVIOUR   101

CHAPTER 6   CULTURE   103
6.1   Introduction   103
6.2   Definitions of culture   103
6.3   The nature of culture   106
6.4   Culture and marketing strategy   108
6.5   Life-styles   112
6.6   Life-styles and social values   116
6.7   Work and play   116
6.8   Social orientation   119
6.9   Security and safety   120
6.10 Women and society   121
6.11 Sub-cultures   123
6.12 Redefinition of products   128
6.13 Summary   129
      References   130
      Review and discussion questions   132

CHAPTER 7   SOCIAL CLASS   133
7.1   Introduction   133
7.2   Social stratification: an overview   133
7.3   Social class measurement   138
7.4   Three principal methods of measuring social class   139
7.5   The Warner Social Class System (USA)   140
7.6   The Hollingshead Social Class System (USA)   141
7.7   New developments in social classification (USA)   142
7.8   Social class classification (UK)   142
7.9   National readership surveys (JICNARS)   143
7.10 Official social class gradings (UK)   147
7.11 Occupational grading system   149
7.12 International Standard Classification of Occupations   150
7.13 EU socio-economic classifications   151
7.14 Harmonizing official and commercial socio-economic
      classifications   152
7.15 Summary   154
      References   154
      Review and discussion questions   155

CHAPTER 8   GROUP INFLUENCE   156
8.1   Introduction   156
8.2   Definition of group   157
8.3   Types of groups   157
8.4   Reference groups   158
8.5   Opinion leadership   162
8.6   Family influences on consumer behaviour: an introduction 167
8.7   Changes in household units and types of families   168

8.8	Marriage and consumer spending habits	170
8.9	Family life-cycle	172
8.10	Family roles and decision-making	176
8.11	Family buying organization	178
8.12	Conflict and compromise in family buying decisions	179
8.13	Children's influence on household purchases	181
8.14	Teenage spending patterns	184
8.15	Summary	185
	References	185
	Review and discussion questions	187

PART FOUR	MODELS OF BUYING BEHAVIOUR	189

CHAPTER 9	CONSUMER BUYING BEHAVIOUR	191
9.1	Introduction	191
9.2	Function of models	191
9.3	Two basic functions of consumer behaviour models	192
9.4	Qualities of an effective model	192
9.5	Types of models	193
9.6	Monadic models of buying behaviour	193
9.7	Multi-variable models of buying behaviour	202
9.8	Conclusions	210
9.9	Summary	210
	References	211
	Review and discussion questions	212

CHAPTER 10	ORGANIZATIONAL BUYING BEHAVIOUR	213
10.1	Introduction	213
10.2	Negotiation	214
10.3	Nature of organizational supplies	216
10.4	Types of organizational supplies	217
10.5	Derived demand	218
10.6	Complexity of organizational buying	219
10.7	Handling risk	220
10.8	The buying centre/decision-making unit (DMU)	222
10.9	Five roles in organizational buying	223
10.10	Multiple influences on buying: research findings	225
10.11	The buyer's dilemma	228
10.12	Research on buying strategy	229
10.13	Concentration of buying power	230
10.14	Models of organizational buying behaviour	232
10.15	Summary	242
	References	243
	Review and discussion questions	244

PART FIVE	STRATEGIC APPLICATIONS	245

CHAPTER 11	INNOVATION	247
11.1	Introduction	247
11.2	Invention and innovation	249
11.3	Early industrial inventors and innovators	250

11.4	Innovation and types of firms	251
11.5	Innovation and risk policies	251
11.6	Classification of innovations	253
11.7	The diffusion of innovations	255
11.8	Five categories of adopters	258
11.9	Empirical evidence of the diffusion of innovation	259
11.10	Five characteristics of innovation	262
11.11	Planning innovation in the firm	263
11.12	Product life-cycle	265
11.13	Project teams	267
11.14	Product champions	268
11.15	The 'make or buy' approach	269
11.16	Market research aids innovation	270
11.17	Summary	270
	References	271
	Review and discussion questions	273

CHAPTER 12 COMMUNICATIONS (1) — 274

12.1	Introduction	274
12.2	Marketing communications	282
12.3	Methods of marketing communications	283
12.4	Planning marketing communications	285
12.5	Eight stages in communications strategy	285
12.6	Marketing communications: four phases	286
12.7	Summary	290
	References	291
	Review and discussion questions	291

CHAPTER 13 COMMUNICATIONS (2) — 292

13.1	Introduction	292
13.2	Models of advertising	292
13.3	Criticism of hierarchical models of advertising	295
13.4	Influence of attitudes on advertising	298
13.5	Advertising influence integrated with consumer buying behaviour	299
13.6	Repetitive advertising	301
13.7	Believability of advertising	303
13.8	Two-step flow of advertising effect	306
13.9	Fear appeals in advertising	306
13.10	Comparative advertising	309
13.11	Women and advertising	311
13.12	Children and advertising	314
13.13	Summary	318
	References	319
	Review and discussion questions	321

CHAPTER 14 MARKETING SEGMENTATION — 322

14.1	Introduction	322
14.2	Nature and purpose of market segmentation	323
14.3	Four decisive factors in segmentation of markets	324
14.4	Types of segmentation	326

14.5	Demographic analyses	326
14.6	Psychographic segmentation	332
14.7	Life-style segmentation	336
14.8	Benefit segmentation	337
14.9	Segmentation by product design	338
14.10	'SAGACITY' segmentation	340
14.11	Geodemographic segmentation	342
14.12	Industrial markets and segmentation strategies	348
14.13	Summary	349
	References	350
	Review and discussion questions	351
CHAPTER 15	**SIGNPOSTS FOR STRATEGY**	352
15.1	Introduction	352
15.2	Social and cultural flux	352
15.3	Social forecasting	356
15.4	Social responsibility of business	357
15.5	Attitudes to advertising in Britain	364
15.6	Effects of gadgetry on viewing of TV advertisements	367
15.7	Advertising under criticism	368
15.8	Mass media trends	369
15.9	Trends in shopping	374
15.10	Healthy, wealthy, and wise	380
15.11	Product liability	382
15.12	Home and leisure	383
15.13	Summary	383
	References	384
	Review and discussion questions	386
INDEX		387

PREFACE TO THE THIRD EDITION

Since 1975 this text has provided management students and practitioners with an integrated account of how the fundamental psychological, sociological, and cultural factors affect the buying decisions made by people in modern economies. In 1985, a second edition, entitled *Marketing: A Behavioural Analysis*, updated some of the material and extended the concepts covered in what was the first British comprehensive text in this field. This third edition retitled *Consumer Behaviour*, incorporates several new inputs as well as adding to the existing coverage of the basic behavioural factors, such as cognitions, attitude theory, and so on. Life-style and psychographic analyses, geodemographic segmentation systems, consumer-involvement theories, and the relationships between moods, attitudes, and behaviour are further explored and updated. Comparative advertising, corporate communications, and attitudes are given extended treatment. The topical issues of women and advertising, the effects of television viewing on young children, environmental problems, and business ethics are discussed at length.

As before, the book is organized in five parts and fifteen chapters; at the end of each chapter there is a full list of references for easy consultation and a set of relevant questions to aid revision.

In writing this new edition, I have, as hitherto, consulted many publications, and I am grateful to the authors and publishers, several of whom have kindly allowed me to use statistical data and diagrams which they originated. I particularly thank Dr Darach Turley, who helped in tracing recent research material and for devising the revision questions.

Once again, I should like to thank the editorial staff of McGraw-Hill for their professional and friendly help over many years. I dedicate this edition to Charles and Georgina, who may, at some future time, even read it.

PART
ONE

INTRODUCTION

THE MARKETING CONCEPT: A REVIEW

Marketing as an activity is not new: it has been practised in rudimentary fashion by traders for thousands of years. But in advanced industrial economies, where specialization of production, labour, managerial talents are widely adopted, marketing has developed as a distinct and important area of management activity and responsibility. It has assumed the role of the entrepreneur in identifying market opportunities and relating these to the skills, productive capacity, and other resources of a company. This has included assessing the nature and degree of risk involved in entering specific product markets. The intimate personal knowledge of their customers' needs which craft workers and small local manufacturers possessed at one time suffered when large-scale production plants generally superseded them. Products were no longer designed and made to suit individual requirements: mass-production techniques demanded uniformity, and at the same time more distant markets had to be developed to take up the vastly increased volume of production. The gap between producer and consumer widened as a result of this industrial and commercial metamorphosis.

Modern economies are developed by individuals acting in their dual roles of producers and consumers. A bewildering variety of goods and services is demanded by those who live and work in countries that have attained economic maturity. Some of these products and services may well be considered to be unattractive or even luxuries by people whose tastes or life-style reflect different cultural and social behaviour. In attempting to satisfy these heterogeneous needs, manufacturers, merchants, builders, bankers, and others organize their resources and apply their skills and energies. All these activities generate the production and availability of goods and services offered for value in exchange (money) to people and organizations in both home and overseas markets. From this manufacturing and trading activity derives the wealth of a nation. The interaction of demand and supply in competitive markets sets the pace of bargaining—a process virtually as old as humankind and one, indeed, which children practise at a very tender age.

About 200 years ago, Adam Smith observed: 'Every man . . . lives by exchanging or becomes in some measure a merchant'.[1] Everyone in some way is involved in the fundamental economic activity of exchange; some are deeply immersed in it, with trading interests spread across the world: others may not be actively in business, but they still require many goods and services for their personal and family consumption. Doctors, lawyers, teachers, shopkeepers, manufacturers, designers, hoteliers, and others are all practising 'marketing' to some extent, because they all form part of the fabric of economic society, to which they contribute by offering specific goods and services for sale. Admittedly, in some cases, like medical expertise available under the British National Health Service, or teaching skills exercised in public authority schools, the exchange process does not involve direct financial settlements. But the practitioners in these types of economic activities are unlikely to prosper unless they adhere to acceptable standards of professional behaviour.

The concept of exchange lies at the heart of economic and social life. Without the facility of exchange, many needs oould not be satisfied, but the specialization of labour and other resources, and organized distribution and selling, result in people and companies having access to a vast array of goods and services.

Exchange, as Kotler notes, assumes four conditions:[2]

1. There are two parties.
2. Each party has something potentially valuable to the other.
3. Each party can communicate and deliver.
4. Each party is free to accept or reject the offer.

Provided these basic conditions are fulfilled, the parties can proceed to negotiate acceptable terms of exchange that will be beneficial to them. Motives to buy will vary considerably, according to influences such as urgency of the need, prestige, safety and security, or aesthetics. Alternative attractive offers may be evaluated: time and other scarce resources will come into the equation of value. Samuelson defined economics, in fact, as 'the study of how men and society choose, with or without the use of money, to employ scarce productive resources, which could have alternative uses, to produce various commodities over time and to distribute them for consumption, now and in the future, among various people and groups in society.'[3]

Marketing (as will be discussed further in this chapter) is a specialized function concerned with the exchange process that underlies the satisfaction of human and organizational needs. As these needs become more sophisticated, production and marketing resources are organized to provide specific types of goods and services. Resources, even of large firms, are limited—at least in the short term—and so management must carefully decide how their corporate resources will be most usefully applied. In markets where there is competitive activity (and virtually all markets today have this common characteristic), firms will need to know a great deal about the nature of demand and the alternative sources of supply related to particular kinds of products and services. The principle of choice is central to a free market economy: buyers demand variety and select according to their criteria of value; suppliers choose to enter certain markets because the prospects of doing business there are more promising than elsewhere. The market mechanism acts as a spur to enterprising manufacturers, merchants, and professional workers to offer attractively designed and priced goods and services in competition not only with home producers but frequently with those from distant lands. The end result, in theory at least, is to add to the economic and other satisfactions enjoyed by individuals and organizations through improved productivity, better standards of living, increased profitability, and higher GNP.

1.1 DEVELOPMENT OF THE MARKETING FUNCTION

Marketing as a separate, identifiable function of management has evolved from the business philosophy which recognizes the importance of the customer to the success of the business. This may seem a very commercial viewpoint, but it is at least realistic, because two parties, as already discussed, are involved in the process of exchange: the supplier and the buyer. In some organized activities, such as medical, legal, or accounting professions, users or buyers are customarily referred to as clients. Art galleries have patrons and visitors; teachers have pupils or students; hospitals have patients; charities have donors. But in every case, a mutually satisfactory relationship has to be established if both parties are to continue their exchange. Without clients or customers, no business or other undertaking can exist for long: as Drucker remarked in 1961: 'The customer is the foundation of a business and keeps it in existence'.[4]

This very basic creed has not always been readily accepted and practised. At one time—in the immediate post-war years in Britain, when there were artificial restrictions on trading, such as furniture and clothing coupons, raw materials licences, and so on—many products were difficult to buy, and a sellers' market operated (when satisfactory sales figures could be achieved fairly easily because people and companies were willing to pay almost any price to obtain goods in short supply). In the early 1950s, the Conservative government of that period held a 'bonfire of controls' which liberated industry and exposed it once more to the brisk atmosphere of competitive business.

Consumer products were the first to experience the decline of a sellers' market and the strong development of a buyers' market. These conditions were world-wide, moreover, and from the early 1950s, companies became increasingly aware of the need to know more about the preferences, prejudices, and buying habits of those who bought their products or services. The days of easy trading were numbered, and no company could expect to survive for very long if customers' needs were not adequately met.

On the whole, manufacturers of consumer products have successfully answered the challenge of the market-place. Some have not survived: others have sought the shelter of larger and more enterprising organizations. Few could prosper in today's harsh economic climate without being aware of the dynamic conditions that operate in most markets, which could significantly affect the demand for their products.

But until comparatively recently, the 'market revolution' appeared to have bypassed industrial and institutional areas of activity. To a considerable degree reluctance to adopt the technique of modern marketing appears to rest on a false premise: that marketing is very suitable, no doubt, for soap, chocolates, and cosmetics, but our products and services are vastly different; 'they don't need all these fancy methods of selling'. Technical cleverness and complexity are thought to be sufficient in themselves: commercial skills, such as marketing, are discounted by such firms.

But economic history has a different story to tell:

> The response of the cotton industry to increased competition and tariffs in the sophisticated export markets (of the late Victorian and early Edwardian period) was not so much to change products or improve design or to cut costs by radical innovation and reorganisation. Rather it was to maintain largely traditional-style products and technology, with slowly improving efficiency, and to rely increasingly on traditional-style markets in India, the Far East and the Empire. The great investment in new mills in Lancashire between 1895 and 1914, based upon the renewed expansion of exports, was in largely traditional technology.[5]

This indictment of what was once the major industry in the British economy and its greatest single exporter, reflects, sadly but truly, the pitiful responses of British management over many industries since that time. In 1970, for example, the Machine Tools Economic Development Committee published the results of a detailed and objective study of the marketing methods of successful firms in the British machine tool industry.[6] Their report, based on a two-year intensive study of manufacturers, merchants, and agents by the PE Consulting Group, stated that it was 'vitally important' for many companies to improve their marketing techniques. Successful firms were characterized by their whole-hearted commitment to serving the needs of their customers. Every executive in these companies—from top management down through the entire management structure—was personally oriented towards the customer. Marketing attitudes generated the specific motivation of these successful companies.

After carefully noting the valuable role played by systematic marketing research and product planning, the report emphasized the responsibility of the selling function. It was felt that many companies could improve their selling methods considerably. Selling effort should be planned carefully and directed at all levels of customers' staff likely to be concerned in the buying decision. This may involve sales staff in patiently analysing and identifying those who are 'key' influences, particularly where complex negotiations are involved. The decision-making processes of modern industry should not be considered in isolation, for they are inextricably linked with human factors that are fundamental in organizational behaviour.

Complacency, therefore, is ill founded in industrial markets. The skills of modern marketing can usefully be applied to *all* types of products or services, wherever they may be offered for sale. The actual techniques used in industrial marketing are not simply transferred from consumer product markets, however: they are adapted for effective use in a vastly different environment. But the fundamental concepts and practices of marketing remain the same, and in 1965 these were cogently expressed by PEP, the independent research organization which investigated 47 British industrial firms' attitudes to marketing:

> Productive efficiency is not the sole criterion of an efficient economy. It is also necessary that the goods produced should be what the consumer requires. Such a simple proposition would need no emphasis, were it not for the fact that in many British firms production is still carried out with small regard for marketing.
>
> The essence of marketing is that a firm will make what it can sell rather than sell what it can make. Marketing therefore required an assessment of consumer needs through market research and the orientation of all the firm's activities towards the satisfaction of those needs.[7]

Further enthusiastic support for the role of marketing in industrial and technical fields appeared in an article in a leading engineering journal:

> Among the old school of businessmen there used to be a saying that 'excellence always tells'; which may have been true once-upon-a-time, but certainly is no longer. In these highly competitive days the marketing man has to *tell* the world about the excellence. He has, also, to tell the engineers what the world wants. Otherwise the engineers's product, however beautifully engineered and however well finished, will gather dust in storage, eating up expensive space, while a flood of inferior products captures all the custom. . . .
>
> Far too many firms are still production oriented instead of market oriented. For historical reasons this is more particularly a vice of engineering. The tradition dies hard that British is necessarily the best and that the world is avid to have it. The disease can strike any firm. . . . Sometimes managements fall so much in love with their own product that they convince themselves it must always remain supreme. A case in point on the large scale was that of steam locomotive manufacturers, quite sure that steam would always hold its own, who suddenly found it displaced by diesel electric engines.[8]

The resistance to accepting marketing as having a purpose in industrial and technical organizations is by no means confined to the UK. In the USA, for example, a director of McKinsey and Co. reported in the *Harvard Business Review* that a capital goods company's management policy was always to sell the largest, highest-powered, most maintenance-free units possible because this suited their manufacturing facilities.[9] However, customers began to prefer smaller, less costly units 'without the rugged engineering characteristics required for maintenance-free operation'. The firm's marketing executives recommended a major redesign of the product line, but they were strongly opposed by the manufacturing and technical experts, who argued strongly that the current product design and cost structure were superior to any competition. All that was needed, they said, was a better selling effort; this was demanded by top management, who accepted the technical experts' views. Only after the company had lost a substantial share of its market was the president willing to reject the opinions of the engineering and manufacturing executives and order the whole range to be redesigned. 'Now that he has, things are looking up. In a situation like this, it is unrealistic, of course, to expect a dramatic turnaround.'

1.2 CHARACTERISTICS OF MARKETING

The gradual evolution of marketing as a specific function of management originates from the basic concept of value exchange. Sensitivity to the perceived needs of the customer or client is the first step towards marketing effectiveness. In Drucker's vivid phrasing: 'Marketing . . . is the whole business seen from the point of view of its final result, that is, from the customer's point of view.'[10]

Marketing has two particular characteristics or qualities: it is a philosophy based on customer orientation and satisfaction, a way of thinking about the business in terms of customer satisfaction. But, as Kotler says: 'It is one thing to exhort a customer orientation and another to implement it. Several steps must be taken by the firm wishing truly to practise a customer orientation'.[2]

Concepts, if they are to be fruitful, have to be applied, so marketing has to be implemented through effective management. Hence, marketing is an activity which, inspired by its basic philosophy, and working closely with other specialist functions of management, helps to stimulate demand for those products and services that can be supplied, profitably, within corporate resources.

So, marketing is not only a message, but also a mission. Like management, it entails thinking and doing. Successful management is not achieved haphazardly; it demands clear, conceptual thought, an analytical approach, and the ability to implement soundly based decisions.

Definitions of marketing are many and often turgid. The Chartered Institute of Marketing definition is as good as most of them: 'Marketing is the management process responsible for identifying, anticipating and satisfying customer requirements profitably'.

From this definition, the first emphasis is on the fact that marketing is a *management* function which, like other specialist managerial functions, has its particular expertise and responsibilities. These responsibilities involve the vital tasks of identifying market needs, of anticipating trends in demand, and of planning to supply, at a profit, acceptable products and services. As entrepreneurs, marketing managers must be seeking new market opportunities; they will be concerned with objective assessment of both present and future market behaviour. Anticipating what may be needed by people and by organizations is, indeed, one of the most difficult tasks facing marketing management. (The subject of innovation is discussed at some length in Chapter 11.)

Satisfying customers or clients should be the guiding principle of all businesses; this is possible only if these conditions are satisfied.

1. Prior research has established the kinds of benefits that were being sought from the purchase or use of a specific product or services.
2. The goods or services provided were designed to give those particular satisfactions. These benefits (as later discussion will show) can be complex and dynamic.

Markets seldom experience static conditions, especially today, when technological change and planned innovation have speeded up the pace of competition. Even successful products have a shorter expectancy of life than a few years ago. The costs of developing new products grow remorselessly each year, while the risk of failure haunts the dreams of entrepreneurs. Lack of success with a new product range may involve a company in substantial financial loss, apart from the social costs resulting from short-time working or closure of manufacturing plants.

Marketing management has therefore the responsibility of identifying customers, of evaluating their present needs, and also of predicting their likely future requirements: management has to live in both the present and the future. Future opportunities must be examined realistically and surveyed critically in the light of the present state of the organization. The enterprise must be kept healthy to ensure that it will live to enjoy the future successes that are planned. Marketing management should aim, therefore, to retain the initiative in their product markets by carefully planning innovative products in collaboration with technical experts. Perhaps the Chartered Institute of Marketing's definition would be acceptable and applied more widely if 'profitably' were replaced by 'efficiently' or 'according to the objectives of the organization'. This would then allow the function of marketing to be seen as relevant to non-profit-motivated organizations, such as the public sector services, charities, sports and recreational clubs, and so on. To function well, these organizations should certainly be responsive to the needs of their clients, patients, and members.

> Private sector businesses and public welfare organisations have different, prime motivations, but they share a common objective: to provide acceptable benefits to members of society. . . . The optimum allocation of scarce resources concerns not only commercial firms but should also be the direct interest of those who formulate policies in public service.[11]

In Britain, the radical restructuring of the National Health Service, for example, has been based not only on fundamental changes in administrative procedures and financial responsibilities, but also on radical behavioural responses by medical and nursing staffs. Patients are even described as customers in some NHS publications, and competitive tendering appears to be among the many business practices now adopted throughout the public health services.

1.3 SERVICE ECONOMY

Britain, in common with the other advanced countries, has an economy which is increasingly dependent for employment opportunities, and national wealth on the service industries. Traditionally, three main sectors of economic activities have been defined: primary, secondary, and tertiary. The first refers to agriculture, mining, forestry, and fishing, which are significant occupations in less developed economies; the second relates to the manufacturing and construction industries which gradually supplant the primary sector as the major source of national wealth; the third concerns the service and distributive trades—sometimes termed 'incorporeal production'—which, as noted, are now the largest generators of economic activity in the UK.

An advanced economy depends heavily on the efficiency of its service industries. These cover vital economic and social contributions, such as health and social welfare, education, banking, law, insurance, technical and professional assistance, transport, energy, electronic communications, and so on. Everyone in an economy is affected to some degree or other by the services provided by the public and private sectors. In many cases, the impact of these services is particularly personal; in other instances, the efficiency of technical and professional services is crucial to the productivity of the manufacturing sector. As is well known, Britain's balance of payments has been given invaluable assistance from 'invisible' exports derived from the insurance, banking, brokerage, and similar services.

Marketing techniques can and should be applied to the service sector industries. Market research, for example, can be most valuable in designing and developing banking, insurance, and other professional services. It has been used effectively in the areas of health and social welfare to identify specific populations and to organize special types of care; for example, for older people or for the disabled. (More detailed discussion occurs in another text.)[11]

In Britain, the service economy has evolved into what is often described as a *mixed economy*, in which the public sector and private sector activities have become largely interdependent. The public services of health, welfare, and education play a crucial part in economic and social life; in addition the public corporations responsible for energy generation and distribution, postal and telecommunications, and rail transport add very significantly to the national economic effort. These public sector undertakings consume vast resources and affect the lives of millions, as well as the overall efficiency of businesses. They too should be market oriented.

1.4 MARKETING IS A TEAM EFFORT

Several management specializations contribute to corporate success: production, design, research and development, purchasing, finance, personnel, and marketing: all have distinctive roles to play in the management team. Individually, their efforts, though valuable, are insufficient, but the whole is greater than the sum of these parts.

Management functions have necessarily become specialized as organizations have grown and the nature of particular responsibilities, such as finance or marketing, has become more sophisticated. Unfortunately, specialization often breeds parochialism; efficiency in a specific managerial function is obviously necessary but, at the same time, cooperation with other management specialists is equally important. Unless the management of an organization works together as a team, little real progress can be expected. As Robert Heller has observed with characteristic clarity: 'You can no longer afford to let designers, manufacturing people and marketers operate as separate, sometimes warring factions, especially when it comes to innovation. In a move led by IBM, companies are thus even putting design and manufacture under combined command.'[12]

The internecine warfare that appears to characterize management behaviour in some organizations should be eradicated: it is counterproductive, personally frustrating, and highly dangerous in competitive environments. Blois has drawn attention to the fact that conflict frequently arises between the manufacturing and marketing parts of a business because of their compartmentalization, and measures of efficiency are related to departmental and not overall effort.[13] There is also disagreement about the relative contributions which marketing and manufacturing make to the success of a business.

1.5 TWIN RESPONSIBILITIES OF MARKETING MANAGEMENT

To avoid misconceptions and misunderstandings about their function in an organization—whether it be in the public or private sector of an economy—marketing management should accept that they have twin responsibilities, if they are to do a first-class job. These dual roles can be described as involving both *interpretation* and *integration*. In real life, these functions are not, of course, discrete and independent; essentially, they are practised as a whole by experienced marketing managers, although at a particular time, concentrated attention might be given to one of these specific responsibilities.

Interpretation involves analysis and evaluation of market behaviour, both present and projected. Market research will be used to collect objective information about the many factors affecting consumption of particular products and services. As further discussion in this text will indicate, there are many influences, other than economic, motivating buyers in consumer and also industrial markets.

Marketing managers should, after identifying and assessing market needs, discuss their findings not only with marketing and sales staff, but also with design, production, financial, purchasing, and personnel specialists. The whole business should be made aware of the market opportunities that are suitable for the company to exploit. This responsibility of marketing management is termed 'integration', i.e. communicating throughout the business and encouraging the full cooperation of everyone in it, so that they are aware of the nature of competition, and the required qualities of products or services, delivery times, pricing policies, and back-up service to win business in certain markets.

Integration involves marketing management in working closely with colleagues in other fields; for example, with design staff in the development of new products, or with production staff in understanding the constraints of manufacture related to particular kinds of products. It also means understanding the problems of purchasing, for example, new types of containers; of discussing with financial experts, the funding necessary to enter new overseas markets or to develop a new system of distribution; or, perhaps, appreciating the inevitable lag in recruiting and training labour to produce a different type or quality of product.

These twin responsibilities should both be accepted and fulfilled by marketing management. Too often, marketing activities seem to be entirely *outside* the organization; there is a crucial role to be played *inside* by effectively communicating and inviting the cooperation of every department of the organization. In this way, businesses can acquire a cutting edge against competition. Implementing the marketing concept entails changing attitudes and encouraging behaviour that is responsive to customers. Marketing can be viewed as a philosophy and also an activity. To make marketing more than an admirable notion, the dual tasks involved in interpretation and integration must be professionally done.

1.6 MARKETING IN A DYNAMIC ENVIRONMENT

Organizations of all types—consumer products and services, industrial and technical supplies, banking and other professional services, and public sector services—should therefore develop their marketing skills. They all use scarce, finite resources which should be organized efficiently so that they provide their customers, clients, or patrons with acceptable products and services. This, as Adam Smith reflected many years ago, is perfectly self-evident and scarcely warrants saying, but what is staring management (and others) in the face is not always seen, as the disastrous decline of the British motor cycle industry so sadly showed. It is no longer safe to assume that certain 'traditional markets' will always remain the preserve of old-established or well-known manufacturers. Vastly improved methods of modern transport have brought competitors nearer to each other and access to markets has likewise become easier. Technologies are now widely dispersed over many countries: Britain is no longer 'the workshop of the world' with unique manufacturing resources and skills developed through generations of industrial activity.

To survive against world competition, British industrialists must become more aware of the need to define closely their trading objectives and to relate their resources to the developing needs of their markets.

> In time of rapid change a business must always be alive to its aims. A major consideration is the type of business to be pursued. Contrast the experiences of two companies. One thought of itself as part of the steel industry and manufactured steel fittings. It suffered competition from asbestos, concrete, aluminium and plastic alternatives. The second company, in a similar business, thought of itself as providing a service in public and private street lighting. In manufactured, or factored, supplies in any material and offered a design and contracting service.[14]

British industrial products, in particular, need a strong infusion of marketing skills. These skills include acquiring a deeper understanding of the principal influences affecting buying behaviour.

1.7 BEHAVIOURAL STUDIES RELATED TO MARKETING

The marketing of goods and services—whether to individuals or to organizations—is not merely an economic activity. Buying behaviour is complex and is influenced by many factors, some of which may conflict with so-called rational decision-making. The interactions of groups and personal behaviour, the interrelationships between attitudes and behaviour, the challenge of authority and status, and the profound, and sometimes subtle, effects of culture on consumption make up, in part, the intricate web of influences which surrounds patterns of consumption.

People's behaviour as consumers of diverse products and services cannot realistically be isolated from their societal roles as parents, workers, students, and so on. Personal consumption takes place in a social and cultural environment; social and cultural norms influence and inhabit personal consumption. As members of society, individuals, by their patterns of consumption, contribute to the overall consumption of society.

Comprehensive, reliable knowledge about buying behaviour, i.e., consumption, should take account, therefore, of the structure of society and the interactions of individuals within the various groups and subgroups which constitute it. Cultural beliefs and values, social aspirations and inhibitions, and the development of the modern welfare society affect consumption habits. The increasing interdependence of the public and private sectors in developed mixed economies has a profound influence in economic and social life. The priorities of economic objectives and social goals, giving rise to fundamental issues, profoundly affect, sooner or later, the pattern of the individual's consumption of goods and services.

Nowadays few, surely, would argue that buying behaviour in general is so very different from other forms of human behaviour that none of the theories and findings from the behavioural sciences is relevant. In fact, in the study of individual and household buying patterns, some of the concepts of sociology and psychology have been used to great effect. Growing interest is now developing in extending social science concepts to the study of industrial buying behaviour.

This willingness to consider the interplay and significance of 'non-economic' influences in business activity was reflected eloquently by the late Andrew Shonfield:

> it is arguable that the disappointment with our current performance in the management of the economy is the result of expecting economics to do on its own a job that requires a joint, and massive, effort by the whole range of social sciences. It is as if one had turned to the surgeons during the early stages of the development of modern medicine, and commanded them on their own to take over responsibility for curing all bodily ailments: no doubt a few more people would have lived; but a lot more would have had their limbs chopped off.[15]

Economic commentators, said Shonfield, talk and write as if the whole area of psychological uncertainty could be ignored. Economics is a very useful science and should not be discarded but it must be acknowledged that it cannot bear the whole burden of 'what might be termed clinical prescription for society whether the subject is the management of money or industrial relations or the drive for exports—or any other of the subjects conventionally labelled "economic".' Shonfield urged that the newer social sciences, social psychology, and sociology in particular, should be used 'to fill out and give substance' to economic studies.

Two hundred years earlier, Adam Smith's[1] sardonic opinion was that the proposals of economic interests

> ought to be listened to with great precaution, and ought never to be adopted till after having been long and carefully examined. . . . It comes from an order of men, whose interest is never exactly the same with that of the public, who have generally an interest to deceive and even to oppress the public, and who accordingly have, upon many occasions, both deceived and oppressed.

In 1984, Sir Douglas Hague, former Chairman of the Economic and Social Research Council, commented:

> I certainly believe that most economists would be better and more effective economists if they took more notice of what sociologists, psychologists and others have to offer. Equally, the other social sciences might be more effective in their own fields if they paid more attention to the working of the economic system and the constraints under which societies have to operate.[16]

Christopher Freeman has observed that economists have an elegant theory which is confronted with a very untidy and messy reality. 'Their theory was and is an important contribution to the explanation and prediction of many aspects of firms' behaviour, but it is not self-sufficient and attempts to make it so can only lead to sterility'.[17] Economists, says Freeman, must pay much more attention to engineers and also to experts from sociology, psychology, and political sciences. Marketing managers who work at the interface of society and business should develop, for example, their knowledge of social values and appreciate how these often tend to confict with economic motivations. Social upheavals have had far-reaching effects on the behaviour and consumption patterns in many markets.

John Kay, a professor of economics at London Business School, has vigorously responded to critics who apparently believe that economics is mostly about forecasting: 'but most economics, and almost all of economics that is of any value, is not about forecasting at all.' Fundamental misconceptions about the nature and scope of economics lead to misunderstandings. Economics 'is about understanding the economy, and although we do not know all, or anything like enough, about how the economy works (any more than we know all, or enough, about how the physical, chemical or biological world works) we do know quite a lot'.[18]

Too many people may have expected too much from economists; but in his fascinating treatise, *Small is Beautiful*, Schumacher warned against the tendency for economics to be viewed as expressing the ultimate wisdom in business and public affairs.[19] There are, he said, few words as final and conclusive as the word 'uneconomic': to brand an activity as such is to question its right to existence. But John Stuart Mill (1806–73) looked upon political economy differently: he saw it 'not as a thing by itself, but as a fragment of a greater whole; a branch of social philosophy, so interlinked with all the other branches that its conclusions, even in its own peculiar province, are only true conditionally, subject to interference and counteraction from sources not directly within its scope'.

Herbert Simon of Carnegie-Mellon University strongly supports this classical view: 'Economics without psychological and sociological research . . . is a one-bladed scissors'. He urges that it should be replaced 'with an instrument capable of cutting through our ignorance about rational human behaviour'.[20]

When organizational buyers enter their office they do not suddenly transform into that curious, completely rational human being dreamed up by early classical economists and fondly termed 'economic man'. Further, they can rarely buy in ideal market conditions. The business environment is complex and real people are exposed to the conflict of economic and social motivations. Although this earlier academic view is now generally discredited, some people still seem reluctant to accept that rationality is not the sole influence in buying situations, particularly those related to organizational supplies.

Drucker has stated that business enterprises have three levels of activities: the physical level, which includes plant, tools, and materials; the economic level, which reflects the activities of producing and distributing products; and the human level, which relates to the activities of individuals working in those organizations.[4] Later discussion will be dealing with the effects of the last category of business activity on the two other levels. Human behaviour has profound effects on the policy and day-to-day operations of organizations of all kinds, so this further reinforces the need to know more about the wants and goals of people; to dig down deeper into the underlying factors affecting behaviour in general; and to attempt to relate these findings to particular market situations. In purchasing food for her family, a woman will be affected by her role as a wife and mother; she will carefully judge the nutritional value of alternative kinds of food. Her personal values and beliefs inevitably contribute to the decisions she makes in the supermarket; these subjective criteria deserve careful investigation and evaluation by marketers.

Marketers accept that products are bought for the satisfactions that customers hope to obtain from them; these benefits are often more than physical. Indeed, it has been said that in economies of affluence consumption tends to place greater emphasis on psychological satisfactions. Food, for example, is eaten not just to quell the appetite and to sustain life: it has assumed significance as an aesthetic experience to be savoured for its colour, texture, and flavour. Frequently it acquires social meanings through being consumed at certain times or in surroundings that lend prestige to the occasion. Similarly, clothing is hardly ever bought solely for its basic function of giving physical protection against climatic variables. On this simple foundation a complex structure of motivations has been erected, and people endeavour to express their personalities by carefully selecting colours to suit their complexions, types of fabric that please them visually and tactually, and styling which is fashionable. It is increasingly evident that these psychological satisfactions are no longer the preoccupation exclusively of women shoppers. Men's clothing, in general, is now subject to the vagaries of fashion to an extent not previously experienced on so wide a scale.

Cultural attitudes and social behaviour undergo changes which have affected, for example, the sales of clothing such as formal suits for men. Some major clothing firms, failing to recognize the trend towards informality and casual wear, nearly went out of business as a result. Inflexible production processes cannot stem a rising trend towards more relaxed social behaviour; like the legendary king, such manufacturers pathetically believed that they had unique powers to halt the inexorable tide.

The large brewery groups significantly underestimated the public's interest in so-called 'real ale'. The Campaign for Real Ale (CAMRA) assumed some of the fervour of a religious crusade and became a real challenge to the nationally distributed, mass merchandised beers. From relative obscurity and without immense resources CAMRA has radically changed beer drinking habits and forced the big breweries to rethink their business strategies. As a result, they have introduced their own special brews and have reintroduced some of the local brewery names which had been suppressed in the mistaken belief that consumers would support nationally advertised brands. Local preferences and loyalties were clearly disregarded by the strategists, who are now in hasty retreat. The traditional public houses of Britain are not drinking dens; they are an intrinsic part of the fabric of local society and their habitués develop strong loyalties that have deep cultural and personal meanings.

In marketing products of many kinds the so-called 'non-rational' factors warrant special study. Consumers may view products very differently from manufacturers, and may not necessarily articulate their needs, aspirations, or fears. Study of customer behaviour should therefore include overt or observable factors and should also attempt to identify the covert less apparent influences which affect consumption habits. The complex interaction of both economic and non-rational factors demands a comprehensive research strategy.

Purchasers appear often to indulge in rationalization of their past decisions to buy some product; they may tend to feel rather 'guilty' about acquiring luxury goods which entail unusually heavy outlays. For reasons of self-prestige, such buyers frequently search for acceptable motivations which would enable them to demonstrate to their families and friends that they carefully weigh the economic consequences of spending large sums of money on what may be considered by others to be frivolous products. Marketers should appreciate that this tendency towards insisting on rational motives, of logical appeals, and of behaviour based on the satisfaction of qualified economic needs, may be influential in the product categories in which they do business. In 1958 Edward C. Bursk wrote:

> for every selling situation the buyer must have some self-approved reason for saying 'yes'—whether the affirmation is in terms of handing over the money or signing on the dotted line, or just feeling agreement with an advertising message. For example, a man may want to buy a new car because it is new and sleek and shiny, but he also needs some rationalisation like 'I'll get a better trade-in if I buy now . . .'. I am convinced this is also true in advertising; that of two advertisements, both of which apply to a product mainly bought for *irrational* reasons, the one that provides in addition some cogent *rational* reason should produce a stronger-reaction than the one that does not. I suspect that one explanation of why the combination of an advertising appeal to the image of masculinity *and* a new crush-proof box worked so well for Marlboro cigarettes is that the box offered a generally acceptable rationalisation.[21]

That message is still applicable today, particularly when the basic product in many markets is now augmented by psychological and other subtle appeals.

The concept of the *augmented product or service* acknowledges that buying often involves complex motivations and needs. More than just the simple or basic satisfaction of use or ownership is demanded by many buyers, whether for their own personal consumption or for the needs of their organizations. Many products often described as commodities—such as popular types of paint, timber, basic chemicals, and so on—are perceived to be identical and it is indeed likely that they provide virtually the same performance irrespective of their origin, therefore price competition will be active in such product markets.

However, around the basic satisfaction related to the core benefit provided by the product or service, additional reasons to buy can be built into a business deal. More attractive service—before, during, and after sale—better styling or more comprehensive guarantees, for example, add extra layers of satisfaction. Several of these added attributes may be based on giving psychological, social, or other benefits. Product or service differentiations can be deliberately designed to attract specific market demand (see Chapter 14).

The augmented product (and service) concept acknowledges that buyers will be sensitive to 'added values'. By utilizing this concept, marketers can avoid being trapped in the commodity classification of products. Building in benefits is sound business sense, because it helps to secure customers who are interested in obtaining more than basic products or services.

Kotler has identified three levels of product (see Fig. 1.1): the core product, the formal product, and the augmented product.[2] Levitt added a fourth dimension: the generic product, the expected product, the augmented product, and the potential product.[22] Both writers, however, are giving the same viewpoint: products which are basically alike, if not identical, can be differentiated by creatively adding new values to the business deal, so that more buying motivations are tapped.

The core benefit is only the first step in the product or service offered: other steps must be taken to attract business; these may involve branding (which helps to reduce perceived risk in buying), distinctive styling (which may include ergonomic design to ensure safety in handling), aesthetically attractive design (which may appeal to certain personality traits), and packaging (which may ensure freshness of contents). Further advantages to the purchaser can include pre- and after-sales service, well-formulated product guarantees, and so on.

Product design linked with effective branding has contributed substantially to the growth of companies such as Dunhill, Hermés, Wedgwood, and Stella Artois, to mention but a few whose quality products and corporate identities are recognized virtually over the entire world. Such premium-priced products are sought eagerly, because they offer subtle satisfactions to those who buy them for their own consumption or as prestigious presents.

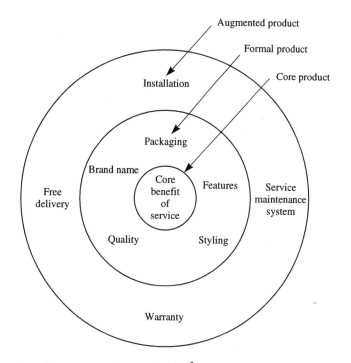

Fig. 1.1 The augmented product concept (*Source:* Kotler)[2]

1.8 RESEARCH INTO BEHAVIOURAL INFLUENCES

To understand buying behaviour and trends in consumption may well seem an unachievable goal: no one would be rash enough to suggest that perfect knowledge is attainable in this or in any other area of study. But this does not relieve those who wish to profit from supplying goods and services to markets of many kinds from acquiring a better appreciation of the multiple factors that influence demand. Any explanation of economic activities which does not also take note of the psychological make-up of consumers, their roles in society, and the cultural background that flavours their orientation towards life is likely to result in unsound business decisions being taken by manufacturers and distributors of a very wide range of goods and services.

Research should therefore aim to acquire comprehensive, reliable knowledge about every aspect of buying behaviour, taking note not only of economic factors but also of the many other complex motivations that may arise from psychological, cultural, and social influences. In real life conditions, these subtle influences may not easily be identified, but this does not mean that they should be ignored. Indeed, Weiner has observed that the determination to explain all economic phenomena with a self-contained model of purely economic factors pushes much of social life to a dimly lit periphery: 'Behaviour not conforming to the assumption of "rational", profit- and wage-earning action is attributed to a catch-all category such as "imperfections in the market"'.[23] Of Britain's economic decline, Weiner notes: 'Strictly, economic explanations have been based on questionable assumptions or have left large space for "residual" factors, which would appear to be social and psychological.'

Successful entrepreneurs seek to acquire sensitive insights into human behaviour; study of the fundamental processes of perception, motivation, attitude formation, learning theory, and sociological factors, such as social class, social mobility, leadership, and reference group theory, adds depth to market investigations. Economic analyses supply the skeletal outline of buyers' needs; behavioural data add fullness and richness to the understanding of market behaviour.

The social sciences are not, of course, to be looked upon as entirely relevant for purposes of marketing analyses. Some aspects of cultural anthropology, for instance, have limited usefulness in this area, while in the field of psychology there are many concepts which are of no direct interest in studying buying behaviour. But there are several useful areas of social science which may be translated into market studies. In the *Harvard Business Review*, Joseph W. Newman once wrote that as marketers had become increasingly aware of how much they had to learn about the nature of buying and consumption, they had turned for assistance to the behavioural sciences, which had provided valuable guides in understanding human behaviour in general.[24]

Research techniques borrowed from other areas of study have been adapted by marketing analysts. Psychological instruments such as attitude scales and projective techniques have proved valuable in marketing research. From social science and quantitative concepts, sampling methodology, questionnaire construction, regression analysis, and Markov processes have contributed to the development of marketing science. That much of the formal content of marketing is drawn from other areas of study is not surprising; what is of particular interest is the degree of success with which these techniques have been adapted and applied in developing a deeper understanding of market variables. In fact, the Marketing Science Institute of the USA, in reviewing the general development of marketing theory, noted its reliance on borrowed concepts and commented: 'Historically, most sciences started by borrowing their conceptual approach and general theoretical ideas from other sciences. Our current state of marketing theory is no different'.[25] At the same time, marketing analysts should be wary of indiscriminate borrowing from other fields of study; care is also needed to avoid swinging from the extreme of explaining all buying behaviour as stemming from the 'rational' explanations offered by economic theory to the other extreme, unduly emphasizing irrational or emotional motivations. Oversimplified psychological explanations based on some personality theory, e.g., Freudian, do not adequately explain buying behaviour. Marketing investigations should be conducted with 'scientific care and conceptual honesty', and the wholesale importing of techniques from other sciences is not likely to result in valuable contributions to marketing theory and practice.

Techniques are not, of course, ends in themselves; managers have the responsibility of applying the data obtained by these modern, and sometimes expensive, methods of analysis to the task of making better decisions. Data gathering should always be undertaken within the defined objectives of disciplined research. Fitzroy[26] has cautioned that marketing as a field of both academic study and actual practice is in a state of transition from speculative thinking and intuitive assertions to a more formal, rigorous, and empirically based study of market variables which are often multi-dimensional. Easy access to computer program packages could result in inappropriate use of multi-variate techniques.

It has also been noted that marketing investigations into customer behaviour often lack the precision of technical data to which top management are accustomed from other areas of management, such as production or finance.[9] Qualitative data, stigmatized as 'soft', tend to be viewed with less confidence than the so-called 'hard data' offered by accountants or production engineers. Although marketing forecasts are also quantified, they inevitably lack the precision of historical data submitted by other departments.

1.9 SYSTEMATIC APPROACH TO THE STUDY OF BEHAVIOURAL INFLUENCES IN MARKETING

A behavioural analysis and study of market variables may usefully be founded on an appreciation of some of the fundamental psychological factors that affect individual behaviour.

These may be listed as: cognitions, learning processes, interpersonal response traits, attitudes, motivations, and personality theories. The interaction of these individual factors and their expression in buying behaviour in both personal and organizational areas requires careful study. Since individuals are also members of a society in which they grow up and by whose standards they are influenced, analysis needs to be extended to include social and cultural aspects of marketing behaviour. Knowledge of the contributions towards buying decisions made by individual members of a family or other social groups demands systematic investigation. Cultural inhibitions may be important influences affecting the diffusion of new products; educational achievements inevitably develop critical appraisal of commercial practices including the methods of promoting products and services. The aspirations of individuals are closely linked with their social and cultural life, and their buying habits and preferences reflect to some degree their personal view of life.

These multiple influences will be discussed at some length in this book so that an insight into buying behaviour affecting both personal and organizational needs may be derived. Leading theoretical explanations of buying behaviour will be examined closely when an overall appreciation of the factors involved has been obtained.

Psychological and other behavioural factors influence not only personal shopping but also organizational buying. Levitt sums up the persuasive effects of behavioural factors in industrial markets:

> When it takes fives years of intensive work between seller and buyer to 'deliver' an operating chemical plant or a telecommunications system, much more is required than the kind of marketing that simply lands the contract. The buyer needs assurance at the outset that the two parties can work well together during the long period in which the purchase gets transformed into delivery.[27]

Over time, a system of reciprocal relationship will be established, but this will not develop satisfactorily without careful marketing. Industrial marketing needs more than technical skills; it requires, in addition, insight into human behaviour (see Chapter 10).

To aid discussion of the multiple influences that bear on buying (referred to in more detail in subsequent chapters), Fig. 1.2 presents a general outline of these interwoven factors. These various behavioural factors—personal and societal—will be examined for their relevance in specific buying situations. Empirical data are quoted wherever they are available to demonstrate the usefulness of some of these behavioural concepts in the marketing of goods and services. More extensive research is necessary to validate certain of the hypotheses offered as explanations of buying behaviour. Environmental variables and personal dispositions and motivations cannot be left as mere speculations, however well informed these may appear to be. The greater general awareness of the contribution that social psychology offers to marketing management in understanding people's behaviour should now be backed up by programmes of research directed to building up a fund of expert knowledge about specific types of product and service markets.

1.10 SUMMARY

The complexity of modern patterns of consumption demands sophisticated understanding; explanations based solely on economic theory are clearly inadequate. The other social sciences—psychology, sociology, and anthropology—can provide extra valuable knowledge of buying behaviour, both personal and organizational.

Marketing, as an important function of management, has the responsibility of interpreting market behaviour to the other key areas of management, so that the whole enterprise is geared to be responsive to customers.

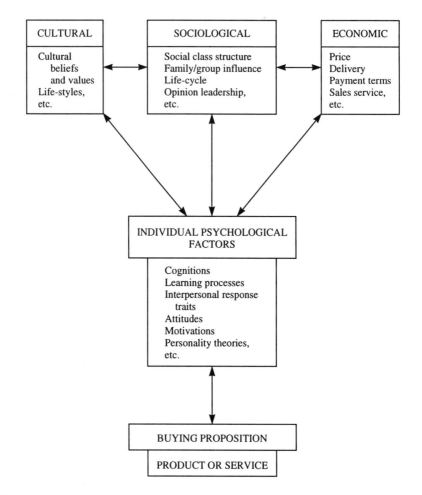

Fig. 1.2 The complex pattern of buying influences

Systematic market research should include both qualitative and quantitative data. In the dynamic environment that characterizes most markets today, marketing management must ensure that their information is complete and up to date.

The outline model of buying influences (Fig. 1.2) will act as a guide to further discussion in this text, and also indicate graphically the complexity inherent in purchase decisions.

REFERENCES

1. Smith, Adam, *An Inquiry into the Causes of the Wealth of Nations* (Carman edn), Methuen, London, 1961.
2. Kotler, Philip, *Marketing Management: Analysis, Planning and Control*, Prentice-Hall, Englewood Cliffs, New Jersey, 1984.
3. Samuelson, P. A., *Economics: An Introductory Analysis*, McGraw-Hill, Maidenhead, 1961.
4. Drucker, Peter F., *The Practice of Management*, Heinemann, Oxford, 1961.
5. Mathias, Peter, *The First Industrial Nation: An Economic History of Britain 1700–1914*, Methuen, London, 1983.

6. Machine Tools Economic Development Committee, *A Handbook for Marketing Machinery*, HMSO, Norwich, October 1970.
7. Gater, Anthony, David Insull, Harold Lind, and Peter Seglow, *Attitudes in British Management:—A PEP Report*, Pelican, London, 1965.
8. Rhodes, Clifford, 'Engineers must be market oriented', *Engineering*, November 1971.
9. Ames, Charles B., 'Trappings vs. substance in industrial marketing', *Harvard Business Review*, July/August 1970.
10. Drucker, Peter F., *Management: Tasks, Responsibilities and Practices*, Heinemann, Oxford, 1973.
11. Chisnall, Peter M., 'Market research', in: *Management for Health Service Administrators*, D. Allen and J. L. Hughes (eds), Pitman, London, 1983.
12. Heller, Robert, 'Pace is faster, but the rules are the same', *Marketing*, 15 March 1984.
13. Blois, K. J., 'The manufacturing/marketing orientation and its information needs', *European Journal of Marketing*, vol. 14, no. 5/6, 1980.
14. Tricker, Ian R., *The Accountant in Management*, Batsford, London, 1967.
15. Shonfield, Andrew, 'Neglect of psychology in managing the economy', *The Times*, 24 February 1971.
16. Hague, Sir Douglas, ERSC Newsletter no. 51, Economic and Social Research Council, March 1984.
17. Freeman, Christopher, *The Economics of Industrial Innovation*, Penguin, London, 1974.
18. Kay, John, 'Crystal ball found wanting', *Daily Telegraph*, 13 September 1992.
19. Schumacher, E. F., *Small is Beautiful: A Study of Economics as if People Mattered*, Harper and Row, London, 1973.
20. Simon, Herbert A., 'Rationality in psychology and economics', *Journal of Business*, vol. 59, no. 4, 1986.
21. Bursk, Edward C., 'Opportunities for persuasion', *Harvard Business Review*, September/October 1958.
22. Levitt, Theodore M., 'Marketing success through differentiation—if anything', *Harvard Business Review*, January/February 1980.
23. Weiner, Martin G., *English Culture and the Decline of the Industrial Spirit, 1850–1980*, Cambridge University Press, Cambridge, 1981.
24. Newman, Joseph W., 'New insights and new progress for marketing', *Harvard Business Review*, November/December 1957.
25. Halbert, Michael, *The Meaning and Sources of Marketing Theory*, Marketing Science Institute, McGraw-Hill, New York, 1965.
26. Fitzroy, Peter F., *Analytical Methods for Marketing Management*, McGraw-Hill, Maidenhead, 1976.
27. Levitt, Theodore M., 'After the sale is over', *Harvard Business Review*, September/October 1983.

REVIEW AND DISCUSSION QUESTIONS

1. In what way is the study of buying behaviour relevant to the marketing concept?
2. Before you have had an opportunity to study consumer behaviour, write out in advance the three main ways in which you hope it will contribute to your study of marketing.
3. How important is the distinction between the BASIC product and the AUGMENTED product for marketers?
4. What contributions do the various behavioural sciences make to the study of consumer behaviour?
5. Taking Fig. 1.2 into consideration, do you feel that consumer behaviour can realistically be called a 'science'?
6. What kinds of data are used in the study of buying behaviour?

TWO

PERSONAL ASPECTS OF BEHAVIOUR

COGNITIONS, PERCEPTIONS, AND LEARNING PROCESSES

2.1 INTRODUCTION

Part Two of this book identifies and discusses the basic personal psychological factors that were shown in Fig. 1.2 (see page 18). This chapter covers cognitions, perceptions, and learning processes, which play a central role in human behaviour. Chapter 3 focuses on needs and motivations, Chapter 4 examines theories of personality, and Chapter 5 deals with attitudes. These four chapters lay the foundation for subsequent discussion in which the individual is viewed as a member of society whose patterns of consumption are affected by group norms, cultural values, and, in many cases, social class.

2.2 DEFINITION OF COGNITION

The term 'cognition' refers to the mental processes of knowing, perceiving, and judging which enable people to interpret the world about them. Persons, objects, and events are perceived by individuals who endeavour to make sense of the stimuli to which they are exposed. Human reactions will be influenced by the ways in which certain kinds of objects are perceived; individuals have a personal view of the world surrounding them which will derive from their environment and their frames of reference. Although an individual's conception of the world will tend to be unique—in the sense that no two persons have precisely the same set of beliefs and attitudes—a certain degree of uniformity will exist because human beings share several basic characteristics. These fundamental features may relate to biological needs such as food and rest, or to psychological satisfaction to be found, for example, in aesthetic pleasures such as listening to music. The more cohesive a community, the more likely its members are to share very similar sets of cognitions.

2.3 COGNITIVE MAP

Individuals' cognitive maps will reflect, therefore a subjective view of the world, but these beliefs are valid and form the core of individuals' personal orientation towards life in general and may profoundly affect their personal relationships. Consumption habits are also likely to be influenced by the cognitions that people hold. These may relate, for example, to the nutritional content of fresh, unprocessed foods compared with tinned foods. Aspects of buying behaviour such as brand allegiance, store loyalty, or distrust of advertising may be evident in some cases. Differences in social status may be reflected in the emphases given to certain cultural activities like attending art exhibitions, symphony concerts, or weekend lecture courses. Deep personal convictions may result in activities dedicated to sponsoring political and religious creeds; to the furtherance of trade unionism; or to the development of birth control clinics. Diverse forms of behaviour are generated, therefore, by the beliefs, attitudes, and value systems that are held by particular people.

The environment in which people live is complex and confusing: there is so much activity; there are so many stimuli competing for attention. Exposed to this bewildering 'noise', people attempt to build some cognitive structure that will enable them to interpret the world about them in a meaningful way.

This cognitive map or structure is determined principally by two kinds of factors: stimulus factors and personal factors. These factors interact to produce an individual's personal set of concepts which affect all economic, social, and cultural activities.

2.4 FUNDAMENTALS OF PERCEPTION

Cognitions and perceptions are closely linked. Markin has described perception as one of the elements of cognition—the processes involved in knowing.[1] Through the stimulation of the senses, perception occurs. 'Perception lies somewhere between raw sensation and the more cognitive term "concept". In short, while perception has sensory data at its core, it in turn has a central role in the cognitive and thinking process.'[2]

The nature of physical stimuli tends to influence the degree of perception; a flashing neon sign, an ordered array of objects on display, a colour advertisement encountered among a series of monochrome pages in a magazine, or a sudden loud noise are almost sure to attract attention. The senses are stimulated by unexpected or unusual objects or events; in the fairly predictable routine of everyday life, an individual tends to seek variety and change. Perception has been described as 'to observe through the senses' and the following model has been given by Young.[3]

	to see	
	to hear	thing
To perceive =	to touch	some event
	to taste	relation
	to smell	
	to sense internally	

The senses tend to be used in combination and, for example, to convey experiences from seeing, smelling, touching, and tasting food; together these senses contribute to perception and opinions are then formed about the quality or other attributes of particular kinds or brands of food.

2.5 FACTORS AFFECTING PERCEPTION

Personal factors modify the effect of the various physical stimuli that influence perception. 'Behind every act of perceiving is the individual's past history of experience. Previous experience has built up a relatively stable cognitive organisation within the individual which determines the meaning of a particular percept.'[3]

The 'span of apprehension' limits the number of objects or concepts to which an individual may pay attention and comprehend at any one time. A myriad stimuli compete for attention; the senses are literally swamped with stimuli jostling for primacy. Obviously only a few can achieve attention, hence the term 'selective attention'. These may do so because of certain characteristics such as level of sound, size, colour, frequency, etc.—all dimensions that are exploited in advertising a wide variety of goods and services.

In addition to being selective, attention is also dynamic: people are continually being bombarded with stimuli of various kinds, and they do not as a rule concentrate for long on the impact made by one stimulus. People tend to switch their attention elsewhere, and the original stimulus soon loses its effect, unless it is re-presented in some attractive way. Re-launches of consumer products occur regularly; on the other hand, consistent brand advertising for one particular product may have developed strong buying habits, so that new products can be introduced under the same acceptable name.

Empirical studies have indicated that there are wide personal differences in the span of apprehension, and that this varies in an individual according to the nature of the objects and events, the personal significance that these may have, and the period of time during which they are under review. Consumers, for example, are exposed to a multitude of promotional messages from marketers of goods and services. Some of these communications will be dismissed as having no personal appeal or interest; the products featured do not offer benefits which an individual is seeking at that time. Of those market communications that are accepted, only a limited number of concepts about specific products or services is likely to be comprehended and become part of the cognitive map of an individual consumer. Attention, therefore, is selectively given, so mere exposure, or (as the advertising researchers' jargon puts it) 'opportunities to see', by no means guarantees that a particular advertisment has actually been perceived.

Furthermore, perception is subjective; individuals tend to interpret information according to their existing beliefs, attitudes, and general disposition. Messages may be distorted by 'sharpening', i.e., adding new elements to make them fit in with existing predispositions and value systems. For example, some people are very interested in diet, nutrition, and health, and may therefore, be unusually sensitive to information, including advertisements, about fresh vegetables, fruit, and vitamins. They may tend to add new dimensions to some of this information to support their beliefs and practices.

'Levelling' may also occur where messages are simplified, perhaps by removing dissonant elements, so that they are acceptable. Warnings against dangers of smoking, which have to be included by government order on advertising and packaging of cigarettes in Britain, are likely to be 'screened out' by habitual smokers.

Perception is subject, then, to thresholds of awareness. Before any sensory experience is possible, stimuli have to attain what is known as the 'absolute threshold'; these will vary considerably for individuals and circumstances. In addition, there is what is termed the 'differential threshold', which refers to the perceived difference between two stimuli competing for attention at the same time. This is a relative measure: the stronger the initial intensity of one stimulus, the greater will have to be the competing stimulus in order to be distinguished. This has been described as Weber's law and is given thus:

$$\frac{\Delta I}{I} = K$$

where ΔI is the smallest amount of extra input to one stimulus that will establish a noticeable difference between the two stimuli

I is the intensity of the original stimulus

K is a constant that varies across the senses.

'Adaptation' describes those situations where people tend to adapt to continued reception of the same stimuli; for example, those, who live near to railways or busy roads often fail to notice the traffic noise which, to a newcomer, would probably seem excessive. If these visitors stayed for long, they would probably adjust to the noise, i.e., it would sink below their threshold of attention. Habitual response blunts perception; advertising has a well-known 'wear-out factor': after a time it ceases to attract the attention of many of those to whom it is projected, so new campaigns have to be planned. Price reductions regularly featured in a store lose a great deal of their impact because they are no longer novel, unless some really swingeing cuts are made which suddenly break through the barrier of indifference. Again, thresholds are not objective measures: different people at various times are likely to have distinct sensitivities to certain stimuli. A hungry person, for example, will be more alert to illuminated signs indicating the site of a restaurant than one who has recently eaten.

Marketing communications are subject, therefore, to selective and distorted perception before being assimilated by consumers. Moreover, the same messages may be interpreted quite differently by individual consumers, although within defined social and cultural groups similar reactions may be expected. Members of a particular culture tend to form similar cognitive systems that direct the social actions of the individual. People may differ quite strongly from one another about an event they witnessed, or in their assessments of the value of a product or service. 'There are no impartial facts. Data do not have a logic of their own that results in the same cognitions for all people.'[4]

Perception of the physical attributes of products is a matter of particular interest to marketers. A classical example of the influence of branding on the perceived taste of beer occurred in an experiment undertaken by Allison and Uhl[5] to test the hypothesis that beer drinkers were able to distinguish between major brands of unlabelled beers. A sample of 326 male beer drinkers (who drank beer at least three times a week) was randomly selected. Each drinker was given a six-pack of unlabelled beer identified merely by alphabetical letters. Each pack contained three brands, one of which was the brand the subject had indicated earlier that he most often drank. Participants were asked to rate the beer for general overall taste on a 10-point rating scale, and to rate it also for specific qualities. After a week, drinkers were given new six-packs which had labels identifying brands in the usual way. As a group, the 'blind' test drinkers were generally unable to distinguish 'their' brand of beer: they rated it about the same as the other brands. But when the packs were labelled (in the second test), they rated all the beers higher and their 'own' beer highest of all. The only condition in the experiment that had been changed was the labelling of the beers, and yet the findings were that most beer drinkers could not identify their favoured brand of beer in a 'blind' taste test.

Hence, perceived differences in products may not necessarily depend on intrinsic qualities; consumers evaluate products against the background of their experiences, expectations, and associations. Perception is seldom an objective, scientific assessment of the comparative values of competing brands of a product. It is a personal interpretation of the information about a specific product which has been successful in attaining a level of significance in a particular consumer's mind.

Perceptions about people and objects may change as more information becomes available to an individual, and as personal needs develop during the course of life. Experiences with a particular brand of a household product may have been disappointing: the service offered in a retail store or garage may be perceived to have deteriorated; a strong personal appeal may have been established by a competitive advertising campaign; or the growing public sensitivity to harmful food additives, for example, may have influenced personal beliefs about the brand of a food product customarily bought. Changing family needs, increased amounts of disposable income, or more sophisticated tastes, may also alter perceptions about some products:

As people acquire new wants, they are led to seek out new information, to learn more. As they learn more about a subject, new wants may be induced, thus impelling them to learn still more. It is also possible, of course, that changes in wants may inhibit the seeking of more information . . . the problems of wants and cognitive change is a complicated one.[2]

Even when provided with new information (which may logically demand change, as in the case of the published data on the dangers of smoking), emotions and personal needs may be so dominant that they preclude change taking place in an individual cognitive structure.

2.6 SUBLIMINAL PERCEPTION

Discussion of thresholds leads to the subject of subliminal perception, which has attracted popular interest because of its alleged powers of hidden persuasion. It has been asserted that consumers have been exposed to some type of 'brainwashing' from messages projected at their subconscious minds. Below the threshold of absolute awareness (see pages 23–24) experiments by James Vicary in the 1950s were reported to have been made in connection with popcorn and Coke advertisements which were flashed on a cinema screen in the USA at speeds well below the audience's threshold. The slogans 'Drink Coke' and 'Eat popcorn', projected subliminally, were said to have increased sales of Coca Cola by nearly 60 per cent and popcorn sales by about 18 per cent over a six-week period in the concession stands. This dramatic event has been subjected to considerable scrutiny over the years, and the general findings of several investigations are that the experiments lacked validity because, for example, there were no adequate controls or provision for replication.

Vicary was, in fact, challenged by the Copy Research Council—a group of research directors and top copywriters in New York—to repeat his reported test. He had little choice but to comply, and a second test was devised, following the same procedures as before. However, no increases in the sales of either Coca Cola or popcorn resulted. In a later interview by *Advertising Age*, Vicary confessed that his 'subliminal' advertising claim was only a ploy to attract support for his failing research organization.[6]

While this particular research can be rejected, the question of subliminal stimuli may not be so readily discarded. While such messages are necessarily brief and personal, perceptual defences may be high—and will certainly vary in strength—and the likelihood of subliminal stimuli being really effective is open to considerable doubt. The Institute of Practitioners in Advertising have condemned such advertising practices in the UK, and the Pilkington Committee on Broadcasting, reporting in 1982, recommended a ban on any subliminal promotions. However, the science correspondent of the *Daily Telegraph* reported in 1981 that subliminal messages, broadcast continuously in a New Orleans supermarket, had ended pilfering that had cost about £40 000 a year.[7]

In another case, it was reported that a machine called Becker's Black Box, devised by the Becker Behavioral Engineering Corporation of Metarie, Louisiana, had raised business considerably in a New York real estate office by whispering continuously: 'My time is valuable . . . dollars now'. The science correspondent viewed with some reserve these and other applications of subliminal messages. Big Brother is not a very nice sort of relative to have around.

2.7 CHARACTERISTICS INFLUENCING COGNITIVE CHANGE

Ballachey has postulated that cognitive change is partly controlled by the characteristics that already exist in a cognitive system. He described 'three main systematic characteristics':

multiplexity, consonance, and interconnectedness.[4] The first of these characteristics refers to the degree of complexity existing within a cognitive system. Some consumers, for example, may have extremely complex sets of beliefs about food: they may elaborate on nutritional values, hygiene attributes, ease of preparation, cultural and social significance, etc. Food is not merely sustenance; it is viewed as a sophisticated subject that has almost endless permutations. The degree to which individuals are able to achieve a balance between these various aspects of a particular kind of food will define their cognitive consonance. The more complex the cognitions in the system, the more difficult it tends to become for consonance to be achieved. The third characteristic—interconnectedness—relates to the degree of relationship between sets of cognitions in an individual structure. For example, the Jewish faith closely integrates personal hygiene and food with religious observances; beliefs and practices are interdependent and result in a distinctive type of cultural behaviour.

Although it is conceded that the impact of multiplexity and interconnectedness of cognitive change 'are complex and little understood',[4] there appears to be a general movement towards attaining an internal harmony or consonance in a cognitive structure. Because individuals vary in their abilities to tolerate strain and imbalance, a general level of consonance does not apply. Some individuals, by their education and professional training, may be able to deal more effectively with situations which may pose serious problems for less experienced people.

Cognitions are not abstract concepts; they are intimately connected to the personal needs and ambitions of individuals, and are intimately associated with perception.

2.8 COGNITIVE DISSONANCE

The theory of cognitive dissonance was propounded by Leon Festinger, Professor of Psychology at Stanford, California, in 1957.[8] It has two underlying hypotheses:

1. The existence of dissonance, being psychologically uncomfortable, will motivate the person to try to reduce the dissonance and achieve consonance.
2. When dissonance is present, in addition to trying to reduce it, the person will actively avoid situations and information which would be likely to increase dissonance.

Individuals strive towards consistence (consonance, agreement, equilibrium) within their cognitive structure (set of beliefs about people, products, events, etc.) and endeavour to reduce tension so as to make life pleasant. Dissonance (disharmony, frustration) is a state of psychological tension which may result from purchasing a product, particularly if it is an expensive one. 'The magnitude of post-decision dissonance is an increasing function of the general importance of the decision and of the relative attractiveness of the unchosen alternatives.'[8]

When a choice has to be made among several products or versions of a product, buyers are likely to experience some anxiety, which will tend to become more intrusive after a commitment to purchase has been made. Buyers may experience some doubts as to the wisdom of their choice, particularly when the qualities of rejected alternative products are brought to their notice, either through advertisements or by word of mouth. The product to which they are now committed may fail to live up to their expectations in some way or other. Its 'negative' features may begin to cause nagging doubts: the buyers are, in fact, experiencing post-decisional dissonance.

According to Festinger's theory, buyers in this situation will endeavour to reassure themselves by seeking information in support of their chosen product, and also by avoiding sources of information which are likely to reduce their buying confidence. They may, in addition, actively collect data which reflect disadvantageously on the alternative products. In order to reduce dissonance, buyers may, therefore, select information favourable to their choice of product, and at the same time, distort or dismiss unpleasant facts. People are selective in their perception, and tend to collect information congruent with their existing beliefs and attitudes.

The reassurance theory of advertising recognizes that buyers may experience dissonance after purchasing some products, and it is suggested that advertising messages should be aimed at present users as well as potential users of products. Various studies have indicated that 'reassurance advertising' has practical value in marketing strategies. Two US researchers were concerned with its impact on car advertising: 'A great deal of advertising, contrary to what one might expect, is read after rather than before the car is bought, and serves to repersuade the reader that he has been wise and practical: Cadillac is well aware of this and its advertisements constantly pat the owner on the back for his good taste and rationality'.[9] Sheth has commented on dissonance theory related to advertising readership data: 'Starch has found that for both non-durable and durable goods, ad readership of a specific brand is higher among users of the brand than among non-users. Brown has noted that 90% of the people who had recently purchased a Ford read Ford advertisements'.[10]

There is some evidence, therefore, that advertisements for certain products tend to be read more after purchase in order, possibly, to reduce dissonance. Of course, the purchaser of a specific brand or type of product will tend to be 'sensitized', i.e., more aware of other owners, but this does not entirely explain the phenomenon. Admittedly, it is difficult to measure the effect of 'reassuring' advertisements, though this could probably be done successfully using some of the techniques of motivation research.

Marketers of many kinds of products should take note of the need to dispel dissonance, otherwise repeat business may not be forthcoming, and existing customers would be unlikely to recommend prospective users to buy their particular choice of product.

Manufacturers can reassure customers through efficient after-sales service. The successful Volkswagen operation in Britain has been built on first-class spares and servicing facilities. Weighbridge manufacturers or switchgear suppliers have consistently backed their products by special after-sales service. In several other industrial product markets, 'package deals' involving the supply, installation, and servicing of equipment help to overcome buyers' legitimate anxieties and confirm their judgement in selecting particular suppliers. Domestic appliance, television, and video manufacturers offer special guarantees as optional extras.

Instruction manuals should contain information that reassures purchasers; the introductory pages may well be devoted to complimenting buyers on their choice. 'Guarantee' cards which are mailed to manufacturers for registration of purchase could be the signal for a letter to be sent to customers offering them advice on the use of the product, details of service agents, and leaflets could also be enclosed which illustrate associated products made by a manufacturer. 'Reassurance' information could also be printed on packaging so that the advertising message is taken right to the point of purchase.

Dissonance reduction should also be an active duty of the sales force. Experienced sales staff realize that unless customers feel happy about the products or services they buy, repeat orders are unlikely. In Chapter 10 on organizational buying behaviour, it will be shown that the manufacturer's salesperson is regarded as a highly reliable and valued source of information. Opportunities obviously exist for sales staff to reassure buyers and to build goodwill for future business.

2.9 CRITICAL REVIEW OF COGNITIVE DISSONANCE THEORY

A critical review of the empirical evidence of cognitive dissonance related to consumer behaviour was made by Cummings and Venkatesan.[11] They identified two categories of studies:

those concerned with the effects of dissonance arousal on attitude change and the tendency to repurchase, and those concerned with the effects of dissonance arousal on selective information seeking by consumers.

It was found that most research had focused on attitude change and the tendency to repurchase as the dependent measure, and in general the findings had supported the theory. However, the evidence related to information-seeking behaviour was held to be questionable. On balance, 'the evidence in favour of the applicability of dissonance theory is more voluminous and somewhat more substantial than the evidence against'. From study of the research that has taken place over a wide range of products, cognitive dissonance theory was said to provide the best single explanation that can account for all the results across these reported cases. But some degree of caution is nevertheless advisable in discussing the supportive evidence because of certain experimental limitations.

2.10 A DISSONANCE STUDY: *WHEN PROPHECY FAILS*

What is now virtually a classic study of the influence of dissonance occurred in the USA in the mid-1950s and was recorded by Festinger et al.[12] Mrs Marion Keech of Lake City, USA, had attracted a group of followers who believed that she had received messages 'sent to her by superior beings from a planet called "Clarion".' These messengers had arrived in flying saucers to warn her of an imminent flood that would 'spread to form an inland sea stretching from the Arctic Circle to the Gulf of Mexico'. This would be accompanied by a cataclysm that would 'submerge the West Coast from Seattle, Washington to Chile in South America'.

Festinger and his colleagues joined the group, who were prepared to abandon their occupations, homes, and friends, and to await arrival of a flying saucer which, it was said, would take them 'to a place of safety in outer space'. The little band of believers waited until midnight of 20 December, when a Visitor had been predicted to call and escort them to safety. But there was no strange visitation or flood; only intense despair and disillusion were experienced by the group. However, Mrs Keech eventually announced that she had since received another message to say that the group's behaviour had so pleased God that the threatened cataclysm had been averted.

By this ingenious 'rationalization', the group was able to explain its behaviour and overcome dissonance. Reality had been distorted so that failure of the prophecy was consonant with group activities. The suppression of unpleasant facts and the promotion (and even invention) of favourable facts have marketing implications, although not necessarily related to space travel.

2.11 LEARNING PROCESSES

Howard has commented: 'Commonsense suggests the importance of learning in buyer behaviour'.[13] Customers buy the same brand of product again because experience (i.e., learning) with the earlier purchase has been satisfactory. If this pattern of buying is consistent over a period of time, a buying habit is formed and brand loyalty develops. Through the learning process, a buyer of goods or services will develop attitudes; if these are unfavourable, then the likelihood of repeat purchases is problematical. Buying situations may, of course, be simple or sophisticated and involve elaborate systems of acquiring knowledge, as in the case of computer installations. Organizational buying frequently entails, acquiring considerable amounts of information about technical specifications, relative qualities of comparative materials, sophisticated pricing techniques, and so on.

The process of learning is a fundamental activity which has been the subject of countless empirical studies affecting both human and animal behaviour. Some of these researches have resulted in contradictory theories and explanations so that there is no general agreement about the nature of learning. Thouless has drawn attention to the fact that a great deal of the 'early experimental investigation of learning was made by means of animals, and the first tendency was to attribute the power of learning to the operation of a few somewhat mechanical laws'.[14] This overlooked that human behaviour is far more varied than animal behaviour 'and the fact that language may be used for the purpose of modifying behaviour introduce obvious differences from the learning even of the most advanced sub-human vertebrates'.

2.12 DEFINITIONS OF LEARNING

From the earliest years, everyone is involved in the process of learning: this is likely to become more formal and sophisticated, until, at least, the stage of maturity. It occurs most intensively in childhood, and 'falls off rapidly with old age'.[14] Learning has been defined as the 'more or less permanent change in behaviour which occurs as a result of practice'; it acts as an 'intervening, unobserved variable linking the two sets of observables'[15] shown in the following model:

Suggested independent variables		*Suggested dependent variables*
Repetition		Trend in behaviour
Activity		Changes in behaviour
Behaviour		Incremental modification
Practice	Learning	of behaviour
Training		
Observation		
Experience		

On the left of the model are descriptions of the 'successive exposure of the organism to the same situation'. The right-hand side contains 'a series of obviously parallel alternatives expressing the idea that learning produces progressive changes in behaviour'.

Markin observes that narrow definitions of learning, such as the acquisition of knowledge or skill received from instruction or by study, are inadequate.[1] He supports a more psychologically based approach which is concerned with the response tendencies, the memory processes, and the acquisition of insight into a situation.

Learning itself cannot, of course, be observed; the 'end product', i.e., behaviour patterns and the changes that may have taken place in them as the result of the learning process, may be observed. Learning, therefore, involves relatively permanent change in behaviour, resulting from experience, insight, and practice.

Britt has pointed out the relevance of the psychological principles of learning to advertising: 'Every time an advertisement or commercial appears, the objective is to have the reader or viewer *learn* something . . . and *remember* what he learned'.[16] Whether or not they recognize it, advertising practitioners are constantly immersed in the principles of learning, which they would do well to understand.

Learning is not confined, therefore, to scholastic endeavours or academic subjects: it is basic to human behaviour, including buying behaviour. If the experience with a product or service is satisfactory, reinforcement takes place which may lead to repeat purchase. On the other hand, if the experience has been disappointing, a negative reinforcement will occur and the likelihood of similar purchases is reduced.

2.13 LEARNING THEORIES

There are many theoretical models of the learning process. Two general schools of thought may be identified: connectionist and cognitive. Within these generic classifications, several variations occur.

Connectionist theories are based on the association between stimulus and response; learning is postulated as being the development of behaviour (response) as the result of a subject being exposed to a stimulus. Perception and insight are not regarded as significant influences in the learning process.

Some connectionists rely on *classical conditioning* as an explanation of learning. Two objects or ideas are connected by the prospect of a reward being given as the result of certain action. Alternatively, some punishment may follow in specific situations. This pleasure–pain theory has been widely researched in laboratory experiments, and is observed in everyday life. For example, children are trained to respond to certain signs of approval or disapproval by their parents or teachers.

Pavlov's experiments on conditioned reflexes in dogs are well known. He had observed that the mere sight of food stimulated dogs to salivate: this he interpreted as an unlearned response, termed an *unconditional* response or reflex (often called an *unconditioned* reflex). He then experimented by introducing a conditioning stimulus, namely a bell that was rung several times immediately prior to food being given. Eventually he was able to get dogs to salivate (a *conditional* reflex but often called a *conditioned* reflex) when they heard the bell and without the actual presentation of food. As the experiments continued, Pavlov discovered that the amount of saliva activated by the bell increased and followed the classical learning curve, flattening out after a certain number of trials had been effected. Hence, it would be necessary to reinforce an unconditioning stimulus to avoid 'extinction' taking place.

Classical conditioning, therefore, has been defined as 'the formation of an association between a conditioned stimulus and a response through the repeated presentation of the conditioned stimulus in a controlled relationship with an unconditioned stimulus that originally elicts that response'.[17]

Conditional responses may have some applications in marketing. For example, the same advertising theme repeated many times is likely to result in extinction of its impact; special offers may lapse but even then satisfied buyers may continue to purchase the specific brand of product because of the strong association formed. How far the salivary glands of consumers could be activated by a secondary stimulus would be open to some interesting speculation. The prospect of reward (or punishment) may stimulate behaviour, of course, such as seeing an inn sign indicating that a certain brew of beer is available, and being tempted to drop in and have a pint or two. The pleasure–pain theory of learning, related to classical conditioning, has had extensive research to support it, although it has been suggested that the extension of the concept of the conditional reflex from the limited field in which it has been established as a useful concept to a wider explanatory principle concerned with all acquired behaviour—of both humans and animals—may have been due more to Pavlov's less critical followers than to his own research findings.[13]

Among the connectionists are some reinforcement theorists including Thorndike, Hull, and Skinner.

Thorndike undertook classical research into the behaviour of cats in puzzle boxes from which they could escape by clawing at a string or lever in order to obtain food.[18] This trial-and-error learning is entirely mechanical: the cats at first made many useless and apparently random movements, before alighting by chance on one that activated the release mechanism. Thorndike's *law of effect* stated that the creation of a strong S–R association depended on the effects (reward or punishment) that followed the response. In further experiments, it was noted that the animals were likely to arrive earlier at the appropriate release movements, because of past experience. Thorndike did not consider that the results of his experiments with cats could be applied indiscriminately. He regarded them as valid merely for those particular animals or for others below their evolutionary level.

Hull extended the law of effect, relating it more closely to motivational factors.[19] He asserted that both association and selective trial-and-error learning occur because they are able to satisfy needs. Hull, unlike Pavlov and the earlier associationists, discarded the principle of sheer contiguity as a sufficient condition for learning. He insisted that learning occurs only if it satisfies a particular need. Hence, the process of learning is influenced by motivation; a response will follow a conditioning stimulus only if the former is likely to result in satisfaction of a need. According to Hull, a reduction of needs is the activator of learning; an organism is stimulated into taking action—perhaps by trial-and-error learning—in an effort to reduce the tension arising from a felt need. (Motivation is discussed in Chapter 3.) Hull's theory of learning based on habit formation had four variables: the number of reinforcements or trials; the magnitude of the reward; the time delay in reception of the reward; and the time elapsed between stimulus and response. Hence, the strength of habit is dependent upon several variables, and the theory is, therefore, rather more sophisticated in its approach than simple S–R learning behaviour.

Skinner introduced the concept of *operant conditioning*, the term 'operant' referring to the fact that, through a system of rewards, punishment and positive reinforcement, the operant 'behaviour' acts on the environment to produce some effect.[20] Hence, the learner is not merely submissive to some unconditional stimulus: action has to be taken. At Harvard, Skinner designed what became known as the Skinner Box, which was used to train animals (rats and pigeons) to learn approximate responses. Inside this sound-proofed environment, buttons or levers could be pressed by the experimental animals; correct responses produced food, water, and escape.

Skinner developed the theory of conditioned reflex by distinguishing between *elicited* and *emitted* responses.[20] The former refer to responses to stimuli (such as Pavlov's dogs salivating at the sight of food), while the latter is of the operant type, i.e., an activity takes place (as in the case of Thorndike's cats pressing levers or pulling strings). It would appear that Skinner's interpretation of the conditioned reflex theory has some relevance to consumer buying behaviour. The stimulus of an advertising message offering a new brand of instant coffee at a special price may induce people to ask for the product at the supermarket. Intervening variables may, however, be influential in modifying or nullifying, the stimulus; hence a simple S–R theory does not seem to be an adequate explanation of buying behaviour. The S–R model was popularized in the advertising business by John B. Watson, whose behaviourism emphasized that advertising messages needed to be endlessly repeated to ensure that viewers were influenced sufficiently to buy.[21] Buying habits related to particular brands of products could become imprinted on consumers' minds by a constant flow of advertising. According to Watson, advertisers by means of repetition and reinforcement were able to etch what impressions they wished on the receptive minds of their audiences.

This view of consumer psychology has obvious limitations. It does not admit that consumers exercise subjective and selective perception and that disappointing experiences with an advertised product are likely to affect buying behaviour. Further, the influence of subconscious motivations is ignored. On the one hand, there is an element of truth in the Watsonian approach to advertising's influence, particularly with relatively low-priced products which are bought regularly. Buying habits tend to develop because they simplify the process of obtaining food and other necessities. Buying 'rules' may be formed: e.g., 'Stick to X brand of instant coffee—the flavour is what we all like', or, negatively, 'Don't buy Y brand of tights—they never last long'. Routine buying tends to encourage habitual patterns of buying behaviour, but these do not become entirely automatic. Reasoned judgement may not actively intervene at the time of purchase, though it would be incorrect to describe the activity as irrational. It tends to be non-rational in the sense that many purchases of this nature may not demand conscious and considered evaluations *every* time they are made. Hence the interest of advertisers in constantly reminding consumers of the advantages of buying specific brands of products. Advertising agencies recommend that their clients should invest in planned *series* of advertisements within a defined period of time. Frequency and recency of exposure are two cardinal tenets of advertising practice.

Operant conditioning differs from the classical S–R (classical conditioning) model of learning, because no natural or unlearned stimulus is introduced to initiate a response. Rather, *unsolicited* responses emitted by the subject are rewarded, i.e., reinforced;[13] these tend to be repeated more frequently. In operant conditioning, learners make a *voluntary* effort to respond, and are motivated by certain needs that they wish to gratify. This may result in positive reinforcement, if the experience is rewarding, or negative reinforcement, if otherwise. In classical conditioning, the learning process is *involuntary*; learners do not initiate responses but are essentially submissive in the experiment.

Both classical conditioning and operant conditioning involve the establishment of an association between stimulus and response, but they do not give insight into the learner, who is, in the simplest interpretation of the connectionist model of learning, regarded as being readily influenced by whatever stimuli (e.g., advertising) may have been applied. Reward and reinforcement are principles of both classical and operant learning; constant repetition reinforces behaviour so that habits become formed. Television viewing may largely be habitual with certain types of consumers; their critical faculties may be little exercised during addictive viewing. Push-button entertainment of this nature demands little or no dynamic activity.

However, Kassarjian[22] has proposed that since most consumer buying decisions tend to be 'unimportant, uninvolved, insignificant and minor', relatively simple explanations derived from behavioural learning theory, instrumental conditioning or operant conditioning, based on Skinner's and Thorndike's classical experiments, might well be considered adequate.

2.14 COGNITIVE THEORIES

Consideration will now be given to the main alternative school of thought on learning; this involves insight and cognitive processes. Cognitivists reject the proposition that human behaviour rests solely on the basis of stimulus–response plus reinforcement. Learning is viewed as the process of restructuring the cognitions of an individual related to specific problems. This perceptual restructuring results in insight, which is a distinctive characteristic of intellectual activity. Problem-solving is the daily preoccupation of consumers; information about products and services may be obtained either deliberately (planned) or accidentally (incidental). Knowledge of products or brands tends to be gained principally as the result of incidental learning through the reception and retention of advertising messages. After reception, advertising messages may be assimilated and stored with other experiences which help to form general attitudes towards the advertised product or brand. At some later time, an event may cause individuals to recall the information which they have 'accidentally' learned, and, provided they have the means and opportunity to purchase, they may buy the product advertised.

Consumers may, of course, also acquire knowledge about products on a planned basis. For example, readers of consumer guidance magazines such as *Which?* tend to approach the purchase of some products on a systematic (planned) learning basis. The qualities of competing products are carefully studied, and such information is usually regarded as highly reliable and objective.

The information gathered from this form of deliberate learning is then added to the existing store of knowledge acquired from past experience and/or from viewing advertisements. This new information may reinforce existing knowledge and so strengthen prevailing attitudes; or, possibly it may cause some dissonance, through being at variance with preconceived ideas about a product. In the latter case, buyers may wish to reduce this tension by seeking (see Sec. 2.8) additional information favourable to their earlier attitudes, or they may reject the dissonant information entirely, or attempt to modify it so that it will fit in with their existing attitude structure. The new model of car which they admire may have rated rather low on safety features compared with less stylish cars. If their personal preferences are still strongly favourable towards the new model, despite its indifferent safety rating, would-be buyers may emphasize more strongly those features (e.g., styling or economy) which help to support their existing favourable attitude. Buyers may consider that, as experienced motorists, the safety features of that particular model of car are not so important as they would be to a novice driver.

Cognitive theories of learning are particularly valuable, therefore, because they take into account the formation and effect of attitudes on behaviour and consumers are viewed as active problem-solvers who are affected by the environment in which their needs develop. Asch has stressed that 'Human actions, even the most lowly, are marked by a quality of intelligence or insight. . . . Our actions are permeated with inferences . . . we may fumble and engage in trial and error, but it almost never has the blind character that associationistic doctrines impute to it'.[23]

The *Gestalt* view of learning, based on Gestalt psychology, is closely associated with the cognitive theory of learning. A group of psychologists, among whom were Wertheimer, Köhler, Koffka, and Lewin, developed a distinctive type of experimental psychology. They postulated that the perceptual field contained individual stimuli which could be segregated from the total field; these they termed *Gestalten* or 'configurations'. Phenomena should be studied as total, organized entities and not just as aggregates of distinct parts. 'Thus if three equidistant dots are placed on a sheet of paper they form a segregated whole of triangular shape. If a large number of similar dots are added, this unification of the three dots may be lost and they may simply be elements in an irregular pattern of dots'.[14] The term 'Gestalt' was used to describe the fact that perception of an object involved an appreciation of its total nature. This derived from its part or configurations, and it in turn gave them meaning.

The basis of this theory is that the whole is more than the sum of its parts: a melody, for instance, is more than any one of its constituent notes. When confronted with a television commercial, the viewer can organize the projected message through the complementary stimuli of vision and sound-track. In a supermarket, a shopper may readily select a particular brand of packaged food, because of a well-organized, overall perception of the product, involving taste, cost, convenience in preparation, and so on.

In the area of consumer behaviour, Wroe Alderson has popularized the Gestalt approach, which supports the cognitive learning theory of the consumer as a problem-solver whose perception of the buying process involves a comprehensive evaluation of all the factors— economic, psychological, sociological, etc. 'Advertising strategy must take account of both gullibility and gumption, of human needs both instrumental and symbolic. In the long-run the odds are in favour of a strategy which takes rational problem solving as a fundamental aspect of human behaviour'.[24]

This view is also taken by Markin, who notes that according to the Gestalt theory of cognitive learning the 'perceptual' or 'cognitive' field of a consumer may be of prime interest to the marketer.[1] By changing or adding to the cognitions held by an individual buyer, the seller may be able to influence product choice. 'This change of the cognitive field is, to the cognitive theorists, learning; thus the seller must more or less "teach" the consumer to prefer his product or brand over those of competitors'.

An associated theory of learning based on the Gestalt viewpoint relates to Lewin's field theory.[25] Joseph Clawson developed a model of buyer behaviour which extends Lewinian theory in particular directions.

2.15 BRIDGING THE GAP

Tolman attempted to bridge the gap between the connectionist and the cognitive theories. He took the simple S–R theory and modified it by introducing an intervening variable. This intervening influence referred to perceptions and beliefs (i.e., cognitions) which act as organizing forces in guiding responses and in selecting stimuli. This may be shown as: S–O–R (O stands for 'organizing force').[26]

Tolman was influenced by the Gestalt school, and he introduced the 'sign-Gestalt' as an explanatory principle in his experiments with rats. Individuals are led to believe that certain kinds of behaviour will be likely to result in the achievement of desirable goals or objectives: their expectations are derived from 'signs' (i.e., stimuli) that suggest the responses likely to result in attaining the objectives in mind. His theory could be applied to marketing behaviour related to advertising or packaging (which are stimuli or 'signs') aimed to persuade the consumer to take action (i.e., to respond by purchasing a particular brand of product). If the product is satisfactory in use, reinforcement is likely to occur and thus may result in further purchases.

Bayton has noted this process:

> When consumption or utilisation of the goal-object leads to gratification of the initiating needs there is 'reinforcement'. . . . This type of behavioural change—increasing likelihood that an act will be repeated—is learning; and reinforcement is necessary for learning to take place. Continued reinforcement will influence the cognitive processes. Memory of the goal-object will be increasingly enhanced; particular sign-expectancies will be more and more firmly established; and the generalisation gradient will be changed in that the psychological distance on this gradient between brand A and the competing brands will be increased.[27]

The influence of intervening variables between stimuli and responses in the psychological field has also been observed by Katona: 'as the result of past experience there exist habits, attitudes and motives which intervene by influencing how stimuli are perceived and how the organism reacts to them. The response then is a function of both the environment and the person'.[28]

2.16 STOCHASTIC LEARNING MODELS

Since the mid-1950s, some researchers have developed particular interest in learning theory related to mathematical models containing stochastic or probabilistic elements. Models of this nature have been originated by Estes[29] and Bush and Mosteller.[30] Kuehn[31] has extended the Bush–Mosteller model of learning. Some of these studies have been applied to the phenomenon of brand switching, an area of research that is still developing.

Consumers, as Fitzroy observes, differ in their buying behaviour because of different attitudes, socio-economic characteristics, etc.;[32] some stochastic models assume heterogeneous populations, while others assume that homogeneity is applicable. Another aspect of these models is the unit of analysis, which is generally taken to be 'the housewife', ignoring, therefore, the effects of intra-household communication. A further point raised by Fitzroy relates to the fact that some products have more than one 'use occasion' and brand choice may not be constant for all these uses.

The basic approach of stochastic learning models rests on the hypothesis that individual consumers learn from their past experiences in buying—the degree of satisfaction (or otherwise) obtained—and these have some influence on their future buying behaviour. The most recent buying experiences with a particular brand or product will have greater effect than those that took place at a more distant time. On this thesis, the Bush–Mosteller model is generally built, but it is also possible to construct a model that will take into account the pattern of experiences over *all* past events.

Over a period of time, it is assumed that the relative frequencies with which a certain brand of a product is purchased by an individual consumer can be analysed and mathematical probabilities calculated. These will be useful in determining the likelihood of a consumer's shifting from one brand to another. If past buying behaviour involved the purchase of other brands, these will be reckoned to have a negative influence on the current brand purchased. As already noted, the model suffers from serious limitations: it is applicable only to 'a closed market with well-established brands having homogeneous product-price relations and good distribution'.[10] There are, therefore, serious constraints in the application of stochastic learning models, although they offer an interesting method for exploring consumer buying patterns in specific product fields. How far these techniques can be developed to be reliable indicators in dynamic market conditions does not appear so far to be determined.

2.17 SUMMARY

Cognitions, perceptions, and learning are fundamental factors influencing human behaviour in general and buying behaviour in particular. Cognitions and perceptions are closely linked: perceptions arise from stimulation of the senses which tend to be used in combination. Personal factors such as the span of apprehension affect perception, which is inherently subjective. People develop individual cognitive maps or sets of knowledge covering persons and objects. They try to attain cognitive harmony, otherwise dissonance occurs, to which Festinger's theory relates. Knowledge of learning processes is important for marketers: two main theories are connectionist and cognitive. Association, reinforcement, and motivation are important factors in learning. Connectionist learning theories are based on S–R, and two versions are classical conditioning and operant conditioning. Cognitive theories of learning are more comprehensive and involve the restructuring of cognitions held by an individual. Tolman's S–O–R theory attempts to bridge the gap between the two schools of learning theory. Stochastic learning models are based on probability theory, but care is needed in using them.

REFERENCES

1. Markin, Ron J., *The Psychology of Consumer Behaviour*, Prentice-Hall, Englewood Cliffs, New Jersey, 1969.
2. Bliss, Perry, *Marketing Management and the Behavioural Environment*, Prentice-Hall, Englewood Cliffs, New Jersey, 1970.
3. Young, Paul Thomas, *Motivation and Emotion: A Survey of the Determinants of Human and Animal Activity*, John Wiley, New York, 1961.
4. Krech, David, Richard S. Crutchfield, and Egerton L. Ballachey, *Individual in Society*, McGraw-Hill, New York, 1962.
5. Allison, Ralph L., and Kenneth P. Uhl, 'Influence of beer brand identification on taste perception', *Journal of Marketing Research*, vol. 1, August 1964.

6. Weir, Walter, *How to Create Interest-evoking, Sales-inducing, Non-irritating Advertising*, Haworth Press, New York, 1993.
7. 'Subliminal messages deter shoplifters', *Daily Telegraph*, 17 February 1981.
8. Festinger, Leon, *A Theory of Cognitive Dissonance*, Stanford University Press, California, 1975.
9. Riesman, David, and Eric Larrabee, 'Autos in America', in: *Consumer Behaviour*, Lincoln Clerk (ed.), Harper, New York, 1958.
10. Sheth, Jagdish N., 'A review of buyer behaviour', *Management Science*, vol. 13, no. 12, August 1967.
11. Cummings, William H., and M. Venkatesan, 'Cognitive dissonance and consumer behaviour: a review of the evidence', *Journal of Marketing Research*, vol. 13, August 1976.
12. Festinger, L., H. W. Riecken Jnr, and S. Schachter, *When Prophecy Fails*, University of Minnesota Press, Minneapolis, 1956.
13. Howard, John A., *Marketing Theory*, Allyn and Bacon, Boston, Massachusetts, 1965.
14. Thouless, R. H., *General and Social Psychology*, University Tutorial Press, London, 1967.
15. Hilgard, Ernest R., and Donald G. Marquis, *Conditioning and Learning*, Appleton-Century-Crofts, New York, 1961.
16. Britt, Stuart-Henderson, 'How advertising can use psychology's rules of learning', *Printers Ink*, no. 252, September 1955.
17. Hilgard, Ernest R., Richard C. Atkinson, and Rita L. Atkinson, *Introduction to Psychology*, Harcourt Brace Jovanovich, New York, 1975.
18. Thorndike, Edward L., *The Psychology of Learning*, Bureau of Publications, Teachers College, Columbia University, New York, 1913.
19. Hull, C. L., *Principles of Behaviour*, Appleton-Century-Crofts, New York, 1943.
20. Skinner, B. F., *Science and Human Behaviour*, Free Press, New York, 1953.
21. Watson, John B., *Behaviourism*, People's Institute Publishing Co., New York, 1925.
22. Kassarjian, H. H., 'Presidential address, 1977: anthroposorphism and parsimony', in: *Advances in Consumer Research*, vol. V., H. K. Hunt (ed.), Ann Arbor Association for Consumer Research, Michigan, 1978.
23. Asch, Solomon E., *Social Psychology*, Prentice-Hall, Englewood Cliffs, New Jersey, 1965.
24. Alderson, Wroe, 'Motivation', in: *Consumer Behaviour*, A. S. C. Ehrenberg and F. G. Pyatt (eds), Penguin, London, 1971.
25. Lewin, Kurt, *A Dynamic Theory of Personality*, McGraw-Hill, New York, 1935.
26. Tolman, Edward C., *Purposive Behaviour in Animals and Men*, Appleton-Century, New York, 1932.
27. Bayton, James A., 'Motivation, cognition, learning—basic factors in consumer behaviour', *Journal of Marketing*, vol. 22, January 1958.
28. Katona, George, *The Powerful Consumer*, McGraw-Hill, New York, 1960.
29. Estes, W. K., 'Individual behaviour in uncertain situations: an interpretation in terms of statistical association theory', in: *Decision Processes*, R. M. Thrall *et al.* (eds), John Wiley, New York, 1954.
30. Bush, Robert and Frederick Mosteller, *Stochastic Models of Learning*, John Wiley, New York, 1955.
31. Kuehn, Alfred A., 'Consumer brand choice as a learning process', *Journal of Advertising Research*, vol. 2, December 1962.
32. Fitzroy, Peter F., *Analytical Methods for Marketing Management*, McGraw-Hill, Maidenhead, 1976.

REVIEW AND DISCUSSION QUESTIONS

1. In which circumstances would marketers of domestic appliances be most likely to witness cognitive dissonance among their customers? What strategies are available to counter such dissonance?
2. What justification is there for marketing students studying learning if learning theorists themselves cannot agree on how learning takes place?
3. Why do you think that some authors have claimed that operant conditioning runs parallel to the marketing concept and that it is particularly useful in developing promotional strategies?

4. How would you react to the view that the variety of what consumers learn cannot be adequately explained by any one theory of learning?

5. From your knowledge of perception theory, how would you advise a marketer of domestic lawnmowers who is devising a trade mark which is also intended for use as a logo on company stationery?

6. Certain UK detergent manufacturers use family branding, others do not. Describe in learning terms the conditions under which family branding is good policy and those under which it is not.

THREE

MOTIVATION

3.1 INTRODUCTION

Human needs and motives are inextricably linked; the relationship between them is so very close that it becomes extremely difficult to identify the precise differences which may characterize them. Terminology, in fact, appears often to be applied somewhat indiscriminantly; as Bayton has observed, 'Some psychologists claim that words such as "motives", "needs", "urges", "wishes" and "drives" should not be used as synonyms; others are content to use them interchangeably'.[1] The absence of clear definitions and the disturbing lack of agreement among researchers and writers has tended to complicate discussion.

The simple model shown in Fig. 3.1 indicates the relationship between needs, motives, and objectives:

Fig. 3.1　Motivation links needs and objectives (behaviour)

Motives initiate behaviour and direct it towards specific types of activities. Hilgard observes that a motivated organism will engage in an activity more vigorously and more efficiently than an unmotivated one.[2] Motivation also tends to focus behaviour.

Wants have been described as the initiating and sustaining forces of behaviour;[3] these may be characterized as 'positive' driving forces that direct wants towards objects, or 'negative' forces such as fears or aversions, which lead wants away from objects.

Motives of fear, for example, may cause some people to avoid air travel unless alternative methods of transport are not available. A strongly developed need for personal security may find expression in the types of investment made; some people may avoid using the telephone for ordering certain products because they prefer personal shopping, which enables them to view and handle goods. Moreover, they may find that shopping expeditions provide them with opportunities for social contacts that would otherwise be denied them. But it is likely that only particular types of stores will be patronized; consumers may deliberately avoid buying from some stores because of past unsatisfactory experiences or, perhaps, because these stores do not appear to be the 'right place' to shop at. By their temperament, certain people seem to be 'risk averse', and so marketers should carefully consider how they could attract these types of buyers, perhaps by special trial arrangements, extended after-sales service and so on.

Needs are of many kinds—from the basic survival needs such as food to sophisticated needs deriving from social, cultural, intellectual, and similar origins that are particularly evident in advanced communities.

Hunger is the motivating force that causes people to seek for means of satisfying this need. But precisely how people's appetite is quelled may vary according to their means, or the company they are in, or the climate, or even their age and social group. On some occasions, individuals may prefer not to eat on account of being overweight or for reasons of religious observance: their behaviour has been modified by strong personal motives which have redirected their energies. Hence, identical behaviour is not necessarily displayed by all who experience a similar basic need.

Food and drink are, as Thouless noted, primarily means of satisfying hunger and thirst, but they also play a much larger part in social life, where they may become the centre of rituals.[4] Civic celebrations inevitably include banquets, yet it would not be right to assume that those in public life have remarkably urgent needs for nourishment.

Over a period of five years, the Institute Cey-Bert of Geneva studied the new preferences of food in the former West Germany, Austria, Belgium, France, the Netherlands, and Switzerland.[5] Among these findings it was reported that modern living conditions created a new food trend in which the bipolar psychological basis is made up of the motivations of 'escape through food', and 'nutritional safety'. The first type of motivation gave rise to exploring new kinds of food with tastes distinctly different from traditional experiences, while the second type of motivation was characterized by 'the ideals of physical and mental health and an attractive body, to be achieved through a balanced diet and fresh natural products'.

Food is, therefore, treated as an aesthetic experience with underlying psychological benefits far removed from its basic function of satisfying a fundamental human need. In affluent communities, the basic needs become the foundation for the gratification of many other types of needs, such as friendship. Bodily needs and social, psychological and cultural demands are not readily distinguished separately: they tend to be linked and interdependent to a considerable extent.

Marketing management is professionally interested in needs; the basic philosophy of marketing rests on the premise that customers' needs are the starting-point from which all other business activities should logically be planned. Because customers—whether they are acting as personal consumers or as buying agents for organizations—experience many kinds of needs, an appreciation of the nature of needs would offer a valuable approach to the study of motivating influences in buying behaviour.

3.2 THE NATURE OF NEEDS

Bayton and other researchers admit that it is difficult to derive a basic list of human needs.[1] Two general categories may be indicated: biogenic and psychogenic.

The biogenic needs, also described as primary, refer to the basic physiology needs which are related to the bodily functions such as hunger, thirst, sex, sleep, and exercise. Most of these needs demand to be satisfied without undue delay or an individual may begin to suffer deprivation. During the time in which they are actively experienced, biogenic needs tend to dominate an individual's attention. Once satisfaction has been achieved, equilibrium is restored to the human organism. Tension has been relieved, allowing individuals to pay heed to other desires which, initially, are less pressing in their pattern of life.

These physiological needs are triggered off by metabolic changes that arouse chemical and neural processes which act as important regulators according to the state of the human organism. Medical researchers found, for example, that patients suffering from Addison's disease had a distinct craving for salt and for foods with high salt content. The term 'homeostatis' has been used by scientists to describe this regulatory phenomenon. The expenditure of energy in some task will result in an imbalance being experienced by an individual. Fatigue will eventually set in as the body temperature falls; this loss of energy will trigger off the stimulus of hunger which will lead to the search for food taking place. According to the personal level of toleration of a state of imbalance, an individual may be willing to expend further considerable effort in order to procure nourishment. Or, as modern food manufacturers suggest, the 'ready-prepared' meal may be the easy solution. Homeostasis is influenced, therefore, by personal factors affecting perception, attitudes, motivation, and so on.

Stafford Beer has pointed out that the big feature of natural, and especially biological, control mechanisms is that they are simply homeostats or control devices for holding some variable between desired limits.[6] This vital principle of self-regulation is evident, for example, in nature; 'the balance of nature' is a well-known phenomenon.

Psychogenic needs—also referred to as emotional, or psychological—reflect the complexity of human behaviour. Apart from the primary needs, which are innate and unlearned, a sophisticated structure of needs relating to social, cultural, emotional, and intellectual interests affects the behaviour of individuals. Primary needs may be modified by psychological needs, as Asch has commented: 'Hunger is a primary need, but there are human ways of eating and human attitudes toward food. Eating becomes under social conditions a developed activity. Food ceases to be something merely to be devoured . . . it becomes connected with social and aesthetic requirements. This development is equally true of all primary needs'.[7]

On many occasions the fundamental need for food has been elevated to reflect social and cultural values. Personal wealth may be displayed by means of the type of food offered to guests, people often display considerable ingenuity in the preparation of special dishes that will give their parties particular appeal. The influence of social and cultural values in buying behaviour will be discussed at some length in Chapters 6 and 7. At this stage, it will be noted that needs develop within the framework of society and are affected by the prevailing culture. Two US marketing scholars have observed:

> In middle-class America, most individuals seem to be attempting to satisfy their love or esteem needs. If advertising at all reflects the American need structure, this becomes evident from a casual perusal of present day advertisements. Seldom does one see an advertisement message like 'Crispy Crackers fill your stomach fuller than other products'; more typically one sees, 'Serve Crispy Crackers with exotic cheese and impress your friends.'[8]

Bayton has suggested that the various formulations of psychogenic needs that have been devised by psychologists and other researchers could be conveniently classified as follows:[1]

1. *Affectional needs*: 'the needs to form and maintain warm, harmonious, and emotionally satisfying relations with others'.
2. *Ego-bolstering needs*: 'the needs to enhance or promote the personality; to achieve; to gain prestige and recognition; to satisfy the ego through domination of others'.
3. *Ego-defensive needs*: 'the needs to protect the personality; to avoid physical and psychological harm; to avoid ridicule and "loss of face"; to prevent loss of prestige; to avoid or to obtain relief from anxiety'.

In offering these classifications of psychogenic needs, Bayton cautiously remarks that an individual may be moved by not merely one need but, more usually, a combination of needs. In this complex of needs, there is often one that is most dominant or 'prepotent'. People may buy a new coat because it protects them against the weather, but their dominant need may be to follow the latest fashion trend in styling and colour.

People, as Maslow has pointed out, are 'perpetually wanting creatures'. Ordinarily the satisfaction of these wants is not altogether mutually exclusive, but only tends to be. The average member of our society is most often partially satisfied and partially unsatisfied in all of his wants'. Human needs appear to be capable of almost infinite extension: 'as soon as one of [these] needs is satisfied, another appears in its place. This process is unending. It continues from birth to death'.[9]

3.3 HIERARCHY OF NEEDS

Maslow has proposed that human needs develop in a sequence ordered from 'lower' wants to 'higher' wants.[9] 'It is true that man lives by bread alone—when there is no bread. But what happens to man's desires when there *is* plenty of bread and when his belly is chronically filled?' Higher needs, states Maslow, then emerge in an endless series. Once hunger is satisfied, it no longer dominates the behaviour of an individual, who is then free to satisfy, for example, social and cultural desires.

This hierarchical sequence of needs is also supported by McGregor[10] in connection with industrial management problems.

Maslow devised the following order of needs, which he divided into five main categories (see Fig. 3.2).

1. Physiological needs, e.g., hunger, thirst, sex.
2. Safety needs, e.g., security and order, protection from both physical and psychological loss.
3. Belongingness and love needs, e.g., affection, sense of being part of a group, affiliation, to love and to be loved.
4. Esteem needs, e.g., prestige, success, self-esteem, status and importance in the eyes of others.
5. Need for self-actualization, e.g., personal fulfilment, self-realization of potential.

Although there appears to be a general lack of empirical evidence to support this sequence of needs, it contains elements of sound common sense which make it of particular interest to marketers. Maier, relating Maslow's theory to the motivation of industrial labour, noted that it does not follow that the satisfaction of lower-level needs ensures the functioning of those at the next level; 'rather potential higher-level needs emerge and influence behaviour only after there is opportunity for satisfaction of lower-level needs'.[11]

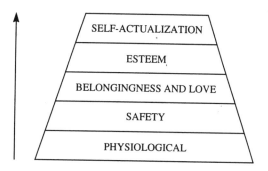

Fig. 3.2   Maslow's hierarchy of needs (*Source*: Maslow)[9]

The strength of physiological needs has already been commented on; the basic economic problem of securing the necessities of life has largely been dealt with satisfactorily by modern industrial communities. Even in times of difficult trading, the standard of living enjoyed by most people is considerably above mere subsistence level.

The effects on behaviour of a chronic shortage of food was studied in an experiment at the University of Minnesota in 1945.[12] Thirty-two volunteers between the ages of 20 and 33 were subjected to semi-starvation for six months, during which time 25 per cent loss of body weight was recorded. The subjects of the experiment became progressively more silent, apathetic, and irritable; sociability suffered and they were inclined to exclude their non-starving friends and the staff of the laboratory from their group feeling. They became easily annoyed about petty incidents, and humour was largely lost as a means of releasing social tensions. Food became the centre of conversation; members of the group found themselves daydreaming about it. Whenever food was given to them, it tended to be treated like gold. Intellectual activities and emotional responses were largely suppressed because the need for food had acquired such potency.

Ballachey records the field study undertaken by A. R. Holmberg in 1950, of the Siriono society, a semi-nomadic Bolivian Indian group. Their food wants were constantly frustrated because of the tropical climate, which made it difficult to preserve and store food, and on account of the very low success they achieved in their daily hunting expeditions. As a result of their harsh way of life, 'art forms, folk tales and mythology are only sparsely developed'. Ballachey summarizes: 'Men who must grub for food cannot want and seek beauty and intellectual understanding'.[3]

In the area of marketing, the consumer whose main preoccupation is obtaining enough food to live on is hardly likely to have much inclination (or money) to devote to other products, and is unlikely, for instance, to be very interested in life assurance policies, or joining an association to foster the arts. However, variations in individual behaviour may occur, and Maslow prudently qualified his theory by observing that some individuals may be influenced by higher motives that achieve prepotency even when lower needs have been entirely satisfied. Partial satisfaction of a particular need may be tolerated: 'it is as if the average citizen is satisfied perhaps 80% of the time in his physiological needs, 70% in his safety needs, 50% in his love needs, 40% in his self esteem needs and 10% in his self actualisation needs'.[13]

This qualification is of interest to marketers, because it allows for characteristic buying behaviour in some areas. For example, cheaper types of food may be bought, or restricted quantities consumed, in order to run a car or to buy fashionable clothing.

Maslow's second category of sequential needs—safety needs—relates to people's desire for protection against both physical and psychological dangers. In a stable society, individuals may develop their education and professional training and enhance their social position. In modern communities, legislation at both the national and regional level protects people against fraudulent trading, dangerous additives to foods, and similar hazards. The rapid growth of the 'consumerist' movement may be attributed to the greater need which consumers feel for protection against highly organized business enterprises. The branding and advertising of products helps to reassure buyers who have a 'very common preference for familiar rather than unfamiliar things, or for the known rather than the unknown'.[9]

Volvo, the Swedish car manufacturers, have consistently promoted safety and also 'durability' as attractive design features of their products; in addition, they have emphasized the high level of service available through their dealer network.

Life assurance and other forms of insurance are other manifestations of the need for safety and security. As human beings have developed, they have attempted to control the environment in which they live. From a primitive conception of life, they have extended their vision so that they become aware of many different kinds of danger. These may relate to occupation, to the fear of redundancy, or to the problems of educating children. (The motivating influence of fear will be discussed later in this text—see Sec. 13.9.)

The third sequential stage of Maslow's hierarchy of needs relates to the fundamental need for love and affiliation: 'If both the physiological and the safety needs are fairly well gratified, then there will emerge the love and affection and belongingness needs'.[9] The need for acceptance by others, to give and to receive love and friendship, is a significant factor in human behaviour and has been seen to extend also to the lower animals. The affiliation want finds expression in the purchase of gifts and in group activities in sports and other cultural pursuits. This may also encourage the development of distinctive styles of clothing or the consumption of particular branded products, e.g., Coke. The strength of the need for affiliation will vary according to personality differences; those who spend their holidays at holiday camps or on popular 'package holidays' may be presumed to have higher needs for affiliation than the solitary bird watcher on a barren coastal mud flat. Emotional needs play a significant part in the decisions which consumers make about many types of products and services; marketing practitioners should endeavour to identify *all* the needs that their customers are seeking to satisfy when they buy a bar of chocolate, a car, or a tube of toothpaste. Kotler quotes Charles Revson, president of Revlon, who when asked what his customers really sought through buying cosmetics, replied: 'In the factory we make cosmetics, and in the drug store we sell hope'.[14]

Maslow's fourth category of sequential needs—esteem needs—refers to deeply rooted desires that are commonly experienced. These he subdivided into two groups. First, there is 'the desire for strength, for achievement, for adequacy, for confidence in the face of the world and for independence and freedom'.[9] The second classification relates to the desire for reputation or prestige, recognition, attention, importance, or appreciation. It has been said that the need for prestige may inspire individuals to accomplish good works, or, on the other hand, it could lead to destructive, antisocial behaviour.[3] Indeed history provides ample evidence of the compulsive power of the need for public esteem and adulation.

McClelland studied in some depth the need that people feel for achievement.[15] What makes individuals and specific cultures economically successful? This may not be directly related to profits or to monetary reward in the business world, or elsewhere. He posed the question: 'Why do civilizations rise and fall?' and he decided that the basis must be psychological. He examined the folk tales from 50 different cultures and also the tales traditionally told to children. Writings from Greek literature, e.g., Homer and Pericles, war speeches, and hymns to the gods, were analysed for their exhortations to high endeavour. Similarly, the European literature of the middle ages was also studied for the way in which it reflected and also influenced people's achievements. He found significant increases in achievement imagery in the fiction of Elizabethan England, and also immediately preceding the industrial revolution. Periods of marked economic success followed in both periods.

In addition, McClelland undertook a series of experiments that endeavoured to measure by means of an 'n-score' (n = need for achievement) the number of times achievement-related ideas occurred in stories written by subjects. He found that people with high n-scores came mainly from the middle class; that the mothers of people with high n-achievement made demands on their children when they were very young and expected them to develop mature behaviour relatively early. High-n people tended to think ahead and to anticipate future events; they attempted to control their environment so that they could exploit opportunities. Their reactions to disaster were superior, and they quickly turned events in their favour.

The contribution of the 'Protestant ethic', originally discussed by Weber in 1904,[16] was also examined by McClelland. After comparing key economic data from a number of countries held to be representative of 'Catholic' or 'Protestant' cultures, he stated that it could 'be concluded with reasonable confidence that, as of 1950, Protestant countries are economically more advanced on the average, even taking their differences into account, than are Catholic countries'. While admitting that there are obvious limitations to empirical findings, McClelland argued that his research was based on systematic investigation, and that 'taken as a whole it tends to support the belief that achievement motivation is an important factor affecting the rate of economic development'. About this conclusion, few business people would disagree; marketing experts in particular tend to have high n-scores. McClelland, in fact, extended his research to investigate n-achievement levels in various type of business occupations over four countries. His 'most general conclusion' was that people involved in sales and marketing had higher n-achievement scores than production, engineering, or finance executives. 'Such a result does not come as a great surprise since the marketing role certainly requires to an unusual degree the kind of entrepreneurial activity (risk taking, knowledge of results of sales campaigns, etc.) that we have found to be characteristic of high n-achievement'.[15]

Critics of McClelland's research findings have commented that, for example, he relied too much on psychological factors and ignored social, political, and historical influences that did not suit his theory. The concept of the 'Protestant ethic' is by no means free of ambiguity and, as one critic has pointed out, it is difficult not to find the Protestant ethic a little parochial as an explanation of the rise of capitalism bearing in mind 'the ubiquitous role of the Jews, or the contribution of the Parsees in India, or the Catholics in Belgium or Italy or the United States, or the Samurai in Japan, or the Chinese in Malaysia, or the Indians in Kenya'.[17] Indeed, the exceptions stretch hard the rule of Protestant supremacy in economic development. It has also been shrewdly observed that there is no control group of failed entrepreneurs to show *their* religious affiliations: bankrupts receive less attention from researchers than successful business people. On the other hand, it has been conceded that there is considerable support for the view that 'any firm religious conviction will be a major determinant of the qualities which make for entrepreneurial success'.[18] However, it would be difficult to assess the precise impact of a specific theological set of beliefs. It is likely that Dissenters in eighteenth-century England were successful not so much on account of their religious beliefs, but because their faith excluded them from a great deal of social life. Causal factors are elusive, although some of the evidence is, at the same time, persuasive even if it is inconclusive.

To conclude, Weber,[16] who is regarded as the generator of the 'Protestant ethic', was admittedly 'not a careful writer who made sure that he was not misunderstood'. He was 'no doctrinaire monist who assigned supreme importance to religion and disregarded political and economic factors'. Projections of his thoughts, rather like Freud's, seem to have been extended—and distorted—beyond his original concepts.

The desire for prestige is often closely associated with the acquisitive and power wants. Thouless has suggested that the ownership of newspapers enables some people to satisfy their self-assertive tendencies, because run strictly as a business 'the capital value of a large newspaper . . . unlike most investments, bears no simple relation to its revenue-producing capacity'.[4] Executives in industry frequently experience considerable satisfaction from the exercise of their authority in making significant decisions. Despite the tribulations of public office, there is no shortage of candidates for parliamentary seats; there may be an element of altruism, but it would be rare to find that this was the sole, or even dominant, need inspiring people to sit in Parliament or other assemblies.

The western industrial communities are based strongly on acknowledging the power of the acquisitive want, which is said to be central to the general orientation of the prevailing culture. This tendency receives social approval because it encourages work and a degree of thrift. In some primitive societies, however, private ownership is strictly limited. 'Rivers has said . . . that amongst some of the peoples of Melanesia there is no private ownership except of such objects, e.g., weapons, as a man makes for himself. Canoes are possessed by a family group, and land is generally held in the same way'.[4]

By assiduously acquiring objects (i.e., products) of various kinds, and by demanding an ever-widening range of services, consumers in modern society endeavour to express their needs for power and prestige. Vance Packard said that many Americans buy antiques because of their symbolic value even when their functional value is dubious.[19] He mentioned the *Chicago Tribune* suburban study which found 'that, if a suburbanite aspires to move up into the "lower-upper class", he will buy antiques—symbols of old social position bought with new money'. People tend to ascend the social ladder by acquiring possessions; they move to houses in the more fashionable districts. By filling their homes with expensive furniture and other products they display their prosperity; the conferred status which generally follows satisfies their developing needs for recognition and prestige.

Critics of this social phenomenon, while no doubt personally enjoying the ownership of camcorders, mobile phones, personal computers, dishwashers, and other 'status' products, condemn the apparently insatiable needs of modern society. For instance, Galbraith declared that consumption has become an addiction, and that consumers are coerced by propaganda to spend more and more until they become captives of the industrial system.[20] His strictures seem to overlook that people, as any marketing manager knows, are not just 'advertising fodder'. They react, and not always favourably, to advertising messages. The influence and limitations of advertising will be considered in some detail in Chapter 13.

Ballachey has underlined the tendency for wants and goals to be developed and organized to enhance and defend the individual.[3] Self becomes 'a nucleus around which the many diverse wants and goals' are centred. Self-esteem is an important part of the psychological make-up of an individual. Most people are concerned to achieve an actual self as similar as possible to an idealized concept, which they have probably been trying to attain since childhood. In pursuit of this desirable self-image, consumption habits may be developed or modified. Certain brands of products may be carefully viewed for the symbolism which they convey. Advertisers frequently present cigarettes, perfumes, cars, or foods in terms that suggest ownership almost automatically confers social and other benefits. Products like these become ego-involved and extensions of the personality of those who buy them. A consumer's self-image tends to be developed and confirmed by the material possessions that are acquired.

Two US researchers found that people who perceive themselves as 'cautious conservatives' were more inclined to prefer small cars because these were convenient and economical; whereas another group, who classified themselves as 'confident explorers', preferred large cars by means of which they felt able 'to control the environment'.[21] (Further reference will be made to self-concept and the ownership of products in Sec. 5.8.)

It will be apparent, therefore, that Maslow's fourth and fifth stages of needs are not easily distinguishable, since in pursuing status an individual may be seeking personal fulfilment. By associating with particular kinds of people—at the golf club or at some prestigious function—aspiring consumers will be affected by the consumption habits of those whose company they wish to share. People may modify their opinions about matters which are held to be of importance; they may even change their religion or their political allegiance. Conformity to group values may entail changes in people's characteristic behaviour; the more desirable they regard membership of a particular social group, the more closely will they be inclined to accept the wants and goals of that group. Social environment helps to fashion habits of consumption; modern industrial society is made up of many interrelated groupings with distinctive patterns of consumption.

McClelland[22] has strongly criticized 'all the leading behavioural scientists', among whom he lists Maslow and Likert, because he alleges that they asked people 'in more or less subtle ways about what their interests were'. People, he declares, are not used to observing themselves systematically and so rationalization is very likely to occur. 'If you interview a successful industrialist he will probably say that he is motivated by a strong need to achieve. It may be totally untrue'. On the other hand, although the profit motive is strongly evident in western society, successful business people 'may not have been motivated by that at all in any true psychological sense'. Self-fulfilment may well be a paramount influence in motivating entrepreneurs to found new enterprises so that they could develop products based, perhaps, on specific technological expertise and/or patent rights. In doing so they may satisfy their needs for recognition as inventive designers and innovators; the prospect of earning significant profits could be a secondary motivation.

Self-diagnosis should be viewed, therefore, as an unreliable method of identifying the many and mixed motives underlying human activities. It would be naive, if not dangerous, to assume that responses to direct questions will be based on objective evaluations of personal behaviour.

The need to improve personal enjoyment of life may cause some people to enrol for educational and recreational courses of various kinds. Through acquiring extra skills and knowledge, an individual may attract social prestige apart from personal satisfaction. Today, there is a more liberal attitude towards those who seek to improve their education later in life. In Britain, the Open University has enabled many adult students to obtain degrees on a part-time study basis. The need for personal fulfilment is powerfully experienced by ambitious people in the professions and in industry.

3.4 MASLOW'S 'SMALLER HIERARCHY OF NEEDS'

Apart from the five sequential stages of needs postulated by Maslow, he also admitted the existence of a smaller hierarchy related to the desire to know and to understand. These cognitive needs should not, however, be considered as separate from the basic needs because 'the desire to know and understand are themselves conative, i.e., have a striving character and are as much personality needs as the basic needs'.[9] This leads to consideration of the curiosity want, which is biologically deep-rooted, although varying markedly in strength among individuals. Environment appears to be a significant influence on the development of the curiosity want, but there also seems to be a 'self-generated' need for a certain degree of excitation. Boredom soon sets in whenever the environment ceases to provide experiences that are interesting to individuals. The nervous system is never really dormant; the brain may indulge in ideas below the level of conscious awareness. This activity may result in new wants, although their fulfilment will largely depend on the resources of the society in which an individual lives. 'In a country without universities, libraries and laboratories, few men will strive to become scholars and scientists'.[3] Their curiosity needs will be poorly served, so that eventually these intellectual ambitions may be discarded. People may 'come to terms' with the limitations imposed on their wants; how individuals may respond would require particular study. Clearly, people have different levels of frustration. Some will be prepared to make considerable sacrifices in order to satisfy their curiosity needs; those who undertake rigorous intellectual training have a highly developed curiosity want.

In marketing activities, it should be recognized that individual consumers tend to vary in the amount and quality of information they require about products and services. Today, there is generally greater insistence by the public on information being given to them on many varied topics. Marketers should endeavour to satisfy the information needs of their customers, and in doing so build up goodwill.

Apart from the need to know and understand, which Maslow associated with his list of sequential needs, he also referred, although somewhat diffidently, to the existence of aesthetic needs: 'Some individuals have a strong aversion to the ugly and a need for the beautiful'.[13] This aspect of human needs is of significance to designers, manufacturers, and distributors of many kinds of products. The increased volume of spending power today is largely in the hands of women, or is heavily influenced by them. By their nature, they are generally more sensitive to colour and fashion styling, and for many years they have been accustomed to a wide choice of well-designed clothing. When they now extend their buying interests into other product areas, such as cars, bathroom fittings, and lawnmowers, they are demanding aesthetic as well as practical satisfaction. Alert manufacturers will welcome this 'invasion', and will ensure that their products have built into them characteristics which will give them 'feminine' appeal. In the early 1980s, a large car manufacturer admitted that they had no woman designer on their staff; although from time to time, apparently, the opinions of women were sought, there was no planned effort to seek this advice.

Over recent years, car manufacturers and distributors have recognized the importance of winning the favour of women motorists, and have wisely adopted design features and promotional messages likely to appeal to the growing number of women buyers.

Design opens up a vast area for the keen marketer to explore. Overheads and other costs rise inexorably: competition is now not only from British firms but also from firms in all parts of the world. The world, in effect, is a much smaller place. An effective design strategy can be the key that unlocks the door to further advance in world markets.

It would be futile, of course, to concentrate design resources on mere external appearance; design responsibilities cover the *whole* product—its satisfactory performance as well as its pleasant styling.

Marketing executives and designers should establish a dialogue that encourages the free and honest exchange of opinions and experience. It would be valuable, for instance, for designers to attend some of the sessions of sales conferences so that they become more personally aware of the reactions of customers and also of the sales force to their latest creations. In addition, it is sound commercial sense to allow designers, from time to time, to accompany selected members of the sales team on their selling trips. Where a company markets its products overseas, designers should visit these territories and see for themselves the conditions under which their products have to operate or be consumed. It would also be useful to study the methods of distributing and presenting these to the final customer. Creative designers cannot fail to return from these explorations with a host of new ideas; their talents will be released with new energy and enthusiasm.

That aesthetic needs are not restricted to consumer products was dramatically illustrated by Theodore Levitt in connection with a testing machine which was presented to a panel of highly qualified laboratory directors.[23] One version of the machine had a front panel designed by the engineers who had developed the equipment; the alternative machine, which was intrinsically identical, was fitted with a control panel designed by professional industrial designers. The latter version 'attracted twice the purchase intentions compared with the engineers' design'. Levitt observed that even scientifically trained and experienced laboratory directors are 'quite as responsive to the blandishments of packaging as the Boston Matron'.

It is apparent that industrial products as well as consumer products need to be well designed both internally and externally. The 'added values' of attractive styling contribute towards favourable buying decisions, and it would be shortsighted of manufacturers to dismiss this product attribute as a superfluous fad. Buyers may not consciously be aware of the influence of attractive styling on their decision to buy a specific product, and they may even strongly deny that aesthetic appeal was a factor influencing their judgement.

Successful industrial produce manufacturers know the sales value of attractive design, as the following example illustrates. A Canadian pump manufacturer approached consultant designers to redesign their range of pumps. Some of their business colleagues were asked why it was thought necessary to have their machines redesigned, because, after all, these only go underground. 'Maybe', the pump manufacturer replied, 'but they are not bought underground'.[24]

Maslow's reference to aesthetic needs reflect the influence of Freudian psychology; he concludes that needs are 'more unconscious than conscious in the average person and that everyday conscious desires are to be regarded as symptoms, as surface indicators of more basic needs'.[13]

3.5 WANTS DO NOT EXIST IN ISOLATION

The various human needs that have been discussed should not be regarded as entirely definitive and absolute. Further, they do not operate in watertight compartments; human beings are highly complex creatures whose needs are varied and growing. Between needs a certain degree of conflict may sometimes be experienced. The tendency towards prepotency of particular needs, such as the basic physiological wants, has already been discussed.

Conflict may arise, for example, because the need for security may be at variance with the desire for prestige and power. Exciting prospects of acquiring substantial capital gain by taking part in a business enterprise may be substantially reduced by the element of a high risk involved which may intimidate some would-be investors. Some consumers avoid buying the latest model of a car until actual road users have had reasonably trouble-free motoring over a period of time. On many occasions, marketers often prefer to follow rather than to lead trends in the styling of their products. They willingly sacrifice prestige needs for the more certain satisfactions obtained from cautious marketing strategies.

People may suffer from conflicting needs in the buying of groceries and other supplies. They may, for instance, desire to buy highly nutritious food like beef, but their needs for economy may dictate that cheaper types of protein should be on their shopping lists. Although human needs are apparently insatiable, incomes are limited, and the pattern of spending may vary considerably between families.

It is clear, therefore, that wants are closely interrelated; that conflict may modify behaviour; and that the influence of needs is felt differently by individuals. Within social groups, however, there is a tendency for common needs to evolve and to receive particular attention. The behaviour of individuals in society finds expression in the goods and services they use; wants are dynamic and Maslow's theory, while not empirically validated, is valuable in pointing out the nature of needs and their relationship to modern styles of living.

3.6 MOTIVATION: AN OVERVIEW

Any discussion of motivation is inevitably related to the study of needs: motives and needs are interdependent; motives actuate and direct actions to be taken in satisfaction of identified needs. Motivation acts as an energizing force which originates, sustains, and directs activities towards diverse objectives. Through the stimuli of motives, people are inspired to achieve success in their professional and private lives; to acquire a host of desirable products; and to satisfy their needs for affiliation, prestige, power, and many of the other wants that have been discussed earlier.

The difficulty of distinguishing clearly between needs and motives in published works has been acknowledged: inevitably, the very close relationship that links these phenomena gives rise to a certain degree of confusion. There is, moreover, some similarity in the classifications adopted for describing motives and needs, which is to be expected since these cannot really be considered for long in isolation. Motives have been classified, for example, as learned or unlearned, rational or emotional, conscious or unconscious, physical (biogenic) or psychological (psychogenic), etc. In 1924, Copeland listed 33 buying motives, classifying them as 'emotional' or 'rational'.[25] The former he defined as those that have their origin in human instincts and emotions, giving rise to impulsive or non-rational responses. He believed that consumer goods were largely bought as the result of instinctive and emotional motivation. Such wholesale listing and classification of buying motives is no longer tenable; it is rarely possible in practice to be so definite about the nature of motivation related to specific products and services. Like wants, motives tend to act in concert and the multiplicity of motivational forces eludes simple analysis. A new car may be bought for many reasons: these may include 'rational' motivations such as reliability and availability of personal transport (the old car tended to break down), or a good trade-in price for the old car which tempted purchase of a new model; 'emotional' motivations may reflect the influence of neighbours and friends who have recently bought new cars, the desire for greater comfort and speed or the symbolic affluence which this purchase may reflect. Katona recalls empirical studies concerned with the purchase of war bonds in the USA during the Second World War.[26] Significant differences in the amounts of bonds held by individuals could not be explained solely on the grounds of income or occupation. 'There were people who, in spite of intensive questioning, mentioned only one reason for their buying war bonds, namely, the patriotic reason "to help win the war".' However, these people bought fewer bonds in each income or occupational group than those who, in addition to patriotic reasons, gave personal financial motivations, such as saving up for a house or to buy a business. Furthermore, when the effect of sale promotion and personal selling of war bonds was investigated, it was found that these methods affected the rate of purchase 'even though the people themselves did not mention solicitation among the reasons for their buying bonds and seemed unaware of the great influence exerted by solicitation'. Those who were motivated to buy bonds because of several reasons and who were also 'solicited to buy' were discovered to be the largest buyers. Katona reflects that the more numerous the forces that drive individuals in the same direction, the greater will be their action. Hence, the success of the war bonds campaign was ensured by advertising several reasons to buy them, and backing up their promotion by personal selling.

Successful marketing of goods and services of all kinds—whether these relate to personal needs or to those of organizations—should be based on a fundamental appreciation of motivation. How people will respond to marketing stimuli, such as price offers, advertising, product attributes, etc., is not always easy to predict. This has led two US researchers to comment: 'Human behaviour is so enormously varied, so delicately complex, so obscurely motivated that many people despair of finding valid generalisations to explain and predict the actions, thoughts and feelings of human beings—despair, that is, of the very possibility of constructing a science of human behaviour'.[27] Systematic, intelligent study and analysis will help to obtain insight into the behaviour of people as consumers of products and services of many types. Of course, perfect knowledge in any science is never attained; but this should not discourage attempts to find out more about the wants of customers and the reasons why they buy particular goods. Products are bought for the benefits which it is anticipated they will give to purchasers. Experienced marketers evaluate their products in terms of customer expectations, and ensure that they build into their merchandise valid reasons why people should buy from them and not from a competitor: this cannot be done successfully without a sensitive awareness of the role of motives in buying behaviour. There is further discussion of the complexity, and occasional conflict, of motives in specific purchasing decisions in Chapters 9 and 10.

Marketers are interested in motivation of their sales staff and distributors as well as those who consume their products. Marketing management is an integrating influence within a company; one aspect of marketing's responsibilities is to motivate designers and production staff to develop and manufacture products which have characteristics likely to make them successful.

3.7 THE QUESTION OF MOTIVATION

The study of motivation is concerned with the question 'Why?' Cognitions, as Ballachey states, guide an individual's actions 'but when we ask why he acts at all, we are asking the question of motivation'.[3] Why, for instance, should people undertake arduous, painstaking research, or risk their lives climbing mountains, or dedicate their energies and professional skills to caring for sick people in some remote corner of the globe? In commercial terms, marketing managers are professionally interested in what motivates or makes people buy (or abstain from buying) certain types or brands of products. Answers to such questions are not easily given, for motives may be complex and mixed; conflict may arise because one motive (for example, safety) may be challenged by another (such as excitement or convenience). Also, there may be times when personal motivations are suppressed or modified in order to meet the needs of others, as in family buying situations.

3.8 THEORIES OF MOTIVATION

Hilgard and colleagues have observed that the term 'motivation' came into general use only in the early years of the twentieth century.[2] Until then, *rationality* had been the accepted view of philosophers and theologians; reason was considered to be the principal influence affecting human behaviour. Classical economic theory stressed the rationality of consumers who were guided in their buying behaviour by objective criteria (see Chapter 1). This mythical creature— 'economic man', whose actions were dominated by rationality—apportioned income to achieve maximum utility. Kotler has called this the Marshallian economic model,[14] after Alfred Marshall, whose theories had a profound effect on the orientation of classical economic science. This view of human economic activities is discussed further in Chapters 9 and 10.

A more mechanistic view was taken by philosophers such as Descartes, Hobbes, Locke, and Hume, who suggested that some human behaviour arose from internal and external forces over which an individual had no control. Hobbes, as Hilgard notes,[2] held that individuals are motivated to experience pleasure and avoid pain, and it is these two factors that underlie all behaviour. As a result, hedonism achieved prominence as a motivational theory.

From the mechanistic approach to motivation, there developed the extreme view that *instincts* were the prime factors in behaviour. Innate predispositions existed which led to certain kinds of behaviour; this was directly contrary to rationalism, which held that people's behaviour resulted from deliberate choice.

Dissatisfaction with the instinct theory of motivation led to a theory of *drive reduction*, which based motivation on the fundamental bodily or visceral needs such as food or rest. These innate or unlearned needs require fairly prompt satisfaction and, until they are met, become prepotent or of prime importance in influencing behaviour. Such biogenic needs (discussed earlier in this chapter) when satisfied restore equilibrium to the human organism.

In the 1950s, the drive reduction theory came to be regarded as deficient, because it ignored external factors as influencing behaviour, and a theory of motivation based on *incentives* was developed. This proposed that motivation should be viewed as arising from an interaction between stimulus objects in the environment and a particular physiological conditions of the organism. External conditions are recognized as important influences on motivation which may, of course, be positive or negative, as noted on pages 40–41.

The incentive theory of motivation recognizes that consumers, for example, are affected not only by their basic tissue needs, but also by the environments in which they live, work, and play. Motivation is not just from within an individual and purely instinctive; behaviour is also guided by factors such as beliefs and attitudes as well as social and group membership. Advertising and other influences in the environment, e.g., shop window displays, may motivate consumer behaviour.

Diverse explanations of human motivation have, therefore, been offered by theorists, 'but as yet there is little consensus'.[2] These various theories have been flavoured 'by the particular philosophy or theory of personality'[8] which researchers have tended to support. Clearly, there is no generally agreed and comprehensive theory of motivation, although in some specific aspects there is a measure of agreement among psychologists. For example, the coincidence of views related to the hierarchical structure of needs and motives held by Maslow and McGregor has already been observed. Howard and Sheth also refer to the 'dominance hierarchy of motives'; because a buyer cannot satisfy equally many motives at any one time, 'the most urgent motive, that is, the one at the "top" of the hierarchy, is satisfied first'.[28] (These researchers use the term 'needs' and 'motives' interchangeably.)

Motivational theories display considerable heterogeneity because psychological phenomena admit of more than one interpretation and different methods of investigation may have been used. Early theorists, such as Charles Darwin (1809–82), projected humans as creatures striving towards goals that were controlled by the environment. He emphasized that in the struggle for survival, human beings differ considerably in intellectual and other abilities. Darwin's biological studies blazed the trail for the extensive researches that were to take place later into animal behaviour. 'When Darwin demonstrated the presence of close relations between the bodily structure of men and other animals, and formulated the principles of variation and natural selection, he realised clearly that the evolutionary process must extend to psychological and social phenomena, that it cannot be restricted to anatomical and physiological facts'.[7] Darwin stressed the importance of instinctive behaviour which, during the course of their lives, human creatures develop and transmit to their offspring.

The *behaviourist* theory of psychology extended Darwin's biological concept of instinctive human behaviour. His adaptive behavioural tendencies were accepted, but the dominance he placed on instincts was replaced by emphasis on the process of learning as a modifying influence.

E. L. Thorndike (1874–1949) was an influential figure in formulating a doctrine of learning in which the process of trial and error was influenced by the stimuli of reward and punishment. Learning theories and their relevance in motivating buying behaviour were reviewed in Chapter 2.

Instinctive theories of motivation were to be re-emphasized by Sigmund Freud (1856–1939) and his associates. His ideas have had profound influence in psychology, sociology, and medical science and have extended to the marketing of products of many kinds. Advertising, in particular, has exploited Freudian concepts in appealing to the emotional, deeply rooted needs of people.

Freud postulated that there are two basic drives or instincts which affect human behaviour: self preservation and procreation. He identified three interacting forces in the personality which produce behaviour: the id, the ego, and the superego. The *id* is the unconscious part of the psyche which consists of instinctual impulses such as aggression, destruction, and pleasure seeking. These, he declared, are present in the newly born child. The id is the source of all the driving psychic energy which makes these instinctive needs of paramount importance in the life of the unrepressed infant. Unrestrained, these impulses are likely to result in antisocial behaviour; the *superego*, therefore, intervenes to impose moral restraints and inhibitions through the agencies of parents and society in general. 'The term "super-ego" has been used for the introjected system of parental prohibitions which is the hypothetical source of pathological guilt'.[4] Cultural beliefs obviously affect the moral standards imposed in particular situations. Freud contended that what he termed the 'dread of society' was the essence of what is called conscience. The *ego* mediates between the powerful, instinctive urges of the id and the inhibitions emanating from the superego. Through the ego, individuals come to terms with reality so that they may organize their energies to achieve personal goals:

> The manner in which the ego guides the libidinal energies of the id and the moralistic demands of the superego accounts for the rich variety of personalities, interests, motives, attitudes and behaviour patterns of people. It accounts for the purchase of a four-door sedan rather than a racy sports-car, the adoption of a mini-skirt, and the use of Ultra-Brite toothpaste.[29]

Freudian psychoanalytic theory has been subject to severe criticism by psychologists and other commentators, largely because many of its projections lack substantial empirical validation. There is no proof, for instance, that the id, ego, and superego really exist. Too great a stress appears to be laid on sexuality as a prime motive in human behaviour, whereas, as Cheskin remarked, it should be obvious that individuals are motivated both socially and libidinously.[30] In fact, Valentine has emphasized that Freud used the word 'sex' in a wider way than it is commonly understood; 'thus the appreciation of curves, the enjoyment of the sense of touch and so forth would come under the heading of sex factors'.[31]

It would be as well to bear in mind, the perceptive words of Professor Karl W. Deutsch of Harvard University: 'It is unfortunately the case that the one-sided formulations of great men are accepted and passed on by their followers far more readily than their more developed and differentiated formulations. There is a kind of Gresham's law, that the primitive propositions of great men tend to drive out their differentiated thoughts.[32]

Freudian theories of motivation are valuable in drawing attention to the existence and significance of unconscious influences in human behaviour. It is recognized that guilt, anxiety, and other conflicting emotions and beliefs may affect human actions. People are not cold calculating machines but creatures of flesh and blood, whose emotional desires should never be ignored. However, some Freudian interpretations related to marketing practice seem to originate more from the fertility of imagination of researchers than from scientific objective inquiry.

Motivation research has largely been developed from the concepts of Freudian psychology, and this topic is discussed in some detail elsewhere.[33]

Because any consideration of motivation must almost inevitably extend to theories of personality, some of the concepts of behavioural science related to personality traits and theories will be discussed in Chapter 4. In this way it is hoped to integrate the study of the diverse motivations to which individuals react in the course of living in modern society.

3.9 NATURE OF MOTIVES

The word 'motive' derives from the Latin root 'move'; thus a motive is a reason for action directed towards a desirable goal, which could be the possession of a washing machine or some other domestic aid. The discharge of tension obtained through the satisfaction of needs has already been noted. Tension mobilizes energy which is directed by personal motivational systems in a certain direction. It has been noted that tension may be caused by physical imbalance; e.g., hunger, or it may largely be psychologically based, as when people notice that one of their best friends is rather more fashionably dressed than they are.

Motivation is subject to personal perception of needs, and until these needs have been stimulated by marketing activities, individual consumers may perceive no reason to buy a particular product. Their need may be latent and so unrecognized, although they may, in fact, benefit considerably from using that product. So-called impulse purchases may frequently result from exposure to stimuli (e.g., shop displays or advertisements) which awaken dormant needs. People's minds are alerted to the existence of certain products, and they may find them sufficiently attractive that they are motivated to buy. Motivation, as the incentive theory proposed, is affected by the environment in which a person lives. In modern societies, there tends to be perpetual stimulation of needs by commercial firms, though the impact of these stimuli are affected by personal differences in perception and meaning (see Chapter 2). Exposure to the same set of stimuli does not mean that all members of the audience will react in the same way. Messages must be *meaningful* to individuals, and suggest that the products or services they are sponsoring are going to help to solve personal needs and desires.

Human motives may lead to complex behaviour. Unlike lower animals, humans have a highly developed set of needs related to their physical welfare and emotional stability: the same motive may result in diverse behaviour by different people. For reasons of prestige, for example, a person may buy an expensive car, or an impressive house, or develop expertise in some art or branch of learning. People may frequent fashionable hotel bars, or even give away large sums of money to charity in the hope of securing public approval or political honours.

On the other hand, the same behaviour may be caused by quite different motives. Some people, for example, appear to be compulsive eaters—they consume food not merely because of the motive of hunger—they may be suffering from loneliness or lack of affection. Food may also be eaten for reasons of social gratification. People may be motivated to visit the theatre or cinema because they really want to see the show; or because they are bored, and find time on their hands in some strange town; or because they are invited to accompany someone whose company is important to them; or they may just want to sit down somewhere and avoid the rain.

3.10 ASPIRATIONS AFFECT MOTIVATION

McClelland's proposition of '*n*-achievement'[15] has already been referred to in connection with human needs. People are motivated by differing levels of aspiration which are reflected in their behaviour. Katona has formulated 'a few generalisations which have been established in numerous studies of goal-striving behaviour':[26]

1. Aspirations are not static; they are not established once for all time.
2. Aspirations tend to grow with achievement and decline with failure.
3. Aspirations are influenced by the performance of other members of the group to which a person belongs and by that of reference groups.

Clearly, social and intellectual aspirations influence people's behaviour and extend to the types of products and services they consume. In Chapters 6 and 7 on social and cultural influences in marketing, the effects of social mobility, opinion leadership, and group membership on consumption habits will be analysed. Because of the insatiability of human needs, consumers accumulate an ever-increasing collection of products. Dissatisfaction soon emerges and change is demanded. The luxuries of yesterday tend, moreover, to become the necessities of modern life today. Society is dynamic and so are its needs and these are reflected in the buying behaviour of consumers.

Technological and scientific invention and innovation have enabled people to lift their levels of aspiration. Transistors, for example, led to the development of home stereo equipment; enabling people to listen to superb orchestral concerts in their own homes. Compact discs have revolutionized the recording of music and their rapid diffusion is increasingly challenging the long-held dominance of long-playing vinyl records. Advances in medical science have resulted in people expecting improved methods of surgery and nursing; what were once considered to be relatively dangerous surgical operations are now regarded as commonplace. Laser technology has been adopted in surgical operations, such as cataract extraction, with remarkable success. Travel has speeded up enormously—jet air travel is not a novelty. Holidays abroad are no longer the prerogative of the wealthy and leisured classes; the problem for some people appears to lie in seeking out distant lands that are not already the target of popular package-deal tourists.

Levels of aspiration are closely associated with other factors affecting human behaviour apart from motivations: the values and beliefs (cognitions) which individuals hold; their attitudes towards life in general and those related to specific aspects of it; their personality traits; and all the character and interests of people in society. Katona has remarked that it is unwarranted to assume that there is a direct relation between need gratification and saturation.[26] Other variables intervene to 'determine what happens following gratification of needs'. Rich industrialists continue to pursue their business activities, despite heavy personal taxation, although they may have no financial need to acquire extra money. Seldom do they seek retirement because of what they declare to be crippling taxation or intolerable trading conditions. The challenge of business enterprise, the opportunities to exercise managerial skills, and the deep satisfaction of exercising power motivate them to achieve even higher production and selling targets. Eventually even these may fail to give personal pleasure, and they may aspire to win acknowledgement by their munificence in funding a new college or medical school in some university.

Marketers should study trends in the markets they do business in: society in general is impatient and demands ready-made solutions to its problems. Consumers are affected by the values and attitudes of modern society. Not all people progress steadily and at the same rate; the problems of innovation will be discussed in Chapter 11.

3.11 SUMMARY

Motivation is the energizing force which stimulates behaviour, including buying behaviour. It is concerned with the question 'Why?' Motives, needs, wants, urges, etc., have been used rather freely, so discussion tends to become difficult.

Two general categories of human needs are biogenic and psychogenic. The former refer to primary or basic needs related to bodily functions such as eating or sleeping. Until these are satisfied, they tend to dominate attention; when satisfied, a higher level of needs—psychogenic—emerges. These needs concern social, cultural, emotional, and intellectual interests. Primary needs may be modified by psychological needs, as with food or clothing.

Motivational forces may also be either positive (attracting) or negative (repelling).

Maslow's 'hierarchy of needs' proposed that human needs progress from lower to higher wants. McClelland studied the need for achievement and developed 'n-scores' as the result of experiments. He suggested that the 'Protestant ethic' was significant in comparative economic development in several countries.

Wants do not exist in isolation; conflict may arise from time to time, over, for example, the need for security and that related to prestige or power.

Various theories of motivation have been offered, e.g., rationalism, drive reduction, incentive. Diverse philophies or personality theories have flavoured these explanations, e.g., Freudian.

Aspirations affect motivation; society is dynamic and human needs seem capable of almost infinite extension.

REFERENCES

1. Bayton, James A., 'Motivation, cognition, learning: basic factors in consumer behaviour', *Journal of Marketing*, vol. 22, January 1958.

2. Hilgard, Ernest R., Richard C. Atkinson, and Rita L. Atkinson, *Introduction to Psychology*, Harcourt Brace Jovanovich, New York, 1975.
3. Krech, David, Richard S. Crutchfield, and Egerton L. Ballachey, *Individual in Society*, McGraw-Hill, New York, 1962.
4. Thouless, R. H., *General and Social Psychology*, University Tutorial Press, London, 1967.
5. Cey-Bert, Robert-Gyula, 'Food preferences reveal a new pattern', *European Research*, September 1974.
6. Beer, Stafford, *Cybernetics and Management*, English University Press, London, 1971.
7. Asch, Solomon E., *Social Psychology*, Prentice-Hall, Englewood Cliffs, New Jersey, 1952.
8. Kassarjian, Harold H., and Thomas S. Robertson, *Perspectives in Consumer Behaviour*, Scott Foreman, Glenview, Illinois, 1968.
9. Maslow, A. H., 'A theory of human motivation', *Psychological Review*, vol. 50, 1943.
10. McGregor, Douglas, M., *Leadership and Motivation*, MIT Press, Cambridge, Massachusetts, 1966.
11. Maier, Norman, R. F., *Psychology in Industry*, Houghton Mifflin, Boston, Massachusetts, 1965.
12. Keys, A., J. Brozek, A. Henschel, O. Mickelson, and H. L. Taylor, *The Biology of Human Starvation*, University of Minnesota Press, Minneapolis, 1960.
13. Maslow, A. H., *Motivation and Personality*, Harper, New York, 1954.
14. Kotler, Philip, *Marketing Management: Analysis, Planning and Control*, Prentice-Hall, Englewood Cliffs, New Jersey, 1967.
15. McClelland, David C., *The Achieving Society*, Free Press, New York, 1967.
16. Andreski, Stanislav (ed.), *Max Weber on Capitalism, Bureaucracy and Religion: A Selection of Texts*, Allen and Unwin, Hemel Hempstead, 1980.
17. Overy, R. J., *William Morris, Viscount Nuffield*, European Publications, 1976.
18. Campbell, R. H., and R. G. Wilson, *Entrepreneurship in Britain 1750–1939*, A. and C. Black, London, 1975.
19. Packard, Vance, *The Status Seekers*, Penguin, London, 1969.
20. Galbraith, J. K., *The Affluent Society*, Penguin, London, 1962.
21. Jacobson, Eugene and Jerome Kossoff, 'Self-percept and consumer attitudes toward small cars', *Journal of Applied Psychology*, vol. 47, August 1963.
22. McClelland, David C., 'An advocate of power', *International Management*, vol. 20, July 1975.
23. Levitt, Theodore, 'The morality of advertising', *Harvard Business Review*, July/August 1970.
24. Pilditch, James, 'Product design for industrial goods', *Marketing*, November 1971.
25. Copeland, M. T., *Principles of Merchandising*, A. W. Shaw, Chicago, 1924.
26. Katona, George, *The Powerful Consumer*, McGraw-Hill, New York, 1960.
27. Berelson, Bernard, and Gary A. Steiner, *Human Behaviour: An Inventory of Scientific Findings*, Harcourt, Brace and World, New York, 1964.
28. Howard, John A., and Jagdish N. Sheth, *The Theory of Buyer Behaviour*, John Wiley, New York, 1969.
29. Kassarjian, Harold H., 'Personality and consumer behaviour: a review', *Journal of Marketing Research*, vol. 8, November 1971.
30. Cheskin, Louis, *How to Predict What People will Buy*, Liveright, New York, 1952.
31. Valentine, C. W., *The Experimental Psychology of Beauty*, Methuen, London, 1962.
32. Deutsch, Karl W., 'Technology and social change: fundamental changes in knowledge, technology and society', *Human Systems Management*, vol. 1, no. 2, September 1980.
33. Chisnall, Peter M., *Marketing Research: Analysis and Measurement*, McGraw-Hill, Maidenhead, 1982.

REVIEW AND DISCUSSION QUESTIONS

1. What are the key distinctions between high and low involvement purchase situations? Outline the implications of these distinctions for marketing activity.
2. Do marketers really need to distinguish between motives, needs, and wants?

3. How might Maslow's need hierarchy be used by a supermarket manager in segmenting customers and in highlighting appropriate store environment features?
4. Describe how motivational conflict might arise for a consumer in the purchase of each of the following: (a) a foreign holiday (b) a whipped ice-cream cone (c) a CD player (d) a children's computer game.
5. Why should marketers incorporate moods and emotions into their marketing strategies?
6. Do you consider that McClelland was justified in giving such prominence to the human need for achievement among consumers?

FOUR

PERSONALITY

4.1 INTRODUCTION

People are often said to be 'characters', to have a lot of 'personality', to have certain personality traits; they are described, rather loosely, as extroverts or introverts. Personality factors seem to be very variable, and are sometimes associated with certain types or brands of products. So, in attempting to understand buying behaviour, an appreciation of the nature and influence of personality would be helpful.

4.2 DEFINITION OF PERSONALITY

Although the word 'personality' is quite widely used in everyday speech, it has specific meaning to psychologists who do not, however, share a commonly agreed definition. It is a complex subject with many variables which has been approached from several theoretical directions. Analysts, while disagreeing about a general definition, as Kassarjian and Sheffett[1] note, tend to 'somehow tie it in to the concept of consistent responses to the world of stimuli surrounding the individual'. Because people tend to be fairly consistent in dealing with events in their everyday lives, 'these generalized patterns of response of modes . . . can be called personality'.

People obviously differ from one another in many ways: physique, intelligence, professional and other occupational training, social and cultural pursuits, etc. Also, they differ in their reactions to environmental influences. Assessment of an individual's personality demands consideration of many factors, since it is shaped by inborn potential, unique experiences, and by cultural and social influences.[3]

Personality is often defined as covering all the ways in which one individual can differ from another,[2] as the characteristic patterns of behaviour and ways of thinking that determine a person's adjustment to the environment,[3] or 'as the substantial, concrete unit of mental life that exists in forms that are definitely single and individual'.[4] Jahoda and Warren defined it as referring to the 'total organisation of internal psychological functioning'.[5] Unlike traits, which are concerned with particular characteristics or aspects of an individual's personality, a personality type embraces all the identified traits of a person.

People obviously differ from one another in many ways: physique, intelligence, professional and other occupational training, social and cultural pursuits, etc. Also, they differ in their reactions to environmental influences. Assessment of an individual's personality demands consideration of many factors, since it is shaped by inborn potential, unique experiences, and by cultural and social influences.[3]

Thouless has observed that 'personality tests' are often distinguished from 'intelligence tests' and refer to tests of characteristics such as aggressiveness or altruism.[2] Used in this restricted way, 'personality' is seen to have virtually the same meaning as what is generally meant by 'character'. If this narrower sense is accepted, personality can be defined as 'the system of emotional dispositions which determine an individual's characteristic ways of behaving in different situations'. Elements of personality that can be measured are termed 'traits' (discussed in Sec. 4.4).

4.3 THEORIES OF PERSONALITY

Personality theories attempt to explain the behaviour of individuals; they share the characteristic of many other psychological theories, for example, motivation, for they are legion and depend largely on the orientation of their authors. None offers a completely satisfactory explanation of personality. The fascinating relationships between behaviour and personality have been studied through the centuries by philosophers, medical researchers, and behavioural scientists and have resulted in diverse speculations, some of which are more remarkable for their ingenuity than feasibility.

Four major theoretical approaches to understanding personality have been given by Hilgard:[3] trait, psychoanalytic, social learning, and humanistic (self-concept). These theories are complex and necessarily demand careful study. However, in order that some insight can be had into the general nature of these models, they will be discussed in outline and related, wherever possible, to marketing situations.

Although for purposes of discussion, the four theories will be treated individually, there will tend to be some 'overflow' between the various models. For example, traits have been developed by some of the neo-Freudian psychologists, such as Horney, and Riesman adopted social typologies which, although discussed in Sec. 4.6 on social learning, also bear on the trait approach to the study of personality.

4.4 TRAIT THEORIES

Trait theories are based on the classification of people into various personality types. Such early theories of personality are to be found in the descriptions of the various temperaments which Hippocrates, the Greek physician, propounded some 2000 years ago. He distinguished four temperaments—sanguine, bilious, nervous, and phlegmatic—and stated that these were determined by the presence in the body of a predominant 'fluid of humour': blood, choler, melancholy, and phlegm. His theories were to persist for about 1500 years, and traces are to be seen, for example, in early English literature.

Many years later, the German psychiatrist, Kretschmer, developed three physical groupings: pyknic (rounded contours of face and body); asthenic (lean, flat-chested, and narrow shouldered); and athletic (large muscles and bones), as bases for theories of temperament.

Other researchers, such as W. H. Sheldon, extended Kretschmer's theories considerably, and also distinguished three types of physique with which were associated corresponding temperaments: endomorphy (relative predominance of roundness in body); mesomorphy (relative predominance of muscle, bone, and connective tissue); and ectomorphy (relative predominance of linearity and fragility). Endomorphs are short, plump, even-tempered and socially relaxed—they are probably good marketing targets for food and drink. Mesomorphs are fond of physical activity and tend to be noisy and somewhat insensitive—good targets for sports equipment, membership of golf and tennis clubs, etc. Ectomorphs tend to be tall and thin, fond of their own company, and are restrained socially—perhaps good targets for booksellers and high quality musical equipment.

These three broad classifications of people closely parallel Kretschmer's typologies. But Sheldon realized that people could not be fitted neatly into such definitive slots, so he devised a seven-point scale for each of the three characteristics to be found in an individual.

The Swiss psychiatrist, Jung, introduced into psychological discussion the concepts of introversion and extroversion. The introverted person tended to be inward-looking and meditative. At the other extreme was the extrovert, who was outward-going, responsive to external stimuli, and impulsive. Obviously, this simplistic model ignores the complex nature of human behaviour. Later, Jung refined this dichotomy by subdividing introverts and extroverts according to the relative dominance of four psychological functions—sensation, thinking, feeling, and intuition.

Jung's original theory has popularly been misunderstood and people are often characterized rather crudely as either extroverts or introverts. But as Thouless[2] explained, individuals can be found along the whole range between the extremes, and there are, however, many more to be found clustered together in the centre of the continuum. Related to buying behaviour, the extrovert may well choose occupations and hobbies which have high social impact, such as selling or show business.

Although physical characteristics may well play some part in an individual's personality, the relationship in reality is far more subtle, and there is comparatively little research evident to support these trait models.

Personality traits have been defined as 'those characteristics that account for differences among people and that are predictive of their behaviour'.[6] These personal differences in response to stimuli tend to be relatively enduring and evolve from heredity, personal experience, and environmental influences. Britt wrote in 1949: 'Everyone has a very personal and unique way of responding to his environment. In fact, our ways of behaving are usually sufficiently unique to enable other individuals to describe us fairly accurately as talkative, shy, bold, timid or otherwise'.[7] These descriptions refer to behavioural traits which have become incorporated into the complete personality of an individual. Traits are ingrained and stable dispositions to respond to certain situations in characteristic ways. These situations may involve people or products and services, or all three. Personality is made up of a set of traits or variables, some of which will be commonly held and others which will be specific to individuals. These traits or factors are measurable in various ways—see later discussion on catalogue of traits.

Differences between traits and attitudes

Traits differ from attitudes in that they are general characteristics which are not directed at anything in particular, whereas attitudes are predispositions to act towards specific people or objects. (These will be discussed in Chapter 5.)

> Aggressiveness . . . might be said to be a general trait of personality—denoting a tendency to be hostile towards all and sundry. However, a 'hostile attitude towards coloured people' is much less global and has reference outside the person to the social object of the attitude. The man in the New Yorker cartoon who declared that he hated everybody regardless of race, creed or colour was referring to his personality, not to his attitude.[5]

Characteristics of traits

Traits differ in the strength in which they are present in individuals; there is not a universal quality in, for example, the trait of activity. Some people are obviously far more active than others. Ballachey distinguishes four significant characteristics that affect personal variations in traits: stability, pervasiveness, consistency, and patterning.[8]

The limited empirical evidence available suggests that the traits of self-confidence and sociability may be relatively stable over a period of time. Competitiveness is a highly pervasive trait, although its strength varies in individuals. Consistency may be of interest in marketing practice: for example, it could be said that the 'bargain hunter' displays a consistent trait which may be related to dominance, i.e., there is an attempt to control the impact of economic phenomena.

Interaction of traits

Traits do not exist in isolation within an individual; they tend to combine and determine the actions taken by a person in both social and economic life. Aggressive traits may be modified by those of sociability and cooperativeness. There is no simple explanation of human behaviour. Strongly argumentative customers may, for instance, possess traits of inferiority which cause them to display a degree of aggression towards suppliers. Experienced marketers look behind the mask of behaviour, and attempt to find out more about their customers' needs and problems.

Catalogue of traits

Personality traits have been described with bewildering prodigality, and are usually associated with specific types of personality measurement techniques. Thurstone's Temperament Schedule measures seven different characteristics: active, vigorous, impulsive, dominant, stable, sociable, and reflective. Edwards's Personal Preference Schedule (EPPS), based on personality needs developed by Henry Murray, takes account of the following psychological variables: achievement, deference, exhibition, autonomy, affiliation, intraception, dominance, abasement, change, aggression, and heterosexuality. The popularity of the EPPS in consumer behaviour studies can be traced to the pioneer research by Evans on car ownership. (The controversial findings of this research are discussed in Sec. 4.9.)

Allport's system has 11 bipolar traits: broad/narrow emotions; strong/weak emotions; ascendancy/submission; expansion/reclusion; persistence/vacillation; extroversion/introversion; self-objectification/self-deception; self-assurance/self-distrust; gregariousness/solitariness; atruism/self-seeking; and social intelligence (tact)/invariability of behaviour in different social circumstances.[4] Some of these factors are closely related to everyday expressions and descriptions of behaviour.

Sophisticated measures of personality have used factor analysis; Cattell[9,10] and Eysenck,[11,12] for example, have developed this particular statistical approach. Cattell, identified 16 factors which he held to be basic traits underlying personality; these bipolar traits are: reserved/outgoing; less intelligent/more intelligent; affected by feelings/emotionally stable; humble/assertive; serious/happy-go-lucky; expedient/conscientious; restrained/venturesome; tough-minded/tender-minded; trusting/suspicious; practical/imaginative; forthright/shrewd; self-assured/apprehensive; conservative/experimenting; group-dependent/self-sufficient; uncontrolled/controlled; and relaxed/tense.

Along a continuum each set of factors is applied to an individual in order to arrive at a personality profile. To facilitate this task, Cattell developed a special personality factor questionnaire.

Eysenck restricted his approach to personality factors to two dimensions: introversion/extroversion and stability/instability. Within each quadrant found from these dimensions, eight personality traits were identified, making 32 in all.

The California Personality Inventory (CPI) has been developed in several studies of innovativeness and opinion leadership (see Chapter 11) with relatively limited success in general.

The Minnoesota Multiphase Personality Inventory (MMPI) was originally constructed to help in psychiatric diagnoses of personality disorders. Unlike the tests based on factor analysis, the MMPI uses a large number of statements (550) concerned with attitudes, emotional reactions, physical and psychological symptoms, and past experiences. Alternative responses can be 'true', 'false' or 'cannot say'; these are scored and related to different kinds of psychological disturbances.

Ballachey classifies response traits into three 'arbitrary categories': role dispositions, sociometric dispositions, and expressive dispositions.[8] Under these headings, traits, which are 'fairly representative' of those identified by investigators, are listed as follows:

Role dispositions	(In parentheses are opposites)
Ascendance	(Social timidity)
Dominance	(Submissiveness)
Social initiative	(Social passivity)
Independence	(Dependence)

Sociometric dispositions	
Accepting of others	(Rejecting of others)
Sociability	(Unsociability)
Friendliness	(Unfriendliness)
Sympathetic	(Unsympathetic)

Expressive dispositions	
Competiveness	(Uncompetiveness)
Aggressiveness	(Non-aggressiveness)
Self-consciousness	(Social poise)
Exhibitionistic	(Self-effacing)

Role dispositions refer to the behaviour of an individual in particular situations. At different times, an individual may fulfil several roles—that of spouse, parent, business executive, or captain of the tennis club. To a considerable degree, people's activities in particular roles will be governed by the expectations of the society of which they are part, as well as being influenced by their personality traits.

Sociometric dispositions concern relationship with other people. In group-behaviour studies, Moreno introduced a method of investigation—*sociometry*—which analysed the personal preferences of individual members of an occupational group for associating with other members of the group.[13] As a result, a sociometric diagram would be prepared which could graphically indicate, for instance, 'isolates' (those individuals whose company was not generally thought to be desirable); 'influential' people would also be noted. In marketing research group discussions, and where members are fairly well known to each other, there may be scope for adopting this technique to identify 'leaders'.

Expressive dispositions relate to the ability of self-expression which an individual may possess when responding to others. Marketing specialists may like to reflect for a little while on the applicability of some of these traits towards building a successful career, and link these with the earlier discussion on needs and motives.

Karen Horney's paradigm

Karen Horney, one of the principal influences in the neo-Freudian psychoanalytic movement, developed a system of classifying her patients according to their predominant interpersonal response trait:[14]

1. Those who move towards people (*compliant*).
2. Those who move against people (*aggressive*).
3. Those who move away from people (*detached*).

Horney summarized her tripartite typology as follows: 'Where the compliant type looks at his fellow men with the silent question, "Will he like me?"—and the aggressive type wants to know, "How strong an adversary is he?" or "Can he be useful to me?"—the detached person's concern is, "Will he interfere with me? Will he want to influence me or leave me alone?"

Compliant individuals seek to be loved, appreciated, and needed. They avoid conflict and do not engage in activities that are likely to antagonize others. For them, important values are sympathy, unselfishness, love, understanding, etc., which help to endear them to their friends.

Aggressive individuals look upon the world as an arena where only the fittest survive. They need to excel and to achieve recognition, to exploit people and situations fully.

Detached individuals are concerned with emotional self-sufficiency and with privacy. They do not want to share or to be troubled by the experiences of others. Independence is of paramount importance to these people. Horney suggested that individuals who were frustrated in either of the other tendencies, or both, may adopt 'detachment' in an attempt to compensate for their lack of success.

Cohen undertook research in consumer behaviour on the basis of Horney's three basic psychological orientations.[15] Although the results were not conclusive, he was able to indicate some findings that are of interest to marketers. As this research tends to be unique in attempting to test the Horney classification of traits related to products, some details will be given.

A questionnaire, incorporating a 35-item Likert-type scale, was administered to a convenience sample of 157 business undergraduates in US colleges, with the objectives of measuring product and brand usage and media preference as well as the CAD (Compliant/ Aggressive/Detached) scale. A wide range of representative products was covered by the inquiry. Cohen found that 'compliant' people preferred recognized brand names, and used more mouthwash and toilet soap. He concluded that high compliant people should be the best targets for advertising these toiletries 'because of their greater concern for possibly offending others'. Aggressive types tended to prefer a manual razor to an electric shaver significantly more than the other types of individuals. They also tended to use more cologne and after-shave lotion than those possessing less aggressive traits. 'Aggressive' people favoured Old Spice deodorant and Van Heusen shirts, whereas 'detached' types showed little interest in such branded goods. On the other hand, no significant patterns of brand usage related to beer consumption, and the number of people who drank wine several times a month (five) was too small for useful analysis. 'High compliants' were found to use Bayer aspirin more than any other type of aspirin compared with the low compliant people.

Horney's paradigm provided an interesting model for Cohen's research, although the findings as a whole are not entirely convincing. He admitted that much more research would be necessary, but 'since much of human action, and probably an even greater segment of human behaviour is interpersonal, Horney's model may have special relevance for marketing'.[15]

Cohen's CAD scale has, however, been viewed by some researchers with a degree of circumspection: 'he admitted to picking and choosing from his data'.[1] Despite these inhibitions, the CAD scale has been applied with some success; for example. Slama, Williams and

Taschian[16] used it in conjunction with the Slama and Taschian involvement scale in research into the shopping habits of undergraduate students at a major western US university. They found that the detached personality type was less involved in purchasing than the compliant or aggressive types.

4.5 PSYCHOANALYTIC THEORIES

Psychoanalytic theories of personality, unlike the traits approach, which is based on self-report, are derived from in-depth study of individuals, whose behaviour is believed to be considerably influenced by the unconscious. In Chapter 3 the instinctive theories of motivation which Freud and his followers originated were referred to; the unconscious influences in personality and motivation are organized around the id, the ego, and the superego.

Freud compared the human mind to an iceberg; the smaller part above the water is termed 'conscious experience' while below it is the far greater mass termed the 'unconscious mind'.

Strong drives and urges emanate from the depths of human nature; conflicts and neuroses complicate the pattern of human behaviour. Some desires appear to be incompatible with other dominant tendencies of the personality, so they are repressed and banished to the unconscious. His emphasis on infantile sexuality and the three stages in a child's development—oral, anal, and phallic—exposed him to severe criticism, and led to Adler, for example, breaking their association. As noted in Chapter 3, Freud's emphasis on the procreative drive—libido or sexual energy—has tended to be misunderstood in popular discussion. In his view, sexuality was not confined to the reproductive processes, but could be related to a wide variety of pleasurable feelings associated with the body and its activities. It could also be sublimated through tenderness and expressions of friendship.

Freudian concepts have been widely adopted in motivation research, and it has already been observed that the indiscriminate application of Freudian psychology has not always resulted in valid marketing research. It should be acknowledged, however, that Freud made a fundamental contribution to the understanding of human behaviour by his challenge to the long-held belief that human beings are completely rational creatures in charge of their own destiny. The complexity of human behaviour is now generally acknowledged, and researchers in marketing have developed techniques to analyse the deeper motivations that influence some buying decisions. Particular attention has been given to the symbolic aspects of products, apart from their economic and functional qualities.

Ernest Dichter, who studied psychology and psychoanalysis in Vienna, went to the USA in 1938, and developed what became known as motivation research. He founded the Institute for Motivational Research with its headquarters in Croton-on-Hudson. His book *The Strategy of Desire*[17] reflected the strong influence of Freudian psychology. He liked to regard himself as a 'cultural anthropologist' who, in depth interviews and group discussions, endeavoured to penetrate people's opinions, motives, etc., related to the purchase and use of specific products. Critics have speculated on how much of Dichter's advice was based on plain common sense or ordinary intuition and how much sprang from the Freudian clinical approach. One example of plain common sense, which any alert advertising agent would support, was Dichter's advice to airline companies who wanted to advertise that air travel was safe, and that people need not be afraid to fly. Traditional advice, when advertising potentially dangerous products, is not to argue that there is danger, but rather to stress the positive qualities. Argument merely helps to reinforce people's anxieties. Dichter recommended that airline advertising should concentrate on the positive fact that flying was speedy and convenient, and that business people using this method of travel would be able to return home faster. This last point would help to overcome individuals' disapproval of their spouses' frequent use of air travel.

Another leading motivation researcher in the USA is Louis Cheskin, whose name has become closely associated with the study of colour as a motivating influence. He has drawn attention to the fact that consumption at one time was mainly of a biological and material nature, but in the affluent economies of modern communities, consumption is largely psychological.[18] Manufacturers should take care to ensure that their products have favourable psychological meanings, because the success of their products will increasingly depend on these subtle appeals.

Pierre Martineau has also emphasized the need to research the hidden motivations of buyers of a wide range of products, and services.[19] The 'psychological label' on the product cannot be ignored; when a product is bought, more than physical satisfaction is sought. The self-concept discussed earlier revealed that through the purchase of products such as food, cars, clothing, or cosmetics, people endeavour to express their personalities as well as obtaining physical benefits. A cigar, a perfume, a shaving lotion, a face powder, a lipstick have a minimum of functional use. Millions of people live just as long, are just as happy without even using them. Physiologically they are completely unnecessary. The product areas and brands are defined almost completely by their subjective meanings.[19]

Some of the more fanciful ideas of motivation research were revealed by Vance Packard's *The Hidden Persuaders* which, in the late 1950s, attracted popular attention and shocked many people by its exposé of methods of investigation into the covert motivations affecting consumer purchase.[20] Packard's book caused some misunderstanding; he went too far by classifying almost the entire activities of advertising practitioners as Freudian depth-oriented. In doing so, he failed to observe that good intuitive copywriting—and there are lots of examples in Victorian advertising campaigns—was not necessarily founded on a depth approach. Of course, he had fun in pointing out some of the more bizarre Freudian interpretations of buying behaviour. He mentioned, for example, the soap manufacturers who received conflicting advice from two leading American motivation research firms on the question of featuring the soap's alleged deodorant qualities. One firm found that people wanted to get rid of their bodily odours, while the other found that people felt subconsciously uneasy at the thought of losing their distinctive body odours. So the unfortunate client just talked about the soap's nice clean smell in his advertisements.

Motivation research techniques are considered in some detail elsewhere.[21]

Freudian psychology was modified by Jung, who objected to the strong emphasis given to sexual impulses, since he believed that people were motivated by many other equally important instincts. In his view, the 'collective unconscious'—a collection of all the memories and patterns of past behaviour—exercised a profound effect on people and predisposed them to act in certain ways. As already observed, Jung originated the personality bipolar traits of extroversion and introversion.

Other neo-Freudians, such as Karen Horney (whose traits model was discussed in Sec. 4.4), stressed that people were shaped much more by their environment than by instincts, which Freud tended to see as dominant factors in personality.

4.6 SOCIAL LEARNING THEORIES

Social learning theories of personality focus on the learning processes by means of which individuals develop behaviour that enables them to cope with the various problems they encounter in life. From these experiences, people develop personality differences.

David Riesman, a social scientist at Harvard University, wrote a distinguished study of the social character of people in US society.[22] His book, *The Lonely Crowd*, stirred some controversy on account of his prognosis of incipient and profound changes which were affecting the American way of life. According to Riesman, human beings could be classified into three types of social characters: tradition-directed, inner-directed, and other-directed. He argued that, depending on economic, demographic, and various cultural factors, a society could generally be said to be made up of one or two of these principal categories. A person may also be found to correspond with any one of these types.

Tradition-directed people guide their behaviour by membership of a particular clan or caste. Riesman believed that there were few, if any, such individuals in the USA today. They would be characterized as generally slow to change, dependent on family and kinship; they have a very low degree of social mobility, and possess a narrowly defined set of values. *Inner-directed* people depend on their own inner values and standards to guide their behaviour in a rapidly changing modern society. They tend to be largely self-reliant, and develop inner strengths to help them combat the strains resulting from insecurity of employment and from the other problems of industrial communities. The *other-directed* people tend to rely on the values of those with whom they associate to guide their actions. In an impersonalized atmosphere created by mass-production techniques and large-scale methods of distribution, other-directed people attempt to find expression for their personality in developing social contacts; other people's favourable reactions become increasingly important for this type of person's emotional satisfaction. 'While all people want and need to be liked by some of the people some of the time, it is only the modern other-directed type who make this their chief source of direction and their chief area of sensitivity'.[22]

Riesman believed that the other-directed person was becoming the predominant type in modern, industrial societies, particularly in areas of high population. Contemporary US society was seen as being in a state of transition from predominant inner-directedness to that of predominant other-directedness, with the middle classes of large metropolitan areas having the greatest numbers of other-directed people. Riesman appeared to think that the population could be projected as somewhere along a continuum from inner- to other-directedness, with very few people to be found at either extreme. He predicted that younger people would be more other-directed than older people; also that those of higher socio-economic groups would be more other-directed than people of lower socio-economic status. His social character typologies were not intended by him for classifying personality; however, his social characterizations have tended to become associated with personality theories.

In 1962, Centers[23] reported research undertaken to test Riesman's theories. Inner- and other-directedness was found to be normally distributed without any appreciable correlation with socio-economic groupings, but with other-directedness being more prevalent in younger people. Centers 'tentatively suggested' that Riesman was correct in believing that other-directedness was increasing in the USA 'inasmuch as younger persons tend to be more other-directed than older people'.

Dornbusch and Hickman[24] conducted extensive research into the effects of other-directedness in consumer goods advertising in the USA. The sample consisted of all 816 issues of the *Ladies' Home Journal* over a 67-year period (1890–1956). This publication was selected because of its 'essentially middle-class orientation' and woman readership. The researchers analysed a random sample drawn from only 41 years' issues because of contraints imposed by time and available funds. It was hypothesized that the proportion of other-directed advertisements would increase through time; six indices of other-directedness were used. These 'fell logically' into two types: endorsements by individuals or groups, and claims that product usage was related to satisfactions in interpersonal relations.

The result of this study showed that the advertising of consumer goods in the USA over the period 1890–1921 had indicated a marked change in orientation which 'was closely related to the sphere of other-directedness'. However, the researchers admitted that after 1940 there appeared to be a decline in this orientation that 'cannot be appropriately evaluated in the light of this first set of data'. They warned against generalizing freely from their restricted field of consumer product advertising to the wider area of US society in general. While they confessed that their original scepticism about the value of Riesman's theories had been replaced by a more credible approach, only further research could reveal the many variables which affect the orientation of advertising appeals.

Kassarjian[25] also researched into the applicability of Riesman's typologies to advertising copy. He prepared 28 pairs of advertisements; one advertisement in each set had an 'inner-directed' appeal while the other had an 'other-directed' appeal; each pair offered the same product or service. The subjects of the test were 200 undergraduates in business administration courses, who, after viewing the prepared advertisements, were asked to complete a questionnaire related to exposure to various advertising media. It was hypothesized that:

1. Inner- and other-directed individuals would prefer advertisements with distinctive appeals of these types.
2. Other-directed individuals would believe that people in general would prefer the advertisements that they themselves liked.
3. Other-directed subjects would have greater exposure to the mass media.

Kassarjian found that other-directed people tended to prefer other-directed advertisements, while inner-directed individuals showed preference for inner-directed advertisements However, both inner- and other-directed individuals felt that, in general, people would be most influenced by other-directed appeals. Different levels of exposure to mass advertising were not found to be significant on the whole. These results, it was stated, confirmed generally the hypotheses 'and may be interpreted as further empirical evidence for several of the Riesman hypotheses concerning social character'. Kassarjian concluded that a social character typology may well be significant in persuasive communication strategies.

Other studies have tended to follow the general pattern of findings: 'a few studies find and a few do *not* find meaningful relationships between consumer behaviour and other measures'.[26]

4.7 SELF-CONCEPT THEORIES

The humanistic theories of personality focus on the individuals' self-image and their urge towards self-fulfilment (self-actualization). Self-concept, developed from Freudian psychological concepts, is of interest of marketers because purchasing behaviour may be significantly influenced by the relationship which products bear to the personalities of buyers. Products and brands tend to be viewed as projections of the self-image of the buyer; their symbolic meanings may give deep satisfactions which superficial analysis will not reveal.

In Chapter 3, some reference was made to the impact of self-image on consumption habits when discussing Maslow's hierarchy of needs. This study will now be extended and related to further empirical studies in the area of personality traits.

The self-concept theories stem from the philosophical projections of Carl Rogers' self theory, which Maslow and other researchers have developed. Individual needs and goals are closely related to the enhancement and protection of 'self'. Individuals develop cognitions about themselves which lead them to actions aimed to maintain and improve their well-being. 'Self' has been defined as 'the sum total of all that a man can call his—his body, traits and abilities; his material possessions; his family, friends and enemies; his vocations and avocations and much else'.[27] This amalgam of physical psychological, and mental attitudes and beliefs which contributes to the concept of 'self' is made up, as Sullivan has remarked, 'of reflected appraisals'. This self-concept also influences the views which an individual holds of others: 'the peculiarity exists that one can find in others only that which is in the self'.[28] Hence, the sort of person that individuals believe themselves to be is based on the reactions of others towards the individual, who then gathers clues as to what sort of person he or she appears to be. This self-concept in turn influences interpersonal relationships, causing individuals to react to their family, friends, or colleagues in ways that become characteristic of their personality needs. But, as Newman has pointed out: 'The image one has of himself, of course, may not be accurate in terms of how he is seen by others'.[29] The individual may have misread the reactions of others: some people appear to lack perception in judging the impact that they have on others. What people are to themselves—their self-concept—is built up of impressions gathered from childhood years of how those with whom they have associated have appeared to evaluate them.

On the basis of this self-image, individuals will be likely to develop an idealized concept of themselves: the sort of person they would like to be. This desirable self-image may never be fully realized but it will stimulate an individual to undertake tasks to improve knowledge, or to develop talents. It may, and usually does, influence consumption habits. Martineau[19] has declared that successful advertising campaigns relate products to the aspirations and emotions of their audiences. People seek products and brands that are 'compatible' with 'what [they] think or want to be'. Products are bought not only for their physical benefits but also to express the moods, feelings, and attitudes of consumers towards society. In many instances, products have acquired curious psychological significances closely concerned with the personalities of consumers.

As observed earlier, aspirations involved in achieving an 'ideal self' may lead to an individual developing a new pattern of consumption in order to gain acceptance by certain groups of people. (The influence of group membership on buying behaviour will be fully explored in Part Three.)

Empirical evidence on self-concept

Birdwell[30] sought to demonstrate that people's perception of their car is essentially congruent with their perception of themselves, and the average perception of a specific car type is different for owners of different sorts of cars. By means of Osgood's semantic differential scaling technique, Birdwell developed a series of bipolar terms to describe the 'self' and the car. The sample of 100 car owners was selected at random from a universe formed by four groups of all the new-car purchasers in Travis County, Texas, who had bought a car during the four-month period prior to the time of interviewing.

The results of the study showed that a close relationship, reflecting a high degree of congruence, existed between the perceptions which car owners had of themselves and their cars. Owners of prestige cars, who are more likely to have substantial purchasing power, tended to identify closely with their cars. 'As one moves down the social and economic ladder, the consumer is more restricted in his ability to buy a car that is truly expressive of self'. Birdwell admitted, however, that his study suffered from certain limitations: the smallness of sample and the fact that it was restricted to only one locale. He also reflected that while it appeared that cars 'are often extensions of the owner's image of self. It should be remembered, however, that what a person wants and likes influences what he sees'. It may be that only after people have committed themselves to a make of car, they begin to perceive it as an extension of their personality. This post-decision reinforcement has been the subject of comment by several researchers, including Kassarjian.[26] Sheth reported that he modified Birdwell's study to obtain perceptions of an ideal car and a 'nonsense' car along with the actual car owned.[31] He found that 'congruence was highest with the ideal car, second with currently owned car, and last with the "nonsense" car'. These findings supported Birdwell's study.

Other research in this field was undertaken by Grubb and Hupp related to Pontiac and Volkswagen ownership.[32] They found that owners of one particular brand of car had 'definite perceptions about the self-concept characteristic' of fellow owners and identified with them, while they saw themselves as significantly different from owners of competing makes of car.

Jacobson and Kossoff[33] also researched the relationships between self-perception and attitudes towards small cars. They found that drivers who perceived themselves as 'cautious conservatives' tended to prefer small cars for their convenience and economy, whereas another group—'confident explorers'—favoured large cars, which were viewed as means of expressing their projected control of the environment.

Dolich[34] also tested the congruency between self-images and product brands; he concluded that greater similarity existed between individuals' self-concept and their most preferred brands than between least preferred brands. Favoured brands helped to reinforce the self-concept.

Green, and other researchers[35] examined further the relationship of image congruity to brand perception and preference for autmobile models, and the relevance of multi-dimensional scaling to this type of research. A convenience sample of 45 business undergraduates were asked to place in rank order 11 brands of cars and to relate these to their own self-concepts. The researchers concluded that preference was *not* positively related to image closeness 'for a number of subjects'; the data reflected 'instances of both proverbs: "Birds of a feather flock together" and "Opposites attract". Congruence between self-concept and product and brand preference requires considerably more study . . . it seems clear to us that the relationship between image congruence and preference is more complex than previous marketing research studies may suggest'. Regarding the applicability of multi-dimensional scaling methods for this type of inquiry, Green *et al.* considered that the methodology would have increasing usefulness, despite its present statistical limitations.

Ross[36] was concerned with studying the problem of whether the consumption of products reflected the actual or the ideal self-concept of an individual. He hypothesized that the latter was more closely related to consumption preferences than actual self-concept when the object of consumption 'is more rather than less conspicuous to others, and conversely, that actual self-concept was more closely related to consumption preference than ideal self-concept when the object of consumption is less rather than more conspicuous to others'. The research involved a convenience sample of 247 female undergraduate and graduate students at Purdue University. Automobiles were selected to represent 'conspicuous' products, and magazines chosen as being products whose consumption was not so conspicuous. Subjects were asked to disregard their present buying habits when ranking the various brands of these products as being more rather than less similar to their own self-concept (both actual and ideal self-concept).

Ross's first hypothesis was 'strongly supported' by the results. 'Subjects preferred brands of products which were more rather than less similar to their own self-concept. The magnitude of the discrepancy between self-concept (both actual and ideal) and brand image (for both magazines and automobiles) increased as a function of a decrease in subjects' preferences for those brands'.

However, the data did not confirm the second hypothesis. Preferences in consumption related more closely, in fact, to the actual self-concept than to the ideal self-concept for each of the six brands of both types of products. Ross speculated on the measures of self-concept used in the research; it could be argued that 'the most appropriate measure of "ideal" self-concept should have been "self as ideally seen by others" rather than "self as ideally seen by self".'

Despite these qualifications, Ross reported that his findings supported in general the researches undertaken by Birdwell and Grubb and Hupp which have just been reviewed.

Further research, and on a wider scale, would be desirable. The studies reported have indicated that self-concept has an influence on buying behaviour, although the exact nature of this varies according to product types. The small size of many of the samples, the nature of the populations from which they were drawn, the lack of replication, and the arguable bases of some definitions used suggest that caution should be used in applying these researches to marketing practice. An interesting example of product image and self-image was reported in connection with Guinness stout.[37] J. Walter Thompson devised a special promotion aimed to widen the appeal of this drink. 'Guinness still has something of an Ena Sharples' ("Coronation Street") image—middle-aged ladies drinking it because they feel it does them good'. Most drinkers of Guinness were found by research to be over 35 years of age. To attract younger consumers, and also those of higher social groups, the product was advertised as being enjoyed by young people, often in modern, sophisticated surroundings.

4.8 SELF-CONCEPT AND SELF-GIFTS

The giving of gifts to oneself is a relatively unexplored aspect of self-concept. Self-gifts may originate as rewards and incentives for personal accomplishments, to celebrate specific anniversaries such as birthdays, graduation, and so on. Such gifts tend to reinforce self-concept and may, as Mick and DeMoss state,[38] 'constitute a sizeable share of self-directed consumer behaviour'. The prospect of self-administered reward may act as an incentive to achieve some challenging goal or to raise existing levels of performance; in some cases, self-gifts may act as compensation for disappointments, bereavement, personal injury, and so on.

The ego-involvement associated with self-gifts suggests that their acquisition provides significant psychological satisfactions. Mick and DeMoss defined self-gifts as: (1) personally symbolic self-communication through (2) special indulgences that tend to be (3) premeditated and (4) highly context bound. Authentic self-gifts are stated to have 'elevated levels' of each of the first three elements, and are characterized by distinct emphasis on the fourth component. As with gift-giving in general, the socio-cultural environment appears to be the 'principal arbitrator' of occasions when gifts, including self-gifts, are acceptable. It might be argued that self-gifts, particularly those of a luxurious or hedonistic nature, reflect some degree of narcissism with overtones of Freudian psychology and self-centredness. Harsher critics may suggest that extended self-indulgence of this kind could, in some cases, be a form of regressive behaviour. Similarly fertile Freudian projections have been made about those who avidly collect stamps, coins, or objets d'art.

Whatever their motivation, self-gifts play a recognizable role in society, adding pleasure, relieving stress, rewarding personal efforts, etc. This form of consumer behaviour is likely to increase in affluent societies, and further systematic research would be worth while. Analyses of promotional strategies related to specific kinds of products would be likely to reveal an increasing emphasis on self-gifting, for example, 'Treat yourself to a . . .' or 'It's time you had a . . .'.

4.9 STEREOTYPES

Walter Lippmann introduced the concept of stereotype related to the perceptions which people obtain about other individuals' objects, and events.[39] 'In the great blooming, buzzing confusion of the outer world we pick out what our culture has already defined for us, and we tend to perceive that which we have picked out in the form stereotyped for us by our culture'. Some leading British researchers[40] have commented that 'National stereotypes are, of course, shameless caricatures based partly on observation, partly on hearsay, and partly (perhaps mostly) on prejudice'.

People are frequently described in terms that greatly simplify, and also exaggerate, some nationalistic tendencies; they are 'stereotype personalities'. Scots may be referred to as mean; the Irish as quarrelsome; the French as romantic lovers; or the English as solid and respectable. Obviously, these shorthand descriptions paint far too simplified a picture of complex human beings from whatever country they may originate. Provided that stereotyping is not carried to absurdity, it may be useful in identifying certain personality traits in customers for some ranges of products. Many products could be described in terms of their customers' general characteristics. Media selection takes account of demographic data and readership figures. Qualitative research could add further valuable information related to personality profiles, and particular traits of significance in the purchase of certain types of products could be identified.

Research at the Massachusetts Institute of Technology[41] indicated that managers in both the public and private sectors of the US economy expressed strong negative stereotypes of their counterparts in the other sector. Such distorted beliefs were inimical to cooperative efforts between the public and private sectors. 'Managers in each sector feel that they have difficult jobs, and their counterparts in the other sector have it quite easy. . . . The only exception to this bilateral myopia is a grudging admission that some demands are unique in each sector'. Even professional administrators, therefore, seem to be quite heavily biased by stereotype projections.

The intrusion of stereotypes was reported as causing the Trades Union Congress (TUC) some concern. A media working party criticized the use in advertising of female stereotypes which were said to be used indiscriminately.[42]

The circulation of the *Guardian*, an influential daily newspaper in the UK, was helped by advertisers' misconceptions fading. 'The idea of the stereotype reader as an earnest young Poly lecturer with a moth-eaten bank balance was brushed aside and by the early 1980s there were few agencies left who thought of the paper's upwardly mobile young bourgeois readers as anything other than a highly profitable marketplace'.[43]

A study of British university students' attitudes towards the stereotype female roles shown in advertisements revealed wide differences but no undue concern.[44] In general, responses reflected a rather cynical attitude; it was acccepted that both male and female stereotypes which were unreal were used in advertisements—but they were discussed as 'part of the advertising game'. This cynicism was in distinct contrast to earlier research in the United States.

A more general study involving an analysis of 317 separate commercials screened in the London ITV area over specific periods during 1981 and 1982 revealed that men and women are portrayed in accordance with their traditional gender roles.[45] Men were projected as having expertise and authority, while women were presented as consumers and occupying roles of dependence in relation to men. It was suggested by the researcher that, contrary to other views, a greater variety in type, style, and tone in commercials would be more likely to bring about an improvement in the portrayal of women in advertisements.

As discussed in later chapters, the role of women in society has markedly changed since the late 1970s. Apart from legislation affecting their employment rights, women as consumers are now recognized to have significant buying power which is by no means confined to routine household supplies. Stereotyping based on gender reflects an inadequate and unimaginative approach, as the London ITV research[45] observed in the early 1980s.

The hit-and-miss attempts of stereotyping has been applied in describing men as well as women: in the mid-1980s a London advertising agency[46] researched 1000 men, across all socio-economic groups and age ranges in order to study their brand choices of 27 types of products, including drink, cigarettes, and toiletries. Groups emerged with labels such as 'untouchables', 'self-exploiters', 'pontificators', 'sleepwalkers', 'token-triers', etc. These various types were described in some detail: for example, 'self-exploiters' were not only entrepreneurial, usually self-employed, hungry for success, but also tending to be resentful of the changes in women's attitudes. They also tended to select brands promoted with the message that buyers knew quality when they saw it. The project commented that at one time they offered people fantasies about a life-style associated with a product, but nowadays people preferred brands which promised to be of some practical use to them

4.10 MARKETING STUDIES RELATED TO PERSONALITY

Several studies have been concerned with automobile brand preferences in the USA. Franklin B. Evans's[47] research results have stimulated considerable controversy ever since they were first published in 1959. He attempted to identify personality differences between the owners of Fords and Chevrolets. He concluded that personality characteristics 'are of little value in indicating whether an individual owns a Ford or a Chevrolet'. Among his critics, Martineau commented that Park Forest, where the research was conducted, was not a representative community. Earlier it had been projected that Ford owners were independent, impulsive, masculine, alert to change, and self-confident, while owners of Chevrolets were conservative, thrifty, prestige conscious, less masculine, and tended to avoid extremes.

In 1960, Ralph Westfall,[48] using a different scaling instrument (Thurstone's Temperament Scale) from Evans, replicated the study. He found that compact and standard car owners did not seem to possess distinctly different personality traits, but that there did appear to be differences in personality characteristics between owners of convertibles and standard versions of cars:

> The characteristics of active, impulsive, stable and sociable appear to have the greatest value as predictors of type of car owned. Individuals who are low in each of the characteristics of active, vigorous, impulsive and sociable are found to be less likely buyers of convertible cars than the average individual. Those who are high in one or several of the characteristics of active, vigorous, impulsive, dominant and sociable are more likely than the average individual to buy convertibles. The characteristic of active is the best prediction of the group.[31]

However, Westfall cautioned against taking these findings uncritically. He referred to the limitations imposed by a sample size (231 respondents), method of sampling used (quota), and the application of probability techniques to data collected by this type of sampling. But the fact that personality differences were discovered between the owners of the two types of cars 'indicates that, at least in some cases, measurable differences do exist between owners of different products serving the same basic function'.[48]

Clearly, further research is necessary before marketers of specific types of products can be in a position to assess the degree of influence of personality variables on their marketing activities. Some pioneer work has been undertaken in certain product areas, but sweeping generalizations should be avoided.

In a 1975 AMA paper, Kassarjian and Sheffett reviewed the results of studies in personality since 1969, by which time about a hundred of these had occurred in marketing literature. In the researchers' opinion: 'review of these studies can be summarized by the single word "equivocal".'[49] The additional studies that have taken place have generally made little contribution to the depth of knowledge, even though they may have expanded it. 'The correlation or relationship between personality test scores and consumer behaviour variables such as product choice, media exposure, innovation, segmentation, etc., are weak at best and thus of little value in prediction'.

Marketing researchers have expanded considerable energies in analysing personality traits such as sociability, emotional stability, aggressiveness, or independence, and have sometimes attempted to explain buying habits related to particular products in terms of these characteristics. As noted earlier, much of the empirical evidence quoted is not very convincing. 'A few studies indicate a strong relationship between personality and aspects of consumer behaviour, a few indicate no relationship, and the great majority indicate that if correlations do exist they are so weak as to be questionable or perhaps meaningless'.[25] This disquieting state of affairs may be due to researchers adopting personality measurements that lack reliability or validity for specific kinds of research inquiries and for the conditions under which they are made.

While it would be naive to attribute to a trait of personality the dominant motive for purchasing some product or service, nevertheless it should be admitted that personality variables may contribute to the final decision to buy. It is surely most likely that personality characteristics do not play their part; their effects, for instance, on selective perception may be significant. People with strong traits of sociability are more likely to patronize social events and to be influenced by the consumption habits of their friends and acquaintances than the detached, retiring person who may prefer more solitary pursuits such as bird watching.

4.11 CONSUMER INVOLVEMENT THEORIES

The psychological concept of involvement was introduced by Sherif and Cantril[50] in 1947 when it was described as the state of an organism confronted with any stimulus that is ego-centred, or when any stimulus is either consciously or subconsciously related to the ego. many different types of involvement are experienced by people, including social, commercial, personal, and buying situations.

Various theories have been advanced in attempts to explain and predict consumers' buying behaviour (see Part Four for extended discussion). Because human needs are many, some of which are sophisticated and others merely mundane and routine, consumer behaviour has been analysed by some researchers as either low involvement or high involvement. The degree of involvement will affect, for instance, the extent to which information will be sought about specific types (and brands) of products and services. Perceived risk, personal interests, and ambitions are other factors likely to influence buying involvement.

Laurent and Kapferer[51] listed four facets of involvement:

1. Perceived importance of the product (its personal meaning).
2. Perceived risk associated with purchase of the product.
3. Symbolic or sign value attributed by the consumer to the product, its purchase, or its consumption.
4. Hedonic value of the product, its emotional appeal, its ability to provide pleasure and affect.

Using a five-point Likert-type scale, 414 housewives were interviewed about their buying habits related to fourteen product categories. The researchers reported that 'as it stands now, involvement theory may be over-simplified'.

While welcoming the contribution to consumer involvement studies made by Laurent and Kapferer, Mittal and Lee[52] felt that they had failed to tackle the question of product-class involvement or brand-choice involvement or both. The former is defined as the degree of interest of a consumer in a product category on an ongoing basis, while the latter refers to the motivation of a consumer in making the right selection from competing brands. For instance, 'a consumer is seldom involved in the washing on an enduring basis, but he/she is likely to be very involved in making the brand selection'.

Mittal and Lee based research on Laurent and Kapferer's four facets but extended them to include both product-involvement and brand-choice involvement. A sample of 78 beer-drinking students was analysed: 'beer was chosen due to its relevance to our respondents'.[51] Results showed good internal reliabilities for perceived importance of brand choice, sign value of the product, sign value of the brand, and hedonic value from the product. The three other facets (perceived product risk, perceived brand risk, and hedonic value at brand level) had modest reliabilities.

It could reasonably be assumed that the involvement factor is high when recreational and hobby products and services are being evaluated. Golf or tennis zealots will most certainly examine thoroughly the design features of a proposed club or racquet before committing themselves to buying new equipment. Skilled DIY enthusiasts become highly involved in the selection of suitable tools, components, and materials to enable them to pursue their dedicated tasks. Competing brands of power tools, for instance, will be subject to detailed evaluation of their various attributes. DIY activities are motivated not necessarily by economic considerations; professional people often enjoy the challenge and diversion of using their hands rather more than their heads in undertaking household improvements and repairs.

The clothing industry, particularly in the women's fashion sector, thrives on the strong interest taken by shoppers in fashion trends, and the high degree of personal involvement in choosing garments whose styling, colours, and textures are judged to be compatible with their personality, self-image, age, and complexion. The fashion industry assiduously cultivates awareness of and interest in its products by regularly changing styling and colours in an attempt to make consumers feel discontented and ill-at-ease with their earlier purchases. This carefully nurtured discontent is also apparent in other product fields, such as cars or bathroom equipment, where styling has been strongly developed as a marketing ploy.

The involvement factor plays a major role in the promotion and purchase of alcoholic and soft drinks, which are projected skilfully to suggest social acceptability, sophistication, and other enticing ambitions. Image-building is a basic constituent of the advertising campaigns run by the companies marketing Martini, Guinness, Bailey's Cream, Bacardi, Courvoisier, Coca-Cola, etc. Consumption of beverages like these confers complex benefits in pyschosocial terms: these may well be more dominant than their thirst-quenching properties. Indeed, 'psychological consumption' appears to be a distinguishing feature of advanced societies.

The distinctions between product-involvement and brand-choice involvement are particularly apparent in the drinks market, where consumers develop strong allegiances to brands of bitter beer, Scotch whisky, or increasingly, lager.

The influence of culture on consumption is discussed in Chapter 6, where life-style approaches are examined. In Chapter 8, the concept of conspicuous consumption, originated at the turn of the century by Veblen,[53] is seen to influence the types and brands of products bought in an attempt to demonstrate social superiority, affluence, and so on. Expensive hand-luggage, 'designer' clothing, or exotic jewellery typify these ego-involved purchases. Further research will doubtless build on the very useful foundations which have been laid by the researchers quoted earlier. There is plenty of scope for development of this aspect of buying behaviour in the design of effective marketing segmentation strategies (see Chapter 14).

4.12 SUMMARY

There is no commonly held definition of personality, but it is often defined as covering all the ways in which one person differs from another. Unlike traits, which are specific characteristics or aspects of personality, a personality type enhances all the identified traits of a person.

Theories of personality are legion: none is entirely satisfactory. Four major theories are: trait, psychoanalytic, social learning, and humanistic (self-concept).

Trait theories go back to Hippocrates; much later theorists have been Kretschmer, Sheldon, and Jung (extroversion–introversion). Personality traits have been described with bewildering prodigality. Edwards, Allport, Cattall, Eysenck, and MMPI are well known, as is Horney's model of interpersonal response traits: compliant, aggressive, detached.

Psychoanalytic theories derive principally from Freudian research into the unconscious mind; Jung and others modified Freud's emphasis on sexual impulses.

Social learning theories focus on environmental influences in developing an individual's personality, while humanistic theories centre on self-image and self-fulfilment: Carl Rogers's 'self-concept' theory and Maslow's 'self-actualization'. Individuals develop an ideal concept—the sort of person they would like to be; this is likely to stimulate behaviour, including consumption patterns.

Stereotypes related to the perceptions that people have about other people, things or events: these projections are distorted and simplistic; nevertheless, they are still widely used in advertising.

Empirical evidence on personality and buying behaviour is equivocal. Some research has been done in certain product areas, but sweeping generalizations should be avoided.

Consumer-involvement theories incorporating both product and brand analyses have potential value in developing effective marketing segmentation strategies.

REFERENCES

1. Kassarjian, Harold H., and Mary June Sheffett, 'Personality and consumer behaviour: an update', in: *Perspectives in Consumer Behaviour*, H. H. Kassarjian and Thomas Robertson (eds), Prentice-Hall, Englewood Cliffs, New Jersey, 1991.
2. Thouless R. H., *General and Social Psychology*, University Tutorial Press, London, 1967.
3. Hilgard, Ernest R., Richard C. Atkinson, and Rita L. Atkinson, *Introduction to Psychology*, Harcourt Brace Jovanovich, New York, 1975.
4. Allport, Gordon W., *Personality and Social Encounters*, Beacon Press, Boston, Massachusetts, 1960.
5. Jahoda, Marie, and Neil Warren (eds), *Attitudes*, Penguin, London, 1969.
6. Howard, John A., and Jagdish N. Sheth, *The Theory of Buyer Behaviour*, John Wiley, New York, 1969.
7. Britt, Stewart Henderson, *Social Psychology of Modern Life*, Holt, Rinehart and Winston, New York, 1949.
8. Krech, David, Richard S. Crutchfield, and Egerton L. Ballachey, *Individuals in Society*, McGraw-Hill, New York, 1962.
9. Cattell, Raymond B., *Personality: A Systematic Theoretical and Factual Study*, McGraw-Hill, New York, 1950.
10. Cattell, Raymond B., *The Scientific Analysis of Personality*, Penguin, London, 1965.
11. Eysenck, H. J., *Fact and Fiction in Psychology*, Penguin, London, 1965.
12. Eysenck, H. J., and S. B. G. Eysenck, *The Eysenck Personality Inventory*, University of London Press, London, 1963.
13. Moreno, J. L. (ed.), *Sociometry and the Science of Man*, Beacon House, New York, 1956.
14. Horney, Karen, *Our Inner Conflicts*, W. W. Norton, New York, 1945.
15. Cohen, Joel B., 'An interpersonal orientation to the study of consumer behaviour', *Journal of Marketing Research*, vol. 4, August, 1967.
16. Slama, Mark E., Terrell G. Williams, and Armen Taschian, 'Compliant, aggressive and detached types differ in generalized purchasing involvement', *Proceedings 15 Conference*, Michael J. Houston (ed.), Association for Consumer Research, 1988.
17. Dichter, Ernest, *The Strategy of Desire*, Doubleday, New York, 1960.
18. Cheskin, Louis, *How to Predict What People Will Buy*, Liveright, New York, 1957.
19. Martineau, Pierre, *Motivation in Advertising*, McGraw-Hill, New York, 1957.
20. Packard, Vance, *The Hidden Persuaders*, Penguin, London, 1957.
21. Chisnall, Peter M., *Marketing Research: Analysis and Measurement*, McGraw-Hill, Maidenhead, 1982.
22. Riesman, David, *The Lonely Crowd*, Yale University Press, New Haven, Connecticut, 1950.

23. Centers, Richard, 'An examination of the Riesman Social Character Typology: a metropolitan survey', *Sociometry*, vol. 25, September 1962.
24. Dornbusch, Sanford M., and Lauren C. Hickman, 'Other-directedness in consumer-goods advertising: a test of Riesman's historical theory', *Social Forces*, vol. 38, December 1959.
25. Kassarjian, Harold H., 'Social character and differential preference for mass communication', *Journal of Marketing Research*, vol. 2, May 1965.
26. Kassarjian, Harold H., 'Personality and consumer behaviour: a review', *Journal of Marketing Research*, vol. 8, November 1971.
27. Hall, Calvin S., and Gardner Lindzey, *Theories of Personality*, John Wiley, New York, 1957.
28. Sullivan, H. S., *Concepts of Modern Psychiatry*, W. W. Norton, New York, 1953.
29. Newman, Joseph W., *Motivation Research and Marketing Management*, Harvard University Graduate School of Business Administration, Boston, Massachusetts, 1957.
30. Birdwell, A. E., 'A study of the influence of image congruence on consumer choice', *Journal of Business*, vol. 41, January 1968.
31. Sheth, Jagdish N., 'A review of buyer behaviour', *Management Science*, vol. 13, no. 12, August 1967.
32. Grubb, Edward L., and Gregg Hupp, 'Perception of self, generalised stereotypes and brand selection', *Journal of Marketing Research*, vol. 5, February 1968.
33. Jacobson, Eugene, and Jerome Kossoff, 'Self-percept and consumer attitudes towards small cars', *Journal of Applied Psychology*, vol. 47, August 1963.
34. Dolich, Ira J., 'Congruence: relationships between self images and product brands', *Journal of Marketing Research*, vol. 6, February 1969.
35. Green, Paul E., Arun Maheshwari, and R. Rao Vithala, 'Self-concept and brand preference: an empirical application of multidimensional scaling', *Journal of the Market Research Society*, vol. 11, no. 4, 1969.
36. Ross, Ivan, 'Self-concept and brand preference', *Journal of Business*, vol. 44, no. 1, January 1971.
37. Dakin, Tony, 'The world's longest pub crawl', *Financial Times*, 2 March 1972.
38. Mick, David Glen, and Michelle DeMoss, 'Self-gifts: phenomenological insights from four contexts', *Journal of Consumer Research*, vol. 17, December 1990.
39. Lippmann, Walter, *Public Opinion*, Macmillan, New York, 1949.
40. Davis, James A., and Roger Jowell, 'British social attitudes: special international report', in: *Social and Community Planning Research*, Jowell, Roger, Sharon Wotherspoon and Lindsay Brook (eds), Gower Press, Aldershot, 1989.
41. Driscoll, James W., Gary L. Cowger, and Robert J. Egan, 'Private managers and public myths: public managers and private myths', *Sloan Management Review*, fall 1979.
42. Rawsthorn, Alice, 'What Katy did wrong', *Marketing*, 9 February 1984.
43. Rawsthorn, Alice, 'Guardian makes it all ad up', *Marketing*, 1 March 1984.
44. Dawson, J. A., 'Responses to sex-role portrayals in advertising', *Advertising*, no. 67, spring 1981.
45. Chappell, Brian, 'How women are portrayed in television commercials', *Admap*, June 1983.
46. Edmunds, Lynne 'Men and the question of image', *Daily Telegraph*, 1 March 1984.
47. Evans, Franklin B., 'Psychological and objective factors in the prediction of brand choice', *Journal of Business*, vol. 32, October 1959.
48. Westfall, Ralph, 'Psychological factors in predicting brand choice', *Journal of Marketing*, vol. 26, April 1962.
49. Kassarjian, Harold H., and Mary June Sheffett, 'Personality and consumer behaviour', *AMA Combined Proceedings*, series no. 37, 1975.
50. Sherif, M., and H. Cantrel, *The Psychology of Ego-Involvement*, John Wiley, New York, 1947.
51. Laurent, Gilles, and Jean-Noël Kapferer, 'Measuring consumer involvement profiles', *Journal of Marketing Research*, vol. 22, February 1985.
52. Mittal, Banwari, and Myung-Soo Lee, 'Separating brand-choice involvement from product-involvement via consumer-involvement profiles', in: *Advances in Consumer Research*, vol. 15, Michael J. Houston (ed.), Association for Consumer Research, 1988.
53. Veblen, Thorstein, *The Theory of the Leisure Class*, Macmillan, New York, 1899.

REVIEW AND DISCUSSION QUESTIONS

1. In which circumstances and for which products and services do you think a consumer's self-concept is likely to affect his or her purchasing behaviour?

2. Why do you think it is that, among personality theories, trait theory has found wider acceptance among marketing practitioners?

3. Which of Karen Horney's three personality types best fits your interpersonal response trait? How do you feel that having this trait affects your consumption of products and services.

4. Select four magazine advertisements promoting goods that relate to the consumer's self-concept. Describe the way in which they attempt to achieve this.

5. Section 4.7 showed that consumers strive to achieve congruence between their self-concept and the personalities or images of the brands they purchase. Use four adjectives to describe the personality of each of the following brands: (a) Ford Fiesta (b) Marks and Spencer (c) McVities biscuits (d) Colgate toothpaste (e) Butlins.

6. Describe any two television advertisements, one of which appeals to the inner-directed personality type, the other to the outer-directed type. Do you feel that personality was the correct way to promote these products? Why?

CHAPTER FIVE

ATTITUDES

5.1 INTRODUCTION

Attitudes influence the lives of everyone, and affect the ways in which individuals judge and react towards other people, objects, and events. While people often mention 'attitudes' in conversation, few, probably, could define precisely what this popular term actually means. Yet the frequency with which references to attitudes occur in discussions of all kinds suggests that they play a very important role in personal and professional life. So much of life is influenced, therefore, by the attitudes—favourable or otherwise—which are held by people that some deeper understanding of their nature and effects is called for.

5.2 DEFINITIONS OF ATTITUDES

As with learning processes, needs, and motives, the definitions of attitudes are many, complex, and often confusing. In 1935, Allport remarked:

> The concept of attitude is probably the most distinctive and indispensable concept in contemporary American social psychology. No other term appears more frequently in experimental and theoretical literature. . . . As may be expected of so abstract and serviceable a term, it has come to signify many things to many writers, with the inevitable result that its meaning is somewhat indefinite and its scientific status called into question.[1]

After reviewing several definitions of attitudes, Allport identified a 'common thread' which could be described as a 'preparation or readiness for response'. The degree of readiness may have several dimensions from the 'most latent, dormant traces of forgotten habits' to motivating influences initiating behaviour. Finally, and after considerable discussion, Allport gave this definition of an attitude: It is 'a mental and neural state of readiness, organised through experience, exerting a directive or dynamic influence upon the individual's response to all objects and situations with which it is related'.[1]

Markin has described an attitude as a mental set or proclivity to respond in a certain way when the appropriate situation occurs.[2]

Lunn has commented that attitudes are generally held to structure the way in which individuals perceive their environment and to guide the ways in which they respond to it.[3]

Thouless refers to the relatively indiscriminate use of the term 'attitude', 'which has sometimes been used in a sense indistinguishable from that of "sentiment".'[4] It has also been used more widely to describe not only specific emotional dispositions, but also non-specific ones, such as tolerance, radicalism, or scepticism. In its 'wider sense', Thouless quotes a definition of an attitude given by Cantril: 'a more or less permanently enduring state of readiness of mental organisation which predisposes an individual to react in a characteristic way to any other object or situation with which it is related'.

Finally, Hilgard and Atkinson present a definition combining features of the definition of Allport, Hovland, Janis and Kelley: 'An attitude represents both an orientation towards or away from some object, concept or situation and a readiness to respond in a predetermined manner to these related objects, concepts or situations'.[5]

Attitudes are characterized, therefore, by a predisposition or state of readiness to act or react in a particular way to certain stimuli. While there is considerable divergence among researchers about the precise nature of attitudes, there seems to be general agreement that they are relatively enduring systems which influence individuals to make certain kinds of responses. They are not innate, but develop with learning; over time, individuals acquire 'a whole inventory of predisposition to act, i.e. attitudes'.[6] Further, an opinion is viewed as the verbal expression of an attitude;[7] hence, opinions and attitudes are closely related.

5.3 ATTITUDES AND MARKETING STRATEGY

Because they are relatively enduring in nature, attitudes have particular interest for marketing strategists. They do not guarantee that certain types of buying behaviour will occur, but they are useful as guides to what buyers are likely to do in certain circumstances.

Since the mid-1960s, interest has become focused particularly on the influence of attitudes on buying behaviour, and researchers have attempted to acquire deeper knowledge of the attitudinal characteristics of particular types of buyers. In advertising research, for instance, the changing of consumers' attitudes toward specific products and services was considered to be a very useful method of assessing the effect of advertising.[8,9] As noted in Sec. 5.2, in the associated area of public opinion formation, Katz has drawn attention to the importance of attitudes:

> the raw material out of which public opinion develops is to be found in the attitudes of individuals, whether they be followers or leaders and whether these attitudes be at the general level of tendencies to conform to legitimate authority or majority opinion or at the specific level of favouring or opposing the particular aspects of the issue under consideration.[7]

In attempting to satisfy their many needs, inherent and also acquired through learning and experience, people develop attitudes that influence their choice of products, brands, stores, methods of payment, and so on. From a tender age, children become aware of brand names—often connected with confectionery—and they quickly form attitudes, based on tasting experiences, towards a particular branded count-line. With other age-groups, whose patterns of consumption will be more complex, attitudes are wide-spanning and not only affect commercial considerations but also are evident in the willingness, for example, to adopt new safety measures such as the installation of domestic smoke alarms. In 1989, the Central Office of Information commissioned a marketing research consultancy[10] to undertake research to gauge changes in attitudes to smoke alarms and to evaluate these in relation to an earlier television advertising campaign. As a result, and also reinforced by an analysis of fire statistics, a new campaign was targeted at the age group 55-plus, especially those of lower socio-economic status. Research had revealed that these older householders tended not to be influenced as much as families with children by the original campaign.

5.4 COMPONENTS OF ATTITUDES

A generally accepted major framework of defining attitudes has been said to be in terms of the cognition–affect–conation paradigm so common in psychology. These three components become mutually interdependent, and their individual natures will now be reviewed.

The *cognitive* component of an attitude refers to the beliefs, i.e., knowledge, about the particular object of an attitude. As Asch has pointed out: 'beliefs depend on available data; therefore differences in beliefs can be traced at least in part to differences in information and knowledge'. Attitudes are directed towards phenomena that are known to exist; an individual cannot have an attitude towards an object if this 'is missing in the natural or social milieu'.[11] People may, of course, invent 'facts' whenever information is sparse or lacking entirely, but they must be aware of the existence of whatever the object of their invention may be. Asch stressed the importance of the cognitive component of an attitude, because the beliefs about an object tend to control the change that may take place in an attitude.

The *affect* or *feeling* component of an attitude relates to the emotional content and arouses either likes or dislikes of a particular object. These feelings may derive from personality traits, motives, social norms, and so on.

The *conative* component or action tendency of an attitude concerns the disposition to take action of some kind; there is a readiness to display particular behaviour towards a specific object. This does not mean that there is necessarily a direct relationship between attitudes and behaviour; that, for instance, a favourable attitude automatically causes behaviour beneficial to the object of the attitude. Consumers may have a favourable attitude towards some manufacturers' products (e.g. Rolls-Royce cars), but may lack the means or need to take buying action.

In their theory of buying behaviour (see Chapter 9) Howard and Sheth defined an attitude as explicitly including only the cognitive component, of which 'affect and conation are derivatives' and are, therefore, only implicitly present.[12]

5.5 CHARACTERISTICS OF ATTITUDE COMPONENTS

Each of the components of an attitude may possess degrees of *intensity* or *valence*, which may take any point along a continuum ranging from very favourable or positive through a neutral area to a position of very unfavourable or very negative. Measuring devices such as Semantic Differential are used to evaluate specific attitudes, and the various types of scales in popular use will be reviewed later. Positive attitudes predispose consumers to react favourably to advertised products or to visit a local store to inspect the range of merchandise. Negative or unfavourable attitudes may lead to consumers avoiding shopping in supermarkets, for example, or discourage the buying of 'own-label' products because it is thought that they are inferior in quality to nationally branded products. In general, available evidence suggests that there is a tendency towards consistency among the components of an attitude; there tends to be a mutual interdependence. For example, highly favourable beliefs about a particular brand of product are more likely to lead to a high degree of action, i.e., purchase. But there may be occasions when personally unfavourable beliefs may not frustrate favourable action. Parents, for example, may have distinctly unfavourable beliefs about pop music, but they temporarily suppress their feelings when they buy pop music records as gifts for their children.

Where there are many elements in the component of an attitude, it is said to *multiplex*; where relatively few exist, the component is described as *simplex*. According to Ballachey: 'Thus, the cognitive component of a man's attitude towards "science" may be multiplex, involving a differentiation between the physical and social sciences, between applied and pure science, between science and scientist, between the theories of science and the data of science'.[13]

Markin has observed that individuals may be favourably inclined towards a certain brand of cigarettes (positive valence), but would not be willing to walk a mile specially to get this brand if there were other brands readily available, because of the multiplex nature of their attitudes.[2]

On the other hand, relatively simple beliefs may be held about some object. To specialists in any field of activity, complex differentiations are made between the objects on which they focus their attention, but to the non-expert these complexities will be of little significance. Packaging, for instance, may be classified in literally hundreds of ways by a technologist in that industry, but the average consumer will be content to describe it in general terms as paper, board, or plastic, or merely as 'wrapping'.

5.6 ATTITUDE CLUSTERS

Attitudes rarely exist in complete isolation, for they tend to be linked in various ways and to form *clusters* that are significant in defining the precise meanings of objects.

> For example, in a study of consumer reactions to the styling of an appliance, two styles were both rated equally 'modern'. While one was thought to represent the 'design of the future' the other was not so characterised. Since being 'modern' clearly has a different meaning in each case, it would have been misleading merely to say that both appliances were equally modern. In order to define in *what way* each appliance was modern, it was necessary to examine the total pattern of attitudes toward each appliance.[14]

5.7 ATTITUDE CONSTELLATION

Individuals tend to organize their attitudes towards the various objects in their world into value systems which guide them in dealing with life's problems. The total collection of attitudes which influence individuals' behaviour is termed their *attitude constellation*. Some peoples 'stock' of attitudes may be substantial; the formation of attitudes will be discussed later in this chapter.

Values have been noted as largely growing out of and being assimilated by the attitudes of an individual . 'As consumers are forced to cope with the continual bombardment of communication stimuli, the repeatedly evoked cognitions, feelings and response dispositions become organised into a set of patterned emotional reactions'.[2] These responses tend to become more complex and in time become values which (as discussed later) form a core part of an individual's personality.

5.8 IMPORTANCE OF INTERRELATIONSHIPS BETWEEN ATTITUDES

Crespi has noted the importance of finding out more about the interrelationships that may exist among attitudes. Three significant aspects of interrelationship were highlighted:[14]

1. How specific or general are attitudes?

Specific attitudes may, for instance, be concerned with the speed and effectiveness of aspirin in relieving pain. However, another consumer may have a very general attitude towards aspirin and be interested in how it should be used.

2. How closely related are attitudes to the individual's value system?

Katz has referred to the fact that when specific attitudes are organized into a hierarchical structure, they form value systems. 'Thus a person may not only hold specific attitudes against deficit spending and unbalanced budgets but may also have a systematic organisation of such beliefs and attitudes in the form of a value system of economic conservatism'.[7] If a woman, for example, identified her role as mother with keeping her home spotlessly clean and hygienic for the sake of the health of her family, her attitude towards a favoured brand of household cleaner will be closely interrelated with her value system. She would be unlikely to change brands solely on account of pride inducements offered by another manufacturer.

3. How central or peripheral to the individual are particular attitudes?

Attitudes to brands of products may be closely related to the whole of a person's orientation towards life. Some people, for example, may be extremely interested in every aspect of home management such as labour-saving appliances, redecoration techniques, food preparation and cooking methods, etc. They will tend to form attitudes related to these personally significant areas of interest. Katz has noted that the centrality of an attitude refers to its role as part of a value system which is closely related to the individual's self-concept.[7] The degree of importance, or salience, of an attitude will be reflected in the position it occupies in the cluster of related attitudes, and also will be influenced by the significance of that cluster in the complete attitudinal structure, i.e., the attitude constellation of an individual. Attitudes possessing centrality, i.e., those that go to the core of an individual's value system, are more resistant to change. It might involve too radical a personality change for any fundamental alteration in an attitude of this type to take place. The whole concept of 'self' may be almost inextricably tied in with strongly held attitudes which have become absorbed into the personality of an individual. (See Chapter 4, where the relevance of self-concept to marketing practice was discussed.)

5.9 FORMATION OF ATTITUDES

Attitudes tend to develop selectively: people pick and choose according to their needs, past and present. As they develop and gain experience of life, increasing their responsibility and acquiring an ever-growing number of needs, attitudes towards persons, products, and other phenomena are likely to change. Products that were at one time considered to be of little personal interest may, at a later stage in life, be regarded favourably and be worth the trouble of personal enquiry. Attitudes towards some products may become less favourable as the life-cycle of the consumer progresses. Clothing styles suitable for teenagers will be thought inappropriate for those past their early twenties, when family responsibilities may preclude heavy expenditure on personal clothing. Attitudes towards saving money are likely to undergo considerable change when, for instance, a young couple start planning to set up home together. Previously, building societies were probably of little interest to them; now, they begin to form attitudes towards these financial institutions. A particular building society may, in fact, be characterized as having a very favourable attitude to young people seeking funds. Attitudes towards other services, such as education, will acquire saliency for parents anxious to ensure that their children benefit from the kind of education they consider to be most suitable. Educational problems are likely to involve the personal standards, i.e., value systems, of individuals. Political, religious, and social beliefs and attitudes may render attitudes towards education highly complex. Other attitudinal targets could relate to the nationalized health service in Britain; to the social welfare of elderly people; to the operations of the City of London and 'big business'; or to the role of the individual in a 'consumer' society.

Attitudes may be formed, therefore, towards people, products, services, political or social systems, distribution methods (e.g., self-service stores or cash-and-carry depots), and a whole number of other phenomena that impinge on an individual's life. Because people associate together in a society, societal influences on personal attitudes cannot be ignored, but it should be noted that each person has a set of attitudes that are unique though some degree of similarity may exist with the individual attitudes held by others.

5.10 SOURCES OF ATTITUDES

Attitudes may be acquired or modified by influence arising from four principal sources: information exposure, group membership, environment, and want satisfaction.

In Chapter 2, the role of cognitions in individual behaviour was discussed; it was seen that personal factors, such as subjective perception, affect the reception of information by individuals. Messages from commercial sources such as advertising may be distorted by 'sharpening' or 'levelling'; people may deliberately avoid exposing themselves to some channels of communication, for example, by making it a practice not to view commercial television programmes.

The cognitive content of attitudes is largely built up from information given by other people and presented, very frequently, through the mass media. Most individuals must rely on information sources of various kinds; some sources will be regarded as highly reliable while others will be highly suspect. In Britain, an article in *The Times* or *The Economist* is generally considered to contain trustworthy information and informed opinion. There are other newspapers whose reports do not inspire the same level of confidence. However, it should be realized that people tend to expose themselves to certain sources of information, and these generally present news and views that are congruent with the beliefs and attitudes of their readers.

Ballachey considers it inevitable that in a complex world, any single individual should have to depend on what 'experts' say. 'The authority may be correct . . . or honestly mistaken . . . or may deliberately falsify facts for his own ends'.[13]

Clearly, marketers need to study *how* their customers obtain information and to research into the depth of knowledge which particular types of customers may have about products and brands of products. Unfavourable attitudes towards dehydrated foods were prevalent in Britain at one time, because many people believed that these foods lacked nutritional value. Wartime food substitutes and shortages were associated with this type of processed food. Exposure to promotional messages together with personal recommendation eventually helped to change attitudes. A new generation of shoppers had also emerged with increased spending power and the willingness to try new products

Learning plays an important part in cognitive activities; the influence of the processes of learning on consumer behaviour was noted in Chapter 2. It may be useful to recall that a great deal of information about products and services is acquired 'accidentally' through advertising. These types of data will be subject, of course, to the limitations of subjective perception. Attitudes may also be generated from information collected in a systematic way, e.g., window shopping or reading *Which*?

If manufacturers fail to communicate accurately with their customers and with those who eventually use their products, people may 'fill in' the gaps in their knowledge about specific aspects of a company or its products by 'inventing facts'. These may be harmful to the reputation of a particular company if they bear little resemblance to the actual facts. Ballachey recalls an attitude study undertaken in the late 1950s in the USA towards the fluoridation of water.[13] Some people voted against it for a variety of bizarre reasons which they had persuaded themselves were facts. Fluoridation was said to be 'rat poison'; to cause hardening of the arteries, premature ageing, loss of memory, and nymphomania; it also ruined batteries, radiators, and lawns. While these so-called facts may evoke amusement, it is important to realize that these beliefs were valid to many of the respondents to this inquiry.

Attitudes also formed from membership of groups to which an individual is affiliated. In a psychological sense, a group refers to a number of people who interact with one another. Detailed consideration of group influence in marketing strategies will be given in Chapter 8. At this stage, a brief review will indicate the contribution of group membership to the formation of attitudes.

The opinions and attitudes of those whose company is shared—either voluntarily or otherwise—affect an individual. Groups have been identified as primary (family, friends, work group) and reference groups (any group with which individuals closely identify themselves so that it becomes a standard for self-evaluation). Groups may include both membership groups (to which a person belongs) and aspirant groups (to which a person aspires to belong).

People tend to belong to groups whose behaviour attracts them; they seek out compatible souls who hold beliefs and have attitudes in sympathy with their own. But an individual may not accept and absorb all the standards of a particular group. People tend to pick and choose— as they do with cognitions—and their attitudes reflect their personal needs. Hence, the influence of groups on the formation of personal attitudes is indirect and complex.

Primary groups are held by many researchers to be of permanent importance in the development of attitudes. From the family, for instance, children acquire attitudes towards society and learn acceptable patterns of behaviour. These tend to be affected by the social class to which they belong. Consumption habits are often found quite early in life; 'family stores' and 'household brand names' are examples of the influence of family attitudes. On many household grocery lists appear brand names which have been 'inherited' from an earlier generation of shoppers. Attitudes towards education, money, sex, religion, and marriage are radically affected by family influences. The customers of joint-stock banks are largely of middle-class status; there tends to be a 'family tradition' to bank, say, at the Midland. Working-class people tend, on the other hand, to use the services of the Post Office Savings Bank or the Trustees Banks, although the latter, in particular, have been notably successful in extending their services over recent years, and have attracted new customers from a wider socio-economic coverage. Perhaps because of lack of suitably designed and projected information, weekly wage earners may have an unfavourable attitude towards the big commercial banks, despite the promotional efforts designed to widen the profile of bank customers.

Individuals may aspire to belong to a group because it is seen as offering them certain professional or social advantages. They will be willing to reject, perhaps, the values and attitudes that influenced their earlier years, and identify themselves closely with those of the group. Attitudes towards the consumption of alcohol, for example, may be modified as individuals seek to mix in certain business and social groups. Group norms lay down acceptable behaviour in certain situations, and the aspiring members anxiously adopt the 'right' kinds of attitudes so as to win approval.

The influence of group norms was dramatically demonstrated by Sherif in a series of experiments.[15] He was concerned with studying the mutual effects of group members upon a particular perceptual experience. A group of subjects was placed in a darkened room and asked to look fixedly at a small spot of light. They were asked, in turn, to say aloud the direction in which they thought the light was moving. At first, they all differed, but soon they started to agree and gradually they began, one by one, to say that the light was moving in the same direction as the people who had spoken earlier had declared. In time, *all* the members of the group stated that the light was moving in the same direction; there was, in fact, complete agreement.

The significant point is that the light actually remained stationary; the illusion of movement was due to the phenomenon known as the autokinetic effect.

This experiment illustrates that where first-hand knowledge is lacking, and in conditions of uncertainty, individual opinions tend to conform to group beliefs and attitudes. Those who were the first to accept group standards could be termed 'easy conformists'; later 'converts' could be classified as 'hard-core independents' or 'high resistors'.

Another set of classical experiments related to group pressure to induce conformity of behaviour was undertaken by Asch.[16] Two cards were prepared; on one card a line 8 in. long appeared, while the other card showed three lines of $6\frac{1}{4}$ in., 8 in., and $6\frac{3}{4}$ in. respectively, the sequence of which was changed in each trial. Individual members of groups of between seven and nine students were asked to judge which set of lines matched that shown singly. At first all the subjects called out the matching line correctly. In one group of eight, seven members were confederates of Asch's and only one genuine subject was present. He was so placed that he gave his judgement after the rest, who had all given false and unanimous answers. The subject 'faced, possibly for the first time in his life, a situation in which a group unanimously contradicted the evidence of his senses'. He had, therefore, the choice of trusting his own senses or of going along with the consensus opinion. What actually happened was that three-quarters of the genuine subjects involved in the experiments distorted at least some of their judgements in favour of the group's estimates. But there were 'extreme individual differences, which indicated the importance of personality factors in yielding to the pressures of group opinion'.[16]

Further experiments by Asch revealed that as the objective differences in the lengths of lines became smaller, individual conformity to group assessments increased, because of the difficulty of judging finer tolerances. Where a subject's opinion was supported by another member of the group, the subject tended to become resistant to the opinions of the rest of the members.

Environmental influences also affect the formation and development of attitudes. A classical and comprehensive study of the effect of environment and group behaviour on attitudes related to Newcomb's researches[17] at Bennington College during the period 1935–9. Bennington College, an expensive US women's residential college, drew its students from wealthy families accustomed to privileged positions in society. When these young women arrived at the college they held conservative political beliefs which had been absorbed from their parents. During their four-year stay at Bennington, they became exposed to an intellectual environment which encouraged the regular discussion of social and political issues. They were also affected by the more liberal attitudes of members of staff and of the senior students. It is important to realize that the Bennington community was largely self-sufficient, and was not near centres of population density. As a result of the new environment, many of the women's own views tended to become progressively more liberal, and this became more pronounced as their stay in college lengthened.

However, Newcomb was interested in finding out more about the minority of students who did not display the tendency to swing towards more liberal views. He found that these were of two kinds: they either had carefully thought through their own attitudes (which remained conservative), or for several reasons they maintained allegiance to family patterns of thought and behaviour. Newcomb also found that senior students of professed liberal views were highly motivated to achieve independence from their families, and to acquire prestige in Bennington because of their close personal involvement with the college's professed standards. It will be apparent that exposure to the curriculum (from which new information would be gathered) also contributed to the development in attitudes.

About 25 years later, a follow-up study revealed that ex-Bennington women and their husbands tended to display more markedly liberal views than a comparable sample of Americans of the same socio-economic class. Ballachey considers that either the influence of Bennington persisted strongly in the lives of former students, and/or that these strong liberal views were reinforced by the husbands and friends chosen in support of these beliefs.[13]

Asch, while critical of some aspects of Newcomb's investigations, considered it was valuable in demonstrating that the formation and change of attitudes 'take place in the setting of significant social and emotional relations'.[11]

Attitudes are also influenced by the wants of individuals, and by the degree of satisfaction that they will tolerate. The multiplicity of human needs was studied in Chapter 3, when it was observed that people are motivated to attain many different objectives. Attitudes will be formed in the course of these activities. In the area of consumer behaviour, attitudes serve needs by helping to simplify, for example, responses to stimuli such as advertising messages. Attitudes will guide buying decisions, and so needs can be satisfied without persistent evaluation of every shopping activity.

When needs are well satisfied, e.g., the family car has been serviced speedily at a local garage, favourable attitudes will be formed about that particular business. Some companies, such as Marks and Spencer, encourage the development of favourable attitudes by their customers through an enlightened trading policy. Corporate image publicity schemes are designed to influence people's attitudes so that favourable opinions will be reviewed later; in general it can be said that developing a favourable image of a company is based on attitude formation, and, perhaps, change. If the consuming public, for example, approves of the methods of trading of a large supermarket chain, they will form favourable attitudes which may lead to their shopping at the local branch.

It is vital for companies to distinguish themselves from competitors: products available from a range of suppliers in the same industry increasingly look alike and may, in the case of generic products such as basic raw materials, be physically identical. 'Most of the major chemical companies, for example, offer similar products to a similar standard of service . . . creating and developing a clear identity is one way of distinguishing a company from its competitors'.[18] (Extended discussion occurs in Chapter 12.)

5.11 CHANGE IN ATTITUDES

In the discussion on motivation in Chapter 3, it became apparent that humans are restless animals whose needs seem to be capable of almost limitless expansion. Immersed in a dynamic society in which technological developments and social and cultural trends affect the whole pattern of life, an individual's attitudes towards many objects and events may undergo considerable change. In Sec. 5.4, the influence of the life-cycle on attitudes towards particular types of products was noted.

The formation and changes that may take place in a person's attitude constellation tend to be closely interwoven. Katona has defined attitude change as 'a finding that at a given time a significantly higher or lower proportion of the population holds certain attitudes than at an earlier time'.[19]

To varying degrees, everyone responds to changes in the world about them; some are able to adjust—'to come to terms'—more readily than others. Personality factors may discourage or even prevent attitudinal change in some directions. People may, indeed, see no reason to change their long-held attitudes and beliefs about some matters of personal importance, for example, the importance of hard work and thrift may be central to their whole way of life. Others may hold deeply rooted attitudes related to trade unionism or to a particular party which form, it may be said, the whole fabric of their being.

The problem of attitude change has been studied at some length. It is a matter of immense importance for those who are trying to influence behaviour; politicians and business people— particularly those in marketing management—should attempt to acquire some understanding of how and why attitudes change, and the constraints which inhibit certain types of attitudinal modification.

Direction of attitude change

Attitudes may change in a direction that reinforces the present attitudinal position: this is termed *congruent change*. It may result in an increase in a positive, approving attitude towards certain phenomena, or in a strengthening of a negative and disapproving attitude. Rosenberg concluded that attitudinal objects which are perceived as means of achieving desirable goals are evaluated favourably, while not surprisingly, those viewed as sources of frustration are evaluated unfavourably.[20] Products or services likely to enhance self-esteem are likely to attract favourable attitudes. A favourable attitude towards a supplier may be reinforced by attentive service to an urgent order placed by a customer. On the other hand, a mildly unfavourable attitude may move to one of distinct disapproval where, for example, a customer in a retail store found that the sales staff, apart from being inefficient, were no longer even courteous.

Incongruent change refers to attitudinal change in the opposite direction to existing attitudes; from positive feelings to negative ones, for example, from opposing the nationalization of building societies in Britain to a radically different attitude supporting this proposition.

Although it has been observed that research evidence of congruent and incongruent attitudinal changes is very limited,[2] it would appear that, other things being equal, there is a tendency for the first kind of attitude change to be more easily secured than the latter.

Reinforcement of existing attitudes and beliefs strengthens the self-concept, particularly where these personality factors are very closely interrelated and serve as fundamental parts of an individual's value system. Cultural traditions and social affiliations will also affect the change which may take place in an individual's attitudes towards some particular product or object. Incongruent change, on the other hand, may demand too great a reorientation of an individual's pattern of behavioural responses, and lead to considerable frustration and cognitive dissonace or imbalance.

Factors affecting attitude change

Not all attitudes are likely to be subject to the same susceptibility to change; variations will be affected by the characteristics of attitudes already held by an individual, and also by the personal characteristics of that individual. Earlier it was observed that attitudes develop selectively according to the needs of individuals.

The following attitudinal characteristics have been noted as important in determining attitude change.[13]

1. *Extremeness*: more extreme attitudes tend to resist change.
2. *Multiplexity*: complex attitudes are relatively easier to move in a congruent direction than simplex, but the latter are more susceptible to incongruent change.
3. *Interconnectedness*: the interrelationships which may exist between some attitudes was discussed earlier. The systematic organization of attitudes into personal value systems may render particular attitudes very difficult to change in an incongruent direction. An isolated

attitude, on the other hand, may be more susceptible to change, because it has no related attitudes to support it.

4. *Consonance*: consistent attitudes tend to be stable; there is mutual support among their components. This theory of consonance was developed by Zajonc, who surveyed the research undertaken by Heider, Osgood and Tannenbaum, and Festinger.[21] He postulated that: 'Common to the concepts of balance, congruity and dissonance is the notion that thoughts, beliefs and behaviour tend to organise themselves in meaningful and sensible ways. . . . Christian Scientists do not enrol in medical schools. And people who live in glass houses apparently do not throw stones'.

   The *concept of dissonance* has already been discussed in Chapters 2 and 3, when reference was made to homeostasis related to the satisfaction of needs. Zajonc, in critically reviewing the relevance of some dissonance studies, has commented: 'There is no question that the concepts of consistency, and especially the theory of cognitive dissonance, account for many varied attitudinal phenomena'.[28] He admits that the various theories of consistency are not, of course, able to provide a full explanation; they are necessarily constrained by the usual preamble '*ceteris paribus*'.

5. *Strength and number of wants served by attitude and centrality of values*: attitudes serving many important needs which are closely related will be less susceptible to change of an incongruent nature. But congruent change would be likely to be more easily effected. Attitudes, which in Katz's terms are 'value-expressive',[7] give expression to individuals' personalities and help to establish their personal identities. Such attitudes go to the core of the personality and are relatively unaffected by change in an incongruent direction. Katona has expressed this tendency in relation to business activities:[19]

   > In studying business behaviour, enduring attitudes are found which have become part of the psychological make-up of practically all businessmen at a given time and country (honesty or concern for profits, for instance). Other attitudes differ from person to person—as, for instance, attitudes toward risk and taking speculation—though they, too, may be acquired in childhood or during early business experiences and may endure over long periods of time. Finally, there are attitudes which vary from time to time and develop in response to change in environment.

In addition, certain personality characteristics also appear to influence attitudinal change:

1. *Intelligence*: Ballachey refers to researches in the USA which have indicated that more intelligent persons are more receptive to new information.[13]
2. *General persuasibility*: there is some evidence related to differences in persuasibility.[22] Some people may be characteristically resistant to persuasive communications, e.g., advertising.
3. *Self-defensiveness*: individuals may protect themselves by refusing to acknowledge unpalatable truths or harsh realities which may upset their self-concept. Katz has referred to the 'ego-defensive' function of attitudes,[7] which has been studied at some length by neo-Freudian researchers. Defence mechanisms may involve subjective perception.
4. *Cognitive needs and styles*: Kelman proposed that individual differences in the need to acquire knowledge (cognitions) affected the attitudinal systems.[23] Katz characterized these people as seeking to understand the events which directly affect their lives.[7] They need to know more about the world about them so that they can construct some standards or frames of reference to guide their behaviour. Attitudes help in this task.
5. *Group affiliations*: the importance of group membership in the formation of an individual's attitudes has already been discussed. The modification and change which take place in an individual's attitudes will be related to the degree of dependence which a person has on group norms. A high dependence will tend to result in resistance to deviations from group norms.[24] Group conformity research findings 'support the general hypothesis that persons

who are most strongly motivated to retain their membership in a group will be most resistant to communications contrary to the standards of that group.'[25]

Communication factors influencing change

Apart from the factors already considered, change may be significantly affected by the method of communicating information. Hovland has referred to the importance of the communicator (*who* says it) and the communication (*what* is said). In addition he includes the characteristics of the audience (*to whom* it is said).[25] (Some aspects of personal and social influences were discussed in Chapter 2.)

The *status of the communicator* appears to be 'often as important in determining the effects of a message as its contents'.[13] The communicator, e.g., the personality of a 'user' of a brand of product featured in an advertisement, should be acceptable to the intended audience and appear to relate closely to that particular type of product. If these criteria are satisfied, people may be likely to associate themselves and their own family problems with the advertiser's personalized message.

Communication also involves *group affiliations* and *opinion leadership*; these topics will be dealt with in later chapters. Now, it can be said that word-of-mouth communication is a subtle and strong influence in social and economic activities. Personal influence may substantially modify—and even entirely frustrate—the persuasive effects of advertising campaigns.

Classic research into the *credibility of communicators* was undertaken by Hovland and Weiss[26] in 1950. They were interested to study the effects on groups of individuals exposed to identical newspaper and magazine articles. One group was told that these articles came from various 'high credibility' sources, while the other group were led to believe that the articles originated from 'low credibility' sources.

The results of this and supplementary surveys showed that immediately following the exposure to 'high credibility' information, subjects' attitudes were far more changed than those who were exposed to the low credibility sources of information. But a particular interesting phenomenon developed, for it was discovered that after a period of four weeks had elapsed, the difference between the groups had dissolved. In Hovland's words: 'The positive effect of the high credibility sources and the negative effect of the low credibility sources tended to disappear after a period of several weeks'.[26]

This so-called 'sleeper effect' suggests that while immediate effects on opinions may be made by information from highly credible sources, over time there is a tendency for audiences to 'dissociate the content from the source and consequently the positive (or negative) influence of the source declines with time'.[27] Apart from supplying 'credible' information to customers, there would appear to be need to repeat the message from time to time in order to preserve the identity of the source and to ensure that the advantages of the original communications are not dissipated.

The sleeper effect has not, however, been accepted universally; its critics have viewed this phenomenon with distinct caution. Capon and Hulbert, for example, have commented that the pattern of findings—either supportive or otherwise—'is far from conclusive'.[28] The research evidence from seven studies was analysed and found to be unimpressive: not only were the designs employed extremely varied, but also they often exhibited methodological flaws. However, their final conclusion was that while there was 'no strong evidence for a generalised sleeper effect', in 'certain subsets of the population' it may be detected.

Sternthal *et al.* have noted that two components—expertise and trustworthiness—characterize source credibility, and they commented that it might be concluded that a highly credible source is more persuasive than a low credibility source.[29] But (as already observed) a rather more subtle explanation is needed. In agreement with Capon and Hulbert and other critics of the sleeper effect, they state that whether it is ultimately demonstrated that the source credibility effect does not persist, because a low credibility source becomes more influential over time or because a highly credible source loses persuasiveness, research connected with the persistence of the source effect shows that with the passage of time the systematic effect of credibility or persuasion is not maintained.

The present state of knowledge about the sleeper effect suggests that there may well be such an influence, but that it would be unwise to accept it as a generalization. Like many behavioural phenomena, it provides useful insight into certain situations, but interpretation should be approached with sensitivity.

However, more recent research findings have resulted in another appraisal of the sleeper effect: 'the central research question is no longer whether a sleeper effect exists, but when it is likely to occur'. This confident declaration by Hannah and Sternthal[30] followed two experiments based on what they termed the 'availability-valence' hypothesis. According to this hypothesis, individuals' attitudinal judgements of a persuasive message 'are determined by the favourableness or valence of the issue-relevant information available in memory at the time of judgement'. Perfect information is unlikely to be stored and readily called up; individuals are viewed as active 'information processors whose attitudinal judgements are determined by how and when they process information'. The researchers defined 'valence' in relative terms: 'Because memory capacity is limited, a change in attitude can occur when information currently held in memory is augmented or supplanted by information that is more or less favourable'. Their experiments, in which students from introductory psychology courses participated, enabled them to declare that the availability-valence hypothesis is 'able to explain the sleeper effect produced in our research and those found in the literature'.

The content of communications aimed to influence people's attitudes and, eventually, behaviour, should also be carefully considered. Hovland has stressed that in order to persuade people to adopt favourable responses, a communicator should use 'arguments and appeals which function as incentives'.[25] He lists as major incentives:

1. *Substantiative arguments* which may lead the audience to judge the conclusions as 'true' or 'correct'.
2. *Positive appeals* suggesting rewards to be gained by responding to a message.
3. *Negative appeals* which suggest 'punishment', e.g., fear appeals.

In commercial areas of communication, the *'pro-and-con' approach* may have limited success. Customers normally expect manufacturers and distributors to present their goods with confidence. The type of appeal made in particular advertisements should, of course, be related to the social and cultural background of potential and existing customers. Highly educated, sophisticated audiences will be able to appreciate a reasoned argument, although perhaps it would be better to use the term 'presentation', as 'argument' suggests a degree of conflict. People are seldom influenced solely by forceful arguments; advertising should be viewed as 'persuasive communication' oriented to the information needs of particular types of customers. Nowadays, of course, there is greater public awareness of mass media techniques; some of the less responsible claims by manufacturers of certain products have been inhibited by legislation and also by public opinion. Consumer publications such as *Which?* have attempted to present the pros and cons of a wide range of products and competing brands. To many subscribers and other readers, this type of substantive argument has proved helpful.

Positive appeals relate to the benefits—physical, psychological, or a mix of both—that customers seek when considering the purchase of products and services. Some attention has already been given to the many motivations that may influence buying behaviour. The prospect of reward may be almost immediate, e.g., entering a restaurant and ordering a meal, or it may entail distant objectives, such as investing money for retirement income in many years' time.

The impact of *negative appeals* such as fear will be referred to in Chapters 12 and 13. This type of approach is generally less acceptable than offering the prospect of a reward. It will be recalled that the perceptual processes are subjective, and that dissonant messages may be 'blocked off', so that they do not have any positive persuasive influence on behaviour. If such messages are dismissed because they are personally distasteful or unacceptable, clearly the approach is at fault. Negative appeals need to be handled with great care; they may merely cause attitudes to harden and also reinforce behaviour in a direction contrary to that advocated by the communicator. A 'boomerang' effect may, in fact, result: the intended audience may focus their intense dislike on the source of the communication, so that not only is the message rejected but also the communicator suffers loss of popularity. Later attempts at communications may be frustrated because the source is considered by the audience to be 'tainted'.

5.12 ATTITUDES AND BEHAVIOUR

Over many years, considerable research has been directed towards the problem of identifying the relationship between attitudes and behaviour. There is almost universal agreement that attitude tends to have only a comparatively low relationship to actual behaviour towards the object of the attitude.

'It is dangerous to assume that a knowledge of attitudes is in itself predictive of behavioural consequences in specific situations. This does not mean, however, that social scientists should renounce the study of attitudes'. What it indicates are 'the complexities of the relationships between attitudes and behaviour'.[31]

An early classic study of the attitude–behaviour relationship occurred in 1934, when La Piere researched the influence of prejudice.[32] He travelled throughout the USA in company with a Chinese couple and visited 230 hotels and restaurants; they were refused service on only one occasion. Later, when questionnaires were sent to these same establishments, over 90 per cent said they would not accept Chinese customers. La Piere also dispatched identical questionnaires to a control group of 100 similar catering establishments, which had not been visited by his party, and the response was similar to his earlier findings.

It should be admitted that La Piere's research has attracted a certain amount of criticism. Crespi, for instance, felt that the study was only superficially convincing; there were several other possible explanations that could account for La Piere's findings without invalidating the verbal expressions of attitude by the hotel owners.[14] Among these alternative explanations, Crespi suggested that the Chinese couple had been accepted because they were accompanied by a white man acting as a 'sponsor'. Fishbein also expressed some doubts about the validity of La Piere's findings. He pointed out that the Oriental couple were well dressed, spoke excellent English, arrived in a car (not so very commonplace in the early 1930s), carried expensive luggage, and were in the company of a Caucasian. Because of these distinctive clues to their social group, Fishbein considered that it was 'not at all surprising' that the behavioural intentions of the hoteliers towards Orientals in general should be 'unrelated to their behaviours with respect to the particular couple'. In particular, Fishbein was concerned to note that La Piere did not attempt to get a 'valid' measure of attitude; he appeared content to measure 'one or two very specific behavioural intentions'.[33]

No doubt La Piere's research will continue to be scrutinized and criticized by later scholars of behavioural studies, such as Wicker, who after extensive study of research studies concerned with attitudes and behaviour, concluded that, taken as a whole, 'it is considerably more likely that attitudes will be unrelated or only slightly related to actions'.[34] However, the debate continued when Wells asserted that attitudes seem to predict behaviour best when the attitudes are very specific, and when the attitude can 'lead to one and only one behaviour'.[35] If the attitude is very general, then behaviour and attitude are likely to diverge. For instance, Wells says that it would be risky to infer the use of bank charge cards from attitudes towards credit, because a consumer, if not paying cash, has a number of credit options open, only one of which is to use a bank charge card.

Sheth has pointed out that 'much of the research [into attitudinal preference as predictor of behaviour] has been correlational in nature: positive associations between attitude and behaviour are obtained and a causal relation has been only inferred, but no direct test of attitude as the cause and subsequent behaviour as the effect has been made'.[36]

Festinger's exhaustive inquiries were unable to find any supporting evidence for the view that changes in attitude are necessarily followed by changes in behaviour.[37] His comprehensive research revealed only three studies, and their evidence was principally negative. For example, foremen who undertook a two-week training course which stressed the principles of human relationships in industry, displayed less consideration for their subordinates when they returned to work compared with an untrained control group. He commented:

> In order to produce a stable behaviour change following opinion change, an environmental change must also be produced which, representing reality, will support the new opinion and the new behaviour. Otherwise, the same factors that produced the initial opinion and the behaviour will continue to operate to nullify the effect of the opinion change.[37]

At this point, it would be pertinent to discuss briefly the tendency in sociological and psychological literature to use the terms 'attitude' and 'opinion' almost interchangeably. Rokeach expressed strong feelings about the looseness of the terminology which is often adopted: 'many writers have ridden roughshod over the distinction between attitude and expressed opinion by using the phrases "attitude change", "opinion change", "attitude *and* opinion change", and "attitude *or* opinion change" more or less arbitrarily and interchangeably in the context of a single discussion'.[38] He quotes, among others, Festinger's paper,[37] as employing the concepts of 'attitude' and 'opinion' indiscriminately. Rokeach felt that some of the research connected with opinion change was not really concerned directly with attitudinal studies. It concentrates 'primarily on the conditions affecting change in the expression of opinion', but does not seem 'to have much to say about the conditions leading to a change in the context or structure of underlying predispositions'. Earlier in this chapter, Katz was quoted as saying that an opinion is the verbal expression of an attitude.[7]

To some extent, the terminological differences to which Rokeach has drawn attention are similar to those which complicate the study of needs and motives. In Chapter 3, it was seen that some confusion exists because there has been a tendency for some researchers to obscure the precise differences between actual needs and the motivational influences which direct the expression of these needs.

In 1985 Wells,[39] whose earlier views on the relationships between attitudes and behaviour have already been given, published the results of a 10-year tracking study of consumer attitudes and behaviour covering a wide variety of topics including dieting, eating-out, travel, entertainment, church, school, and finances. A consumer mail panel of about 1500 men and 1800 women, matched to the consumer population by demographics, has enabled significant insights to be gained into trends in attitudes and behaviour, to observe how attitudes and behaviour diverge, and also to note when and how they coincide. Perhaps the most important finding, Wells states, is that abstract trends do not predict. 'After having examined about one hundred attitudes and values, including all of the attitudes and values espoused by prominent futurists, we found *not one* that would pass the straight-face test of predictive power'. However, it appeared that in a 'very small number' of cases these phenomena 'tracked fairly well' over the short term; for example, the statement 'I would be willing to pay more for a product with all natural ingredients' reflected the well-acknowledged concern about food additives and preservatives, and the reported increased purchase of natural snack-food bars. But there were 'many more cases' where attitudes went one way and behaviour went another, as instanced by the statement 'Meal preparation should take as little time as possible', contrasted with data showing a *decreasing* use of frozen dinners over the same period of time.

There are 'at least three reasons' why abstract trends do not track behaviour: (1) an attitude can be enacted in many different ways; (2) many things can interface between an attitude and its behavioural consequences; (3) a trend can change at any time. In the first instance, women showed a flat response trend over time to the statement 'I like to feel attractive to members of the opposite sex', whereas data revealed an increased use of home permanents but a decrease in use of hair colourants. An example of the second reason could relate to favourable attitudes to home ownership but the inability to buy a house of one's own. The third reason is the alleged instability of trends, and Wells gives an example of attitudes towards the energy shortage; the earlier feeling in 1975 that 'The energy shortage is a hoax created by the government, utilities and corporations' declined until 1979 when a sudden upturn occurred, to be followed by a gradual drop in 1980 and 1981. From 1981, another change of direction took place. Wells comments that any *prediction* based on extrapolation of this trend would have been wrong at least four times in ten years.

Since high-level abstractions cannot be depended upon to predict or even track consumer behaviour, Wells then turned to considering how low-level, specific questions, like those on intentions, performed. He reported 'some pretty good correlations that held up over time'. For example, intentions to buy a CB radio or video cassette recorder within the next two years correlated well with later purchases. Intentions to buy specific products seem to result in actual purchases because they 'allow the respondent to assess the impact of things that become feeling and doing', and also 'incorporate attitude change if change has already occurred'.

Wells raises the crucial question that if intentions track behaviour and attitudes do not, why trouble to measure attitudes? The answer seems to be that when attitudes and behaviour diverge, a search for the causes of disagreement should reveal factors which have influenced the eventual outcomes. Wells refers to Katona's[19] observation in 1960 that consumer behaviour is the result of three concurrent causes: (1) attitudes; (2) enabling conditions; (3) precipitating circumstances. It is asserted that these last two factors combine with attitudes to produce behaviour.

Fishbein, a social psychologist in the University of Illinois, has made a major contribution to the study of attitudes related to behaviour. His proposition is that attitudes and behaviour should not be regarded as the sole problem: 'rather, we must concern ourselves with at least four things: attitudes, beliefs, behavioural intentions and behaviour. Our problems thus becomes the investigation of the interrelationship among all of these four concepts'.[40] His trenchant view is that 'in general we have made a very bad assumption for 75 years, namely that attitudes towards a product or towards objects have some direct link with behaviour. I do not think this is true, and I think there is now sufficient evidence to say that it is not true'.

Instead of considering beliefs and behavioural intentions as part of attitude, Fishbein preferred to define them separately and to regard them as 'phenomena that are related to attitudes'.[33] It will be observed that in doing so, Fishbein has rejected the traditional definition of attitude as being made up of the three components—cognitive, affective, and conative. He preferred to view attitudes as a relatively simple unidimensional concept connected with the amount of affect or feeling for a particular object. In support of this argument, Fishbein commented that although attitudes are frequently said to have three components, many popular measuring instruments are restricted to evaluating the affective component; further, 'there is considerable evidence' that this single affective score has high relationship with the beliefs held by an individual about the object of an attitude. He offers, therefore, a definition of an attitude, which is 'consistent with Thurstone's original definition', as 'the amount of affect for or against some object'.[40] It is based on a set of beliefs about an object and is reflected in the 'totality of behaviour with respect to the objects'.

Fishbein acknowledged that although an individual may hold many beliefs about a given object, 'there are probably no more than 7 ± 2 beliefs that serve as primary determinants of an attitude at a point in time'.[40] He refers to various research in information processing, span of attention and apprehension (see Chapter 2) which indicate that the human organism can handle only about five to nine pieces of information at a time. These will be the salient beliefs which are influential in forming attitudes towards certain people, products, etc.

He expressed his basic mode by the following equation:

$$A_o = \sum_{i=1}^{n} B_i a_i$$

where A_o = attitude toward object 'o'

B_i = strength of belief 'i' about 'o'

a_i = evaluate aspects of B_i

n = number of salient beliefs

In discussing this model, Fishbein[40] pointed out that $\Sigma B_i a_i$ is not an attitude *per se*, but merely the cognitive basis for attitude; in other words, 'a person's beliefs are not his attitude, but his attitude is based on his beliefs'. If people's beliefs are known, then it becomes feasible to tell what their attitudes are. Since beliefs are interrelated and form systems (see Chapter 2), changing one belief may affect others. For example, if consumers are told that a certain product is significantly reduced in price, they may be led to believe that its quality has also fallen.

Fishbein emphasized that behaviour does not automatically follow from holding certain attitudes. However, he stressed that behavioural intentions deserve special investigation because they are a direct lead to behaviour. If specific behavioural intentions are measured and too much time does not elapse between the measure of intention and observation of behaviour, behaviour can usually be predicted quite accurately.[41] Many kinds of behaviour can be engaged in; for example, a consumer may, in addition to buying or not buying a certain product, discuss it with friends, recommend it (or warn them against it), read advertisements about it, make special shopping trips to find it, borrow it, and so on. 'The fact that A's attitude towards the product is more favourable than B's merely indicates that he will engage in more of these favourable behaviours'.

According to Fishbein, there are two kinds of factor underlying an intention to buy a certain product. One of these refers to attitude, not towards the product but concerned with the behaviour which an individual is contemplating in relation to that product. 'What the Fishbein model does is to switch the object that we are looking at'.[40] The second factor relates to 'social normative beliefs', i.e., what influence certain social norms may exercise on specific behaviour; other people's opinions as perceived by an individual. 'More often than not, we intend to do things that others who are important to us think we should do'.[41]

From these two components—attitudes to the act and normative belief—Fishbein proposed that an estimate could be formed of a person's intention to buy a particular product. In some instances, the first factor may have more influence than the other, and analysis should be directed towards obtaining information about the relative importance of these factors in specific buying situations.

Fishbein then developed his basic model into what is termed the Extended Fishbein Model, because he recognized that one of the factors that contributes to an individual's intention to act in some way is the attitude towards taking that action, and not the attitude towards the object of the behaviour.[41] Hence, the following equation was formulated:

$$A_{\mathrm{act}} = \sum B_i a_i$$

where B_i = beliefs about the consequences of a particular act

  a_i = evaluation of those consequences

  A_{act} = attitude towards specific act (e.g., booking an overseas holiday).

Fishbein's theories have naturally attracted critical appreciation. A helpful analysis and application of Fishbein's original attitude theory appeared in the *Journal of the Market Research Society* during 1970.[42] The researchers considered that 'the Fishbein approach to describing or defining the concept attitude is a sensible and practicable one. The distinction between attitude and belief is an important one'. In addition, it is valuable to know both what 'a person thinks about something in terms of a given characteristic and also how favourably he views that characteristic'. There would be little point, for instance, in finding out that an individual rated a certain model of car very highly on 'performance', if this characteristic was not really influential in the decision to buy; economy, styling, and price may be more significant factors. Before Fishbein's intricate method of measuring attitudes could be universally adopted, further work would be needed to test it out thoroughly in a variety of product markets.

Sampson and Palmer in 1975 noted that 'despite the hysteria extended to the Fishbein model in England' related to research on baked beans and detergents, it had been disappointing as a general prediction model for market research purposes.[43] The best results encountered had concerned a very specific problem, i.e., research among general practitioners in connection with drugs for a particular kind of arthritis. in this particular case, there were four factors that contributed to likely accurate behaviour prediction from attitudes: (1) homogeneous 'involved' population, (2) high interest attitude object, (3) specific situation nominated, and (4) more rigorous data collection methods. Such conditions would be unlikely in a broad sample of housewives when predictions are needed for 'What *brand* of fruit juice they will buy when half of them couldn't care less about fruit juice anyway, and a half of the interviewers couldn't care either'.

Sampson has also tackled Fishbein's Extended Model, and while he applauds the continued emphasis on the belief and evaluation components of attitudes, he states that, in his opinion, what people say they intend to do and what they actually do are usually quite different, and frequently have no relevance to their attitudes.[44]

Several other notable researchers have commented on the complexity of attitudinal change and behavioural change. Bird and Ehrenberg felt that 'the interplay between attitude change and behavioural change is as yet very unclear despite the large and increasing amounts of money and effort put into the assessment of consumer attitudes and motives. There is in fact little data available on the relation between change in attitude and changes in behaviour'.[45]

In 1988, Richard Bagozzi[46] of the University of Michigan critically reviewed attitude research approaches including Fishbein's model. He felt that while there have been considerable advances in the measurement of attitudes, such as conjoint analysis, common factor analysis, and factor analysis, developments 'have seemingly stagnated in the conceptual side of attitude research'. While the Fishbein model has had 'a pervasive and lasting impact in psychology and marketing', it is possible to identify 'certain shortcomings'; for example, the model explains reasoned actions, such as problem-solving, but not *unreasoned actions*, such as impulse buying, habitual purchases, or acting out of fear or coercion. It also ignores the possibility that beliefs, evaluations, and attitudes may 'form separately toward the consequences of both *success* and *failure* to achieve a goal, or experience an outcome': all these responses are, in fact, subsumed in a single index. Further, the *processes* leading to behavioural performances are neglected; the focus is only upon the anticipated consequences of behaviour. The steps between intentions and behavioural performance are likewise disregarded; 'it rather assumes that intentions inevitably produce their implied effects'. Finally, the model fails to give adequate consideration to the effects of post-behaviour and other 'mindless' processes on intentions and on subsequent behaviour. Bagozzi also observes that although the Fishbein theory holds that intentions transform atittudes into action, research has found 'that attitudes sometimes directly affect behaviour without necessarily or fully working through intentions'.

Joyce also discussed the relationship between attitudes and behaviour in the context of advertising influence.[47] 'Obviously, there is no point in setting out to influence attitudes if they do not influence behaviour—but do they?' Dissonance theory, Joyce felt, had rather led some people to believe that 'purchasing behaviour affects attitudes towards products and that the reverse is not true'. He suggests that the relationship between attitudes and buying behaviour, i.e., purchase, was a two-way one: 'Attitudes influence purchasing, but purchasing influences attitudes as well. Using research to establish the precise links between the two may therefore be difficult'. The model proposed by Joyce is

$$\text{Attitudes} \rightleftharpoons \text{Behaviour}$$

This mutual relationship has a strong appeal to common sense. Behaviour is reinforced by the satisfactory performance of some product and it is likely that repeat purchases will be made. Favourable attitudes towards that brand of product are strengthened: all this is very much in agreement with learning theory. Dissonance theory has also indicated that consumers seek to obtain reassurance about the products they have chosen, and that this in turn influences their attitudes.

Finally, this discussion will have revealed some of the difficulties surrounding attitudinal influence. As has been said many times before, buying behaviour is complex and it would be naive to expect to find simple relationships between variables. Patient objective research may be successful in adding to the fund of knowledge that is slowly being acquired.

5.13 MOODS, ATTITUDES, AND BEHAVIOUR

In common with many psychological terms, such as personality, the word 'mood' has many meanings and applications. It is often used, for example, to describe the City's views of economic trends, ranging, perhaps, from euphoria to despondency. At election times, the so-called mood of the country is evaluated by politicians and media commentators. Opinion polls are said to track the changing moods of the electorate. Trade unions are judged to be in a less belligerent mood because of the rising levels of unemployment. It is rare to read a newspaper or view television news and reports without the intrusion of that useful word 'mood'.

Of the various definitions used, one refers[48] to an individual's subjectively perceived affective state that is general and pervasive, as contrasted with feelings directed toward specific objects, e.g., the affective component of brand attitude. Intrinsically, moods are transient states of feeling, and differ from emotions, 'which are usually more intense, attention-getting, and tied to a specifiable behaviour'.

Thouless[4] notes that moods may have physiological causes; the mood of pleasure, for example, may be the result of good health. Psychological causes may also be responsible for some moods, and lead to psychoneurotic behaviour where a sense of guilt or a state of extreme fear or anxiety is evident. Simplistically, moods could be classified as positive (e.g., cheerful) or negative (e.g., depressive), but research has not yet resulted in much insight into the effects of specific moods and 'common models of consumer behaviour do not explicitly recognize the role of mood states'. On the other hand, research in psychology shows that mood states are important influences on behaviour, judgement, and recall.

The effects of moods on consumers' attitudes and behaviour deserve recognition, since they are likely to affect many buying decisions; for example, those in good moods may be more readily persuaded to try new products or to complete a market research questionnaire, while those in bad moods may, in fact, deliberately go on a buying spree, perhaps to cheer themselves up (see Sec. 4.8). Mood-oriented approaches by marketers could include advertisements deliberately designed to generate moods of self-indulgence, or conversely, altruism and pity related to specific charitable causes. Mood development may be evident in point-of-purchase displays, demonstrations, and background music. Banks and other financial institutions may find that their clients, existing and potential, respond to particular kinds of 'mood-inducing' messages in their promotional activities; several have redesigned their premises so that they offer clients a more relaxing atmosphere in which to transact business. The merchandise in many retail stores is similar and sometimes identical, while prices and after-sales service are virtually the same. To differentiate their businesses, store managers have attempted to create a mood of excitement by stimulating shoppers' senses through colourful displays, focused lighting, and novel display units. 'Atmosphere' may well be the most effective means of positioning a store competitively; this strategy has been followed very successfully by leading stores like Harrods. Many years ago, a highly experienced stores operator reminded his staff that retailing was essentially like show-business: it had to offer glamour and excitement, not just products, to shoppers.

The extent to which moods influence product, brand choice, and favoured shopping location deserves further research related to specific buying situations. Moods seem to be inseparable elements of human behaviour, and their subtle and endemic effects should not be studied solely in consumer markets. As will be discussed in Chapter 10, the organizational buyer is motivated by both personal and organizational goals, and personal psychological factors (including moods) will affect the style and outcome of negotiations.

5.14 SUMMARY

Definitions of attitudes are many, complex, and confusing. Generally, attitudes are viewed as predispositions to specific kinds of behaviour related to certain objects, people, or events: they can be favourable or unfavourable and can be held with degrees of intensity (valence). Three components have been identified: cognitive, affect or feeling, and conative or action tendency.

Multiplex attitudes have many components; simplex attitudes have relatively few. Attitudes tend to be organized into 'constellations' which form value systems.

Attitudes are formed selectively, according to people's needs; they are not innate. They may be required or modified by information exposure, group membership, environment, and want satisfaction.

Attitude change may be congruent or incongruent; how far attitudes may be changed depends on their extremeness, multiplexity, interconnectedness, consonance, strength and number of wants served, and centrality of values.

The so-called 'sleeper effect' appears to be influential in communications and attitude change.

Considerable discussion has centred on relationships between attitudes and behaviour. Fishbein has made notable contributions with his theories, which have aroused significant interest and criticism.

The influence of mood-states on marketing phenomena, including buyer behaviour, retail store strategies, and promotional campaigns, warrants specific investigation. The effects of moods on consumers' attitudes and behaviour also deserve evaluation.

REFERENCES

1. Allport, Gordon W., *Handbook of Social Psychology*, C. Murchison (ed.), Clark University Press, Worcester, Massachusetts, 1935.

2. Markin, Ron J., *The Psychology of Consumer Behaviour*, Prentice-Hall, Englewood Cliffs, New Jersey, 1969.

3. Lunn, J. A., 'A review of consumer decision process models', ESOMAR, Helsinki, 1971.

4. Thouless, R. H., *General and Social Psychology*, University Tutorial Press, London, 1967.

5. Hilgard, E. R., and R. C. Atkinson, *Introduction to Psychology*, Harcourt, Brace and World, New York, 1967.

6. Bliss, Perry, *Marketing Management and the Behavioural Environment*, Prentice-Hall, Englewood Cliffs, New Jersey, 1970.

7. Katz, Daniel, 'The functional approach to the study of attitudes', *Public Opinion Quarterly*, vol. 24, summer 1960.

8. Adler, Lee, Allan Greenberg and Donald B. Lucas, 'What big agency men think of copy testing methods', *Journal of Marketing Research*, November 1965.

9. Boyd, Harper W., Jnr, and Michael L. Ray, 'What big agency men in Europe think of copy testing methods', *Journal of Marketing Research*, May 1971.

10. Brace, Ian, 'From doll's house to dying: alarmingly effective research', in: *Research Works*, Derek Martin and John Goodyear (eds), NTC, Henley-on-Thames, 1992.

11. Asch, Solomon, *Social Psychology*, Prentice-Hall, Englewood Cliffs, New Jersey, 1965.

12. Howard, John, A., and Jagdish N. Sheth, *The Theory of Buyer Behaviour*, John Wiley, New York, 1969.

13. Krech, David, Richard S. Crutchfield, and Egerton L. Ballachey, *Individual in Society*, McGraw-Hill, New York, 1962.

14. Crespi, Irving, *Attitude Research*, American Marketing Association, Chicago, 1965.

15. Sherif, M., 'A study of some social factors in perception', *Archives Psychology*, no. 187, 1935.

16. Asch, Solomon E., *Readings in Social Psychology*, E. E. Macooby, T. M. Newcomb, and E. L. Hartley (eds), Carnegie Press, Preston, 1952.

17. Newcomb, T. M., *Personality and Social Change: Attitude Formation in a Student Community*, Dryden, New York, 1943.

18. Rawsthorn, Alice, 'Controversy by design', *Financial Times*, 16 November 1989.

19. Katona, George, *The Powerful Consumer*, McGraw-Hill, New York, 1960.

20. Rosenberg, M. J., 'Cognitive structure and attitudinal effect', *Journal of Abnormal and Social Psychology*, vol. 53, 1956.

21. Zajonc, Robert B., 'The concepts of balance, congruity and dissonance', *Public Opinion Quarterly*, vol, 24, summer 1960.

22. Hovland, C. I., and J. Janis (eds) *Personality and Persuasibility*, Yale University Press, New Haven, Connecticut, 1958.

23. Kelman, H. C., 'Process of opinion change', *Public Opinion Quarterly*, vol. 25, 1961.

24. Kelley, H. H., and E. H. Volkart, 'The resistance to change of group anchored attitudes', *American Sociological Review*, vol. 17, 1952.

25. Hovland, C. I., I. L. Janis and H. H. Kelley, *Communication and Persuasion*, Yale University Press, New Haven, Connecticut, 1953.

26. Hovland, C. I., and W. Weiss, 'The influence of source credibility on communication effectiveness'. *Public Opinion Quarterly*, vol. 15, 1951.

27. Kelman, H. C., and C. I. Hovland, ' "Reinstatement" of the communicator in delayed measurement of opinion change', *Journal of Abnormal Social Psychology*, vol. 48, 1953.

28. Capon, H., and J. Hulbert, 'The sleeper effect: an awakening', *Public Opinion Quarterly*, vol. 37, fall 1973.

29. Sternthal, Brian, Lynn W. Phillips, and Ruby Dholakia, 'The persuasive effect of credibility: a situational analysis', *Public Opinion Quarterly*, vol. 42, fall 1978.

30. Hannah, Darlene B., and Brian Sternthal, 'Detecting and explaining the sleeper effect', *Journal of Consumer Research*, vol. 11, September 1984.

31. Jahoda, Marie, and Neil Warren, *Attitudes*, Penguin, London, 1966.

32. La Piere, R. T., 'Attitudes vs actions', *Social Forces*, vol. 13, 1934.

33. Fishbein, Martin, 'The relationships between beliefs, attitudes and behaviour', in: *Cognitive Consistency*, Shel Feldman (ed.), Academic Press, New York, 1966.

34. Wicker, A. W., 'Attitudes vs actions: the relationship of overt responses to attitude objects', *Journal of Social Issues*, vol. 25, 1969.

35. Wells, William, 'Do trends in attitudes predict trends in behaviour?', in: *Attitude Research Enters the 80s*, Richard Olshavsky (ed.), American Marketing Association, Chicago, 1980.

36. Sheth, Jagdish, N., 'A review of buyer behaviour', *Management Science*, vol. 13, no. 12, August 1967.

37. Festinger, Leon, 'Behavioural support for opinion change', *Public Opinion Quarterly*, fall 1964.

38. Rokeach, Milton, *Beliefs, Attitudes, Values: A Theory of Organisation and Change*, Jossey-Bass, San Francisco, 1968.

39. Wells, William, D., 'Attitudes and behaviour: lessons from the Needham life style study', *Journal of Advertising Research*, vol. 25, no. 1, February/March 1985.

40. Fishbein, Martin, 'St. James and St. Martin: a comparison', Tony Twyman (ed.), *Admap*, September 1972.

41. Fishbein, Martin, 'Attitude, attitude change and behaviour: a theoretical overview', in: *Attitude Research Bridges the Atlantic*, Philip Levine (ed.), American Marketing Association, Chicago, 1975.

42. Sampson, Peter and Paul Harris, 'A user's guide to Fishbein', *Journal of the Market Research Society*, vol. 12, no. 3, 1970.

43. Sampson, Peter, and John Palmer, 'Attitude measurement and behaviour prediction: some alternative beliefs', in: *Attitude Research Bridges the Atlantic*, Philip Levine, (ed.), American Marketing Association, Chicago, 1975.

44. Sampson, Peter, 'The technical revolution of the 1970s—will it happen in the 1980s?, *Journal of Market Research Society*, vol. 22, 1980.

45. Bird, M., and A. S. C. Ehrenberg, 'Consumer attitudes and brand usage', *Journal of the Market Research Society*, vol. 12, no. 4, 1970.

46. Bagozzi, Richard P., 'The rebirth of attitude research in marketing', *Journal of Market Research Society*, vol. 30, no. 2, April 1988.

47. Joyce, Timothy, 'What do we know about how advertising works?', *Advertising Age*, May/June 1967.

48. Gardner, Meryl Paula, 'Mood states and consumer behavior: a critical review', *Journal of Consumer Research*, vol. 12, December 1985.

REVIEW AND DISCUSSION QUESTIONS

1. What relationship, if any, is there between consumers' attitudes and their subsequent purchasing behaviour? How does the nature of this relationship impact on market research and marketing strategy?

2. A manufacturer of a new kitchen appliance commissioned an attitude survey of housewives in May 1990. Of those surveyed, 85 per cent indicated a positive attitude. In October 1991 the appliance was launched. In the following eighteen months it reached only 15 per cent penetration of its projected market. What factors might explain this discrepancy between the housewives' attitudes and their subsequent behaviour?

3. How would you react to the criticism that expenditure by companies on attitude surveys is a waste of valuable resources?

4. How useful would Fishbein's basic attitude model be as a framework for an advertising campaign designed to change consumer attitudes to a brand of women's clothing?

5. In what ways might a multi-attribute approach to attitude measurement (e.g., Fishbein) have richer strategic implications for marketing than the traditional three-component approach?

6. Recount four instances where your purchasing behaviour was at odds with your pre-purchase attitudes. Explain why this was so.

GROUP ASPECTS OF BEHAVIOUR

SIX

CULTURE

6.1 INTRODUCTION

Parts One and Two identified and examined the basic personal psychological factors such as cognitions, perception, learning processes, attitudes, and motivation. Part Three discusses group aspects of behaviour which consider individuals as members of society with distinctive patterns of culture.

Cultural beliefs and values influence, sometimes profoundly, the economic decisions made by individuals either as personal consumers or when they may be acting for an organization. Interaction takes place between individuals and their environment; they are affected by the society of which they are members. Nearly 400 years ago, John Donne,* the English metaphysical poet, wrote these memorable lines: 'No man is an Island, entire of itself; every man is a piece of the continent, a part of the main. . . . Any man's death diminishes me, because I am involved in Mankind; And therefore never send to know for whom the bell tolls; It tolls for thee.'

To understand the behaviour of people, some knowledge of the influence of cultural norms and values is necessary. Study of environmental factors such as cultural and social influences will help to construct what may be termed the mosaic of behaviour; from these many variables—personal and environmental—the intricate pattern of human behaviour will become apparent.

Before it is possible to discuss the influence of an environmental variable—or indeed any variable, as in the case of the personal psychological factors—it would be helpful to define what that variable is and to understand something about its structure and the extent of its impact on an individual's behaviour. With this precept in mind, the influence of cultural factors in buying behaviour will start with an examination of the definitions of culture.

6.2 DEFINITIONS OF CULTURE

As with practically every variable so far considered, there are several definitions of culture which have been offered by psychologists, anthropologists, historians, and other writers.

* 'Devotions upon Emergent Occasions', no. XVII.

Howard and Sheth viewed culture as 'a selective, man-made way of responding to experience, a set of behaviour patterns'.[1] In their interpretation, culture consists essentially of traditional ideas and, in particular, the values that are attached to these ideas. They postulated that cultural influences affect motives, brand comprehension, attitude, and intention to purchase.

Linton defined culture as 'the total way of life of any society, not simply . . . those parts of this way which the society regards as higher or more desirable. Thus culture, when applied to our own way of life, has nothing to do with playing the piano or reading Browning'.[2] Culture is not a narrow view of human activities, exclusively concerned with listening to symphony concerts or visiting art galleries. It extends to include *all* the activities that characterize the behaviour of particular communities of people. 'This totality also includes such mundane activities as washing dishes or driving an automobile'. Linton elaborated his definition of culture as follows: 'A culture is the configuration of learned behaviour and results of behaviour whose component elements are shared and transmitted by the members of a particular society'. By 'configuration', Linton implied that 'the various behaviours and results of behaviour which compose a culture are organised into a patterned whole'. He accented the learning process in the acquisition of cultural behaviour; although some degree of instinctive behaviour was apparent it could not be regarded as part of culture 'in spite of [the] obvious influence upon culture'. For example, although eating fulfils a basic need, the way in which individuals eat, and the types of food they consume, will depend on how they have learned to eat. Linton used the term 'behaviour' to include all the activities of an individual, 'whether overt or covert, physical or psychological'. The phrase 'shared and transmitted' underlines the essential quality of culture: that it refers to certain types of behaviour which are common to two or more persons; individual idiosyncrasies are not part of the culture of a society, until such time as they may become diffused to other people and affect their patterns of behaviour. Linton cautioned against believing that 'sharing' a cultural belief necessarily meant that *every* member of a particular society would have to share in that belief. 'Actually, it would be impossible to find any element of culture which had been shared by all members of a society throughout that society's entire duration'.[2]

Cultural patterns change; new values emerge to challenge old-established behavioural patterns. Within national cultures, sub-cultures develop with distinctive ideas and values, some of which may be antagonistic to traditional beliefs. In modern industrial communities, sub-cultures develop to satisfy the needs of an individual for affiliation and identification with those who share similar views and whose behaviour is compatible with personal standards. 'Modern subcultures are almost as numerous as the interests of researchers dictate':[3] the old-wealth elite, café society, the jet set, teenagers, disadvantaged minorities, students, etc. In Sec. 6.11 more detailed discussion will consider the influence of sub-cultural groups on marketing strategies.

The concept of culture, although difficult to define precisely, 'serves to point to the fact that, despite border-line cases, there are large numbers of people who are alike in customs, language and rituals, yet clearly different from their neighbours who, in turn, are similar to each other'.[3]

Each culture, as McCracken observes,[4] 'establishes its own special vision of the world'; this incorporates 'understandings and rules' that have particular significance for its members. Culture derives, therefore, from a group of people *sharing* and *transmitting* beliefs, values, attitudes, and forms of behaviour that are held in common and regarded as important to that society.[5] Although some people may, from time to time, deviate from these accepted patterns of thought and behaviour, the essential core of a culture continues to be influential, because its roots are deep and firmly embedded. In times of cultural change, cherished beliefs and traditional behaviour are likely to be challenged; how far the old culture can assimilate new sets of values will be discussed later.

Wherever people have lived and multiplied, as Schumacher observed, some form of culture has been created.[6] 'Always and everywhere they have found their means of subsistence and something to spare. Civilisations have been built up, have flourished, and, in most cases, have declined and perished.'

Culture, as seen by Ballachey, refers to 'distinctive modal patterns of behaviour and the underlying regulatory beliefs, norms and premises'.[7] These help members of a society to cope with many problems that arise during the course of their lives. People learn patterns of behaviour which simplify these problems, and some of these solutions may become established as cultural norms. But the relationship is not one-way: individuals are influenced by the culture of their society and also contribute to that culture. In time, people's personal behaviour may infect the actions and reactions of their associates, and result in some change in the cultural values of a particular society. Culture, therefore, is not a static concept; in modern communities, cultural changes reflect the dynamic nature of industrial societies and have significant repercussions on the goods and services which are demanded.

The radical differences in cultural outlook on life have been described vividly by Banton:

> Backward societies look to the past. Each generation learns its roles from its fathers and continues to regard them as teachers and exemplars. People strive to be as worthy as their fathers were, not to surpass them. Frequently they are caught in the vicious circle by which poverty breeds apathy and apathy keeps people poor, but culturally these societies are characterised by their intellectual self-sufficiency. Industrial societies look to the future. They see history as the story of progress up to their present elevation. Children learn at school things that their parents could never teach them, but the emphasis is not so much upon being better people as upon doing greater things. . . . the cultural characteristic of industrial societies is their need to believe in the future.[8]

Hence the fundamental orientation of culture in a modern industrial society is towards achievement and the attainment of increasing levels of satisfaction. McClelland's theory of high n-achievement as a motivating influence has already been seen to have a profound influence on the behaviour of certain types of individuals and to exercise a far-reaching effect on national culture patterns and economic development.[9] The industrial and technological revolutions have dramatically changed the behaviour of individuals who now live and work in densely populated areas, where they frequently experience social and psychological tensions because of the impersonal nature of their work and the environment in which it is done. As they adjust to the pace of modern life, people may seek to modify some of the old beliefs and values, such as thrift, held by earlier generations. Credit buying no longer carries a certain social stigma; societal norms have undergone some modification and a 'credit culture' has evolved as a strong feature of modern societies. In Britain, the spectacular growth of bank credit cards, e.g., Access, has been possible because of this fundamental change in attitudes and cultural values.

As far back as 1966, Claude Lévi-Strauss, the French anthropologist, characterized western societies as 'hot societies', which 'willingly accept, indeed encourage, the radical changes that result from deliberate human effort and the effects of anonymous social forces'.[4] In such dynamic societies, change is endemic and even demanded; cultural values are subject to almost continuous challenge. 'Hot' societies breed restless environments where patterns of consumption are complex, individualistic, and dynamic. Lévi-Strauss's typology seems to be a particularly apt description of present-day western societies, where the growth of materialism has been nurtured by changing sets of cultural values which are rapidly disseminated through the mass media. Many advertisements, plays, and novels tend to reinforce this trend towards materialistic consumption, as seen, for example, in the widely dispersed American television programmes *Dallas* and *Dynasty* (youth sub-culture is discussed in Sec. 6.11).

A striking commentary on modern industrial culture was contained in an article which appeared in *Industrial Marketing Management*:

> Kenneth Boulding, the distinguished American economist, has characterised the modern 'super-culture' as built upon the culture of 'airports', throughways, skyscrapers and artificial fertilisers,

birth control and universities'. This culture is based then upon technical innovation, innovations often made without any form of social control and without examination of the consequences.[10]

The last part of this extract tends to be a rather sweeping condemnation of innovation, whereas in the severely critical atmosphere generated by various pressure groups such as consumer associations, and the constraints increasingly imposed by legal sanction, manufacturers' activities are drastically curtailed.

Today, trading policies and practices are being openly debated and challenged; the mass media, which are quick to spot new areas of interest, have made the consuming public aware of many things that had previously failed to attract general interest. For example, people have been made aware of certain additives to food which could be harmful to health; the dangers of pollution have been discussed at almost inordinate length.

The influence of public attitudes on commercial activities has been noted by Levitt: 'When Pittsburgh's steel mills shut out the sun at high noon 30 years ago, the need for pollution control was obvious. But there was no market then: nobody thought of doing anything about the smog, even though techniques for controlling it were available'.[11]

Ansoff has drawn attention to the 'vigorous public debate' that has been going on for some years about the role of the business firm in society.[12] The issue for the business firm, he declares, is two-sided: 'How far should the firm be constrained by society from actions that are inimical to the public good—even if such actions are essential to making a profit? Should business management voluntarily assume obligations for pursuing social purposes in addition to, or even in place of, economic purposes?' There is no doubt, Ansoff concludes, that companies will remain activated by profits, but their activities 'will be strongly affected by an awareness of social consequences'.

Further discussion of 'consumerism' as a cultural factor occurs in Chapter 15, but it will be apparent from this brief review that change is a built-in feature of modern culture systems. In keeping with the hierarchy of needs, as proposed by Maslow[13] (discussed more fully in Chapter 3), cultural values are affected by the ambitions and interests of members of a particular society. They reflect people's beliefs, attitudes, and motivational systems; the slow pace of change evident in primitive communities is no longer tolerated by those who are exposed to the dynamic, competitive atmosphere of industrialized society.

6.3 THE NATURE OF CULTURE

It will be evident that culture manifests itself in diverse ways. Societies of all kinds form traditional behavioural characteristics that identify them to other communities and to individuals within those groups. Materialism appears to be a predominant feature of western culture; material progress is rewarded and approved in general. That brilliant and reforming economist, Barbara Wootton, once wrote that two adjectives are frequently applied to contemporary western societies—'affluent' and 'permissive'. To these she added a third—'acquisitive'—which she viewed as describing 'an even more dominant characteristic of the world in which we live'.[14]

Some of the motivational theories and explanations of personality differences that were mentioned in Chapters 3 and 4 may be usefully studied in conjunction with the present discussion on cultural influences. People's behaviour is bound up with the culture of their communities as well as being affected by their personal differences in perception, motivation, personality traits, and attitudes. As individuals develop in the society in which they live, they tend to learn the habits and values that are generally regarded as desirable. They become acculturated through the process of socialization or enculturation; the values of that particular society are then integrated into their personality and their consumption habits are likely to be affected. 'Diet, uses of energy, patterns of worship, work and play partly and rightly reflect a vast and precious variety of cultures and social purposes'.[14]

Although the basic psychological factors affect all people, irrespective of their race or residence, there are cultural inhibitions, traditions, and values that influence the ways in which, say, the fundamental need for food is satisfied. Why, for example, reflect Wind and Douglas, should a Frenchman not satisfy his drive for hunger with a hamburger just as much as an American?[15] Cultural differences may position products differently, as in the case of hot, milk-based drinks, which in the USA and the UK are bedtime drinks, whereas in Latin America, a hot milk drink like chocolate caliente is a morning drink 'or a nice way to start the day'.[16]

Cultural norms are those standards of behaviour that have gradually established themselves as guides to conduct in certain situations. They may have considerable influence on social behaviour or on the methods of transacting business. Norms regulate or prescribe particular kinds of behaviour which may be reinforced by the pressure of public opinion apart from mandatory restrictions.

Two kinds of norms have been identified by sociologists: *folkways* and *mores*. The former refer to relatively minor social conventions such as 'dressing for the occasion'—wearing an evening-dress suit at a formal dinner, for example. Folkways—or the ways which people in a society like to acknowledge as acceptable standards of behaviour—are also referred to as 'customs'. Conformity to the customary behaviour of a particular community helps strangers, for instance, to win acceptance by established members. At one time, women in western communities generally accepted that trousers were not an appropriate style of clothing for them, though of course this cultural inhibition no longer applies. Mores, the second category of norms, relate to standards of behaviour that are generally considered to be central to the prevailing culture. These include religious and moral beliefs associated with family life, national feelings of patriotism, and so on. Deviations are strongly discouraged and are frequently punished by social ostracism or legal penalties. It would seem that this division between norms is to some degree arbitrary, particularly when a society is in a state of flux, and long-held values are being openly challenged. A more tolerant view is taken of those, for example, whose marriages have ended in divorce. Men's clothing and hairstyles have completely overthrown the traditional culture restraints that had been imposed for many years on tailors and hairdressers. Informal clothes are tolerated in many business firms, whereas at one time the bank clerk or the shop assistant had to be formally attired.

Markin noted that many of the folkways and mores of a culture become so much a part of the fabric of that society that they became known as 'institutions'.[17] These embody a whole set of beliefs, customs, values, and norms related, for instance, to churches, schools, governments, and retail stores. In the UK, for example, Harrods is virtually an 'institution' and not just a retail store, while at a more popular level, Marks and Spencer have achieved unique cultural acceptability as 'Marks and Sparks'.

All individuals are products of the culture of their society, which affects very considerably the actions and decisions which they take every day.[18] Individuals may react quite differently to the same situation, according to their cultural background and general experience. Norms of behaviour tend to regulate the way people live. Acceptable patterns of behaviour become identified with particular social groups and with specific occupations. Bank managers are expected by the society in which they live to be reliable, honest, and serious-minded individuals. Public entertainers may be excused some personal idiosyncrasies and flamboyant habits, whereas similar behaviour by a solicitor or a minister of religion would not be tolerated by their clients or members of their flock. some deviation may be tolerated, but certain limits appear to be acknowledged as restraints to excessive behaviour. Society imposes its regulatory constraints—more implicit than explicit—and inhibits the conduct of those who wish to continue to be members and to enjoy the benefits of that society.

6.4 CULTURE AND MARKETING STRATEGY

Consumption habits, which are part of the behaviour patterns of individuals, are deeply affected by the prevailing culture of the society in which people live: 'A culture is a kind of adhesive which binds together men of similar ideas, values and behaviour'.[17] All societies develop distinctive cultures which reflect the many facets of human behaviour that have been learned and accepted by groups of people so that these form part of their traditional way of life—their life-style. A culture is transmitted in innumerable ways, some of which are obscured by generations of folklore and defy rational explanation.

Cultural norms affect eating habits, and these may reflect the regional differences in living styles. In his fascinating study of patterns of consumption in Britain, David Allen has reflected on the regional variations in this island, some of which are still apparent today.[19] The 'chip butties' of the north-west or the oatcakes of the Potteries are distinctive gastronomic experiences. In Lancashire, the traveller, on asking for afternoon tea, may still be given a menu listing 'high tea', equivalent to the southerner's evening meal.

Cultural anthropology is concerned with finding out about how people's lives are affected by the environment in which they live and work; it investigates the meaning of symbols, rituals, and taboos; and it attempts to study the significance of national culture patterns. Comparisons of methods of dealing with problems, such as the assimilation of ideas from other cultures, would be made across national boundaries and also within the sub-cultures existing in a community.

From being closely identified with primitive societies and their cultural development, anthropologists have now focused their professional skills on to the problems of modern industrial communities. Anthropology has tended to suffer 'from an unhelpful aura on the one hand of the jungle and the tom-tom, and on the other of the armchair and carpet slippers'.[19] It has popularly been linked with the habits of some distant islands in the Pacific, and has attracted an image 'romantic and intriguing (even, indeed, faintly salacious)'.[20]

The cultural influences affecting human behaviour should not be regarded as merely of academic interest: some esoteric branch of studies which has more significance for students of history and sociology than for business executives. This is far from the truth, because the cultural values of a society find expression in the products and services that are demanded; the acceptance of new products, for example, may be very dependent on the cultural implications involved in changing some pattern of consumption. (The particular problems of innovation related to cultural factors are discussed in Chapter 11.)

Products, as McCracken stresses,[21] are 'vehicles of cultural meanings' and consumers may be viewed as 'more or less sophisticated choosers and users of these cultural meanings'. Products and marketing strategies should, therefore, be designed to take account of the cultural meanings that are perceived to be important to an identified type of consumer. A five-step approach to integrating cultural values into products and services is given as:

1. *Research*: identify present and also possible symbolic elements and cultural meanings in consumers' lives.
2. *Product development*: ensure that every aspect of the product—design, physical properties, packaging, etc.—reflects the identified cultural meanings.
3. *Marketing*: devise promotional campaigns that reflect and transfer cultural meanings.
4. *Copy testing*: to determine whether cultural meanings inherent in promotional campaigns were transferred successfully.

5. *Final stage of research*: to track what effect these cultural transfers have had on consumers' perceptions, attitudes, buying habits, and so on.

Cultural beliefs and values are extremely important in human society. Underlying many human actions (and these include buying behaviour) are a multitude of superstitions, fears, aversions, myths and fables, which, although seemingly 'irrational' so some observers, exercise profound influence. The pervasiveness of cultural constraints was noted by Levitt in an article in the *Harvard Business Review*:

> The sea may harbour a huge food supply, but the consuming public is not likely to embrace any great fondness for strange new foods. Food habits are among the most difficult of all to change, even in the face of extraordinary deprivation. No better and no more discouraging examples are the singular disappointments suffered in recent years by companies that have created new, low-priced, high-protein foods for consumption by under-nourished masses in South America and India. . . . Thousands of wretched people starve daily in India amidst the world's largest roving supply of edible cattle. The capabilities of technology form perhaps the least realistic basis for predicting what we will consume or how we will live.[11]

The close link between cultural beliefs and practices and economic activities was observed in a study of French peasants, whose rural society was completely transformed in the 1950s mainly as a result of the introduction of hybrid corn.[22] Officials tried to convince the peasants of the productivity advantages of switching to hybrid corn from the traditional type, but since the former required more space and care, they needed additional land, tractors, insecticides, and fertilizers. As a result, they had to obtain bank loans and become more money conscious; this led them to be more concerned with food prices and powerful peasant unions developed. 'Thus, this sector of French society was totally transformed as the result of a minor change. . . . Culturally, economically, politically, everything had changed in the attitudes and the situation of these peasants and in their relations with environment'.

The intrusion of cultural values into economic activities affects, in particular, export marketing strategies. No company is likely to be successful in overseas countries if it ignores or offends cultural behaviour patterns. Kotler has referred to the cultural taboos that may affect the sales of some products in certain countries; it would, for instance, be 'the height of folly to try to merchandise cosmetics on a mass scale in the Middle East or hamburgers in India'.[23] Examples have occurred in Britain when American-owned companies have attempted to popularize food products based on US lifestyles. Cake mixes or canned soups, although backed by major companies' promotional campaigns, have failed to win widespread acceptance because their recipes were not suited to British palates or the methods of preparation were unusual. Different patterns of behaviour in some overseas markets may mean that products which are perfectly acceptable in a manufacturer's home market may not be successful when offered elsewhere and without any attempt at modifying the flavouring, consistency, packaging, or perhaps, the method of distribution to suit national preferences and habits.

A cautionary tale about the significance of cultural taboos concerned an official exchange of gifts many years ago. King Ibn Saud of Arabia had presented Churchill and Eden with expensive rings and jewelled swords following a meeting in Cairo at the end of the Second World War. Churchill thereupon ordered a 'particularly luxurious Rolls-Royce to be built and sent out to Jedda'. This superb vehicle was duly delivered, 'specially fitted with a gun-rack, long wide running-boards for six bodyguards and a vast armchair in the back'. The King inspected his present and seemed satisfied, but then suddenly told his brother, Emir Abdullah, that he could have the car. It appeared that the King had observed it had a right-hand drive; on long journeys he preferred to sit in the front seat of a car. 'But by oriental convention it would be an intolerable humiliation to sit on the driver's left.[24] So this prestige car proved to be an unacceptable gift because of a cultural constraint.

Cultural differences exist even between the precise meanings of some English words as used by Americans and as understood by British people. Margaret Mead has commented upon the different meanings which the word 'compromise' carries for American and British speakers.

> In Britain, the word 'compromise' is a good word, and one may speak approvingly of any arrangement which has been a compromise, including very often, one in which the other side has gained more than 50% of the points at issue. . . . Where, in Britain, the compromise means to work out a good solution, in America it usually means to work out a bad one, a solution in which all the points of importance (to both sides) are lost.[25]

At times, there may be genuine misunderstanding as apparently 'occurred at the 1962 Geneva Disarmament Conference, when the British delegation wanted to table a motion which enjoyed American support. When the Americans were told the proposal they disagreed with surprising vehemence. Not until much later did the British discover that to table in America means "to reject or set aside".'[26]

Cultural development within markets deserves special consideration by would-be exporters. The Single Market in Europe by no means implies uniformity of cultural and social behaviour, buying preferences, and so on. Europe is not a cultural entity with identical patterns of thought, attitudes, and behaviour. While a degree of globalization of products, such as teenage fashions, jeans, fast-food outlets, and sports equipment has occurred in some consumer markets, it cannot be said that a single European market will result in identically similar consumer tastes or habits.

Mark Abrams described three Europes: the 'new Europe' of big cities like Paris, London, Hamburg, Stockholm, and their conurbations, together with areas of high-density population such as Switzerland and north-west Italy. The 'emerging Europe' of his second classification is composed of areas such as the semi-urbanized hinterlands of southern France, northern Italy and south-west Germany. His third grouping, termed 'old Europe', refers to the 'marginal' farming lands to be found in parts of Spain, Portugal and the north-west of Scotland.

Cultural groupings may not necessarily be limited by national boundaries, and so the adoption and diffusion of products should be viewed by marketers with a more sophisticated appreciation of cultural boundaries. Asa Briggs,[27] referred in 1972 to the inherent cultural and economic differences that would continue to distinguish Europe:

> The younger generation are already far more 'integrated' than any generation before—through fashion, through entertainment, through education, above all through travel. Yet there will remain differences, some of which will not correspond to national boundaries and will rather reflect sub-cultures and economic sub-groups—with religion continuing in some sense to influence the first and with the latter including not only pockets of poverty but occupational groupings. . . . Europe may be integrated, but it will never in my view become completely 'homogenised'. It will always have variety, which is the essence of its inheritance, and the variety will be expressed in attitudes as much as in local circumstances.

Some products may have a strong international appeal to certain age groups, e.g., Coca-Cola, the promoting of which has deliberately fostered an international image. But it would be dangerous to assume that standardization of products and methods of presentation (e.g., advertising copy) across world markets is the answer to successful exporting.

Dichter suggested in 1962 that world markets could be based on the relative position and influence of the middle classes which may be seen to be particularly significant in modern countries compared with less developed countries.[28] He declared that the 'restless middle-class is the most important factor in the constructive discontent which motivates people's desires and truly moves them forward'.

The status of women in particular cultures may affect the consumption of certain types of products, such as domestic labour-saving equipment. Singer found that in selling machines in Middle East countries, the husband rather than the wife had to be approached with the argument that the ownership of a sewing machine would make his wife more efficient and useful, and not merely save her personal trouble and time.

An anthropological survey into the development of irrigation in two southern Indian villages found that this had affected family and sex roles.[22] In the first village, the peasants began to replace the traditional subsistence crops with sugar cane, which gave them a progressively increasing income. This enabled them to extend and diversify their farming activities, and since some of these activities, such as raising poultry and cattle, and selling eggs and milk, were traditionally regarded as women's roles, the economic freedom and family status of women were enhanced.

In addition, since the peasants had to sell their cane to publicly owned factories, certain constraints became influential: each peasant had to be treated equally, and not more cane than could be consumed would be bought. Hence, selling quotas were imposed on every family; this encouraged peasants to settle their eldest son on an independent plot at a much earlier time in their family life, and so irrigation assisted the earlier economic independence of the rising generation.

At the same time, however, the irrigation programme 'reinforced rather than eroded, the traditional system of culture. The new crops brought extra income, the surplus of which could be loaned to the less well-off, thus increasing the disparities of income between the castes of peasants, though all become richer after irrigation'. The peasants and the Untouchables became more closely interdependent than ever before; although the latter could not afford to buy land, they shared in the general prosperity which resulted in better employment opportunities, while also improving their relationships within their own cultural group, because they were no longer competing among themselves for limited work opportunities. Also, the peasants needed to devote more time to the cultivation of cane than had been necessary with traditional crops; having less time to visit the near-by city, they became more closely involved in village life.

The powerful effect of ritual and taboos has been eloquently observed by Lewis Mumford in *The Myth of the Machine*. He says that just as ritual is 'the first step towards effective expression and communication through language, so taboo was the first step towards moral discipline. Without both, man's career might have ended long ago, as so many powerful rulers and nations have ended their lives, in psychotic outbreaks and life-depressing perversions'.[29] He reflects that ritual, dance, totem, taboo, religion, magic 'provided the groundwork for man's later higher development'. The important and unique contribution of ritual is also cogently expressed by Michael Argyle: 'Ritual can be regarded as a kind of language which expresses the things that cannot easily be put into words'.[30]

Pursuing his theme of the cultural meanings attached to products, McCracken[4] states that often the donor selects a gift because it is perceived as having 'meaningful properties', which it is desired to transfer to the receiver. Hence, the exchange of gifts enables donors to 'insinuate certain symbolic properties' into the lives of recipients. Gift-giving is likely to include attractive packaging and the ritual of presentation. The whole event is, therefore, full of symbolic significances and may signify the status of both the donor and the receiver.

In many product markets, gift-giving is an important buying motivation; for example, tea and coffee sets, expensive pens, exotic perfumes, flowers, or dining-out in fashionable restaurants. Gifts like these resonate with psychological and cultural meanings, and they should, of course, be acceptable to those who receive them. On many ocasions, gifts may be given in order to attract particular responses, such as the continuation of friendship, the encouragement of scholarship, or to cement business relationships. Anthropologists refer to rites of passage associated with significant steps in a person's life, for example, birthday, coming-of-age, engagement, marriage, or retirement. Special celebrations and gifts mark such occasions, which bring together families, friends, and colleagues. Throughout human history—

in advanced and primitive societies alike—the rituals of gift-giving are observed with dignity and ceremony, adding colour and vitality to everyday life.

6.5 LIFE-STYLES

The concept of life-style refers to the distinctive or characteristic ways of living adopted by certain communities or segments of communities. It relates to the general attitudes and behaviour towards the allocation of time, money, and effort in pursuit of objectives considered desirable by particular types of individuals. Life-styles do not remain unchanged in modern society; they may undergo significant alterations, as has been witnessed in the upgrading of merchandise in many groups of stores to cater for the more sophisticated tastes of their customers.

People of a given occupation or income group tend to associate with each other and to spend their money in characteristic ways. They 'come to think of themselves as a group, and finally, develop a set of values that is a special variant of the national culture'.[31]

Life-style research and psychographics

This type of psychologically based research uses data related to the activities, interests, beliefs, and opinions of consumers, as well as demographic analyses. It is applied in the segmentation of consumer markets (discussed in Chapter 14). Life-style research was developed by the Leo Burnett Agency in Chicago and the University of Chicago. It is 'concerned with those unique ingredients or qualities which describe the style of life of some culture or group, and distinguish it from others. It embodies the patterns that develop and emerge from the dynamics of living in a society'.[32] Life-style, therefore, adds depth and understanding to investigations of consumer buying behaviour.

The major elements of life-style research were identified by Plummer as activities, interests, opinions, and demographics;[33] this approach was identified as AIO and, with related methods, became known as psychographics. Under each of these dimensions, several factors were listed. For example, 'activities' covered work, hobbies, social events, vacation, entertainment, shopping, sport, etc., while 'opinions' included social, personal, political, business, education and products.

In 1970, Daniel Yankelovich, one of the foremost US market researchers, founded the Monitor Survey which tracks over 50 trends in people's attitudes towards time, money, family, self, institutions, the future, and many other factors affecting their life-styles. Prominent companies subscribe to the Monitor Survey which, among many research projects, claims to have identified the trend towards white wine and light alcoholic drinks. Yankelovich and his associates researched the 'baby-boom' generation in the USA and classified this as *self-starters* (independent-minded consumers); '*materialists*' (influenced by advertisements featuring eager, active shoppers); and '*nesters*' (family-centred, concerned with traditional values and products offering satisfaction).

Another American pioneer in psychographic research was the advertising agency Needham, Harper and Steers (now known as DDB Needham), who developed ten life-style categories bearing imaginative titles, such as Thelma, the old-fashioned traditionalist, Candice, the chic surbanite, and Fred, the frustrated factory worker.

Based on the research foundations laid by Arnold Mitchell in the 1970s, the Stanford Research Institute (SRI) developed VALS (values and life-styles), a typology which initially characterized people as 'survivors' and 'sustainers'; survivors were perceived as struggling for survival, typically elderly, distrustful, and with buying habits focused on basics; sustainers, though only slightly better off, hope that in time things will get better and so do not despair;

their buying is price-conscious. VALS further segmented consumers into 'inner-directed' and 'outer-directed', derived from the sociological analyses of David Riesman (see Chapter 4). Inner-directed consumers are classified in three subgroups as: '*I-am-me*' (very young, individualistic, often confused about goals in life, and tending to be impulsive buyers); *Experiential* (seek direct experience; includes some maturing from being the ego-centrics of the 'I-am-me' group; utility of a product considered more important than the possible projection of personality); *Societally conscious* (largest of inner-directed types; concerned about simple, natural living and with social issues; discriminating buyers, interested in environmentally sound products).

Consumers typified as 'outer-directed' are divided into three subgroups: *Belongers* (largest of VALS groups—38 per cent conservative, conforming, hard-working, and not innovative buyers); *Emulators* (10 per cent of US consumers, regarded as upwardly mobile, ambitious, more status conscious than Belongers, and are 'conspicuous consumption' buyers); *Achievers* (21 per cent successful business executives and professionals, competent, confident, comfort-loving, materialistic, and avidly seek the trappings of success like expensive cars, holidays, and so on).

A 30-item VALS questionnaire results in client companies having their product markets profiled by VALS types. Respondents are asked to agree or disagree with statements like: 'What I do at work is more important to me than the money I earn'. Clients can then develop products, packaging, and advertising appeals targeted at specific consumer groups.

While VALS has attracted considerable patronage from leading companies in the USA, mostly in consumer products and services, and is used by large advertising agencies in planning advertisements for television and the press, the rather neat pigeon-holing of consumers into one of the eight classifications listed, seems to ignore that people may well be made up of a mix of these psychographic types. They may also lack consistency in buying, perhaps becoming more indulgent on one shopping expedition than on another, when their moods have changed (see Chapter 5). However, it should be noted that SRI concede that these life-style categories are not fixed or immutable, and acknowledge that many people, as they grow up and gain experience of life, may progress from one level to another.

While recognizing the valuable contributions made by psychographics to knowledge about consumer behaviour, concern has been expressed about the reliability of the scales used, the measurements applied, and the methods of analysis used; it is urged that special care should be exercised to ensure that the research methods involved are fully reliable and appropriate.[34]

Life-style research was conducted by Annette Horne into owner-occupied and council-tenanted housing in the UK.[35] The questionnaire contained over 200 statements covering a wide range of activities, interests, and opinions, such as: 'I take a real interest in politics'; 'Most women need a career as well as a family'.

'Dramatic differences' were found in the responses between owner-occupiers and council tenants 'which immediately establish a separate lifestyle for each group'. For example, owner-occupiers felt more secure and more confident about themselves than council tenants; they tended to be innovators and were not afraid of taking on responsibilities. House owners had a much wider range of interests than council tenants, who were less likely to want to change traditional patterns of behaviour. The typical female owner-occupier is more interested in a varied diet for her family, and regarded herself as a skilful shopper.

Another life-style research attempted to distinguish 'prestige hierarchies' related to the purchase of cars, clothing, and place of residence in the Chicago suburbs.[36] The resultant data confirmed that hierarchies existed but 'they are not as clear and straightforward as the national hierarchies for occupational prestige', which led the researchers to suggest that 'the present state of evidence conflicts with the commonsense expectation that public opinion has a clear image of of the prestige hierarchy' for the 'important examples of visible consumer behaviour' which they had adopted in their survey.

International life-style comparisons were studied by Linton and Broadbent, who point out that life-style research is one of several psychographic methods which draws a portrait of a group of people: 'it describes what they are like in terms similar to those you would use to describe a neighbour or a colleague'.[37] The researchers admitted that the major problem in multi-country research is translation: 'not only a question of words having the same meaning, but also the same associations'. By its very nature, a life-style questionnaire focuses on exactly 'those points which are most local in character and with subtleties difficult to export'. There were 'some broadly similar results' by country; for example, more young people than older women like parties; women of all ages take pride in cooking, but with older women this is more marked.[37]

The life-styles of what has been termed the 'affluent middle-aged' has also attracted attention. Wendy Gordon declared that it is clear that people reaching middle age—accepted as beginning some time between 45 and 55 years of age, with 50 being the most popular choice—have needs and behaviour patterns that are markedly different from younger groups.[38] They are relatively affluent because, most major financial commitments being finished, their disposable incomes are quite high. As might be expected, the middle-aged and middle class and the middle-aged working class tended to have different attitudes to this phase of life and to perceptions of affluence. The former seemed to be more optimistic about the future, while the latter appeared to be extremely bitter about 'the state of Britain today', and were pessimistic about their retirement prospects.

The spending and saving patterns of the 'affluent middle-aged' were researched by Buck, who defines these as 'households where the children have ceased to be dependent, where the husband and wife are normally both working, where the housing payments are relatively low and where outstanding debts are few'.[39] He feels that to define older age groups as 45–64 is not particularly helpful in understanding their buying propensity; statistics for 'all over-55s', for example, confuse those who are in well-paid occupations with retired people, 'who genuinely have little disposable income'. The older age groups have immense *potential* spending power; in some markets this is well marked: 45–65-year-old women are relatively heavier buyers of fragrances and hair-care products than younger women, although they buy fewer cosmetics, skin lotions and deodorants. Buck concludes that while it may be more exciting for advertisers to aim their campaigns at the 'swinging young', they should not neglect the 'staid and elderly', for these have cash available to spend.

Research Bureau Ltd, a leading British marketing research agency, investigated life-style patterns within the UK.[40] Through a combination of factor and cluster analyses, the following eight groups of housewives were classified from a representative sub-sample of 3500 housewives under the age of 45.

Cluster 1 'The young sophisticates' (15 per cent)
These were characterized as: extravagant, experimental, non-traditional; young, ABC1 social class (see Sec. 7.9), well educated, affluent, owner-occupiers, full-time employed; interested in new products. Sociable. Cultural interests.

Cluster 2 'Cabbages' (12 per cent)
Conservative, less quality conscious, not obsessional; demographically average, but more full-time housewives. Middle class, average income, education; lowest level of interest in new products. Very home-centred; little entertaining.

Cluster 3 'Traditional working class' (12 per cent)
Traditional, quality conscious, unexperimental in food, enjoy cooking; middle-aged, DE social group (see Sec. 7.9), less educated, lower incomes, council house tenants; sociable; husband and wife share activities; betting.

Cluster 4   *'Middle-aged sophisticates'* (14 per cent)

Experimental, not traditional, less extravagant; middle-aged, ABC1 social-class, well educated, affluent, owner-occupiers, full-time housewives; interested in new products; sociable; cultural interests.

Cluster 5   *'Coronation Street housewives'* (14 per cent)

Quality conscious, conservative, traditional, and obsessional; DE social class, live relatively more in Lancashire and Yorkshire ITV areas, less educated, lower incomes, part-time employment; low level of interest in new products; not sociable.

Cluster 6   *'The self-confident'* (13 per cent)

Self-confident, quality conscious, not extravagant; young, well educated, owner-occupiers, average income; no distinctive features.

Cluster 7   *'The homely'* (10 per cent)

Bargain seekers, not self-confident, houseproud; C1C2 social class (see Sec. 7.9). Tyne Tees and Scotland ITV areas, left school at early age, part-time employed; average level of entertaining.

Cluster 8   *'The penny pinchers'* (10 per cent)

Self-confident, houseproud, traditional, not quality conscious; 25–34 years, C2DE social class, part-time employment, less education, average income, betting, saving, husband and wife share activities, sociable.

To some extent, life-style may be a nebulous concept that lacks the crispness of demographic measurements. But there are aspects of human life that cannot be explained merely by a set of statistics. Cultural values (as noted earlier) are pervasive, deep rooted, and not always easy to identify or classify. To say that everyone in a developed economy such as the UK is middle class today is simplistic: it equates income with family behaviour patterns and ignores significant differences in cultural values. For instance, professional and non-manual workers are more likely to have had full-time further education and to have attained higher level qualifications (above GCE 'A' level).

In the age group 20–24, nearly one in three from a professional home background was receiving full-time education compared with fewer than one in thirty from homes where the father was a manual worker. This association is even more marked in the 16–19 group, where three out of four from a professional background were continuing their education compared with only one in four from the homes of semi-skilled or unskilled workers.

Later in life, the socio-economic bias becomes highly visible: more than 90 per cent of economically active men aged 25–69 who had studied full time at university held professional, managerial, or intermediate non-manual jobs, compared with about 30 per cent whose full-ime education ended at school, college, or polytechnic. Manual occupations were predominantly held by those who had no formal educational qualifications.

Various cultural orientations have influenced the behaviour, including consumption patterns, of people. Earlier in this chapter, modern society was described as materialistic, affluent, permissive, and acquisitive. Western industrial communities have experienced not only economic upheaval but also far-reaching cultural reorientation. The younger generation, as always, have challenged—and often flouted—traditional standards of behaviour: the Flower People, the Hippies, New Age Travellers, and other expressions of the so-called 'alternative society' have, in their turn, introduced new and sometimes startling cultural practices. Some of these influences have had more permanent effect on society in general, and seem to have coincided with fundamental economic and social changes. For example, attitudes to work, leisure and pleasure, saving and spending, security and safety have all undergone change; some of the characteristics of these cultural realignments will now be discussed.

6.6 LIFE-STYLES AND SOCIAL VALUES

The relationships between life-styles and social values are close, complex, and, to some extent, confusing. Since the early 1980s, Taylor Nelson have conducted an annual survey of social changes in the UK, based on seven social value groupings: self-explorers; social resisters; experimentalists; conspicuous consumers/achievers; belongers; survivors; and 'aimless'. This Monitor service is now operated by Applied Futures Ltd, which runs a large-scale survey with questions derived from psychographic procedures involving, for instance, group discussions and depth interviews (see also Sec. 15.3).

The highly regarded Target Group Index (TGI) research service offers a specialized system called *TGI Outlook* involving a six-variable cluster analysis based on TGI data covering 192 life-style statements about people's attitudes and opinions related to products, brands, and media usage. These 'Outlook' groups are distinctively, if somewhat imaginatively, known as: Trendies (15 per cent of sample); The Indifferents (18 per cent); Social Spenders (14 per cent); Pleasure Seekers (15 per cent); Working-class Puritans (15 per cent); and Moralists (16 per cent).

Notable research into changes in life-styles and social values has been developed for some years by the International Research Institute on Social Change, which conducts annual surveys in twelve European countries, North America, Brazil, Argentina, and Japan, through randomly selected samples of about 2000 respondents aged 15 and over.

6.7 WORK AND PLAY

Attitudes towards work have changed significantly since the Second World War. Like life itself, it was, once, often accepted to be brutish, laborious, and sometimes dangerous. Little respite was expected from the harsh daily toil which consumed most of the waking hours and often resulted in disease.

The uncritical adoption of Weber's doctrine of the so-called 'Protestant ethic' (see Chapter 3) encouraged the belief that salvation was attained through hard work, self-discipline, and thrift by those who toiled in Blake's 'satanic mills'.

Economic turbulence has added to the cultural reorientation towards work; industry in the UK has undergone fundamental restructuring. The declining industries of coal, iron and steel, shipbuilding, and heavy engineering have given place to those founded on electronics and the so-called knowledge-based technologies. The expansion of the financial and technical service sectors of the economy has also contributed to the new working environment. Strongly unionized work forces have been successful in securing shorter working hours, vastly extended paid holidays, and other improvements in the conditions of employment.

With rising living standards (despite inflation) and generally better standards of housing, health, and diet, large sectors of the population are now avidly seeking ways in which to spend their leisure hours. Apart from 'passive' leisure, such as TV viewing, there is increased participation in all kinds of sport, such as sub-aqua activities, organized hill climbing, hang-gliding, pot-holing, and so on. Planners in the public sector are having to face increased pressure to accommodate the virtually insatiable needs of those who wish to use their leisure time fully.

Sport is now a sizeable industry as well as a social and recreational activity, with many thousands of sports clubs across all social classes. The Sports Council estimate that around 21 million adults and 7 million children take part in sports or active recreation on a regular basis in Britain. Snooker, pool, and billiards were revealed in the *General Household Survey* of 1987 as the most popular sports with 15 per cent of people participating. Higher socio-economic groups were more likely than others to take part in a wide range of sports, particularly cycling, jogging or running, and swimming or diving. Spectator sports are significant recreations: nearly 19 million spectators attended Football League matches in England and Wales during 1990/91, while over 5 million attended greyhound race meetings and, although 1 million fewer than in 1981/82, this form of spectator sport remained the second most popular.

Others dedicate their leisure hours to self-improvement: the Open University (OU), founded in 1969, is a singular British educational success. It has over 250 study centres throughout the UK; 57,000 adults already have OU degrees. Associated with it is the Open Business School, which was launched in 1983 and graduated its first 211 distance-learning MBAs in 1992; also offered are certificate and diploma courses in business management subjects. The Open College is another offshoot providing tuition at non-degree level. In its earlier years, OU students were predominantly from the teaching profession, housewives represented only 10 per cent and unemployed people a mere 2 per cent of enrolments in 1971. However, in 1989 the former accounted for 17 per cent and the latter for 10 per cent of enrolled students.

In 1959 Reuel Denney wrote an article entitled 'The leisure society', in which attention was drawn to the growing trend towards shorter working hours resulting in market opportunities for 'efficient supplies of entertainment'.[41] However, according to data in the 1984 edition of *Social Trends*, the basic weekly hours worked, for instance, by full-time male employees fell gradually during the 1970s and on average were only 0.8 hours fewer in April 1982 than in April 1970. Overtime accounted for over 10 per cent of the 44.1 hours worked each week in April 1982 by the average male manual worker, compared with 3 per cent of the 38 hours worked by non-manual workers. *Social Trends* 1992 indicated[42] that four out of five male employees worked between 35 and 45 hours per week, excluding meal breaks and overtime. Half of all female employees worked for fewer than 35 hours per week, while 40 per cent worked between 35 and 40 hours weekly. However, manual workers worked shorter basic hours and received more paid holidays than ever before: in 1991, 92 per cent were entitled to four weeks or more paid holiday.

Very few self-employed people worked short hours: 25 per cent of all self-employed women worked more than 45 hours per week, and 25 per cent of self-employed men worked more than 60 hours weekly. Self-employment has increased dramatically since 1980, after little change during the 1970s; between 1980 and 1990 there was an average increase of almost 60 per cent.

Average working hours per week in the twelve EC countries during 1989 totalled 37.7, with 40.6 for men and 33.3 for women. The UK weekly total was very similar to those of France, Germany, Italy, and Ireland, rather more than Belgium, Denmark, and the Netherlands, but less than Spain and Portugal. The trends in actual working hours seem to echo the earlier views of Levitt, who doubted that leisure time itself would provide bigger markets for the sales of sports equipment. Greater spending power was likely to be more influential than reduced working hours.[11]

Affluence and the desire for leisure are obviously closely related; the former permits the latter orientation towards life. Labour-saving equipment in homes, convenience foods, sports and other leisure activities, high-tech equipment, and so on, have all developed rapidly over the past few years.

Official statistics[43] show the following significant trends: in 1977, 57 per cent of UK households enjoyed the availability of a car, and nearly 10 per cent had two cars; in 1989, almost two-thirds of UK households had a car, and 18 per cent had two cars. In 1977, just over half of UK households were centrally-heated; in 1989, this figure had increased to nearly 80 per cent. In 1977, 75 per cent of UK households had a washing machine; in 1989, over 85 per cent had one. In 1977, telephones were in 57 per cent of households; by 1989 they were in 86 per cent of homes. Virtually all homes had refrigerators and television sets by 1989.

Sales have been helped by dual income families. Between 1971 and 1990, the number of women in the labour force rose by 3 million, while the number of men increased by only 300 000. In 1990, there were 12 million economically active women in Britain; the trend in female employment is projected[42] to continue and result in 12.8 million by the turn of the century, constituting 45 per cent of the total civilian labour force. In 1990, 36 per cent of women in the 16–59 age group worked on a full-time basis and 28 per cent worked part-time.

Hobby pursuits and do-it-yourself activities offer marketers valuable and expanding markets. DIY, in particular, has now become a major spare-time activity and a source of growth for suppliers of equipment, raw materials, etc.

The tremendous sums of money freely spent on recreational interests have some interesting social aspects; working-men's clubs in Britain are frequently luxuriously appointed and concerts are held at which leading television personalities often appear. The old 'spit and sawdust' image is only a distant memory for many of the miners and millworkers of the old industrial areas.

Associated with the desire for increased leisure are new shopping centres which are planned to offer consumers a comprehensive range of merchandise. Parking sites allow easy access to the pedestrianized precincts where shopping can be pursued without traffic hazards.

Astute marketers may take advantage of people's preference for leisure by ensuring that their stores are sited where the public can reach them without a great deal of personal effort.

Patterns of holiday-taking have changed markedly; in 1990, 42 per cent of DE adults took at least one holiday annually compared with 79 per cent of the AB group. Between 1981 and 1990, the number of overseas holidays taken by British residents increased by over one half to 20.5 million, though this figure was 0.5 million less than in 1989. *Social Trends*[42] comment that 'Research in the US suggests that during economic recession people travel smaller distances, use their cars instead of flying, visit friends and relatives less, and leave the children at home more'. Similar, though not identical, travel behaviour may be evident in the UK. In 1981, 13.4 per cent of the average UK household's expenditure was on leisure (television, radio, holidays, sports equipment, hobbies, alcoholic drink consumed outside the home); by 1986 it was 16 per cent but fell slightly to 15.6 per cent in 1989.

The hedonistic approach to life has overthrown some ingrained cultural values: postponed gratification is largely replaced by immediate satisfaction. No longer is it considered reprehensible to be in debt—at least not in debt to a bank or as a 'subscription account' customer. The 'credit culture' has swung into Britain with the exponential growth of credit cards, and the rapid expansion of hire-purchase selling. In 1989 in the UK, 43 per cent of men and 33 per cent of women held credit cards; two-thirds of all adults and four-fifths of all current account holders now possess some kind of plastic card. In 1976, there were under 1 million cards in circulation compared with 7 million in 1981, and 28 million in 1988.[42] The widespread use of automated teller machines (ATMs) for cash withdrawal by personal customers has contributed significantly to this trend, as well as to the fact that wages and salaries are increasingly being paid directly into bank or building society accounts.

The ominous rumblings of atomic and chemical warfare appear to have a cultural reaction: 'Enjoy life while you can'. As noted in Chapter 3, Hobbes held that people are motivated to seek pleasure and avoid pain, and as a result hedonism arose as a motivational theory.

In discussing the nature of needs in Chapter 3, it was noted that food, a basic and common need, is no longer consumed in advanced societies merely to sustain life: it has significant social and psychological functions. It can be used, for example, as an expression of group acceptance, affection, prestige, and wealth. Exotic foods are served at expensive eating-houses which have proliferated since the 1960s. Added to this trend are the vastly increased demands for 'slimming' foods, 'health' foods, and special diets to titillate jaded palates. When the rich and leisured over-eat they can retire to some expensively equipped 'health farm', where they expose their corpulent bodies to a form of pleasurable masochism.

An interesting pilot study of the sexual polarization of attitudes towards food items and food dishes appeared in 1977.[44] The researchers felt that while there was general agreement that 'the gap between traditional male and female roles is becoming increasingly blurred', men do differentiate between 'male appeal' and 'female appeal' related to food. 'Fussy/foreign' or 'pale and tasteless' dishes were viewed as feminine preferences. However, women did not think that their own food tastes were very different from men's. This apparent contradiction, the researchers suggested, may be explained either because the 'liberationist' sees no good reason why there should be any differences in food tastes between men and women, or that those 'anxious to preserve the traditional female role' may argue that women are particularly concerned to satisfy male tastes in food, and are, therefore, prepared to allow their own tastes to fall in line with their menfolk. The researchers suggest that food advertisers should be careful not to reinforce the 'more liberated aspects of women's roles at the expense of the traditional elements of wife and mother'. Women prefer to see themselves in a variety of roles, hence food advertising should probably continue to depict women as food providers.

Some observers would see the wide acceptance of birth control to be a logical expression of a hedonistic orientation towards life. Popular journals have described modern communities as 'the Pill culture', which appears to have strong affinities to that other expressive cultural description: the permissive society.

6.8 SOCIAL ORIENTATION

In Chapter 4 Riesman's social character typology was examined: he classified three types of social character: tradition-directed, inner-directed, and other-directed.[45] Other-directed people—sociable individuals who are influenced by the behaviour of the society in which they mix—are concerned to identify themselves with their fellows. As Kassarjian has said:

> His path to success is not by way of producing a more competitive product but by merchandising a pleasing personality. Getting along with others is the magic key to accomplishment, depending less on what he is and what he does than on what others think of him and how competent he is in the art of being manipulated as well as manipulating others.[46]

Riesman forecast that in modern communities the other-directed person would become more influential. Close personal contacts would be developed; social appeals in advertising should be particularly effective, but at the same time the subtle influence of 'word-of-mouth' communication would be likely to grow. Other-directed consumers are more willing to seek the opinions of their contemporaries, and advertisers should ensure that their products perform as well as the advertising copy promises. The VALS system of psychographics was seen earlier to utilize Riesman's typologies.

Social interaction may encourage conformity of behaviour. In Chapter 4, Karen Horney's three groupings of personality traits were also reviewed.[47] It was observed that 'compliant' people—those who 'move towards others'—tended to be affected by what other people thought of them. They were anxious to conform to the standards of behaviour of their particular society; this could manifest itself in the brands and types of products they bought. (The influence of group behaviour will be discussed more fully in Chapter 8.)

Keeping up with the Joneses is not, however, just a modern tendency. Perkin notes that it was observed by Defoe in the early eighteenth century,[48] when he wrote that 'the same flourishing pride has dictated new methods of living to the people; and while the poorest citizens live like the rich, the rich like the gentry, the gentry like the nobility, and the nobility striving to outshine one another, no wonder all the sumptuary trades increase'. Social emulation is clearly not confined to the twentieth century.

Conformity to group norms bring social approval and reassurance to an individual. But there are many people who deliberately seek to express their personalities by diverging from behavioural norms. This tendency may be seen in the clothing fashions that individualists may adopt. The marked development in specialized products and methods of distribution for these types of consumers offers marketers profitable opportunities. Not everyone wants to shop at the big High Street stores; the boutique, specialist food store, or exclusive restaurant appeal to those who are unwilling to become immersed in what J. B. Priestley in *Journey Down the Rainbow* (1955) once called the 'Admass' culture. With his customary pugnacity, he stated that most Americans, though not all, had been Admassians 'for the last thirty years; the English, and probably most West Europeans, only since the war'. However, he reflected that it was better to live in Admass than to have no job at all, although 'the whole system of increasing productivity, plus inflation, plus a rising standard of material living, plus high-pressure advertising and salesmanship, plus mass communication, plus cultural democracy and the creation of the mass mind, the mass man' deludes consumers into thinking 'everything is opening out when in fact it is narrowing and closing in' on them. Today, probably more would agree with his eloquent indictment of modern consumption tastes and life-styles (see Chapter 15).

6.9 SECURITY AND SAFETY

In Chapter 3, reference was made to Bayton's formulation of psychogenic needs and to three classifications of which 'ego-defensive needs' represented 'the needs to protect the personality, to avoid physical and psychological harm', etc.[49] Maslow also included 'safety needs' in his hierarchical structure and gave them second priority.[13] The need for safety and security is deep-rooted; people differ in the amount of risk they are prepared to accept. Innovators generally find risk taking congenial, and their specific characteristics will be fully discussed in Chapter 11 on innovation in marketing.

In the 'Welfare State' of Britain, health, social, and unemployment benefits have been planned to reduce the insecurity of life for people of all classes. But the drastic restructuring of many industries and of firms within them, has often resulted in public apprehension about the future career opportunities which now lie open to people. In the early 1970s, a comparative study of the economic environment in the USA and several European countries revealed that 'every third household head in the United States, Britain and Holland opts for security as for most important criterion of an occupation'.[50] In Germany, the figure rose to 70 per cent, which the researchers felt indicated the 'prevailing German concern with the preservation of the progress already achieved'. Since the time of this survey, economic and social problems have increased rather than diminished the instinctive motivation for survival and security.

High status and security of tenure are distinguishing characteristics of many of the professions; the self-assurance fostered by these features tends to find expression in independent behaviour. Bourne, for example, found that, when interviewed privately, men with very high status and security were willing to differ from earlier group decisions and felt perfectly free to express their deviation publicly.[51] Personal status is frequently associated with high income;

these may combine to form an exclusive stratum of consumer society which is discriminating and able to indulge fully their desires for prestige and personal fulfilment: Maslow's ladder of needs has been almost effortlessly climbed.

But there are many people for whom the insecurity of life looms large. They desperately seek personal reassurance through the products and services they buy. Job redundancies, short-time working, the fear of growing old and being unable to follow some occupations, the effects of illness on working efficiency, and the crushing worries of mortage repayments bear heavily on certain sections of society.

People may feel that shopping for the needs of their families has become increasingly risky. Prices rise with stunning regularity; store shelves are filled with a bewildering assortment of products and brands of products. Pack sizes vary so much that comparisons of value are difficult to make easily.

Security and the need for protection encourages the sale of branded products. A recognized trade or brand name reassures consumers; it helps manufacturers to launch new products under the protective umbrella of an established brand. Memorable and acceptable brand names are the ammunition of successful marketers. Large firms with substantial advertising budgets are able to promote their products and services and to build up confidence and brand loyalty. Alfred Politz wrote in 1960 of the 'familiarity principle': 'Something that is known inspires more confidence than something that is unknown'.[52] Research tests have shown that leading branded products are generally preferred to unfamiliar brands. Recognized and favoured brand names communicate with consumers; render their buying decisions easier to make, and reduce the tensions and anxieties which contribute to the insecurity of life.

The growth of life-assurance business can be clearly associated with the fundamental human desire for security. Other forms of insurance, for example, private health schemes such as BUPA in Britain, have attracted increasing patronage. People join motoring organizations like the AA or the RAC to reduce the element of risk in driving both at home and overseas. In business undertakings, and in many public utilities, premises and cash transit are protected by commercial 'security' forces.

One of the unfortunate developments recorded by *Social Trends*[42] is that of rising crime in Britain. Crime statistics need careful evaluation because the 'definitions of crime vary as society changes. The complexity of society tends to increase the range of activities labelled crime. . . . Moreover, changes in the law re-define crime'. Furthermore, the relationships between so-called true and recorded crime are complex: the latter depends on several factors such as the incident being reported to the police and accepted by them as genuine, and also judged to be likely to result in a successful prosecution. The British Crime Survey reported that the number of burglaries rose by 17 per cent between 1972 and 1987; it has been estimated that 45 per cent of burglaries committed ended as recorded offences in 1972, but by 1987 there was a dramatic increase to 73 per cent. Little wonder then, that more homes, as well as industrial and commercial pemises are fitted with burglar alarms and other security devices.

Other examples of the growing interest in making life as safe and secure as possible relate to improved guarantees, more attention to after-sales service, and the emphasis on safety standards in the design and operation of various mechanical and electrical appliances.

6.10 WOMEN AND SOCIETY

The role of women in economic, social, and cultural life in western communities has changed radically since the 1950s. In an article in the *Journal of the Market Research Society* in 1972, the authors reflected that 'the groundswell of the women's lib movement is changing the cultural background of our society every day'.[53] They argued that although a great deal of marketing activity is concerned with providing goods uniquely related to the needs of one sex or the other for biological reasons 'most markets are related to sociologically developed sex differences in which men or women could *essentially* be the purchasers'. Marketers need to appreciate that cars, lawnmowers, and similar products are bought by women as well as men. Women's purchasing influence has most certainly extended beyond the supermarket or clothes shop.

Equal pay has existed in the professions for several years and is rapidly extending to commercial and industrial occupations. In Britain, discrimination against the employment of women is a statutory offence.

The notable trends in the employment of women in the UK have been mentioned earlier; their employment rate of 52.9 per cent in 1989 was one of the highest in the EC, and exceeded only by Denmark (60.8 per cent). Better educational facilities for girls have opened up new career opportunities which were previously reserved exclusively for men. Apart from personal emancipation, women have acquired economic independence on a scale never before experienced. The wide acceptance of birth control practices, smaller families, and vastly improved medical attention have allowed women to become significant factors in the economic structure of society.

In 1972, *Ad Weekly* reported from New York on the 'U.S. Women's Consumer Revolt'.[54] The traditional housewife-and-mother role has been radically affected by the growth of dual roles for women—'careerists' and home builders. More women are taking an active part in public life and making their voices heard in claims against manufacturers. Despite all these activities, the *Ad Weekly* report stated that companies 'failed to recognise the modern woman's change of lifestyle', and many advertisements still blatantly disregarded the new status of women in society. Since that report, many consumer product manufacturers and distributors have recognized, although tardily, the importance of attracting women as buyers in their own right of an increasingly extended range of goods and services.

A nationwide study of US women was conducted in 1975 to examine life-style differences between those who preferred the 'traditional feminine orientation' and those who opted for a 'modern orientation'.[55] Approximately 90 per cent of the 2000 sample responded to questions on interests and opinions, activities, product use, and media use. While 45 per cent of respondents indicated that they preferred a traditional marriage, with the husband responsible for providing for the family and the wife running the house and looking after the children, 54 per cent preferred a marriage where husband and wife shared responsibilities more, and 1 per cent preferred 'some other arrangement, such as staying single or living with a group of other persons'. From demographic analyses, the most striking contrast was in the proportion of working women preferring the modern orientation (56 per cent) against those preferring the traditional orientation (26 per cent). While preference for egalitarianism declines with age, it is not predominant until 55 plus.

Women who opted for the modern feminine life-style were found to be

> more liberal in their attitudes towards life, events and business; have more cosmopolitan interests; financially optimistic but careful spenders; pragmatic about major purchases; very interested in their physical appearance; and were more optimistic about the future. However, their basic value structure is similar in kind, but not degree, to that of the traditionally oriented women.

It was also reported that whereas in 1967, 60 per cent of adult women in the USA generally or definitely agreed with the statement: 'A woman's place is in the home', less than a decade later, only 26 per cent supported this view.[55]

Research on the life-styles of women in the USA, the UK, and France in 1977 revealed some striking similarities: in all three countries the basic pattern of life-style centred around women's acceptance or rejection of their traditional home-making role.[56] This dimension appeared to be closely linked with conservative and traditional moral attitudes. While some women rejected the 'home factor', all, none the less, defined their personal and social positions with regard to it. The researchers suggest that this exploratory research into multi-country life-styles may help in developing appropriate international market segmentation and positioning strategies.

Understanding the role of affluent housewives in Latin America proved vital for a survey of household food expenditure: only belatedly did the researchers find out that upper-income women knew very little about daily food purchases—the maids did all the family grocery buying.[16]

Another aspect of female cultural influence on buying relates to demographic trends. While the phenomenon of elderly women living alone was fairly widespread in the 1950s, thirty years later more than 50 per cent of all women aged 65 and over lived like this. In general, one-person households are increasing; in 1990 they represented more than one-quarter of all British households and rose from 12 per cent (1961), 18 per cent (1971), 22 per cent (1981) to 26 per cent (1990). Of these, 7 per cent (1961), 12 per cent (1971), 14 per cent (1981), and 15 per cent (1990) were pensioner households. Mintel predict that single-person households will increase to 6.8 million by 2001, compared with 4.6 million (1981) and 5.9 million (1991).[57]

This large segment of the elderly population are not likely to buy in bulk, but they *will* probably be interested in small packs of quality foods, security devices, and so on.

6.11 SUB-CULTURES

A national culture is made up of several sub-cultures that have their own distinctive characteristics, some of which may be very different from the total pattern of culture. These subgroups in a society may be based on the cultural traditions emanating from ethnic, religious, physical, or social sources. Sub-culture groups enable individuals to satisfy their needs for affiliation and personal relationships. By closely associating themselves with particular types of cultural activities, people tend to reinforce their beliefs and attitudes about the events in their lives, so that a commonality of values emerges.

In modern society, numerous sub-cultures develop: they are of significance to marketers because of their influence on the brands and types of products and services demanded by their members. Overall marketing strategies should be constructed after careful analysis of the demands from market segments which may derive from sub-cultural needs. The closer an appeal can be made to cultural desires, the more likely are marketing communications to be accepted and acted on. Discussion of sub-cultural trends should therefore expand the preceding evaluation of the role of culture in marketing activities, and indicate the value of a micro approach to the study of national cultures.

Youth

This sub-culture, based on the adolescent age group, has had an incredible influence on national life. The 'pop culture' exploded in western society in the 1960s, bringing with it radical changes in styles of clothing and entertainment. 'Teenage' markets have been developed in fashion clothing, food, beverages, records, and sports. The relatively high spending power of youthful members of industrial societies has attracted manufacturers to compete fiercely for their patronage. Special boutiques dedicated to teenage fashions boomed in the High Street throughout the land; 'Miss Selfridge' in Oxford Street, London, spearheaded the marketing of stylish fashion clothing to the rising generation of independently minded young women. But demographic trends eventually slowed the pace of teenage fashion shopping. 'Chelsea Girl', a chain of fashion-stores launched in the 1960s and targeted at the teenage and early twenties market, shrewdly switched their trading name and range of merchandise in 1990; now known as

'River Island', they aim at the 20–35 age group, offering fashion clothing designed to appeal to more discerning tastes. The ambience of the River Island stores is deliberately designed to give an air of relaxation and informality: 'the idea is to create a cross between a Long Island beach house and an English country house'[58] (see discussion in Chapter 5 on the influence of moods on buying). This repositioning strategy will keep Lewis Shops, the private business involved, at the forefront of the dynamic fashion trade. The Chelsea Girl name will be retained and used through licensing agreements.

A survey by J. Walter Thompson (published in 1982) reported that some of the older men and women interviewed thought that modern youngsters expect more stimulus and entertainment to be provided for them externally; they are less prepared, and less able, to generate their own amusement, having been accustomed to 'push-button' entertainment.[59] Today, young people are said to 'think twice before rushing into marriage and starting a family: many are keen to spend a few years enjoying life to the full first'. Early in their teens, youngsters were reported to want to follow their own leisure preferences; they are spurred to independence by their peers. Sports are competitively pursued by boys especially, providing an approved outlet for their abundant energy. Young teenagers; while demanding more social freedom; 'tend to be desperately short of money'. Youth clubs, special interest groups, and listening to records, are typical pastimes. The natural gregariousness of youth emphasizes their need to belong to an identifiable group; the popularity of pubs and parties further illustrates this behavioural trend.

The number of children in the public sector nursery and primary schools fell by 22 per cent over the period 1976–86, reflecting the reduced birth rates in the late 1960s and 1970s. But the number of enrolments increased slightly each year between 1986 and 1989; projections to the year 2000 indicate a slight fall and then a steady increase. In public sector secondary schools, numbers fell between 1981 and 1990, but increases are projected from 1992 until at least the end of the century.[42] The effects of demographic trends are already evident in many product and service markets, and also affect employment opportunities.

The cultural influence of youth has deeply affected the total pattern of culture within industrialized communities. In many business undertakings, youthfulness is highly valued and executives are rapidly promoted in the early stages of their careers. The physical energy and attractiveness of youth have inspired promotional campaigns featuring products 'for the young in heart'; vitamin tablets, hormone replacement therapy, plastic surgery, and various formulations of cosmetics promise to restore some of the faded glories of youth. Clothing fashions for middle-aged people follow the trends set by the teenage market; 'the trickle-down theory seems to have been replaced in many product markets by a process of filtering and absorbing the ideas and styles of younger consumers. The economic power of teenagers has been instrumental in changing the socio-cultural behaviour of society at large.

Yuppies, Sloans, and Dinkies

The Yuppie (young urban professional) was bred from the affluence and conspicuous consumption of the 1980s, with this decade's emphasis on 'hedonism, ostentation and status-seeking materialism'.[60] Exactly who and what this egocentric creature is remains somewhat obscure, although, in 1984, *The Yuppie Handbook* was apparently the source of this bizarre acronym which has been enthusiastically adopted by the mass media. In the USA, Yuppies were defined in 1984 by *Newsweek* as aged between 25 and 39 years, earning at least $40 000 or more in professional or managerial positions. Estimates of their numbers in the USA vary between 1.2 million and 12.2 million, but are likely to be around 4 million. Their numbers are, however, of less importance than their influence as a reference group affecting patterns of consumption more generally (see Chapter 8).

Yuppies—of either sex—hotly pursue luxury products and services that project conferred status. Distinctive brand names like Rolex, Burberry, Gucci, and Cartier are greatly prized. The so-called Sloane Ranger, which also had its handbook in the 1980s, evolved from an article in *Harper and Queens* in the mid-1970s. It soon became a popular label for 'all vaguely upper and upper-middle class girls and chaps'.[61] The cultivated accents and frenzied laughter of the Hooray Henrys and the Henriettas echoed in the boutiques and wine-bars of Sloane Square and Kensington; Laura Ashley skirts and pearl necklaces became favourite fashion styles; soon pseudo-Sloanes emerged to emulate these trends: the whiff of snobbery was in the air, as popular fashion stores and women's magazines endorsed the life-style. In the harsher economic climate of the 1990s, the Sloane Ranger appears to have become the Lone Ranger.

Although consumption behaviour in an avowedly classless society may be less stridently class-conscious than formerly, egocentric life-styles, though muted, linger on. Self-esteem and self-actualization, as Maslow proposed, are still likely to influence the consumption habits of the wealthy communities of the western world (see Chapters 3 and 5). Materialistic consumption, it has been wisely observed,[61] peaks and troughs; though fluctuations occur, the overall trend is in the direction of increased materialism.

Yuppies may eventually settle as 'Dinkies' (dual income, no kids households). Other subgroups of young consumers have sprouted from the Yuppie roots, such as 'buppies' (black), 'guppies' (gay), 'huppies' (Hispanics), or 'preppies' (school students who often evolve into yuppies). The proliferating catalogue of acronyms tends to stretch credulity.

Opals

Demographic trends clearly indicate that there are increasing numbers of older people not only in the UK population but also in most developed countries. Euromonitor data[62] indicate that across the EC, in 1983, 9 per cent of the population was in the age-group 60–69 and 9.6 per cent were 70-plus, compared with 9.7 per cent and 10.1 per cent in 1992. Chronological age itself is, of course, an imperfect measure of people's interests and abilities; good standards of nutrition, improved housing, and wide leisure facilities, plus, in many cases, fairly significant pensions, have contributed to the general enjoyment of life by elderly people. Socio-economic, educational, and psychological variables all tend to affect the ways in which people perceive themselves, and their willingness to view themselves as elderly is subjective. The boundaries of middle age and old age tend to be elastic in many cases. (The incidence of family life-cycle is considered in Chapter 8.) It is certainly a fact that disposable income is greater in the 55-plus age group than with younger age groups committed to mortgages and the bringing-up of children.

It should be noted, however, that because women tend to live longer than men and marry men rather older than themselves, the over 60 population in the UK is largely female and accounted for nearly 60 per cent in 1988. The growth of one-person households has been noted earlier; more than 40 per cent of women over 60 years of age live alone compared with about 20 per cent of men of that age group. The Office of Population Censuses and Surveys (OPCS) projections are that the number of state pensioners will be likely to increase significantly over the next thirty years or so, and that by 2021, those in the age-group 60-plus would represent at least one-quarter of the population.

In the USA, 'Opals' (older people with active life-styles) signify older consumers who are relatively affluent, healthy, and are active socially. These 'golden-oldies', sometimes and rather pejoratively described as 'wrinklies', have substantial spending power, as marketers have gradually come to recognize. The negative images of this important sub-cultural group of consumers are at last being discarded; for example, special holiday packages—sometimes luxurious and expensive—are being offered by astute travel agents. Extreme old age inevitably, and sadly, reduces mobility, but there are many at what might be termed the threshold of old age who have the energy and means to enjoy many years of travel and other leisure experiences.

Ethnic cultures

Within many large communities, small sub-cultures based on different nationalities often occur. Some ethnic cultural differences may be reflected in the brands and types of products consumed. In some cases, ethnic and religious influences combine to form distinctive behavioural patterns, as in the case of Hindus.

Thouless[63] has noted that the fundamental class divisions in the USA are based on racial distinctions. 'Particularly strong is that between those of pure white blood and those known to have any negro ancestors'. Physical characteristics have assisted the groupings which have resulted. The class distinction existing between whites and blacks is based partly on occupation, because high-status occupations are not usually held by blacks.

In the late 1950s, Milton Alexander studied New York consumers and identified four major ethnic groups: Italian, Jewish, Negroid, and Puerto Rican.[64] He found that 'despite all countervailing socio-economic pressures, ethnic food habits continued to prevail in Greater New York'.

In 1965, Bauer and colleagues published an article entitled 'The marketing dilemma of negroes'.[65] They commented on the basic problem that faced blacks in the USA—'whether to strive against odds to attain these middle-class values (and the goods which come with them), or to give in and live without most of them . . . certainly it is the consensus of both negro and white students of the American negro that negroes have accepted white middle-class values'. However, they are at a disadvantage in securing these, hence the tendency to spend relatively heavily on clothing, furniture, and alcoholic drink to indicate their desired high status. The authors of the article quoted *Chicago Tribune* panel data (1961) which revealed that blacks drank at least 25 per cent of the Scotch consumed in the USA, although they represented only 11 per cent of the population. Almost 17 per cent of black families said they bought Scotch compared with 9.3 per cent of white families. Apparently the distributors of White Horse Whisky found that the average black Scotch drinker said he drank almost twice as much per week as the average white Scotch drinker. Following a series of questions, it appeared that blacks associated the drinking of Scotch whisky with high status.

Another inquiry related to the car-buying habits of blacks and whites in the USA.[66] It was found that the former tended to buy a significantly higher percentage of more expensive cars than white consumers.

Later research into the black market in the USA was reviewed by Bauer and Cunningham in 1970.[67] During their detailed review of the status of blacks in US society, they pointed out that the differences in black–white spending patterns needed to be interpreted carefully. 'Thus high expenditures on clothing may be associated with either a desire for display and immediate "kicks", or with striving toward respectability. And high expenditures on alcoholic beverages may be associated either with retreat from the present world, or with striving for social status'.

A review of black buyer behaviour appeared in the *Journal of Marketing* in 1972.[68] The black market was seen to be diverse, with 'at least two major segments: those consumers who are able to live a middle-class life, and those who are not because they live at a subsistence income level. Income level is the primary determinant of these segments'. Therefore, at the top end of the black market, differences between black and white consumption patterns tend to be negligible and are diminishing rapidly. Lower-income blacks represent a large market which 'those marketers who can offer economic and reasonable quality' products should carefully analyse.

How far a specialized market will develop in the UK to meet the cultural needs of sections of the immigrant population has not been determined. Many years ago, Italian immigrants, for example, set up their own specialized food shops which are to be seen wherever their fellow Italians form cultural groups. In many British towns and cities, greengrocers and supermarkets regularly stock a range of fruit, vegetables, spices and other producrs which were originally demanded by the Afro-Caribbean communities.

In 1982, Catherine Stott reported in the *Sunday Telegraph* that an American multi-millionaire, John Johnson, 'one of the few Establishment blacks in the United States', was hosting a lunch at the Dorchester Hotel in London to launch a range of black cosmetics, called, ironically perhaps, 'Fashion Fair'.[69] Mr Johnson built up a 'vast black publishing empire', which includes *Ebony*, the biggest black circulation magazine in the world. In 1991, Spiegel, the largest US direct-to-home mail order company, announced a partnership with *Ebony*, to produce a new catalogue with clothing especially developed for black women.

In the UK, as the *Advertisers Annual* 1991/92 shows, there are over thirty publications catering for ethnic minorities. These include the *Asian Times*, a weekly journal founded in 1983, with a circulation of 21 000; the *Daily Jang*, established in 1971, with an ABC certified circulation of 19 427; the *Gleaner*, established in 1951, with ABC circulation of 13 361, and owned by the Gleaner Group of Jamaica. *Tan*, a monthly established in 1990, has a circulation of 15 000. In 1992, the *Weekly Journal*, the first broadsheet newspaper aimed at the growing number of young black middle-class people, was published with a target readership of 1.1 million. This launch was by the publishers of *The Voice*, a middle-market tabloid, which was being challenged by *Black Briton*, a middle-market tabloid started in August 1991. Within ethnic minorities, it is clear that competitive activities exist.

> Black models are more frequently used in fashion shows and advertisements; special radio and television programmes now cater for Afro-Caribbean and Asian listeners and viewers; the professions are increasingly populated by practitioners from ethnic minorities; special schooling arrangements have been made in centres where there are high densities of, for example, Muslims.

In Britain, the ethnic minorities population is generally much younger than the white population: one in twenty of ethnics is over 60 compared with one in five of whites. Two-thirds of the ethnic minorities population under the age of 16 were born in the UK. Over the period of 1987–9, it was estimated[42] that of the 54.7 million population in the UK, 2.6 million (4.75 per cent) were ethnic minority groups. Of these, the largest group was Indian (779 000), followed by West Indian/Guyanese (482 000), and Pakistani (433 000).

How far and how soon cultural assimilation will take place in the UK, now described as a multi-cultural society, is open to speculation. Diverse consumption patterns may include dress, language, food, and family behaviour. Cross-fertilization of cultures within the UK may occur: there are already indications of this phenomenon in, for example, music.

A study of the cultural assimilation of Mexican-Americans in the south-west of the USA was assessed by comparing their food consumption patterns with those of income-matched Anglos in the same region and those of income-matched Mexicans in Mexico City.[70] Results suggested that 'the assimilation process is more than a simple linear progression from one culture to another'. Mexican-American consumption patterns are not a simple blending of Mexican and Anglo food habits. Instead, a unique cultural style appears to have emerged. The researchers advise advertisers and marketers who are trying to reach assimilating immigrants to note that what will work before and after the assimilation process might not work during the process. They also suggest caution where immigrants' behaviour patterns for a product are different from the culture of the origin and the culture of the residence; in such cases it is important to determine the means and values that immigrants associate with that type of product.

Religious groups

Significant sub-cultural behaviour may be related to religious beliefs. Mormons, for example, do not drink tea, coffee, or alcoholic liquor or smoke tobacco. Christian Scientists have strong views on medical care. Orthodox Jews buy Kosher or other traditional foods which are of particular importance in the observation of their cultural traditions. They need to buy two fridges and two dishwashers, to ensure that milk and meat products do not come into contact with one another. Muslims are forbidden to eat pork, but this meat is consumed extensively by the Chinese. At one time, Roman Catholics did not eat meat on Fridays and certain other nominated days in the year: to the dismay of fishmongers, Pope John XXIII rescinded this prohibition.

Perkin has given a fascinating insight into the influence of religion, which 'provided the nearest approach in the old society to overt class attitudes'.[48] He traces this influence from the Restoration period 'when the Puritan aristocracy and gentry finally opted for the Church' and left the dissenting sects to 'their social inferiors'. What emerged was the 'familiar sandwich' in the social structure of English religion with Anglicans at the top and bottom and Dissenters in the middle. The close associations of capitalism and Puritanism have popularly been explained as Weber's theory (see Chapter 3). But, as Perkin observes, not all Dissenters were capitalists; some were yeoman farmers and textile workers. 'Dissent flourished in precisely those groups which both wished and could afford to be somewhat independent of the paternal hierarchy'.[48]

In Chapter 3, the economic consequences of the 'Protestant ethic' were compared with achievements in Catholic countries, although *within* countries having significant 'mixed' populations no research appears to have been reported. Dichter suggested that the middle classes are dominant influences in developing markets,[28] and so it may be hypothesized that the importance of religion as a sub-culture group affecting the consumption of products is likely to be subservient to that of socio-economic groups, particularly in view of the decline of formal religious observance in many countries, including the UK.

Data from *Social Trends*[42] indicate that in the UK between 1975 and 1990, the total adult membership of the Trinitarian churches (those believing in the unison of the Holy Trinity in one Godhead) fell by 16 per cent to 6.8 million. But membership of non-Trinitarian churches, including Mormons and Jehovah's Witnesses, increased significantly; the former from 10 000 to 15 000, and the latter from 8 000 to 12 000. However, the greatest increase in religious membership was in other religions, including Muslims (40 000 to 90 000); Sikhs (12 000 to 39 000); and Hindus (10 000 to 14 000).

6.12 REDEFINITION OF PRODUCTS

Cultural trends have tended to redefine the uses of certain products. The male toiletries market has expanded rapidly since the late 1970s and male cosmetics have emerged. Irving White commented in 1959:

> Advertising must take account of the current values and product-definition of the society (or sub-society) in which it intends to operate . . . the social values implied by the concept 'perfume' are such that its users are necessarily considered feminine. . . . Advertisers of male cosmetics . . . have discovered that they must carefully conceal the feminism and narcissism involved in colognes.[71]

The male toiletries market in the UK is booming: between 1985 and 1994 sales have doubled to £360 million per annum, two-thirds of which is accounted for by after-shave and similar 'male fragrances'. From a stumbling start in the early 1960s cosmetic companies like Estée Lauder have successfully introduced the brands of Aramis, Clinique for Men, and Roc Pour

Homme. The Body Shop and Boots are offering ranges of cleansing and grooming products aimed at this growing market segment. Male skin-care products are mostly repackaged female lines, using more 'masculine' colours and with robust packaging because of the general tendency for men who use these types of products to travel frequently on business. In 1991, Taylor Nelson undertook research among 1250 men, who kept a diary about their toiletry habits over a six-month period. As a result, 'heavy users' (any man who used four or more products forty or more times over a two-week period) were found to be 30 per cent of the sample, while 'light users' (three or fewer products per fortnight) accounted for 40 per cent. Most of the former were in the age-group 17–34; however, almost one-third of heavy users were aged 45–64.

This particular manifestation of hedonism is late in achieving acceptability: it has involved the changing of attitudes which (as shown in Chapter 5) often takes a long time, particularly where self-concept and cultural traditions are concerned. Today, there is a more permissive attitude towards the use of such products, but, as White[71] pointed out, marketers accept the limitations of the prevailing culture when they attempt to 'create new expectations for the consumer'. Advertising may influence cultural developments so that certain products expand their appeals. In the USA, for example, Marlborough cigarettes were considered to be a 'woman's brand' at one time, until the manufacturers extended their market by showing these cigarettes being smoked by tattooed 'he-men' in their advertisements. At one time the UK florists' trade association ran a publicity campaign featuring a tough-looking man who patronized the Interflora flower service.

These and similar campaigns are aimed to restructure consumers' cognitions and attitudes about products which have traditionally been associated with, for example, feminine tastes. In the past, many products have acquired sexual definitions which, in today's more liberal interpretation of the roles of men and women in society, now seem strangely out of date.

Pursuit of this point of view to its logical extreme has resulted in the unisex approach in the marketing of some products and services. Obviously there are limitations imposed, for instance, by physical characteristics related to the styling of clothing, and how far this trend will develop remains to be seen. Unisex hairdressing salons are now more common in Britain, although these have not yet supplanted the traditional establishments.

6.13 SUMMARY

To understand human behaviour, including buying behaviour, cultural values must be appreciated. Several definitions of culture have been given; although difficult to define precisely, it derives from a group of people *sharing* and *transmitting* beliefs, values, attitudes, and behaviour patterns which are held in common and regarded as important to a specific society. Cultural norms refer to those standards of behaviour which have gradually established themselves as guides to conduct in certain situations; they are of two types—folkways and more—the former relate to minor social conventions and the latter form the cultural core.

Life-style research attempts to give insight into attitudes and behaviour patterns of specific sectors of populations: it covers activities, interests, opinions, and demographics, such as the 'affluent middle-aged' or 'teenagers'.

Cultural orientations are affected by many variables, such as age, sex, social group, education, aspirations, professional interest, ethnic origin, religious observance, and so on.

All societies develop cultures which affect deeply their economic and social progress. Culture gives people an identity and social cohesion. it may also profoundly affect consumption behaviour.

REFERENCES

1. Howard, John A., and Jagdish N. Sheth, *The Theory of Buyer Behaviour*, John Wiley, New York, 1969.
2. Linton, Ralph, *The Cultural Background of Personality*, Appleton-Century, New York, 1945.
3. Bliss, Perry, *Marketing Management and the Behavioural Environment*, Prentice-Hall, Englewood Cliffs, New Jersey, 1970.
4. McCracken, Grant, 'Culture and consumption: a theoretical account of the structure and movement of the cultural meaning of consumer goods', *Journal of Consumer Research*, vol. 13, June 1981.
5. Bennett, Peter D., and Harold H. Kassarjian, *Consumer Behaviour*, Prentice-Hall, Englewood Cliffs, New Jersey, 1972.
6. Schumacher, E. F., *Small is Beautiful: A Study of Economics as if People Mattered*, Harper and Row, New York, 1973.
7. Krech, David, Richard S. Crutchfield, and Egerton L. Ballachey, *Individual in Society*, McGraw-Hill, New York, 1962.
8. Banton, Michael, *Roles: An Introduction to the Study of Social Relations*, Tavistock, London, 1968.
9. McClelland, David C., *The Achieving Society*, Free Press, New York, 1961.
10. Sinclair, Craig, 'Technological change = social change', *Industrial Marketing Management*, vol. 2, 1973.
11. Levitt, Theodore, 'Think before you leap'. *Harvard Business Review*, May/June 1969.
12. Ansoff, H. Igor, *Business Strategy*, Penguin, London, 1972.
13. Maslow, A. H., *Motivation and Personality*, Harper, New York, 1954.
14. Wootton, Barbara, *Contemporary Britain*, Allen and Unwin, Hemel Hempstead, 1971.
15. Wind, Yoram, and Susan Douglas, 'Some issues in international consumer research', *European Journal of Marketing*, vol. 8, no. 3, 1974.
16. Chandran, Rajan, and Sigfredo. A. Hernandez, 'Marketing research problems in Latin America', *Journal of Market Research Society*, vol. 24, no. 2, 1982.
17. Markin, Ron J., *The Psychology of Consumer Behaviour*, Prentice-Hall, Englewood Cliffs, New Jersey, 1969.
18. Britt, Stuart Henderson, *Consumer Behaviour and the Behavioural Sciences*, John Wiley, New York, 1966.
19. Allen, David Elliston, *British Tastes: An Enquiry into the Likes and Dislikes of the Regional Consumer*, Collins, London, 1969.
20. Allen, David Elliston, 'Anthropological insights into customer behaviour', *European Journal of Marketing*, vol. 5, no. 2, summer 1971.
21. McCracken, Grant, 'Culture and consumer behaviour: an anthropological perspective', *Journal of Market Research Society*, vol. 32, no. 1, January 1990.
22. Boudon, Raymond, 'Why theories of social change fail: some methodological thoughts', *Public Opinion Quarterly*, vol. 47, no. 2, 1983.
23. Kotler, Philip, *Marketing Management: Analysis, Planning and Control*, Prentice-Hall, Englewood Cliffs, New Jersey, 1980.
24. *Sunday Telegraph*, 29 April 1963.
25. Mead, Margaret, 'The application of anthropological techniques to cross-national communication', *Trans. New York Academy of Science, Series II* vol. 9, no. 4, February 1947.
26. *Daily Telegraph*, 30 August 1973.
27. Briggs, Asa, *Advertising Quarterly*, no. 33, autumn 1972.
28. Dichter, Ernest, 'The world customer', *Harvard Business Review*, vol. 40, July/August 1962.
29. Mumford, Lewis, *The Myth of the Machine*, Secker and Warburg, London, 1967.
30. Argyle, Michael, *Bodily Communication*, Methuen, London, 1975.
31. Kahl, Joseph A., *The American Class Structure*, Holt, Rinehart and Winston, New York, 1961.
32. Lazer, William, 'Lifestyle concepts and marketing', in: *Towards Scientific Marketing*, Stephen A. Greyser, (ed.), American Marketing Association, Chicago, 1963.
33. Plummer, J. T., 'The concept and application of lifestyle segmentation', *Journal of Marketing*, January 1974.

34. Edris, Thabet A., and A. Meidan, 'On the reliability of psychographic research: encouraging signs for measurement accuracy and methodology in consumer research', *European Journal of Marketing*, vol. 24, no. 3, 1990.

35. Horne, Annette, 'Housing and lifestyle', ESOMAR, Helsinki, 1973.

36. Felson, Marcus, 'Invidious distinctions among cars, clothes and suburbs', *Public Opinion Quarterly*, vol. 42, no. 1, 1978.

37. Linton, Anna, and Simon Broadbent, 'International lifestyle comparisons: an aid to marketers', *Advertising Quarterly*, no. 44, summer 1975.

38. Gordon, Wendy, 'The lifestyle of the affluent middle-aged', *Admap*, February 1981.

39. Buck, S. F., 'The affluent middle-aged: spending and saving patterns', *Admap*, March 1981.

40. Lunn, Tony, Sally Baldwin and Jackie Dickens, 'Monitoring consumer lifestyles', *Admap*, November 1982.

41. Denney, Reuel, 'The leisure society', *Harvard Business Review*, vol. 37, May/June, 1959.

42. *Social Trends 22*, HMSO, 1992.

43. *Annual Statistics*, Central Statistical Office, 1992.

44. Dickens, Jackie, and Brian Chappell, 'Food for Freud? A study of the sexual polarisation of food and food products', *Journal of Market Research Society*, vol. 19, no. 2, 1977.

45. Riesman, David, *The Lonely Crowd*, Yale University Press, New Haven, Connecticut, 1950.

46. Kassarjian, Harold H., 'Riesman revisited', *Journal of Marketing*, vol. 29, April 1965.

47. Horney, Karen, *Our Inner Conflicts*, W. W. Norton, New York, 1945.

48. Perkin, Harold, *The Origins of Modern English Society, 1780–1880*, Routledge and Kegan Paul, London, 1969.

49. Bayton, James A., 'Motivation, cognition, learning: basic factors in consumer behaviour', *Journal of Marketing*, vol. 22, January 1958.

50. Katona, George, Strumpel Burkard, and Ernest Zahn, *Aspirations and Affluences: Comparative Studies in the United States and Western Europe*, McGraw-Hill, New York, 1971.

51. Bourne, Francis S., 'Group influence in marketing and public relations', in: *Some Applications of Behavioural Research*, Rensis Likert and Samuel P. Hayes (eds), UNESCO, New York, 1957.

52. Alfred Politz, 'The dilemma of creative advertising', *Journal of Marketing*, vol. 25, no. 2, October 1960.

53. Turle, J. E., and R. Falconer, 'Men and women are different', *Journal of the Market Research Society*, vol. 14, no. 2, 1972.

54. Brenna, Tony, 'U.S. women's consumer revolt', *Ad Weekly*, 29 September 1972.

55. Reynolds, Fred D., Melvin R. Crask, and William D. Wells, 'The modern feminine lifestyle', *Journal of Marketing*, vol. 41, no. 3, 1977.

56. Douglas, Susan P., and Christine D. Urban, 'Lifestyle analysis to profile women in international markets', *Journal of Marketing*, vol. 41, no. 3, 1977.

57. *British Lifestyles 1992*, Mintel, London, 1992.

58. Urry, Maggie, 'Chelsea Girl deserts to River Island', *Financial Times*, 8 March 1990.

59. Fuller, Linda, 'Going out: how people spend their leisure time out of the home', J. Walter Thompson, London, 1982.

60. Belk, Russell W., 'Yuppies as arbiters of the emerging consumption style', in: *Advances in Consumer Research*, vol. 13, R. J. Lutz (ed.), Association for Consumer Research, 1986.

61. Hardman, Robert, 'There'll always be a Henrietta', *Daily Telegraph*, 15 January 1992.

62. *1992: The Single Market Handbook*, Euromonitor, London, 1990.

63. Thouless, R. H., *General and Social Psychology*, University Tutorial Press, London, 1967.

64. Alexander, Milton, 'The significance of ethnic groups in marketing new-type packaged foods in Greater New York', *Proceedings of the American Marketing Association*, Chicago, 1959.

65. Bauer, Raymond, A., Scott M. Cunningham, and Lawrence H. Wortzel, 'The marketing dilemma of negroes', *Journal of Marketing*, vol. 29, July 1965.

66. Akers, F., 'Negro and white auto-buying behaviour', *Journal of Marketing Research*, vol. 5, August 1968.

67. Bauer, Raymond A., and Scott M. Cunningham, 'The negro market', *Journal of Advertising Research*, vol. 10, no. 2, April 1970.

68. Sexton, Donald E. Jnr, 'Black buyer behaviour', *Journal of Marketing*, vol. 36, October 1972.
69. Stott, Catherine, 'That new black magic', *Sunday Telegraph*, 10 October 1982.
70. Wallendorf, Melanie, and Michael D. Reilly, 'Ethnic migration, assimilation and consumption', *Journal of Consumer Research*, vol. 10, December 1983.
71. White, Irving S., 'The functions of advertising in our culture', *Journal of Marketing*, vol. 24, July 1959.

REVIEW AND DISCUSSION QUESTIONS

1. Which cultural factors affecting consumer behaviour should UK exporters consider when exporting to other EU countries?
2. What are the principal differences between consumers' values and their attitudes? Describe what you consider to have been the three most significant changes in British values over the past ten years. What are the likely consequences of these value changes for marketing practice?
3. What should marketers do to avoid errors in marketing in an unfamiliar culture?
4. Which cultural values might influence the volume and manner of consumption of the following goods in different cultures: (a) beer (b) pedal cycles (c) male cosmetics (d) Post Office savings certificates.
5. Describe an instance in which you transgressed a cultural folkway. Were you aware of any sanction or pressure from other people to alter your behaviour?
6. Consult any US consumer behaviour text. Locate the chapter on culture and find three consumption-related values that seem to be more/less prevalent in the culture in which you live.

CHAPTER SEVEN

SOCIAL CLASS

7.1 INTRODUCTION

Social class is not a new concept, although sophisticated methods of classification are relatively modern. Social class awareness is often said to be one of the more enduring characteristics of British life. Some might deny that social stratification exists at all in modern Britain: that egalitarianism has spread widely since the Second World War and eroded social class distinctions. Others, equally trenchant in their views, declare that while the old social barriers may have fallen, new criteria of distinctive social and economic behaviour have replaced them.

In this chapter, social stratification and its effects on patterns of consumption will be considered. This will augment the discussion on cultural aspects of behaviour in Chapter 6.

7.2 SOCIAL STRATIFICATION: AN OVERVIEW

Wherever people congregate, a class order seems to emerge rapidly. As Berelson and Steiner observed:

> Every known human society, certainly every known society of any size, is stratified. . . . The hierarchical evaluation of people in different social positions is apparently inherent in human social organisation. Stratification arises with the most rudimentary division of labour and appears to be socially necessary in order to get people to fill different positions and perform adequately in them.[1]

The roots of social class discrimination lie in antiquity and are recorded in history; the Romans, for example, used the term 'classis' to differentiate people according to property and taxation. 'Ranks', 'degrees', and 'orders' were traditional features of medieval society. Property and patronage were essential elements of feudal England.

Social discrimination may be based on the caste systems as in India, or in Sri Lanka, which was reported to have so complicated a caste system that everyone, except the very top Brahmin caste, is inferior to someone else.[2] The Sinhalese regard the Tamils, who represent 30 per cent of the population, as inferior, but within the Tamils themselves there are innumerable degrees of inferiority and superiority. More subtle distinctions, which seem to be largely covert and difficult to identify readily, may be present in old-established industrial communities such as Britain.

Social order is endemic and it seems to evolve naturally as people in a community accept varying responsibilities during the development of society. Different occupations call for degrees of specialized skills, education, and personality attributes; some trades and professions have a more immediate impact on the community at large and they may attract social prestige and authority. The criteria of social status are frequently complex, and are not always directly related to income. Furthermore, there is some diversity among the stratification criteria used by various researchers.

People tend to classify occupations, perhaps distinguishing between those who earn money by physical labour—the class of workers some economists termed the 'hard-handed' labourers—and those who have been termed 'soft-handed' workers. In factories, class distinction may be signified by the type of overall worn: the blue overall of a machine operator contrasts with the white jacket of the shop-floor management.

Social stratification is more evident in countries where strong ethnic groups exist in particular societies. Superior and inferior rankings develop, and occupational mobility means that the lowest ethnic arrivals in a community start at the bottom of the social ladder by taking on the least desirable jobs. This phenomenon was noted by Hollingshead in an analysis of the ethnic origins of the inhabitants of New Haven in the USA.[3] He discovered that one-third were of Italian origin, followed in relative importance by: Irish, Russian, Polish and Austrian Jews; British-Americans; Germans; Poles; Scandinavians; negroes. 'Although all of these groups have been in the community for at least half a century, they are keenly aware that their ancestors were English, Irish, Italian, Russian, German, Polish or Negro'. Each group kept its identity and developed occupational specialities. The last wave of immigrants had to undertake the 'dirty' jobs in the community. In Britain, there has been some evidence of this tendency in post-war years, as the immigrant population has increased.

This 'pecking-order' has been observed by students of comparative biology. Schjelderup-Ebbe revealed that hens display a certain type of social awareness: 'There are no two hens within the same community who do not exactly know who is superordinate, and who is subordinate'.[4] Lorenz also noted this phenomenon in his study of jackdaws,[5] and De Haan also reported similar behaviour among captive monkeys.[6]

Thouless writes that social stratification implies not only that some people regard themselves as socially superior to others, but also that this difference and its resultant obligations are accepted by the others.[7]

Economic and social historians relate the emergence of the term 'social class', as it is generally used today in Britain, to the rapid transformation from a rural to an urban society which was one of the most distinctive features of the industrial revolution. Only one in five of the population had lived in a town of over 10 000 inhabitants at the beginning of the nineteenth century; 50 years later, one in three lived in towns, and by 1851, over 50 per cent of the population was described as 'urban'. Rapid population growth also characterized these years of intense industrial activity. The first census of 1801 recorded almost 9 million people in England and Wales and almost 2 million in Scotland; by 1851, the English population had doubled, and the Scottish one increased by 50 per cent, and there were over 6 million inhabitants in Ireland. The population grew between 12 and 18 per cent each decade, so that in 1911 the total UK population was over 45 million.[8]

The new middle classes that emerged from the industrial revolution emphasized the increasing class consciousness of the Victorians. Political power passed from the aristocracy and old landed gentry, as the result of the Reform Bills, and the rising middle class, aided by the railways, aimed to distance themselves from the working classes. 'The London General Omnibus Company was founded in 1855 to carry the middle classes from the new estates to the West End at a leisurely pace—an hour from Islington. . . . In 1863, the first stretch of the Underground was opened from Paddington to Farringdon Street'.[8]

Despite the Founding Fathers' dramatic assertions that all men had been born equal and had equal rights, social divisions also exist on the western side of the Atlantic. Further, a perceptive American writer has noted that the idea that barriers between classes were breaking down has not held up to scrutiny: 'myths often prove more durable than truth'.[9] The 'affluent society' has been notable for the continuing degree of inequality and wealth and income. 'In fact, the long-term trend has been towards greater, rather than the less, inequality since the very first days of the nation'.

Members of particular social classes tend to restrict intimate friendship to those whom they regard as 'equals', i.e., members of their social class. Group norms are reinforced by this tendency which confers on individuals the benefits of psychological—and even physical—protection. In older cities, there is evidence of this in the localized concentration of ethnic groups in certain districts.

Money and occupation may be basically important in linking the social significance of people, but other factors are influential. In 1954 Alan Ross published an article in which he coined the terms 'U' and 'non-U' to describe respectively the language used in everyday conversation in Britain by the 'upper class' and those who 'are not of the upper class'.[10] Later this essay was included in a book entitled *Noblesse Oblige*, edited by Nancy Mitford, which attracted popular interest. It was suggested that the habitual use of certain phrases could be taken as a guide to social class origins or ambitions. Socially aspirant people were advised to adopt 'U-type' phraseology which would speed their social advancement.

Byron, it is said,[11] hated Keats essentially for reasons of class rather than rank. Keats was 'allegedly one of the "Cockney poets"—writers who were disposed to rhyme "dawn" with "morn".' The boundaries of snobbery seem to stretch to all manner of petty accusations, some vindictive and others rather droll, as instanced in the use of diminutives. 'Bertie is the upper-class version of Albert, while Bert is the lower-class version. William becomes Willy or Billy in U-speak, but Bill is non-U. Robert is an acceptable U-name, but Bob is not (Robbie or Bobby or even Bobbity being U). Alexandra should not be diminished to Alex but to Xandra'.[11] Evelyn Waugh, John Betjeman and other literati have delighted in the opportunities offered by the nuances of class-related language.

The influence of the 'Establishment'—a rather pejoratively biased description of the vague mix of institutions, such as the Monarchy, Parliament, the Civil Service, the Church of England, the Law, public schools, Oxbridge, select media, etc., which are perceived (and often accused) of exercising influence and authority, imposing traditional values and the status quo in Britain over many generations—has been the target of radical writers and speakers. Perceptions (as noted in Chapter 2) tend to be subjective and, in this case, likely to be coloured by the personal status of individuals. Change is certainly taking place; the old guard is losing its traditional dominance, for example, in the higher ranks of the Civil Service; the BBC, moulded in the solid, deferential role imposed on it by John Reith, is now often accused of seeking to undermine the traditional values it once stiffly upheld. Popular entertainment and the mass media have contributed with gusto to the 'disestablishment' of the old order. Paradoxically, the *arrivistes* are peculiarly prone to seek admission to the haunts of those whose social power has been freely criticized and challenged.

With the better educational facilities now more generally available, social mobility has developed strongly, and people in western society are able to move up the social ladder rather more easily than earlier generations. The emergency of the 'meritocracy'—a telling description of the professional and business leaders who have attained prominence through their intelligence and diligence, which was invented by Michael Young in 1958[12]—reflects the dynamic nature of modern society. But, as Sampson noted in 1971, Britain changed rather differently from Young's prognosis of a new meritocratic ruling elite with the lower classes left with rudimentary education until rebellion in 2033.[13,14] While the 1960s had seen the 'apotheosis of the clever grammar-school boy' who had broken the hold of the public schools and the old boy network of the ruling families, the products of the comprehensive schools now eclipsed those of the grammar schools which, as the result of legislation, had largely disappeared. This social revolution, Sampson commented, has affected the Labour Party as well as the Tories: many prominent Labour politicians today are graduates with middle-class values and life-styles, few are working class who have 'come up the hard way'.

Today, elite positions of influence in public and commercial life are held by those who have been able to secure, at an early age, good educational and professional qualifications. Nepotism will always be present in human society, but its influence is certainly constrained by the abrasiveness of modern life.

These social trends should be noted by marketers. Social mobility brings with it new needs: 'new styles of life tend quickly to become habitual. Consumption patterns that at first seem indulgent and discretionary tend to become routine and necessary'.[15] As income rises—or in anticipation of higher earnings, very often—expenditure tends to grow to meet it. The influence of social mobility will be referred to again in Chapter 8 when opinion leadership is discussed. Society has been said to be in a state of almost perpetual flux. 'Neither the "who" of each class nor what motivates them' are matters for assumption; careful and continued market monitoring is necessary to ensure that marketing decisions are based on reliable information.[16] The sharp divisions in the consumption habits between 'white-collar' and 'blue-collar' workers are fast disappearing. Both in the USA and in Britain, the old barriers separating the factory worker and the office worker are largely swept away as the economic power of the former class of worker has strongly increased. Products and services that were once considered 'middle class' are now bought across a far wider spectrum of society. Miners, dockers, building-site workers, and factory workers take their holidays abroad, enjoy drinking wine with their meals, and patronize restaurants. The wearing of a white collar is no longer a reliable indication of economic influence in society: 'every year the white-collar line is breaking down further. More blue-collar workers are becoming middle-class as well as middle income and modern'.[16] Even among white-collar workers there are many grades of economic activity requiring significantly different educational and professional qualifications.

But while the old working class may be fading away, and new consumption habits are being formed that in many instances follow the traditional pattern of the middle classes, it should not be assumed that complete integration is taking place between these social strata. Ownership of consumer durables, such as washing machines, does not mean that the significant social and cultural orientations which have distinguished these segments of society have also been dissipated. The formation of attitude is closely linked with social environment, and it was observed in Chapter 5 that attitudes do not change suddenly, and their influences may in fact extend throughout life. With increased spending power, it is relatively easy to 'upgrade' through purchasing some of the products whose ownership was largely restricted to those up the social ladder, but it does not follow that fundamental social attitudes and habits are transformed.

As a whole, the joint-stock banks are still little used by working-class people; book shops generally have a middle-class clientele; private education is the highly controversial interest of the middle classes; the 'consumerism' movements are largely generated and supported by middle-class professionals; the age at which full-time schooling ends remains considerably influenced by social class membership. In Chapter 6 the imbalance of the UK student population with regard to social class origin was noted: full-time university students are disproportionately from the higher socio-economic groups. Differences in personal and family values are reflected in people's life-styles, and it may take more than one generation for middle-class standards to be completely assimilated by those aspiring to upgrade their social status. Some degree of tension may result: there may not be a consistency of interest shown towards all the products and services consumed by middle-class society and marketers should recognize that the edges of their markets will be somewhat 'ragged': clearly defined segments based on social class membership may be unreliable. Refrigerators, for instance, are now in virtually all British homes, but life assurance policies or fine wines are still predominantly of upper- and middle-class concern.

As people ascend the social ladder, their awareness of life enlarges; they tend to broaden their horizons. As Levy has said: 'The higher one is in the social scale, the more comprehensive are one's values; there is a greater sense of participation in the community, as well as an increase in self-expressive attitudes. Self-fulfilment is more valued and more pursued as a real possibility'.[17] It would be relevant to relate this concept to Maslow's theory of 'self-actualization' (see Chapter 3).

As people expand their views of life, their needs tend to increase. Cognitions and attitudinal structures become more complex and are influenced by cultural values. More sophisticated satisfactions are sought in many cases: 'Going up the social scale, one finds that food tends to be regarded and used in increasingly symbolic fashion, and going down the scale, one discovers that it is consumed more and more pragmatically'.[17] The biogenic needs (as already observed) tend to become elaborated. Some people are prepared to go to great trouble in hunting out unusual brands of a product or to cultivate tastes for exotic foods in order to demonstrate their sophisticated styles of living; perhaps they see themselves as trend setters. These types of consumers will be discussed in Chapter 11, where personality factors related to the diffusion of new products and services will be examined.

At one time, trade unionism was almost exclusively a working-class phenomenon, although NALGO (local government workers) and the NUT (teachers' union) have been active for many years. White-collar worker unions have had a catalytic effect on middle-class attitudes towards conditions of employment. In 1972 it was noted that the 'basic distinction' between the middle classes and the working class was that the latter advanced as 'a result of group activity', whereas those above them socially moved 'forward by individual initiative'.[18] However, this distinction is becoming blurred, and may well cease to be applicable in modern Britain.

But certain disagreeable distinctions remain in contemporary Britain and which have not been radically changed by significantly improved earnings: these differences relate to factors such as sickness, life expectation, infant mortality, and general health. Between the social classes there are still unpalatable patterns; for example, the higher socio-economic classes tend to live longer, suffer fewer chronic and acute illnesses, and experience fewer still-births than those lower down the scale. Unemployment, particularly long term, is also disproportionately distributed.

The so-called *embourgeoisement* of the working classes, as Breach and Hartwell propose, could easily be called the proletarianization of the middle and upper classes, and a broadly unified culture has emerged.[19] However, a rather different view is taken by a leading US social researcher, Richard Coleman, who reflects that it was often thought that the affluence which blue-collar workers in the USA experienced in the 1950s and through to the 1970s would 'surely have produced a change of attitudes and values: the phrase for this hypothesised change is "embourgeoisement".'[20] However, research has usually proved the contrary: essentially no value change occurred. Limited horizons, sharp sex-role perceptions, centrality of family, etc., have been little affected by ownership of cars, telephones, or television. Possessions, not wider social contacts or new ideas, satisfied these people's need for modernity and change. But very different behaviour has characterized the life-styles and self-concepts of the higher echelons of the US population over the same period of time. In many cases, less conspicuous consumption has motivated behaviour, self-expression is more prized; more time is being volunteered for charities of various kinds.

Coleman summarizes by saying that the economic and social upheavals since the 1950s have not obscured 'the fundamental continuity of the class structure' which has persisted despite life-style variations within each class.[20] '*Ne plus ultra*' may well seem an appropriate reflection.

Pierre Martineau observed in 1957 that a rich man is not simply a poor man with more money which, if he were given it, he would spend in the same way: 'Where he buys and what he buys will differ not only by economics but in symbolic value'.[21]

Martineau summarized his research findings as follows:

Middle class	*Lower status*
1. Pointed to the future.	1. Pointed to present and past.
2. Viewpoint over long expanse of time.	2. Live and think in short expanse of time.
3. More urban identification.	3. More rural identification.
4. Stress rationality.	4. Essentially non-rational.
5. Well-structured sense of the universe.	5. Vague and unclear structuring of the world.
6. Horizons vastly extended or not limited.	6. Horizons sharply defined and limited.
7. Greater sense of choice making.	7. Limited sense of choice making.
8. Self-confident, willing to take risks.	8. Very much concerned with security and insecurity.
9. Immaterial and abstract in their thinking.	9. Concrete and perceptive in their thinking.
10. See themselves tied to national happenings.	10. World revolves round their family and body.

Bearing in mind the date of this survey, most of these points essentially reflect differences between attitudes and expectations that seem valid today. Perhaps the third aspect noted—urban/rural identification—may not be so widely representative, at least in British society.

Martineau (using the Warner Social Classification, to be discussed in Sec. 7.5) noted that there was a 'fundamental difference in attitudes between the two lower classes'.[21] Upper-lower individuals view their home as their castle: 'he loads it down with his hardware', which act as symbols of security. But the lower-lower person is 'far less interested in his home', and prefers to spend his or her money ostentatiously on 'flashy clothes or an automobile'. The 'hardware' today is likely to include a personal computer.

Social class membership continues, therefore, to influence buying preferences to some degree, even though levelling up (or down) of society has occurred. Personal psychological factors are still influential, as Martineau observed: 'Everything we buy helps us to convey to others the kind of people we are, helps us identify ourselves to the world at large'.[21] The concept of ideal self and its influence on consumption habits has, of course, already been observed earlier in this book.

Marketing executives have a professional interest in the structure and distribution of social classes. Marketing strategies are frequently concerned with the demands of the mass market: the substantial majority of consumers who form the 'middle wedge' of total consumer demand. Since marketing executives and researchers tend to be from the higher income and social grades, it is all the more important that they should analyse and understand the personalities, motivations, and cultural values of those who constitute the audiences at which the bulk of their promotional activities are aimed.

7.3 SOCIAL CLASS MEASUREMENT

In the late 1940s, Richard Centers undertook some extensive researches into US social class structure.[22] Dissatisfied with occupational groupings as bases for social behaviour, Centers probed deeper. He asked respondents what were the significant factors that helped them to decide a person's class—as to whether or not they belonged to the particular social group of an individual respondent. He concluded that social classes could be described as 'psychosocial groupings' whose interests in political, social, and economic areas tended to coincide and whose socio-economic situations were broadly similar. This reference to psychosocial factors is of interest to marketers in segmenting markets. Centers's research resulted in the following criteria for class membership (see Table 7.1).

Table 7.1 Criteria for class membership other than occupation

	% (approx)
Beliefs and attitudes	47
Education	29
Family	20
Money	17
Other answers	6
Don't know	9

Note: Some respondents attributed class to more than one factor.
Source: Centers.[22]

7.4 THREE PRINCIPAL METHODS OF MEASURING SOCIAL CLASS

Various methods have been devised and used to measure the social class structure of communities. Three of the principal methods will be outlined.

Reputational method

This system has been popularized by the pioneer researches undertaken by Lloyd Warner into US society. Social class is defined in terms of how members of a community view one another and place their associates in the social structure: 'those who interact in the social system of a community evaluate the participation of those around them . . . members of a community are explicitly or implicitly aware of the ranking and translate their evaluations of such social participation into social class ratings'.[23] Howard and Sheth, in their definition of social class, have noted that 'these classes can be ranked according to the views of its members as to the value of each class in terms of its contribution to the society as a whole'.[24]

This method of classifying individuals is largely restricted to relatively small, compact communities where people are well known to one another, e.g., the typical English village where 'everyone knows everybody'.

Subjective method

Individuals are invited to classify themselves related to the community of which they are members, and from such answers an overall view of the stratification is achieved. Obviously, individual ratings may be heavily biased.

Objective method

Objective criteria are decided upon which are relevant to particular communities; these may include income, occupation, education, location of residence, etc. Individuals are classified against these types of criteria by social scientists. Following his earlier research, Warner and his associates developed a social classification in 1960 which has been widely adopted in social and marketing research inquiries in the USA.[23] The variables noted by Warner related to income, source of income, education, occupation, and neighbourhood. Another objective method of classifying social classes was devised by Hollingshead and Redlich in 1958. Some details of these two systems will now be given, and it will be seen that they share certain basic attributes.

7.5 THE WARNER SOCIAL CLASS SYSTEM (USA)

W. Lloyd Warner and his associates produced six main classifications of US society:[23]

Upper-upper – Aristocracy ('Social Register')
Lower-upper – New rich ('nouveau riche')
Upper-middle – Professionals and managers
Lower-middle – White-collar workers
Upper-lower – Blue-collar workers
Lower-lower – Unskilled labourers

The top group—the 'Social Register' set—represent the families who have distinguished themselves not only by wealth but also by occupying high status positions in a community over several generations; the wealth of such a family has been owned for many years, and they possess unique influence in society, although constituting a minuscule proportion of the total population

The lower-upper group are those individuals who have wealth but are not fully accepted socially. They aspire to membership of the cherished top status group 'but they are consciously aware that their money is too new and too recently earned to have the sacrosanct quality of wealth inherited from a long line of ancestors'. Meanwhile, they must groom their families so that one day they may be admitted to the upper reaches of society, and so they avidly pursue philanthropic causes while building up their finances.

The upper-middle class are the well-educated professional people who are usually leaders in their communities: 'the solid, highly respectable people who get things done and provide the active front in civic affairs for the classes above them'. Warner estimated that the three social groups so far analysed represented about 13 per cent of the total population in the USA.

The lower-middle class is made up of clerks and other white-collar workers whose ambitions are limited. They generally live in unfashionable districts; some of them are successful members of ethnic groups. In Vance Packard's terminology: 'they are the non-commissioned officers of our society'.[25]

The upper-lower class are the 'poor but honest workers' with, at one time, severely limited incomes and abilities.[23] These blue-collar workers are the largest class—about 40 per cent of the total population. It is important to recall the earlier observations on the gradual erosion of the 'collar division' as far as earning power is concerned.

The bottom of the social pile—the lower-lower class—are the unskilled, casual labourers and their families who are despised by the rest of society. Although their general behaviour is considered reprehensible, Warner pointed out that research 'shows many of them guilty of no more than being poor and lacking in the desire to get ahead'.[23]

Martineau, in reviewing Warner's typology, referred to critics who had held that the basis of these investigations had rested on studies of smaller cities in the USA (10 000–25 000 population), and therefore the same classification may not be applicable to metropolitan centres of population.[26] Further, Warner's studies had been mainly concerned with 'the differences in the broad patterns of living, the moral code, etc.' and they did not specifically relate to marketing problems and buyer behaviour.

In the mid-1950s, an intensive study of about 4000 households in the metropolitan area of Chicago was conducted under the direction of Martineau and Warner and sponsored by the *Chicago Tribune*. Families were classified in the following social classes, which were related to Warner's typology:

	Percentage of population
Upper and upper-middle	8.1
Lower-middle	28.4
Upper-lower	44.0
Lower-lower	19.5

The study showed that there were distinct differences in shopping habits and patterns of spending over the various social groups.

Closer relationships were found to exist between the choice of store at which people shopped, patterns of spending, and social class membership. 'People are very realistic in the way they match their values and expectations with the status of the store. . . . The shopper is not going to take a chance feeling out of place by going to a store where he might not fit'.[26] This tendency was also noted by Levy, who pointed out that shopping habits, choice of media, and advertising exposure were linked to individual characteristics and class membership.[17] Packard also referred to the 'pride, pleasure and prestige' that many women feel in patronizing a high-class store, and in the satisfaction they obtain in 'looking down on the customers of the lower-class store'.[25]

Two US researchers discovered that the higher the social status of a woman shopper, the more quickly she wished to complete her shopping.[27] The lower the status of the shopper, the higher the proportion of 'downtown' shopping. However, they drew particular attention to the changes in income distribution, education, leisure time, and suburban living, which have 'tended to obscure the social class distinctions that were prominent at one time'. Although the geographical area covered by their investigations was necessarily limited the researchers felt that their findings suggested a fundamental change was taking place in the shopping and consumption habits of all social classes.

The differential responses of social groups to advertising and their media habits will be discussed in Chapters 12 and 13; which deal with behavioural aspects of communication.

7.6 THE HOLLINGSHEAD SOCIAL CLASS SYSTEM (USA)

The other method of classifying social class in the USA was developed by Hollingshead, who established five major social classes based on a weighted combination of three factors: residence, occupation, and income.[28] He took the view that the home 'mirrored' the family's living-style, that the level of occupation reflected its skill and social power, and that its tastes were affected by the type of formal education received. Hollingshead's classification is as follows:

	Percentage of population
Old families Top businessmen } the social elite	3.4
Business managers Lesser professionals } those 'on the way up'	9.0
Various salaried admin. posts Small business owners } average incomes	21.4
Semi-skilled and skilled manual employees } below average incomes	48.5
Unskilled and semi-skilled Poorly educated } low incomes	17.7

Warner's and Hollingshead's classification of social class have certain similarities and are based on the objective method of social class measurement. The mass markets of general interest to marketers can be seen in Hollingshead's third and fourth groups, representing 70 per cent of the total population, and are also reflected in Warner's third, fourth, and fifth social groups, which account for about the same proportion of the general population.

7.7 NEW DEVELOPMENTS IN SOCIAL CLASSIFICATION (USA)

Coleman has reported on a study in the 1970s sponsored by the Joint Center for Urban Studies of MIT and Harvard, in which a representative sample of 900 residents from Boston and Kansas City metropolitan areas were surveyed on their social status perceptions, using a reputational and behavioural approach.[20] This research found three principal and approximately equal groupings of Americans—'people (like us) in the middle', 'people above', and 'people below'—with economic status as the main differentiating factor, followed by education and behavioural standards. This Coleman–Rainwater model is said to reflect popular imagery and observation of how people interact as equals, superiors, or inferiors, and is claimed to be 'the latest look' at social class from a Warnerian social-psychological perspective. The researchers are conscious of the danger that lies in oversimplification and 'thumbnail sketches and three-card thematic summaries, because of the great variety of behaviour to be found within every status group'.

Another model, developed by sociologists Gilbert and Kahl, which views US class structure as 'essentially a matter of style, social networks and personal prestige reputation', is based on a series of qualitative economic factors and their symbolic meanings.[20]

7.8 SOCIAL CLASS CLASSIFICATION (UK)

One of the notable pioneers of social research in the UK was Charles Booth, a Liverpool businessman, whose massive statistical survey *Labour and Life of the People of London over the Period 1886–1902* used a framework of eight socio-economic classes in order to measure working-class conditions: four below and four above the poverty line.[29] He labelled these from A to H: Class A were from the 'lower depths' of society—'casual labourers, street sellers, loafers, criminals, and semi-criminals'; Class B were the 'very poor, ill-nourished, poorly clad'; and so-on to Class H: 'the servant-keeping class'.

From this early attempt at social classification other researchers, such as Rowntree, developed social categorization.[30] In addition, the official censuses and surveys conducted in the UK have contributed most valuably to socio-economic classification (these are discussed in detail later in this chapter).

7.9 NATIONAL READERSHIP SURVEYS (JICNARS)

A widely used classification for socio-economic groupings in Britain is that originally introduced by the National Readership Survey (NRS) to measure readership of certain magazines and newspapers. Informants are classified into social grades, which have become widely adopted by marketing researchers generally.[31]

Readership surveys were pioneered in the UK by the Hulton Readership Surveys, which were made annually between 1946 and 1955 inclusive. In 1956 the NRS was taken over by the Institute of Practitioners in Advertising (IPA), which published the NRS until 1967. From 1968, the NRS has been jointly administered by the Joint Industry Committee for National Readership Surveys (JICNARS) under the aegis of a committee representing the Newspaper and Periodical Contributors Committee, the Institute of Practitioners in Advertising and the Incorporated Society of British Advertisers.

In 1992, Michael Mander, chairman of the NRS, announced a new board structure as follows:[32] excluding the chair and managing director, four members from the Newspaper Publishers' Association (NPA), four from the Periodical Publishers' Association (PPA), three from the IPA, one from the Incorporated Society of British Advertisers (ISBA), and one from the Association of Media Independents (AMI).

Since its inception, the NRS has classified social groups into six principal categories (see Table 7.2) The various socio-economic groups are described briefly by JICNARS as follows.[31]

> *A – Upper middle class:* 'the head of the household is a successful business or professional man, senior civil servant, or has considerable private means. A young man in some of these occupations who has not fully established himself may still be found in Grade "B", though he should eventually reach grade "A".
>
> In country or suburban areas, "A" grade households usually live in large detached houses or in expensive flats. In towns, they may live in expensive flat or town houses in the better parts of town'.
>
> *B – Middle class:* 'In general, the heads of "B" grade households will be quite senior people but not at the very top of their profession or business. They are quite well off, but their style of life is generally respectable rather than rich or luxurious . . . non-earners will be living on private pensions or on fairly modest private means'.
>
> *C1 – Lower middle class:* 'in general it is made up of the families of small tradespeople and non-manual workers who carry out less important administrative, supervisory and clerical jobs, i.e., what are sometimes called 'white-collar' workers'
>
> *C2 – Skilled working class:* 'consists in the main of skilled manual workers and their families: the serving of an apprenticeship may be a guide to membership of this class'.
>
> *D – Semi-skilled and unskilled working class:* 'consists entirely of manual workers, generally semi-skilled or unskilled'.
>
> *E – Those at lowest levels of subsistence:* 'consists of old age pensioners, widows and their families, casual workers and those who, through sickness or unemployment, are dependent on social security schemes, or have very small private means'.

JICNARS provide their interviewers with detailed examples of the occupations that relate to the groups quoted above. Informants are placed in a socio-economic classification ranging from A to E which indicates to buyers of advertising media the types of consumers covered by certain publications.

Table 7.2   Socio-economic classification (JICNARS)

Social grade	Social status	Head of household's occupation	Approximate percentage of families
A	Upper middle class	Higher managerial, administrative or professional	3
B	Middle class	Intermediate managerial, administrative, or professional	10
Cl	Lower middle class	Supervisory or clerical and junior managerial, administrative, or professional	24
C2	Skilled working class	Skilled manual workers	30
D	Working class	Semi-skilled and unskilled manual workers	25
E	Those at lowest levels of subsistence	State pensioners or widows (no other earner), casual or lowest grade workers	8

Definitions
1. A *household* consists of either one person living alone or a group of persons, usually but not always, members of one family, who live together and whose food and other household expenses are managed as one unit.
2. The *head of household* is that member of the household who either owns the accommodation or is responsible for the rent, or, if the accommodation is rent free, the person who is responsible for the household having it rent free. If this person is a married woman whose husband is a member of the household, then the husband is counted as the 'head of the household'.
3. *Chief wage earner* is the senior working member of the household. Normally the oldest related male of 21 years of age or over in full-time employment. If there is no male of 21 years or over then the oldest related female of 21 years and over in full-time employment is taken. Non-related persons living in the household cannot count as chief wage earners.

Source: JICNARS.[31]

From July 1992, some changes took place affecting the significance of 'head of household' and 'chief wage earner' in defining the socio-economic status of respondents.[32] Briefly, these meant that the social grade of the informant's household was no longer based on the 'head of household' but on the 'chief income earner'. Up to the time of this change, the head of household (as defined in Table 7.2) was a significant factor, except where this person was dependent solely on state benefit, in which case 'chief wage earner' was used.

Under the new arrangements, the chief income earner is defined by this question: 'Which member of your household would you say is the chief income earner, that is the person with the largest income, whether from employment, pensions, state benefits, investments or any other sources?' If two persons claim to have equal income, interviewers classify the elder as the chief income earner (see pages 145–146).

From time to time, criticism of the NRS social gradings has been made on the grounds that since these socio-economic groupings are based on the occupation of the head of the household, they do not accurately reflect the propensity of consumers to purchase certain types of products.

The socio-economic groupings listed in Table 7.2 were certainly devised at a time when society appeared to be more stable and consumption patterns were largely class based. As noted in Chapter 6, the concept of life-style behaviour does not necessarily coincide with social group membership. Disposable income will vary for several reasons, such as middle-class life-styles with their emphasis on long-term objectives like housing and education policies, and so on. Also, the old social stratifications based on income have been eroded by the bargaining power of industrial and technical unions, and 'working wives', now a permanent feature of the UK labour market, whose extra earnings have added to family incomes, as discussed in Chapter 6. A marked weakness of the A–E classification was its reliance on the occupation of the head of the household. A printing operative or oil rigger are likely to be as well paid as a barrister, but their patterns of expenditure may well be very different.

However, the new procedures[33] by which the definition of a household was based on the chief income earner, instead of the head of household, should improve the quality of the NRS. Four principal reasons were given for the change: first, the traditional definition of head of household was increasingly objected to by both respondents and interviewers, particularly because a husband was given preference over his wife, even though she might be fully or partly responsible for the accommodation; second, interviewers experienced growing difficulties in applying the relatively complicated questioning procedures involved in defining 'head of household' and 'chief wage earner'; third, the market research industry was keenly interested in interviewers having a simpler and more acceptable method of identifying socio-economic status; and fourth, a chief income earner definition is consistent with most survey practice in Europe and elsewhere.

A pilot survey by NRS in October 1991 revealed that about 15 per cent of women were classified as chief income earners who, under the existing procedures, would have been recorded as 'wife of head of household'. It was reported that, as far as could be judged, the effect on the social grade profile was slight; there was, as expected, a bias towards ABC1s.

Discretionary expenditure on, for example, hobbies, may be disproportionate to income. Rising expectations and patterns of consumption are evident in a mobile society; the consumption of wine, for example, is no longer restricted to professional households. It should be added, however, that social class membership *is* closely associated with the ownership of some products, e.g., Rolls-Royce cars, or the use of certain services, such as domestic telephones. But generalization of the relationships between social groups and the consumption of products should be avoided, because there is growing evidence that in many instances, only tenuous relationships exist. The disposable income of the 'blue-collar' family may be as high as that of the professional family, yet they will be classified quite differently. An established barrister is classified as A together with a bishop of the Church of England. A teacher aged under 28 is a C1, but above that age transforms into a B. A self-employed London taxi-driver or a plumber is classified as a C2 type, whereas an articled clerk is considered to be C1. Skilled workers in industry are only C2, but small shopkeepers, who probably earn less, appear in group C1.

These curious anomalies are further complicated by the growth of literacy, greater opportunities for education without regard to family income or social status, and the fact that social groups do not necessarily display consistent behaviour.

In studying socio-economic groupings, it would be advisable to refer to the earlier chapters which have demonstrated the importance of understanding the psychological make-up of an individual. The NRS classifications should be considered as valuable in providing useful initial analyses of social groupings which now need to be used in conjunction with behavioural data. To ignore attitudes or personality traits renders socio-economic grading of limited real value to marketers. The so-called irrational factors which influence buying behaviour should not be overlooked; group influences (to be discussed in Chapter 8), family traditional behaviour, motivations, and perceptual processes all contribute to the decisions to buy certain products and services. Buying behaviour has been acknowledged to be complex, and to rely exclusively on a method of socio-economic grading originated over a generation ago is to rest content with comparatively superficial assessment of market behaviour.

Readership surveys merely give information about what periodicals certain social groups looked at; they do not offer explanations of behaviour—they deal with the 'what' and omit the 'why'. Further, the term 'readership' has never really been satisfactorily defined; it is not an absolute concept. Some advertisements tend, therefore, to look quizzically at the readership figures quoted by larger media owners.

Newer methods of consumer classification based on household and location (ACORN), and socio-economic groupings related to life-cycle and occupational mobility (SAGACITY) will be discussed in Chapter 14, which covers market segmentation. Further details of the NRS survey process are published elsewhere.[34] Income figures are associated with the various social groups, but these have not been quoted in Table 7.2 as they tend to become outdated fairly quickly.

In addition to the procedural changes[32] in the NRS affecting the significance of the chief income earner, other amendments from July 1992 concerned two questions related to the definitions of 'housewives' and 'other shoppers': the classification 'housewives' was replaced by 'main shoppers'. The traditional NRS 'housewives' question—'Who in your household would you say is mainly responsible for, or shares the household duties such as shopping or cooking?'—was replaced by the new 'shoppers' question: 'We would like to know about your personal involvement in shopping for your household's food and groceries'. (This question is followed by enquiries about types of shops, amounts spent, etc.)

NRS gives the following reasons for replacing 'housewives' with 'main shoppers':

1. The concept of a sole housewife is no longer appropriate, because members of households tend to be involved in different degrees with household duties.
2. The degree of involvement can readily be measured from responses to the new questions.
3. NRS will still be able to analyse the data in terms of female (or male) 'housewives' by including only those who claim to do half or more of the shopping.
4. The shopping question is much more precise and provides degrees of involvement.
5. Little difference exists in estimated population figures for female housewives and female main shoppers—a not-unexpected overlap exists.
6. The male main shopper definition results in a much more realistic marketing figure.
7. NRS readership figures for females of either definition are not significantly affected, and actually improve with the main shopper definition among males.

Research on JICNARS classification

Research Services Ltd,[31] at the request of JICNARS, investigated the NRS social grading system. Among their comments were the following points:

> Although the historical development of social grading based on occupation is well established, the precise reasons for the choice in pre-war studies are not well documented. It would appear that occupations were first used because in the more rigid social order that existed the occupation of the head of the household was a simple and efficient method of deriving income categories. As the relationship between occupation and income has lessened, occupation has remained the background of social grading because no better methods have been found, and because it has still remained a powerful and useful stratification factor, even though the interpretation has become more complex ... social grading analyses used in published tables of the NRS are to a large degree chosen because:
>
> (a) From a technical standpoint occupation is relatively stable and reliable at the data collection stage.

(b) It is a reasonable 'general purpose' classification in that it is useful for most product fields without necessarily being the most ideal for particular product fields.

These findings, published in 1970, generated further debate and concern continued to be expressed about the efficiency of the JICNAR social classification.

In 1979, a working party of the Market Research Society under the chairmanship of Peter Sampson concluded that the present system needed modification or replacement, and commissioned special research to investigate the validity of social grading as a discriminant of buying behaviour. 'The requirements of an acceptable system' were specified as follows:

(i) It should provide discrimination across a wide range of product areas with respect to at least one of three basic parameters: (a) product field image; (b) weight of usage; (c) brand (or equivalent) usage.

(ii) It should be capable of simple, consistent application over different data sources and collection methods, and it should be stable.

(iii) There should be no other measure capable of collection with the same facility providing stronger but similar discriminatory ability.

(iv) Both users and suppliers of data should have confidence in the measures they are using.[35]

The research evidence, on the whole, was not reassuring, although it was concluded that social grades, as used in the National Readership Survey, the Television Consumer Audit, and Target Group Index, continued to be a powerful discriminator.[36] However, it was stressed that the present system should be used intelligently; some leading market researchers[37,38] have expressed reservations about these general findings.

7.10 OFFICIAL SOCIAL CLASS GRADINGS (UK)

Apart from commercially inspired systems of socio-economic classification, there is considerable interest in grading the social and economic characteristics of consumers for purposes of government administration and in disseminating information to assist trade and industry.

The Census Reports of the Registrar General give 17 main socio-economic groupings:

1. Employers and managers in central and local government, industry, and commerce—large establishments.
2. As above—small establishments.
3. Professional workers—self-employed.
4. Professional workers—employees.
5. Intermediate non-manual workers.
6. Junior non-manual workers.
7. Personal service workers.
8. Foremen and supervisors—manual.
9. Skilled manual workers.
10. Semi-skilled manual workers.
11. Unskilled manual workers.
12. Own account workers (other than professional).
13. Farmers—employer and manager.
14. Farmers—own account.
15. Agricultural workers.
16. Members of armed fores.
17. Indefinite.

In addition to the above socio-economic groupings, the Registrar General recognizes five social groups: I, II, III(N), III(M), IV, and V. It will be seen that group III has been divided into N (non-manual) and M (manual).

The classification of occupations into social classes is very complex because of the vast number of occupations. The *Official Classification of Occupations* (1970) lists more than 20 000 separate occupational titles grouped into 223 occupational units. The official view is that each socio-economic group should contain people whose social, cultural, and recreational standards and behaviour are similar, but since it is not practicable to ask direct questions about such matters in a population census, employment status and occupation are taken as guides when allocating people to socio-economic groups.

The Registrar General's social classes provide the foundation of all official and sociological class classifications in Britain. From time to time, certain occupations have been reclassified; for example, aircraft pilots and navigators were transferred from social class III to II and draughtsmen from II to III, reflecting relative changes in the economic and social structure.

Society and Community Planning Research (SCPR), an independent, non-profit institute specializing in surveys, regularly publishes reports, including *British Social Attitudes*. It is interesting to note that they usually collapse the six social classes given by the Registrar General, into four groups: I and II, III(N), III(M), IV and V. The remaining respondents are grouped as 'never worked/not classifiable', but are shown in the tables produced in reports.

SCPR have also developed five-digit Occupational Unit Groupings:

1. Salariat (professional and managerial).
2. Routine non-manual workers (office and sales).
3. Petty bourgeoisie (self-employed, including farmers, with and without employees).
4. Manual foremen and supervisors.
5. Working class (skilled, semi-skilled and unskilled manual workers, personal service and agricultural workers).

There is 'a residual category of those who have never had a job or have given insufficient information, but this is not shown in any of the analyses in reports'.[39]

The *General Household Survey*, which is an inter-departmental survey sponsored by the Central Statistical Office (CSO), was introduced in 1973, and designed to measure, on a continuous basis, household behaviour related to factors such as housing, health, employment, and education. The socio-economic groupings used are based on the first fifteen main classifications as defined by the Registrar General but these are 'collapsed' so that six classifications emerge. Table 7.3 indicates the coverage of the six categories related to the Registrar General's main classifications. It will be noted that useful cross-references are to the Census groupings, while the six 'collapsed categories' can fairly readily be related to the JICNAR groupings.

The *Household Food Consumption and Expenditure Survey* of the Ministry of Agriculture, Fisheries, and Food groups households into eight classes based on the ascertained or estimated gross income of the head of the household, or of the principal earner in the household if the weekly income of the head is less than the amount defining the upper limit of the lowest income classification (D). These main groups are as follows:

A1, A2, B, C, D, E1, E2, OAP (old age pensioners)

From the beginning of 1980, agricultural workers, formerly in group C, were allocated to an income group entirely on the basis of their income.

The *Family Expenditure Survey* of the Department of Employment bases the occupational classification used in the report on the Registrar General's socio-economic groupings, but with

Table 7.3 Collapsed categories of Registrar General's socio-economic groupings as used in the *General Household Survey*

Collapsed categories	Approximate percentage of population	RG Socio-economic groupings
1. Professional	4	3, 4
2. Employees and managers	14.6	1, 2, 13
3. Intermediate and junior non-manual	20.0	5, 6
4. Skilled manual	33.4	8, 9, 12, 14
5. Semi-skilled and personal services	19.5	7, 10, 15
6. Unskilled manual	6.6	11
Never worked	2.0	

Source: General Household Survey (CSO).

certain adjustments. The separate groups analysed are: professional and technical workers; clerical workers; shop assistants; manual workers; and members of HM Forces. Where an individual has more than one job, the classification is related to the most remunerative occupation.

7.11 OCCUPATIONAL GRADING SYSTEM

The Department of Employment have issued a list of key occupations for statistical purposes, which has 18 principal classifications as shown in Table 7.4. There are approximately 3500 separately identified occupations together with some residual occupations; they are analysed on a four-tier system of classification which comprises 378 unit groups, 73 minor groups, and 18 major groups. Hence, it is possible to refine the types of occupation shown in the main groups given in Table 7.4. This occupational classification is said to be 'broadly compatible with other national and international classifications'.[40]

The occupations listed in Table 7.4 are clearly different from the Registrar General's social class and socio-economic groups, but it is possible to segment the working population thus: non-manual (groups I–IX) and manual (groups X–XVIII), which would allow some basic comparisons to be made with the RG classifications.

Consumer memory for the name of a product. May also be activated by relating it to the advertising. The total package of association brought together

Table 7.4 List of key occupations for statistical purposes as issued by the Department of Employment

Group

I	Managerial (general management)
II	Professional and related supporting management and administration
III	Professional and related in education, welfare, and health
IV	Literary, artistic, and sports
V	Professional and related in science, engineering, technology, and similar fields
VI	Managerial (excluding general management)
VII	Clerical and related
VIII	Selling
IX	Security and protective service
X	Catering, cleaning, hairdressing, and other personal service
XI	Farming, fishing, and related
XII	Materials processing (excluding metal) (hides, textiles, chemicals, food, drink and tobacco, wood, paper and board, rubber and plastics)
XIII	Making and repairing (excluding metal and electrical) (glass, ceramics, printing, paper products, clothing, footwear, woodworking, rubber and plastics)
XIV	Processing, making, repairing, and related (metal and electrical) (iron, steel, and other metals, engineering (including installation and maintenance) vehicles and shipbuilding)
XV	Painting, repetitive assembling, product inspecting, packaging, and related
XVI	Construction, mining, and related not identified elsewhere
XVII	Transport operating, materials moving and storing, and related
XVIII	Miscellaneous

Source: Department of Employment.[40]

7.12 INTERNATIONAL STANDARD CLASSIFICATION OF OCCUPATIONS

The International Labour Office (ILO) in Geneva issued an International Standard Classification of Occupations in 1969 which was a revised version of the occupational information that originated in 1949.[41] Its objectives were to provide a systematic basis for presenting occupational data related to different countries and to facilitate international comparisons. There are 10 major groups, plus the armed forces, as shown in Table 7.5. Of these groups, there are 4 levels: 8 major groups, 83 minor groups, 284 unit groups, and 1506 occupational categories. These give 1881 titles in total.

Table 7.5 International Standard Classification of Occupations

	Definitions of titles
Major group 0/1:	Professional, technical, and related workers
Major group 2:	Administrative and managerial workers
Major group 3:	Clerical and related workers
Major group 4:	Sales workers
Major group 5:	Service workers
Major group 6:	Agricultural, animal husbandry and forestry workers, fishermen and hunters
Major group 7/8/9:	Production and related workers, transport equipment operators and labourers
Major group X:	Workers not classifiable by occupation
Armed forces:	Members of the armed forces

Source: ILO.[41]

7.13 EU SOCIO-ECONOMIC CLASSIFICATIONS

Socio-economic status groups in the EU contain 14 classifications (see Table 7.6). Most marketing research firms in Britain who undertake inquiries in EU countries tend to use the British National Readership Survey socio-economic groupings as a basis for consumer analysis. In some cases the analysis is reduced to the three main socio-economic groupings: upper class, middle class, and lower class, corresponding to AB, C1C2, and DE.

In a multi-country consumer survey in the EU, Social Surveys (Gallup) used the following classifications of the occupation of the head of household:

Code
1. Farmer/trawler owner, etc. (own account only).
2. Farm worker.
3. Businessman, top manager.
4. Executive; professional.
5. Skilled tradesman, artisan, craftsman.
6. Salaried, white collar; junior executive.
7. Worker.
8. Student.
9. Housekeeper.
0. Unemployed; retired.

Table 7.6 Socio-economic status groups of EC

Community code	Socio-economic status
1.	Farmers.
2.	Other agricultural workers.
3.	Employers in industry, construction, trade, transport, and services.
4.	Own-account workers in industry, construction, trade, transport, and services.

5.	Employees and own-account workers in liberal and related professions.
6.	Managers, legislative officials, and government administrators.
7.	Employees with liberal and related professions.
8.	Foremen and supervisors of manual workers (employees).
9.	Skilled and semi-skilled manual workers (employees).
10.	Labourers (employees).
11.	Supervisors of clerical workers, sales workers, and service staff; government executive officials.
12.	Clerical, sales, and service workers.
13.	Armed forces (regular members and persons on compulsory military service).
14.	Economically active persons not elsewhere classified.

Source: Document 3065/76E (1981 Community Census of Population Programme).

7.14 HARMONIZING OFFICIAL AND COMMERCIAL SOCIO-ECONOMIC CLASSIFICATIONS

It will be readily apparent that some diversity exists in the socio-economic classifications adopted by various official investigations. The Registrar General's main groupings are largely utilized, although in the case of the *General Household Survey* and the *Family Expenditure Survey* certain adjustments are made to accommodate the needs of those particular inquiries. The type of information sought—its complexity and refinement—largely influences the structure of the socio-economic groupings that are used in individual surveys. Even where different groupings are in use, it is generally possible to compare these with related classifications and to obtain a reasonably adequate total appreciation of consumer activity in the areas covered by these surveys. But it would obviously be very helpful if marketing research data could be easily or readily related to official socio-economic groupings.

The Head of Marketing Research at the Mirror Group of Newspapers has suggested that since it seems unlikely that the OPCS would adopt the socio-economic groupings used by marketing researchers, the latter should consider analysing data by one or other official classification in addition to the customary A–E analyses.[42]

In 1980, the European Society for Opinion and Marketing Research (ESOMAR) set up a working party to deal with harmonization of demographics, especially in connection with international research. It is interesting to read from their report that 'the major part of the committee's work has been devoted to the problem of defining, and working with, social class'.[48] It was stated that across and within several countries, widely different meanings attach to 'social class'. From their considerable deliberations, the Committee drawn from nine European countries developed what they considered to be a 'rather good, workable system' (see Table 7.7).

Reviewing the ESOMAR working party endeavours, Sampson reflected that many market researchers view the concept of social class 'as outdated and lacking the power to discriminate between consumers nowadays'.[44] After bearing in mind the MRS working party's research findings, which were outlined earlier, Sampson concluded, however, that measurement of social class 'will continue to be made and continue to be found useful'. There is no single, simple way of classifying consumers, and while a general system, such as social class, is useful on many occasions, in some cases it will be necessary to develop specific 'customized approaches'. The trick is to combine 'the best of the general with the most useful of the specific'.[44]

Table 7.7   Projected Pan-European demographic scale

1. Employment categorization

(a) *Self-employed*

Farmer with less than 15 hectares (small farms)	1
Farmer with 15 hectares or more (large farms)	2
Owner of shop/company with up to five employees	3
Owner of shop/company with six or more employees	4
Professionals (i.e., jobs requiring qualification of degree standard such as doctors, accountants, lawyers, etc.)	5

(b) *Employees manual*

With completed apprenticeship or equivalent (i.e. skilled worker)	6
Unskilled	7

(c) *Employees non-manual*

Professionals working in their actual profession	8

(d) *In a managerial/senior capacity with a company, organization, civil service, or other public authority*

Responsible for up to five employees (reporting to him/her)	9
Responsible for six or more employees	0

(e) *Middle management*

Middle management responsible for up to five employees	X
Middle management responsible for six or more employees	Y

(f) *Other employees*

Other employees mainly office-based	1
Other employees not office-based	2

(g) *Non-working*

Unemployed	3
Housewife (exclusively working in the house, not receiving pension or other income)	4
Student, still at school or college/polytechnic/university	5
Retired, old age pensioner	6

2. Terminal education age

Received no education at all/did not finish education	1
Finished their full-time education at 16 years or younger and received no further education	2
Finished their full-time education between the ages of 17–19 and received no further education	3
Received further education, but not at university, polytechnic, or with a professional institute	4
Received further education at a university, polytechnic, similar college, or with a professional institute	5

Note: Since the UK appears to be unique in having some professions (e.g., solicitors, accountants, etc.) qualify by the process of articles, followed by examinations set by the relevant professional institute, unless such a proviso is made at codes 4/5, these respondents could possibly be coded at 2 or 3 and the points allocation be wrong.
Source: Røhme and Veldman.[43]

7.15 SUMMARY

Social stratification is endemic; it is particularly evident in countries where strong ethnic groups exist. A new meritocracy is one of the hallmarks of industrialized societies like Britain. As people ascend the social ladder, their awareness of life enlarges, their horizons broaden, and their needs increase; cognitions and attitudinal structures become more complex and are influenced by cultural values, as in the consumption of food.

Social class measurement tends to be made by: the reputational method, the subjective method, and the objective method. In the USA the Warner Social Class System is adopted widely. In the UK, JICNARS socio-economic groupings (A–E), despite their obvious shortcomings, are still used in market research surveys. Official bases of social classification are diverse and complex; the Registrar General's social categories underlie most: it would clearly be desirable to harmonize official and commercial socio-economic classifications.

Consumption of products and services may not be directly related to socio-economic status; care is needed in applying the JICNARS classification and in interpreting the findings of specific surveys. In a mobile industry society, where dual household incomes are well-established features of the economy, 'blue-collar' jobs may be imperfect indicators of a household's propensity to consume. But more money does not necessarily mean that middle-class behaviour norms will be accepted.

REFERENCES

1. Berelson, B., and G. A. Steiner, *Human Behaviour: An Inventory of Scientific Findings*, Harcourt, Brace and World, New York, 1964.
2. Kenny, Mary, 'All racists under the skin', *Sunday Telegraph*, 26 February 1984.
3. Hollingshead, August B., 'Trends in social stratification: a case study', *American Sociological Review*, vol. 17, no. 6, December 1952.
4. Schjelderup-Ebbe, T., 'Social behaviour of birds', in: *Handbook of Social Psychology*, C. Murchison (ed.), Clark University Press, Worcester, Massachusetts, 1935.
5. Lorenz, K. Z., *King Solomon's Ring*, Harcourt Brace Jovanovich, London, 1952.
6. De Haan, J. A. B., *Animal Psychology: Its Nature and Problems*, 1948.
7. Thouless, R. H., *General and Social Psychology*, University Tutorial Press, London, 1967.
8. Fraser, W. Hamish, *The Coming of the Mass Market*, Macmillan, London, 1981.
9. Parker, Richard, 'Fact and fancy about America's "classless society"', *Business and Society Review*, no. 10, summer 1974.
10. Ross, Alan S. C., 'U and non-U', *Encounter*, 1954.
11. Casey, John, 'U turns and non-U-turns', *Sunday Telegraph*, 8 December 1991.
12. Young, Michael, *The Rise of the Meritocracy, 1870–2033*, Thames and Hudson, London, 1958.
13. Sampson, Anthony, *The New Anatomy of Britain*, Hodder and Stoughton, London, 1971.
14. Sampson, Anthony, *The Changing Anatomy of Britain*, Hodder and Stoughton, London, 1982.
15. Levitt, Theodore, 'The new markets—think before you leap', *Harvard Business Review*, May/June 1969.
16. Coleman, Richard P., 'The significance of social stratification in selling', in: *Marketing: A Mature Discipline*, Martin L. Bell (ed.), American Marketing Association, Chicago, 1961.
17. Levy, Sidney, J., *On Knowing the Consumer*, Joseph W. Newman (ed.), John Wiley, New York, 1968.
18. Shanks, Michael, *The Stagnant Society*, Penguin, London, 1972.
19. Breach, R. W., and R. M. Hartwell, *British Economy and Society 1870–1970*, Oxford University Press, Oxford, 1972.
20. Coleman, Richard P., 'The continuing significance of social class to marketing'. *Journal of Consumer Research*, vol. 10, December 1983.
21. Martineau, Pierre, *Motivation in Advertising*, McGraw-Hill, New York, 1957.

22. Centers, Richard, *The Psychology of Social Classes*, Princeton University Press, New Jersey, 1949.
23. Warner, W. Lloyd, Marchia Meeker, and Kenneth Eels, *Social Class in America*, Harper and Row, New York, 1960.
24. Howard, John A., and Jagdish N. Sheth, *The Theory of Buyer Behaviour*, John Wiley, New York, 1969.
25. Packard, Vance, *The Status Seekers*, Penguin, London, 1969.
26. Martineau, Pierre, 'Social classes and spending behaviour', *Journal of Marketing*, vol. 23, October 1958.
27. Rich, Stuart U., and C. Jain Subhash, 'Social class and life cycle as predictors of shopping behaviour', *Journal of Marketing Research*, vol. 5, February 1968.
28. Hollingshead, A. B., and F. C. Redlish, *Social Class and Mental Illness*, John Wiley, New York, 1958.
29. Booth, C., *Labour and Life of the People of London over the Period 1886–1902*, Macmillan, London, 17 volumes, 1889–1902.
30. Rowntree, B. S., *Poverty: A Study of Town Life*, Longman, Harlow, Essex, 1902.
31. Monk, Donald, 'Social grading on the National Readership Survey', Research Services Ltd, Joint Industry Committee for National Readership Surveys (JICNARS), 1970.
32. 'NRS definition changes: housewives or shoppers?', *Market Research Society Newsletter*, July 1992.
33. 'Major definition change in social grading on NRS', *Market Research Society Newsletter*, June 1992.
34. Chisnall, Peter M., *Marketing Research: Analysis and Measurement*, McGraw-Hill, Maidenhead, 1982.
35. Sampson, Peter, 'The Market Research Society working party on socio-economic grading: a progress report', *Admap*, February 1980.
36. Higgins, A., 'A review of social grade', Market Research Society, London, 1980.
37. Twyman, Tony, 'Re-classifying people: the Admap Seminar', *Admap*, November 1981.
38. Bermingham, John P., 'Have you been de-classified recently?', *Admap*, November 1981.
39. *British Social Attitudes: The Seventh Report*, Roger Jowell, Sharon Witherspoon, and Lindsay Brook, with Bridget Taylor (eds), SCPR, Gower, Aldershot, 1990.
40. Department of Employment: Classification of Occupations and Directory of Occupational Titles (CODOT), HMSO, Norwich, 1972.
41. International Labour Office (Geneva), *International Standard of Classification of Occupation* (revised edn, 1969).
42. Ault, Brian, 'The future of social and economic classification', *Admap*, May 1979.
43. Røhme, Nils, and Tjarko Veldman, 'Harmonization of demographics', 35th ESOMAR Congress, Vienna, 1982.
44. Sampson, Peter, 'Consumer classification: the art of the state', *European Research*, vol. 10, no. 4, 1982.

REVIEW AND DISCUSSION QUESTIONS

1. Outline the benefits and drawbacks of social classification as a variable for segmenting consumer markets in Britain. Might income be a more appropriate variable for some product areas?
2. A UK marketer of home wine-making kits has been told that social classification might be a useful means of isolating and segmenting markets. In pursuing this advice she discovered that besides the traditional measures of social classification, there were also a number of more recent measures. From your reading of this chapter, how would you advise her?
3. From a marketing perspective, what would you consider to be the principal advantages and drawbacks of determining a family's social class exclusively based on the occupation of the head of the household?
4. What do you consider consumers have in their minds when they talk of their social class?
5. From your study of marketing, do you feel that it is realistic to treat social classes as viable market segments?
6. In a society with a wide mixture of social classes, do you find it acceptable to see products marked exclusively to the upper classes?

EIGHT

GROUP INFLUENCE

8.1 INTRODUCTION

In the preceding chapters the influence of groups has been considered in relation to motivation, personality traits, and attitude formation and change. It was seen, for example, that affiliation needs may cause some individuals to be motivated to buy particular types and brands of products in order to associate themselves closely with certain kinds of people. Riesman's 'other-directed' people were observed to be affected by the behaviour of others whose society was attractive to them. In attitude formation, the influence of groups was shown to be significant; people tend to belong to groups of many kinds, and the norms of those groups affect individual attitudes. Individuals also subscribe to the formation of group attitudes according to their status within the group. The empirical evidence supplied by Sherif, and also Asch, on the power of group norms was studied; in addition, Newcomb's research into the environmental influences of Bennington College on student's personal attitudes was noted.

In Chapter 7 the tendency for individuals in particular segments of society to form close friendships with those of equal social status was referred to; this led to the formation of groups with members having similar sets of values and interests. Personal values become closely related to the standards of the group, which in turn impose on the individual certain levels of conformity.

As Thouless has observed: 'Modern civilised society is a complex system of interrelated social groupings'—from the intimate family circle through to national and even international groups.[1] In contemporary society, an individual may belong to a great variety of groups: professional and occupational, social and political, recreational and religious. People may be members of the local Law Society, golf club, Townswomen's Guild, Rotary Club, Women's Voluntary Service, or they may be a member of an occupational group, as a school teacher or doctor. Groups consist of a number of people—as few as two—who interact with one another. This mutual social interaction influences individuals and the group of which they are members. The reciprocal nature of group activity gives it unique influence in society. 'Group interaction is seen as a major determinant in attitude formation and attitude change, as well as for other phenomena (satisfaction of social needs) of importance to the individual'.[2]

Katona has drawn attention to the fact that many major economic decisions are 'arrived at by consultation or give and take among group members'.[3] The group consensus exerts a powerful influence in economic life, though not all economic decisions are always group decisions.

8.2 DEFINITION OF GROUP

A group is a social entity that allows individuals to interact with one another in relation to particular phenomena. As a result of this frequent social interaction, a group social structure is evolved.

Brodbeck has given this definition of a group: 'A group is an aggregate of individuals standing in certain descriptive (i.e. observable) relations to each other. The kinds of relation exemplified will, of course, depend upon, or determine, the kind of group, whether it be a family, an audience, a committee, a labour union, or a crowd'.[4]

Groups may be 'natural', e.g., family groups; they may be specially formed to achieve certain objectives, e.g., steering committees; they may evolve because some individuals feel the need for sharing intellectual or other interests; they may result from occupational responsibilities, e.g., work groups.

In Chapter 5 it was pointed out that individuals may not necessarily adopt all the norms and attitudes of groups to which they belong. They will tend to adopt only those that are important in indicating agreement with the core beliefs and attitudes of those groups. The degree to which group standards are accepted and adhered to by individuals will depend on the dependence of individuals on group membership (e.g., membership of a professional association or institution may be vital for an individual's career) and the nature of membership (voluntary or obligatory). Where 'closed shops' operate in some factories, membership of a trade union is obligatory but not all members will feel entire personal commitment to the union's activities. But membership of the works' sports club is voluntary, and an entirely different group feeling is likely to be evident. The attraction of the group to members is also important. Where membership is highly valued by individuals, they will tend to conform precisely to group behavioural norms. Members will be attracted by the objectives of particular groups, e.g. civic societies have been formed in many towns in Britain by individuals who share concern for the developmental and environmental problems of their neighbourhoods. In such instances, groups develop high cohesiveness, where members will be expected to adhere closely to group norms and to further actively the objectives of the group. Where groups exhibit a lower level of cohesion, pressures to conformity of behaviour by individual members will tend to be significantly reduced and a greater degree of deviation would be tolerated.

8.3 TYPES OF GROUPS

Two generic types of groups may be identified: primary and secondary.

Primary groups refer to those intimate, personal associations by which relationships of a regular nature are built up between two or more persons. These groups have a primary influence on the individual member's personal development; they include the family, friends, or working colleagues, and involve an individual in direct and frequent interaction with other members. The saliency of primary groups in the development of an individual's attitudes was discussed on pages 79–90.

Secondary groups have been differentiated by some researchers as those groups to which an individual may belong by more deliberate choice than could be exercised with being a member of a primary group, e.g., membership of a political party compared with family membership. However, some of these distinctions tend to become rather blurred.

Groups may also be classified as formal or informal. Formal groups have defined organizational structures and the duties and rights of members are specified. Informal groups have less rigid structures, although their objectives may be pursued as avidly as those of formal groups.

8.4 REFERENCE GROUPS

These refer to groups with which individuals closely identify themselves so that they become standards of evaluation, and the sources of their personal behavioural norms. As was noted in Chapter 5, groups may include both membership groups (to which a person belongs), and aspirant groups (to which the person seeks to belong). Some leading US researchers have commented:

> In social psychological theory, it has long been recognised that an individual's *membership groups* have an important influence on the values and attitudes he holds. More recently, attention has also been given to the influence of his *reference groups*; the groups in which he aspires to attain or maintain membership. In a given area, membership groups and reference groups may not be identical. They are identical when the person aspires to *maintain* membership in the group of which he is a part; they are disparate when the group in which the individual aspires to *attain* membership is one in which is is not a member. It has been widely asserted that both membership and reference groups affect the attitudes held by the individual.[5]

Origin of reference group theory

The concept of reference group was originated by Herbert Hyman in 1942 to describe the kind of group used by an individual as a point of reference for his own judgements, beliefs, and behaviour.[6]

In a paper which was published 20 years[7] after the production of his theory, Hyman reflected that 'behind the concept lay an old vigorous tradition of thought in social psychology', to which several eminent researchers had contributed valuably during the course of their investigations. Reference group theory has now become assimilated into social science. 'On the common-sense level, the concept says in effect that man's behaviour is influenced in different ways and in varying degrees by other people—reference-group influence represents an unrealistic truism which has long been recognised'.[8] This view is also shared by Venkatesan, who researched into the effects of group norms on consumer behaviour. 'Although knowledge about conformity to group norms in the marketplace is slight, common-sense would lead us to conclude that consumer decision making takes place in an environment where conformity is a major force'.[9] He added that empirical evidence was needed to validate this hypothesis. In a controlled laboratory experiment, Venkatesan investigated whether in the absence of objective criteria individual consumers would tend to conform to the group norm or collective opinions of those with whom they associated. This experiment involved a group of university students who were asked to evaluate and choose the *best* suit from three identical men's suits labelled *A*, *B*, and *C*. The subjects were told that these suits were from three different manufacturers, that they were of differing qualities, that previous studies in which clothing experts took part had indicated that the *best* one could be picked out, and that the present investigation was concerned to establish whether consumers would be able to pick the best suit.

In the first stage of the experiment, subjects were allowed two minutes each to examine the suits and then, individually, to indicate their choice on a special form. These evaluations provided base data for later comparisons of group influence.

The next stage of the research involved groups of four individuals, three of whom were confederates of the experimenter; the other was a subject. The confederates had been instructed to choose *B* as the best suit. After examining the suits, the subjects returned to their seats and each person was then asked to announce his choice publicly. It was arranged that the confederates always gave their judgement before the subject in their group, thus ensuring that a group norm had been established before the latter was asked to respond.

In the absence of any group pressure, it was found that subjects distributed their judgements evenly over the three suits, whereas exposure to group pressure resulted in individual subjects conforming to the group norm.

Venkatesan admitted the limitations of his study, but indicated that the findings were supported by other investigations into the influence of group pressure on conformity. 'In many buying situations there exists no objective standard independent of others' opinions'.[9]

While the theoretical concept of reference groups was evolved in the early 1940s, the actual behaviour it described seems to be a fairly fundamental aspect of human behaviour. Emulation of admired or respected people, living or dead, has long fired the imaginations and aspirations of those who seek to share in their success. Behind many successful advertising campaigns lies the reference group theory: products and specific brands are frequently promoted in social terms, for example, in attractive surroundings in which people of a certain social class and age-group are portrayed as delighted consumers. Life-style marketing entices buyers to use particular brands of toilet soap, to acquire a certain make and style of car, or to go on holiday to some inviting location (see Chapters 3, 4, and 6).

Section 8.5 will consider the role of opinion leadership in reference group behaviour.

Two-way influence of reference groups

Reference groups may influence behaviour in two principal ways:

1. By affecting levels of aspiration, hence contributing to either satisfaction or frustration.
2. By affecting the types of behaviour through establishing conventional patterns of personal expenditure, thus producing either conformity and also contentment, or otherwise.

An example of the first type of influence would be a couple who anxiously plan a dinner party that will be up to the standards of those to which they have been invited over recent months. The second type of influence may involve certain social taboos that restrict the personal spending habits of some groups, e.g., ostentatious living-styles might be considered 'bad taste' in some highly cultured communities. This indicates that reference group norms may lead to 'avoidance' behaviour by individuals wishing to conform. Ambitious young executives may deliberately avoid very modern styles of clothing because their seniors may have displayed strong feelings about their staff wearing unconventional clothes at the office.

Stafford has identified 'three general dimensions' of reference behaviour: knowledge, affectivity, and sanctions which are interrelated variables.[2]

Individuals must be aware of the existence of a referent and of its prevailing norms and values. Sanctions are of two kinds—positive (rewards) or negative (punishment, active or passive). Affectivity 'relates to the degree of identification a person has for a particular group'.[2] Where there is considerable personal involvement, the norms of the group will be particularly influential. Marketers would need to assess the extent to which consumers, for example, identified with the behavioural patterns of certain sections of society. Venkatesan has noted, however, that 'few individuals would care to be complete conformists in their consumption patterns'.[9] They often like to have 'an acceptable range of alternatives within a given norm. We all know cases where individuals conform to the group norm by buying a product, but each individual purchased a different colour, brand, etc., thus maintaining a feeling of independence'. Marketing managers should carefully consider how much variety within their product ranges is necessary in order to satisfy consumers' needs for self-expression when buying mass-produced products.

Bourne posed three basic questions related to the practical value of reference group theory for marketing.[8] He identified these as:

1. *Reference group relevance*: in particular marketing situations, how is reference group influence assessed?
2. *Reference group identification*: how are particular reference groups or individuals in certain marketing situations to be identified?
3. *Reference group identification and effective communication*: how is effective communication with identified groups or individuals achieved?

Because many influences affect buying decisions, it is not easy to assess the contribution made by reference group influence. Bourne considered the conspicuousness of a product was probably the most general indicator to its susceptibility to reference group behaviour. Conspicuousness has two aspects: the product should be conspicuous in the literal sense of being perceived and identified by others, and it should be conspicuous in having certain uniqueness. If every man wore a top hat, this type of headgear would no longer attract attention. Bourne analysed various products to ascertain whether reference groups influenced the purchase of a product, the choice of a particular brand or type, or both. The possible susceptibility of a range of products and brand buying to reference group influence was studied by the Bureau of Applied Social Research at Columbia University. Figure 8.1 shows that a particular item may be susceptible to reference group influence in three different ways.

$$\text{Brand} + \text{Product} \quad - \quad \text{(Upper left cell)}$$
$$\text{Brand} + \text{Product} \quad + \quad \text{(Upper right cell)}$$
$$\text{Brand} - \text{Product} \quad + \quad \text{(Lower right cell)}$$

Only in the case of 'minus–minus' (lower left cell) items was the influence of the reference group considered not to be involved *at the time the research was undertaken*. It will be realized that products change their significances over time; a black-and-white television is no longer a significant reference group product. Radios and refrigerators have moved into the classification of product − brand − through near saturation in ownership. Clothing (product − brand +) has no reference group influence as far as the product is concerned, but the *type* of clothing *is* subject to considerable reference group appeal. Instant coffee (product + brand −) in this

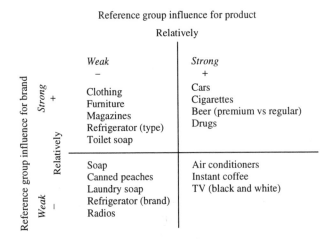

Figure 8.1 Products and brands of consumer goods analysed by reference group influence (*Source:* Bureau of Applied Science, Columbia University).

analysis is dependent on the social acceptability of it as a product, whereas brand is largely a matter of personal judgement.

In general, reference group influence is likely to be effective when products reflect personal taste; where little is known about a product, the more effective is reference group influence on an individual consumer.

Bourne has suggested that research should be undertaken on individual products or brands, and he offered the following guidelines to marketers when they had identified the reference group influence on the products.[8]

(i) Where neither product or brand appear to be associated strongly with reference group influence, advertising should emphasise the product's attributes, intrinsic qualities, price and advantages over competing products.

(ii) Where reference group influence works, the advertiser should stress the kinds of people who buy the product. This involves learning what the stereotypes are and what specific reference groups are influential, so that appeals can be effectively slanted.

However, Bourne recommended that 'the popular image of the product's users' should be projected as 'broad as possible' without reducing its appeal to significant segments of the market. This could possibly be done by using separate advertising media to communicate with potential new users.

Bourne's theme that reference group influence is significantly affected by a product's conspicuousness, was developed by Bearden and Etzel.[10] 'Uniqueness' was projected in terms of luxuries and necessities, the former having a degree of exclusivity while the latter are owned by virtually every one. 'Visibility' was projected in terms of *where* a product is consumed: 'brand decisions involving products which can be noticed and identified are more susceptible to reference group influence'. To test these theories, the researchers collected data from 645 members of a consumer panel in South Carolina during 1979, and also 151 respondents took part in a follow-up study. After preliminary research involving a convenience sample of 57 non-student adults, four products were selected as representing each of four product categories: (1) public luxury; (2) public necessity; (3) private luxury; (4) private necessity. Typical examples of these categories are (1) golf clubs, snow skis; (2) man's suit, woman's dress, motor-car; (3) pool table, video game, automatic icemaker; (4) refrigerator, blanket, mattress.

Respondents were asked to evaluate product decisions against each of the following reference group criteria:

1. *Informational*: from whom would information be sought about a prospective purchase.
2. *Value-expressive*: the likely enhancement of self-image or perceived attachment to the group.
3. *Utilitarian*: whether prospective purchase would be approved by group members and seen to be complying with group norms.

The research resulted in the identification of 'substantial differences' in reference group influence across the four classes of products surveyed, and the findings were reported to be 'consistent with Bourne's framework'.[10]

Multiple reference groups

It would be as well to bear in mind that people generally belong to several different groups, just as their activities during the day will also vary. Reference group influences may, therefore, originate from separate sources affecting particular kinds of products and services, e.g., household goods, food, entertainment, fashion, education. Individuals do not have to be members of a specific group for the norms of that group to influence their behaviour.

8.5 OPINION LEADERSHIP

Hyman, the originator of reference group theory, later drew attention to the need for more attention to the reference *individual* against over-attention being given to the reference group. 'In my original research I stressed both concepts, since over half the subjects gave evidence that they used particular other individuals—rather than large categories or groups of people—as reference points for appraising their status'.[7] Hyman referred to the influence of the 'opinion leader' and the 'influentials' in certain product fields, such as agricultural, drugs, women's fashions, and voting behaviour.

The concept of opinion leadership emerged from research undertaken by Lazarsfeld, Berelson, and Gaudet in connection with the 1940 US election campaign.[11] It was discovered that friends, co-workers, and relatives were influential in voting decisions; these sources of influence existed in every social group and stratum and were not confined to the upper social groups. 'Common observations and many community studies show that in every area and for every public issue there are certain people who are most concerned about the issue as well as most articulate about it. We call them the "opinion leaders".'

Group leadership studies have attracted considerable interest. Stafford has commented: 'Informal structuring tends to occur in all groups after a period of time during which the members have interacted with one another'.[2] Individuals acquire a certain rank or status that will largely decide their social influence over others. When someone has high status within the group, that person tends to be considered as the group leader. Rogers noted, however, that opinion leadership is not dichotomous: that people are or are not leaders. 'Influence is a matter of degree and should properly be viewed as a continuous variable, rather than a dichotomy of "leaders" and "followers". Some individuals are looked to for advice by many of their peers; others are asked for their opinions about an innovation by only a few'.[12]

Katz and Lazarsfeld undertook a classic study into the effects of opinion leadership related to marketing.[13] They researched the buying behaviour of 800 women in Decatur, Illinois, in the areas of films, fashion, public affairs, and food shopping. They found that personal influence was significant, 'although the fact that a woman is a leader in one area has no bearing on the likelihood that she will be a leader in another'. But their findings were challenged by Marcus and Bauer, who re-analysed the research data and declared that there were significant overlaps in opinion leadership for fashion and public affairs, fashion and food shopping, and food shopping and public affairs.[14]

The phenomenon of 'opinion bandwagons', as projected by Lazarsfeld, Berelson and Gaudet,[11] was felt by Marsh and O'Brien[15] 'to have been inadequately conceptualised in most past research'. They conducted in May 1988 an experiment related to Britain's membership of the EC. Four questions were put to respondents selected by random sample from British Telecom's market research database, BRUTUS, and by means of CATI (computer-assisted telephone interviewing) technology. A final sample of 1202 adults was achieved; responses were suitably weighted. Of the four questions, one was concerned with whether public opinion is moving towards Britain staying in or getting out of the EC, or whether public opinion is not changing. Another question asked how the respondent felt about the EC. Between these questions, respondents were deliberately told by interviewers that 'recent opinion polls have shown that public opinion is moving towards Britain / staying in / getting out / of the Common Market'. The researchers reported that information about public opinion has 'a conspicuously stronger effect on those who did not have strong prior views for or against the EEC than among their more opinionated peers', and that 'anti-marketeers seem more moved by the information than the pro-marketeers'.[15]

While acknowledging that further experiments are desirable and would be undertaken, the researchers felt that this particular research indicated that a moving bandwagon appears to be a decisive influence on some people, who subsequently change their views in the direction of the bandwagon (see Asch's experiments on group pressure in Chapter 5). It is apparent from this specific research that knowledge of and interest in a topic encouraged tenacity in the case of the anti-marketeers.

Classes of opinion leadership

Merton classified opinion leaders in two ways: monomorphic and polymorphic.[16] He described the former as the experts in a limited field whose influence 'does not diffuse into other spheres of decision'. Other opinion leaders—and this includes a good number of the top influentials—are polymorphic, i.e., they extend their influence in a variety of areas, some of which appear to be unrelated. He also showed that some individuals could fill the role of monomorphic opinion leaders for some groups and polymorphic opinion leaders for others.

Charles W. King directed a survey of new product adoption in Marion County (Indianapolis) to measure opinion leadership overlap across six types of consumer products, including packaged foods, household cleaners and detergents, women's fashions, cosmetics and personal grooming aids, drugs and pharmaceutical products, clothing materials, and large and small appliances.[17] The major conclusions of this study were as follows:

1. Only 31 per cent of the 976 respondents did not qualify as opinion leaders in any of the six product categories.
2. Opinion leadership overlap across product categories is widespread.
3. Opinion leadership overlap is highest between related product categories.
4. High opinion leadership overlap across all combinations of product categories suggests that a generalized opinion leader exists in consumer product groupings.

Clearly, further research is needed into opinion leadership and its influence in specific product markets.

The two-step flow of communication

Katz and Lazarsfeld showed in their Decatur study that opinion leaders are more likely to be exposed to the mass media than those whom they influence.[13] (The particular significance of this exposure with relation to specific types of products will be examined in Chapter 11, which covers innovation.) It was proposed by these researchers that marketing communications should be aimed at the opinion leaders in the various segments of each social class likely to be interested in particular types of products. From these opinion leaders, messages would be transmitted to other members of their groups. Opinion leaders act, therefore, as intermediaries between marketers and the mass markets that they wish to influence. This 'trickle-down' theory has attracted criticism: King rejected it as applicable to the fashion adoption process and proposed instead a 'trickle-across' flow of influence.[17] This horizontal flow of adoption within strata was supported by empirical evidence related to women's millinery 'the innovators or early buyers in the fashion season were not an "elite esotery" of upper class consumers. Nor were the early buyers the dominant personal influentials in the adoption process. In contrast, the fashion influentials were concentrated in the late buyer group'.

Sheth, in reviewing the 'trickle-down theory' has remarked that the most logical objection to it would seem to be based on the fact that individuals tend to temper their aspirations with reality in order to avoid constant frustration.[18] They may note some of the consumption habits of those in superior positions, but realize that, in many instances, it would be impracticable for them to imitate this buying behaviour, perhaps from lack of funds. It cannot be presumed, therefore, that the 'trickle-down' effect is automatic in all markets.

Interpersonal communication takes place *within* social strata, and it appears that some people fulfil the role of Hyman's 'reference individuals'.[7] Social interaction processes tend to be ignored by the 'trickle-down' thesis. (This aspect of communications will be discussed in Sec. 12.1.)

Gabriel Weimann[19] of the University of Haifa applied the Strength of Personality Scale (PS), developed by the Allensbach Survey Centre in Germany for testing self-perceived levels of personal influence, to two Israeli samples. The first involved a random sample of 650 Jewish adults; the second was of 270 inhabitants of an Israeli kibbutz community, whose personal communication network was subjected to sociometric mapping (see page 63). Cross-cultural comparisons of the efficiency and validity of the PS scale were made between earlier research in Germany and the Israeli survey. In both populations, it was found that a person of higher socio-economic status is more than three times as likely to be ranked as having strong personal influence than a lower-status person. However, the researchers observe that 'this relationship does not indicate direction of causality: opinion leaders may achieve their leadership through social acknowledgement of their education, income, occupation, and popularity, but they may also achieve higher social positions because of their stronger personality'. Weimann points out that opinion leadership was originally theorized to be a combination of personal and social factors, which the PS scale recognizes in its design. The findings of the survey show that 'influentials are not the opinion leaders according to the original definition but fit better the more sophisticated characterization that stemmed from the growing criticism of early studies on opinion leadership'.[19]

Finally (as noted in Chapter 6), emulative social spending has always seemed to be part of society. A leading social historian has observed that the Victorian 'common people' wore a conscious imitation of the dress of their immediate superiors, excepting items such as top hats.[20]

Methods of measuring opinion leadership

Three basic approaches to measuring opinion leadership may be identified.

Sociometric method Sociometric analysis[21] has already been outlined in Chapter 4. Sociologists frequently use a graphic tool—a sociogram—to demonstrate the extent of interaction among members of a group. It is possible to identify 'influentials', i.e., those who are likely to act as opinion leaders. The method is suitable for small-scale investigations but would be cumbersome for extensive field research. One interesting application was concerned with a group of doctors in a small New England community.[22] The pattern of interaction between these physicians was examined in relation to the adoption of a new drug. Three significant social sub-cultures were discerned, a small group of 'neutrals', and two 'isolates'.

Key informant This method entails asking individuals in specific groups to identify those who influenced them in particular product markets.

Self-report method Respondents are asked to make a personal evaluation of their influence on their peers. This self-designation approach was used by a US researcher who studied food preparation ideas, and, at another time, automobiles.[23] In the food preparation survey, this basic question was asked: 'Would you say other people seem to come to you for ideas about recipes and food, or that you seem to go to other people for ideas?'

Where respondents described themselves as people to whom associates come for advice on this topic, they were classified as opinion leaders. This method of identifying opinion leaders could lead to bias, since most people would like to think that their advice is sought on certain topics. Conceivably, others may underrate their influence on those with whom they associate. This particular research, concerned with food preparation ideas, involved 299 respondents in a sub-sample of female 'heads-of-household' distributed among New York, Chicago, Los Angeles, Philadelphia, Houston, and Atlanta.

The findings were that 'a small segment of consumers appears to exist in virtually every socio-economic group and to influence that group's ideas about product-related ideas'.[23] Although these people seem to be demographically indistinguishable from their associates (except for higher incomes and occupational levels), compared with other members of their groups, opinion leaders involve themselves more with news items and activities related to the specific new products.

In the same article an interesting reference was made to the relationship between the ultimate success of a new product and its early adoption by opinion leaders. A Los Angeles motor speedway included a coupon in its introductory campaign to sell tickets. The first 50 purchasers were recorded and subsequently interviewed by telephone; this research included a self-report measure of automotive opinion leadership. Of the 'early adopters', 60 per cent were characterized by the research findings as automotive opinion leaders, compared with 17 per cent in the general population of Los Angeles, as an earlier research had revealed. 'It appeared that 17% of the Los Angeles residents were probably responsible for 60% of the advance ticket sales'. It was suggested that this research study had indicated that 'other types of new product research—including concept studies and test market surveys—could use self-report to obtain indicators of a product's potential early adoption among opinion leaders as well as the general public'.

A further example of the influence of associates on buying behaviour was given by Katona, who referred to research by Eva Mueller in connection with the information-seeking habits of buyers of large household appliances (television sets, refrigerators, washing machines, and cookers). It was found that

> more than half of the buyers turned for advice to acquaintances and in most instances also looked at the appliances used by them. A third of the buyers bought a brand or model that they had seen in someone else's home, often the house of relatives. Information seeking through shopping around in stores appeared to be of lesser importance than information seeking from relatives, friends and neighbours.[3]

Katona also referred to studies of purchases and purchasing intentions related to tumble-driers, dishwashers, freezers, air-conditioners, and rubbish disposal. When a representative urban sample was asked 'Do your friends have any of them?' more than 60 per cent answered yes at a time when less than 25 per cent of the urban population actually owned at least one of these products. Katona surmised that some respondents may have wanted to show off, but a strong correlation was found to exist between affirmative answers to this question together with another question asking whether their friends liked the new appliances, and actual intentions to purchase specific types of these products.[3]

Regular research into the characteristics of opinion leaders has been undertaken since 1968 to evaluate the communication strategy of the Continental Can Company in the USA.[24] The self-designating method of identifying opinion leaders was applied to a sub-sample of 556 respondents from the same socio-economic area. It was found that leaders were 'involved to a greater degree in organisations', that they had higher levels of aspiration, and belonged to a higher socio-economic class than non-leaders. The researchers concluded that the self-report method of identifying opinion leaders 'tends to discriminate in favour of qualities generally accepted to be associated with leadership—i.e., organisation membership and offices held; higher education; income and stock ownership; greater mobility in employment, residence and investment portfolio; and personality oriented toward achievement rather than security'. Summing up, these researchers favoured this system of identifying leaders because of its economy, reduction of interviewer bias, and because it can be used in conjunction with random samples.

Opinion leaders are trendsetters in the mass markets that volume production and distribution methods are dependent on for continued prosperity. An indication has been given of the significant influence of leadership in consumer product markets. Opinion leaders may be identified by the selfsame method discussed in some detail; marketers should make some systematic effort to understand more about the social influences which affect the sales of their products. Katona would not have marketers forget, however, that 'groups are formed and led by individuals who, although they occasionally submerge in groups, remain the basic units of behavioural studies'.[3] But no real analysis of the motives, attitudes, and decisions of individual consumers is possible unless the societal framework within which an individual lives is recognized and understood.

Coleman has drawn attention to a subdivision of 'upper Americans' that sociologists and demographers have recently identified; these are a combination of 'media influentials' (people with roles in TV and the press) and 'non-profit professionals' (experts employed by government, schools, and foundations).[25] These 'new class' Americans tend to be anti-capitalist and anti-bourgeois; they infuse into the educational system their particular values and styles of consumption which set them apart from the middle American classes. This form of opinion leadership—the mass media commentators and entertainers—is not confined to the USA, as various demonstrations have indicated in the UK and elsewhere.

In the USA, the General Electric Company (GEC) has interviewed national samples of adults by telephone every three months (quarter) since 1964, in order to alert management to changes in public opinion.[26] From 1972, questions were included to identify respondents whose opinions might change earlier than the total sample, and for this purpose the Katz–Lazarsfeld approach was adopted.

Two assumptions were made:

1. When faced with an unclear situation requiring some reaction, people turn to friends and relatives to define it in terms that allow them to act.
2. For any given subject, there are some individuals to whom others are more likely to turn for advice. The latter are described in the literature in various ways: innovators, trendsetters, influentials, opinion givers, and so on.

As the result of two questions, respondents were subdivided into recent advisers, potential advisers, and non-advisers. Political participation questions covering six government activities were asked each quarter over 1975–8. It was possible to identify recent advisers (opinion leaders) whose opinions changed from three to fourteen quarters earlier than non-advisers. In addition, there were demographic differences within groups: 'in at least one case, recent advisers among those with a high school education or less changed earlier than college-educated respondents'.

Joan S. Black, manager of Survey Operations for GEC, concludes that although non-advisers who changed later may have been influenced by those who changed their opinions earlier, they may just be 'responding to the media at a slower pace'.[26] She observes that the 'controversial concept of two-step communication introduced by Lazarsfeld, Berelson, and Gaudet[11] in 1948 has not been resolved yet'.

Opinion leadership and the diffusion of innovation (discussed in Chapter 11) and reference group theory appear to have particular relevance to fashion clothing. Although empirical evidence is sparse, there has been a traditional belief that fashion trends operate in a hierarchical way. Nystrom was probably the first to suggest that fashion 'trickles down' from the higher social classes to the lower.[27] But this historical view (as noted earlier) has been rejected by King, who declares it to be out of date because of the vast social changes that have taken place over the post-war years.[17] He suggests that these significant changes and the impact of the highly organized mass media have resulted in a fashion change becoming a horizontal 'trickle across' the social strata. The breakdown of the traditional social processes, aided by the mass media and promotional techniques, is also held by Carman to have resulted in a more rapid diffusion of fashion.[28] However, he disagrees that the vertical flow of group influences has now been replaced by the horizontal flow postulated by King.

Although both these researchers are concerned with North American society, it would be reasonable to assume that similar influences have been active in Britain.

The growth of the 'pop culture' over western society has largely emancipated youth from the opinion leadership of their forebears. The 'trickle-down' theory of product acceptance may be supplanted by a new theory of product assimilation, starting with the younger age groups and gradually moving upwards to achieve market saturation. Clothing styles, including colours, tend to be strongly influenced by the 'pop culture' of modern urban societies.

McCracken[29] has suggested that 'the groups responsible for the radical reform of cultural meaning are those existing at the margins of society, e.g., hippies, punks or gays'. Because of their non-traditional life-styles, such sub-cultural groups are more radical and innovative than the conventional society of present-day North America. Another group of 'change agents' are stated to be fashion journalists and social observers, i.e., journalists who study and note new social developments and serve more or less as gatekeepers, reviewing innovations and assessing trends in the arts, entertainment, fashions, etc. In doing so, they act as 'influentials' 'even before an innovation passes to its early adopters'.

Midgley researched the male fashion market and found that early adopters were younger than later adopters; there was a 'strong relation between innovativeness and age'.[30] The earlier adopters were also of lower social class (70 per cent were either C2 or DE social groups). He concluded that 'fashion is a phenomenon of the young', who had a favourable attitude to change and who actively sought it, in the sense of looking at more shops, paying attention to fashion styles and advertisements, etc.

In general, therefore, the scarcity of empirical evidence makes it difficult to make an objective assessment of the 'trickle-down' theory of fashion; the emancipation of youth with its relatively high disposable income, willingness to try new experiences, and less inhibited approach to fashion styles and colour may be viewed as a sociological and cultural expression which has affected consumption patterns across society. Both duchesses and secretaries wear jeans today.

8.6 FAMILY INFLUENCES ON CONSUMER BEHAVIOUR: AN INTRODUCTION

The family occupies a unique place in society; it is the fundamental social unit. 'The norms and sentiments that rule it have their sources partly in the wider community; the community is, in part, the repository of family ideals and a source of family stability'.[31]

The influence of a family on its members is pervasive; the effects of family traditional attitudes, interests, and motivations not only will be felt in the formative years but also are likely to extend throughout life. During their early years, children may acquire consumption habits—including learning brand names of certain types of products—which become part of their way of life. Old-established firms cherish their 'household brand names' which may have been built up over several generations of family buying behaviour. Certain types and brands of products acquire particular significance to individuals because they form part of the family pattern of life ('We *always* have Cooper's Oxford marmalade at breakfast time').

The family embraces so much of life; it is a sub-cultural group within society, and at the same time it is an important economic unit. Its members, especially its working members, contribute to the production and distribution of national resources. It is a complicated purchasing organization supplying the needs, perhaps, of two or more generations. Buying behaviour is substantially affected by the nature of the family, and its responsibilities may generate demand for a diverse range of products and services. The household budget includes expenditure on housing, food, durable products, education, clothing, transport, holidays, and so on.

The influence of culture on consumption has been discussed in Chapter 6, when life-style approaches were examined. The life-style of a family largely sets its status in society. Veblen, and later researchers, have commented on the social influences on patterns of consumption assumed by individuals and families.[32] He maintained that the 'leisured classes' aspired to status by their consumption habits; conspicuous consumption being their objective. This particular concept of leisured living does not seem entirely acceptable or credible in the more egalitarian society of modern industrial cultures. However, people's aspirations, professional opportunities, general behaviour, and expectations are deeply affected by the traditional living styles of their families, and (as observed in Chapter 7) social class patterns of consumption are still discernible in some product and service markets.

Through the family, individuals are introduced to society; they learn acceptable standards of behaviour. Within the family, cultural values are transmitted, and specific roles are assumed in the household. Members of a family interact with one another, and this may lead to conflict on occasions, particularly when those in authority constrain the behaviour of dependants. A mother may decide that she knows best what style of clothing to buy for her young children, and refuse to purchase some garment which she thinks to be unsuitable, e.g., because it would not stand up to heavy wear.

Definition on family

The term 'family' is used to describe several kinds of households. Sociologists have specific ways of describing certain types of families; a brief review of this terminology will be given.

Nuclear family refers to the immediate 'family circle' made up of father, mother, and children who live together.

Extended family describes the nuclear family together with other relatives, such as grandparents, uncles and aunts, cousins, and in-laws.

Family of orientation or origin is the family that individuals are born into, the family of their origin or birth, in which they are reared.

Family of procreation or marriage refers to the family founded by marriage. The family of origin is also a family of marriage in its own right, but when the children grow up and leave the family home to get married, it then becomes the family of origin for these adult offspring.

Research carried out in 1993 shows that, the number of one-parent families with dependent children has increased to over one in seven (about 1.6 million families). Step-families—mixed households of parents with children from earlier marriages—are becoming a fairly prominent feature of the last years of the twentieth century. The social dominance of the traditional nuclear family is now challenged by the 'horizontal' family of step-children and step-parents.

8.7 CHANGES IN HOUSEHOLD UNITS AND TYPES OF FAMILIES

Before discussing family buying behaviour, it would be helpful to review briefly the changing nature of households in Britain as a result of demographic, cultural, and social factors. In some cases, the effects are radical both in terms of personal life and also in patterns of consumption: 'the idea that every family depends on a single breadwinner is as old-fashioned as unsliced bread'.[33] Some of these changes, such as 'working wives', have already been alluded to when it was observed that the employment rate for women in Britain is one of the highest in the EU. It is estimated that there are now two or more workers in many households, and nearly one-quarter of married women work 30 hours or more per week outside the home.

The following key indicators from official reports indicate the general trends observed in Britain today:

The population of Great Britain is peaking; in mid-1990 it was 56 million; by the end of the century it is expected to be about 58 million.

There were 944 000 live births in the UK in 1961, 902 000 (1971), 731 000 (1981), 788 000 (1988), 777 000 (1989); the 'baby boom' years are well and truly over.

In 1990 28 per cent of all births were out of wedlock compared with 4–5 per cent in the early 1950s.

The 55-plus population accounted for almost 33 per cent of adults in 1986; this sector is projected to increase to 34 per cent by 2006 and to over 38 per cent by 2021.

The 55–64 age-group of 6 million (1986) will fall to 5.6 million (1996), and then grow significantly to 7 million (2011) and 7.8 million (2021).

The 65-plus age-group represented 15.7 per cent of the population in 1989; by 1996 it is likely to be 15.8 per cent and then decline to 15.7 per cent in 2006.

The 75-plus population will increase from 3.7 million (1986) to 4.1 million (2001); after this time, the trend will be likely to flatten out and then start curving upwards between 2016 and 2021, to reach 4.4 million.

The disproportionate relationship between males and females in older age-groups will change: in 1986, among the 55–64 age-group there were 1.1 women to every man; in the 65–74 age-group, the ratio was 1.27 to 1, and in the 75-plus group, the ratio was 2 to 1. However, projections up to 2021 indicate a narrowing gap, almost to parity in the 55–64 group, 1.2 for 65–74, and 1.75 in the 75-plus group.

The average household size was 3.09 (1961), 2.64 (1982), and 2.46 (1990); increasing numbers of one-parent and step-families are now evident.

There has been a dramatic increase in one-person households: 12 per cent (1961) to 26 per cent (1990), and projected to reach 6.8 million (2001).

In 1990, 15 per cent of all households were occupied by pensioners. More than 50 per cent of all women aged over 65 live alone. Life expectation for women is 78.8 years and for men 73.2 years; in the early 1950s the comparative figures were 71.2 and 66.2.

Public sector nursery and primary school pupils declined between 1976 and 1986, due to reduced birth rates in the 1960s and 1970s. But enrolments increased slightly 1986–9, and will fall somewhat to 2000, after which a steady increase will be apparent. In secondary schools, numbers fell between 1981 and 1990, but increases are projected from 1992 to the end of the century.

A sharp decline will be evident in numbers of teenagers and 20 year olds: the proportion of 15–19 year olds will fall from 6.8 per cent of population (1990) to 6.1 per cent (2000), while 20 year olds will fall more dramatically from 16.1 per cent to 12.3 per cent. The Youth Culture is at an end after 30 years or so.

Divorces have increased dramatically since 1961: in England and Wales, divorcees represented 2.1 per thousand of married people in 1961, 6.0 in 1971, and 12.7 in 1989. Many eventually remarry. In 1989, marriages between bachelors and spinsters accounted for 66 per cent of all marriages compared with 86 per cent in 1961.

Self-employment has increased significantly since the 1980s (2 million) and in 1990 totalled about 3 million.

Ethnic minorities represented about 5 per cent of the British population in 1987–9, and are clustered, particularly in London, Birmingham, Manchester, and Bradford; they comprise 17 per cent of the Greater London population and 5 per cent of Greater Manchester's.

Between 1990 and 2000 30 year olds will increase from 7.7 million to 8.9 million (15.4 per cent of population); the 30–39 age-group is also likely to grow and reach 9.1 million by 2001.

The British work force is estimated to be around 28 million—the second highest in the EU—and has increased with the entry of more women workers, who represent over 40 per cent of the workforce and are estimated to grow to 45 per cent by the year 2000.

Examination of these selective and interrelated factors reveals the fundamentally altered profile of the UK family and household since the early 1960s. More people live alone; divorce and single parent households have increased significantly; the average household size is smaller; the age structure of the population has changed; the 'traditional' family household is declining; working wives are a well-established feature of the economy; more very old people will be in the population.

The effects of these changes are evident in public sector provision of education, housing, health, and social welfare services, as well as in consumer goods and service industries. What affects the family also affects industry; in some cases the effects may be lagged but in others, such as groceries and clothing, the impact is more readily apparent.

8.8 MARRIAGE AND CONSUMER SPENDING HABITS

In western societies, marriage generally leads to a new household being established; new housing, furniture, and kitchen equipment are required. The impact on consumer needs is therefore considerable. If a new home is not immediately set up, and the newly married couple live with, for example, the bride's parents, a different pattern of spending will result. In a study published in 1968, J. Walter Thompson found that, in 1964, 50 per cent of all married women under the age of 35 started their married lives in one of the parental homes,[34] a later report indicated that this figure had fallen to 27 per cent in 1973.[35]

Although the reports are now somewhat dated, they give interesting insights into family living patterns in the UK in the late 1960s. it is evident that the trend towards the young couples sharing one of the parental homes declined markedly, and it is no longer a significant factor in researching family spending behaviour.

With middle- and upper-class families, there is a greater tendency for young people to set up their own homes on being married. Where this is not done, the most likely arrangement is for the young couple to share the home of the wife's parents. The JWT survey found that maternal influence over the young housewife was marked in the early years of her marriage; a third of married women under 35 lived within walking distance of their parents, and over a half of young housewives saw their mothers at least once a week. The JWT survey asked young housewives whom they would turn to for advice on certain matters: on baby care and in buying groceries the wife's mother was clearly an important source of advice; her influence extended to new recipes or arranging a party, but these activities were also influenced by friends, and even the husband. The latter is likely to be 'major' source of advice for consumer durables such as washing machines, cookers, or refrigerators. As the young housewife acquires experience and self-confidence, the influence of her mother as chief adviser tends to decline.

These research findings are supported by a study of young housewives made by Joyce.[36] Housewives in the age group 16–34 were asked about their buying behaviour and the persons of whom they would seek advice. With groceries, 29 per cent of these young wives would turn for advice to their mothers, 18 per cent to their husbands, and 21 per cent to their friends. If they were considering the purchase of an important item for their homes, 82 per cent would seek advice from their husbands, 4 per cent would ask their mothers and 3 per cent would turn to a friend. Joyce also found that the importance of a mother as a dominant source of advice diminished as a young housewife developed her own expertise in shopping; friends play an increasingly important role.

Further evidence of the dependence of certain classes of consumers is given in research findings from MIT and Harvard,[37] which 'demonstrated with astonishing clarity how the socio-geographic horizons of working-class Americans differ from those of the middle class. A representative sample of 1000 men and women in the metropolitan areas of Houston, Dayton, and Rochester was asked where the 'physically closest' of their relatives lived and how this might have influenced their non-residential location. It was found that 55 per cent of the lower-class and 45 per cent of the working-class respondents occupied a house or apartment within a linear mile of where a parent, sibling, in-law, aunt, uncle, cousin, grandparent, or grown child resided, whereas only 19 per cent of middle-class and 12 per cent of upper-class Americans lived so near to any of their relations.

Working-class Americans have been described as 'family folk' who are heavily dependent on relatives for economic and social support; this long-held view has been supported by several research studies. Relatives are looked to for job opportunities, advice on purchases, and as sources of help and solace in times of trouble.

Working-class horizons, as Coleman observes, are much more limited than those of the middle and upper classes.[25] There are significant social and psychological differences apart from geographic ones: 'In almost every aspect, a parochial view characterises this blue-collar world'. (See Chapter 7 for Martineau's research on class perspectives.)

In the mid-1950s research studies concerned with family and kinship in east London by Young and Willmott found that 'the wider family, far from having disappeared, was still very much alive in the middle of London'.[38] A high proportion of working-class young married couples shared the house of one set of parents, usually the wife's. There was a distinct tendency for daughters to set up home near to their mothers, so that a matrifocal orientation influenced the development of these new families of marriage. This may influence the consumption habits of the new young couple, and tend to reinforce past behavioural patterns affecting, for instance, the types of food consumed and the times at which it is eaten. The social and cultural environment of the 'extended family' will, as Elizabeth Bott has remarked, 'exert consistent informal pressure . . . to conform to the norms', and also to offer mutual help to members.[39] This clustering of families spanning several generations has undoubtedly had a profound effect on the behaviour of individuals. Strong family links may discourage the adoption of new life-styles; patterns of personal expenditure may be inhibited by the cultural traditions and taboos of the 'tribal family'.

Of course, social mobility is easier these days and new consumption habits can be learned—the transport driver may confidently order scampi at the motorway restaurant—but his basic orientation towards life, and many of his consumption habits, will have been formed during the early years of family life. In addition, young people have had disproportionate wage and salary increases over the past few years, so that they are able to gain a measure of economic independence at an earlier age than the preceding generation. J. Walter Thompson's research has noted that from the early teens onwards, children tend to develop their own interests and start to pursue these separately rather than join in family activities.[40]

In seeking economic and social independence, young members of a family may, not altogether surprisingly, challenge some traditional values and behaviour:

> Prior to the 1960s the idea of young people forming the cultural and commercial vanguard was unthinkable for most people, particularly their parents. But films like *Love on the Dole* and *Saturday Night, Sunday Morning*, and the growth of popular music in the 1960s, challenged the assumption that sons would follow fathers and daughters their mothers. That challenge to the authority of their elders ushered in a period when young people set the consumer agenda for the rest of society as mods, rockers, hippies, smoothies, skin heads, punks and new romantics.[41]

This desire for freedom may be carried on into marriage, and many couples (particularly the younger generation) are said to enjoy going out separately as well as together. This move to greater independence can disrupt family unity by breaking down traditional patterns of behaviour. The relatively high proportion of 'working wives' has also added to the greater independence within families.

The personality characteristics of the housewife will also affect the rate at which she is able to become independent in her shopping behaviour. Her motivational influences—for example, the strength of her need for achievement, or for dominance—are likely to contribute significantly to her style of housekeeping. The earlier discussion on personality traits, attitudes, motivations, and cultural environment should be related to the consumption habits of young housewives in particular. The innovation of new products depends largely on the rate of acceptance by the younger age groups of consumers, since these are generally more receptive to new ideas. Again it would be relevant to consider how much this depends on the strength of the curiosity aspect of behaviour which may cause some housewives to be willing to experiment with new brands and/or new recipes of food products. At all times, study of consumers should be comprehensive because buying behaviour is complex.

8.9 FAMILY LIFE-CYCLE

The concept of life-cycle has been borrowed from sociology and applied usefully to the study of the consumption habits of families. The stages at which families find themselves during the course of their lives affect the nature of goods and services they demand, and there are likely to be marked changes in the volume of expenditure on specific products. Decisions are also likely to be arrived at in different ways during the family life-cycle.

The stages of the family life-cycle have been described as follows:

> beginning with the simple husband–wife pair it becomes more and more complex as members are added and new positions created, with the number of interpersonal relations reaching a new peak with the birth of the last child, stabilising for a brief period to become less and less complex subsequently with the launching of adult children into jobs and marriage. . . . as the group contracts once again to the dyadic composition of the family changes, so do the age-role expectations for occupants of the positions in the family, and so does the quality of interaction among family members.[42]

Various formulations of the typical family life-cycle have been offered by researchers; as a result, it is sometimes difficult to make cross-comparisons of data from different studies. In addition, some families may not fit neatly into any of the prescribed life-cycle stages.

Lansing and Morgan have conceptualized the life-cycle of families in the USA as follows:[43]

1. Bachelor stage: young single people.
2. Newly married couples: young, no children.
3. The full nest: young married couples with dependent children.
4. The full nest II: older married couples with dependent children.
5. The empty nest: older married couples with no children living with them.
6. The solitary survivor: older single people.

A similar model has been projected by Wells and Gubar, although they prefer to subdivide stage 3 into those parents with children below the age of 6 and those having children above that age.[44] They also subdivide stage 5 into two categories: those where the head of household is still working and those where they have retired. Stage 6 is also subclassified into (a) still working, and (b) retired.

The Wells and Gubar model has been criticized by Murphy and Staples because 'non-traditional' families are excluded.[45] Their 13-stage model is unique in recognizing both divorce and childlessness. To date there are no comparative data related to the predictive ability of the Wells and Gubar and the Murphy and Staples models.

In their report on leisure activities, J. Walter Thompson have taken life-cycle in five stages.[46]

1. Young, single people: 'solo'.
2. Young married couples with no children: 'homebuilders'.
3. Couples with young children (youngest under 10): 'learner parents'.
4. Couples with older children (youngest 10–15): 'practised parents'.
5. Over 35, no children under 16 at home: 'free again'.

Another JWT report that focused on how women entertain at home, while acknowledging that men are obviously involved in the decision as well as the style of home entertainment planned, concentrated on interviewing women in various life-cycle stages which were defined as follows.[46]

1. Single women under 35, with no children under 16.
2. Married women under 35, with no children under 16.
3. Women with children, youngest child under 10.
4. Women with children, youngest child aged 10–15.
5. Women aged 35–64, with no children at home.

Wagner and Hanna,[47] in researching family clothing expenditure in the USA, based their life-cycle variables on the modernized family life-cycle proposed by Murphy and Staples,[45] to take account of both 'changing demographic trends and non-traditional flows through the family life cycle'. However, the Murphy and Staples model was modified in three ways:

1. All single household heads, whether divorced, widowed, or never married, were given the same status. (The never-marrieds or prematurely widowed were not included in the Murphy and Staples model.) In their revised family life-cycle, Wagner and Hanna assumed that the clothing expenditure patterns of all single household heads are similar.
2. Child-bearing and child-rearing stages were defined by the age of the oldest—not youngest—child.
3. Infancy was defined as ending at 2 years of age.

Wagner and Hanna's revised family life-cycle eventually had 18 stages, as follows:[47]

	Age of household Head
Young single adult	18–34
Young single parent I	18–34 with oldest child up to 11 years
Young single parent II	18–34 with oldest child up to 17 years
Young married adult	18–34
Young married parent I	18–34 with oldest child up to 2 years
Young married parent II	18–34 with oldest child up to 5 years
Young married parent III	18–34 with oldest child up to 11 years
Young married parent IV	18–34 with oldest child up to 17 years
Mature single adult	35 or older and employed

	Age of household Head	
Mature single parent I	35 or older and employed	with oldest child up to 11 years
Mature single parent II	35 or older and employed	with oldest child up to 17 years
Mature married adult	35 or older and employed	
Mature married parent I	35 or older and employed	with oldest child up to 5 years
Mature married parent II	35 or older and employed	with oldest child up to 11 years
Mature married parent III	35 or older and employed	with oldest child up to 17 years
Older single adult		
Older married adult		
Other		

Wagner and Hanna observed that although the Murphy and Staples model classifies more families than the traditional Wells and Gubar model, the revised version used by them is even more successful and only 0.8 per cent were categorized as 'other' compared with 8.4 per cent in the traditional family life-cycle typology.

As a result of their researches into family clothing expenditures using the revised model based on Murphy and Staples, Wagner and Hanna concluded that increasing the number of family life-cycle stages to include non-traditional families does not improve the predictive ability of family life-cycle models, at least as far as clothing expenditures are concerned. While family life-cycle affects clothing expenditures, 'the importance of stage in the family life cycle in determining expenditures has been exaggerated'.[47]

Katona has pointed out that all items of consumer durables are bought by a larger proportion of younger than older families, and that 'in the last few years the frequency of purchases was highest when the head of the household was between 25 and 35 years old. . . . Usually the dividing line between young and old is set at 45 years', although Katona admitted that some of the differences in consumption habits may be attributable more to income than positions in the life-cycle.[3]

Four arbitrary age groups have been linked with stages in the family life-cycle:

Young adulthood: 20–35 years old.
Middle years: 35–50 years old.
'Free' years: 50–65 years old.
Senior citizenship: 65-plus.

These groups may be studied in relation to the life-cycle stages given earlier, although it should be realized that differences may exist in social classes. At one time, for instance, professional men used to marry at a later age than working-class men, and so they assumed family responsibilities some years after the average age of husbands down the social scale. Further, the working-class man is likely to have achieved the peak of his earning capacity far earlier in his life than the professional or business man. Different cultural backgrounds and social environments will also be reflected in the distinctive buying behaviour of these types of consumers. Consumption habits are partially explained by the family life-cycle, but to rely entirely on this concept for an explanation of consumer buying behaviour would be very inadvisable. Certain types of products, of course, can readily be seen as appropriate to particular stages: the early years of marriage are concerned with mortgages, life assurance policies, baby foods, push-chairs and clothing; toys and games become more 'educational' as the baby develops. Holidays will tend to become more personally expensive after the children have been reared, and 'eating out' may be possible for two, whereas this may have been prohibitively expensive with the children as well.

In considering the family life-cycle, it is also necessary to keep in mind the effect of dual incomes. Earlier, the impact of 'working wives' was alluded to; it may mean that there will be extra money available at a comparatively early stage in the family's life. The income derived from 'working wives' may help to provide luxuries which would be outside the scope of the earnings of the 'head of household'. The aspirations of socially conscious parents may be met by their combined resources, e.g., providing for private education for their children, or taking them on expensive holidays overseas.

Many household durable goods are now increasingly bought from the dual incomes of husband and wife. This joint decision-making has implications for marketing strategies. Personality factors of both parties may be significant influences in the choice of a particular brand of a product.

A life-cycle analysis should, therefore, be sophisticated and allow for variables of age group, marital status, number and ages of children, social class, source of income, and so on.

In 1987, Granada Television commissioned the British Market Research Bureau (BMRB) to conduct a survey of adults because of their concern over the increasing media coverage devoted to the so-called North–South divide in Britain. About 1400 adults—700 in the London TV area and 700 across the rest of Britain—were sampled and findings weighted to provide a national picture. In this research, BMRB developed six distinct groups of life-stage, based on age, marital status, working status, and presence of children: 'we have described each as a different "power" group. . . reflecting their spending power in terms of disposable income'.[48] The following groups were identified:

1. *Granny Power* (14 per cent): people 55–70 years of age, in households where neither the head of the household nor the spouse works full-time; no children and no young dependent adults (16–24) live with them.
2. *Grey power* (12 per cent): people 45–60, in households where either the head of the household or spouse works full-time; no children and no young dependent adults.
3. *Older Silver Power* (18 per cent): married people with older children (5–15) but no under 5s.
4. *Young Silver Power* (16 per cent): married people with children 0–4 years.
5. *Platinum Power* (7 per cent): married people aged 40 or under, with no children.
6. *Golden Power* (1.5 per cent): single people aged 40 or under, with no children.

These groups account for 82 per cent of all adults; the remaining 18 per cent are a 'miscellaneous assortment of adults' who do not fall into any of the categories.

In the first stage of their extensive research, BMRB reported that social class and life-stage are 'powerful discriminators' of people's consumption behaviour, whereas life-style groupings—of which they developed five clusters derived from a factor and cluster analysis—were generally less effective. They concluded that the life-style categories could be condensed by combining Golden with Platinum Power, and Older with Young Silver Power. BMRB declared their intention to use life-stage as a standard classification, because

1. It can be applied consistently at an international and cross-cultural level.
2. It can be effectively carried out with relatively small samples.
3. It does not become outdated.
4. It can be used readily with standard demographic data.
5. The collection of life-stage data, unlike social class inquiries, is regarded more tolerantly by would-be informants.

The Granny Power group, as might be expected, has a high house-ownership rate; this suggests that many families are likely to receive a major inheritance at some time between middle life and the retirement of the chief income earner. This new source of wealth may be used to pay off mortgages, take an expensive holiday, or acquire sizeable financial investments apart from house-ownership and pension rights, or, perhaps, be passed further down the family. It has been estimated that, in Britain, assets worth £9 billion a year will be inherited from the 1990s to the year 2000; this could present a lucrative opportunity for alert financial services marketers. (Further consideration of family life-cycle is given in Chapter 14, where SAGACITY segmentation is described.)

8.10 FAMILY ROLES AND DECISION-MAKING

The assignment of roles to specific members of a family has an impact on its social development and on its buying behaviour. Hill has described the family as 'a small group system, intricately organised internally into paired positions of husband–father, wife–mother, son–brother and daughter–sister. Norms prescribing the appropriate role behaviour for each of these positions specify how reciprocal relations are to be maintained, as well as how role behaviour may change with changing ages'.[42] The sensitive interplay of roles is to be seen in buying behaviour, and in particular in the areas of influence occupied by husband and wife.

The duty of providing funds for the welfare of the family is customarily assumed by the husband; and wife tends to be the custodian with responsibilities particularly related to purchasing food and household goods.

Bales and others have identified 'task behaviour' and 'socio-emotional' or expressive behaviour.[49] The first category is directed towards solving a specific problem; it is goal-oriented behaviour in which an individual acts in an instrumental role. The latter category is concerned with the degree of integration within the group; it gives emotional support, releases tension, and an individual filling this role provides reassurance and reward.

In buying behaviour related to family needs, these different roles may be reflected in the relative influence of husband and wife.

Field has given the analyses shown in Table 8.1 based on studies undertaken by researchers over a number of years.[50] Field identified three dimensions which 'seem the most obvious in determining' the relative influences of husband, child, and wife:

1. *Discernment*: 'technical know-how, judge quality, ability to discriminate within product field, to select outlet'.
2. *Price*: 'expensiveness, whose earnings go to make payments, who can pay, get credit'.
3. *Satisfaction*: 'who gets most use, benefit, value, enjoyment, out of the purchase'.

Field cautioned against too rigid an interpretation of this scheme because it could be affected by variables such as the quality of produce involved.

Sampson has suggested that it may be useful to devise some 'product hierarchy' that could serve as a guide to the extent and degree of influence exercised by members of a family on purchases, apart from any contributions to buying decisions made by persons outside the nuclear family group.[51] He felt that a dividing line would have to be 'drawn somewhere' between housewife purchases (which required definition) and 'household' or 'family' purchases. Table 8.2 relates to Sampson's proposal.

The hierarchical concept of product influence in family buying decisions deserves careful attention. It may provide the foundation for extended research to discover more about the interactions of members of a family in specific product areas. Sampson has referred, in fact, to the possibility of adopting sociometric techniques of analysis (Moreno's technique was

Table 8.1   Products and husband/wife purchase decision patterns

	Husband	Mainly joint	Wife
Population sample (USA) (Gisler)			
Plugs, tyres, oil	+	0	0
Alcoholic drinks	+	0	0
Shaving goods	+	0	0
Insurance	+	+	0
Heating	+	+	0
Cars	+	+	0
Vacation	0	+	0
Washing machine	0	+	0
Refrigerator	0	+	0
Vacuum cleaner	0	+	+
Toaster	0	+	+
Aspirin	0	0	+
Soft drinks	0	0	+
Shampoo	0	0	+
*Difference between matched working and non-working wives (Nye and Hoffman)			
Food, shopping	+		0
Medical care	+		0
Furniture	0		+
Cars	0		+
House purchase	0		+
Vacation	0		+
Insurance	0		+
Financial matters	0		+
Really important decisions	0		+
Purchase decisions in general (Foote)			
Families with pre-school children	+	+	0
Younger couples	0	+	0
Lower social grade	0	0	+
Middle social grade	0	+	0
Upper social grade	+	0	0

*This section of the table shows the direction of the differences. For example, the husbands of working wives play an increased part in shopping and medical care compared with the husbands of non-working wives. Working wives play an increased part in other purchasing spheres compared with non-working wives.

Source: Field.[50]

discussed earlier in this chapter) to determine individual preferences and dislikes which may be related, for example, to breakfast cereals, detergents, shampoos, or analgesics.[51]

Field has proposed that it may be possible to construct a two-dimensional typology of British households with reference to particular product fields.[50] His three main types of household are outlined as:

1. *Instrumental housewife, communicative household*: the housewife initiates thinking, discussion and demands *and* is non-selectively responsible or obedient to what the household communicates.
2. *Instrumental and perceptive housewife*: the housewife initiates *and* is selective in her responses to her household's communications.
3. *Expressive and perceptive housewife*: the housewife gives general support to household, rather than initiating thinking discussion or demands, *and* is selective in her responses to her household's communications.

This typology would obviously require validation, and it would be unlikely that it could be applied generally. It may be possible, however, to identify particular buying situations where this typology would be of value. Extended research in specific product areas would be necessary to test this approach to analysing household buying behaviour. Studies would need to be made of the methods of communication *within* families: to know more about how buying propositions are generated; the extent of influences of individuals on product type and brand choice; the degree to which shoppers are willing to respond to the influence exerted by their spouse and/or children. It would also be valuable to learn about the relative values that shoppers attach to certain products, e.g., that margarine may be better for health than butter, or that cornflakes are not as nourishing as porridge.

Table 8.2   Proposed hierarchy of products for family needs

(a)   Low unit price/high purchasing frequency items (e.g., food products, cleaning products, toiletries).

(b)   Low unit price/low purchasing frequency items (e.g., some proprietary pharmaceuticals, home decorating materials, certain 'speciality' food and drink items not normally on the 'weekly shopping list').

(c)   High price/low purchasing frequency items (e.g., consumer durables, furniture, furnishings, floor coverings).

(d)   Very expensive items of low purchasing frequency, such as holidays.

(e)   Major items of 'capital expenditure', such as houses, home extensions, central heating, motor cars, etc.

Source: Sampson.[51]

8.11 FAMILY BUYING ORGANIZATION

The family could be viewed as a buying organization resembling that of a commercial firm. In Sec. 10.8 the concept of a buying centre is discussed.

Five roles in the buying process can be identified:

Gatekeeper—User—Influencer—Buyer—Decider

These roles are sometimes undertaken by the same person, although very often it happens that different people are active in these various roles and influence the buying of particular products or services.

This approach could be adopted in the study of family buying behaviour. It would encourage analyses of the role of members of a family, so that comprehensive knowledge would be attained. A mother, for example, may delegate some of her buying responsibilities because of her other commitments. She may not specify a particular brand or product; new brands may be introduced by younger members of a family. The role of gatekeeper may vary: with grocery and household products, the main shopper is likely to be most important in collecting information, e.g., reading advertisements, visiting neighbours, and discussing shopping problems, or scanning the posters on supermarket windows. In the case of overseas holidays, the initiative may come from the parents, but teenage children may organize the collection of information. Their media habits and preferences would deserve analysis.

The person who actually decides to buy will vary according to the nature of the product. Some aspects of role differentiation related to products have already been discussed. Joyce's research indicated that although many consumer durables commonly involved joint decisions to buy made by the couple, this did not extend to car buying, which remained essentially a man's province.[36] In the intervening years since this study was made, many women own their own cars apart from being significant in the purchase of family cars.

As earlier discussion has emphasized, the greater economic, political, professional, and social freedom of women will undoubtedly change traditional views on the buying of some products.

An IPC survey published in 1981 showed that women are the main consumers of 10 out of 17 alcoholic drinks bought for home consumption; 65 per cent of liqueurs, 62 per cent of port and sherry, 57 per cent of vodka and 55 per cent of gin are consumed by women, while men consume mainly whisky, dark rum, and beer.[52] Whatever alcoholic drink is preferred for home consumption, both men and women prefer to buy it in a supermarket.

Dual incomes may mean that the dominant role of the husband as sole income producer will be challenged. Greater participation in an ever-widening area of buying may be expected, and marketers should not be content to rest on a few generalizations about the buying habits of those who consume their products. Society is dynamic; marketing practitioners should keep their information up to date.

8.12 CONFLICT AND COMPROMISE IN FAMILY BUYING DECISIONS

As with individual buying behaviour, family decision-making involves emotions as well as rational thought. It is further complicated because more than one person's views, attitudes, and opinions are likely to have to be taken into account. Discrete responsibilities tend to be assumed by individuals, often because of their family roles, for example, father, husband, and breadwinner, or on account of their specific skills and family tasks, such as a wife and mother acting in a parental and housekeeping role.

In traditional families, these roles and responsibilities were well understood, but fundamental economic and social changes have occurred in the family structures; patterns of employment, educational facilities, and rising expectations have contributed to the dynamic nature of modern societies. The sharing of accommodation and of a widening variety of goods and services such as food, domestic equipment, insurance, and holidays tends to render decision-making far more complex than when only an individual consumer is involved. Members of a household have probably well-developed perceptions, interests and opinions related to specific kinds of products or brands. These may be influenced by such factors as motivation (see Chapter 3) and cultural values (see Chapter 6).

It is not surprising then, that a degree of conflict may often be experienced in family buying decisions, especially when the anticipated purchase will be likely to affect all members of a family; for example, deciding on the style and location of a new family home, or the acquisition of a video cassette recorder. Other products may not impinge so directly on all members of a household, but are, nevertheless, likely to be of great importance to one or more individuals, as with the purchase of a dishwasher or a motorized lawnmower.

The high participation of married women in the labour force has resulted in extra household income being available for discretionary spending. This career orientation by women is increasingly evident in most developed countries and is still growing in Britain. One of the outcomes of 'working wives' is to reinforce the trend towards shared financial responsibilities in household expenditure and the related decisions. The once staunchly held views about the distinct roles of men and women in running a home have been challenged and largely supplanted by the more modern and enlightened perception of a partnership, sharing in domestic duties and also the full range of family decision-making. In many cases, incomes are jointly banked and allocated by mutual agreement; tasks connected with the processes of decision-making may be distributed according to the personal and professional competences of an individual. For example, collection of information concerning specification, price, and availability of proposed new purchases such as a microwave oven or a personal computer may be the accepted tasks of a specific member of a family, perhaps a gadget-conscious teenager. On the other hand, the extent and nature of financial savings and investments are likely, in this 'sharing' model, to be fully discussed and agreed by both partners before any commitments are made. These instances typify an organized, democratic approach that attempts to reduce discord and, more positively, encourages participation by fully recognizing the value of shared inputs to family decisions concerning a diverse range of goods and services.

This more sophisticated behaviour contrasts happily with that characterized by C. Whan Park[53] as a 'muddling through' process, where husbands and wives appear to know little about one another's likes and dislikes and the ways in which decisions are made. Partners avoid conflict by approaching matters requiring decisions carefully, in what Park described as 'conflict-avoiding heuristics'. Because of the lack of insight into one another's perceptions, attitudes, and so on, the decision-making process is full of ambiguities. Park found, in a limited study of the decision strategies of joint buyers of homes in a mid-western university town in the USA, that 'three major heuristics' were used:

1. *Common preference levels on salient objective dimensions*: securing agreement on key dimensions, such as home-style, number of rooms, etc.
2. *Task specialization*: where one partner has specific interests and expertise, such as in kitchen layout, the other will be willing to leave decisions of that kind to that partner.
3. *Concessions based on preference differences*: one partner is willing to concede on some aspect of the home for which the other has strong views, such as four bedrooms instead of three.

'Thus, each spouse follows his or her own decision strategy (enhancing one's own utility) while attempting to minimize conflict, which often involves groping through a recursive, discontinuous process'. Park's research 'appeared to support this conceptualization', although he warned against generalizing freely because, for instance, 'the subjects were essentially self-selected and their educational distribution was not representative of the larger population'.[53]

Earlier, Sheth[54] had adopted March and Simon's inter-conflict strategy in proposing four modes of resolving family conflict in buying situations: problem solving, bargaining, persuasion, and politics. He contended that conflicts arise because of differences in buying objectives and also different perceptions about decision alternatives.

To avoid conflict and achieve desirable decisions in buying for family needs often demands considerable tact and subtlety. Spiro[55] identified five distinct ways in which partners applied influence when attempting to get agreement to buy certain products:

1. *The low-level influencers* (60 per cent of sample) only infrequently attempted to influence their partners, but when attempts were made, these were well organized and tended to be supported by detailed information.
2. *Subtle influencers* (20 per cent) also rely on an expert influence approach but reinforce this by adding a 'reward/referent' element, based on one partner's offering an inducement to the other or by appealing to their feelings for one another.
3. *Emotional influences* (7 per cent) were found to be in a small but distinctive group which made full use of a range of emotional ploys, such as tears, anger or sullenness, plus the reward/referent strategies of group 2.
4. *Combination influencers* (10 per cent) used a variety of approaches, almost as the mood took them.
5. *Heavy influencers* (7 per cent) made frequent use of each of the influence strategies.

Spiro's research revealed that there was a tendency for both partners to use the same type of influence strategy; however, if one spouse did not adopt an influence strategy in order to minimize or eradicate disagreements, the other was also unlikely to do so. It is piquant that when spouses were asked to describe the influence ploys used by their partners during the decision-making process, neither men nor women could accurately identify them. Although partners may not have been able to describe precisely the strategies used by their spouses, Spiro reported that no less than 88 per cent of the married couples surveyed admitted that they had encountered disagreements when considering purchases, and that to avoid conflict they had been obliged to adopt some type of influencing stratagem.

Douglas[56] has drawn attention to the fact that, over recent years, research into family decision-making 'appears to have shifted emphasis from the study of the roles played by different family members in various family decisions to a focus on the decision-making process itself, and the strategies used by the families to arrive at decisions'. With this reorientation in mind, she suggested that research should be concerned with:

1. Decision-making processes across the many highly complex range of decisions, which are often interrelated, rather than concentrating on one isolated decision.
2. The influence of third parties on partners' family decisions should be acknowledged, by extending, for instance, research to children, sales personnel, etc.
3. Increased attention should be paid to environmental influences, such as time pressures, mood, fatigue, in-store displays, and accompanying family members.
4. Increased use of 'in situ' research techniques like observation or 'collection of in-store protocols', in order to overcome the limitations of self-report, the potential reactivity of 'laboratory' research, and the influence of environmental variables.

8.13 CHILDREN'S INFLUENCE ON HOUSEHOLD PURCHASES

Clearly, children influence many buying decisions, but the research at present available does not provide adequate data for general guidelines for marketing strategies. Increasingly, modern society is child oriented, and in this trend Britain seems to have accepted some of the North American cultural norms. Apart from toys and other products obviously designed for children's consumption, there are, it would appear, many household goods that are influenced by the behaviour of children.

A US market research firm found that advertisers who wished to promote home computers to families should concentrate on the 12–14 age-group, because they had special interest in and knowledge of this type of equipment. Another survey highlighted the importance of children in family decisions to subscribe to cable television services. Fast-food outlets, such as the McDonalds' hamburger chain, breakfast cereal makers like Kelloggs, or Pepsi-cola drink suppliers, are all keenly aware of the power of children in persuading their parents and others to patronize their branded products. From a tender age, children recognize and demand favoured brands of confectionery like Mars bars, and can readily recall advertising jingles. Children tend to be fairly heavy television viewers, so they are natural targets for promoting recreational facilities for the family, including, perhaps, visits to Disneyland.

Research aimed at *age group* behaviour is needed; children display very considerable differences in interests and persuasive tactics over the years, and it would be invidious to approach this problem in a very general way. Social trends indicate that children are being given greater freedom by their parents in the type of clothing they wear; the mass media have exposed children from an early age to the fashion styles of 'pop' stars and other entertainers. Parents may find that their authority is being challenged because of the pressures exerted on their children from these trendsetters in the entertainment world.

Peter Cooper has argued that there is a 'shift in opinion-leading in the direction of Youth. Correspondingly, the skills and sagacity of age have tended to lose their status'.[57] He viewed 'teenage' and parental values as now existing 'on the basis of equal power and validity, thus being a source of some confusion for the orientation of the individual'. In some product fields, e.g., fashion clothing, pop records, or cosmetics, the teenage culture has led to new market segments being opened where novelty, excitement and self-expression are dominant influences. In diluted form, some of these products may reach the adult market and become integrated into general patterns of consumption. 'The probable changes in the future are that the new Cults (Teenage) will be taken as reference points for adult opinion, rather than vice versa as in the past'.

As discussed in Sec. 8.5, the 'trickle-down' theory of product acccceptance seems, in many cases, to be supplanted by a new theory of product assimilation, starting with the younger age-groups and gradually moving upwards to achieve more general acceptability. There is evidence of this phenomenon in casual wear like colourful, patterned anoraks, ski-pants, and T-shirts; these uninhibited fashion styles reflect, perhaps, what has been termed the 'classless society' of the present times.

In the late 1960s, Berey and Pollay researched the influence role of children in family decision-making.[58] They hypothesized as follows:

1. The more assertive a child is, the more likely will the mother be to purchase the child's favourite brand of breakfast cereal.
2. The more child-centred the mother, the more likely she will be to purchase the child's favourite brand of breakfast cereal.

The results, in fact, showed that although the child-centredness of the mother may increase her receptivity to being influenced by the child as 'far as cereals were concerned', there is apparently the stronger effect of the mother being in strong disagreement with the child over what brands to purchase. Highly child-centred mothers displayed a tendency to buy their children's favourite cereal less frequently. The mother acts as a 'gatekeeper' who may reject some marketing communications that are ostensibly aimed at the child consumer. The researchers commented:

> Given that the mother is not only a purchasing agent for the child but also an agent who superimposes her preferences over those of the child, it is clear that a lot of advertising would be well directed at the mother, even if the mother is not a consumer of the product. Without such

advertising, the child's influence attempts may be largely ignored if the mother thinks the brand desired is an inferior food.[58]

Berey and Pollay's research findings require careful interpretation, because their sample, carried out in the USA, was limited to 48 children in the age range 8–11 years who were at a private school in an urban community. In addition, 'child-centredness' should be clearly defined.

Two other US researchers studied the influence of three variables on children's purchase influence attempts and parental yielding: demographics, parent–child interaction, and mother's mass media habits.[59] Mothers were asked to indicate the frequency of their child's attempts at influencing buying for 22 products over 5 categories: 'relevant foods' (breakfast cereals, soft drinks, etc.); 'less relevant foods' (bread, coffee, pet food); 'durables for child's use' (toys, clothing, bicycle, camera, etc.); 'notion toiletries' (toothpaste, bath soap, shampoo, aspirin); and 'other products' (laundry soap, automobile, gasoline brand, etc.). All products were extensively advertised but there were considerable variations in price, frequency of purchase, and relevance to the child's personal needs.

It was found that children frequently attempted to influence food purchases, 'but these attempts decreased with age'. There were marked attempts to influence the purchase of durables; young children (5–7 years old) frequently attempted to influence their mothers for games and toys, older children (11–12 years old) frequently sought to influence the buying of clothing and record albums. In general, across the four main categories of products studied, attempts by children to influence purchase seemed to decline with age. The researchers noted that 'influence attempts may be part of a more general parent–child conflict'. Personality characteristics appeared to play their part: 'furthermore, mothers who restrict viewing [of television] are not likely to yield to purchase influence attempts' by their children.

Finally, the family is instrumental in the socialization of its young members and in influencing their patterns of consumption. It is within the family environment that children first become aware of the means of satisfying their basic needs for food, drink, warmth and so on. In this process of seeking gratification, young children became conscious of choice; they are often invited by their parents and others to choose between one or more types of food, confectionery, or entertainment. They gather clues concerning family norms and traditions, which may influence their selection, perhaps to please someone for whom they have a special regard. Parents may encourage their children to develop selectivity in buying, for example, by patronizing certain stores which, like the John Lewis Partnership or Marks and Spencer, have established enviable trading reputations. Such parental influence will, inevitably, decline as children grow up and begin to exercise their own preferences, influenced, probably, by their peers and popular entertainers.

In their early years, children learn quickly about modes of consumption in their families and, until they socialize more widely, may well believe that these consumption patterns are universal. Gradually they accumulate new consumer experiences through visits to other relatives, friends, and during holidays, perhaps overseas. The mass media, particularly television, are of prime importance in alerting children to new types and brands of products, as well as presenting inviting images of new life-styles, with projected promises of social success associated with buying, for instance, a branded mouthwash. This learning process may be affected by family discussions about the practicalities of buying certain kinds of advertised products and services, and although some degree of argument may be expected, the family plays a powerful mediating role in such circumstances. An element of 'bargaining' or 'trading' may characterize these interchanges.

Children's buying behaviour may be projected as part of an important socializing process that starts at a very early age and continues throughout their formative years, influenced by the flow of communication existing between parents and children in a household; further research is recommended.[60]

8.14 TEENAGE SPENDING PATTERNS

One of the largest and most significant social changes that have affected young people in the UK since the late 1950s has been the growth in education, especially in the tertiary institutions. In 1988/89 there were nearly 580 000 full-time UK students in universities and public sector higher education establishments. Another factor is the high rate of teenage unemployment, and the sad fact that unemployed teenagers are much more likely than employed teenagers to have no formal academic qualifications.

These factors have inevitably restricted the economic and social freedom that youngsters generally are restive to achieve. They are, as the JWT survey on leisure noted, spurred to independence by their peers and demand freedom to follow their own leisure-time interests early in their teens.[40] Up to then, they have, willingly or otherwise, joined in the family activities such as country walking, visiting relatives, or trips to the seaside.

Richard Eassie of Mintel considers that from the marketing viewpoint, the term 'teenager' is not very helpful; the 13 year old is vastly different from the 19 year old.[61] Some teenagers will challenge, deliberately or otherwise, family norms by adopting exotic or bizarre styles of clothing, and seek to associate themselves, at least vicariously, with various unconventional sub-cultures. The adolescent years can be a 'troublesome period'; in addition to physical changes, psychological, social and cultural adjustments have to be made both by young people themselves and by their families.

It is almost quixotic, that because of the falling numbers of the under-25s, Levi Strauss, whose jeans were to be seen everywhere as virtually a symbol of adolescent rebellion, have had to turn their attention to other market segments in order to ensure continuity of sales. In common with UK demographic trends, US teenagers are fewer on the ground and 15–24-year-old males will have dropped from 20.2 million (1985) to 17.4 million (1995). Levi Strauss have targeted the over-25 age group, offering a new-style of jeans—rather smarter and more liberally cut than those sold to teenagers—in an endeavour to offset declining demand from the segment that has been the mainstay of their business since the 1950s.[62]

Many teenagers have part-time jobs, but up to the age of 14 or so pocket money is the major source of income, supplemented by birthday and other presents; within the teenage population as a whole, two-thirds of income derives from earnings. Although teenagers generally do not have large incomes, if they are living at home with their parents they will enjoy a fairly high level of discretionary spending power, certainly far more than if they were still being educated. This discretionary income will enable them to follow fashion, hobby interests, and sports activities relatively freely. Later, as they save up to set up their own homes, savings schemes will be carefully assessed, and advice may be sought from parents and friends. The handling of financial affairs becomes increasingly critical for young people: banks and building societies have become far more active in attracting funds from teenagers and particularly in offering banking facilities to students. Since banking accounts are rarely transferred, the policy of 'catch 'em young' is a sound common-sense strategy.

Young women spend considerable sums on cosmetics and clothing. As 70 per cent of teenagers' mothers are in the 35–44 age-group, marketers should devote special attention to the buying preferences and general behavioural characteristics of this important yet minor (16 per cent) sector of the adult female population. Although teenagers may initiate the idea of buying appliances (e.g., videos, home computers, or expensive items of clothing), it is often the parent who has the last word, and such purchases may have to satisfy both generations.[61] As in most things, expectations rise, and the younger generation's innate optimism may often be at variance with the competing needs of the family.

It was noted earlier that there will be a sharp decline in the numbers of teenagers and 20 year olds in the UK population: 15–19 year olds will fall from 6.8 per cent (1990) to 6.1 per cent of the population by the end of the century; the numbers of 20 year olds will show an even greater fall, from about 16 per cent to around 12 per cent. Manufacturers and retailers catering specifically for these market segments in clothing, confectionery, records, and sports activities, face strong challenges from these demographic trends (see Chapter 6).

8.15 SUMMARY

Modern society is a complex system of interrelated social groups; these range from family circles, regional, national, and even international groupings of people. Groups may be primary or secondary, also formal and informal. Reference groups are important in individual and social behaviour; there may be membership groups and aspirant groups. Opinion leadership springs from reference group theory; opinion leaders may be monomorphic or polymorphic. The two-step flow of communication was originated by Katz and Lazarsfeld: this 'trickle-down' theory has been challenged by an alternative model: 'trickle-across'.

The family is a unique sub-cultural group in society which has profound psychological social, cultural, and economic influences. Various types of households have been identified by researchers: nuclear family, extended family, family of orientation or origin, and family of procreation or marriage. Significant demographic, cultural, and social changes have occurred in the UK which have affected the nature of households. Many of these factors, such as divorce and single-parent households, are interrelated.

Marriage generally leads to setting up a new home: this affects consumption habits over many products and services.

Family life-cycle stages generate changes in demand for various products and services; several models of family life stages have been devised.

Family decision-making assigns roles to specific members of a family; some conflict may be experienced, particularly with modern attitudes towards child behaviour. Child-orientation may encourage freer spending, particularly by working wives. Teenage spending patterns will be affected by further education and demographic trends.

REFERENCES

1. Thouless, R. H., *General and Social Psychology*, University Tutorial Press, London, 1967.
2. Stafford, James E., 'Effects of group influences on consumer brand preferences', *Journal of Marketing Research*, February 1966.
3. Katona, George, *The Powerful Consumer*, McGraw-Hill, New York, 1960.
4. Brodbeck, M., 'Methodological individualism definition and reduction', *Philosophy of Science*, vol. 25, 1958.
5. Siegel, Alberta Engvall, and Sidney Siegel, 'Reference groups, membership groups and attitude change', *Journal of Abnormal and Social Psychology*, vol. 55, 1957.
6. Hyman, Herbert H., 'The psychology of status', *Archives of Psychology*, no. 269, 1942.
7. Hyman, Herbert H., 'Reflections on reference groups', *Public Opinion Quarterly*, fall 1960.
8. Bourne, Francis S., 'Group influence in marketing and public relations', in: *Some Applications of Behavioural Research*, Rensis Likert and Samuel P. Hayes Jnr (eds), UNESCO, New York, 1959.
9. Venkatesan, M., 'Experimental study of consumer behaviour conformity and independence', *Journal of Marketing Research*, vol. 3, November 1966.

10. Bearden, William O., and Michael J. Etzel, 'Reference group influence on product and brand purchase decisions', *Journal of Consumer Research*, vol. 9, September 1982.
11. Lazarsfeld, Paul F., Bernard Berelson, and Hazel Gaudet, *The People's Choice*, Colombia University Press, New York, 1948.
12. Rogers, E. M., *Diffusion of Innovations*, Free Press, New York, 1962.
13. Katz, Elihu, and Paul Lazarsfeld, *Personal Influence*, Free Press, New York, 1955.
14. Marcus, A. S., and R. A. Bauer, 'Yes: there are generalised opinion leaders', *Public Opinion Quarterly*, vol. 28, winter 1964.
15. Marsh, Catherine, and John O'Brien, 'Opinion bandwagons in attitudes towards the Common Market', *Journal of the Market Research Society*, vol. 31, no. 3, July 1989.
16. Merton, R. K., *Social Theory and Social Structure*, Free Press, New York, 1957.
17. King, Charles W., 'Fashion adoption: a rebuttal to the "trickle-down" theory', *Towards Scientific Marketing*, Stephen A. Greyser (ed.), American Marketing Association, Chicago, 1964.
18. Sheth, Jagdish N., 'A review of buyer behaviour', *Management Science*, vol. 13, no. 12, August 1967.
19. Weimann, Gabriel, 'The influentials: back to the concept of opinion leaders?', *Public Opinion Quarterly*, vol. 55, pp. 267–79, 1991.
20. Perkin, Harold, *The Origins of Modern English Society 1780–1880*, Routledge and Kegan Paul, London, 1969.
21. Moreno, J. L. (ed.), *Sociometry and Science of Man*, New York, 1956.
22. Menzel, H., and E. Katz, 'Social relations and innovation in the medical profession: the epidemiology of a new drug'. *Public Opinion Quarterly*, winter 1955–6.
23. Corey, Lawrence G., 'People who claim to be opinion leaders: identifying their characteristics by self-report', *Journal of Marketing*, vol. 35, October 1971.
24. Fenton, James S., and Thomas R. Leggett, 'A new way to find opinion leaders', *Journal of Advertising Research*, vol. 11, no. 2, April 1971.
25. Coleman, Richard P., 'The continuing significance of social class to marketing', *Journal of Consumer Research*, vol. 10, December 1983.
26. Black, Joan S., 'Opinion leaders: is anyone following?', *Public Opinion Quarterly*, vol. 46, no. 2, summer 1982.
27. Nystrom, P., *Economics of Fashion*, Ronald Press, New York, 1928.
28. Carman, J., 'The fate of fashion cycles in our modern society', in: *Science, Technology and Marketing*, R. Haas (ed.), AMA Conference Proceedings, 1966.
29. McCracken, Grant, 'Culture and consumption: a theoretical account of the structure and movement of the cultural meaning of consumer goods', *Journal of Consumer Research*, vol. 13, June 1981.
30. Midgley, D. F., 'Innovation in the male fashion market, the parallel diffusion hypothesis', ESOMAR Fashion Research and Marketing, December 1974.
31. Asch, Solomon E., *Social Psychology*, Prentice-Hall, Englewood Cliffs, New Jersey, 1965.
32. Veblen, Thorstein, *The Theory of the Leisure Class*, Macmillan, New York, 1899.
33. Rose, Richard, 'Oceans of affluence spotted with islands of poverty', *Daily Telegraph*, 2 April 1984.
34. J. Walter Thompson Co. Ltd, 'The new housewife', J. Walter Thompson, London, 1968.
35. J. Walter Thompson Co. Ltd., 'Consumer change in the mid-70s', J. Walter Thompson, London, 1976.
36. Joyce, Timothy, 'The new housewife: a comprehensive social study', ESOMAR Congress, Vienna, 1967.
37. Coleman, Richard P., 'Attitudes toward neighbourhoods: how Americans want to live', Working Paper no. 49, Joint Center for Urban Studies of Massachusetts Institute of Technology and Harvard University, 1977.
38. Young, Michael, and Peter Willmott, *Family and Kinship in East London*, Penguin, London, 1957.
39. Bott, Elizabeth, *Family and Social Network: Roles, Norms and External Relationships in Ordinary Urban Families*, Tavistock, London, 1957.
40. J. Walter Thompson Co. Ltd., 'Going out: how people spend their leisure', Linda Fuller (ed.), J. Walter Thompson, London, 1982.
41. Leadbeater, Charles, 'Dancing to a maturer measure', *Financial Times*, 4 January 1990.
42. Hill, Reuben, 'Patterns of decision-making and the accumulation of family assets', in *Household Decision-Making*, Nelson N. Foote (ed.), New York University Press, 1961.

43. Lansing, J. B., and J. N. Morgan, 'Consumer finances over the life cycle', in: *Consumer Behaviour*, vol. 11, L. H. Clark (ed.), New York University Press, 1955.

44. Wells, W. D. and G. Gubar, 'Life cycle concept in marketing research', *Journal of Marketing Research*, November 1966.

45. Murphy, Patrick E., and William A. Staples, 'A modernised family life cycle', *Journal of Consumer Research*, vol. 6, June 1979.

46. J. Walter Thompson Co. Ltd., 'Having people in: how women entertain at home', Linda Fuller (ed.) September 1981.

47. Wagner, Janet, and Sherman Hanna, 'The effectiveness of family life cycle variables in consumer expenditure research', *Journal of Consumer Research*, vol. 10, December 1983.

48. O'Brien, Sarah, and Rosemary Ford, 'Can we at least say goodbye to social class?', *Journal of the Market Research Society*, vol. 30, no. 3, July 1988.

49. Bales, R. E., 'The equilibrium problems in groups', in: *Working Papers in the Theory of Action*, T. Parsons *et al.* (eds), Free Press, New York, 1953.

50. Field J. G., 'The influence of household members on housewife purchases', Thomson Medals and Awards for Advertising Research, 1969, Thomson Organisation, London, November 1968.

51. Sampson, P., 'An examination of the concepts evoked by the suggestion of "other members of household" influence over housewife purchases', Thompson Gold Medal Awards for Advertising Research, 1968, Thompson Organisation, London, November 1968.

52. IPC Magazines, 'Alcoholic drink in the home: who buys what?' David Trown (ed.), IPC, London, 1981.

53. Park, C. Whan, 'Joint decisions in home purchasing: a muddling-through process', *Journal of Consumer Research*, vol. 9, September 1982.

54. Sheth, J. N., 'A theory of family buying decisions', in: Models of Buyer Behavior: Conceptual, Quantitative and Empirical, J. N. Sheth (ed.), Harper and Row, New York, 1974.

55. Spiro, Rosann L., 'Persuasion in family decision making', *Journal of Consumer Research*, vol. 9, March 1983.

56. Douglas, Susan P., 'Examining family decision-making processes', in: *Advances in Consumer Research*, R. P. Bagozzi (ed.), vol. 10, Association for Consumer Research, 1983.

57. Cooper, Peter, 'The decline in the status of houshold decision making', *British Journal of Marketing*, vol. 2, autumn 1968.

58. Berey, Lewis A., and Richard W. Pollay, 'The influencing role of the child in family decision making', *Journal of Marketing Research*, vol. 5, February 1968.

59. Ward, Scott and Daniel B. Wackman, 'Children's purchase/influence, attempts and parental yielding', *Journal of Marketing Research*, vol. 9, August 1972.

60. Moschis, George P., 'The role of family communication in consumer socialization of children and adolescents', *Journal of Consumer Research*, vol. 11, March 1985.

61. Eassie, Richard, 'Money at a mixed up age', *Campaign*, 25 February 1983.

62. Rawsthorn, Alice, 'Looking beyond the teenage market', *Financial Times*, 20 July 1989.

REVIEW AND DISCUSSION QUESTIONS

1. How does the extent of reference group influence on consumers vary according to characteristics of the reference group and the particular product or service in question?

2. Examine the problems involved in identifying opinion leaders and indicate the strategies that marketers can utilize to harness opinion leadership as a source of consumer influence.

3. In which ways do families make buying decisions differently from individuals? What are the marketing implications of these differences?

4. In the light of recent demographic changes in the UK, evaluate the use of the family life-cycle as a variable to segment markets.

5. Evaluate the importance of opinion leadership to the marketer of a new quality ultra-sonic

car alarm. What problems is she likely to encounter in isolating opinion leaders for this product and how might opinion leadership be incorporated into her marketing strategy?

6. Describe any three print or television advertisements which utilize the family life-cycle concept. Which particular life-cycle do they address and how are the products/services featured made relevant to the respective life-cycles?

MODELS OF BUYING BEHAVIOUR

CHAPTER NINE

CONSUMER BUYING BEHAVIOUR

9.1 INTRODUCTION

In Parts One and Two, discussion focused on personal and group aspects of behaviour. Study of the individual psychological factors has been extended into the environmental influences of culture, social class, and groups. As creatures of society, whose expectations are dynamic, human beings have acquired many sophisticated needs and are motivated in complex ways. In Part Four, some explanatory models of buying behaviour will be identified and explored. This chapter will be concerned with consumer buying behaviour models, and Chapter 10 will deal specifically with organizational buying behaviour.

9.2 FUNCTION OF MODELS

A model is an abstract conception of reality; it is a simplification of complex variables—'a blue print which shows the essential elements of a larger system' and 'which cannot be regarded as anything more than a rough approximation to a complicated reality'.[1]

A model represents, therefore, a theoretical construction of phenomena that are thought to be interrelated and significant in influencing the outcome of a specific situational problem; in this particular instance, the buying process. It is a useful framework and guide to researchers into marketing problems, such as the role of advertising in the overall marketing strategy. A model endeavours to clarify relationships between inputs into the buying situation—stimuli arising, for example, from advertising exposure or from the attractive styling of products—the mixed motivations which affect purchase decisions, and the resultant outcome or output (purchase or rejection of a product or service).

The traditional approach of economists to problems of pricing is to construct a theoretical model as a fundamental basis on which further studies including testing of hypotheses are extended. In marketing studies, the scientific approach of economic theorists has been adopted in attempts to obtain more reliable knowledge about buying behaviour. Models of buying behaviour, varying in complexity and orientation, have been developed since the 1940s.

Hague has observed: 'The businessman can hope to understand the situations facing him only if he can analyse them clearly and state them simply. Simplified representations of reality—models—are his only hope of drawing out what is essential and what is inessential to particular problems in a complex modern business world'.[2] He goes on to say that business problems are hardly ever purely economic, purely human, or purely technical, but a mixture of the three.

Theoretical approaches and business pragmatism may seem to be antipathetic, but, as is commonly observed, there is nothing so practical as a good theory. In everyday living, as Lunn points out, theories are used all the time: to prepare a meal, catch a train, secure a sale, or buy a new car.[3] These activities all entail some views about how things work. From past experience, some kind of theory has been developed; admittedly, this may not be 'spelled out', let alone put down in some formal equation, but there will probably be a set of constructs that can be called upon to help in solving particular problems. In developing a model, managers have to identify market variables and assess their impact and interrelationships. This process demands clear analytical thinking; it rejects ambiguity and subjectivity. Because markets are dynamic, models of buying behaviour need to be continuously reviewed and updated if they are to be useful in planning marketing strategies. A static conception of the world in which a business operates is obviously unrealistic and highly dangerous, particularly where demand conditions are prone to change. For example, new habits of consumption, rising expectations, more critical attitudes, changing customer profiles, new methods of distribution, and price competition have all contributed to the volatility of many markets, both consumer and organizational. Marketers should develop sensitivity to the changes affecting the consumption of the products and services they offer.

9.3 TWO BASIC FUNCTIONS OF CONSUMER BEHAVIOUR MODELS

From the introductory discussion, it will be apparent that models of buying behaviour have two basic uses for marketing managers:

1. They describe in simplified form the market parameters or characteristics affecting purchase of certain types of goods or serivces.
2. They allow predictions to be made of the likely outcomes of specific marketing strategies.

These dual objectives of description and prediction will involve quantitative and qualitative assessments, so that a fuller understanding of customers, both present and prospective, is achieved. The process of modelling brings the underlying assumptions about a market 'out into the open in the form of a structure': once this structure has been made explicit, 'it is then open to understanding, criticism and—most importantly—checking'.[4]

9.4 QUALITIES OF AN EFFECTIVE MODEL

In order to be useful, a market model should have the following qualities:[4]

1. *Relevance*: it must be as closely linked as possible to real marketing situations.
2. *Comprehensibility*: decision-makers cannot use models which are vague and poorly constructed.
3. *Validity*: within reasonable limits, the model should be as similar to the real world as possible; it should be verifiable. But how well any model is capable of validity reflecting real market conditions is by no means easily determined. Model building inevitably entails some degree of bias in the selection of and the emphasis given to certain variables.

These key criteria should guide in the design of models and avoid the trap of producing highly sophisticated structures that cannot be understood by management. Models are meant to aid decision-making, not to make it more difficult. Lunn feels that researchers have too readily developed models 'either in terms of mathematical equations or abstruse socio-psychological concepts, or both'; with the result that they cannot be communicated to those who are supposed to use them.[3] While a model should describe a market adequately, a degree of selectivity is advisable. Otherwise too many phenomena will be crowded in and only cause confusion.

9.5 TYPES OF MODELS

Micro-economic models

Various theoretical approaches have been adopted in the design and development of buying behaviour models. Earlier attempts have largely been derived from one discipline (e.g., economics). These *monadic models* were, in time, supplanted by more complex models which took account of research findings from psychology, sociology, and cultural anthropology as well as economics. These *multi-variable models* reflect what Lunn has termed the *eclectic approach*, which attempts to synthesize relevant knowledge from the various behavioural sciences.[5]

9.6 MONADIC MODELS OF BUYING BEHAVIOUR

Monadic models were often based on microeconomic theory, such as the classical principle of utility or satisfaction which asserts that a consumer acts rationally and with knowledge of all products of a type when buying quantities of these products. *Homo economicus* was held to be motivated in all activities by purely economic considerations: objectives in buying were theorized to be the pursuit of maximum overall satisfaction. This curious, completely rational 'economic man' fitted in neatly to the artificial environment in which, it was alleged, 'perfect competition' ensured that buying preferences could not be based on differentiation in the design or quality of specific products.

Such theories failed, of course, to recognize the complexity of buying behaviour, which is subject to so many influences other than those emanating from simplistic economic theory. Constraints of time, effort, and imperfect knowledge together with the seeking of emotional and social satisfactions are factors in real buying situations which should not be ignored (see Chapter 1). Subjective values and personal tastes may, for instance, overthrow the price elasticity of demand relationship which, stated simply, says that as price falls, demand tends to rise, and vice versa. If a small change of price results in a large change in demand or supply, then demand or supply respectively is said to be elastic. On the other hand, if a large change in price has only a slight effect on demand or supply, then demand or supply respectively is inelastic. But the theory fails to account for consumers often preferring to pay higher prices for branded goods, or for their willingness to assume that price is an indicator of quality. Furthermore, it is very difficult for shoppers to keep up to date with changing prices, particularly those of fast-moving consumer goods, and they may well continue to buy at a particular store even though some of its lines may be priced a little higher than elsewhere, provided that prices are perceived to be 'about right'. This approach is similar to a *trade-off model* which accepts that when consumers have a series of choices to make between different amounts of a set of attributes, they realize that they cannot achieve a theoretically ideal product combination, so a compromise is reached. By this realistic acceptance, consumers 'satisfize' rather than 'optimize'. The resultant buying behaviour is probably very close to real life in many cases; for instance, higher prices may be set against convenience of location, quality of service, car-parking facilities, and so on.

The psychoanalytic model

Another type of monadic model projects buying behaviour as irrational, as distinct from the rationally based microeconomic viewpoint. The *psychoanalytic model* was significantly influenced by Freudian concepts (see Chapter 4) which were developed by Dichter and others in motivation research techniques. Again, the reliance on one source of theoretical knowledge resulted in an unbalanced view of buying behaviour. Because human needs and motives are so complex (see Chapter 3) this limited approach cannot contain such sophisticated behaviour and is therefore seriously deficient.

Perceived risk model

Yet another monadic model of buying behaviour[6] is based on research undertaken at the Harvard Business School in the mid-1960s by Bauer[7] and Cox.[8] Consumption behaviour was theorized to depend upon an individual's subjective perception of the risk inherent in particular buying propositions. Bauer's concept of perceived risk stresses the subjective nature of perception (see Chapter 2). Different people will tend to view risk according to their personality, experience, etc. In other words, risk is relative, not absolute, and tolerance to risk will vary. Furthermore, an individual's perception of risk is unlikely to be constant; it will tend to vary according to the nature of the problem, situation, product, or service and will be affected by a variety of factors, such as the economic, political and social environment. Bauer hypothesized that consumers adopt risk-reducing strategies when they buy only at well-known stores or restrict their purchases to branded products.[7] However, others may perceive risk at a lower level or be more willing to accept it, so they may, for instance, shop in cut-price stores or buy unbranded goods. (Also see Chapter 11.)

Cox theorized that risk is a function of two elements: uncertainty and consequences.[8] The former relates to the buying goals; these may involve a choice between a luxury product for personal use (jewellery) and a functional product (a carpet). The latter refers to the likelihood that a given product or service will satisfy expectations. A consumer will weigh up carefully the risks involved in purchasing particular products or brands and, according to Cox, select the one that minimizes perceived risk. Of course, as Sternthal and Craig point out, some people may be risk seekers and others risk averters, so precise measurement is not feasible.[6]

In general, risk may be viewed[9,10] by consumers as having several elements or aspects affecting their buying decisions; these can be financial, performance, physical, psychological, social, and time-loss. Different sets or combinations of these elements are likely to be present in specific situations, and decisions will be affected by personal assessments of the total risk involved. For example, psychological risk may be perceived because a product or brand might conceivably be inconsistent with the prospective purchaser's self-image (see Chapter 4); physical risk may be perceived when considering the purchase of a particular kind of product, such as an electric hedge-cutter or a novel type of food-mixer; time-loss risk may arise from fears that a purchase might not live up to its expectations, perhaps resulting in annoying waste of time in taking, for instance, a home computer back to the suppliers for adjustment or replacement.

With some products (for example, matches) risk is slight while for others the uncertainty and consequences are likely to be the same for the various alternatives considered, for example, cars of a certain class; this theory of buying behaviour thus appears to have restricted application.

At the same time, it gives valuable insight into an aspect of consumer behaviour, and has been included in more sophisticated models discussed later in this chapter.

Research into consumers' preferences for methods of reducing risk in buying was undertaken by Roseluis,[10] who mailed a questionnaire to 1400 housewives in a commuter suburb of Denver, Colorado; 472 effective responses were obtained. Several generalized risky buying situations were presented; in order to avoid bias, these were not related to specific products or methods of buying.

Attitudes towards various 'risk relievers' (i.e., ways of reducing perceived risk, such as being brand loyal or relying on guarantees) were measured on a five-point scale: almost always helpful; usually helpful; sometimes helpful; rarely helpful; almost never helpful. In all, methods of risk relief were selected for their representativeness, applicability to various methods of purchase, and applicability to kinds of products.

Respondents' perceptions of the kinds of loss they might suffer in risky buying situations were defined in the questionnaire as time loss, hazard loss, ego loss, and money loss.

It was found that buyers generally preferred some risk relievers to others, depending upon the kind of loss applicable. Time, ego, and money losses are countered by a 'reasonable variety' of risk relievers, whereas for hazard loss (products perceived as dangerous to health or safety when failure occurs), the choice among risk relievers is restricted: brand loyalty, major brand image, and government testing evoked clearly favourable responses.

In general, brand loyalty was viewed more favourably than all other risk relievers; the second favourite was major brand image. Other types of relievers, such as store image, free sample, word of mouth, or official testing, which generally attracted a 'neutral' or 'slightly favourable' response, could not be discriminated clearly in statistical tests. Likewise, endorsements, money-back guarantees, and private testing, which evoked 'slightly favourable' or 'neutral' responses, failed to reveal consistent patterns of differences as the result of Chi-square analysis. The least favoured strategy to reduce risk was to buy the most expensive model of a product.

As Bauer and other researchers have noted, risk relievers were influenced by personal perceptions which varied according to types of buyers.

Roseluis suggests that a seller should first determine the kind of risk perceived by the customers, and then design a mix of risk relievers suitable for particular kinds of buyers and types of loss. A creative approach to risk reduction would benefit both buyers and sellers.[10]

A fairly basic and commonsensical approach would be to ensure that consumers have ready access to information about the types and varieties of products and services on offer, through well-designed brochures and, of course, from sales staff who are sensitive to the anxieties which may be experienced in some buying situations. Also, the availability of efficient after-sales service and guarantees associated with products should help to reduce perceived levels of risk (see Sec. 2.8).

The 'black box' models

The so-called 'black box' model of buying behaviour (Fig. 9.1) is based on the psychological approach which projects the human being as the processor in a system with outputs (behaviour) that are the results of inputs. What exactly happens inside the 'black box' has been the subject of speculation, theory, and experiment for many years. This elementary model is a start, however, to more sophisticated study of the many variables in the decision process, as reflected in multi-variable models, which are discussed later

Subjective verbal models

These refer to relatively simple descriptions of a specific buying situation as viewed by individuals, who are encouraged to articulate their feelings and reactions to the various

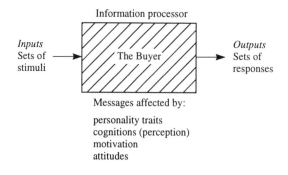

Fig. 9.1 The 'black box' model of buying behaviour

problems they encountered when buying a particular product or service. While this approach lacks the objectivity of formal research, it may nevertheless be useful in providing supporting data to that obtained by other methods of enquiry. Shoppers for example, could be asked to describe their typical approach to buying some items of groceries for their family. They would be invited to state the criteria they apply for judging the freshness of vegetables or bread, or the governing influences affecting the choice of brand of coffee or baked beans. The degree of brand awareness and loyalty may become evident in certain product markets; price sensitivity or hygiene attraction may be revealed as important factors. This micro analysis may be helpful to marketers in predicting the buying behaviour of the macro market.

Decision-process, or logical-flow models

These analyse the buying process as a series of sequential steps which a buyer takes. At each of these stages, problems may arise, and these should be noted by suppliers to a market so that a fuller understanding of the needs and aspirations of their customers is achieved. Marketing opportunities may be identified as the result of analysing buyers' behaviour at each stage of the decision process.

The steps in the buying programme of activities have been variously described. Kotler's[11] analysis and a comparative model devised by Engel, Kollat and Blackwell[12] are given in Fig. 9.2.

Although, as will be seen later, these types of models have certain deficiencies, they provide the basis for developing discussion of consumer buying behaviour, which will cover six aspects: *problem recognition*; *search*; *evaluation*; *decision processes*; *use behaviour*; and *post-purchase activities*.

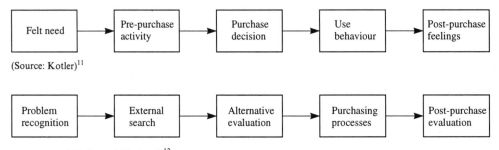

(Source: Kotler)[11]

(Source: Engel, Kollat and Blackwell)[12]

Fig. 9.2 Comparative decision-process models of buying behaviour

Problem recognition The starting-point is a felt need or recognition of a problem. Needs may also be described as wants, wishes, motives, or drives (see Chapter 3). These needs may be clearly defined, as in the case of requiring a meal, although the means of satisfying hunger may entail search for acceptable food or venues, whereas other needs involving, perhaps, rather vague notions about taking a holiday abroad, may not be so easily articulated or satisfied. Whatever the nature of the prospective purchase, buyers seek to satisfy *end-goals*; these may be relatively simple or, alternatively, fairly complex and even abstract, as with psychogenic needs (see Chapter 3). Further, end-goals may result in 'positive' behaviour, such as purchase of specific types or brands of products, or 'negative' or 'avoidance' behaviour because of strong aversions or fears related to the consumption of certain products or services like investment in stocks and shares, air travel, or food allergies.

Search Prospective purchasers search for ways of reducing the tension caused by an activated need; this pre-purchase activity is likely to involve them in varying degrees of search for products, services, and also brands, which hold out the promise of satisfying the aroused need. In some cases the search processes may be extensive and protracted, while in others, searches may be short, simple, and hardly apparent. Negotiating for a house or apartment, for example, will typically entail many months—even years—of exhaustive (and exhausting) visits to estate agents, viewing of properties, arrangement of mortgages, and so on, contrasted with the majority of the groceries obtained weekly at the local supermarket, or buying petrol at the filling station.

Wilkie and Dickson[13] reviewed research in the USA on consumer information search and found that a significant percentage of consumers showed very little evidence of information-seeking behaviour, often visiting only one store, considering only one brand, and consulting only a few information sources before durable goods; however, some consumers undertake considerable search before purchase; generally, there is a 'surprisingly low' reported information about search efforts. Wilkie and Dickson undertook a national study of US consumers' search behaviour related to major domestic refrigeration and laundry appliances; the overall results of this extensive research admittedly presented 'a rich and sometimes puzzling picture of consumer behaviour leading to the purchase of a major household appliance'. However, it was found that although many consumers may not be certain, at first, about their precise needs, almost all were able to indicate what models of appliances they would not buy. The researchers suggest that consumers are 'fairly to very certain about what they want. This certainly reduces the need to search for information to make the choice. It also dramatically reduces the number of appliance models that consumers will consider and shop for'.

Evaluation This stage of the buying process involves critical evaluation of the various products and services that have been discovered in the search procedures. Buyers of household goods, for instance, will carefully consider the attractions of new competitive brands, but might be reluctant to switch from their favoured brands, unless they are offered some special enticement, such as trial packs or significant price advantages. But brand loyalty may so strongly influence them that they are virtually resistant to change (see Chapter 2). These buyers have well-developed preferences—even prejudices—which form what has been termed the *evoked set*,[14] made up of a few brands of specific brands of products that have won approval through their performance over periods of time, sometimes many years. This repertoire of trusted brands simplifies search and facilitates buying decisions. Opinion leadership may influence brand choice, and even encourage 'experimental' buying of, for example, alternative brands of packaged coffee or detergents (see Chapter 8). The opening of a new supermarket may attract shoppers, motivated by curiosity and the zest for bargains, to make some trial purchases, perhaps including own branded products, which they will evaluate and compare

Choice criteria	Rating score
Styling/appearance	☐
Easy to use	☐
Value for money	☐
After-sales service	☐
Availability	☐

Fig. 9.3   Choice criteria rating evaluation

with their customary purchases. In this process of critical evaluation, consumers will tend to develop criteria which influence their selection; these *choice criteria* are likely to be affected by many factors, for example, their perceptions, and the other psychosocial and cultural phenomena outlined in Fig. 1.2 and also explored in some depth in later chapters. Essentially, choice criteria are concerned with expectations covering standards of performance, price levels, unique design features, availability ex-stock or delivery promises, etc. Attributes of competing brands will be assessed with varying degrees of rigour.

Some buyers may have significant professional knowledge of technical equipment like personal computers or sophisticated hi-fi systems, and are probably particularly stringent in their evaluations of these products. The components of what may be termed a battery of choice criteria related to a specific product will tend to attract different responses from individual consumers; some may give special emphasis to efficiency in use or the ready availability of after-sales service, while others may be primarily influenced by stylish design or competitive pricing. The relative importance of these product features could be assessed by adopting some well-tried marketing research techniques like rating scales. A representative sample of typical buyers would be asked to rate attributes of a specific product or brand on a five-point or ten-point scale, or any other intervals. The highest score would indicate, for example, 'very important'. From analyses of their responses, the relative values of buying criteria could be readily assessed. See Fig. 9.3 for a typical application covering a small domestic appliance, perhaps a washing machine or a vacuum cleaner.

Another method might use semantic differential scales which usually involve a number of five-point or seven-point scales that are bipolar with each extreme defined by an adjective or adjectival phrase such as new/old; usual/unusual; modern/old-fashioned; high price/low price. Alternatively, descriptive phrases are often effective in measuring the acceptability of a product or service. The 'image' that products acquire can be analysed, and the contribution made by individual features can be quantified. Competing brands can be subjected to the same evaluative criteria, and their profiles compared.

The methodology is remarkably flexible and has many applications: perceptions of supermarkets, cars, foreign business practices, and charitable organizations are a few examples. Figure 9.4 relates to competitive brand profiles of a fruit-flavoured soft drink. (Fuller discussion of scaling techniques occurs elsewhere.)[15]

Some prospective purchasers may (as indicated in Chapters 2 and 5) consult consumer guidance journals such as *Which?* presenting test results of a wide range of competing products and brands.

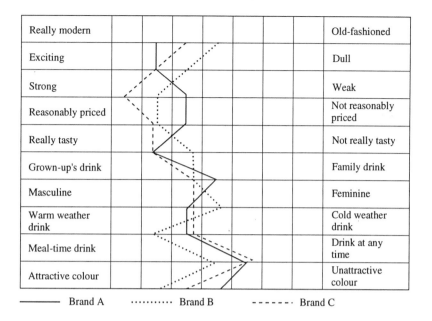

Really modern								Old-fashioned
Exciting								Dull
Strong								Weak
Reasonably priced								Not reasonably priced
Really tasty								Not really tasty
Grown-up's drink								Family drink
Masculine								Feminine
Warm weather drink								Cold weather drink
Meal-time drink								Drink at any time
Attractive colour								Unattractive colour

——— Brand A   ·········· Brand B   - - - - - - Brand C

Fig. 9.4 Brand profile fruit-flavoured soft drink[15]

The theory of consumer-involvement influences the search and evaluation processes of buying behaviour (see Chapter 4). Products have been classified as either high-involvement or low-involvement, according to their particular psychological significance to buyers. In the former case, consumers are more likely to spend considerable time and energy in collecting and evaluating information about these ego-involved products, while the latter, largely habitual, low-value purchases, will be decided on with much less effort. The significance of particular end-goals will, therefore, influence the search for acceptable alternative brands of products and services. On some occasions consumers may seek to 'optimize' and even be fortunate enough to find an 'ideal' solution to their consumption problems, but at other times they may be willing to follow a policy of 'satisfizing', which provides a reasonable level of satisfaction without all the expense and trouble of extended search.

Decision processes It will be apparent, therefore, that decisions to purchase are made up of several sub-decisions which may cover specific attributes and aspects of a product, such as price, method of payment, quantity, favoured brand, and place of purchase. These separate decisions require individual evaluations before the final decision to buy a specific brand of product is arrived at. Consumers' decision-making has been recognized as involving many facets of human behaviour, and entails search and evaluation of various levels of intensity and complexity. If every shopping expedition covering many types of consumer products were subject to elaborate decision-making, it would very soon become a very burdensome task. To avoid having to start virtually from zero, shoppers tend to adopt ready-made guides or decision-rules, particularly when buying routine supplies—'the necessities of life'. These useful guides, known as heuristics, simplify shopping; for example, 'Always buy X brand of toilet soap or Y brand of detergent', or, with the increasing awareness of adulterated foods, 'Avoid food products which contain certain additives regarded as harmful or undesirable'. Brand awareness reinforced by satisfactory product performance contributes vitally to the 'memory bank' of a shopper, who is able to buy confidently, and within acceptable levels of risk, favourite brands of chocolate, washing-up liquid, or cordials.

With other products, involving relatively large financial responsibilities and which tend to be bought infrequently, decisions are less likely to be substantially influenced by heuristics, although, of course, many types of durable products are branded and relatively expensive, for example, DIY power tools. The search processes for products of this nature are generally fairly extended before sufficient information is available to make a decision one way or the other. Perceived risk is a salient factor with purchases of, for instance, domestic heating systems, washing machines, or security installations. Family buying influences were discussed in Chapter 8, and were seen to affect decisions concerning the acquisition of many products and services, adding further to the complexity of such decisions.

Use behaviour This stage of the buying sequence is concerned with studying the behaviour of buyers who have purchased a particular product or adopted a specific service. The consumption habits of consumers warrant systematic research not only to establish their present needs but also to form some reliable guides as to their latent and future needs. Life is dynamic; people's wants grow and new levels of satisfaction are sought. Through monitoring the markets in which they operate, marketers may collect valuable information about consumption trends, competitors' activities, and distributors' policies which will aid their own decision-making. Eating habits, for instance, have changed over the past few years and have affected the consumption of certain kinds of foods; 'working wives' (see Chapters 6 and 8) have significantly influenced the sales, for example, of easily prepared foods, microwave ovens, and other products that help to lighten the burden of running a home. Buying motives may sometimes be complex, and marketers may make wrong assumptions about their market opportunities unless they keep closely in touch with those who actually buy and use their products.

Effective market segmentation strategies can be developed from marketing research investigations, which should make full use of the range of methodologies available.[15] These include personal interviewing, postal and telephone questionnaires, consumer panels, and observational techniques. New products, improved versions of existing products, and better packaging can result from systematic, well-devised inquiries into attitudes towards shopping, problems of running a home, use of various labour-saving devices, methods of decorating, and so on. Spray-on polishes, for example, were developed in this way. Group discussions, 'depth' interviews and other qualitative techniques are used successfully to identify and analyse consumers' perceptions, attitudes, motivations, brand preferences, and other influences on their consumption habits. Non-reactive research measures like observation may be used to study shoppers' typical behaviour in supermarkets and other stores; it was discovered, for instance, that a new style of labelling of a particular product had a negative effect on sales because shoppers were observed to experience difficulties in recognizing its new format. Sometimes 'hidden hardware' such as concealed cameras or tape recordings are adopted to study unobtrusively consumers' characteristic buying behaviour.

Post-purchase activities Post-purchase evaluation—the final stage of the decision process—will be critical for the successful long-term marketing strategies of suppliers. Unless customers feel satisfied about the particular product that they bought in expectancy of receiving certain benefits, they will be reluctant to buy the same brand again. This stage of the buying programme underlines the necessity, for example, of adequate after-sales servicing arrangements for domestic equipment, motor cars, lawnmowers, and many other products on which buyers tend to rely heavily for their comfortable and efficient style of living. Festinger's theory of cognitive dissonance (see Chapter 2) appears to have particular relevance to this final stage of buying behaviour.

There will be opportunities for marketers to reassure customers, and to make their decision-making as free from worry as possible. Package holidays, guaranteed after-sales service, reliability and durability of products established by popular usage, and reputation of the supplying organization are all factors contributing decisively to the success of products and services which involve customers in deliberate and anxious evaluation before committing themselves.

Assessment of logical-flow buying models

While the various sequences outlined in these models are generally acceptable, particularly, perhaps, because their elements endorse practical experience in buying many goods and services, very considerable elaboration is required before they can be of real value in actual marketing situations. The commentaries for each of the six stages have attempted to give insight and guidance in considering the issues related to these steps. The sequential approach tends to be an oversimplification of the behavioural influences involved in buying, and a more comprehensive approach to explaining consumer behaviour is clearly desirable. Further, the decision-process models do not have the support of substantial validation; no single decision process has applicability across all product markets; individual brands of products may be approached very differently. The rate of movement through the stages is not likely to be the same for all types of products and services. Some purchases, probably those of low cost with a strong element of routine buying (such as sugar, matches, tea, or cocoa) are unlikely to entail a great deal of deliberation every time they are bought. Marketers of frequently purchased consumer goods attempt to establish brand recognition and loyalty through extensive promotional campaigns. Once brand loyalty has been achieved, shoppers tend to pass almost automatically through the early stages of the decision without making conscious evaluations every time they wish to buy these types of products.

From preceding chapters and also the commentaries in this chapter, the complex nature of buying influences has been fully recognized: simplistic assumptions should be discarded. Social and cultural changes have far-reaching effects on people's patterns of consumption; the impact of harsher economic conditions encourages increased price sensitivity; new concerns over health and safety may trigger off legislation and result in more stringent expectations from consumers. Regular marketing research should be used by manufacturers and distributors to ensure that their products and services are acceptable to those who buy them.

In the specialized field of advertising research, logical-flow models have been popular techniques used to explain the influence and effectiveness of media publicity. In Chapter 13, several of these models are discussed, but particular mention will be given here to a model of customer behaviour developed by Du Pont[16] during their investigations into the effects of advertising. Their model (shown in Fig. 9.5) involved an explicit analysis of the elements in the purchasing behaviour of prospective customers and the logical relationships existing among those elements. Du Pont researchers identified the series of steps which they considered were taken by 'a hypothetical group of customers'. The model was also adopted as a useful approach for researching the ways in which advertising *might* affect the consumer's behaviour. An extensive field experiment was then conducted to determine how advertising affected behaviour at each stage in the customer decision process. As a result of this research programme, Du Pont developed a multiple regression equation as a tentative guide to the profitable allocation of advertising expenditure.

Classic research in the area of advertising effectiveness utilizing elaborate statistical models was undertaken by Palda, who researched the influence of advertising on the sales of Lydia Pinkham's Vegetable Compound over the period 1908 to 1960.[17] Because of certain unique features—e.g., this product had no close substitutes and the company consistently spent between 40 and 60 per cent of its sales revenue on advertising—Palda was able to indicate the value of certain equations in measuring the carry-over effects of Pinkham's advertising.

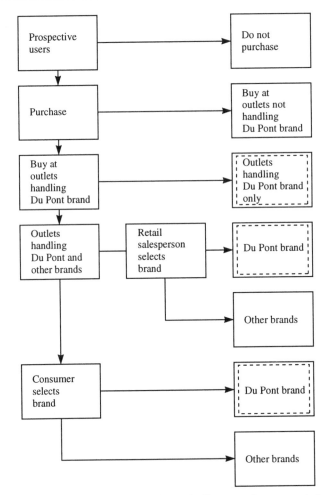

Fig. 9.5 E. I. Du Pont de Nemours and Co. Inc. schematic diagram of customer behaviour model

Obviously, the unusual marketing situation enjoyed by Pinkham's product makes this research of limited general usefulness, although the systematic method of inquiring into and identifying buying influences such as advertising illustrates the development of marketing theory and its applications.

Formalizing a model of buying behaviour by setting it down in equation form would be the ultimate ambition of marketers. The difficulty lies in obtaining reliable data from which to construct such an equation, and of being reasonably confident that it includes an adequate expression of *all* the factors in a particular buying situation. Equations tend to have an air of finality that may be misleading. Considerable research should be undertaken over a period of time considered to be long enough to give sound knowledge of market behaviour affecting specific products. Any equations found as the results of this objective programme of research should then be subjected to further testing and validation.

9.7 MULTI-VARIABLE MODELS OF BUYING BEHAVIOUR

These more comprehensive models endeavour to formalize the multiple influences that affect purchase decisions and to show the extent of their interaction. The consumer is typified as a problem-solver aroused by some stimuli who has to cope with information and inputs from a variety of sources. Information is processed; economic, socio-cultural, and psychological influences are evaluated; and the result leads to purchase—immediate or postponed—or to rejection of a particular product or brand of product.

Since the 1950s many theories have been advanced as explanations of consumer behaviour. Sheth has remarked: 'The existing variety of formulations resembles the variety of responses of seven blind men touching different parts of an elephant and making inferences about the animal which necessarily differ from, and occasionally contradict, one another'.[18] He recommends concentration on the individual buyer's problem-solving processes which include psychological and environmental factors. This view is also taken by Robert D. Buzzell: 'Since prediction of market behaviour is the fundamental technical problem in model-building, it seems likely that applications of behavioural science concepts and findings are the most fruitful avenue for improvement in the future'.[16]

Well-known theoretical models of consumer buying behaviour have been produced by Howard and Ostlund; Engel, Kollat, and Blackwell; Nicosia; and Andreasan. These theoretical explanations of buying behaviour will be surveyed and an appreciation given of their general applicability.

The Howard–Ostlund model

In 1963, John Howard of Columbia University developed a comprehensive model of buying behaviour;[19] this was expanded and refined by Howard and Sheth in 1969,[14] and further defined by Howard and Ostlund in 1973, when it claimed to have greater predictive capability than the earlier versions.[20] It is also claimed to be applicable to industrial and institutional as well as consumer behaviour. The model (see Fig. 9.6) is comprehensive, complex, and not easy to describe or understand.

McCracken[21] has somewhat sardonically observed that: 'Every consumer behaviour textbook offers an elaborate diagram filled with boxes and arrows . . . resembling nothing so much as the wiring instructions for an unusually complicated piece of electronic technology'. There is certainly a lot of truth in this rather acerbic observation, but it will, nevertheless, be useful to examine the various elements of Howard's model which made a pioneering contribution to the development of consumer behaviour studies.

The exogenous variables include the institutional environment, societal environment, and personal characteristics (shown at the top of the diagram). According to the nature of purchases, information from institutional and societal sources together with personality factors may influence buying decisions, as for example, in house buying, where estate agents, banks, building societies, and personal and family preferences are likely to be involved to varying degrees.

Information processing then takes place; this is likely to involve perceptual bias (see Chapter 2). Complete, objective evaluation of market sources of supply is most unlikely, and this is recognized in the model by, for example, 'time pressure' which restricts search.

The next stage of the model is concerned with the cognitive and purchase processes; this starts with motives, which are characterized by content and intensity. The former refers to the goals which the buyer is trying to attain; the latter relates to the relative importance of each goal. Motives are influenced by personality, the societal environment, and by information; in turn, a buyer's motives influence personal and situational attitudes (i.e., those belonging to others who are significant in the buying process). Personal and situational attitudes and brand comprehension are also affected by information recalled.

After all these activities, the intention to buy may follow. When a purchase has taken place, reinforcement may occur if buying expectations have been fulfilled, and so confidence is built in a particular brand of product; repeat purchase is then likely.

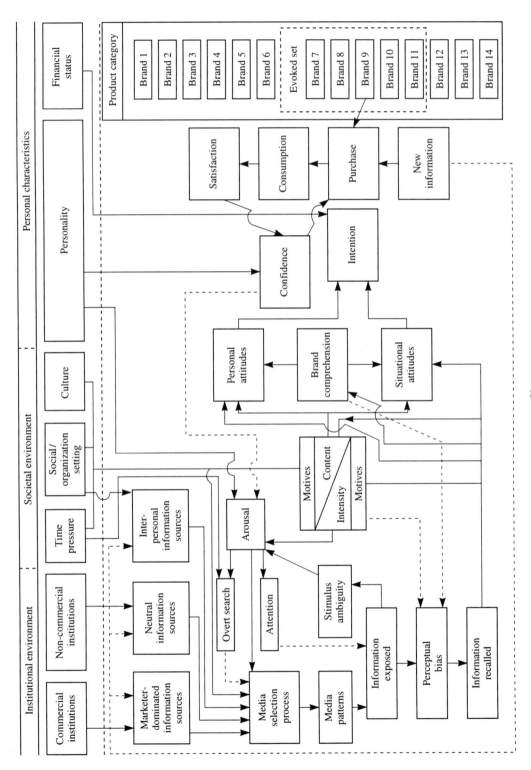

Fig. 9.6 The Howard–Ostlund model (*Source:* Howard and Ostlund)[20]

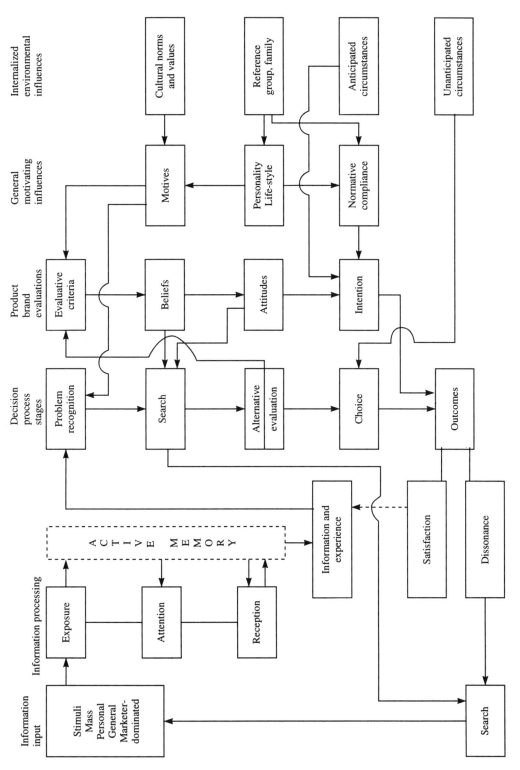

Fig. 9.7 The Engel–Kollat–Blackwell model (*Source*: Engel *et al.*)[22]

Although (as noted earlier) this is a very comprehensive model, it is not easy to follow, and this is made more difficult because variables are of two types: content variables, which deal with *what* the buyer thinks (brand comprehension, personal and situational attitudes, intention and confidence), and structural variables which deal with *how* the buyer thinks (e.g., media selection process and perceptual bias). Although, as Sternthal and Craig comment, content variables may be measured directly, structural variables require inferences to be made from observation and from questionnaires.[6] They are critical of Howard and Ostlund in their admission that securing such adequate measures might be considered as a desirable goal rather than an achievement.

The Engel–Kollat–Blackwell model

This comprehensive model of buying behaviour originated in 1968, and was revised in 1973 and 1978[22] (see Fig. 9.7). The core of this model is a five-stage decision process which starts with problem recognition, followed by a search for information so that the problem can be dealt with satisfactorily. Sources of knowledge, internal and external, are used to generate alternative solutions from which a choice is made, resulting in satisfaction or dissonance.

Information input depends on stimuli from the mass media, personal contacts, and general market sources plus 'active memory', or store of knowledge gained from past searches and experience.

This model also recognizes 'general motivating influences', such as personality and life-style, which affect the decision process. In addition there are 'internalized environmental influences', such as cultural norms and values, and group influence. Also 'unanticipated circumstances' have a direct bearing on the selection process.

Although the Engel–Kollat–Blackwell model presents a very helpful projection of consumer buying behaviour, it is not, in the view of Sternthal and Craig,[6] an adequate theory because it does not specify the preconditions under which certain outcomes will emerge. 'Strategists are much more concerned with knowing whether the outcome under certain conditions will be positive or negative than knowing that there is a strategy-outcome relationship'.[6]

The Nicosia model

This model, originated by Francesco Nicosia, is based on the technique of computer flow charting with feedback loops.[28] Nicosia believed that simulation techniques are effective in explaining 'in greater depth the structure of a consumer decision process', and are useful in predicting consumer behaviour.

Lunn states that Nicosia must be regarded as one of the leading figures in the eclectic approach to model building.[5] 'A distinctive feature of Nicosia's approach is the shift of emphasis away from the purchasing act itself, and towards the decision processes which both precede and follow this act'.

Briefly, Nicosia identified four basic 'fields' in his flow chart; these are shown in Fig. 9.8. It is assumed that neither the firm nor the consumer has had any previous experience directly related to a specific product or brand; the starting-point is truly zero. Each of the four 'building blocks or fields' should be viewed, according to Nicosia, 'As a subprogram of the overall computer program' throughout which 'a number of invariant cognitive and other psychological activities' (e.g., physical and cognitive perception, selective exposure) take effect.

Field one covers the flow of a message from its origin (the firm advertising a product) to the ultimate reception and 'internalization' of the message by the consumer. This field of activity has two subdivisions: subfield one, which includes the attributes of the company and its products, media characteristics, target audience, etc., and subfield two, which is concerned with environmental factors, personality characteristics, and cognitive factors affecting the reception

FIELD ONE: From the source of a message to the consumer's attitude

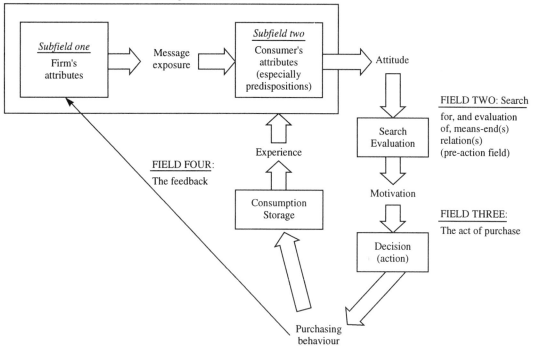

Fig. 9.8 The Nicosia model: a structure of consumer behaviour (*Source:* Nicosia)[23]

of the message. The communication aimed at a target audience will be modified by perceptual influences which may distort the intended message. From this interaction an attitude towards the product and brand may emerge, and this will become an input into field two. In field two, data search and comparative evaluation take place. Nicosia differentiated between *internal* and *external* search processes. Internal search relates to the consumer's conscious and unconscious associations with the product, brand, etc., while external search refers to information gathered from the environment, e.g., from advertisements or from family and work groups. In the evaluation process, data from both internal and external sources are weighed up by the consumer, who will endeavour to achieve some acceptable degree of consistency or balance in the beliefs (cognitions) and attitudes concerning the specific product and brand advertised. The input from this area into field three may be a motivation to buy the brand advertised, but this may not occur if the evaluation stage resulted in an unfavourable attitude being formed towards that branded product.

Field three covers the 'possible transformation of the motivation into an act of purchase'.[23] This outcome will be affected by several factors, such as the availability of the particular brand advertised. If purchase occurs, field four will consist of storage and use of the product; the output is feedback which may or may not result in repeat purchases. This feedback closes the 'consumer's loop' by linking field four and subfield two of field one. Likewise, the output of field three (purchase decision) is also the input into field one, subfield one, thereby closing the 'firm's loop'.

Nicosia elaborated the field and subfield processes, and related many research findings to his model, e.g., Markov processes. His model is based on a very restricting example of advertising and product acceptance (where earlier experience was lacked by both buyer and seller), and this tends to limit the usefulness of his theory of buyer behaviour. The adaptability of the Nicosian model to mathematical techniques makes it particularly valuable for further research. Nicosia believed that his analytical approach showed clearly the strategy to be adopted for gaining insight into consumer buying behaviour: 'first, to study relatively simple structures of consumer behaviour by analog computer, and then to study progressively more complex structures by digital computers'.

Lunn feels that some criticisms could be levelled at Nicosia's work 'and he would be the last to regard it as definitive'.[5] He cites, for instance, the tendency to represent the search and evaluation process as 'over-rational', which no doubt applies to infrequently purchased high-cost products, but is far less likely with frequently purchased low-cost goods. Also, definitions of attitude and motivation 'seem unsatisfactory'. However, despite such short-comings, Nicosia is regarded as having made an invaluable pioneering contribution to consumer modelling.

The Andreasan model

This develops a 'general model of customer (buyer) choice behaviour built upon several conceptions about attitude formation and change drawn from social psychology'.[24] Alan R. Andreasan, the originator of the model, stated that the key to attitude change is exposure to various kinds of information. This exposure may be voluntary or involuntary: 'the entire process from stimulus to outcome comprises an information-processing cycle' which involves four stages: input stimuli, perception and filtration, disposition changes, and various feasible outcomes.

Andreasan developed his theory from a simplistic model towards a model of complex decision-making processes (shown in Fig. 9.9). He contended that two principal strategies are adopted by marketing practitioners in order to attract favourable purchasing decisions; these are market segmentation and product differentiation. The former strategy 'seeks to make marketing efforts (product design, distribution program, etc.) fit existing attitudes and behaviour'; the latter attempts 'to change attitudes so that customer will accept existing product, outlets and so on'. Andreasan believed that his model of buying behaviour should be useful 'as a detailed organising concept for marketing decision makers who must take customer decisions explicitly into account when employing either or both of these strategies'.[24]

Attitude formation and change are central concepts of Andreasan's model. Selective perception and distortion of product information may occur, effectively changing or eliminating the communication planned by the marketer. Because information must pass through this perceptual barrier, and in doing so may lose some of its original character, Andreasan drew particular attention to the important role of attitudes in influencing buying decisions.

> the beliefs, feelings and dispositions an individual holds about a class of complementary products or brands, such as General Electric small appliances, typically affect his attitude toward new members of that class, such as a new G.E. electric knife sharpener. Similarly, *changes* in attitudes towards some one product in a class, say a more favourable belief in its reliability, may affect attitudes towards other products in the same class.[16]

Marketers who seek to influence attitudes towards their products should also bear in mind that channels of communication themselves are subject to perceptual judgement.

Andreasan considered that his model of buying behaviour could be viewed as a useful guide for the integration of much of the diverse literature in behavioural studies, and as an attempt to develop a theoretical basis for studying customer behaviour. In evaluating Andreasan's model, it would be advisable to remember that the relationship between attitude and behaviour is complex, and a unidirectional influence should not be assumed.

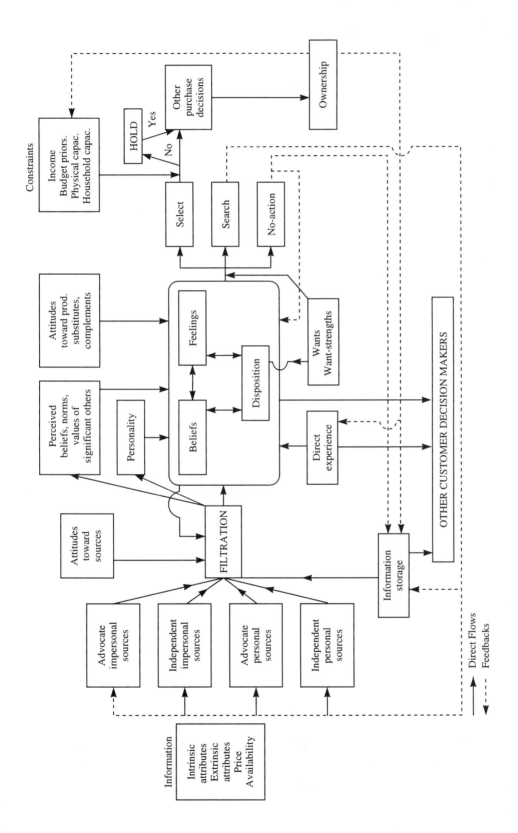

Fig. 9.9 Andreasan model of complex customer decision (*Source*: Andreasan)[24]

9.8 CONCLUSIONS

Of the many formal models of buying behaviour, the multi-variable approach is the most acceptable one so far available. The Engel–Kollatt–Blackwell and the Howard–Ostlund models have much in common, including their somewhat confusing diagrams; both are eclectic in their approach, drawing their concpts from a wide range of the behavioural sciences. Consumer behaviour is projected as information acquisition and processing, moderated by psychological, social, and cultural influences. Both models view the purchasing process as a series of steps that lead either to buying or to rejection of the proposition involved.

Empirical validation of these comprehensive models is clearly desirable. So far they have given highly valuable insight into the factors that affect consumer buying behaviour, although, as noted earlier, some degree of difficulty and ambiguity surrounds certain characteristics of the models.

In essence, the consumer is viewed not as a pawn in the business game, but as an active processor of data who has the ability to reject as well as to accept products.

The multi-variable models emphasize that many decisions to buy, even those reputedly based on purely economic considerations, are subject also to so-called non-rational factors. People's needs and motivations (see Chapter 3) are complex and they are likely to seek satisfactions at an economic level and also at deeper levels, involving emotions, cultural norms and values, group affiliations, etc. The interdisciplinary approach of the multi-variable models is clearly superior and more valid than the restricted base of the monadic models. These offer partial explanations of buying behaviour which need to be amplified before they can be accepted as useful guides for developing marketing strategies and tactics. In a highly critical review of microeconomic theory, Kamarck has observed that the assumption that consumers are rational, selfish, know what goods will satisfy them best and spend their money accordingly, does not stand up to close examination.[1] It is not possible to 'be so confident that consumption levels are completely determined . . . there is an inherent lack of precision in consumer preference orderings'. Consumers may, for example, take pleasure in 'randomly varying' their patterns of consumption; they may maintain the same buying preferences, despite a change in circumstances, because of security or comfort derived from buying certain products or services. Moreover, a consumer 'may get pleasure by sacrificing his otherwise desired consumption pattern for others', perhaps due to family preferences or so as to contribute to charitable causes.

Kamarck rejects as too simplistic the usual economic assumption 'that consumers aim to maximise satisfaction within the limits of their incomes'. Rather than the single motivation of the desire for satisfaction, there are three motive forces of behaviour: the desire to relieve discomfort, the desire for stimulation to relieve boredom, and 'the desire for the pleasure that can accompany and reinforce both'.[1] This is certainly a long way from the monadic model approach, and reflects instead the richness and diversity of human behaviour, of which buying behaviour is an essential part. Economic theory, though valuable, cannot be expected to provide more than a skeletal framework of the consumer buying process.

9.9 SUMMARY

A model is an abstract concept of reality which essentially simplifies complexity and is a rough approximation to real life. Construction of a model assists understanding of problems, because situations have to be analysed clearly and variables identified.

Consumer buying behaviour models have two main uses: descriptive and predictive. They should possess the attributes of relevance, comprehensibility, and validity.

Two main types of models are identified: monadic and multi-variable. The former derive from one principal theoretical source, e.g., microeconomics, and have a restricted approach to buying behaviour. Another single theoretical source might be the psychoanalytic concepts of Freud which emphasize the irrationality of behaviour as distinct from the rationality of microeconomic theory; or the perceived risk model based on Bauer and Cox's researches.

Multi-variable models, on the other hand, are eclectic, drawing from across the behavioural sciences. These more comprehensive explanations of buying behaviour have been developed by Howard–Ostlund and Engel–Kollat–Blackwell, and offer valuable insights into the complexity of buying behaviour which is inadequately dealt with by monadic theoretical models.

Nicosia and Andreasan have also made valuable contributions to the understanding of consumer buying, deriving concepts freely from social psychology and other sources.

The multi-variable models require empirical validation, and also some degree of redefinition of criteria of their constructs.

The various elements such as cognitions, attributes, and life-styles in these models can be identified readily from the discussions in preceding chapters. No model can really offer a complete explanation of buying behaviour that is universally applicable; they need interpretation and sophisticated understanding before they can be of value to marketing management.

REFERENCES

1. Karmarck, Andrew M., *Economics and the Real World*, Basil Blackwell, Oxford, 1983.
2. Hague, D. C., *Managerial Economics: Analysis for Business Decisions*, Longman, Harlow, Essex, 1977.
3. Lunn, Tony, 'Consumer modelling,' in: *Consumer Market Research Handbook*, Robert Worcester and John Downham (eds), Van Nostrand Reinhold, Wokingham, 1978.
4. Westwood, Dick, Tony Lunn, and David Beazley, 'Models and modelling Part 2: modelling and structures', *European Research*, July 1974.
5. Lunn, J. A., 'Review of consumer decision process models', ESOMAR, Helsinki, 1971.
6. Sternthal, Brian, and C. Samuel Craig, *Consumer Behaviour: An Information Processing Perspective*, Prentice-Hall, Englewood Cliffs, New Jersey, 1982.
7. Bauer, Raymond A., 'Consumer behaviour as risk-taking', in: *Dynamic Marketing for a Changing World*, R. S. Hancock (eds), American Advertising Association, Chicago, 1960.
8. Cox, Donald F. (ed.) *Risk Taking and Information Handling in Consumer Behaviour*, Harvard Business School, Boston, Massachusetts, 1967.
9. Jacoby, Jacob, and Leon Kaplan, 'The components of perceived risk', in: *Proceedings of the Third Annual Conference of the Association for Consumer Research*, M. Venkatesan (ed.), Chicago, 1972.
10. Roseluis, Ted, 'Consumer rankings of risk reduction methods', in: *Perspectives in Consumer Behaviour* (revised), Harold H. Kassarjian and Thomas S. Robertson (eds), Scott, Foreman, Glenview, Illinois, 1973.
11. Kotler, Philip, *Marketing Management: Analysis, Planning and Control*, Prentice-Hall, Englewood Cliffs, New Jersey, 1967.
12. Engel, James F., David J. Kollat, and Roger D. Blackwell, *Consumer Behaviour*, Holt, Reinhart and Winston, New York, 1968.
13. Wilkie, William L., and Peter L. Dickson, 'Shopping for appliances: consumers' strategies and patterns of information search', in: *Perspectives in Consumer Behaviour*, Harold H. Kassarjian and Thomas S. Robertson (eds), Prentice-Hall, Englewood Cliffs, New Jersey, 1991.
14. Howard, John A., and Jagdish N. Sheth, *The Theory of Buyer Behaviour*, John Wiley, New York, 1969.
15. Chisnall, Peter M., *Marketing Research*, McGraw-Hill, Maidenhead, 1992.
16. Buzzell, Robert D., *Mathematical Models and Marketing Management*, Graduate School of Business Administration, Harvard Business School, Boston, Massachusetts, 1964.

17. Palda, Kristian S., *The Measurement of Cumulative Advertising Effects*, Prentice-Hall, Englewood Cliffs, New Jersey, 1964.
18. Sheth, Jagdish N., 'A review of buyer behaviour', *Management Science*, vol. 13, no. 12, August 1967.
19. Howard, John A., *Marketing Management, Analysis and Planning*, Richard D. Irwin, Homewood, Illinois, 1963.
20. Howard, J. A., and L. Ostlund, *Buyer Behaviour: Theoretical and Empirical Foundations*, Knopf, New York, 1973.
21. McCracken, Grant, 'Culture and consumer behaviour: an anthropological perspective', *Journal of the Market Research Society*, vol. 32, no. 1, January 1990.
22. Engel, James F., David J. Kollatt, and Roger D. Blackwell, *Consumer Behaviour*, Dryden Press, New York, 1978.
23. Nicosia, Francesco M., 'Advertising management, consumer behaviour and simulation', *Journal of Advertising Research*, vol. 8, no. 1, March 1968.
24. Andreasan, Alan R., 'Attitudes and customer behaviour: a decision model' in *New Research in Marketing*, Lee E. Preston (ed.), Institute of Business and Economic Research, University of California, Berkeley, 1965.

REVIEW AND DISCUSSION QUESTIONS

1. How would you answer the criticism that consumer behaviour models are of practical use to teachers alone?
2. A number of models of buying behaviour were reviewed in this chapter. Which of them do you think would be most valuable to the marketing practitioner? Why?
3. What would you consider to be the major drawbacks of the multi-variable models of consumer behaviour examined in this chapter?
4. Describe any informal models of buying behaviour that you might have used to understand consumers before reading this chapter.
5. What are the main advantages of multi-variable models compared to the more traditional monadic models?
6. How does the concept of risk affect buying behaviour, and in what ways is it likely to impinge on the prospective purchase of a new type of food-mixer?

CHAPTER TEN

ORGANIZATIONAL BUYING BEHAVIOUR

10.1 INTRODUCTION

Business organizations are of many kinds: one way of viewing them would be to use the traditional analysis of economic activities which differentiates the primary, secondary, and tertiary industries. The primary or extractive sector covers agriculture, mining, forestry, and fishing; the secondary or manufacturing sector relates to industrial manufacturing and construction; the third sector covers the service and distributive activities of the economy. In all advanced economies, there has been a shift from growing products to making products, and then to providing services that are often closely related to particular products. The tertiary sector has become the major source of employment, and Britain, along with other advanced countries, has what is termed a service economy. This reflects a relatively wealthy society, in which increasing emphasis is given to the provisions of professional, technical, and personal services, while the older industrial activities, like coal-mining, shipbuilding, and textile manufacture, are replaced by sophisticated products, such as those based on electronics, computer technology, and other 'knowledge-based industries'.

A distinctive feature of post-war Britain was the establishment and growth of nationalized industries covering, for example, energy generation, coal-mining, and telecommunications. The culture of state industries and state-controlled corporations was directly challenged by the Conservative government of 1979, and a radical programme of privatization and de-regulation was vigorously pursued. The gas supply industry, for instance, monopolized by the British Gas Corporation, was privatized as British Gas plc; the ten water authorities of England and Wales were transformed in 1989 into public limited companies; the Central Electricity Generating Board was split up into two companies, National Power and Powergen, with the National Grid becoming jointly owned by a number of private-sector distribution companies, which evolved from the former area electricity boards. British Telecom plc emerged from the transformation of telecommunications in the 1980s, and after privatization in 1984, faced the challenge of competition from a new entrant, Mercury Communications. In addition, far-reaching changes continue to influence the policies and practices of the health, education, and welfare services of Britain.

Private sector industries and the public sector services together formed the 'mixed economy', which once appeared to be a permanent though, at times, precarious characteristic of developed economies such as Britain's. While widespread changes have taken place, some industries are still virtually dependent for their home market sales on contracts, placed either by government departments and local authorities, or by a very limited number of privatized organizations covering, for example, motorway construction, bridge-building, railway and coal-mining equipment, and supplies for steel making and telecommunications. Concentrated buying power inevitably leads to considerable bargaining with suppliers; a power-dependence relationship evolves from the interaction between buyers and sellers. For this to be satisfactory, both parties have to cultivate patterns of negotiating behaviour that are likely to result in mutual benefits. Cooperation, not conflict, should be the objective of such negotiations, as discussed later in this chapter (pages 239–242) when reviewing specific research by the IMP Project Group.

10.2 NEGOTIATION

Successful business people are usually good negotiators, or employ someone who is skilled in this vital tool of management. Negotiation is a two-way process of communication. In the language of sociology, it is an interpersonal behaviour event in which people fulfil distinctive roles, such as buyer and seller. In negotiation, buyers and sellers are motivated by both economic and personal factors; successful sellers aim to discover the relative importance of these various motivations so that they can present their propositions in terms that are attractive to their buyers.

Words are the tools of communication; negotiations have often failed because negotiators have been unable to present their ideas clearly and attractively. In negotiation, it is important to learn something about the other party's frame of reference, because this may vitally affect the interpretation that is placed upon the words used. 'We tend to forget how circumscribed our own experience is and we take for granted that whatever the word means to us it will mean the same to everyone else'.[1] The golden rule is to stay within the working vocabulary (which is likely to include professional and trade jargon) of the negotiating parties, avoiding words that do not communicate their intended meaning unambiguously.

But in addition to spoken communication, there is the powerful influence of non-verbal communication which affects the outcome of negotiation. Facial expressions, gestures, intonation, delivery, and body language all contribute to the negotiation and help to create the favourable psychological atmosphere that is critical in establishing a satisfactory reciprocal relationship.

In negotiation, marketers should be constantly alert to the reactions of their customers. These reactions may also be non-verbal: nods, grunts, yawns, and restless movements may well indicate more accurately than words the impact that selling propositions are having on them. Some people are not particularly articulate, or they may not wish to cause offence or embarrassment, and so their words by themselves may be poor indicators of their real feelings. Marketers should endeavour to 'hear between the lines', to listen with a 'third ear', so that they develop deeper knowledge of their customers.

Michael Argyle has developed the concept of bodily or non-verbal communication and, with helpful examples, has indicated its value in social and business contacts.[2] In particular, he has emphasized the cultural and social implications attached to certain bodily signals. In Chapter 6 of this book, cultural norms and values were seen to have significant effects on human behaviour. Argyle points out that cultures develop rules and conventions which apply to such universal functions as eating a meal, working in a group, or buying and selling; these norms 'may vary greatly—consider buying and selling in Britain and North Africa'; or in Japan, where non-verbal communication is said to have a greater degree of subtlety than elsewhere, partly because of Zen teaching about the value of silence and perception without speech, partly due to the cultural homogeneity of the Japanese and the development of a code of prescribed behaviour, and partly because most social behaviour takes place inside small, closely knit groups, where people know each other extremely well.[2]

Drucker has vividly discussed the need to appreciate cultural norms in negotiation.[3] When, for example, the westerner and the Japanese talk of 'making a decision', they mean different things.

> With us in the west, all the emphasis is on the answer to the question. Indeed, our books on decision making try to develop systematic approaches to giving an answer. To the Japanese, however, the important element in decision making is defining the question. The important and crucial steps are to decide whether there is a need for a decision and what the decision is about. And it is in this step that the Japanese aim at attaining 'consensus'. Indeed, it is this step that to the Japanese is the essence of the question . . . (what the west considers the decision) follows its definition.
>
> During this process that precedes the decision, no mention is made of what the answer might be. This is done so that people will not be forced to take sides; once they have taken sides, a decision would be victory for one side and a defeat for the other. Thus the whole process is focussed on finding out what the decision is really about, not what the decision should be. Its result is a meeting of minds that there is (or is not) a need for a change in behaviour.
>
> All of this takes a long time, of course; the westerner dealing with the Japanese is thoroughly frustrated during the process. He does not understand what is going on. He has the feeling that he is being given the runaround.

Drucker quotes the case of Japanese people negotiating with Americans for licensing agreements. They

> keep on sending new groups of people every few months who start what the westerner thinks are 'negotiations' as if they had never heard of the subject. One delegation takes copious notes and goes back home, only to be succeeded six weeks later by another team of people from different areas of the company, who again act as if they had never heard of the matter under discussion, take copious notes, and go home.

In fact, Drucker explains, the Japanese are behaving quite seriously.

> They are trying to involve the people who will have to carry out an eventual agreement in the process of obtaining consensus that a licence is indeed needed. Only when all of the people who will have to carry out the agreement have come together on the need to make a decision will the decision be made to go ahead. Only then do negotiations really start—and then the Japanese usually move with great speed.

Japanese people place particular emphasis on the need to establish warm personal relationships as an essential preliminary stage to the negotiation of business deals. Entertainment and the exchange of gifts are part of this important cultural approach. Cultural behaviour also influences the style and progress of negotiations in Japan.

> It is important for foreigners, particularly Americans, to recognize that the Japanese have a custom of being silent for what seems to westerners as an excessively long time. The westerner should not become excited or feel a compulsion to speak during these periods of silence because it often results in a concession on a disputed point by the westerner when he simply tries to keep the conversation going.[4]

Negotiation includes not only the transmission of information through words, but also the establishment of an acceptable emotional environment. 'Emotions are more reliably communicated in a face-to-face situation where gestures and facial expressions . . . can supplement language and where the responses can be observed directly, and corrected if a mistake should be made by either party'.[5] This highly flexible method of communication—words and non-verbal signals—has the universal benefit of immediate feedback which written communication lacks. Even in an electronic age, business deals will still demand expert personal negotiating skills. People may live in greater comfort and have more sophisticated patterns of consumption, but their psychological and social characterizations are basically unchanged. As noted in Chapters 2, 3 and 5 on cognitions, perceptions, attitudes, and motivations, people are not just rational, decision-making automata; they do not leave outside the conference room their prejudices, inhibitions, and ambitions. They can, therefore, be complex, contradictory, and infuriating at times. Successful negotiators need to have adequate knowledge of their products and also be sensitive to the behavioural aspects of business deals.

Negotiation has been observed to be characterized by four Cs:[6]

1. Common interests (something to negotiate for).
2. Conflicting interests (something to negotiate about).
3. Compromise (give and take on points).
4. Criteria or objectives (determining the objectives or criteria for its achievement).

These four characteristics deserve reflection: both parties enter into a bargaining situation which involves a buyer–seller relationship. 'Bargaining is negotiating, comparing, making choices and arriving at an agreement with a partner—a supplier or customer—who himself has been negotiating, comparing and making choices'.[7]

Trust is the foundation of satisfactory business agreements. But the concept of trust is not easily measured in objective terms; certainly, past performance ('track record') can give valuable clues as to likely future behaviour, assuming, of course, that earlier experience is relevant. Apart from this—and sometimes in place of it—judgement has to be based on other criteria and these tend to be subjective. The perceptual processes described in Chapter 2 are at work, although their influence may be described as insight, flair, or nous.

Both present and long-term effects of negotiation should be carefully evaluated; dramatic negotiating successes may begin to tarnish when the full impact of certain conditions imposed during hard bargaining filters through a business. The RB 211 débâcle is a sobering example of tremendous negotiating optimism that failed dismally and accelerated the trend towards government intervention in business.

10.3 NATURE OF ORGANIZATIONAL SUPPLIES

In many cases, the products and services demanded by organizational buyers will be similar to those bought by consumers, but the *reasons* for their purchase will be different. For example, paint, stationery, heating fuels, cars, insurance and banking are supplied to both sets of customers. However, the products and services used by industry, commerce, and the public sector are bought because they are related to the objectives of these organizations, and these constraints will affect buying behaviour. In the case of industrial and commercial transactions, products and services will be required because they will be expected to contribute to the profitability of an enterprise by enabling production and distribution to be undertaken efficiently. As Ansoff[8] has observed: 'A firm seeks its objectives through the medium of profit and, more specifically, through conversion of its resources into goods and/or services and then obtaining a return on these by selling them to customers'.

However, a great deal of buying takes place in organizations which are not motivated by profits. Vast sums of money are disbursed by the purchasing agents acting for local authorities, health and welfare organizations, police, and public transport systems. In these circumstances, the responsibilities of the purchasing agent may primarily be concerned with servicing the organization. Budgetary constraints inevitably will affect the using of specific types of goods or services, but since income largely has not to be generated from profit-making activities, the orientation of the public service towards its suppliers and its markets tend to be vastly different from that of an industrial or commercial undertaking.

Although organizational buyers in the public service and in industry may differ in the nature of their primary motivation, they share the same responsibilities: to procure goods and services for use in their organizations as opposed to personal consumption.

While many products and services bought by organizations are similar to those purchased in consumer markets, there are also many instances when distinct differences are observable, and this applies particularly to capital equipment. For example, computer installations, oil rig construction, or aeronautical engineering are complex, sophisticated products which have relatively extended durability, low frequency of purchase, and very high cost. On the other hand, many industrial supplies may be limited to low-cost items such as components.

Special types of supply arrangements may also characterize organizational markets: for example, reciprocal trading (where two firms agree to inter-trade in certain types of products), consortia (where companies may form voluntary associations for a limited period in order to secure large contracts which they could not handle individually, as in major construction projects), project management—also known as 'turnkey operations' (civil engineering contracts where a 'turnkey contractor' has total responsibility for both design and construction, coordinating the inputs made by specialized subcontractors)—or licensing and joint venture operations (such as Pilkington's float glass licensing).

10.4 TYPES OF ORGANIZATIONAL SUPPLIES

Although there is much in common between the goods and services provided for consumer and organizing needs, there are also considerable differences which influence significantly both demand and supply.

Various attempts have been made to classify organizational supplies: generally it has proved difficult to fit these neatly into exclusive groupings. In the late 1960s, the Industrial Marketing Research Association (IMRA) adopted a system of classification which progressed logically from basic raw materials to semi-processed products, components, and eventually to finished equipment.[9] They identified the following three categories of products (and services):

1. *Capital goods*: 'sold as an inherent whole to further production, in machines, accessories, or components'.
2. *Primary products*: 'basic materials like steel, chemicals or aluminium bars sold to manufacturers'.
3. *Intermediate products*: 'such as tubes, castings, or building materials which have to undergo some major change of form'.

Other researchers, such as Stanton,[10] have observed that 'Industrial goods are those intended for use in making other products, or for rendering a service in the operation of a business or institutional enterprise'. He classified industrial products into five categories based on the broad uses of products, in contrast to the classification of consumer products on the basis of buying habits. These are Stanton's classifications and his descriptions of the products within them:

1. *Raw materials*: these are 'industrial goods which will become part of another physical product and which have received no processing at all, other than necessary for economy or protection in physical handling', e.g., minerals, land, wheat, cotton, tobacco, fruit and vegetables, livestock, and animal products such as eggs and raw milk.
2. *Fabricating materials and parts*: 'these become actual part of finished product; already

processed to some extent. Fabricating *materials*, e.g. pig-iron, or yarn, will undergo further processing. Fabricating *parts* will be assembled with no further change in form, e.g. spark plugs, fan belts, buttons, etc.'

3. *Installations*: these are 'manufactured industrial products—the long-lived expensive major equipment of an industrial user, e.g. large generators, factory building, jet aeroplanes for airline. The differentiating characteristic of installations is that they set the scale of operation in a firm'.

4. *Accessory equipment*: this is 'used to aid production operations of an industrial user, but it does not have a significant influence on the scale of operations in a firm; does not become actual part of finished product. Life is shorter than installations (3) and longer than operating supplies (5), e.g. office equipment, small power tools, forklift trucks'.

5. *Operating supplies*: these are 'convenience goods' of industrial field. They are short-lived, low-priced items usually purchased with minimum of effort. They help a firm's operations but do not become part of a finished product, e.g., lubricating oils, stationery, heating fuel.

From the above product classification, it will be seen that the use to which a product is put inevitably affects its classification; spark plugs, for example, could fall in category 2 as original equipment, but might be considered within category 5 as replacement items for fleet owners.

10.5 DERIVED DEMAND

A significant characteristic of industrial supplies refers to the fact that demand is mostly directly dependent on trends in end-use markets. For example, a supplier may provide components or packaging which are used in the final product made by their customers. The demand for these finished products will affect the patterns of demand for component products and services. Dyers of textiles, for instance, are inevitably affected by the general level of demand for finished textiles which, in turn, is influenced by the makers-up, who themselves are subject to the vagaries of the fashion trade, where consumer preferences are often extremely difficult to forecast with any degree of certainty. Hence, even in industrial markets, personal, psychological, social, and cultural influences make their presence felt. The large fibre producers have consistently researched at several levels of the textile fashion market in order to plan their production and marketing.

The demand for capital equipment is also largely subject to the prospective demand for the goods which the plant is able to produce. Because of the lead times involved in the design development, and production of new capital equipment, problems of assessing likely future demand for the resultant products tend to be particularly marked. Industrial marketers of food processing equipment, for example, should clearly study patterns of consumption of the products manufactured on their types of machinery: demographic trends, changes in consumer tastes, shifts in attitudes related to certain kinds of foods, etc., are all factors which are vital for them to know about so that they can anticipate behaviour in their own markets. An interesting example of consumer advertising to popularize the use of glass bottle packaging was undertaken by the trade association connected with glass-container manufacture. This type of market intervention has also been notably practised by Australian wool producers under the famous 'Woolmark' symbol.

It is important that industrial marketers understand fully the applications or end uses of their products. Hakansson has observed that suppliers have to be experts in their own product field and should also have a thorough grasp of the processes of production involved in making the final product to which they are contributing.[11] Industrial marketing involves contacts at several levels in an organization, and marketers must be competent to discuss technical as well as commercial aspects.

A further aspect of derived demand is that relatively small price reductions are unlikely to affect sales. Buyers may, in fact, hold off buying for a time in the expectation of further price cuts. On the other hand, increases in price may lead to greater demand from buyers anxious to stock up before prices rise significantly. This price—demand relationship is clearly different from the general theory of price elasticity of demand, where price variations tend to influence inversely levels of consumption. It is feasible for price reduction in industrial supplies to be followed by reduced business, if the general level of demand in the final market is falling. There may be occasions when shortages of raw materials have so raised price levels that substitutes are sought, for example, plastic in place of timber, or synthetic fibres instead of natural fibres in carpet production.

This brief review of derived demand indicates that although the behavioural factors discussed in earlier chapters may seem to be quite unrelated to industrial supplies, they do, in fact, influence these markets. After all, people are the final consumers and their buying behaviour has been seen to be affected by economic, physical, psychological, social, and cultural factors. At some time—admittedly, sometimes lagged by years—consumer preferences in a market economy will be felt by firms engaged in supplying raw materials, components, finished products, and services of various kinds. No supplier can afford to ignore what is going on in the big wide world populated by people whose main interest is to satisfy their myriad needs.

10.6 COMPLEXITY OF ORGANIZATIONAL BUYING

Organizational buyers are subject to complex influences in the daily routine of servicing the needs of their companies and other institutions. The complicated pattern of influences and relationships involved in purchasing decisions defies simple explanation. Both within an organization and external to it, buyers are subject to diverse motivations; furthermore, these may from time to time be in conflict. Organizational buyers have to deal with demands arising within their own organization and imposed by other functional managers, and those emanating from negotiation with suppliers of a very wide range of goods and services.

Michael Shanks expressed this dilemma as follows:

> The majority of businessmen are motivated by a complex mixture of considerations. They want to make as much money as they can, certainly, but they want other things as well. . . . Besides the desire for profit, therefore, there is the desire for prestige, for self-satisfaction, for service, leisure or a whole medley of other emotions—good, bad and indifferent.[12]

(The complex nature of motives was discussed in Chapter 3.)

Organizational buying is, therefore, complex in that it deals with supplies often far more sophisticated in nature than most consumer products; the process of buying is seldom settled entirely by one person's decision; the scale of purchases is mostly substantial; and the repercussions from purchasing a specific product such as capital equipment may be profoundly felt both within an organization and inside the market it serves. Fully automatic machines, for example, may be bought for a textile factory; these will represent considerable capital investment to be absorbed over a given period of trading. This modern equipment may result in cost economies and give the manufacturer concerned a special marketing advantage; at the same time, there are bound to be reduced demands for labour, and redundancies may occur. Hence the effects of an organizational purchase may be diverse and very extensive.

10.7 HANDLING RISK

In attempting these dual goals, corporate or organization people endeavour to satisfy the objectives of their institution while at the same time being interested in enhancing their own career. This concept of self-preservation and improvement influences the decisions which they take in day-to-day business transactions. They are likely, for instance, to avoid excessive risk in decision-taking, not only for their company's sake but also for their personal reputation and advancement. As David C. McClelland has observed: 'A great part of the efforts of business executives is directed towards minimising uncertainties'; therefore, buyers will carefully assess the degree of risk related to specific purchase decisions.[13]

Maslow's well-known 'hierarchy of needs' (see Chapter 3) place safety needs immediately after the satisfaction of basic physiological needs. The desire for protection against physical and psychological dangers was observed to affect personal behaviour, patterns of consumption, and occupational choice.

The theory of perceived risk was referred to in Chapter 9, when it was seen to depend upon subjective perception. It was hypothesized by Bauer that consumers adopted certain buying habits related to the risks attached to particular transactions. Not surprisingly, risk strategies are also evident in organizational markets, as research by David J. Wilson has indicated.[14] He studied the decision-making styles of industrial buyers among 132 purchasing agents and manufacturers in chemical, petroleum, and light and heavy manufacturing industries in South Ontario.

Three personality traits were considered during the study:

1. *The need for certainty*: the response to uncertainty was considered to be an important element in purchasing decisions.
2. *Generalized self-confidence*: this referred to the degree to which an individual's ideal and actual self corresponded; self-confidence was hypothesized to be a significant influence in purchasing decisions.
3. *The need to achieve*: this described the orientation which purchasing agents had towards work or play. Those experiencing a high need for achievement aspire to undertake difficult tasks, maintain high standards, and are willing to work towards distant goals.

During the course of five simulated purchasing problems, purchasing agents' choices were compared with their measured personality traits, and groups were formed from these. Because 'most business decisions are eventually evaluated in monetary terms', Wilson chose an expected monetary value model as the standard against which the groups' average scores on the personality tests were evaluated. 'Subjects who generally made choices close to those of the model were classified as having normative decision styles'. Those who avoided uncertainty and persistently made non-normative choices were described as conservative. A small group who initially made normative but later changed to conservative choices were classified as switchers.

Wilson concluded that the style of decision-making, based on research into the personality traits of purchasing agents, may offer a useful method of market segmentation. Industrial sales staff may be able to emphasize different persuasive arguments which have appeal to known personality characteristics of particular buyers. This depends, of course, on sales staff either being given this information in advance of their interviews or on their ability to recognize decision styles. As Wilson says: 'Additional field research is needed to implement analysis of decision styles in business situations'.[14] These research findings, although not significant over all the classifications of decision styles, suggest a valuable field in which extensive research may be usefully undertaken.

Hakansson and his associate researchers noted that interpersonal contacts enabled information to be exchanged which helped to reduce certain types of risk that are perceived by contracting parties. For example, 'environmental uncertainty may arise because a buyer is unfamiliar with the economic climate or supply situation prevailing in the industrial sector or country of a supplier. Contact patterns can help provide the framework in which questions about that environment can be posed directly or inferred from other information'.[11] These researchers also observe that the risk perceived by buyers in placing an order for a specific product or service is due to the uncertainty and possible adverse consequences surrounding that decision. The more complex the product, the greater the uncertainty for both buyer and seller. (See Chapter 2 for a discussion of cognitive dissonance.) As noted in Chapter 9, some buyers, both personal and organizational, may be risk seekers while others are risk averters; these characteristics will be discussed more fully in Chapter 11.

Risk is a factor that has such pervasive influence that marketers should give it particular attention, and ensure that their products and services are offered within acceptable parameters of risk. This may, for example, entail the development of training facilities for customers' staff and post-sales servicing arrangements. Industrial buyers have learned to offset the risks of interference in supplies of essential raw materials and components through dual sourcing, i.e., allocating their buying orders over two or more suppliers.

Suppliers also need to check carefully the degree of their dependence on particular industries and specific customers. 'Portfolio' planning applies not only to the range of products marketed, but also to the organizations whose custom is sought.

On the lines of financial portfolio planning, where a balanced range of investments is aimed for, market portfolio planning is a risk-control strategy with the objective of securing an optimal mix of products, markets, and customers. As will be discussed in Chapter 11, the introduction of new products and services inevitably carries risk; this needs careful assessment so that it can be carried within the resources—human and organizational—of a business.

In overseas marketing, the risks inherent in developing and maintaining demand can be significant, so a carefully planned risk policy is advisable. The ability to tolerate risk has been seen to be related to a firm's size and liquidity and to the self-confidence of its management. Some businesses are distinctly high-risk enterprises—for example, ethical pharmaceuticals, or oil drilling; other businesses customarily operate under low-risk conditions—the pace of innovation is slow, plant is unlikely to become obsolescent quickly, their products are not subject to widely fluctuating demand, and research and development costs are fairly small, for example, nuts and bolts manufacture.

Douglas and Craig proposed that risk in overseas marketing should be assessed against factors such as the number of expropriations, rates of inflation, and foreign exchange fluctuations.[15] Opportunities could be based on GNP per capita, GNP growth and demographic trends. Three kinds of risk policy—applicable to both home and export markets—have been classified: risk avoidance (reduction of vulnerability) risk minimizing (draw up 'risk profiles' of market opportunities), and risk bearing (planned dispersion of risk through licensing, joint ventures, systems selling, consortia, etc.).[16]

Writing in the *Harvard Business Review*, Henry B. Arthur has commented on the multi-faceted aspects of buying:

> It is true that more and more competitors today seek to be chosen on dimensions other than just price. But this trend, while it may be more prominent, is not something new—it is as old as trading. The traders of old leaned heavily on personal relationships, human psychology and the arts of persuasion, as well as on pricing, quality and convenience, to win the customer's preference.[7]

Levitt has underlined the fact that because industrial buyers tend to become heavily dependent on the performance of their suppliers, 'both sides will make entirely new concessions. But instead of concessions being made in the old-fashioned atmosphere of personal bargaining, they will occur in a tight process of business-like sophisticated bidding.'[17] These bidding proposals will have to stipulate a great deal more than price itself. 'The ability to perform the logistics of tightly scheduled delivery, will become fully as salient an issue as price, and Levitt states that this will lead to 'a de facto legal recognition' that what is bought is not just a tangible product, but a 'whole cluster of related benefits, services and values', i.e., the augmented product (see Chapter 1).

Since price by itself is always a hazardous way of holding business, suppliers should aim to provide non-product advantages—to build round their products a constellation of buying motives in order to attract interest in their products. Moreover, there is seldom just one effective price operating in a market for a specific type of product, a price that is the final influence in decisions to buy. Generally, there will be found to be a range of prices for particular products of a certain quality, and the industrial buyer, like the personal shopper, will not necessarily puchase the lowest-priced product. There are occasions, in fact, when an unusually low price may arouse suspicion and discourage the placing of business. Better-known firms which have established reputations for reliability of quality and service may be able to capitalize on their trading names when quoting for supplies. Because mutual confidence between organizational buyers and their suppliers may be the fruit of satisfactory transactions over a long period of time, this experience will give a valuable dimension to negotiations which is not likely to be eroded by the price-cutting tactics of some kinds of competitors.

Organizational buyers recognize that the true value of products and services is made up of many parts, all of which require careful investigation. It is the responsibility of purchasing agents to ensure that specifications relating to specific products cover *all* the values or benefits considered to be necessary. The relative importance of intrinsic qualities and the various 'added values'—the 'augmented product'—should be carefully analysed. Included in this assessment will be the 'non-rational' factors, such as the pleasantness (or otherwise) of doing business with particular firms, for buyers tend to be persuaded by a sales person whose personality is acceptable to them, provided, of course, that the product meets their needs.

Also of significant interest will be the back-up service which is becoming increasingly important with some technical products. After-sales service may extend to the selling of complete package deals, as with computer systems, where everything is taken care of, from training of staff, design of the system, installation of the machine, through to supply of software. Comprehensive services of this nature are extending in both industrial and consumer markets; buyers need make only one decision which will automaticlly ensure that they receive a complex of benefits, without the responsibility of having to make a series of separate evaluations and decisions. This comprehensive marketing approach is often referred to as 'systems selling'. It would be advisable to use market research to identify and evaluate buying motivations which could be 'built into' products and services.

10.8 THE BUYING CENTRE/DECISION-MAKING UNIT (DMU)

Apart from the mixed motivations that influence organizational buyers, it is also important for marketers to study *how* buying decisions are taken. *Who*, in fact, is the key figure in deciding to buy a particular product or service, and what is the contribution made by other members of the organization?

A pioneer study of the various influences on purchasing decisions over 11 major industries in the USA was made by the journal *Scientific American* in 1950. This was updated in 1970, and in 1978 Erikson focused on the chemical industry.[18] These various studies confirmed that several departments were typically involved in buying decisions. The purchasing department played a key role, in buying materials, components, and equipment, particularly where price negotiations, new sources of supply, and selection of suppliers were concerned.

Stemming from the pioneer research in the USA, the concept of the decision-making unit (DMU) was introduced into British marketing literature in 1967, when a report *How British Industry Buys* was published jointly by the Institute of Marketing and Industrial Market Research.[19] In this survey, Hugh Buckner indicated that industrial buying was essentially a team effort; actual responsibilities varied according to products and the nature of organizations. This research was updated in 1974 with the publication of a further report that confirmed the complexity of industrial buying arrangements.[20]

Brand, in research published in 1972,[21] showed how UK companies employing over 250 people reached their purchasing decisions; these were shared, equally or, in some cases, to a greater degree, between general/technical managers and purchasing executives. More recently, the *Financial Times* commissioned the Cranfield School of Management to investigate industrial purchasing practices over a range of British industries: plant and equipment, commercial vehicles and trailers, company cars, materials, component parts, office equipment including microcomputers and mainframe and/or minicomputers.[22]

A pilot study of 300 firms was undertaken in early 1983 followed by the main survey over the period May to September 1983. Dun and Bradstreet's detailed computerized list of key British enterprises provided the sampling frame from which a stratified random sample of 2963 companies was drawn. This research again indicated that buying responsibilities were shared by management and were significantly influenced by the type and cost of specific products, the size of the organization, and the degree of specialized management skills available.

In 1985, a multinational research study[23] was concerned with one key element of industrial buying behaviour—the buying process itself—and was based on a randomly selected sample of 1632 purchasing managers in the pulp and paper, chemical and allied products industries spread over Australia, Canada, the UK and the USA. By means of postal questionnaires (40 per cent response rate), it was found that

> managers *do* differentiate between the various stages of the buying process and the responsibilities for these are assigned to different functional areas or departments within the company. Another important finding was that the industrial buying process is more concerned with *what* is purchased than with any national characteristics. The buyer–seller relationship is of paramount importance, and the various roles in buying appear to be much the same wherever business is being transacted.[24]

10.9 FIVE ROLES IN ORGANIZATIONAL BUYING

Five roles are typical of organizational buying processes, and form what is termed the 'buying centre':[25] gatekeeper, influencer, user, decider, and buyer. These roles are sometimes undertaken by the same person, but very frequently different people are active in these various roles and are influential in the buying process. Between the members of the buying team there will be a complex interplay of personal and organizational motivations and objectives that will influence their behaviour and the purchase decision eventually taken.

Information on the various responsibilities and activities in the buying process should be gathered in systematic market research. This analytical approach to tracing the influence of those who jointly subscribe to purchasing decisions will help in planning effective marketing strategies. The tendency for several persons to participate in the buying process varies greatly according to the type of industry, size of firm, and nature of the product. Research has indicated that informal meetings of executives often result in buying decisions 'in many cases quite important decisions are influenced by an ad hoc committee which meets once a day at lunchtime in the management dining room'.[26] Most business executives have had some experience of this type of influence, and some organizations go so far as to draw up lunchtime agenda for discussion among senior members of staff.

The various roles of the decision-making unit will now be reviewed; the functions described are not always discrete, but they are discussed individually so that the complexity of organizational buying will be fully recognized.

The role of *gatekeeper* in the buying team requires careful study. Who, in fact, collects the information on which buying groups will depend largely for appraisal of competitive bids? What is the status of this individual in the firm: perhaps the gatekeeper is only a junior executive whose responsibilities are solely concerned with sending out routine enquiries and collecting quotations for standard equipment and stores. In more complex business situations involving the purchase of new types of machinery or systems, the role of gatekeeper may be undertaken by a senior engineer or technical expert. From the marketer's viewpoint, the gatekeepers for specific types of products should be identified so that information could be channelled to them at the appropriate time. As with other responsibilities in the buying team, the role of gatekeeper may be merged with that of influencer or purchasing agent on some occasions.

Influencers are not always easily identifiable. In consumer product fields a great deal of research has been undertaken into the role of personal influence in product and brand choice. Social scientists, basing their studies on Katz and Lazarsfeld's original inquiries recorded in their book *Personal Influence*,[27] have shown that personal influence is active in group behaviour. Society is a system of interconnected groups holding common beliefs about the world in general and also, perhaps, about the consumption of certain goods and services. These groups, it is hypothesized, have leaders who appear to be very influential in setting behavioural patterns which tend to be followed by the less active or less prestigious members of a community. But the difficulty lies in identifying these leaders or influencers in specific situations, such as organizational transactions. They seem to act unobtrusively and are not readily distinguishable, but this does not mean that their subtle influence can be dismissed.

In some companies, *users* will have decided influence on the type of product and the brand bought, particularly where technical suppliers are involved. Satisfactory performance will be considered to be of paramount importance to users of products under consideration; price, discount terms, and related matters will be 'left to the commercial people to sort out'. In one case 'it was found that the works manager wanted a product to have long life, the safety officer wanted one that carried no risk, while the buyer looked for the cheapest product'.[24] Such a divergence of objectives indicated the need for marketing management to develop specific promotional and sales campaigns aimed at attracting support of these sectional interests.

The roles of *buyer* and *decider* are sometimes combined in the same executive, but the degree to which buyers actually influence and decide on purchases varies considerably. With some consumer products, buyers tend to identify themselves closely with brands which become extensions of their personality, their self-image. They become, in psychological terms, ego-involved. This has been seen to influence the purchase of cars, cigarettes, beverages, and clothing. In some industrial buying situations, ego-involvement may also affect decisions to purchase.

Firms usually prefer their suppliers to be recognized generally as making reliable products backed by dependable service. Production engineers, for example, may recommend the purchase of new equipment which carries the name of a leading manufacturer. They may consider that their own technical expertise is reflected in the specification of certain makes of production equipment. Their own professional reputation will be built up by the success with which, in the past, they have justified the selection of specific suppliers' products by their subsequent satisfactory performance. Furthermore, they will, no doubt, experience pride and satisfaction in equipping their workshops with machinery made by leading manufacturers.

Their recommendation to purchase specific machines will be based on their productive efficiency compared with competitive equipment, but other variables will also be likely to affect their judgement.

Highly specialized functions of management increasingly feature in industrial and commercial firms, and also non-profit organizations such as national charities. Functional specialists in research and development, information technology, or computers have specific professional knowledge and expertise which can significantly affect buying decisions. A survey[28] of industrial buying behaviour in high technology laboratory instrumentation revealed that technical staff played a major role in purchasing decisions, and final selection was materially affected by technical and sales-service back-up and product reliability; price was reported to be relatively unimportant.

Internal politics may also be active in some buying propositions involving technical products, as was found in the purchase of a computer system, when the 'gatekeeper' deliberately filtered and amended the flow of information to suit personal objectives.[24]

The complexity of these motivations may be usefully related to the behavioural theory of the firm postulated by Cyert and March.[29] Their research identified four classifications of buying determinants:

1. Individual
2. Social (interpersonal).
3. Organizational (formal).
4. Environmental.

Within these four kinds of determinants , task and non-task variables interact in complex ways.

Task variables refer to the so-called rational factors influencing purchase, such as price, quality, and delivery—the basic 'hard data' of most marketing research inquiries. Non-task variables refer to the non-economic factors, such as motivation, personal values, political and cultural activities, and social influences—in fact, the nebulous influences in buying usually characterized as 'soft data' by marketing researchers. Task factors relate directly to the industrial buying situation and appear to be paramount in decisions to purchase many types of products. However, the influence of non-task factors should not be ignored. Environmental influences, for example, are becoming increasingly important and society's attitudes towards the responsibilities of business enterprises extend beyond mere economic boundaries. Trading policies and practices in many companies are being openly debated and challenged.

Consumerism, anti-pollution lobbies, the growing public awareness of the possible harmful biological and genetic effects of some food additives, and some of the practices of mass advertising have had their influence on the purchase decisions taken in industry. Business generally is far more complex and open to public criticism than it was a few years ago: inevitably, buying behaviour will reflect public attitudes because corporate success relies heavily on the acceptability of products and the company 'image' they project.

10.10 MULTIPLE INFLUENCES ON BUYING: RESEARCH FINDINGS

Complex production techniques are almost inevitably associated with sophisticated buying procedures. Functional specialists influence the choice of supplier far more than the buyer, who is frequently little more than an approved signature on the order form. The intricate process of organizational buying has been studied by several researchers.

Alexander, Cross, and Cunningham reported that a study of 106 industrial firms revealed that three or more persons influenced the buying processes in over 75 per cent of the companies examined.[30]

McGraw-Hill, in a special investigation of British engineering firms, reported that in companies with between 400 and 1000 employees, there were more than five buying influences, and in companies of over 1000 employees, more than six persons were involved in the buying decision.[31]

Professor Frederick E. Webster Jnr of Dartmouth College, USA, undertook a survey of 58 purchasing agents and other executives involved in buying by means of a non-probability sample of New England manufacturing firms.[32] These firms covered a variety of industries in 14 cities and towns in Massachusetts, New Hampshire and Vermont.

The findings were strongly consistent with hypotheses which had been formulated earlier, and although the research design is open to criticism, the survey indicated certain leading influences in industrial buying behaviour:

1. Informal communications in industrial markets may be much less common than in consumer markets. If specific information is needed quickly, buyers may telephone others, usually to enquire *where* to buy and seldom *what* to buy. Many respondents said they would be reluctant to divulge information about newly purchased products which may give their companies some competitive advantage. In consumer markets, there is a recognized tendency for buyers to seek out others in order to reduce dissonance following the purchase of some products. No such motivation appeared to be evident in industrial buying situations.

2. The manufacturer's sales staff are highly valued as a reliable source of information. They are largely important due to their 'flexibility' as communicators: they can provide the right kind of information relative to the needs of individual buyers. Distrust of sales staff was not widespread. In fact, 26 out of the 50 respondents said that the manufacturer's salesperson was the most *trusted* source of information. The implications for selection, training, motivation, and supervision of sales forces are clearly evident.

3. Only 2 out of 50 respondents indicated that there were certain companies to which they consistently looked as guides to their buying decisions. Hence, opinion leadership in industrial markets seems largely ineffective. Most companies argued that specific companies were not important; companies have *particular* problems and it would be very unlikely for an individual manufacturer to find precise coincidence of needs and experience elsewhere. The two respondents who looked to opinion leaders shared the following views: that companies who were opinion leaders were of large size, committed to new product development, financially successful, and 'growth' companies with progressive top management. In fact, it is particularly interesting to note that this specification embraces the characteristic qualities which research has shown to be identified with 'innovativeness'.

4. At the 'awareness' stage, trade journals were slightly more important than sales personnel.

Webster stated that his conclusions were entirely consistent with the results of a national probability sample of 200 purchasing managers in 1966. He concluded that word-of-mouth communication (from external sources) does not appear to be significant in industrial markets; the manufacturer's salesperson exercises the key influence with buyers. The findings of Webster's interesting research are summarized in Table 10.1.

It is relevant to note that Webster's research focused only on *inter-firm* dimensions of word-of-mouth communications. He ignored the *intra-firm* aspects; word-of-mouth communication within firms was studied by John A. Martilla.[33] His findings were based on research undertaken in three industrial markets from which he was able to show 'that word of mouth communication *within* firms is an important influence in the later stages of the adoption

Table 10.1   Percentage of respondents finding each source important, by stage in buying process

	Awareness	Interest	Evaluation	Trial	Adoption
Manufacturers sales staff	84	90	64	70	56
Trade journals	90	38	22	16	8
Buyers in other companies	18	22	28	16	8
Engineers in other companies	26	34	44	20	18
Trade associates	42	24	14	4	8
Trade shows	76	38	16	12	4

Notes

1. Respondents were asked to indicate any source that was useful to them at each stage of buying process.
2. No requirements were placed on the number of sources—it was possible for a respondent to indicate that all sources were important at all stages or that none was useful at any stage.
3. Out of a possible 30 responses (6 sources × 5 stages), the average respondent indicated 10.
   Source: Webster.[32]

process. Opinion leaders were found to be more heavily exposed to impersonal sources of information than other buying influentials in the firm'.

Martilla studied the paper-buying practices of 106 converting firms, including 38 envelope converters, 37 business form converters, and 31 greeting card publishers, with annual sales ranging from $1 million to over $200 million. Although he had to use a judgement sample, because of the lack of an adequate sampling frame, the findings of the postal survey were checked against a series of personal interviews and were found to be very similar.

'Contrary to Webster's findings, buying influentials in the converting markets also reported seeking information and opinions about paper from persons in competing firms, in much the same way as within the firm'. Martilla further commented that generalization across all industrial markets about the amount of information passed between firms is dangerous, 'since this may be in part a function of the degree of product differentiation and market isolation'. In many industries, as experienced executives will doubtless know, a surprising amount of information is circulated through formal and informal meetings which are regular features of industrial activities. Some industries are characterized by their attitude of friendly cooperation with competitors at trade federation level and through personal contacts at senior executive level.

Martilla also confirmed that industrial opinion leaders were difficult to identify, but that in paper converting firms, they were found to be 'exposed more frequently and in greater depth' to impersonal sources of information such as trade advertisements, editorials, product literature, sample books, etc., than the other executives who took part in the buying process. Martilla speculated that if this pattern of impersonal communication applied to other industrial markets, it would suggest that substantial advertising may be advisable to ensure that new products, for instance, were brought to the attention of 'buying influentials,' who had no direct contacts with manufacturers' salesmen.

Research on the dimensions of interactivity within the buying centre was undertaken by Johnston and Bonoma in connection with capital equipment and services.[34] Based on 60 individual buying examples, they examined the following characteristics:

1. *Lateral involvement*: number of departments involved.
2. *Vertical involvement*: number of levels involved.
3. *Extensivity*: number of individuals involved.
4. *Connectedness*: degree to which members of a buying centre are communicating with each other.
5. *Centrality*: degree of central influence exerted by purchasing managers.

The average time taken in the buying process was found to be about six months, with the longest time extending over several years. It was also found that in the search for a supplier of services, the prime criterion was the reputation of the vendor. In purchasing capital equipment, bids were often invited which formed a basis for negotiation; this was often a long and painstaking process. It was concluded that the sellers should take note of the degree of lateral involvement in customers' buying arrangements, and also the centrality factor, because this indicated the power of the purchasing manager.

10.11 THE BUYER'S DILEMMA

With highly technical products, e.g., electronic equipment, and in dynamic market conditions, buyers are at a disadvantage. They cannot possibly be specialists in such areas, although there is a tendency to appoint specialist buyers in some large organizations who have the opportunity to develop expert knowledge over a narrower field of purchasing activities.

In general, organization buyers in specialist markets tend to find themselves in a difficult position. They are responsible, at least nominally, for the external sources of materials and services that are essential for the efficient operation of their organization. Some of these buying decisions will have been taken without consultation: the buyer will have been used merely as the routine channel along which buying requisitions are passed to be translated into orders to suppliers. As professionals, buyers will regard this limitation of their authority with some disfavour, and as individuals they may feel that they have suffered some loss of status in the organization. Their personal feelings may well become more evident in those buying situations where their power as a buyer is unchallenged. By insisting on the detailed observance of buying conditions related to orders placed for routine stores, they may attempt to assert their authority in the competitive structure of the managerial system. In more extreme situations buyers may, as Marrian pointed out, 'impose "punishments" upon executives or dependants who bypass their procedures, by means of delaying order processing and execution'.[35]

That this view of the buyer is no illusion can be seen in a survey of 47 firms undertaken in the mid-1960s by PEP under the patronage of the Nuffield Foundation.[36] They reported (among many other points): 'Within the management hierarchy it often appeared that the buyer was a relatively unimportant member of the firm and sometimes he was no more than a senior clerk with direct responsibility to a senior member of management, who might be the accountant, the works director or the commercial manager'. The accountant of a large earth-moving equipment firm held an attitude typical of many senior managers: 'Buyers to my mind fulfil a clerical function only. They're told what to buy and how much to buy, and what time it's got to be in by. They're told all that by the production control department. They've then got to buy in the best market. They've got to know these markets. They've got to know who to talk to'. None the less, this executive pointed out that buying was becoming a more professional activity.

The buyer's status may be further affected by contracts for some strategic supplies being decided at board level. Buyers may, therefore, experience professional dissatisfaction from having large and vital areas of decision making taken from them, apart from those involving highly technical matters.

Unless buyers' positions are made clear to other executives in the organization, they may well become 'whipping boys' for the inevitable faults, delays, and other shortcomings of suppliers. They should be encouraged to take an active part in discussions concerning technical component parts, so that they can build up expert knowledge of these markets. Their professional buying experience may well result in considerable economies in negotiating terms. They should not be expected to act merely as a 'chaser', without real knowledge of the technical aspects of the goods ordered.

With close working arrangements with other executives, the buyer will become of greater value to the organization. There will be a ready flow of information between the various departmental heads, and the buyer will be encouraged to refer sellers' representatives to individual technical specialists for an appraisal of their particular products. In turn, the technicians will provide buyers with accurate data so that they can obtain competitive quotations and they may also, from time to time, discuss with them possible alternative specifications which may effect economies.

This more enlightened and cooperative approach to buying was highlighted in a report by the British Productivity Council of 16 case studies in value analysis, which showed clearly that significant advantages were obtained from discussing problems jointly with suppliers' representatives, company technicians, and the buyers.[37] This type of cooperation will obviously grow with the development of more complex methods of production. The acceptance of risk is inevitable in business: it has been observed that buyers will wish to minimize their risk while achieving maximum efficiency. It will be to their professional advantage to bring together all those who are interested in a particular transaction so that the final decision is made with the agreement of all of the parties involved in the negotiation.

10.12 RESEARCH ON BUYING STRATEGY

George Strauss,[38] Professor of Business Administration at the University of California, Berkeley, made a detailed study of buying agents in 142 firms, biased strongly towards large engineering companies, 'since agents in these firms face the most complex problems'. By suggesting alternatives in specifications, quantities, substitute materials, etc., buyers were able to keep the initiative; they no longer felt that they were 'at the end of the line'. Although conflict with other departmental chiefs may arise, the buyer could skilfully reduce this by using formal and informal techniques to influence the buying requisitions. This demanded an appreciation of the needs of engineering, production, and other functional specialists.

Strauss found that most buyers used a variety of techniques, depending on the problem, to keep their status in the organization:

1. *Rule-oriented tactics*: keeping to the formal rules of the organization.
2. *Rule-evading tactics*: passive resistance.
3. *Personal-political tactics*: 'informal' relations played a less important role than was expected.
4. *Educational tactics*: persuasion.
5. *Organizational interactional tactics*.

'Expansionists' favoured informal tactics 'such as indirect persuasion, inducing others to make changes in the work flow, and inter-departmental politics'. They had long-run strategies and sought to influence buying considerations at an early stage. Their general approach was characteristically flexible; they used, with success, both formal and informal tactics to achieve their objectives. Successful 'expansionism' seemed to depend on: the technology of an industry (complex production offered the greatest opportunities); management philosophy (one remarkably successful agent was in a company which had just introduced a new management and where all relationships were in flux); and education (better education seemed to develop the use of informal techniques and the ability to secure advantages in committee deliberations).

These subtle strategies have been further discussed by Bonoma and Shapiro,[39] who identified five bases of power which influence buying decisions:

1. *Reward power*: the exercise of patronage which could be in terms of monetary, social, psychological or other benefits.
2. *Coercive power*: punitive control over certain individuals who may seek to obtain special supplies, etc.
3. *Attraction power*: exercise of persuasion to win support from others in the organization.
4. *Expert power*: based on technical expertise and experience.
5. *Status power*: derived from rank and authority within organizations.

10.13 CONCENTRATION OF BUYING POWER

It has been observed that transactions covering the supply of goods and services for organizations tend to be more specialized than in consumer markets. In addition the actual number of buyers for specific products is smaller, and there tend to be greater differences between buyers. Buying power is frequently concentrated geographically, and may also be dominated by a relatively small number of companies in a specific industry. In the past, industries have tended to cluster in certain geographic areas, e.g., pottery in Stoke-on-Trent, printing and hosiery in Leicester and Nottingham, cutlery in Sheffield, and motor-car manufacture in Coventry and Birmingham.

It is interesting, perhaps, to recall that the concentration of industry is by no means a modern phenomenon. In the early years of industrial growth in the UK, a distinctive pattern of industrial concentration was observable as this fascinating extract reveals:

> The Strutts with their 1500–1600 workers at Belper and Milford, not counting their factory at Derby, were the largest of the country manufacturers, though Robert Owen came to a close second with a total labour force of 1600–1700 at his mill at New Lanark; there were some large country colonies in Scotland and one in Wales employing more than 800 and others between 250 and 500, including Styal; but the number of 'cotton lords' was actually very small compared to the host of petty employers with their scores of workers. In 1816, when steam had begun to bring the industry into towns, there were only nine mills—six of them in Manchester—with more than 600 workers but there were 85 with less than 200. Altogether the large firms accounted for 14,000 out of the 60,000 cotton factory operatives at that time, and they never failed to draw a distinction between themselves and their smaller and less reputable competitors.[40]

In addition to geographical concentration, industrial markets are frequently dominated by a limited number of enterprises whose aggregate output accounts for the bulk of the output of a specific product market. Industrial mergers and reorganizations have characterized many industries, such as brewing, shipbuilding, carpet production, and electronic engineering, and large-scale centralized buying has developed strongly. The operation of the 80/20 rule has greater significance for marketers than in the 1950s, and 1960s. Car manufacturing in Britain is centred around a very small number of high-volume production plants; the telecommunications industry is largely represented by a few large companies with substantial experience in the design and production of sophisticated equipment.

Research by Channon on UK industrial concentration in the period 1970–8 showed that there was an overall trend towards higher concentration.[41] By 1978, 55 (35.2 per cent) of 156 industry segments had a five-firm concentration ratio greater than 60 per cent. (This ratio relates to the percentage of net output for the industry segment which is represented by the five largest enterprises.) This significant trend clearly affects buying negotiations; only 34 (21.4 per cent) of 149 industry segments had this level of concentration in 1970.

Buying power can range from monopsony, where there is one buyer but many sellers, to oligopoly, where there are few producers but many buyers. An example of virtual monopsonistic demand would be British Rail's recruitment of locomotive drivers and engineers in the UK. At the other extreme, oligopolistic conditions clearly limit buyer power, because no one buyer is able to dictate the terms of business; a typical example might refer to the supply of replacement tyres and motor accessories. However, two types of oligopolistic supply can be identified and affect buying behaviour: *perfect oligopoly* relates to homogeneous or largely undifferentiated commodity products such as cement, where price leadership is often apparent; and *imperfect oligopoly*, where some degree of differentiation is perceived to exist between the products of alternative suppliers. Differences may be based on actual physical characteristics, such as the intrinsic design, or perhaps, largely limited to the power of a well-established brand name. In such circumstances, price-competition is likely to be present and buyers will exercise substantial leverage in bargaining, although, as already observed, their behaviour may be inhibited because of the perceived risks involved in purchasing, for example, innovative products and also in opening accounts with new suppliers. Reliance on one supplier for an essential component is a high-risk strategy, which has encouraged the adoption of 'dual sourcing'.

Since the early 1980s however, manufacturing programmes based on 'just-in-time' (JIT) methods have placed new responsibilities on both buyers and suppliers. JIT methods are also used by supermarkets to save on staff costs and warehouse space. Under this synchronized system of supply, specific components and other products are dispatched in a sequence of deliveries to coincide with the needs of flow-line production programmes. In the North of England Nissan, for instance, have established special relationships with their suppliers, many of whom have set up plants within easy travel distance of the Nissan plant. The logistics of this type of operation are clearly critical to ensure continuous production at the major manufacturing centre.

High concentration of buying power inevitably leads to demands for special terms, priority in deliveries, and other preferential treatment from suppliers to these large organizations. There is a substantial danger, of course, that component manufacturers, for example, may become 'captive suppliers' to their very big customers; marketing strategists should carefully evaluate the risks of accepting contracts for very high proportions of their total output. The withdrawal—or threat of withdrawal—of a large-volume business may effectively limit suppliers' initiative in their market.

Concentration in industry and commerce is a phenomenon not restricted to potential and existing customers: suppliers are also likely to be affected by the current trend to large-scale operations. This may result in restricting very significantly the choices of supply open to an organizational buyer seeking specific types of products or services. It could lead to some prime-product manufacturers acquiring main suppliers in order to safeguard their own production flows, or extending their purchases beyond home-based sources of supply. This tendency is already apparent in several industries: it leads to buyers assuming a global-scanning approach to the problem of ensuring adequate supplies for their organizations.

The implications of industrial clustering are widespread: the dependence of very large industrial units on a comparatively small number of suppliers will encourage the development of standards of negotiation that recognize that bargaining is not the same as fighting, because suppliers made weak by systematic, unfairly based contracts represent a real danger to the long-term profitability of the firms with which they do business.

The role of buyers in organizations will be affected by their own personality, and the success that they are able to achieve in purchasing negotiations, both within and outside their company or institution, will largely be determined by the skill with which they can manipulate the managerial system. As Sayles has wisely remarked: 'When the organisation is viewed as a complex series of interlocking patterns of human relationships, work-flow patterns, and control patterns, the opportunity for the individual to innovate and shape his own environment becomes apparent'.[42]

10.14 MODELS OF ORGANIZATIONAL BUYING BEHAVIOUR

Various models have been offered of the buying processes in procuring organizational supplies. As with consumer buying models, those projected in relation to organizational purchases range from relatively simple descriptive models based on a sequential approach to the act of purchase to more sophisticated attempts to explain buying behaviour in terms of economic, social, cultural, and psychological motivations. Three types of models are described: verbal descriptive models, logical flow (decision process) models, and behavioural models.

Verbal descriptive models

This simplest, and probably most subjective, model could consist of a generalized account of the ways in which buyers may typically approach problems of purchasing goods and services for their organizations. By means of free-style interviews, market researchers could collect information about a range of purchases, and also the factors influencing selection of suppliers, evaluation of competitive products, extent of internal collaboration with other departments, consultative discussions with technical experts, and so on. These types of inquiries are often useful when designing further market research investigations.

Logical-flow (decision process) models

These are basically the same as those already examined in consumer buying behaviour, which, it will be recalled, contained many assumptions. From the early stages of identification of a need, progress is made by specifying products or services which may be capable of satisfying particular needs, then identifying suitable sources of supply, evaluating their offers, and finally selecting a specific supplier (or suppliers). The MSI model is a typical example of this step-by-step approach; many other formulations exist which share the type of framework, which will now be discussed in some detail.

Marketing Science Institute (MSI) industrial buying model   The MSI industrial buying model originated by Robinson, Faris, and Wind is based on the 'Buygrid' conceptual framework, which analyses industrial buying situations into three 'buyclasses' and eight 'buyphases' as shown in Fig. 10.1.[43]

The 'buyphases' follow a sequential approach similar to the decision-process models used in consumer marketing studies, and outlined in Chapter 9.

These phases are set against three alternative Buyclasses which are likely to modify significantly buying practices. At different points in the buying sequence, contributions to the decision process may come from several of the distinct functions of management within organizations.

Phase 1 has two elements: the recognition of a problem and the awareness that solution may be obtained through purchasing a specific product or service. Industrial problems may be

		BUYCLASSES		
		New task	Modified rebuy	Straight rebuy
B U Y P H A S E S	1. Anticipation or recognition of a problem (need) and a general solution			
	2. Determination of characteristics and quantity of needed item			
	3. Description of characteristics and quantity of needed item			
	4. Search for and qualification of potential sources			
	5. Acquisition and analysis of proposals			
	6. Evaluation of proposals and selection of supplier(s)			
	7. Selection of an order routine			
	8. Performance feedback and evaluation			

Fig. 10.1   The 'Buygrid' analytic framework for industrial buying situations (*Source:* Robinson *et al.*)[43]

Notes
1. The most complex buying situations occur in the upper left portion of the 'Buygrid' matrix, when the largest number of decision-makers and buying influences are involved. Thus, a new task in its initial phase of problem recognition generally represents the greatest difficulty for management.
2. Clearly, a new task may entail policy questions and special studies, whereas a modified rebuy may be more routine, and a straight rebuy essentially automatic.
3. As buyphases are completed, moving from phase 1 through 8, the process of 'creeping commitment' occurs, and there is diminishing likelihood of new vendors gaining access to the buying situation.

caused by levels of stocks being diminished, by customers demanding new specifications of existing products supplied to them, or by the demand developing for entirely new versions of products; other causes may be triggered off by plant breakdowns and similar unplanned events.

Phase 2 and *phase 3* cover activities that are of crucial importance to marketers. Depending on the nature of the 'buyclass' related to a specific product need, marketers may be able to exert considerable influence on those members of the decision-making team who are involved in specifying the characteristics considered desirable. Consultation, leading to mutual exchange of information, may become the foundation on which future business is built. The role of the industrial salesperson in these critical phases of the buying process has already been commented on (see Webster).[32] The salesperson needs to identify the various buying influences, and to form a careful opinion of the relative importance of these to the final act of purchasing. Successful industrial negotiators are well aware of the need to analyse the buying team's power structure: this strategic approach has already been reviewed.

Phase 4 concerns the search for and evaluation of potential sources of supply for a specific product or service. Buying criteria may be affected by many factors which suppliers should endeavour to identify in relation to industries and individual firms within those industries. Marketing research should be useful in systematically analysing these needs, so that products are designed which are capable of providing the benefits explicitly or implicitly sought by application of buying criteria.

Phase 5 and *phase 6* include requests for sources of supply to submit proposals (quotations) to the prospective purchasing organization, on evaluation of which, one or more offers are accepted. During the course of submitting prices and specifications affecting quality, delivery, etc., prospective suppliers' activities in phases 4 and 5 are likely to overlap and, to some degree, become almost indistinguishable.

Phase 7 starts with the act of purchase and continues through to monitoring the activities of a selected supplier until delivery is made and the specific product or service is in use. The satisfactory completion by suppliers of customers' order requirements leads to the next stage of the MSI model.

Phase 8 relates to the long-term evaluation of a specific product's performance. At this stage, the importance of 'users' in the buying team's decision process assumes significance for suppliers. Feedback of performance will be demanded before repeat purchases are generally made; on the list of buying criteria, reliability, quality, and similar characteristics are likely to be ranked high. In fact, these features were shown to be significant influences in research findings concerning one of the largest UK manufacturers of machine tools.[44] Moreover, because of the infrequency of purchase of these products, information about machine performance may be derived from experience gathered over a period of years stretching back some considerable way. Past experience by users play an important part in the decision process for capital items of equipment such as those investigated. Suppliers of industrial equipment are dealing in products that represent investment decisions; prospective buyers will approach with caution, and post-purchase evaluation will be thorough and influential in future buying decisions.

This last phase is likely to witness the impact of post-decisional dissonance (see Chapter 2), so the provision of efficient technical advice and adequate servicing arrangements will be critical inputs into effective marketing strategies.

Relationships between phases Close interrelation will exist between the various phases in the buying process; they are not likely to be watertight compartments. In fact, it may be difficult, and even unnecessary, to identify exactly the limits of each phase. As with consumer products, the rate of progress of individual buyers through the different stages in the buying sequence may be considerably affected by the type of product: this aspect of buying deliberation is reflected in the three 'buyclasses' shown in Fig. 10.1. Routine items of stores, such as cleaning rags or nuts and bolts, are unlikely to occupy a great deal of time in the middle steps of the buying ladder, whereas installation of a filtration plant or a computer system will call for very extensive activities in drawing up specifications, evaluating competitive offers, and similar complex matters. Finally, particular attention will be given by customers to ensuring that contractual obligations of this nature are fulfilled adequately by the chosen suppliers.

The MSI model incorporating the 'Buygrid' framework offers a useful method of analysing organizational buying processes on a linear basis. As the model does not specifically identify the complex influences affecting purchase decisions, 'it is more a skeletal framework than a fully integrated and complete model of the decision processes in organisational buying'.[24] The activities of the executives involved in the various stages of the decision process are discussed in some detail, but from the viewpoint that they are almost exclusively motivated by economic factors. The inputs to the buying process may arise, as has already been observed, from social, cultural, and psychological sources as well as economic ones: 'clues are given as to their identity', but, in essence, the model is deficient.

The MSI model was critically assessed by Bellizi and McVey, who applied it in research on the commercial construction industry in America.[45] From a postal questionnaire sent to a sample of 650 general contractors, 140 usable responses (21.5 per cent) were obtained. They found that the MSI 'buyclass' variable was of little value in explaining or predicting buying behaviour, although it appeared to have some relationship to the amount of information sought by buyers and the number of alternatives considered by them. This latter finding is not surprising, bearing in mind that 'buyclasses' differentiate between first-time purchases and repeat purchases.

While 'buyclass' variables were stated to lack significance related to buying behaviour in the construction industry, *product type* was declared to be a meaningful variable. It was found—again not surprisingly, perhaps—that the influence of top managers varied as cost and nature of the goods purchased moved from inexpensive operating supplies to expensive capital equipment. The former tended to be within the influence of construction site superintendents, shop foremen, and other building trade workers, while the latter became increasingly the focus of senior management's attention.

The researchers expected that top managers could exert more influence than lower echelons of staff under 'new buy' conditions. 'Surprisingly, the opposite was found. Although the findings are not statistically significant, the direction of the scores is somewhat perplexing. It is further surprising to find the "buyclass" variable statistically non-significant'.[45] Hence, the researchers, as noted earlier, felt that the 'buyclass' variable of the MSI model had little explanatory or predictive value.

In evaluating these critical findings, the restricted coverage of the survey and the relatively low response rate should be borne in mind. As Bellizi and McVey say, further research in the influence of the 'buyclass' variable is called for.

Behavioural models

This third type of buying model has also been discussed in Chapter 9; it attempts to recognize and study the complex interplay of economic factors, and socio-cultural and emotive influences in buying decisions. The conflict that may arise from these mixed motivations has been noted earlier, and it has been seen that the organizational buying transaction is by no means immune from those influences often typified as non-rational.

A comprehensive model of organizational buying behaviour endeavours, in general terms, to reflect all the factors that are thought to be significant in obtaining goods and services. The precise relationships of these multiple influences will be affected by the nature of specific products, and individual interpretation of their effects should be based on objective research findings.

Jagdish Sheth has constructed a model of industrial buyer behaviour based on the format and classification of variables used in the Howard–Sheth model which was discussed in considerable detail with reference to consumer purchases. Sheth's integrative model of industrial buyer behaviour is depicted in Fig. 10.2[46] and, like the consumer model, it requires systematic testing over a range of supplies and with particular types of organizations. Sheth points out that this industrial buyer behaviour model, unlike the more general model devised by Howard and Sheth, is limited to organizational buying; it describes the joint decision-making process as opposed to the individual decision process, and it contains far fewer variables.

Three distinct aspects of organizational buyer behaviour are identified:

1. The 'psychological world of the individuals involved in organisational buying decisions'.
2. The 'conditions which precipitate joint decisions among these individuals'.
3. The 'process of joint decision-making with the inevitable conflict among the decision makers and its resolution by resorting to a variety of tactics'.

Sheth includes several social and psychological factors, of which 'expectations' about suppliers and brands are of prime importance. Since organizational buying processes frequently

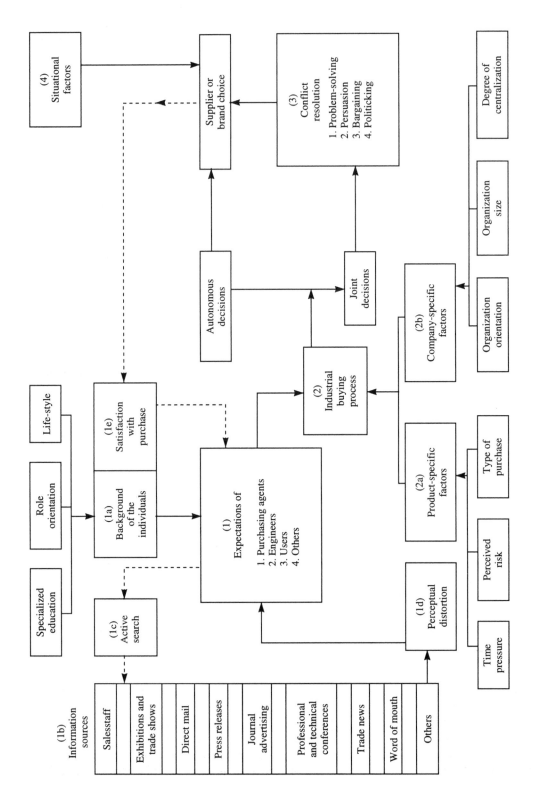

Fig. 10.2 Sheth's integrative model of industrial buying behaviour (*Source*: Sheth)[46]

involve 'at least three departments'—most probably executives from the purchasing, quality control, and manufacturing activities—it is important to form some appreciation of the 'differential expectations' among these individuals. Five different influences are seen to be active: the background of the individuals; information sources; active search; perceptual distortion; and satisfaction with past purchase.

The individual contributors to the organizational decision process will tend to set different objectives which are to be met by a supplier of a particular product or brand. These differing criteria may result in conflict: in general, users tend to be interested in prompt delivery, satisfactory installation, and efficient servicing arrangements; purchasing agents pay particular attention to maximum price advantage and transport facilities; and engineers are preoccupied with standards of quality, performance, and product standardization.

Sheth argues that these different criteria are substantially the results of personal backgrounds, life-styles, professional training, etc.; exposure to sources of information ranging from word of mouth to commercial advertising; the responsibility for 'active search' which tends to be considered as the responsibility of purchasing agents; the effect of perceptual distortion and retention of the various messages received by individual executives; and, finally, the degree of satisfaction with past buying experiences with a specific supplier's product. It is highly likely that purchasing agents, engineers, and production executives may experience different levels of satisfaction, because of the difference criteria that they use as measures of acceptability.

Marketing research techniques such as psychographic scaling and factor analysis would be valuable in obtaining data on the critical differences in perception of a product or brand by the various contributors to the organizational buying process.

The second characteristic aspect of organizational buying behaviour identified by Sheth—determinants of joint as opposed to autonomous decisions—refers to the vital need for suppliers to be able to identify the *nature* of the buying decision, i.e., does it depend on a single, autonomous decision or is it the product of a joint process of deliberation and agreement? Sheth considers that there are six primary factors affecting the nature of specific buying decisions. He classifies these in two categories: product- or service-specific factors and company-specific factors. These components are shown at the bottom of Fig. 10.2, and it will be observed that product-specific factors include perceived risk, type of purchase, and time pressure. Company-specific factors are seen to be organization orientation, organization size, and degree of centralization.

Sheth admits that although there is considerable research evidence in general organization behaviour to support these six factors, research is needed in industrial buying situations relating to their influence.

The third characteristic of organizational buying behaviour—the process of joint decision making—contains the core of the model projected by Sheth. This aspect of organizational buying behaviour has already been discussed at some length. Conflict in organizational decision-making where several parties are involved appears to be inevitable. It may, in fact, be a creative influence in acting as a catalyst, developing managerial effectiveness and contributing to the quality of the final decision taken. The ways in which conflicts are *resolved* are matters of real interest, because these affect the substance of buying decisions. Where buying conflicts degenerate into the 'tactics of lateral relationship' typified by Strauss, and noted earlier, the whole process of decision-making will be imperilled.[38]

Conflict may arise in many ways: from bad communications within an organization, lack of mutual trust, interdepartmental rivalries which have been allowed to exert abnormal pressures on the work-style of staff, differing expectations of executives taking part in decision processes, lack of breadth of experience by some executives, etc. Many buying decisions in organizations are subject, therefore, to an almost Machiavellian process of wheeling and dealing.

Sheth draws attention to the influence of 'ad hoc situational factors', such as temporary price controls, trade recessions, industry strikes, and merging of supplying firms, which 'ample empirical evidence suggests' may be particularly influential in some industrial buying decisions. 'In other words, similar to consumer behaviour, the industrial buyers often decide on factors other than rational or realistic criteria'.

It is admitted by Sheth that where buying decisions are based strictly on a set of situational factors, theorizing or model building will not be relevant. In these circumstances, systematic studies should be made of the ad hoc events which intervene to spoil the theorized relationships in a specific buying decision. Sheth's model is valuable in offering a framework that highlights the multiple nature of organizational buying influences and presents these factors in a methodical manner. 'How far they relate to actual buying situations is a matter for objective investigation'.[24]

The Webster–Wind model This projects industrial buying as 'a decision-making process carried out by individuals, in interaction with other people, in the context of a formal organisation', which, in turn, is influenced by several environmental variables.[25] Four classes of variables are noted by these researchers: environmental, organizational, social, and individual. Within each class, two broad types of variable—task and non-task—are found (see Sec. 10.9). These four factors are projected to be influenced by task and non-task variables as shown in Table 10.2.

Webster and Wind realistically comment that it is rarely possible to identify a given set of variables as exclusively task or non-task; both dimensions are likely to be present, but one may be predominant. 'For example, motives will inevitably have both dimensions—those relating directly to the problem to be solved and those primarily concerned with personal goals'.[25] The researchers add that these motives 'overlap in many important respects and need not conflict; a strong sense of personal involvement can create more effective buying decisions from an organisational viewpoint'. (It may be as well to compare this opinion with the discussion in Sec. 10.6 on complexity and conflict in buying situations.)

Table 10.2   Classification and examples of variables influencing organizational buying decisions

	Task	Non-task
Individual	Desire to obtain lowest price	Personal values and needs
Social	Meetings to set specifications	Informal, off-the-job interactions
Organizational	Policy regarding local supplier preference	Methods of personnel evaluation
Environmental	Anticipated changes in prices	Political climate in an election year

Source: Webster and Wind.[25]

Webster and Wind's model (see Fig. 10.3), like Sheth's, list a great number of factors which, to varying degrees, influence industrial buying behaviour; it is presented 'as a comprehensive view of organisational buying that enables one to evaluate the relevance of specific variables and thereby permits greater insight into the basic processes of industrial buying behaviour'. The various roles in buying (discussed in detail Sec. 10.9) are a notable feature of Webster and Wind's model, which includes the individual psychological factors of cognitions, motivations, personality, and learning processes; group influences are also included. However, useful though

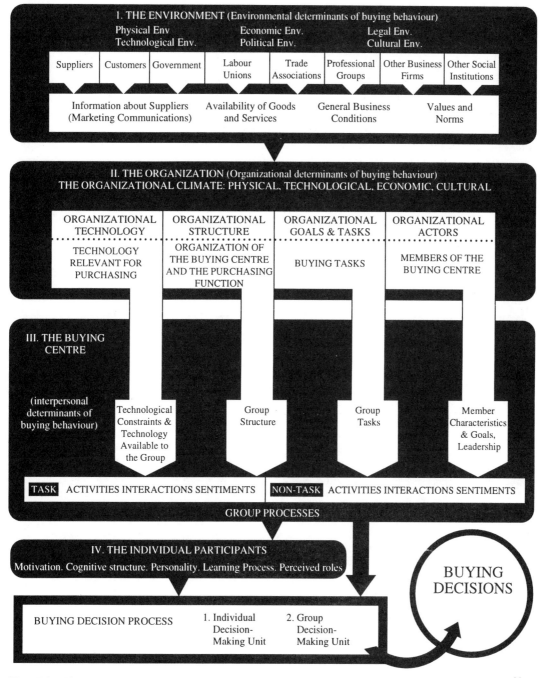

Fig. 10.3 The Webster–Wind model of organizational buying behaviour (*Source:* Webster and Wind)[25]

this general model of organizational buying behaviour is, it does not detail how buyers process and use the information derived from the multiple sources listed.

The interaction model This model, developed by the IMP Project Group and based on research by Hakannson and others,[16] focuses on the interactions that take place in the process of negotiations (see Fig. 10.4). The research project covered industrial buying and selling

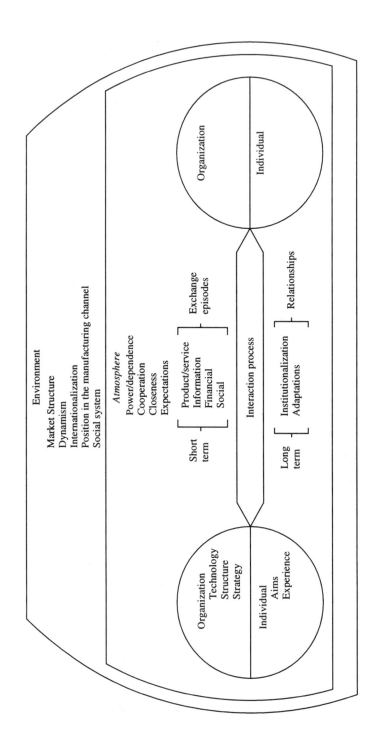

Fig. 10.4 The Hakansson interaction model of industrial marketing and purchasing (*Source:* Hakansson)[11]

behaviour in France, Italy, Sweden, Germany, and the UK, and both quantitative and qualitative data were collected as the result of 900 'operative interviews'. Six research institutes collaborated—including the University of Manchester Institute of Science and Technology (UMIST) and the University of Bath in the UK—in this research whose underlying theoretical base is derived from two sources: inter-organizational theory and the new institutional economic theory. It is also said to be directly related to evolutions in marketing literature, particularly those emphasizing inter-company relationships.

Four basic elements are said to contribute to the interaction between buyers and sellers: the interaction process, the participants, the interaction environment, and the atmosphere created by the interaction. From Fig. 10.4, these four sets of variables will be noted, and it will also be seen that there are several subdivisions of these basic factors. For example, in the interaction process there are 'episodes', which may be 'individual' and refer to the placing or delivery of a specific order. These kinds of activities give rise to expectations by both parties which tend to become institutionalized in time. The interaction process is favoured by both relationships and episodes (see Fig. 10.5).

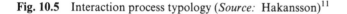

RELATIONSHIPS

		Limited	Extensive
	Simple	I	III
EPISODES			
	Complex	II	IV

Fig. 10.5 Interaction process typology (*Source:* Hakansson)[11]

Cell I of the matrix relates to situations typified by simple problems and limited previous relationships between the two parties to a business transaction. Hakansson declares this to be the 'classical' model of exchange situations, where the buyer freely selects from existing alternatives; decision-making is relatively simple in these conditions, and marketers are said to have very limited scope because 'almost everything is standardised'.[11]

Cell II (complex episodes/limited relationships) refers to situations when two companies are about to transact business for the first time. While the relationship is likely to be of limited duration, the negotiation will probably be complex, as with major capital equipment. It is vital, therefore, for mutually advantageous relationships to be established at an early stage in the negotiations, which will involve several people—technical, financial, production, etc.—whose professional inputs will require effective coordination so that negotiations proceed satisfactorily.

Cell III (simple episodes/extensive relationships) typifies many business transactions which have become virtually routinized. However, both parties should be sensitive to changed circumstances that may cause 'episodes' to become more complex.

Cell IV (complex episodes/extensive relationships) may result from a crisis or need for change in a relationship, emanating, perhaps, from technical or commercial changes affecting product developments or involving new ownership of the company.

Hakansson's model stresses that buying and selling establishes relationships to which both parties have contributed. It is stated that this concept is held to be 'in contrast to the more traditional view of marketing which analyses the *reaction* of an aggregate market to a seller's offering. This comment would certainly surprise experienced executives who know that business negotiation is a dynamic process dependent on developing mutually agreeable relationships (see Sec. 10.2).

The interaction model accepts that behavioural factors are influential in organizational buying and selling; it stresses that both formal and informal contacts help in establishing productive relationships; and it emphasizes the need for executives to develop insight into human behaviour if they are to be successful in negotiations. Relationships need to be fostered both *within* organizations as well as externally; sometimes, organizations seem to be in danger from internecine warfare rather than from the assaults of competitors.

The IMP project[11] spanned several countries, so it is not surprising that attitudes towards participation and authority were found to be 'quite different' in France and Germany compared with Sweden, but it was felt that more extensive research would be required before this cultural phenomenon could be definitely accepted.

Arm's-length trading vs. Alliances

The degree to which 'arm's-length' trading arrangements between buyers and sellers in industrial markets could be effectively supplanted by 'alliances' involving closer ties and newer types of close working cooperation was studied by two US researchers.[47] From a random sample of 1157 firms drawn from three major SIC (Standard Industrial Classification) groups, a final sample of 155 respondents was achieved; these covered a variety of components, including fabricated metal parts, electronic sub-assemblies, and finished components such as motors and power units. All respondents were asked to complete a postal questionnaire with reference to a self-selected supplier about whom they were knowledgeable, in order to assess the nature and degree of close working relationships between buyers and their suppliers.

The research findings tended to challenge the view that closer relationships were 'a universally desirable idea': 'bilateral governance' (the term used to describe close relationships) was declared to be 'useful only when specific assets and uncertainty evoke a need to protect and adopt'. It was also found that selling is 'not simply the "flip side" of purchasing', and different safeguards are necessary for the parties concerned. Buyers and sellers were reported to have 'different incentives for developing close relationships, but their approaches to developing alliances may differ'. The rather indeterminate nature of these findings reinforces the researchers' recommendations for further empirical studies in this area.

10.15 SUMMARY

Negotiation is at the heart of business deals: both buyers and sellers are motivated by personal and organizational factors. Cultural norms, personal psychological factors, and group influences are likely to contribute to successful negotiations.

Organizational supplies are sometimes similar to those bought by consumers, but the *motives* for purchase will be different. But in many cases, distinctly different products and services are demanded, such as capital equipment and sophisticated technical services. These kinds of products are characterized by extended durability, low frequency of purchase, and substantial cost.

Various categories of organizational supplies have been developed: IMRA's has three 'sequential' classes: capital goods, primary goods, and intermediate products.

Derived demand is a significant factor in industrial marketing; end-use analysis is imperative.

Risk is an inherent feature of life, and particularly evident in business deals. Risk policies should be carefully thought through.

Organizational buying is complex and research has indicated the influence of decision-making units (DMUs). Five roles in buying have been identified: gatekeeper, influencer, user, decider, and buyer.

Buyers may develop distinctive role strategies so as to maintain their power in their organizations.

Models of organizational buying behaviour include MSI (decision process); Sheth, and Webster and Wind's (behavioural); also the contribution based on IMP Group's research, focusing on the interaction processes in buying and selling.

REFERENCES

1. Oppenheim, A. M., *Question Design and Attitude Measurement*, Heinemann, Oxford, 1968.
2. Argyle, Michael, *Bodily Communication*, Methuen, London, 1975.
3. Drucker, Peter F., 'What we can learn from Japanese management', *Harvard Business Review*, March/April 1971.
4. Keegan, Warren J., *Global Marketing Management*, Prentice-Hall, Englewood Cliffs, New Jersey, 1989.
5. Jackson, K. J., *The Art of Solving Problems*, Heinemann, Oxford, 1975.
6. Kapoor, Ashok, 'MNC negotiations: characteristics and planning implications', *Columbia Journal of World Business*, vol. 9, no. 4, winter 1974.
7. Arthur, Henry B., 'On rivalry in the market place', *Harvard Business Review*, September/October 1972.
8. Ansoff, H. Igor, *Corporate Strategy*, Penguin, London, 1968.
9. Industrial Marketing Research Association (IMRA), 'Regulations', Lichfield, 1969.
10. Stanton, William J., *Fundamentals of Marketing*, McGraw-Hill, Kogakusha, 1978.
11. Hakansson, Hakan (ed.) *International Marketing and Purchasing of Industrial Goods: An Interaction Approach*, John Wiley, Chichester, 1982.
12. Shanks, Michael, *The Stagnant Society*, Penguin, London, 1972.
13. McClelland, David C., *The Achieving Society*, Free Press, New York, 1961.
14. Wilson, David T., 'Industrial buyers' decision-making styles', *Journal of Marketing Research*, vol. 8, no. 4, November 1971.
15. Douglas, Susan P., and C. Samuel Craig, *International Marketing Research*, Prentice-Hall, Englewood Cliffs, New Jersey, 1983.
16. Wormald, Avison, *International Business*, Pan, London, 1973.
17. Levitt, Theodore, 'The new markets—think before you leap', *Harvard Business Review*, May/June 1969.
18. Erickson, Robert A., 'How industry buys—an update,' in: *The Challenge of the Eighties*, ESOMAR, Brussels, September 1979.
19. Buckner, Hugh, *How British Industry Buys*, Hutchinson, London, 1967.
20. *Financial Times*, 'How British industry buys', 1974.
21. Brand, Gordon, *The Industrial Buying Decision*, Cassell, London, 1972.
22. *Financial Times*, 'How British industry buys', 1983.
23. Banting, Peter M., David Ford, Andrew C. Gross, and George Holmes, 'Generalisations from a cross-national study of the industrial buying process', *International Marketing Review*, vol. 2, no. 4, winter 1985.
24. Chisnall, Peter M., *Strategic Industrial Marketing*, Prentice-Hall, Hemel Hempstead, 1989.
25. Webster, Frederick E. Jnr, and Yoram Wind, *Organizational Buying Behaviour*, Prentice-Hall, Englewood Cliffs, New Jersey, 1972.
26. Desoutter, Michael, 'Industrial advertising', in: *Marketing of Industrial Products*, Aubrey Wilson (ed.), Hutchinson, London, 1968.
27. Katz, Elihu, and P. F. Lazarsfeld, *Personal Influence*, Free Press, Glencoe, 1955.
28. Abratt, Russell, 'Industrial buying in high-tech markets', *Industrial Marketing Management*, vol. 15, 1986.
29. Cyert, Richard M., and James G. March, *A Behavioural Theory of the Firm*, Prentice-Hall, Englewood Cliffs, New Jersey, 1973.
30. Alexander, R. S., J. S. Cross and R. M. Cunningham, *Industrial Marketing*, Richard D. Irwin, Homewood, Illinois, 1961.

31. McGraw-Hill, 'Special report on the buying and selling techniques in British engineering industry', McGraw-Hill, Maidenhead, 1963.
32. Webster, Frederick E. Jnr, 'Informal communications in industrial markets', *Journal of Marketing Research*, vol. 7, no. 2, May 1970.
33. Martilla, John A., 'Word of mouth communication in the industrial adoption process', *Journal of Marketing Research*, vol. 8, no. 2, May 1971.
34. Johnston, W. J., and T. V. Bonoma, 'Purchase process for capital equipment and purchases', *Industrial Marketing Management*, vol. 10, 1981.
35. Marrian, Jacqueline, 'Marketing characteristics of industrial goods and buyers', in *The Marketing of Industrial Products*, Aubrey Wilson (ed.), Hutchinson, London, 1968.
36. Gater, Anthony, David Insull, Harold Lind, and Peter Seglow, 'Attitudes in British management', PEP report, 1965.
37. British Productivity Council, 'Sixteen case studies in value analysis', British Productivity Council, 1964.
38. Strauss, George, 'Tactics of lateral relationship: the purchasing agent', *Administrative Quarterly*, Cornell University, September 1962.
39. Bonoma, T.V., and B.P. Shapiro, *Segmenting the Industrial Market*, Lexington, Kentucky, 1983.
40. Chambers, J. D., *The Workshop of the World*, Oxford University Press, Oxford, 1968.
41. Channon, Derek, 'Industrial structure', *Long Range Planning*, vol. 15, no. 5, 1982.
42. Saylés, Leonard, *Managerial Behaviour*, McGraw-Hill, New York, 1964.
43. Robinson, Patrick J., Charles W. Faris, and Yoram Wind, *Industrial Buying and Creative Marketing*, Allyn and Bacon, Boston, Massachusetts, 1967.
44. Cunningham, M. J., and J. G. White, 'The determinants of choice of supplier', *European Journal of Marketing*, vol. 7, no. 3, winter 1973/4.
45. Bellizi, Joseph A., and Phillip McVey, 'How valid is the Buy-grid model?', *Industrial Marketing Management*, vol. 12, no. 1, February 1983.
46. Sheth, Jagdish N., 'A model of industrial buyer behaviour', *Journal of Marketing*, vol. 37, no. 4, October 1973.
47. Heide, Jan B., and George John, 'Alliances in industrial purchasing: the determinants of joint action in buyer–supplier relationships', *Journal of Marketing Research*, vol. 27, February 1990.

REVIEW AND DISCUSSION QUESTIONS

1. How would you react to the view that industrial buying behaviour should be treated as a separate topic as it is not adequately catered for by consumer buying behaviour?
2. Assess the role and importance of the buying centre in organizational buying behaviour.
3. A firm wishes to select the most appropriate sales strategy to market fax machines to businesses in a certain city. How might an understanding of organizational buying behaviour assist in the design and conduct of a survey to determine which strategy should be used?
4. Compare and contrast the notion of the buying centre as it applies to organizational and family purchasing behaviour.
5. How many of the buyphases mentioned in Sec. 10.14 might be applicable for a firm (a) buying a fax machine for the general office (b) hiring a consultant to hold a sales seminar for staff (c) purchasing biscuits for the staff canteen.
6. How might an organization's decision process change depending on whether the purchase in question was a straight rebuy, modified rebuy, or a new task decision?

STRATEGIC APPLICATIONS

ELEVEN

INNOVATION

11.1 INTRODUCTION

In Part Five, strategic applications of marketing will be considered and related to the personal aspects of behaviour (Part Two) and group influences (Part Three), together with the models of buying behaviour described in Part Four. This chapter deals with the vital function of innovation, assessing it particularly from the behavioural viewpoint. Subsequent chapters will cover communication and market segmentation strategies. The final chapter identifies and evaluates significant trends in patterns of consumption attributable, perhaps, to certain attitudinal, social, and cultural changes that have taken place or which may well become apparent later.

Innovation is an essential constituent of successful marketing strategies. Organizations of all sizes and across the complete spectrum of industrial and commercial activities need to plan for the systematic development of new products and services. These efforts should be directed by experienced executives who have the authority to search out new ideas and pursue them with energy and intelligence. In this vital task, they should have the explicit encouragement and practical support of senior policy-making management who, while not directly intervening in the research and development programmes, will exercise skilful judgement in assessing prospects for the commercial exploitation of developed products.

The need for innovation is perennial; few companies can exist for long without a flow of new products or services which invigorate it and bring new opportunities for profitable expansion. Innovation is at the heart of advancement in modern societies: this can be seen to have dramatic effect in, for example, medical science, computer and information processing, micro-technology, petrochemicals, nuclear energy, bio-technology, and agricultural science. In these spheres, there is a hum of excitement as new products and processes flow from the inventive minds of professional and technical experts. As the president of the Massachusetts Institute of Technology remarked:

> One thing is clear. We haven't run out of important problems. There is an urgent need for continuous innovation, both to improve the quality of life and to further economic development (for some people these may be synonymous goals). But even more important, we must continue to innovate just to keep the system we now have working properly, to retain what has already been

achieved, and to insure that the quality of life doesn't drastically deteriorate because technical and industrial capabilities cannot keep up with our changing needs and resource base.[1]

The marketing environment for practically every business has changed rapidly since the early 1980s. Social and economic developments have altered people's orientation towards life; there is increasing pressure exerted by these environmental factors on business undertakings of all kinds.

> In every sphere of human endeavour, change is seen to be accelerating. Compare the phenomenal advances in medicine over recent years with the hundreds of years it took to develop even the simplest surgery. . . . It took man thousands of years to develop from flint axes to bows and arrows. It was hundreds of years before he made the cannon. In half a century he has moved from an inability to fly to the ability to orbit the globe in spacecraft. The rate of technological process accelerates and is now reaching dizzy speeds: anti-missile replacing missile—anti-anti-missile replacing anti-missile.[2]

With his customary incisiveness, Drucker has said that the purpose of a business is to create a customer and that marketing and innovation are the two basic functions of any business enterprise. Innovation, he observes, goes right through a business. 'It may be innovation in price or in service to the customer . . . in management organisation or in management methods . . . or a new insurance policy'.[3] All businesses have opportunities for innovation in their markets; for some, such as fashion clothing manufacturers and distributors, it is the vital life blood of their organizations.

Like a tidal wave, micro-electronics has swept through industry with devastating effects on the design and production of cars, watches, measuring instruments, cameras, washing machines, photocopiers, television sets, numerically controlled machine tools, wordprocessors, calculators, etc. The list is almost endless: yet micro-technology is an industry that did not exist until fairly recently. Now, its impact is dramatic on innovation in other industries. In a breathless race for technological supremacy, the microchip has revolutionized production, and in its own industry the dynamics of change are unparalleled.

The transistor, first applied commercially in the early 1950s, made the vacuum tube seem as cumbersome as an elephant and resulted in more compact and reliable computers, televisions, radios, etc. Yet, it is well to remember that radar, television, sound amplifiers, etc., were all dependent originally on the same basic invention, the wireless valve. In 1961, further progress was achieved with the introduction of the integrated circuit; four years later, one chip could accommodate 10 transistors, while 15 years on, the number of transistors that could be put in to one chip was no less than 100 000. This meteoric advance continues; almost as soon as one version of a chip has been marketed, it is out of date. It has been estimated that it costs between £3 million and £4 million to set up a production plant for microchips but the expected lifespan is no more than four years. Such inexorable growth clearly carries great risk.

Technological obsolescence has now reached frightening proportions. Lead time has virtually evaporated, and competition from across the world has challenged home producers. When Du Pont invented nylon in the 1930s, it had virtually no competition for many years, but when it introduced delrin in 1960, Celanese followed with a rival product within a year.

The merciless rate of attrition is particularly evident in consumer product launches, where the probability of success is devastatingly low. GAH, a London-based consultancy 'tracked almost 3,500 new product launches in Britain between 1982 and 1986, and as well as the poor survival rate found that even fewer introductions succeeded in recouping their investment costs'.[4] The consultants also referred in their report to similar trends in the USA, 'where only 1% of new food products ever achieved annual sales of 15 million dollars'. In the mid-1960s, a study of 20 large US companies showed that about '30–90% of products introduced in the market failed to produce a satisfactory rate of return'.[5]

Because innovation is difficult and expensive, and the pay-off uncertain, companies should plan to tackle this problem methodically. Ansoff has suggested that in a highly dynamic market environment a firm will obtain better growth and profitability if a small staff has the responsibility of searching out new products and markets, performing exploratory market research, and evaluating opportunities.[6] This planned approach to innovation will be examined more fully later. In the complex conditions of modern trading, where barriers to international competition are largely swept away, marketers cannot afford to misjudge the reactions of their customers to new products or services. Three characteristics are said to distinguish successful innovators: luck; the presence at the head of the business at a crucial stage of someone with the characteristics of an entrepreneur; and, 'third and most important'; coordination of all the various facets of management so that research and development, finance, production, and personnel work together to a coherent plan or strategy articulated by a chief executive.[7]

11.2 INVENTION AND INNOVATION

Before taking the subject of innovation further, it would be as well to clarify the terms 'invention' and 'innovation'; which tend to be used with a certain lack of specificity. In general, leading management writers view innovation as *applied invention*; however, Schumpeter stated that although most innovations could be traced back to some theoretical or practical discoveries, it was possible to innovate 'without anything we should identify as invention'.[8] Also, invention of itself does not necessarily produce any 'economically relevant effect'. Mansfield, who conducted notable research into industrial innovation, regarded innovation as applied invention which had no economic significance until it was commercially exploited. He felt that regardless of whether there exists a clear distinction between invention and innovation, the key to exploiting fully an invention lay in successful innovation.[9] An interesting view of innovation is taken by Roger, who stressed that newness of an idea related to an individual's perception: 'It really matters little so far as human behaviour is concerned, whether or not an idea is "objectively" new as measured by the amount of time elapsed since its first use or discovery'.[10]

Technological innovation, according to the 1968 report of the Central Advisory Council for Science and Technology, may be defined in several ways, but in the report it 'is used in a general sense to denote the technical, industrial and commercial steps which lead to the marketing of new manufactured products and to the commercial use of new technical processes and equipment'.[11] At one extreme innovation can imply simple investment in new manufacturing equipment or any technical measures to improve methods of production; at the other it might mean the whole sequence of scientific research, market research, invention, development, design, tooling, first production, and marketing of a new product.

A study of industrial innovation undertaken at the Science Policy Research Unit of the University of Sussex (Project SAPPHO) accepted that innovation entailed 'a complex sequence of events, involving scientific research as well as technological development, management, production and selling'.[12] The report stressed that it had been concerned with studying *innovation*, not invention. Innovation was seen to involve 'the commercial application of the results of previous inventive work and experimental development'. This definition was in agreement with the Central Advisory Council Report quoted earlier.

In general, there seems to be agreement that the process of innovation applies in commercial terms the fruits of invention. It reaches back to research and development and goes forward to the market-place through a complex series of integrated management activities. From the marketer's viewpoint, successful innovation of products and services results in improved market performance: increased profitability, improved market share, expanded market opportunities, and so on. Exploitation of inventions sets in being the process of innovation, without which 'an inventive idea . . . is quite useless'.[8] Innovation may derive from dramatic inventions such as micro-technology, or it may emanate from improving existing products: the process of 'incremental advance' will be discussed later.

11.3 EARLY INDUSTRIAL INVENTORS AND INNOVATORS

Economic history is richly stocked with the names of pragmatic inventors who, with variable success, added to the impetus of the industrial revolution in Britain. Crompton, for example, was said to be an inventor of genius who was temperamentally quite unable to create a successful firm, whereas Arkwright, the skilful adapter of other people's prototypes, exploited most profitably the factory production of roller-spun cotton yarns.[13]

Steam power was the new energy source developed in the late eighteenth century by pioneers such as Thomas Newcomen, James Watt, and Richard Trevithick, but of these, only Watt could claim formal scientific training. Early industrial innovators were largely pragmatists who looked for profit-earning opportunities; they were often inspired amateurs or brilliant artisans with limited theoretical knowledge but great persistence whose high natural intelligence was stimulated by intense curiosity. Goodyear, who successfully vulcanized rubber, lacked theoretical knowledge; the automatic telephone dialling system was invented by a Kansas City undertaker.

Chance also played its part in successful invention: serendipity led to several important discoveries including penicillin, which might have eluded scientists for many years. Fibre metallurgy resulted from a bunch of steel wool being dropped accidentally in a hot plastic mix by a researcher, frustrated in his attempts to find a new epoxy resin plastic for automotive applications.[14] Galvani, a physiologist, had left a dissected frog hanging by its legs on a set of different metals. His observation of the contraction of the frog's legs, due to the generation of electric spark, led to the development of the electric battery. Roentgen discovered X-rays by chance while experimenting with electrical discharges in high vacuums. An employee of General Motors accidentally mixed iodine into gasoline and, much to his surprise, paved the way to the discovery of antidetonants. 'As the result of fundamental research into the behaviour of chemicals at very high pressure, ICI invented polythene which, at first, was thought to be primarily useful as a very superior insulant. Its applications, in fact, proved to be diverse: packaging, household products, cold water piping, etc.'.[15] Finally, Teflon was a chance development by a Du Pont chemist who was attempting to make an improved refrigerant.

Burns and Stalker have referred to the accidental nature of much of inventive genius and industrial applications: 'Invention was seen as the product of genius, wayward, uncontrollable, often amateurish; or if not of genius, then of accident and sudden inspiration'.[16] However, they felt that this haphazard though often successful approach was no longer tenable in modern industry. The intimate atmosphere of small firms which fostered social relationships among members of their staff has largely been replaced by large impersonal organizations. 'It was still possible, in the years between the wars, for a major innovation like the gas turbine to be developed in ways reminiscent of the classic days of nineteenth century back-parlour inventions. The jet engine's invention depended on an individual's persistence and enterprise'.

The indifference shown by some leading industrial firms towards new product concepts was critically observed by Jewkes and his researchers in their classic text, *The Sources of Invention*.[17] The list of rejections is shattering: RCA resisted Armstrong's idea of frequency modulation; the Sulzer loom was offered to and declined by the leading textile manufacturers; the established aircraft companies did not believe that the retractable undercarriage had any potential; in 1925, the Marconi Company told Baird that they had no interest at all in television; and the invention of the gyro compass could not attract the backing of the navigational equipment makers. Paul Eisler, a prolific inventor of, among many products, the printed circuit, showed an early version of this outstanding innovation to Plessey, but they rejected it because it would threaten the jobs of women workers on production lines wiring and assembling electrical circuits.

11.4 INNOVATION AND TYPES OF FIRMS

In 1959 Carter and Williams declared that there was 'no great difficulty' in classifying firms according to the 'degree of technical progressiveness' attained by them.[18] They were:

1. 'Those which are in the forefront of discovery in applied science and technology, quick to master new ideas and to perceive the relevance of work in neighbouring fields'.
2. 'Those which are quite uninterested in science and technology, and are perfectly content to continue with traditional methods without even examining the alternatives'.
3. 'A large middle group, neither outstanding leaders in technology nor wholly uninterested in it'.

From research, these authors concluded that technical progressiveness was related 'to the general quality of the firm; and attention to other aspects of its general quality—for instance, to management efficiency or to salesmanship and market research—helps to create the conditions for technical progress'.[18] Those firms in category 1 are clearly entrepreneurial and quick to perceive market opportunities, whereas group 2 are complacent and alarming in their lack of entrepreneurial energy; the last group seem to be the large 'middle wedge' who are certainly not leaders but who may be reluctant followers.

In innovative strategy, firms are either leaders or followers. Ansoff typified firms as: *reactors*, which wait for problems to occur before attempting to solve them; *planners*, which anticipate problems; and *entrepreneurs*, which anticipate both problems and opportunities.[19] These latter do not wait for a specific trigger but conduct continual research for strategic opportunities, so that they can quickly take profitable advantage of market developments. Exploitation is not likely to succeed without adequate research and planning, although companies must always be on the guard against internal 'red tape' slowing down the whole process so much that opportunities are seized by competitors. Timing is one of the crucial factors in the success of new products. Some reasonable balance should be aimed at, so that in adopting planned innovation strategies companies do not lose their essential flexibility and management flair.

Ansoff's planners and entrepreneurs are often described as 'proactive': they anticipate change and plan to take advantage of it, unlike those firms adopting a reactive posture. The entrepreneurs compare closely with Carter and William's technological leaders in group 1.

11.5 INNOVATION AND RISK POLICIES

Being a market leader inevitably entails relatively high risk; innovation and risk are inseparable. Products may fail for many reasons; sometimes because they are 'before their time', or require a radical alteration in the ingrained habits of consumption or traditional ways of behaving (see Chapter 6). Examples occur from time to time in grocery products. For instance, instant mashed potato was a relative failure when it was marketed commercially in Britain some years ago, partly because it was then associated too closely with wartime 'substitute' foods. Today, it is achieving very considerable success, helped no doubt by the changed attitudes of shoppers, a new generation of consumers for whom wartime restrictions are not personally meaningful, and probably because of the higher family incomes enjoyed generally. Although branded instant mashed potato has been extensively promoted, this alone would not have made it a highly successful product today. Another example is tea bags for domestic use in Britain; they are now extremely popular and are the growth section of the rather depressed demand for tea in general. Yet, it took nearly 20 years for these 'American' tea-making habits to be adopted by British families in any significant numbers. Largely through the catering trade, the idea of using tea bags has infiltrated into British homes.

This market inertia may also be noted with some durable products, but (as noted in Chapter 6) significant changes in consumption have occurred: the new generation of home-makers now regards, for instance, central heating as virtually essential—eight out of ten UK homes now have it. Other durable products, once considered expensive luxuries, now contribute to the comfortable life-styles of many; for example, washing machines are in 85 per cent of British homes, telephones in nearly 90 per cent, refrigerators in almost every home (compared with 42 per cent in 1965). Television sets and sound equipment of various levels of sophistication abound. Sales of these types of products have grown as consumers seek to satisfy their rising expectations, including comfort in their homes, greater awareness of food hygiene, and labour-saving devices to ease the tasks of housekeeping. Highly competitive prices have also influenced the adoption of these products: refrigerators and freezers have greatly increased acceptability because modern homes are usually built without the old-style larder.

The acceptance and diffusion of products through markets will be referred to again; opinion leadership was discussed in Chapter 10 and this phenomenon will now be linked more closely with innovation strategies. Those who adopt new products and services will be analysed, and their personality characteristics will be identified in an attempt to obtain a fuller understanding of the personal factors that affect the acceptability of new ideas and products. Companies of all kinds depend heavily on customers who are willing to innovate—to give new products a trial—so some knowledge of the innovator-customer is clearly desirable.

Constant surveillance of markets is becoming increasingly important for manufacturers of all types of products. Risk taking is an essential function of management, and there is no denying that innovation strategies often bear a strong element of financial, physical, or social risk—or some combination of all these three types. But businesses cannot stand still in a dynamic environment: there is the lurking danger of stagnation leading to final extinction. As the result of considerable research into industrial innovation and the diffusion of new products, Mansfield noted that

> there seemed to be definite 'bandwagon' or 'contagion' effect. As the number of firms in an industry using an innovation increases, the probability of its adoption by a non-user increases. This is because, as experience and information regarding an innovation accumulate, the risks associated with its introduction grow less and competitive pressures mount. Moreover, in cases where the profitability of an innovation is difficult to assess, the mere fact that a large proportion of a firm's competitors have adopted the innovation may prompt the firm to consider it more seriously.[9]

The risks attached specifically to industrial innovations were researched over the period 1953–73 across major industrialized countries.[20] It was found that 13 per cent of products from 'a broad spectrum of industries' were withdrawn; less than two-thirds of 'significant innovations' achieved profitability, and repeat business was less than 50 per cent. Just over 40 per cent of successful innovations became standard products.

An instance of dramatic product failure was given by *Fortune* magazine in 1980:[21] it concerned Polaroid—'an innovative enterprise with a stunning history of technological and marketing success'—whose instant movie camera, 'Polavision', has proved to be an extremely costly failure. 'Polaroid misread the market . . . demand fell off just as it was gearing up to produce them'. Video cameras, which were challenging the 8 mm movie camera market, were ignored by Polaroid. Instead, they simply distributed 'Polavision' as widely as an earlier model, and also failed to arrange for adequate point-of-purchase demonstrations. It was admitted later that: 'We learned we didn't know how to sell it. People don't go into a drug-store to buy such a big-ticket item'.

RJR Nabisco spent $500 million over a period of seven years in developing its so-called 'smokeless' cigarette, 'Premier', which heated rather than burned tobacco and resulted in almost no smoke. But in March 1989, RJR withdrew it from test markets because of the strongly unfavourable reactions experienced. It was said that they could not market 'Premier', which had sharply reduced tar intake, as a 'safer' smoke on account of the potential risk of liability law-suits. Also, if 'Premier' were claimed to be 'safe', then other RJR products might be unfavourably compared, so the promotional message for the new cigarette focused on the fact that it eliminated 'side-stream' smoke, a source of annoyance to some non-smokers. In addition to these limitations, 'Premier' encountered 'intense hostility from regulatory authorities keen to stamp out smoking altogether'.[22]

The Seven-Up Company in the USA had been tremendously successful with their first product to use the 7-Up name—Cherry 7-Up—and this led them to develop another soda drink, 7-Up Gold. But the innovation was a disastrous flop, despite $10 million spent on network television advertising. Among several explanations of this fiasco, it was observed that the company's main product was promoted as the 'Un-Cola', but the new product was of a reddish-brown hue like a cola; it also had caffeine added, regardless of Seven-Up's earlier advertising theme 'Never Had It. Never Will'. The advertising campaign for 7-Up Gold apparently not only failed to attract the targeted audience of teenagers, but also failed to reach an equally important market sector—mothers of young children. Earlier, over-optimism had curtailed test-marketing operations; fuller tests might have revealed that consumers had confused perceptions, because 7-Up Gold clashed with the strongly developed image of Seven-Up products: 'clear and crisp, and clean, and no caffeine'. The chairman's honest summing up was 'You think you learn your lessons and practice intelligent marketing, but you can be side-tracked'.[23]

Even market leaders, it seems, are prone to make mistakes from time to time. The need to develop a risk policy has already been discussed in Chapters 9 and 10; in innovation strategies it is certainly important to assess realistically the nature and extent of risk in producing and marketing new products. An inherently good product may be unsuccessful because of timing, lack of appreciation of customer preferences, insufficient attention to 'product education', etc. Felix Wankel spent years developing the rotary engine, which promised to be a serious challenge to the ordinary piston engine fitted in cars, but it has an excessive appetite for fuel. This innovation suffered a severe disadvantage because its commercial introduction was closely followed by the international fuel crisis of the 1970s.

11.6 CLASSIFICATION OF INNOVATIONS

Innovations have been classified in various ways; some of these ways will now be considered.

Robertson has classified innovations into three basic groups: continuous, dynamically continuous, and discontinuous.[24]

1. '*A continuous innovation* has the least disrupting influence on established patterns. Alteration of a product is involved, rather than the establishment of a new product, e.g. fluoride toothpaste; new model automobile changeovers; menthol cigarettes'. To use these products, consumers do not need to change their behaviour at all, or only very slightly.
2. '*A dynamically continuous* ' *innovation* has more disrupting effects than a continuous innovation, although it still does not generally alter established patterns. It may involve the

creation of a new product or the alteration of an existing product, e.g. electric toothbrushes; the Mustang automobile; Touchstone telephones'.

3. '*A discontinuous innovation* involves the establishment of a new product and the establishment of new behaviour patterns, e.g. television; computers'. When they were first marketed, dehydrated foods diffused slowly because they entailed changes in values and in food preparation habits.

Many marketing innovations relate to new formulations of existing products and fall into Robertson's first category. At a later stage of development and acceptance in markets, it would seem that the two other types of innovatory products 'gravitate' to the status of continuous innovations.

The non-stick frying pan might be classed as a continuous innovation, although it certainly has elements of Robertson's third category of innovation since 'coated' pans have radically changed some kitchen habits. According to a report in *The Times*, the inventor of the first non-stick frying pan, Karl Kroyer, has more than 200 patents to his name.[25] Other significant innovations include video tape, radial tyres, transistors, printed circuits, hi-fi equipment, package holidays, and tufted carpeting.

Innovations have also been described as *revolutionary* or *evolutionary*. The former include jet engines, Xerox dry-copying process, or float glass, an invention which has been commercially exploited by Pilkington with marked success. It is interesting to reflect that this success was achieved only after vast expenditure on research and development in which a senior member of the Pilkington family was personally involved. This high-risk strategy paid off, and the royalties from the float glass process, which has been licensed all over the world, have represented between 40 per cent and 74 per cent of Pilkington's pre-tax profits since 1974. However, as *Fortune* observed, competitors are now challenging Pilkington's right to control the technology and have sold licenses for their own modifications of the float process.[26] With 'tapering royalties', the company has spent many millions on R&D since the mid-1970s in efforts to find other successful innovations.

A truly revolutionary innovation came from the gifted mind of Paul Eisler, who invented the printed circuit and precipitated the development of modern electronics. His genius was reputed to be both theoretical and practical:

> not only did he see that the tangled mass of wires which characterised electrical circuits in the first half of the century could be replaced by metallic tracks bonded on to an insulating layer, his experience in printing technology led him to develop a manufacturing method, foil etching, which is still in use today. His work led to miniaturisation, to the integrated circuit or silicon chip and, most important, to the low-cost mass production of electronic circuitry.[27]

The more customary mode of innovations is one of *gradual evolution*: products are improved by numerous small advances in technology. Together, these incremental innovations help to keep a company in an attractively competitive position. Sir John Harvey-Jones, the former dynamic leader of ICI, has commented on the 'valuable lesson' he was taught about technological inventions and their commercial pay-offs:

> Technologically proud and able companies always want to make big inventions. Big leaps forward are much more satisfying than small incremental changes. Yet, making money from a great invention is notoriously slow and difficult. It is the small innovations, targeted directly to someone's needs, that produce the quick and generous pay-back.[28]

The critical role of incremental, or what may be termed 'sequential', innovation has been advocated by many researchers and, in his fascinating economic history of Britain, Mathias[29] has stated that every major innovation is developed not only on fundamental advances by famous individuals but also on innumerable smaller developments made by unknown people.

Further, it is rare for something entirely new to be developed without the concept, at least, originating in some earlier product. Even the pocket calculator had its origins in the mechanical adding machines and calculators of a generation ago; but micro-technology so radically transformed the product that it bears little resemblance to its forebears.[30]

Langrish identified two basic models of innovation, *discovery push* and *need pull*, from research based on a sample of 51 innovations.[31] These two main types were further divided as follows:

1. *Discovery push*
    (a) 'science discovers, technology applies'.
    (b) 'technological discovery'.
2. *Need pull*
    (a) 'customer need'.
    (b) 'management by objective'.

Langrish admitted that it was not easy to fit innovations into any one of these models 'in a clear and unambiguous manner'. Leaving innovatory ideas to the market can be dangerous since customers are known to adhere closely to existing and familiar products and technologies. Their ability to think outside their own immediate experience is likely to be distinctly limited, whereas 'science or discovery push', by its nature, is attempting to put forward more technically demanding, fundamental, and riskier projects. Basic research is, of course, very expensive; many firms have deliberately opted for a policy of being followers, watching and waiting, ready to jump into the market which others (leaders) have opened up.

Successful technical innovations have been said to be mostly the outcome of a synthesis between interpretation of market needs ('need pull') and recognition of technical possibilities ('delivery push'), which, on reflection, seems a well-balanced mix.[32]

A further classification of innovations was given by Myers and Marquis based on research over 1963–7 in US industries.[33] Two broad groups were identified, the *defensive* and the *offensive*. The former, as its name suggests, aims to protect market share and corporate growth, while the latter refers to a product/market strategy positively planned to secure new business. Again, in real-life conditions, a blend of these approaches is highly likely.

11.7 THE DIFFUSION OF INNOVATIONS

From the discussion on the nature of innovations it will be evident that in some cases new products may entail changes in customer's behaviour, and it is important, therefore, for marketing managers to acquire an understanding of the process of diffusion.

The spread of ideas and practices among diverse culture has been studied by anthropologists for many years. Gabriel Tarde (*The Laws of Imitation*, 1903) was the first to draw attention to the fact that the process of diffusion takes the shape of the normal curve. A few people adopt the innovation at first; then the majority follow suit, and finally the rest join in (see Fig. 11.1).

Rogers defined diffusion as the process by which innovation spreads through a particular society.[10] Katz, Levin, and Hamilton, in a review of research on the diffusion of innovations, defined diffusion as: (1) the acceptance (2) over time (3) of some specific item—an idea or practice, (4) by individuals, groups or other adopting units, linked to (5) specific channels of communication, (6) to a social structure, and (7) to a given system of values, or culture.[34] These researchers commented that 'the diffusion of innovations is one of the major mechanisms of social and technical change'. Various studies have been undertaken covering many disciplines, but in both the fields of anthropology and sociology, 'diffusion studies came to a halt by about

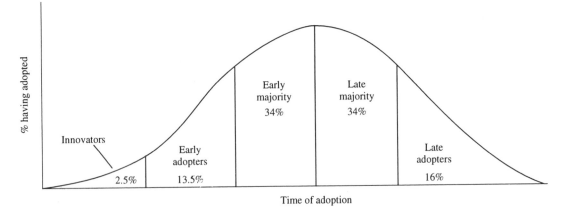

Fig. 11.1 Five stages of the diffusion of innovations

1940. In anthropology, attention shifted to the closely related problem of acculturation. . . . It is less clear why diffusion studies failed to hold the interest of sociologists'.

Rogers acknowledged that although a product or idea may be adopted, the process of diffusion may sometimes end in rejection. From exhaustive research studies ranging from the adoption of new drugs by doctors to the buying of bulk milk tanks from US farmers, Rogers distilled several important generalizations about the diffusion of new ideas. He identified the following significant factors:

1. The nature of the innovation.
2. The method of communication used.
3. The social environment in which adoption takes place.
4. The time dimension.

Communication and diffusion processes are closely linked; informal communication was found to be instrumental in the adoption and diffusion of air-conditioning equipment in a middle-class community of younger white-collar workers in the USA. Ownership tended to be clustered around certain housing blocks and could be directly traced to the social interactions between the children of the neighbourhood as well as that of their parents.[35] The subtle influence of personal informal communication was discussed in Chapter 8 with specific reference to opinion leadership: within groups or communities, certain individuals were significant in providing guidance and information for the majority of the group. They tended to act as intermediaries between the mass media promotional messages and the group in general.

Webster has emphasized that the communication and diffusion processes in industrial markets 'are somewhat different from the same processes in other social systems such as a local medical community, or a farm community, or a neighbourhood because of the unique features of industrial markets'.[36] Industrial buying decisions frequently involve several people who are motivated by both personal and organizational goals. The whole environment in which industrial decisions are taken is vastly different from the social environment of the individual consumer. Furthermore, the volume of investment which a new product may represent—and hence the risk involved—is almost certainly very much greater than with consumer spending (see Chapter 10).

Mansfield studied the rate of diffusion of twelve innovations in four industries: bituminous coal, iron and steel, brewing, and railways.[9] He hypothesized that the probability that a firm will introduce a new technique is an increasing function of the proportion of firms already using it and the profitability of doing so, but a decreasing function of the size of the investment required. The following findings emerged from his research:

1. Diffusion of a major new technique is a fairly slow process—often 21 years or more before all major firms adopted it, seldom less than 10 years.
2. There seemed to be a 'bandwagon effect' (see Sec. 11.5).
3. The rate of imitation or diffusion tended to be faster for more profitable innovations and for those requiring relatively small investments. Rates of diffusion also varied among industries; there was 'some slight indication that it is higher in less concentrated industrial categories'.
4. Study of 'intra firm rate of diffusion of diesel locomotives suggest that there are great differences among firms in the rate at which they substitute an innovation for an older method'.

Mansfield's studies lead him to suggest that 'there exists an important economic analogue to the classic psychological laws relating reaction time to the intensity of the stimulus'. The prospect of profit acted as a stimulus and seemed to control the speed of a firm's response both in using an innovation and the rapidity with which older methods were discarded.

The industrial adoption process was also studied in the USA by Ozanne and Churchill,[37] who took as their model the five stages of adoption as outlined by Rogers:[10] awareness, interest, evaluation, trial, and adoption (or rejection). Ozanne and Churchill's inquiries concerned the adoption of a new automatic machine tool ($35 000–$70 000) by a sample of mid-western industrial firms. The machine was not a radical innovation, but its automatic control system and certain other features represented readily observable improvements.

They interviewed a total of 90 decision-makers in the 39 firms that eventually cooperated in the survey. Two or more persons were found to participate in 79.5 per cent of the adoptions. Groups were analysed over the following variables: size, age, education, cosmopoliteness (degree to which individuals' orientation is external to their immediate social system), commitment to status quo, technical orientation, professional affiliation, and level in hierarchy. Firms were analysed by age, numbers of employees, and proportion of elite personnel.

Five factors affecting industrial innovation adoption were identified:

1. *Activating factors*: changes in a company's external or internal environment that may set in motion the industrial adoption process:
   (a) Capacity problems.
   (b) Skilled labour problems.
   (c) Equipment obsolescence.
   (d) Purchase replacement decision ('make or buy').
   (e) New task or problem.
   Large firms and those with more technical and scientific decision-makers tended to mention a new task or product as the determining factor. Smaller firms were more likely to mention skilled labour problems.
2. *Purchase-directing factors*: factors that influenced choice of a particular supplier of an innovation:
   (a) Quick delivery.
   (b) Cost-benefit comparisons.
   (c) Special product attributes.
   (d) Personal selling.
   (e) Past experience.
   It was found that firms with more technical and scientific executives in their policy-making group were now likely to specify cost/benefit comparisons as the primary motivation for placing business.
3. *Duration of the industrial adoption process*: the researchers concluded that 'the most meaningful element of duration is the time between initial awareness and interest arousal'.

4. *Alternatives considered*:
   (a) Groups with greater technical orientation tended to investigate more substitutes.
   (b) Groups with many professional affiliations also tended to consider more offers to supply.
   (c) Groups with higher educational attainment tended to appraise more machines.
   (d) Groups with older members tended to examine fewer substitutes.
5. *Information use*: personal and impersonal. It was significant that groups whose members travelled widely used many more sources of information. Cross-classification of educational level and number of information sources suggested that design groups with well-educated members used more information sources. Ozanne and Churchill concluded that the industrial adoption process is: 'exceedingly complex, far more so than the individual's adoption process'.[37]

Sheth was interested to investigate the effect of word-of-mouth influence in the adoption of 'low-risk' innovations.[38] He noted that existing research indirectly implies that word of mouth will not be important in less radical or low-risk innovations, at least not to the same extent as in radical or high-risk cases. Further, existing research 'explicitly suggests that word-of-mouth is not very important in informing buyers about the new product although it is very important in influencing them'. In addition, the influence of word of mouth may build up as messages are passed on. However, Sheth believed word-of-mouth influences to be influential with low-priced product innovations. He cited stainless steel blades which were introduced to the market in 1964 without mass media advertising 'for a considerable period of time'. More than 900 male respondents were interviewed; 36 per cent said they were made aware of stainless steel blades by a personal source; 48 per cent stated they were influenced to adopt the new blades by a personal source; 18 per cent stated that they had influenced someone else after their own adoption; and 48 per cent adopted the new blades immediately on becoming aware of their existence.

Sheth found that word-of-mouth communication was effective in this low-priced product market, and that there was a strong relationship between awareness and influence of word of mouth. There also seemed to be support for Katz's subsidiary proposition, i.e., that personal sources may, in addition to informing the public, also influence and reassure them, thus encouraging purchase of a new product.[39]

11.8 FIVE CATEGORIES OF ADOPTERS

In Fig. 11.1, five categories of adopters in the process of innovation diffusion were observed. Rogers's five categories of adopters are typified as follows:[10]

1. *Innovators*: venturesome (2.5 per cent).
2. *Early adopters*: respect (13.5 per cent).
3. *Early majority*: deliberate (34 per cent).
4. *Late majority*: sceptical (34 per cent).
5. *Laggards*: tradition (16 per cent).

These types were described by Rogers as 'ideal' and are 'conceptualisations that are based on observations of reality and designed to institute comparisons'. He declared that no pronounced divisions actually occurred; innovativeness could be viewed as a continuum similar to that found in social classification.

Roger's studies, from which he developed this sequential approach to the adoption of an innovation, resulted in a normal curve of distribution (as shown in Fig. 11.1). He was principally concerned with the adoption of an innovation by farmers over a period of time. His model appears to be supported by the research on industrial innovation undertaken by Mansfield (discussed in Sec. 11.2). Other studies will be examined later; at this stage it should be said that Rogers's paradigm requires and deserves more extensive validation related to marketing practices. It may offer a most valuable tool for product innovation strategy.

'Innovators are venturesome; they are eager to try new ideas'.[30] Those who buy products first are, inevitably, exposed to some element of risk. The phenomenon of risk has already been reviewed in connection with theories of motivation (Chapter 3) and in buying models (Chapters 9 and 10), and it also was seen to be significantly influenced by perception (Chapter 2).

Knowledge, experience and the degree of self-confidence of individuals clearly varies, and so will their ability to tolerate risk.[40]

In general, innovators appear to be well educated, to be self-confident, and to have ready access to information both nationally and locally. They are willing to change their habits of consumption (and may switch brands more readily than later adopters). But it would also seem that there is no 'general innovator' for all products and services. As with personal influence, different individuals seem to be effective in particular areas of innovation. 'High mobility' was another distinctive characteristic of early adopters. These individuals tend to move around a lot; they are experimental and welcome new ideas. At each move they tend to upgrade their house and its equipment. Vance Packard has referred to the 'exploitation' by advertisers of this upgrading urge of people.[41] Advertisers, it is said, have a vested interest in 'upward' mobility. (The effects of levels of aspiration on consumer behaviour were discussed in Chapter 3.)

But what of the 'laggards', those generally defined as the last group or segment of a market to adopt a new product or service? Unlike the non-adopters or non-users, they finally accept a new idea and follow the trail blazed by the innovators. In general, the problem of marketing to laggards has had little attention. They would appear to exhibit a marked reluctance to accept risk—this may relate to financial or other forms of risk. Marketers should consider how reassurance could be built into their promotional messages for new products: guarantees, 'money-back' offers, after-sales service, etc. Laggards, as Rogers described them, 'tend to be frankly suspicious of innovations, innovators and change agents'.[10] In general, laggards appear to stick to products they know about, and they avoid products that appear to be too new, unproven, and therefore risky. Brand loyalty would seem to be a strong characteristic of this type of consumer. According to Rogers's normal distribution model of innovation adoption, half of the total market may be represented by those who adopt later. This very significant proportion of a market obviously requires infiltration by mass-merchandisers if volume sales are to be achieved.

11.9 EMPIRICAL EVIDENCE OF THE DIFFUSION OF INNOVATION

In 1957, Coleman, Katz, and Manzel undertook a study of the acceptance of a new drug among a group of doctors.[42,43] A sample of 216 physicians in 4 cities was interviewed. They were able to isolate certain demographic and personality characteristics of the physician-innovator. These were briefly: younger age, larger number of subscriptions to medical journals, and closer association with medical institutions outside the local community. It was also found that doctors who shared a surgery tended to introduce the drug about two to three months sooner than their colleagues who practised alone: 'the doctor needs all the reassurance he can get from his fellows to lessen the uncertainty which he faces'. The researchers used sociometric analysis to identify sources of influence among doctors in a district. Their results suggested that 'networks of informal relations among doctors were highly effective as chains of information and influence in the diffusion of this innovation'. Social influence was significant first at a professional level, and then spread through friendship networks.

The first diffusion research in marketing was undertaken by the US Opinion Research Corporation (ORC) in 1959.[44] During this survey, 105 household heads were interviewed about their first use of a number of consumer products, with the objective of identifying 'taste makers' or innovators. The hypothesis was: 'The central thread of our modern society is mobility. The leadership elite is that group of people who possess this quality in greater degree than do other people'. Respondents were classified on a scale of mobility: high, medium, and low. High mobility criteria were: level of education, occupational mobility, social levels of contact, breadth of intellectual interests, economic status, etc. ORC concluded that about 27 per cent of the population could be classified as 'high mobiles'; these were considered to be the leaders of the US economic system. They were the first to adopt credit cards, electric blankets, hi-fi equipment, etc. This particular research—now rather old—was based on a limited sample in a middle-class community in the USA. It would be valuable to extend this type of research, and to relate it to motivational theories and to the more fluid structure of society today.

Robertson investigated the diffusion of the Touch-Tone (push-button) telephone in a middle-class suburban community in Illinois.[45] Innovators were defined as the first 10 per cent to adopt the system; the sample size was 100. Criteria measured were: venturesomeness, social integration, cosmopolitism, social mobility, and privilege. The only unconfirmed hypothesis referred to 'cosmopolitism'. Innovators, in fact, were found to be less cosmopolitan and to be 'somewhat more oriented toward their local community'. However, Robertson suggested that this may 'make sense' because if the individual is closely integrated socially with a local neighbourhood group, this may inhibit wider social contacts. Robertson's research findings led him to suggest that 'Advertising and sales strategies based on these variables would appear to stand the best chance of success'.

A study of a community antenna television system (CATV) in Laurel, Mississippi, found that 55 per cent of those who first subscribed to the service were in professional, managerial, or proprietorial occupations compared with 41 per cent of the later adopters and 22 per cent of all those in that socio-economic grouping in the community investigated.[46] It would appear that the risk factors already discussed had a significant influence, as the financial loss would be more easily borne by the more affluent consumers. Occupational mobility was significantly greater for consumer innovators than for these who adopted the service later. Almost 25 per cent of first adopters had changed jobs at least once between 1964 and 1968 compared with 16 per cent of later adopters. This 'high-mobility' factor coincides with the ORC study. Another shared characteristic related to social affiliations; consumer innovators scored significantly higher than later adopters on 10 out of 18 scales of the California Psychological Inventory: dominance; capacity for status; sociability; social presence; self-acceptance; sense of well-being; tolerance; achievement via conformance; achievement via independence; intellectual efficiency.

From research connected with 5 grocery product groups involving 142 housewives in a suburban area of Maryland,[47] it was found that new products that are not seen to be significant departures from those previously offered may be tried more readily by shoppers because the 'risk' involved appears to be less. Hence, these products tend to experience a faster rate of diffusion. Marketers may like to reflect on the old adage 'something of the old with the new': the novelty stimulates interest and curiosity while the recognizable features reassure and reduce the element of perceived risk.

That the degree of newness of a product is a major factor in determining acceptance was also demonstrated by research into purchases of 20 new supermarket products.[48] The sample comprised 250 housewives in Lexington, Kentucky. Products were classified by the researchers and trade experts as 'artificially new', 'marginally new', and 'genuinely new'. 'The results of the study seem to indicate that different groups of individuals may be "innovators" for different products depending on the products' attributes, specifically, how similar or dissimilar the product is relative to previous offerings'. Hence, the thesis discussed earlier (that innovation adoption relates to specific types of products and is not a universal orientation) appears to be supported by this study. Perceived risk is also seen to be a significant factor in accepting new products.

Research into the adoption characteristics of the personal computer market in the USA was conducted in 1980 based on 1669 in-home interviews.[49] As a result, 212 sets of respondents were classified as 'early adopters', and the remainder as 'possible late adopters'. 'Since only 5 of the early adopters were women, they, and all other women, were excluded from the sample'. Hence, the research findings cover 207 male 'early adopters' and 729 male 'possible later adopters'. Respondents were given 3 sets of independent variables—general attitudes, demographics, and sociographic—and asked to report on these.

Early adopters were characterized as follows: not frequent watchers of spectator sports; college educated; twice as many credit cards as possible late adopters; enjoy complex problem-solving; less likely to play tennis or golf; likely to own tape-deck equipment; more venturesome in being among first to buy and use new products; less likely to watch television; about twice as likely as possible later adopters to own video games; more likely to own a microwave oven; familiar with computers and disagreeing that 'computers control people'; more than twice as likely to travel for business purposes; aged about 30 years, 10 years younger than possible later adopters; more likely to be able to type; about $12 000 invested compared with $5000 of possible later adopters; and, less likely to believe they are 'victims' of the energy crisis.

The distinctly different profile of early adopters and possible later adopters of personal computers gives valuable clues as to advertising copy, media selection, and channels of distribution. Since the time of this research, the personal computer market has experienced considerable growth.

The adoption and diffusion processes involve both economic and non-economic factors; they are by no means confined to industrial, commercial, or consumer products and services, and deserve to be studied in relation to the health, education and social welfare services. 'Myths, fears and fables often inhibit the adoption of new ideas, as an attitude study which was concerned with the fluoridation of water revealed some years ago in the US'.[15] (The important factor of compatibility is discussed in Sec. 11.10.)

Research into laggard behaviour has been relatively limited. Some US researchers noted 'that over 1,000 studies in more than five disciplines have examined diffusion of innovations, but most have been devoted primarily to innovators, and/or their importance'.[50] Specific research was directed, therefore, to examining 'laggards', based on a sample of 541 households in Cedar Rapids, Iowa, and related to the initial purchase of 16 new grocery products. From data obtained, approximately 24 per cent of buyers were classified as laggards (cf Rogers's 16 per cent), 16 per cent were innovators, and the remaining 60 per cent were 'merely termed other-adopters'. The researchers noted that the exact boundaries between the various categories of adoption were not clear-cut. This observation coincides with Rogers's concept of innovative-ness as a continuum.[10] Conclusions from the study were that the major differences between laggards and innovators appeared to be income and brand loyalty. 'Families with laggard food buyers were found to have significantly lower incomes than families with innovator food buyers'. This inhibited the buying of new products; laggards preferred to wait until other more affluent buyers had tested out these innovations. Brand loyalty was, therefore, more evident with laggard buyers. It was suggested that marketers seeking to influence late adopters should stress 'not the newness of their products, but their proven acceptance and use'. Trial offers may be one way to attract these particular buyers.

The relationship between innovativeness and opinion leadership was researched by surveying the buying behaviour of 972 housewives in Marion County, Indiana, with relation to products covering domestic appliances, packaged foods, household cleaners and detergents, women's clothing fashions, and cosmetics and personal grooming aids.[51] The data suggested that no strong relationship existed between innovativeness and opinion leadership for consumer products in general. Degrees of relationship differed among types of products, ranging from correlations of 0.35 for women's clothing fashions to 0.17 for small appliances. Greater overlap seemed to occur with products of related interest, e.g., correlations of 0.25, 0.23, and 0.30 respectively were recorded for packaged food products, household cleaners and detergents, and cosmetics and personal grooming aids. These findings would tend to confirm that innovation and also opinion leadership are substantially constrained by personal interests and involvement with certain types of products.

The significance of value orientations in the adoption of innovations was examined in relation to the introduction of television in Britain. Katz and his associates have referred to research which established 'that even when class membership is held constant, different value orientations characterise early and late adopters. The former seemed to be more present-oriented while the latter were more future-oriented and perhaps inner-directed'.[34]

11.10 FIVE CHARACTERISTICS OF INNOVATION

Rogers identified four key elements in the analysis of the diffusion process, one of which referred to the characteristics of the innovation itself.[10] These characteristics will now be considered with regard to five main factors that affect acceptance of innovation in general.

1. *Relative advantage*: this is a complex matter that involves perception of the advantages of an innovation from the user's viewpoint. New products should have features that will give them distinct advantages over competitive products. Research would enable products to be designed having these relative advantages. Relative advantages may be economic or social, e.g., lower cost of production with improved machine tool, or significant social benefits from ownership of the latest kitchen equipment. For music lovers, the compact disc (CD) gives far superior reproduction than the traditional vinyl LP. It has another relative advantage in that the CD is not played with a stylus, which causes wear and results in sound imperfections, but with a laser beam that 'reads off' digital information from a metal surface. This is protected from casual damage by a transparent plastic coating. In theory at least, the CD will never wear out. Relative *dis*advantages are the cost, which is significantly more than the most expensive LP, recordings are on one side only, so playing time is limited to about an hour, and special playing equipment has to be bought. Despite these constraints, CDs have been so enthusiastically adopted that they have virtually ousted vinyl LPs from the lists of leading recording companies. But the irresistible pace of innovations in this dynamic market continues with Philips's introduction of the digital compact cassette (DCC), a slimmer, more durable type of cassette with the quality of sound found in a compact disc. Another challenge comes from Sony's launch of the mini disc, which can record up to 74 minutes from another source. In both cases, special listening equipment will be needed, which may slow the rates at which these ingenious products achieve popularity, although the need for laser players did not seem to be a serious barrier to the sales of CDs.

2. *Compatibility*: in Chapter 6, the importance of cultural norms in the adoption of products was seen to be significant. If a new product is not compatible with cultural beliefs and values it is not likely to be diffused rapidly. An attempt was once made to get Kentucky farmers to raise pickles instead of growing tobacco; it was resisted because the growing of cucumbers was perceived to be a feminine type of enterprise which was at variance with the farmers' perception of themselves at work. Another interesting case involved 'Analoze, a cherry flavoured pill that combined analgesic-antacid qualities and could be used without water'.[52] It was judged by a panel of consumers to be clearly superior to competing products, yet despite professional marketing, Analoze was abandoned after unsuccessful

test marketing in five cities. It was concluded after careful analysis that the fatal flaw was the slogan 'works without water': 'Headache sufferers consciously or unconsciously associated water with a cure, and consequently had no confidence in a tablet that dissolved without water'; it was inconsistent with their existing values.

Rogers illustrated the compatibility need of innovations by reference to the failure of an intensive campaign to boil drinking water in a small Peruvian village.[10] Although persistent efforts were made by medical workers to popularize this innovation, most families would not accept it. According to their cultural norms, only sick people should need to use hot water; healthy ones drank only cold water. Conflict may arise in marketing because of the different professional orientations of management. Production engineers, for example, may lay great stress on maintaining traditional standards of product design, durability, etc., whereas the marketing staff may be seeking to satisfy their customers' changed needs, perhaps for a lightweight version of a popular machine.

3. *Complexity*: this refers to the degree to which a product innovation is capable of being understood and sold. Graham researched the diffusion rates of canasta and television; canasta was found to have a lower level of diffusion because it required explanation. 'Unlike television, canasta cannot be adopted simply by purchasing an apparatus'.[53]

4. *Divisibility*: to what extent can an innovation be tried on a limited basis? Some products—e.g., computer systems, bulk transporters, air-conditioning equipment—pose problems in trial, whereas consumer products may frequently be bought in small trial sizes. This characteristic of innovations suggests that marketers of new products should examine whether they could help the diffusion of innovations by arranging for special terms for trial purchases.

5. *Communicability*: this refers to the success with which the results of innovation can be communicated to other members of a group. In some cases, the results are demonstrable, e.g., decorated rooms in which a new-style emulsion paint has been used. However, difficulty was experienced in convincing some farmers of the virtues of pre-emergent weed killers which are sprayed on to fields before weeds appear. The product has been adopted slowly because there was little immediate evidence (i.e., dead foliage) to demonstrate the effectiveness of the treatment. Aerosol fly sprays immediately take effect, whereas other types of deterrents are not perceived to be so directly effective.

11.11 PLANNING INNOVATION IN THE FIRM

The Central Advisory Council for Science and Technology Report (see Sec. 11.2) stated categorically:

> any firm, or indeed any country, engaged in world trade in advanced industrial products, must repeatedly modernise its manufacturing processes and introduce new or updated products if it is not to lose markets and go out of business because of competition from advances elsewhere. Hence the constant need for market awareness and for technological innovation.[11]

Five dominant factors were identified as making for success in technological innovation:

1. Direct links between research and development (R&D) activities in the organization as a whole.
2. Framing of planned programmes of innovation.
3. Management which is not only effective technically but also market oriented.
4. Capable of achieving short lead-time from initial project to marketing stage.
5. Productive capacity and market size related to launching costs of the project.

Pessemier referred to McGraw-Hill's survey of firms engaged in industrial research and development work.[54] Just over 40 per cent of respondent firms indicated that the primary purpose of their R&D programmes was to 'improve existing products'; for slightly less than 50 per cent it was to produce 'new products'. Only 11 per cent of firms considered that 'new processes' were of prime interest. In response to a question about the pay-off period envisaged from their research activities, 39 per cent gave less than three years; 52 per cent said three to five years; and only 9 per cent expected to have to wait six or more years. Longer pay-off periods appeared to be associated with major innovations. Most R&D work was designed to obtain recovery of the investment in under five years.

Problems of lead-time and product life-cycle are closely associated. Pessemier has drawn attention to the fact that the shorter the product's life and the longer the lead-time, the more difficult becomes the problem of ensuring a continuous flow of new products. A definite policy should be drawn up to guide the activities of a company so that it is able to keep abreast of market developments. In Japan, the problems of lead-time loom large: within one year of its introduction, Sony's TR-55 camcorder faced competition from rivals who offered an equally compact, if not smaller, product. One of Toshiba's technical executives commented that 'The time between you launching a product and your competitor's launch is getting shorter, because very similar basic research is being done all the time in all the big companies'.[55]

Research at McGill University into the new product success rate of industrial firms in Canada, based on a 69 per cent response from a sample of about 200 firms 'known to be active in new products', suggested that there was no obvious and direct link between the volume of R&D expenditure and the effectiveness of firms' new product programmes.[56] 'The implication is that while R and D spending does indeed generate sales via new products, it does so in an inefficient manner. The R and D dollars spent by several low R and D firms *will generate more sales* than the same R and D dollars spent in a high R and D firm'. It is suggested that there is strong evidence of rapidly diminishing returns. While technological and production factors were related to the magnitude of output, marketing resources are the key to success in new product performance. In this research, 'success' was defined as the degree to which a product exceeds (or fails to achieve) the minimum acceptable profitability for this type of investment.

Pessemier has proposed a systematic approach to new product development:[54]

1. *Search*: this entails actively searching for potential profitable new lines to add to a firm's product range. It is a positive, methodical vetting of ideas and products that appear promising.
2. *Preliminary economic analysis*: this is an initial screening process to check a potential new product against agreed criteria; e.g., comparability with company's objectives; productive and marketing plans and strengths; legal and other constraints; etc.
3. *Formal economic analysis*: extended research on product ideas which have passed the initial screening stage. Detailed examination would be made of all the aspects of the proposed new product, and its probability of success in defined markets. The decision is then made to go ahead to development stage, to reject entirely the proposition, or to defer it for later consideration.
4. *Development*: the proposition is translated into a tangible product, and submitted for evaluation to the new product development team.
5. *Product testing*: products (probably more than one version) are submitted to some form of test marketing. Marketing research techniques will be used to measure reactions of buyers (both trade and final consumers). Products may need to be amended after market reports have been examined.
6. *Commercialization*: after satisfactory clearance of market tests, production and market plans need to be carefully synchronized and an overall plan worked out in detail. Phased

marketing may be advisable to allow production lines to 'warm up'. Whatever strategy is adopted, it is vital that there should exist the very closest agreement on the objectives.

GAH, a London-based consultancy (see Sec. 11.1),[4] identified several managerial inadequacies in their study of new product launches by the food industry in the UK:

1. Few companies integrate new product development into their overall business strategy.
2. New products, while individually successful, are, therefore, unlikely to make an 'ideal fit' with overall corporate strategy.
3. There is a lack of effective direction at top level.
4. As a result, a project-by-project approach tends to be adopted instead of innovation activities being fully integrated and encouraged by top management.
5. There is a lack of new product development portfolios which results in inconsistent methods and standards of evaluation.
6. Customers are rarely consulted by companies when product improvements and innovations are considered.

11.12 PRODUCT LIFE-CYCLE

The concept of the product life-cycle has direct relevance to the task of innovation in marketing strategies. Products of all types have limited lives during which they retain profit-earning capacity. The span of useful life will vary according to the nature of products and the market conditions. In fashion clothing, pop records, or other products that are subject to volatile market demands, the pattern of life-cycle will be significantly different from, for example, household furniture. The pop record may zoom up the popularity charts, and within a few weeks it may have exhausted its appeal. Yo-yos, hula-hoops, and skateboards are other examples of products which, like rockets, make dazzling entries and soon burn out.

In domestic textiles such as carpets there is some evidence of a quickening in the pace of change; new textiles and new methods of production have enabled carpet manufacturers to follow general fashion trends more readily. This has been encouraged by the attitudes of many young home-makers who appear to prefer stylish colours and patterns before durability.

The product life-cycle (PLC) can be charted as showing a typical five-phase sequence, from introduction through to a period of growth, followed by a period of market maturity (when volume stabilizes, although unit profits may begin to fall off), on to the saturation stage (when further market development in that particular segment is most unlikely), and finally passing to the decline or obsolescence period. In time, all products tend to reach their terminal stage in particular markets. Some overseas markets in developing countries may, for instance, continue to be profitable outlets for semi-automatic equipment, which is now outdated in highly industrialized communities. Products may arrive at the obsolescence stage for various reasons.

1. The need for them may disappear or be greatly reduced, e.g., nylon stockings have largely been replaced by tights.
2. Substitute products may appear, e.g., emulsion paints as opposed to distemper.
3. A vastly superior product may have been introduced into a market, e.g., fully automatic domestic washing machines, or stainless steel razor blades.

Although the PLC concept has attracted sharp criticism—which is not altogether surprising in view of the unsophisticated way in which it has sometimes been projected—the underlying theme is simply that products tend to have a finite existence as profit earners. This general tendency is more readily observable in certain product markets, while in other markets there are products and brands which appear to have survived for generations without radical change.

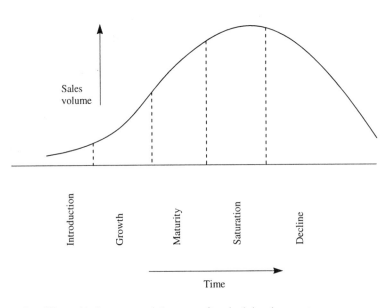

Fig. 11.2 The product life-cycle: five sequential stages of typical development

Hence, the general acceptance and application of a 'normal curve' model of PLC would be naive and unrealistic. The general pattern of product life-cycle is shown in Fig. 11.2, but the curve will vary according to types of products and market conditions.

The life-cycles of products tend to change significantly. Markets in general are more volatile; successful products soon attract competition and sophisticated equipment tends to be outdated far sooner than previously. Manufacturers should objectively analyse their product ranges and establish where various products lie in the life-cycle sequence. One electronics company 'suddenly found itself with two products late in the growth phase, none in the maturity or obsolescence phases, and none in introduction or early growth'.[57] As the result of rapid development and acquisition strategies, the company was able to obtain the new products needed for survival.

Product life-cycle strategies will vary through the various sequences outlined in Fig. 11.2. Before the introduction phase, considerable product development and testing will have taken place and considerable effort will have been expended to give a product every opportunity to be successful when it is floated on the market. The introductory period may involve test marketing in representative regional markets or, if confidence is high, a national launch may be feasible. Over this period and the subsequent growth period, substantial promotional costs are likely to be incurred. This calls for sales forecasts of anticipated demand. When sales indicate that the product has achieved a profitable level of acceptability, advertising will be pulled back, and a holding campaign will be devised to ensure that customers are kept aware of the particular brand of product when they are in a buying situation. The extent of this advertising will be affected by the frequency with which certain products are purchased.

Inevitably, the decline phase will become apparent, and manufacturers may decide to 'milk' the product dry, or to withdraw it from sale. By this time new products should have been phased in, so that the initiative is retained in the market. Product life may be extended by four basic methods: finding new users; encouraging existing customers to extend the product's use; motivating customers to increase their consumption of the product in its present application; and finding new uses for the product.

Rank Xerox redesigned their photocopying machines so that performance was substantially improved. 'This process, which is really no more than the application of standard product life extension techniques, has enabled us to keep pace with current change on equipment whose basic design is now several years old'.[58]

In some cases, pruning or rationalization of product lines may be advisable. Sevin, who has undertaken notable research into marketing productivity analysis, has categorically stated: 'Manufacturers and wholesalers generally do not know reasonably accurately the dollar marketing costs and the dollar profit (or loss) contributions of each of their products, customers, sales territories, and other segments of their business'.[59] As the result of controlled market experiments a company was able to eliminate 592 out of 635 unprofitable products, many of which, it was discerned, were viewed by their customers as not being substantially different from standard and profitable items in the product line. As the result of this rationalization programme, Sevin reported that 'long run sales volume was increased and marketing costs were reduced substantially, while the dollar net profit contribution was increased by almost 24%'.

This brief review of the concept of product life-cycle enables the role of innovation to be viewed within the overall marketing strategy of a company. Marketing management has the responsibility of planning new product introductions so that the whole product line maintains an equilibrium. Each product should be analysed for its contribution to total sales and profits, and target figures should be set, related to the various sequences in the life-cycle. This appraisal should include assessing the degree of risk attached to particular product opportunities; where life-cycles are likely to be short, early recovery of development and other costs should be planned.

11.13 PROJECT TEAMS

The appointment of an innovation manager, free from routine managerial duties, whose principal task would be leading a project team that has access to all departments of a firm, is recommended by business strategists. 'There is something about men united in a common cause of a one-time effort, which turns a job into a mission and a mission into a crusade. . . . Historically, most of the great victories from all fields of endeavour had characteristics of project management present'.[60]

Project teams should be carefully selected and be given terms of reference as guides to the area activities they have responsibility for investigating. Within the project group, however, the innovation manager should have freedom of action or otherwise the whole purpose of independent search and analysis may be frustrated.

In multi-tiered management structures, there is often an inbred resistance to risk taking. 'When "doing more of the same" patently no longer works, "doing more of the same with more muscle power" is often the strategy best suited to the managerial hierarchy'.[61] To tackle this corporate blocking, a project or venture group approach is advisable.

This method of organizing innovation was also confirmed in research findings from a random sample survey of 18 US firms with annual sales ranging from under $1 billion to over $5 billion.[62] 'Classical, top-down management structures are too bureaucratic and rigid. One- or two-man shows do not command sufficient interdisciplinary resources to meet the needs of an innovative task'.

Harry L. Beckers, former director of research for Royal Dutch Shell, states that innovations often start with someone who knows about market needs and opportunities and is also aware, through colleagues, of new scientific developments. He advocates the '1:3:9' principle: for every three inventors, one supporting colleague is needed to keep them informed of the latest scientific developments; a further three colleagues are needed for every inventor, to develop concepts into marketable products or processes. 'Incidentally, I suspect that in Japan the 1:3:9 approach to invention is much more widely accepted than elsewhere, which perhaps explains Japanese success in the field of technological innovation'.[63]

11.14 PRODUCT CHAMPIONS

Schon has argued strongly that innovation requires 'product champions' to overcome the built-in inertia of organizations.[64] In some industries, 'resistance to change goes underground', and it then 'becomes capable of destroying most product innovation'. In many large organizations the screening process appears to be operated virtually to kill new ideas.

The SAPPHO Project researchers found that the presence of a 'product champion' was important where this person was also the 'business innovator'.[12] 'Thus our results did not support the somewhat romantic view that the product champion can overcome the defects of an unsuitable organisation or a weak business innovator. However, they provide strong confirmation for the view that innovative success is closely linked with the power and enthusiasm of the key decision-maker'. It was of interest to note, however, that SAPPHO's analysis 'suggested a slightly better performance by firms which showed capacity to modify their organization and give greater freedom to innovators'. It follows, therefore, that merely setting up a project team is not likely to be the complete answer to the problem of innovation: there should be definite commitment and interest displayed by senior management in the activities of the innovation team, who should be given authority to obtain data both internally and outside the company.

The vital role of product champion was assumed by Sir Alistair Pilkington in the development of float glass, as noted earlier in this chapter:

> Developing this process was a big financial gamble . . . over 100,000 tons of unsaleable glass costing $3.6 million were produced in the pilot plant. Month after month, Alistair Pilkington faced the firm's directors with a new request for $280,000 of operating funds . . . for a company with net profits of about $400,000 per month, this was a major risk.[65]

Saleable glass was finally produced in 1958, and the company has since reaped large royalties. However, as a Harvard researcher points out, the credit for this remarkable success must be shared; in addition to a product champion 'Harry Pilkington, the entrepreneurial chairman of the board . . . absorbed the risks' and the result was 'a classic example of the entrepreneur and the champion working in unison'.[65]

Another outstanding example of project teamwork occurred in 1947, when the transistor was developed at the Bell Telephone Laboratories at Murray Hill, a few miles south of New York. This revolutionary invention ('No great invention, it has been asserted, has done so much good and so little harm')[66] has radically changed communication systems and has had profound effects on medical, radio and television, and recording equipment.

Before the Second World War, Bell Laboratories had realized that their future development in the telephone network system of the USA was impeded by the radio valve, a cumbersome, comparatively fragile component with a large appetite for power. Immediately after the war, William Shockley of Bell 'began to assemble a brilliant team that in little more than two years turned a curiosity called germanium into an amplifier of electric currents'. Since that time, other successful innovations, e.g., the solid-state TV camera, have followed. The secret of Bell Telephone's success was said to be 'that Murray Hill had always been left alone to find its own problem'.[66]

However, informality in product development has been known to pay off:

The IBM disk memory unit, the heart of today's random access computer, is not the logical outcome of a decision model by IBM management. It was developed in one of their laboratories as a bootleg project—over the stern warning by management that the project had to be dropped because of budget difficulties. A handful of men ignored the rules. . . . They risked their jobs to take on a project they believed in.[64]

11.15 THE 'MAKE OR BUY' APPROACH

In industrial production, 'make or buy' decisions are fairly routine: whether to make specific components in the firm's factory or to purchase them from an outside supplier, usually a specialist producer. For example, IBM's first personal computer was assembled largely from components supplied by outsiders; the same policy is followed for other products. In innovation strategies, a related approach would be possible. This could involve taking over a successful 'innovatory' company, merging it with another company that has distinct skills in innovation, joint-venture operations, buying developed products or product ideas from inventors and/or successful 'innovating' companies, or obtaining the rights of manufacture under licence.

Ansoff has pointed out that there are two primary factors influencing the choice between these major alternative strategies of innovation.[19] These key factors are start-up cost and timing.

Licensing deals are attractive because risk in development is minimized while the need to make heavy investment in research is avoided. A licence deal frequently allows adopting companies to take almost immediate advantage of inventive skills. In addition, some products may already be protected by patents in specific markets, and the only effective method of marketing in these areas would be to acquire a manufacturing or patent licence. It would be advisable to enquire fully into territorial restrictions, degree of exclusive use in specific market, access to technical services of the sponsoring company, precise financial commitment involved (i.e., initial down-payments and subsequent royalties), and options related to future developments affecting the products now under licence.

One of the most successful joint ventures of recent years has been that of Rank Xerox, whose photocopying equipment sales have added very appreciably to the profitability of the British end of the venture. It is, perhaps, instructive to recall[15] that when the Xerox 914 copier was originally subjected to independent market evaluations by three highly reputable firms in the USA, two advised against marketing it, while the third believed that it had some vague chances of success but strictly limited sales potential. These pessimistic projections were discarded by Xerox's top management because they declared that such forecasts largely ignored the effect of a consumer learning curve: when people discovered that quality reproduction of documents was readily available, then demand would develop strongly. This perceptive prognosis proved correct; the impact and importance of learning on consumer buying behaviour should never be underestimated (see Chapter 2).

The plastics and petrochemical industries have made extensive use of international licensing agreements: 40–45 per cent of the world's manufacturing capacity of low-density polyethylene is based in the original ICI development, and half of the total capacity is believed to have been installed through licensing deals.

There appears to be a trend developing among large industrial concerns with substantial research units to concentrate on the development of new ideas which have been bought in, thus cutting back the lead time significantly. This trend was noted in the report of the Central Advisory Council for Science and Technology: 'Several firms and countries have prospered through a policy of avoiding long lead-times and heavy development costs by buying other people's technological knowledge and by concentrating on the commercial application of imported inventions and innovations'.[11] The report emphasized that Britain had fallen far behind some of her international competitor countries in this profitable strategy; even in the USA it was common practice to buy other people's technical knowledge. An American source was quoted as stating that 15 of the 25 major innovations made by Du Pont came from inventions made outside this large science-based organization.

11.16 MARKET RESEARCH AIDS INNOVATION

Market research has a very useful role to play in the identification and profitable exploitation of new product ideas. (Discussion of specific techniques occurs in a specialist text.)[67]

Knowledge is called for so that sound decisions can be taken; sustained systematic inquiries are necessary in order to reduce the risk involved in new product development. This means constant monitoring of the market in which a firm operates (or plans to operate), so that trends are identified and market gaps related to the company's resources. Creative flair is not to be frustrated, of course, but the basic analytical approach should be applied to the productive ideas of 'brainstorming' and related creative sessions.

In evaluating market opportunities, the behavioural factors discussed in Parts Two and Three should be recognized. Experienced marketers know that what people say they want and what they will actually buy often fail to coincide. But skilful researchers do not expect to obtain guarantees of future behaviour; they will aim for insight into patterns of consumption and levels of satisfaction and aspiration related to particular kinds of products and services.

11.17 SUMMARY

Innovation is crucial to corporate success, but it is difficult and expensive and the pay-off is uncertain. Innovation is viewed as applied invention. Serendipity or chance has sometimes resulted in spectacular discoveries, such as penicillin.

Firms have been characterized as reactors, planners, or entrepreneurs. Risk taking is an essential part of management decision-making, particularly related to innovation.

Innovations have been classified variously, e.g., as continuous, dynamically continuous, and discontinuous; or as revolutionary and evolutionary.

Innovation diffusion takes the shape of the normal curve. Five categories of adopters have been identified: innovators, early adopters, early majority, late majority, and laggards. Also, five characteristics of innovation affect acceptance: relative advantage, compatibility, complexity, divisibility, and communicability.

Product life-cycle theory has direct relevance to innovation in marketing strategies; five stages of PLC have been noted.

Innovation is often the result of project teams, as SAPPHO has indicated. 'Product champions' frequently play major roles.

Licensing and other production/marketing strategies help to control risk and speed diffusion of innovations.

Market research can be used effectively in identifying new consumption trends and possible market opportunities.

Innovation strategies must always take note of behavioural factors which may well speed or retard diffusion of new products and services.

REFERENCES

1. Wiesner, Jerome B., 'Is innovation in decline?', *McKinsey Quarterly*, winter 1979.
2. Tricker, R. Ian, *The Accountant in Management*, Batsford, London, 1967.
3. Drucker, Peter F., *The Practice of Management*, Heinemann, Oxford, 1955.
4. Parkes, Christopher, 'Time for management to get a proper grip', *Financial Times*, 30 March 1989.
5. Sheth, Jagdish N., 'A review of buyer behaviour', *Management Science*, vol. 13, no. 12, August 1967.
6. Ansoff, H. Igor, *Business Strategy*, Penguin, London, 1972.
7. Shanks, Michael, *The Innovators*, Penguin, London, 1967.
8. Schumpeter, Joseph A., *Business Cycles*, McGraw-Hill, New York, 1939.
9. Mansfield, Edwin, *Industrial Research and Technological Innovation*, W. W. Norton, New York, 1968.
10. Rogers, Everett M., *Diffusion of Innovation*, Free Press, New York, 1962.
11. Report of the Central Advisory Council for Science and Technology, 'Technological innovation in Britain', HMSO, Norwich, 1968.
12. Science Policy Research Unit, University of Sussex (Project SAPPHO), 'Success and failure in industrial innovation', Centre for the Study of Industrial Innovation, London, February 1972.
13. Campbell, R. H., and R. G. Wilson, *Entrepreneurship in Britain 1750–1939*, A. and C. Black, London, 1975.
14. Sahal, Devendra, 'Invention, innovation and economic evolution', *Technological Forecasting and Social Change*, vol. 23, 1983.
15. Chisnall, Peter M., *Strategic Industrial Marketing*, Prentice-Hall, Hemel Hempstead, 1989.
16. Burns, T. and G. M. Stalker, *The Management of Innovation*, Tavistock, London, 1966.
17. Jewkes, John, David Sawers, and Richard Stillerman, *The Sources of Invention*, Macmillan, Basingstoke, 1969.
18. Carter, C. F., and B. R. Williams, 'The characteristics of technically progressive firms', *Journal of Industrial Economics*, March 1959.
19. Ansoff, H. Igor, *Corporate Strategy*, Penguin, London, 1968.
20. Chakrabarti, Alok K., Stephen Feinman, and William Fuentevilla, 'Industrial product innovation: an international comparison', *Industrial Marketing Management*, vol. 7, no. 4, 1978.
21. Bernstein, Peter W., 'Polaroid struggles to get back into focus', *Fortune*, 7 April 1980.
22. Buchan, James, 'Smokeless cigarette fails to set world alight', *Financial Times*, 2 March 1989.
23. McGill, Douglas C., '"Sure-fire" idea flops at Seven-Up', *International Herald Tribune*, 15 February 1989.
24. Robertson, Thomas S., 'The process of innovations and the diffusion of innovation', *Journal of Marketing*, vol. 31, January 1967.
25. Walker, Christopher, 'Inventor of the non-stick frying pan turning his efforts to pollution', *The Times*, 30 October 1972.
26. Kinkead, Gwen, 'The end of ease at Pilkington', *Fortune*, 21 March 1983.
27. Cane, Alan, 'Printed circuit pioneer', *Financial Times*, 3 November 1992.
28. Harvey-Jones, Sir John, *Getting it Together*, Heinemann, Oxford, 1991.
29. Mathias, Peter, *The First Industrial Nation: An Economic History of Britain 1700–1914*, Methuen, London, 1983.
30. Jones, Trevor (ed.) *Micro Electronics and Society*, Open University Press, Milton Keynes, 1980.
31. Langrish, J., M. Gibbons, W. G. Evans, and F. R. Jevons, *Wealth from Knowledge: Studies of Innovation in Industry*, Macmillan, London, 1972.
32. Ferrari, Achille, 'Innovation: myths and realities', *Industrial Marketing Management*, vol. 2, 1973.
33. Myers, Sumner, and Donald G. Marquis, 'Successful industrial innovations: a study of factors underlying innovation in selected firms', National Science Foundation (NSF 69–17), 1969.
34. Katz, Elihu, Martin L. Levin, and Herbert Hamilton, 'Traditions of research on the diffusion of innovations', *American Sociological Review*, vol. 28, April 1963.
35. Whyte, William H. Jnr, 'The web of word of mouth', *Fortune*, vol. 50, November 1954.
36. Webster, Frederick E., Communication and diffusion processes in industrial markets', *European Journal of Marketing*, vol. 5, no. 4, 1971.

37. Ozanne, Urban B., and Gilbert A. Churchill Jnr, 'Five dimensions of the industrial adoption process', *Journal of Marketing Research*, vol. 8, no. 3, August 1971.

38. Sheth, Jagdish N., 'Word-of-mouth in low-risk innovations', *Journal of Advertising Research*, vol. 2, no. 3, June 1971.

39. Katz, Elihu, 'The two-step flow of communication: an up-to-date report on an hypothesis', *Public Opinion Quarterly*, vol. 21, 1957.

40. Bauer, Raymond A., 'Consumer behaviour as risk taking', in: *Dynamic Marketing for a Changing World*, R. S. Hancock (ed.), American Advertising Association, Chicago, 1960.

41. Packard, Vance, *The Status Seekers*, Penguin, London, 1969.

42. Coleman, James, Elihu Katz, and Herbert Menzel, 'Social processes in physicians' adoption of a new drug', *Journal of Chronic Diseases*, vol. 9, no. 1, January 1959.

43. Coleman, James, Elihu Katz, and Herbert Menzel, 'The diffusion of an innovation among physicians', *Sociometry*, vol. 20, December 1957.

44. Opinion Research Corporation, 'America's tastemakers', *Research Report of the Public Opinion Index for Industry*, vol. 17, no. 4, April 1959.

45. Robertson, Thomas S., 'Consumer innovators: the key to new product success', *Californian Management Review*, vol. 10, winter 1967.

46. Boone, Louis E., 'The search for the consumer innovator', *Journal of Business*, April 1970.

47. Donnelly, James H., Jnr, 'Social character and acceptance of new products', *Journal of Marketing Research*, vol. 7, February 1970.

48. Donnelly, James H., Jnr, and Michael J. Etzel, 'Degrees of product newness and early trial', *Journal of Marketing Research*, vol. 10, August 1973.

49. Danko, William D., and James M. MacLachlan, 'Research to accelerate the diffusion of a new invention: the case of personal computers', *Journal of Advertising Research*, vol. 23, no. 3, 1983.

50. Uhl, Kenneth, Roman Andrus, and Lance Poulsen, 'How are laggards different? An empirical inquiry', *Journal of Marketing Research*, vol. 7, February 1970.

51. Summers, John O., 'Generalised change agents and innovativeness', *Journal of Marketing Research*, vol. 8, August 1971.

52. Schoor, Burt, 'The mistakes: many new products fail despite careful planning, publicity', *Wall Street Journal*, vol. 159, 5 April 1961, quoted in Steven J. Stein, 'Behavioural science offers fresh insight into product acceptance', *Journal of Marketing*, January 1965.

53. Graham, Saxon L., 'Class and conservatism in the adoption of innovations', *Human Relations*, vol. 9, February 1956.

54. Pessemier, Edgar A., *New Product Decisions*, McGraw-Hill, New York, 1966.

55. Bradshaw, Della, 'The camcorder cut down to size', *Financial Times*, 19 April 1990.

56. Cooper, Robert G., 'New product success in industrial firms', *Industrial Marketing Management*, vol. 11, no. 3, 1982.

57. Clifford, Donald K., Jnr, 'Managing the product life-cycle', *European Business*, July 1969.

58. Hughes, Michael, 'Increasing penetration in industrial markets', in: *Long Range Planning for Marketing and Diversification*, Bernard Taylor and Gordon Willis (eds), Bradford University Press/Crosby Lockwood and Sons, Bradford, 1971.

59. Sevin, Charles H., *Marketing Productivity Analysis*, McGraw-Hill, New York, 1965.

60. Staudt, Thomas A., 'Higher management risks in product strategy', *Journal of Marketing*, vol. 37, January 1973.

61. Van Mesdag, Martin, 'The dangers of playing safe', *Marketing*, 8 March 1984.

62. Souder, William E., 'Effectiveness of product development methods', *Industrial Marketing Management*, vol. 7, no. 5, 1978.

63. Beckers, Harry L., in: *Milestones in Management: An Essential Reader*, Henry M. Strage (ed.), Basil Blackwell, Oxford, 1992.

64. Schon, Donald A., 'Champions for radical new innovations', *Harvard Business Review*, March/April 1963.

65. Maidique, Modesto A., 'Entrepreneurs, champions and technological innovation', *Sloan Management Review*, winter 1980.

66. Fishlock, David, 'The world's smallest big invention', *Financial Times*, 21 December 1972.

67. Chisnall, Peter M., *Marketing Research: Analysis and Measurement*, McGraw-Hill, Maidenhead, 1992.

REVIEW AND DISCUSSION QUESTIONS

1. Much attention is paid to early adopters in launching market innovations. Which product characteristics will increase the likelihood of this group adopting such innovations?
2. Discuss the relevance of consumer adopter categories for a firm about to launch a new do-it-yourself cholesterol test kit.
3. In 1980, 1 per cent of UK households owned a video cassette recorder. By 1988, this figure had risen to 51 per cent of households. How might an understanding of diffusion theory help explain such a high adoption rate?
4. A large manufacturer of patent medicine and personal grooming products wants to introduce a new brand of upright dispenser toothpaste in addition to the brand that it already markets. Evaluate for the firm what information might be used for innovation studies to guide introduction of the product.
5. For each of the following, state whether it represents an innovation, and if so, what type of innovation: (a) wine in cardboard boxes (b) compact disc players (c) a wholly organic bran cereal (d) an anti-plaque mouthwash (e) Lycra cycling shorts.
6. From a consumer behaviour perspective, what exactly is 'diffused' during the diffusion process?

TWELVE

COMMUNICATIONS (1)

12.1 INTRODUCTION

Every organization, however it is constituted or whatever its aims, needs an effective and integrated strategy of communications, so that its objectives and activities become known to those whom it is attempting to serve. In addition, it will seek to obtain approval of its policies and to encourage the formation of favourable attitudes. By creating this receptive environment, organizations plan to propagate their activities; these are diverse, ranging from religious, political, cultural, and social interests to those concerned with promoting foods and services in industrial and consumer markets.

The strategic plan of communications should embrace all the varied forms of publicity available in modern communities. For example, it should include media advertising, editorial comment, and public relations activities of various kinds, suitable for the particular organization's needs.

Corporate image

This frequently invoked phrase may have attracted a degree of odium, perhaps because people suspect that they may be manipulated by slick public relations campaigns on behalf of large, wealthy corporations with relentless ambitions to dominate their markets. Fortunately, in a free market economy, consumers are unlikely to be bamboozled; many innovative products and services (as noted in Chapter 11) have failed despite massive promotional expenditure. Some of them had the backing of world-famous brand names, but they suffered devastating defeat at the hands of shoppers, who may be willing to try but certainly not rebuy products unless they live up to expectations.

Most people could recite brand names associated with products they use or which, perhaps, they buy for their families or friends. The list is often long and (as observed in Chapter 8) will cover many types of products, such as food, household goods, electronic products, entertainment and travel facilities, toiletries, drinks, and confectionery, and probably includes such favoured brand names as Kelloggs, Nescafé, Persil, Fairy Liquid, Sony, Philips, Kodak, British Airways, Colgate, Coca-Cola, Bacardi, Canada Club, McDonalds, Mars, and Lego.

All these highly successful brands have prospered because they enable consumers to identify products and services that they can trust; originally, they may have found them through family usage or have been influenced by the consumption habits of friends or colleagues (see Sec. 8.5).

Massive investment over many years has been made in these globally recognized brand names by the companies that own them. Creatively developed and jealously guarded, these powerful brand names provide their owners with unique market leverage. Vigilance and sensitivity to the perceptions and needs of their users and of society at large are at the heart of successful marketing strategies and tactics; it is desirable to consider at some length the nature and purposes of corporate image or identity. As the co-founder of the Sony Corporation, Akio Morita, succinctly stated: 'I have always believed that the company name is the life of an enterprise. It carries responsibility and guarantees the quality of the product'.[1]

An organization is an entity, with a personality that it has acquired as the result of past behaviour and of the messages that it has given to those it serves, and also to members of its staff. Communication is influential, therefore, within an organization and external to it in building up the image and reputation that become an integral part of the organization.

This corporate identity exists whether or not it is acknowledged by those who are responsible for the policy and executive decisions within the organization. The public with whom the organization is dealing—in the case of a commercial company, its past, present, and potential customers—and also members of its staff will have formed opinions about the organization. These beliefs and attitudes may appear to be subjective—to have some degree of personal bias—but to those who hold them, they will be valid and act as guides to behaviour. All individuals possess a cognitive map—a set of beliefs—that influences their personal orientation towards life and towards the many activities in which they are involved. Perception is seldom an objective, scientific assessment of phenomena; it tends to be a personalized interpretation which may at times be radically different from what it was planned, for instance, to communicate (see Chapter 2). Attitudes depend on personal needs and interests for their formation and possible change (see Chapter 4). People have sets of attitudes that are unique to them although there may be some common elements among individual attitudinal structures.

These beliefs and attitudes are likely to be of two kinds: general and/or specific, and the latter category will be concerned with particular aspects of an organization which are of significant interest to individuals. From these specific views an overall impression will be developed. This overall impression provides an 'image' of an organization to individuals who deal with it; for a trading company a favourable image subscribes to that intangible asset known as good will. This valuable asset is not acquired haphazardly; it derives from all the factors about an organization's behaviour which add up to its total personality or image—*as seen by its public.*

'Companies are inclined to believe that their internal defects are invisible to the outside world. For most observers they are. Yet curiously, the customers on whose goodwill a business's livelihood depends, are one group of people with private insight into operations, and they are uniquely placed to make comparisons with its competitors'.[2] To gain this valuable insight, customer attitude surveys are well worth while. Only objective inquiry by independent researchers can really provide information that reflects how customers, both present and prospective, perceive a particular supplier.

One company was surprised to find as the result of a survey that it was seen to be an honest and technically competent organization, but one that lacked marketing aggressiveness because of its perceived behaviour towards customers. For example, the company was considered to be bureaucratic in its attitudes and responses to customers; key personnel changes were not notified to customers; technical proposals were also viewed as deficient. Although the firm's products were rated high in terms of performance, reliability, and ease of maintenance, customers were concerned about 'its overall capability to manage a product development effort and still maintain cost and schedule credibility'.[3]

Paradoxically, as Peter Hutton, a widely experienced marketing researcher, shrewdly notes, 'most companies pay very little attention to their image in the world outside them and yet, in quite a large proportion of cases, the customers of those same companies are quite strongly influenced by their own view—their image—of their suppliers'.[4]

The reputation of commercial organizations depend on many factors (the quality of products and services, pricing policies, methods of distribution, promotional strategies, after-sales service, etc.) which attract customers to do business with it. Practically everything a company does communicates to its customers the type of business it is; that is why it is important to integrate all the activities of a firm because the corporate image is constructed from the activities of production, financial, personnel, and marketing staff. It is commonly said that a chain is as strong as its weakest link: it would be advisable to have an independent check made of the strength of the individual links in the chain of organization. For instance, the sales of products can be severely obstructed because of the inefficiency of the after-sales service department; or the accounting department may irritate customers by their frequent mistakes in invoicing, or by pressing for payment of goods which were returned as being faulty. If complaints about products do not receive proper attention, customers feel annoyed, and are less willing to place further business with that company.

Communication responsibilities extend to trade distributors, for they are the link between manufacturer and consumer that needs to be strongly forged. Unless dealers are willing to support the expensive advertising campaigns of manufacturers by displaying ranges of their products, it is unlikely that those campaigns will be effective. Dealers should therefore be kept informed by marketing management of the policies of their companies. New products should be introduced in time to let orders be placed (and delivered) before advertising starts. If products have technical features, dealers' sales staff should be invited to visit the company's plant to receive adequate product knowledge, including, if necessary, training in servicing particular types of equipment, e.g., washing machines. By involving dealers in marketing strategies, personal responsibilities will be developed for the success of a manufacturer's range of products.

Another important aspect of communications relates to the suppliers to the marketing company of raw materials, component parts, packaging, and services of various kinds. These should not be neglected; successful companies depend heavily on the efficiency of their suppliers to maintain delivery schedules. They should be encouraged to cooperate fully in this task by being told by senior management of the contribution which their product or service makes to the eventual product which is marketed. Many finished products are largely assembled from components made by outside suppliers, and the reputation of the marketing company rests heavily, therefore, on the standards of quality maintained by component manufacturers. In some instances, the company marketing the products has no direct manufacturing responsibilities; Marks and Spencer have established a unique trading reputation for the reliability of the products sold in their stores. This has been earned over generations by meticulous attention to the quality of the products on sale; they set exacting standards to which their suppliers have to adhere consistently.

A successful corporate communications strategy takes account also of the cultural and social environment in which a company makes and sells its products. In Chapters 6, 7, and 8, the individual consumers's behaviour was seen to be influenced by cultural norms, social habits, group membership, and so on. Organizations too cannot live in isolation. They are inevitably drawn into the fabric of society and contribute in some way to the culture of that society. Today, the role of the commercial firm in society is openly debated and challenged. Ansoff (see Chapter 6) discussed this trend in the mid-1960s when he drew attention to the 'greatly expanded explicit and implicit restrictions' which companies would need to face 'in the form of anti-trust, labour and public domain laws (for example, water pollution, strip mining) as well as informal public and social pressures from the local community and the government'.[5]

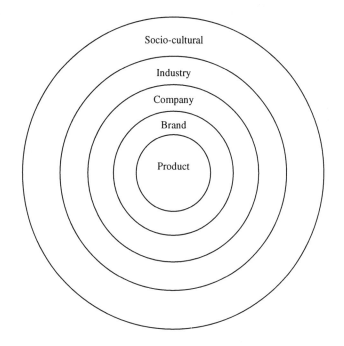

Fig. 12.1 Levels of corporate image (*Source*: Hutton)[4]

Peter Hutton[4] has referred to the '*levels of corporate image*' that surround products (see Fig. 12.1). The '*outer level*' covers significant socio-cultural influences that affect opinions and attitudes towards industry and commerce. The '*industry level*' relates to perceptions about specific economic activities, such as chemicals, insurance, telecommunications, and energy supplies, in which companies operate. The '*company level*' pertains to particular companies, such as Ford, Esso, Heinz, Proctor and Gamble, Rank-Xerox, and Volkswagen: this is the level at which many key contacts are made with a wide range of people and organizations, i.e., employees, investors, suppliers, and competitors. The '*brand level*' is clearly associated with certain well-known companies, although some brand names are more popularly known than those of the companies that own them. At the core of the corporate image diagram lies the *product* itself, the performance of which finally decides the future of the company: the corporate image of a company is largely determined by its products and their brand images. The various levels of corporate image development are interrelated, as are the influences on buying behaviour discussed in earlier chapters.

Consumers are increasingly aware of their power in the market-place; they can no longer be treated in an offhand manner by companies seeking their patronage. The public's attitude towards business has undergone a subtle change which manufacturers cannot ignore, or do so at their peril.

The impact of 'consumerism' on marketing strategies and, in particular, on advertising practices will be considered in Chapter 15. Meanwhile, it will be evident that businesses operate in a far more critical climate today than a few years ago. The traditional freedom experienced under a free-enterprise economy has been radically curtailed: the age of accountability has replaced the era of *laissez faire*. Enlightened communication policies have been adopted increasingly by public and private sector organizations in attempts to gain the confidence of their users, but many organizations still need to tell the public, their customers, and their suppliers what their objectives are. Ann Burdus has noted that the companies that are skilled in communicating what they are doing for society are those which are clear about their own identity and, over time, are able to sustain an indentifiable stance which truly reflects what they are. 'I.C.I. advertising reflects what I.C.I. is. They are not trying to adjust a misconception. They are talking about themselves and their industry in a positive way'.[6] Actions are said to speak louder than words; but words are also needed to tell people about the actions a company takes, for instance, in looking after its employees, or in maintaining standards of quality.

In their communication strategies, companies should take heed of the wider issues which society has clearly shown it holds to be of importance. Communications links should be established, therefore, with government departments, local authorities, and trade associations which are likely to influence the development of the particular industrial and commercial activities of specific companies. In these cases, personal methods of communication will be used instead of the mass media, which, obviously, would be unsuitable.

Large organizations like ICI are fully aware of the need to keep track of public opinion, and have used an annual large-scale survey since 1969: the MORI Corporate Image Survey provides companies with an objective assessment of public attitudes towards business and industry in general, specific industries and companies, and issues of particular concern to them.[7]

These 'tracking surveys' are particularly valuable in providing trend information: for example, changes in people's perceptions of an industry or of a particular firm can be evaluated over time. Since 1975, ICI have investigated the effect of ICI plants on local communities; analysis revealed that it not only raised awareness, but also improved 'image': a case of familiarity breeding favourability.

Apart from being useful in publicity, these attitude surveys have been important in briefing ICI's management on the state of public awareness, perception, and attitudes and in relating these trends to corporate policy. These appraisals are not restricted to planners, but where the findings are considered relevant, edited versions are distributed to operating divisional staff.

Communications with the financial investment world are also important for the development of companies. Stock exchange confidence will assist in the long-term financing of companies seeking to attract, for example, investors to subscribe to a new share issue. Financial journalists are influential sources of information to investors. Hence, it is important that companies should not only tell their customers about new products and improved techniques of manufacture, but also inform the financial press, so that their activities are brought to the notice of those seeking to invest in progressive companies.

MORI and other leading survey organizations also undertake special studies of MPs, business and financial journalists, editors of specialist magazines (such as women's interests, motoring, and broadcasting), general secretaries of the trades unions, and other influential centres of opinion leadership (see Chapter 8).[7]

The recruitment of well-qualified staff is a matter of great importance for the continued prosperity of companies. Communication programmes should include, therefore, regular contacts with universities, polytechnics, and other centres of advanced education, so that promising young men and women know of an organization's career opportunities. Many smaller and medium-sized companies could benefit from making such contacts.

The responsibilities of a company's communications strategy are, therefore, diverse and far-reaching. Top management should ensure that the various facets of communication which have been outlined are integrated in a comprehensive programme. To restrict market communications to media advertising would reflect a narrow conception of the role of effective communications in modern organizations. Direct product promotion, such as advertising, is likely to be far more effective if it is supported by other publicity tactics which are appropriate to specific tasks of communication.

Designing corporate image

It is intriguing that in a largely literate society, signs and symbols are increasingly adopted by organizations of many kinds to project themselves to their customers, suppliers, and the world at large. Many of these logos are now so well-established that they insinuate their presence at an almost subconscious level of perception. Instant recognition—without confusion—is one of the vital qualities of an effective logo; it should also provide a strong and reassuring impression that is compatible with the organization's corporate policies. To be able to convey so much in so small a space challenges the ingenuity of designers like Wally Olins of Wolff Olins, one of the foremost firms engaged in corporate logo development. He declares that corporate identity is not a new concept, but a new name for an old idea: 'everything from a new nation to a new religion has chosen signs and symbols to express identity'.[8] National flags, the Christian cross, regimental badges, and the multi-starred emblem of the European Union, all possess dynamic qualities of communication; people are instantly aware of the organizations represented by such images; their store of memories is stirred, perhaps, by the sight of these logos, so that they recall experiences that have affected their present perceptions and influenced their sets of attitudes. In the case of commercial logos, responses may be favourable and lead to brand loyalty.

Like virtually everything, logos age as fashions in design and typography change over time. Sometimes, the modifications are so subtle and gradual that they escape immediate notice, as has happened with some family brands like Marmite and Bisto. In 1989, British Petroleum's green and yellow shield, which had featured BP since the 1920s, was subject to sensitive updating. In empathy with the increasing interest in environmental issues, the area of green in the design was enlarged, while the initials were italicized and given a slight bias towards the right, reflecting, according to BP, a new source of movement in a growing company. BP set up an 'identity committee', which developed a visual standards manual to ensure that the new logo was fully integrated into all aspects of the company's operations. In the late 1980s, ICI spent £7.5 million in redesigning their corporate logo and all the widespread commitments involved in diffusing this modification throughout their extensive organization. In essence, the design changes were relatively minimal; the familiar 'wave' on the roundel was softened, and a simpler style of lettering was used; the overall design was intended to symbolize a modern industrial undertaking.

Rather more fundamental changes occurred when the Prudential Assurance Company sought to escape from being known popularly as 'the Pru', and approached Wolff Olins Consultants. Following investigations, these design specialists found that the word 'Prudential' (but not its popularized abbreviation) brought positive reactions and suggested 'safety' and 'honesty'. A radically new design was developed, derived from the traditional images of Prudence reflecting wisdom, foresight, and similar admirable qualities. Despite initial resistance from directors, the novel logo was launched and has resulted in fundamental changes in the perceptions and attitudes of clients and staff about the company.

Another organization that undertook a challenging task in reorienting their corporate identity was Woolworth Holdings, which changed its name in 1989 to Kingfisher and also adopted a matching symbol. Although the new title attracted hostile reactions from the City and Fleet Street, the company secured the full support of its shareholders at an extraordinary general meeting. It was cogently argued that the old identity reflected perceptions of the rather outdated stores of the 1950s and 1960s, and failed to acknowledge the revitalization that had taken place in the Woolworth's chain, and also ignored the whole new range of merchandizing activities connected with ownership of B&Q, Comet, and Superdrug stores. Operating companies retained their distinctive trading titles, while the group identity of Kingfisher projected a virile retailing organization.

Doubts may linger about who benefits most from all these feverish design activities; even

Wally Olins was reported as saying: 'If you take a lousy, low-profile company and give it a new corporate identity, you will turn it into a lousy, high-profile company. There is no reason the public should be anything but sceptical. What do they get out of it? Just a logo to look at'.[9] In his stimulating text, *Corporate Identity*,[8] he takes a rather more managerial viewpoint, arguing that the trend towards globalization of industry and commercial activities means that corporate identity issues will become more salient in the future.

Researching corporate image

It has been seen that the boundaries of corporate behaviour are extensive, sometimes spanning the world, and incorporating many cultures among their customers, suppliers, local and national authorities, and members of their staff. Clearly, it is advisable, if not imperative, that corporate communications should be professionally monitored to check their effectiveness. Examples of systematic inquiries involving, for instance, tracking studies, have already been given, and in this section some further aspects of researching corporate image will be reviewed.

During the late 1980s, Courtaulds commissioned a design consultancy service to evaluate perceptions of the company and its business prospects. More than 200 respondents from top management, opinion formers, and major customers were interviewed at length about this large and diversified group's corporate behaviour; from these probing inquiries, it was evident that there was a strong desire for a central culture. Courtaulds were said to have spent £1 million over nearly two years in developing a semi-abstract symbol known as the C-mark, and in a coordinated programme to improve the ways in which the 70 main subsidiaries in 26 countries dealt with their customers.[10]

In 1988, having been owned by Philips for over 60 years, Mullard decided to change their name to Philips Components Limited. Before this happened, a survey firm was asked to check any negative perceptions that might be related to the Philips name or result from dropping the Mullard one. They were also requested to collect information that might be useful in planning the proposed announcements and other publicity efforts. Mullard's competitive profile was already regularly assessed; the new research, by telephone survey among customers and distributors in key areas, aimed to 'establish the image of Philips in general and on a number of relevant dimensions'.[11] During these inquiries, the name of the sponsoring company was not revealed. In addition, depth interviews were conducted with a selected number of Mullard's most important customers, and in these instances, 'it was neither possible nor useful to keep Mullard's identity concealed'. From the findings of this carefully planned research, Mullard were given information and guidance, which enabled them to proceed with the proposed changes without causing misunderstandings and problems.

Organizations of all kinds need effective means of communicating with their clients, customers, patrons, and adherents. Since the time when they were founded, these entities have gradually acquired corporate personalities or identities that have influenced their progress in specific spheres of activities. How they are perceived is largely within their own control, although, of course, the perceptual processes have been observed to be intrinsically subjective (see Chapter 2). But the organizations can and *should* avoid misinterpretations of their behaviour by adopting a policy of 'open communications' with a wide range of audiences.

Charity organizations have specially urgent needs to communicate: they are dependent on voluntary support from donors and workers who have developed favourable perceptions and attitudes about the nature of the tasks tackled by these bodies. The Samaritans, founded in 1953, has a nationwide network of volunteers 'offering sympathetic caring and confidential support to anyone feeling suicidal or despairing'.[12] Their precarious financial position—being utterly dependent on voluntary contributions—led the Samaritans in 1989 to consider how they might increase fund-raising, so as to continue their dedicated work. It was suspected that many people might not realize it was a charity; if this supposition was correct, then it would be vital to change, first of all, the public's perceptions before launching a wide-scale appeal for funds. Another aspect that needed clarification related to the perceptions about the actual role of the Samaritans: were they solely concerned with the suicidal or pre-suicidal, or did they fulfil a wider role, as a 'listening post' for other human problems?

The Samaritans commissioned two leading market research organizations who undertook a telephone omnibus survey of 1023 adults aged over 15 and also extensive interviews of 1966 adults in their homes. (For details of such methodologies refer to specialist text.)[13] The key findings were that: first, awareness of the Samaritans as a charity dependent on public support was extremely low, although 91 per cent of respondents knew *something* about them; second, perceptions about the roles of the charity were confused and inadequately reflected their real activities; and third, elderly, young and unemployed people and those of low social status were significantly less aware of the Samaritans than the rest of the sample.

As a result of these rather disturbing findings, it was evident that some radical changes were necessary. The management structure was reorganized; fund-raising activities were more fully integrated and closely associated with events to publicize the objectives of the charity; closer links were established with other organizations to coordinate activities aimed to help specific groups; sponsored 'outreach' teams working in the community were developed to promote awareness of the Samaritans, and to target those who may be in need of special help. In order to clarify overall efforts, particular attention was given to all forms of communication, to ensure that misconceptions about their activities were minimized; this concern with effective communication was reflected in the compilation of a list of recommended and non-preferred words to be used, or avoided, in all communications so as to encourage the development of clear and favourable perceptions. The Samaritans' research initiative provided them with insights and practical guidelines for long-term planning, as well as day-to-day operations.

Corporate images can be measured in various ways, but essentially they should be comparative assessments based on objective inquiries. For instance, MORI, a leading market and opinion research organization, has accumulated particularly relevant experience in this type of research (as discussed earlier in this chapter). Of the methodologies that could be applied, rating scales are popularly used; for instance, companies could be rated on a five-point scale related to specific criteria, such as the extent to which they are well known or, indeed, unheard of; or, perhaps, indicating attitudes ranging from 'very favourable' to 'very unfavourable' (see Chapter 9 for qualitative techniques used in brand evaluations).

From an evaluation of comparative scores, the relative positions of companies could be plotted on a two-dimensional scatter diagram, as shown in Fig. 12.2.[4] Scrutiny of this reveals that company A, for instance, occupies a very favourable position, being well known and well regarded, whereas company B is in a far less desirable position and is probably very vulnerable. Above the statistical line of 'best-fit' is where the better known and better regarded companies are located.

In 1983, a major survey was conducted by AGB among 155 large UK companies over all sectors of business; 101 of these firms were from the 155 companies tested as leading media advertisers in *Campaign*, and the remaining 54 were from *The Times* 1000 list of leading UK firms.[14] Of the 155 companies covered in the survey, 123 were manufacturers; over half were in consumer goods and about 20 per cent were in service industries. Although the survey resulted in some ambivalent responses, marketing was perceived to be the principal function of public relations (PR). 'Over 80% of consumer goods and service companies rated customers as a major target audience. They barely expressed an interest in reaching the financial community, politicians, or "opinion formers".' However, industrial manufacturers took a wider view of the

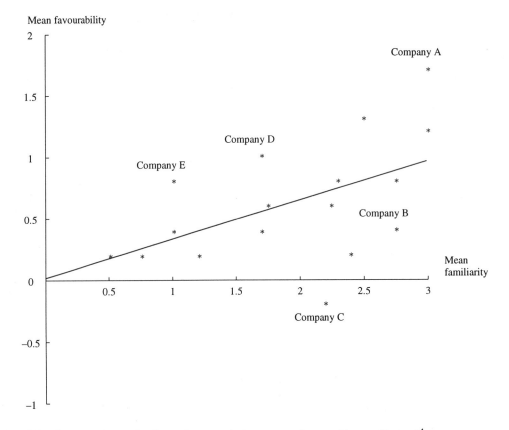

Fig. 12.2 Comparative evaluations of companies' corporate images (*Source*: Hutton)[4] (Scores allocated 0–3 for 'familiarity', and −1 to +2 for 'favourability')

value of PR, and regarded communicating with financial and political audiences to be almost as important as reaching customers. Not surprisingly, most pharmaceutical companies viewed government relations as prime targets for their PR campaigns. Of particular surprise was the apparent low value placed by consumer goods and service companies on PR to staff: 'not one retailer mentioned staff relations as important'.

Non-advertisers, chiefly in the industrial sector, were likely to be committed to PR and used it to communicate with several target audiences. The respondences to this survey were defined as the most senior personnel responsible for PR in their companies, and it appears from the findings that many of them have distinctly limited horizons for their PR communications programmes. Over 60 per cent agreed that it was difficult to assess the effects of PR activities, while equal candour was shown by the 17 per cent who offered no opinion as to whether PR was the most cost-effective way of reaching specific target audiences.

12.2 MARKETING COMMUNICATIONS

The dissemination of information about a company's products and services forms an important part of the overall strategy of communications. In isolating product promotion for extended discussion, it is not intended to suggest that it should be divorced in practice from other forms of publicity.

12.3 METHODS OF MARKETING COMMUNICATIONS

There are five principal ways in which a company can communicate with its market:

1. Media advertising (commercial television, newspapers, periodicals, poster, cinema and commercial radio advertising, direct mail).
2. Public relations activities.
3. Selling.
4. Merchandising (point-of-purchase promotion).
5. Packaging.

An effective product promotional strategy reguires systematic planning on similar lines to other areas of management responsibility. The first stage, therefore, is to define clearly the objectives; the second is to design a promotional strategy that will be most likely to achieve those objectives.

Promotional strategies vary in their objectives according to the needs of individual companies. Objectives are frequently classified as long term or short term.

Objectives, whether long or short term, should always relate to the needs and circumstances of particular companies. Individual companies in different industries will require promotion tactics to achieve tasks which may vary quite considerably. Some possible objectives are listed below:

1. To make an immediate sale.
2. To inform the market about the availability of a product or service.
3. To develop primary demand for a type of product or service.
4. To introduce special terms, e.g. price concessions.
5. To create brand awareness and build brand loyalty.
6. To increase market share.
7. To increase frequency of use of a product or service.
8. To encourage distributors to stock and actively sell the product.
9. To promote new uses for a product.
10. To create the corporate image of a company.
11. To announce new servicing arrangements.

The list of possible objectives could be extended, of course, and it will readily be seen that promotional strategies frequently include multiple objectives, one usually being predominant.

Direct buying as the result solely of advertising would be unusual; it tends to occur with mail-order shopping more than in most other kinds of buying situations. In general, other marketing stimuli intervene to influence buying behaviour, e.g., visits to stores to inspect the quality of products advertised, or 'window shopping' as the result of reading an advertisement in a newspaper. The type of action triggered off by viewing an advertisement is more likely, therefore, to lead to behaviour which *may* eventually result in buying the promoted product rather than immediate purchase of it.

Different promotional tactics may make up the total marketing promotional strategy. The 'promotional mix' will be designed to achieve optimum efficiency in the use of the company's financial and other resources. In some particular cases, budgets may prevent heavy expenditure on media advertising, and so this may be compensated for by offering distributors special discounts, organizing attractive point-of-purchase displays, and running some type of consumer competition. Two principal kinds of promotional strategies have been identified: 'push' and 'pull'. The latter is effective where marketers have adequate funds for heavy consumer advertising which is planned to generate a strong demand for those products at retail level. Company sales staff have to ensure that retailers' stocks are sufficient to meet the anticipated demand. The alternative strategy was outlined earlier: dealers are encouraged to stock products by special price incentives—a limited amount of consumer advertising may be undertaken, primarily to influence trade buyers. These main promotional strategies tend to be used in combination. It has also been known for distributors to be induced to over-stock as the result of a strong selling campaign linked with a 'saturation' type consumer promotional strategy. The resulting heavy inventories may then act as a spur to distributors to sell the advertised product.

An important function of advertising is to support the sales force's activities. In industrial markets, this function assumes particular significance. Morrill undertook considerable research into the effectiveness of advertising in industrial markets.[15] Over a period of four years, Morrill's company held nearly 100 000 interviews and investigated 1000 advertising schedules for 26 different product lines sold in 90 product markets at 30 000 different buying locations. The objectives of this extended study were as follows:

1. To examine two computer-matched samples of a product's buyers, one exposed to its advertising, the other unexposed.
2. To estimate the attitudes of the two groups towards the product's competing manufacturers.
3. To determine how much each group buys from competing suppliers advertising at different levels.
4. To correlate exposure and market share.

The industries studied included 'a basic chemical sold in quantity to a tight market of 500 processors'.[15] Of the three major manufacturers, only the leader did any advertising. Research also covered three manufacturers 'who all make a low-priced electrical device used in quantity in all kinds of industrial plants'.[15] Competition in this product market is fierce.

The results of this research showed that industrial advertising was influential with buyers for these reasons:

1. 'It improves the buyer's opinion of the manufacturers' which 'means a larger share of the market by the manufacturer'.
2. 'It acts as valuable introduction for the salesman to his prospective customer'.
3. 'Although qualitative factors are doubtless of great importance to a program's success, lack of frequency of advertising is the single most common cause of program failure. Out of several hundred failures studied, more than 90% ran fewer than five pages of advertising in one magazine in a 12 month period. As a general rule . . . a frequency of five pages per year is needed to turn the scales in favour of a product or product line'.
4. 'Given adequate frequency, most industrial advertising appears extremely profitable. Total cost of selling to groups exposed to the advertising often drops by 10% to 30%'.
5. 'The non-advertiser stands at a serious disadvantage in a well-advertised market. His cost of selling to groups exposed to his competitors' advertising may actually increase 20% to 40%'.
6. 'There is no question that a company can sell without advertising—but advertising certainly increases profitability'.
7. 'Apart from increasing a company's market share, perhaps the greatest value of a well-planned advertising program is that it can reduce the overall costs of selling by multiplying the effectiveness of the individual salesman far more than it increased direct selling costs'.

The last of these research findings should be considered in relation to Webster's survey of industrial buying behaviour (see Chapter 10).

12.4 PLANNING MARKETING COMMUNICATIONS

There are many ways of communicating with customers, clients, or consumers. Personal negotiation (discussed in Chapter 10) is a highly flexible method of communication that is indispensable in many personal and business situations. But, of course, it is limited to fairly small numbers of people at one time and tends also to be relatively expensive. In order to communicate more widely and speedily, some method of mass communication is adopted, particular by large-scale producers. However, it is vital to remember that advertising is merely another way of *communicating* and, as observed already, its effects are limited by many factors, some of which are of psychological, sociological, and cultural origins.

Advertising by itself rarely results in sales; it is essentially an element in the total 'communications mix' which contributes to the efficiency of the marketing strategy. Hence, marketers should approach the task of communicating with their customers in a systematic way: eight main areas of decision-making occur, as discussed in the next section.

12.5 EIGHT STAGES IN COMMUNICATIONS STRATEGY

1. Define target group(s) of customer/consumers which marketer seeks to influence.
2. Study how these defined groups arrive at purchase decisions related to the specific products to be promoted.
3. Define the type and the extent of information which these target groups need; determine nature of appeals to be made to customers—existing and potential.
4. Draw up objectives for communications.
5. Allocate tasks of communication to specific tactical resources, e.g., selling, advertising, point of purchase.
6. Estimate overall budget and agree distribution over components of 'promotional mix'.
7. Decide how communications tasks will be divided between marketer and distribution channels.
8. Integrate promotional strategy into general marketing strategy.

It will be evident from this sytematic approach to forming a communications strategy, that research will be needed into the characteristics of particular markets, not only to establish the extent of usage and product preference, but also to investigate buying motives, personal attitudes, social groups' influence, and the many other factors affecting buying behaviour that have been discussed in this book. Promotional messages must be acceptable in order to be persuasive; hence the crucial role of behavioural studies in acquiring a deeper knowledge of buying activities. Media should be selected for their effectiveness in communicating with *particular kinds* of people, not merely socio-economic groups, but defined in terms of sociological and psychological characteristics. 'Communications that are thought to represent some particular interest or characteristic of the audience are more influential on opinion than general undifferentiated sources. Thus, communications directed to particular audiences are more effective than those directed to the public at large'.[16] Marketers should demand much more sophisticated data from media owners, so that advertising expenditure may be most effectively distributed.

These stages are given in brief outline, but they deserve and should receive considerable attention by marketing executives. In addition to these stages, an effective method of measuring the effectiveness of advertising should be devised, consistent with the agreed objectives. This feedback tends to be neglected in practice. Marketing and advertising plans should be closely meshed, so that media advertising is linked with the activities of the sales force, ensuring, for example, that 'gatekeepers' (see Chapter 10) are covered by the media selected for a specific product or service campaign.

12.6 MARKETING COMMUNICATIONS: FOUR PHASES

Marketing communications are not received raw and unchanged from their sources; they are subject to processing in which the psychological factors of perception, learning, attitudes, and motivation (see Chapters 1–5), and the social and environmental influences of social class, group affiliation and culture (see Chapters 6–8) also modify the messages projected to specific types of audiences.

As Sheth observes, this processed information is likely to vary significantly from 'the information packaged by the communicator'; consumers take the information provided and combine it with other experiences and their existing store of information to make judgements about the product or brand advertised.[17]

In Fig. 12.3, four phases of marketing communications are outlined. On the left, the source of the communication is shown as the sender or marketer of a product or service. From this source, communication inputs, i.e., marketing messages, are fed into the market environment via selected media, which may be personal (selling or word of mouth) or impersonal mass advertising. These various types of messages are directed towards defined target groups of customer/consumers who receive, although perhaps in a biased way, these marketing communications.

However, this sequential flow of communication is affected by three factors which have been included in the outline model: encoding, decoding, and 'noise'. *Encoding* refers to the communicator's design of the message in terms which, it is planned, should enable the intended meaning to be conveyed to the receiver. In marketing, consumer messages should be designed to offer attractive benefits from purchase of a particular product, and these satisfactions should be related to identified needs. *Decoding* relates to the interpretation of the message that the communicator has aimed at the specific target audience. In both cases, subjective factors may intervene to distort the meaning of particular messages. Social and cultural experience, for example, may cause certain elements in a message to be misunderstood, misinterpreted, or, perhaps, render them incomprehensible. These factors in communication are of vital importance to marketing management. Consumers, for instance, want to know about products and services in terms that are meaningful to them; they do not want to be immersed in the technological problems that surround the development of these products and services. The automatic push-button camera enables them to take photographs with the minimum amount of

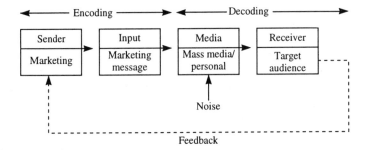

Fig. 12.3 Marketing communications outline model

risk and the highest probability of achieving professional standards; these are the kinds of facts that should be transmitted in marketing communications.

Perception (see Chapter 2) is a personal interpretation of phenomena. Not all marketing communications will be significant for individuals; people tend to select from the myriad stimuli to which they are exposed those that appear to be relevant to their needs. Information will be filtered through the mesh of personal interests, attitudes, motivational structure, social background, and cultural influences. Existing personal cognitive structures will also affect the admissibility and the extent of influence of information about, for instance, a new food product. 'People tend to see and hear communications that are favourable or congenial to their predispositions. They are more likely to see and hear congenial communications than neutral or hostile ones. And the more interested they are in the subject, the more likely is such selective attention'.[16]

In Chapter 10, the importance of personal factors in negotiation was discussed; success was seen to hinge on establishing mutually agreeable relationships in which both verbal and non-verbal modes of communication were used.

Referring again to Fig. 12.3, it will be observed that a *'noise'* factor intervenes in the transmission of communications. This influence or interference modifies or even entirely frustrates the effectiveness of certain messages. 'Noise' emanating from personal factors such as subjective perception has already been discussed. External 'noise' refers to environmental influences, e.g., the activities of competitors who may launch a promotional campaign aimed to divert attention from the marketing propositions of a particular firm; price-cutting tactics, special 'bonus offers', or the opening of a branch store adjacent to competitors. These events may affect the reception of a marketing communication. An international or national disaster may so preoccupy people's minds for a time that they feel unable to entertain some types of commercial proposals. Other factors, perhaps some news item about fire damage, may alert householders to pay particular attention to messages advising them to check their fire insurance cover. The atmosphere in which people read their newspapers may affect their receptivity to advertising messages; at some times they may tend to be more relaxed than others. Perhaps their level of commitment to a particular journal may also influence communication: a regular reader of, say, the *Financial Times*, is likely to be a different kind of person from one who casually scans the paper in a waiting room. Women's journals may be read in a more relaxed manner than a daily newspaper; there may be greater willingness on the part of readers to receive communications from marketers. Weekend television commercials may be viewed more 'tolerantly' than those transmitted on working days, when marketing messages may even irritate rather than persuade.

The significance of 'noise' factors in communication warrants research related to specific types of products and services.

Figure 12.3 also shows a feedback mechanism which should be used by marketers. Some systematic inquiries should be made to establish the effects of communications designed for certain target audiences. Some of the potential objectives of advertising strategies were outlined earlier. The feedback in communications should devise techniques of measuring the effectiveness with which these relevant objectives have been achieved.

Messages will flow both ways: from the marketer to the customer/consumer and back again. Marketing feedback may be registered by volume of purchases of a particular brand of product being promoted, by measuring changes in buying attitudes, by checking the number and type of complaints about merchandise or service, or by the nature of competitive reaction to a promotional campaign. Advertising themes have sometimes been swiftly modified or dropped entirely because monitoring revealed that unfavourable attitudes towards the communicator were being formed, as the earlier reference to Du Pont demonstrated.

Urwick Orr and Partners, one of the leading management consultancies, surveyed British and other European companies' advertising strategies related specifically to evaluating the extent of formalized advertising objectives and the feedback technique applied.[18] They found that the majority of consumer-product firms declared that they selected objectives for advertising, although often these were described in elementary terms. 'The majority of the companies which admit to having no advertising objectives at all market industrial goods'. Most spend comparatively little on advertising. 'Banks and hire-purchase companies seemed to occupy a unique position. Their advertising budgets are on the increase; but none could point to clearly defined goals'.

The following methods for measuring the effectiveness of advertising messages were ranked as follows:

1. 'Sort and count', e.g., coupon response.
2. Group or panel discussions.
3. Recall tests.
4. Comparison of sales results (monthly, quarterly, or annually).
5. Psychological depth interview (see Chapter 14).
6. Folder tests.
7. Sales staff's monthly reports.
8. Annual market research survey.
9. Dealers' reports.
10. Mathematical models (few companies used these 'and even such companies were not entirely clear about what precisely they were trying to measure').

The survey revealed that a common failure among companies was to 'dovetail' the measurement methods with the specific objectives; for instance, the psychological depth interview method was used by one company to measure attitude changes, although the advertising objective it gave on the questionnaire concerned 'informing the public of a product's availability'. It appeared from the findings of the survey that 'even progressive companies which have formulated clear advertising objectives do not always use the most relevant methods to evaluate results'.[18] This topic will be discussed again when models of advertising are considered in Chapter 13.

Feedback of the effect of marketing communications should not be confined to messages via the mass media. Personal methods of communication, such as selling, also call for objective evaluation. Yet the performance of sales representatives as marketing communicators tends to receive limited attention. It is conventional to compare sales figures per territory with targets, which collectively make up the company's overall sales forecast, but apart from this measurement, the contributions that representatives make to corporate communications are largely ignored. Since face-to-face communications are recognized to be extremely important in business, it would be logical to extend feedback measurements to include comprehensive assessments of the effectiveness of representatives. In appointing representatives to certain territories, the communication tasks selected to specific types of customers should be carefully analysed and criteria of success could be agreed. This more sophisticated approach to evaluating the efficiency of the sales force acknowledges that in some markets fairly difficult 'missionary' work may have to be undertaken before orders start flowing in. Responses to marketing communications may differ considerably over various product markets. The immediate response, in some cases, may be lack of interest or even hostility. Some industrial representatives may have to build up personal acceptability over a fairly long period of time before they are in a position to discuss business. Costs are obviously incurred in these negotiations; feedback measurements attempt to apply the principles of cost–benefit analysis to this admittedly difficult area of business negotiation.

Other methods of product promotion also deserve assessment. Point-of-purchase display material, for example, serves to reinforce the communication from advertising at the critical physical place of decision-making. It reminds consumers of the impressions they received from the advertisement they saw on the television screen or in a periodical. It is a continuation of the process of communication. Experiments could be devised to test the sales effectiveness of different kinds of displays in comparable selling areas. If store demonstrators are employed by some manufacturers, their relative efficiency should be rated. These members of staff are likely to be the only direct personal link with consumers; they will be regarded by the public as reliable sources of information about the products being promoted. Marketing management should take particular care in the selection, training, and supervision of their store demonstrators, and view them as more than just sales assistants.

Packaging was also listed among the principal methods of communicating with customers. A pack is not only a handy container for a product, but also contributes to the personality and influences the acceptability of products of many types. With some products, e.g., cosmetics, packaging is an indispensable part of the product mix. It adds glamour and excitement to a lipstick or to a face powder; it gives psychological satisfactions that are of importance to life. Through the medium of packaging, marketers communicate the quality of their particular brand of merchandise. It may suggest exclusivity and sophistication, and suggest that cultural and social satisfactions are to be derived from consuming that brand of product.

The design of packaging should be a blend of functional values, such as durability, and aesthetic satisfactions. With modern methods of distribution, many products have to 'sell themselves' when on display in self-service stores. The overall design of a package and its labelling should assist a shopper to identify the brand among the many other competing products. The following guidelines would be useful in designing packaging. The packaging should:

1. Arrest shoppers' attention.
2. Arouse interest.
3. Readily impart the brand name and suggest the nature of the product.
4. Invite action (purchase).

Package design should not be considered solely as a single unit, because packages of branded products tend to be displayed in bulk. *En masse* they form a pattern of shape and colour that may be particularly effective in attracting the attention of the shopper. Package designs should, therefore, embody features of design that will give mass displays strong visual appeal. In the case of canned soups, for example, it was found that where multicoloured printing was used it produced a distinct optical diffusion that inhibited the human eye from focusing on the brand name or the illustration of the product. Designers have simplified the display faces of packs considerably in order to overcome these difficulties.

In addition, packaging designs should be related to promotional campaign strategies. For example, the colours should be checked for reproduction in media advertising, such as television or magazines. The well-designed pack is essential for successful television appearances; colour reproduction should be as accurate as possible so that the advertised product will be recognized in the shops. Brand names should be clearly projected on packaging.

Post-decisional dissonance was discussed in Chapter 2; marketers should take full advantage of packaging to reassure customers about the qualities of their products and, perhaps, to give them helpful instructions regarding their applications. Packaging can help to build customer loyalty. One vitamin pill manufacturer found that the old-fashioned container in which the product was packaged tended to make consumers reluctant to use them at meal times. A completely new range of packs was designed so that they looked like 'attractive condiment jars': they were kept 'not in the medicine chest but on the table with flowers and salt shakers. Such a redesign created more interest in the product'. An eyedrop maker created a single unit package dispenser to replace a pack that was considered by frequent users to be unattractive and awkward to use.[19]

When Golden Wonder originally tackled the market leader, Smiths, who had been firmly established for generations in the UK potato crisp market, they used packaging as a creative marketing tool. Instead of the traditional glassine bags used by the rest of the industry, they introduced double-walled cellulose film bags that not only gave the contents longer shelf-life, but also could be printed in multicolour with highlight reflection, thus adding considerably to their attraction.[20]

The significance of packaging as a medium of communication was strongly confirmed by research findings in the USA:

> In one instance, a manufacturer of frosting mix 'improved' the package by changing the illustration of the frosted cake to what was thought to be a much more realistic, more appetising version—only to find that the brand's market share was cut in half. Interviews from the customers who had switched away from the brand revealed that although the new package 'looked just fine', the colour of the frosting had changed just enough to signal a difference in the type of chocolate flavour. Although the product was unchanged, there was enough difference in the two photograph renditions to result in a 100% sales differential. Both packages were carefully designed by professionals, but the subtle visual difference . . . was not detected prior to actual sales tests and subsequent interviews with consumers.[21]

Packaging may suggest modernity, although the contents may be little changed, e.g., flip-top crushproof cigarette packs. New types of products have been developed as the result of innovations in packaging, such as aerosol-spray furniture polishes. Product differentiation may largely depend on the style of packaging adopted to suggest, perhaps, luxury, as in the case of some toilet soaps, bath salts, or even razor blades.

Colours used in packaging should be checked for their cultural implications in some overseas markets. White, for example, signifies mourning in Japan; green is the colour of happiness in Pakistan, but it could suggest ill-health or immaturity in Switzerland.

Packaging offers marketers an extremely versatile and effective method of communicating with particular types of customers/consumers. It deserves special attention in the development of the total communications strategy of a company, so that marketing appeals at the point of purchase are consistent with media advertising campaigns.

12.7 SUMMARY

Every organization needs to communicate with its customers or clients. Corporate images or personalities are built up from perceptions gathered by customers and others: these are largely subjective assessments. A favourable image assists corporate development in many ways. Organizations should foster goodwill by planning enlightened communication policies; 'tracking studies' are used by leading firms such as ICI to monitor trends in attitudes, perceptions, etc.

Organizations have a mix of communications at their disposal; systematic planning covers eight sequential stages which need expert attention.

Packaging is an auxiliary form of market communication which can be used creatively.

Marketing communications are subject to distortion from various sources: encoding, decoding, and 'noise' influence the reception of messages. Perception is subjective and affected by personal and enviromental factors.

Systematic feedback to check the efficiency of advertising is strongly recommended.

Advertising and other forms of promotion should be closely linked with overall marketing efforts, otherwise wastage will occur.

REFERENCES

1. Morita, A., *Made in Japan (Sony)*, E. P. Dutton, London, 1986.
2. Alberge, Maurice, 'What the customer saw', *Management Today*, March 1980.
3. King, William R., and David I. Cleland, 'Environmental information systems for strategic marketing planning', *Journal of Marketing*, vol. 38, no. 4, 1974.
4. Hutton, Peter, 'Corporate image', in: *Researching Business Markets*, Ken Sutherland (ed.), Industrial Marketing Research Association (IMRA), Kogan Page, London, 1991.
5. Ansoff, H. Igor, 'The firm of the future', *Harvard Business Review*, vol. 43, September/October 1965.
6. Burdus, Ann, 'Communicating confidence: will the big corporations please speak up?', *Advertising*, no. 64, summer 1980.
7. Worcester, Robert, and Ian McIntyre, 'Strategic decision research: its communications and use at ICI' in: *Applied Market and Social Research*, Ute Bradley (ed.), Van Nostrand and Reinhold, Wokingham, 1982.
8. Olins, Wally, *Corporate Identity: Making Business Strategy Visible*, Thames and Hudson, London, 1989.
9. Jardine, Cassandra, 'What is the difference between these two emblems? A £171 million', *Telegraph Weekend Magazine*, 4 November 1989.
10. Chisnall, Peter M., *Strategic Industrial Marketing*, Prentice-Hall, Hemel Hempstead, 1989.
11. McDonald, Colin, *'Corporate Image' survey*, Market Research Society, London, 1988.
12. Buss, Nicky, Mike Leibling, Michelle Jacobs, and Ricky Wright, 'The Samaritans: reaching out with research', in: *Research Works*, Derek Martin and John Goodyear (eds), NTC, Henley-on-Thames, 1992.
13. Chisnall, Peter M., *Marketing Research*, McGraw-Hill, Maidenhead, 1992.
14. McLaughlin, Nicola, 'PR's place in the sun', *Marketing*, 23 February 1984.
15. Morrill, John E., 'Industrial advertising pays off', *Harvard Business Review*, March/April 1970.
16. Berelson, Bernard, and Gary A. Steiner, *Human Behaviour: An Inventory of Scientific Findings*, Harcourt Brace and World, New York, 1964.
17. Sheth, Jagdish N., 'How consumers use information', *European Research*, July 1979.
18. Majaro, Simon, 'Advertising by objectives', *Management Today*, January 1970.
19. Schlackman, William and John Dillon, 'Packaging and symbolic communication', in: *Consumer Market Research Handbook*, Robert Worcester (ed.), McGraw-Hill, Maidenhead, 1972.
20. Pilditch, James, 'The place of packaging', *Marketing*, February 1972.
21. Twedt, Dik Warren, 'How much value can be added through packaging?', *Journal of Marketing*, vol. 32, January 1968.

REVIEW AND DISCUSSION QUESTIONS

1. Using Fig. 12.1 as a framework, what problems do marketers face in (a) developing effective marketing communications, and (b) evaluating marketing communications?
2. Evaluate the various procedures available to marketers to gauge the effectiveness of their advertising communications.
3. Examine the different types and sources of 'noise' likely to interfere with reception of a television advertising communication for a washing detergent.
4. In what ways can packaging assist marketers as a vehicle for communicating with customers?
5. Describe any instance with which you are familiar where a marketing communication has been decoded by consumers in a manner not intended by the sender.
6. In what ways can corporate image affect a company's business performance?

THIRTEEN

COMMUNICATIONS (2)

13.1 INTRODUCTION

Mass communication inevitably involves advertising; media available in a developed economy like Britain are diverse and highly organized. The 'mechanics' of advertising—preparation of art work, copy writing, etc.—are outside the scope of this book, and these professional aspects of advertising practice are well covered by specialist texts, details of which could be obtained from the Chartered Institute of Marketing, the Communications, Advertising and Marketing Foundation (CAM), or the Advertising Association. In this chapter, discussion on behavioural factors related to advertising will be continued and some theoretical models of advertising influence will be examined. Professional competence in the production of advertisements is, of course, very desirable, but the foundation for effective communication is derived from the behavioural sciences.

13.2 MODELS OF ADVERTISING

In Chapter 9, logical-flow models of buying behaviour were discussed, and it was mentioned that this type of model has been used quite widely in the specialized field of advertising research.

There are several variations of a basic hierarchical approach to the influence of advertising which have been offered by researchers and practitioners. The number of stages and the terminology involved tend to vary, but their common theme is concerned with indicating that the influence of advertising is a sequential process.

One of the pioneers of advertising measurement, Daniel Starch, commented in 1923 on the role of advertising:[1]

An advertisement to be successful:

must be seen
must be read
must be believed
must be remembered
must be acted upon

292

Later, Starch outlined 'the behaviour of advertising' as follows:[2]

1. 'Advertising calls attention to and informs people about products and services via mass-communication media'.
2. In fulfilling the function (1), 'advertising establishes a favourable or preferential association link between a need and a brand name, so that when the need arises the name will come to mind with a favourable or preferential image established (a) through repeat advertising and (b) through satisfactory use performance of the product itself'.
3. 'Hence, advertising leads to buying action because of (a) the existing preferential image, (b) the attention-directing and reminding process, and (c) the persuasive-activating power of the message'.

Starch identified 'two sets of forces' that constantly affect the influence of advertising: 'one set tends to weaken the associative links' through the processes of either forgetting or fading of memory, and also because of competitors' counter-advertising strategies; the other set may strengthen the associative links through the power of repetitive advertising, and by satisfaction continuing to be given to those who purchased advertised products. Starch admitted that his verbal model was 'to be sure, . . . theory, but in the final analysis, it is likely to be the most accurate description of reality'. It is certainly more comprehensive than his earlier explanation of the success of an advertisement; it draws attention in particular to personal environmental factors as well as product experiences which affect the function of advertising in marketing strategies.

A popular flow-model of advertising termed DAGMAR (Defining Advertising Goals for Measured Advertising Results) was developed by Colley:[3]

All commercial communications that aim at the ultimate objective of a sale must carry a prospect through four levels of understanding:

1. (From Unawareness to) Awareness — The prospect must first be *aware* of the existence of a brand or company.

2. Comprehension — He must have a *comprehension* of that the product is and what it will do for him.

3. Conviction — He must arrive at a mental disposition or *conviction* to buy the products.

4. Action — Finally, he must stir himself to action.

Colley admitted that 'this formula, perhaps in different words, is as old as advertising, selling, and other forms of persuasive communication'. The first task of advertising, then, is to strive for product awareness by the target audience. The next step is to ensure that certain attributes of the advertised product are known; for example, brand name, size of pack, where it can be seen or bought, etc. The third stage involves convincing a consumer, for instance, that the particular brand of beer advertised is really worth a trial. The 'action' stage occurs when a consumer 'has made some overt move toward the purchase of the product'. This could involve a visit to the local store to inspect the merchandise advertised, but it does not necessarily follow that a purchase will be made. Other factors may intervene: price too high, product not in stock, lack of visual appeal, and so on.

Colley viewed the role of advertising as helping to move the consumer 'through one or more levels in the spectrum' leading to the final act of purchase. He regarded advertising as performing 'certain parts of the communicating job with greater economy, speed and volume' than could be affected by other means.[3] It was essentially an economical method of communicating with mass markets, and its specific tasks varied according to the needs of individual organizations. (For some of the primary tasks of advertising, see Chapter 12.)

Colley described his simple model as 'applied common sense'; it views the advertising process as a series of 'logical and comprehensive steps' along the path trodden by the consumer who had been exposed to some advertising stimulus. Colley did not, however, offer empirical evidence for his model; he appealed to experience and common sense. An advertising message cannot be comprehended before an individual becomes aware of its existence; until an advertisement has been perceived and related to a consumer's needs, the consumer will not be in a position to reject it or take some positive action such as enquiring further about the advertised product. Clearly, Starch's original model and Colley's DAGMAR model share a common approach; they also have the disadvantage of relying on rather nebulous descriptions of consumer's reactions to advertising.

Another widely quoted model, AIDA, has been adopted in analysing buying behaviour, including the influence of advertising.[4] It has also been popularized in sales training programmes.

A ttention
I nterest
D esire
A ction

A similar formulation was outlined by Rogers in his studies of the process of innovation, i.e., awareness, interest, evaluation, trial, adoption or rejection (discussed in Chapter 11).[5]

Lavidge and Steiner postulated that people move up a series of steps impelled by the force of advertising.[6] These steps are also similar to the phases described by Starch, Colley, Rogers, and others: awareness, knowledge, liking, preference, conviction, purchase. Lavidge and Steiner indicated that these steps are not necessarily equidistant. Some products are approached more slowly; these are likely to have a greater psychological and/or economic commitment, i.e., the risk factor is more evident. Other products may be regarded as less serious, and their purchase will not be likely to involve a great amount of conscious decision-making. Once brand loyalty has been established for such 'low-risk' products, the threat from other brands will tend to be considerably less than with ego-involving products. Branding assists, therefore, in establishing simple 'decision rules' which eliminate a great deal of conscious decision-making every time a frequently used product is bought.

Lavidge and Steiner related their six steps of advertising influence to a three-phase psychological model based on the theory that an attitude has three elements (see Chapter 5), as follows:

Conative
     Purchase
     ↑
     Conviction
     ↑
     Preference

Affective
     ↑
     Liking
     ↑
     Knowledge

Cognitive
     ↑
     Awareness

The first two steps (awareness and knowledge) relate to information or ideas; to 'intellectual, mental, or "rational" states'.

The second two steps (liking and preference) are concerned with the formation of favourable attitudes or feelings towards the product which is advertised.

The final two steps (conviction and purchase) relate to action, i.e., the purchase of the advertised product.

Lavidge and Steiner declared: 'This is more than a semantic issue, because the actions that need to be taken to stimulate or channel motivation may be quite different from those that produce knowledge. And these, in turn, may differ from actions designed to produce favourable *attitudes* towards something'.[6]

13.3 CRITICISM OF HIERARCHICAL MODELS OF ADVERTISING

The linear sequential approach ('step-by-step persuasion') has attracted sharp criticism from several writers. Palda regarded these hierarchical concepts as 'sketchy views of the internal psychological process the typical consumer is supposed to go through on his way from the perception of an ad to purchase'.[7]

Lavidge and Steiner's model assume that attitude change precedes behavioural change, which ignores the complexity of the relationship between attitudes and behaviour (discussed at some length in Chapter 5). Festinger, Fishbein, Ehrenberg, Joyce, and others have all stressed that the link between these two factors is by no means fully understood. The generally held view is that there is a reciprocal relationship between attitudes and behaviour. However, it must be admitted that although the sequential or hierarchical approach to advertising influence has been regarded as inadequate, the paradigm, in general, offers a useful framework which should not be entirely discarded. Advertising research has tended to rely heavily, in fact, on recall and recognition techniques which are associated with the hierarchical concept of advertising.

Critics like Haskins have rejected what has been termed the FIFO process (facts-in, facts-out). Haskins admitted that learning and recall of factual information from mass communication media occur, but he felt strongly that the recall and retention methods adopted widely in advertising research seemed 'at best, irrelevant to the ultimate effects desired, the changing of attitudes and behaviour'.[8] Factual advertisements that could easily be remembered by an audience were, according to Haskins, relatively easy to design; indeed, the emphasis on role memorization was encouraged by the contemporary educational system. 'As the products of that system, we consciously or unconsciously build that approach into our efforts at mass communication'.

Colin McDonald has also forcefully commented on the inadequacy of viewing the advertising process as one of causality: pushing otherwise passive consumers to buy following exposure to advertised products or services. 'The myth has extensively influenced advertising jargon; it is said that advertisements must make an *impact* (like a ball striking another ball), or people must receive *impressions* (like wax), or messages are *hammered home* (like nails)'. Such naive projections were, at first, 'kept relatively simple, as in DAGMAR, but then elaborated into great complex diagrams with feedback loops more difficult to follow than the wiring diagram of your car, and finally, when reality defeated even this much subtlety, retreated into the ultimate confession of ignorance, the "black box".[9] McDonald emphasizes that the approach to researching advertising should start by acknowledging that people respond to advertising, not that consumers are subject to it.

The viewer of advertisements is not, then, someone passively waiting to be stimulated into buying; the mind is not a *tabula rasa* on which impressions can be etched at will. This simplistic and offensive view of the consumer lacks reality and credibility. Psychological research into cognitions, learning processes, attitudes, and motivation (see Chapters 2–4) clearly shows that people discriminate, distort, and actively participate in their reception of advertising messages. Attention is selective, perception is subjective, while retention and recall are fallible and also selective.

Herbert Krugman, who for years was manager of corporate public opinion at the US General Electric Company, has strongly urged that 'we should not speak of captive audiences "watching" TV advertising but also of active audiences "monitoring" the advertising and distributing their attention selectively, with closer attention to involving commercials, with less to the others, and preserving a certain economy of effort overall, i.e., by limiting their attention'.[10]

In Chapter 12, it was observed that market communications are affected by three factors: encoding, decoding, and environmental noise. The concept of the learning process is particularly faulty in these linear models of advertising. It is suggested that people will 'take in' a certain amount of information which advertisers hope will then encourage them to move up the ladder towards the final step of purchase. Haskins is severely critical of this naive view,[8] and furthermore, classical learning theories, such as those based on simple S–R models, have been seen to be inadequate: a cognitive and organizing influence affects human behaviour (see Chapter 2). While learning from advertising messages may be largely accidental compared with planned systematic learning, it does not follow that viewers are gullible and readily manipulated. Through their perceptual and cognitive filters, advertising messages will be subject to some degree of distortion.

Despite the acknowledged shortcomings of the linear models of advertising, recall is widely used as a measure of advertising effectiveness, although an experienced English advertising practitioner has remarked: 'Recall is such a complex process, involving perception, memory suppression and verbalisation, that few psychologists feel happy when using it as a measure of attention although the depth of their feeling is dependent upon the precise nature of the measurement'.[11]

Lannon and Cooper aptly describe the various models and theories of the advertising process as falling into three main categories: 'hammer and nail' theories, 'conversion' theories, and 'hierarchy of effects' theories; a major oversight of all of them is 'that they make little allowance for the participation of the receiver of the communication in the process'.[12] They have reflected on the durability of the 'primitive but enduring linear sequential models', and have suggested several explanations:

1. They lend themselves so readily to measurement. 'At each stage of the process a piece of research can be designed to provide a measurement of the advertisement, embryonic or completed, in achieving some set of pre-determined objectives'.
2. The major US marketing companies in Europe who are 'typical exponents of this sort of thinking' are very successful. Consumers continue to buy highly promoted products because they offer excellent quality and many shoppers 'quite sensibly infer' that because a great deal of money has been spent on their launch, they must be good. On the other hand, Lannon and Cooper suggest that it could be argued that product excellence maintains sales despite a style of advertising 'known to be disliked by women these days sensitive to being hectored, patronised and portrayed firmly tied to the kitchen sink'.
3. Simple conditioning, in that such advertising, although perceived to be unappealing and old-fashioned, may nevertheless be associated so firmly with consistently high-quality household cleaning products that the relationship is 'simply associative and mechanical' in women's minds.
4. 'Perhaps the simplest reason': the language of the linear-sequential models is close to the imperative language used in marketing, e.g., 'moving into markets', 'mapping-out strategies', 'devising tactics', etc.

Lannon and Cooper draw attention to the emergence in Britain of the 'sophisticated consumer of advertising who is able to enjoy some advertisements for their creativity (but not necessarily being persuaded to buy the products in question), while rejecting other advertisements as patronising and/or conventional'. These researchers conclude that more appropriate theories of advertising influence are needed: 'language and concepts more in tune with the intuitive and mystical creative process, than the rational, logical organisational process'.[12] They propose that the perspective should be that people use advertising rather than advertising using people. Products and brands are endowed by consumers 'with meanings over and above their sheer functional value'. Research should endeavour to distinguish between the 'ostensive or face value aspect of brands and their *latent* or symbolic values' (see Chapter 3).

Lannon and Cooper offer 'a humanistic view' of advertising and branding; brands are held to have practical, rational values, but it is their symbolic values that give them distinction and uniqueness. Advertising is said to operate more effectively at the symbolic, intuitive level of consciousness. To research at this level requires a 'holistic cultural' model which reflects the inherent complexity of buying behaviour. They conclude that the 'holistic cultural' model should be developed so that it fits 'more firmly into the pragmatic requirements of organisations'.

This perception of the viewing behaviour of mature, sophisticated consumers also seems to coincide with theories of consumer involvement (discussed in Chapter 4). Researchers have analysed consumer behaviour in terms of either low-involvement or high-involvement. Although research in these areas has still plenty of scope for development, the concept of consumer-involvement appears to have particular relevance to promotional campaigns and their effects on consumers. For instance, people who are thinking about buying a new washing machine or car will be particularly sensitive to information about these high-involvement products. Their searches will include scanning of advertisements featuring these products, critically evaluating the various competing offers, and rating these products on specific attributes. In addition, they may also consult their friends and colleagues in this pre-purchase activity (see Chapter 9 for typical patterns of buying behaviour, especially risk-handling). A high level of cognitive activity is entailed when advertisements featuring high-involvement products are viewed by those who are considering purchase in the near future. The reverse seems to happen with low-involvement products, where elaborate and extended search is untypical.

Advertisements evoke, therefore, very complex and variable responses; moreover, the power of advertising is limited by several factors. It 'is not strong enough to be the main driving force in market or social change; but if other forces are driving a change, advertising will help to shape the way it comes about'.[13] If certain conditions exist, for example, increasing concern about health and safety and growing interest in relevant products and services, then advertising can contribute to the successful marketing of these. Without this societal support, advertising will have an uphill battle. 'Most of the limited evidence supports the view that, in competitive markets, advertising does not seem to have an effect in making the market as a whole grow, unless it was set to grow anyway'. It is, however, 'a powerful force in establishing and sustaining market share'. The defensive role of advertising is a well-recognized function, particularly in fast-moving consumer product markets. While it is generally accepted that advertising plays a major role in establishing brand awareness in highly competitive markets, its power is inhibited. 'Advertising's role is much less to create demand than to show people how to satisfy the demands they have. It does this by fuelling the competition between brands in a market . . . [its] main economic function can thus be seen as the lubrication of competition'.[13] The power of advertising is also affected by factors affecting the reception of promotional messages, which are subject to distortion at the various stages of communication (see Chapter 12).

13.4 INFLUENCE OF ATTITUDES ON ADVERTISING

That attitudes are significant in assessing the influence of advertising was clearly shown in the findings of two studies published in the USA.[14,15] Five measures of advertising effectiveness were rated (awareness, recognition, recall, attitude, and buying predisposition) by 40 top-billing US advertising agencies in 1964, and also by 39 of the largest European advertising agencies about five years later. Their ratings of the five advertising measures are given in Table 13.1, from which it will be noted that 'recognition' was least favoured while 'attitude' attracted substantial support, because it was felt that advertising campaigns are concerned with changing consumers' attitudes towards specific products and services. A favourable attitude does not automatically lead to purchase of a product or specific brand of product; further, an unfavourable attitude may not, in some instances, hinder purchase. Personal attitudes may be repressed, for example, when gifts that would not be bought for personal use are chosen to appeal to the tastes of friends.

It would be logical to include attitudinal measures when formulating advertising models. 'Rather than assume that advertising's function is to affect sales directly or to have an effect on a level of the hierarchy, it would seem more functional to assume that advertising can maintain or shift attitudes with respect to salient product characteristics and their ratings'.[16] Attitudes towards the consumption of some products have undergone change over recent years; margarine, for example, is no longer viewed merely as a substitute for butter for those whose budgets are severely limited: it has acquired significance as a 'health' food and is eaten by middle-class families who are concerned about the dangers of high animal fat content foods. Social influences help to form and affect the direction of change of attitudes.

Joyce's theory[17] of the relationship between attitudes and behaviour, which he developed within the context of advertising influence, indicated the interdependent nature of this association (see Chapter 5). Favourable attitudes towards a specific branded product may be reinforced by acceptable performance; repeat purchase is, therefore, most likely. Conversely, unsatisfactory performance will probably change attitudes adversely and result in switching to another brand when purchase of that type of product is necessary; further advertising of the rejected brand will have reduced effectiveness.

Cox has suggested that 'a great deal of advertising must function either to *reinforce* existing attitudes and behaviour (e.g., maintenance of brand loyalty), or to stimulate or activate people who are already predisposed to act in the desired manner'.[18]

Consumption habits tend to be affected, therefore, by the attitudes that individual consumers have towards food, clothing styles, recreational activities, etc. Advertisers should take note of changing attitudes which may affect the pattern of consumption of their products. In their communications to specific market segments, advertisers would benefit from emphasizing those characteristics (physical and/or psychological) of their products that are salient to the present attitudes held by their existing and prospective customers. For instance, car manufacturers today tend to give greater prominence in their advertising campaigns to the safety features of their products; they are in tune with the public's growing sensitivity to the dangers inherent in motoring.

Advertising may assist in developing trends in consumption that have become apparent in certain markets. Through the mass media, large numbers of consumers are made aware of products and services that fit in with their contemporary attitudes; these messages will be congruent and are likely, therefore, to be acceptable. Persuasive communications should attempt to 'catch the mood' of their audiences by presenting them with information in an agreeable context. Dissonant messages are likely to be 'screened out', while 'sharpening' and 'levelling' may also occur so that the content of some marketing communications may be

Table 13.1   Ratings of five measures of advertising effectiveness

	USA 1964		Europe 1969	
	Highest value or real value	Some value or minor value	Highest value or real value	Some value or minor value
Awareness	24	13	23	15
Recognition	6	33	8	31
Recall	16	22	16	23
Attitude	30	9	31	8
Buying predisposition	24	13	20	19

Source: Boyd and Ray.[15]

radically different from planned messages (see Chapter 2). 'Since attitudes reflect perceptions, they inevitably indicate predispositions. Thus, they permit advertising strategists to design advertising inputs which will affect perceptions and thereby change predispositions to respond or behave'.[16]

The hierarchical models of advertising so far considered would be more useful if they were to articulate the behavioural factors that influence the customer's/consumer's progress through the various stages outlined. Advertising will not have the same effect on every type of product; a very substantial proportion of total advertising expenditure is concerned with promoting frequently purchased branded food products. Advertising is directed to building brand awareness and loyalty; it does this chiefly through reinforcing the attitudes that consumers have towards particular brands of products as the result of past experience.

13.5 ADVERTISING INFLUENCE INTEGRATED WITH CONSUMER BUYING BEHAVIOUR

In Chapter 1 a model of the complex pattern of consumer buying influences was offered as a useful basis for studying interactions that influence the consumption of a wide variety of goods and services. This model is now extended to include the process of advertising. From Fig. 13.1 it will be seen that advertising does not operate in a vacuum. It influences and is influenced by personal factors and by environmental factors such as cultural norms, family life-cycle, opinion leadership, etc. Economic factors, such as price or availability, also modify, perhaps considerably, the effect of advertising. The significance of these factors will be related to the nature of the products advertised. In preceding chapters, the interaction of these variables has been repeatedly stressed. Since advertising cannot be successful without an audience of some kind, and it is generally acknowledged that different 'target' audiences tend to have distinctive orientations towards the consumption of certain types of products, advertising strategists should analyse these behavioural characteristics.

In Fig. 13.1, advertising influences are shown at five levels: awareness, perception, evaluation, enquiry, and purchase decision. The effect of advertising diminishes; hence the diagram utilizes an inverted triangle which reflects the fact that exposure to an advertisement does not mean that buying of the promoted product will follow as simple stimulus–response theory would imply. It suggests, instead, that Tolman's S–O–R theory (see Chapter 2) is a more valid interpretation of the influence of advertising. The intervention of variables between the stimulus of advertising and the response of buying is likely to be distributed at different

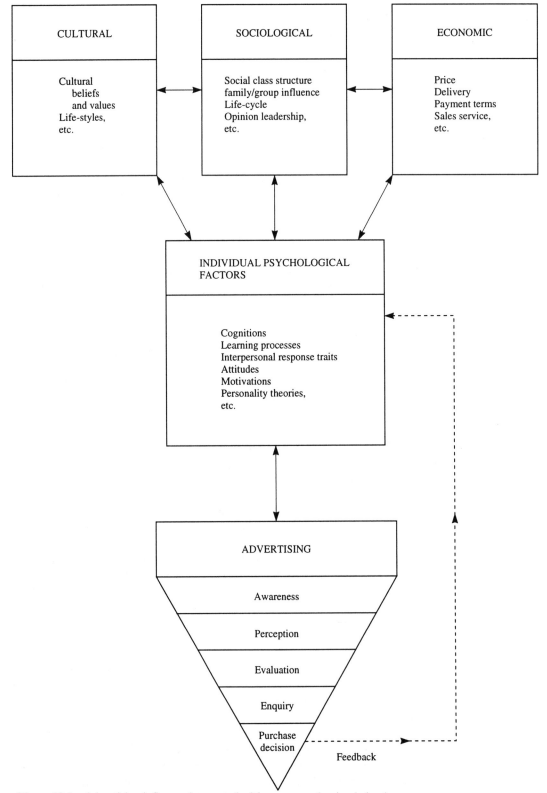

Figure 13.1　Advertising influence integrated with consumer buying behaviour

levels of the 'advertising ladder'. It is suggested that the formation of attitudes and, perhaps, their modification, take place at the 'evaluation' stage of the advertising process outlined in Fig. 13.1.

A feedback mechanism also operates to relate product experience and individual factors such as cognitive structures and attitudes. There is therefore constant activity in the market-place. Bauer[19] has suggested that many marketing communication failures have arisen because the 'initiative of the audience has been recognized only reluctantly by marketers. He proposed that communications should be viewed 'as a transactional process in which both audience and communicator take important initiative. A successful communication is a good "deal" in which each party gives and takes in some pattern that is acceptable to them'. The exchange of values in communication, says Bauer, may not always be equitable; deception may take place either arising from subjective perceptions by audiences or even malpractice by a communicator. However, since an 'audience enters into the relationship in expectation of a square deal', deliberate deception by an advertiser would fail in the long run.[19]

This viewpoint is supported by David Lowe Watson, who suggested that the advertising process should be 'seen as part of a network of relationships, linking the buyer, the seller and the product advertised'.[20] This new emphasis on 'total communication' entails coordination of every aspect of the communications programme (a point which received particular attention in Chapter 12). Watson declared that the 'relationship theory exposes the fallacy of the "economist's view" of advertising as a kind of intelligence service to buyers in a market place where decisions between brands are made on a strictly rational basis'. It is, commented Watson, comparatively easy to show that the majority of advertising 'is wasteful and inefficient by this yardstick', because the information it gives 'is selective, incomplete, and frequently obviously exaggerated'. Watson concluded that the buyer/seller relationship, which was primarily established through advertising, could play a positive role in society by reducing the 'level of confusion, distrust, dissatisfaction and disappointment which would otherwise exist'.

13.6 REPETITIVE ADVERTISING

John B. Watson's S–R model of advertising (discussed in Chapters 2 and 3) stressed the importance of frequency and recency of exposure to advertisements by target audiences. He believed that buying habits could be instilled by a constant flow of advertising of branded products which became etched on the receptive minds of consumers. To this end, repetitive advertising strategies should be designed to imprint indelibly brand awareness and related advertising messages.[21] While there are elements of truth in Watson's advertising theory, it ignores personal factors such as subjective perception, which may considerably modify the influence of advertising. Nevertheless, his theory is an acceptable explanation of how advertising may be used to provide consumers with convenient 'guidelines' which simplify buying of many goods, generally those bought frequently. Most consumers can spontaneously recall a 'battery of brands' related to specific types of products, and while they may not necessarily have gathered this information from advertising alone, it is highly likely that frequent exposure to advertised brands has contributed significantly to their store of knowledge.

Carrick investigated the problem of why repetitive advertising is necessary.[22] He first evaluated some of the conventional arguments in favour of repeat advertising. 'Traditionally, continued advertising is explained by the need to educate the young, the rate of forgetting, or the character of the learning process'. These theories were rejected by Carrick as being inadequate for the following reasons.

1. The 'tremendous impact of personal influence' in forming behaviour patterns is ignored. 'Youths acquire most of their learning from [these] intimate groups'; this extends to brand preferences.

2. Early psychological experiments assumed that the rate of forgetting was a 'simple function of time or intervening events'. But people are capable of remembering something that is 'functionally useful for them to know and this seems more appealing both intuitively and empirically'.

3. Learning does not depend on merely accumulating 'associated bits of information'. 'It consists of movement from one functionally meaningful cognitive organisation to another by sudden discrete insights'. Cognitive restructuring does not depend on frequent repetition.

Carrick agreed that in actual buying problems it is often difficult and costly for buyers to obtain full information about certain types of products. Hence, to save time, money, and effort 'a limited number of an object's discriminable characteristics are taken as indicators of its significance. There is not a one-to-one correspondence between an individual's conception of the real world and what is actually there'.

These discriminating features may relate to colour, size, shape, texture, or a trade mark. Simple indicators or 'cues' may be useful guides to buying decisions. For example, the ripeness of fruit 'may be judged relatively accurately by colour or feel'. However, bread may have chemical additives to render it 'squeezable' as a cue to freshness. A different sort of cue may relate to price: frequently consumers use price as an indicator of quality. (This observation may be usefully related to Gabor's researches into pricing strategies.)[23] Buyers tend to have price ranges in which they are willing to purchase certain products; there tends to be a level of confidence associated with positions in the price range. A further cue relates to trade marks, brand names, and house symbols. Carrick stated that although a high correlation does not exist between superior quality and extent of advertising, attitude surveys in the USA have revealed that 'consumers believe nationally advertised products are superior' to non-advertised, own-label brands.

Two views 'consistent with the evidence' emerge as tenable: brand names acquire significance mainly through advertising; frequency of advertising is an indicator to consumers of brand superiority. Carrick commented: 'A brand's significance properties are assumed to vary directly with advertising frequency. Frequency is computed as the number of impressions over a relatively short preceding time. The differences in advertising frequency for two products must be relatively large before it is assumed that significance properties differ'.[22] He stated that the degree of 'significance information' from advertising was limited mostly to acquiring knowledge of brand names, and advertising frequency reinforced this learning process. Increasing familiarity with particular brand names encouraged consumers to regard them as relatively superior products. This view coincides with Politz's 'familiarity principle' (see Chapter 6).[24]

Kelvin, a British psychologist, also attacked the 'widely held assumption' that repetitive advertising acted by merely 'stamping in' a memory. For advertising messages to be retained (and therefore, to be persuasive) communication should be in terms which are meaningful to particular kinds of people: meaningless, constant repetition will be wasted advertising. 'A stimulus which is meaningless, or becomes so with constant exposure to it, simply becomes one of the many stimuli to which we cease to pay attention'.[25] But repetitive advertising may be effective, Kelvin conceded, because of the intervention of chance, referring to statistical probability. Repetition of an advertisement means that an individual's chance of being exposed to it increases, particularly when he may be experiencing needs which could be satisfied by the promoted product. Repetitive advertising may function, therefore, on a probabilistic basis.

Stewart's researches into advertising effects included an assessment of the power of repetitive advertising.[26] He conducted a controlled experiment in Fort Wayne, Indiana, which involved two products: Lestare, a prepacked dry bleach, and Chicken Sara Lee, a premium-priced, frozen chicken dinner in a ready-to-cook pack. In four districts, which were reasonably the same, different levels of newspaper advertising were undertaken over a twenty-week period. The same advertisement was given twenty, eight, or four exposures; in addition, no advertising at all occurred in one area. Nearly 6000 housewives were interviewed during the experiment, which included brand awareness measurements, attitude surveys, etc. One curious finding related to the advertising for the packaged bleach: after a series of repetitive advertisements (four, eight, or twenty exposures), a smaller percentage of respondents purchased the brand than those who had been exposed to no advertising at all. This phenomenon may be partly attributable to the design of the Lestare advertisement; it also indicates that the power of advertising has definite limitations. The advertisement in question may have lacked strong personal appeal; it may not have been noticed by many shoppers; and for other reasons the offer may not have been attractive. With the other product, a close relationship was observed between the level of advertising and trial purchases.

Ehrenberg[27] noted that the role of repetitive advertising in well-established brands is predominantly defensive, to reinforce the already developed repeat buying habits of consumers. He asserts that consumers tend to notice advertising for the brands that are being bought by them; repetitive advertising enables the buying habit to continue in face of competition. This view of the role of repetitive advertising is said to be 'consistent with the fact that advertising by itself is generally not very effective in creating roles or changing attitudes. It also explains why most people feel they are not personally affected by advertising'.[27] Ehrenberg summarizes by observing that most mass media advertising is for competitive brands and is used as a defensive tool, which is necessary if the producer is to stay in the market. Most consumers have a repertoire of brands of products which are fairly regularly purchased, and they choose according to some general feeling about a particular brand, or perhaps because that brand is perceived to have certain attributes that suggest it will satisfy their needs rather better than other available brands. Past experience may reinforce buying loyalty, although brand switching may occur either because of the disappointing performance of earlier purchases or just for the sake of variety. By keeping the brand name salient in dynamic market conditions, repetitive advertising encourages existing consumers of the brand to maintain their purchasing habits. Research has shown that there is a 'fading effect' after an advertising campaign has ended; this could be severely aggravated if a competitive campaign was run soon afterwards. Reinforcement advertising messages are therefore essential for the maintenance of profitable sales.

13.7 BELIEVABILITY OF ADVERTISING

Cynics believe that the relationship between advertising and truth is remote, if not antipathetic. Some Victorian copywriting would not be allowed today, but neither would some of the conditions under which people had to work be tolerated in modern industry. Expectations are dynamic and influenced by many factors, including public opinion and legislation. In Britain, advertisers are inhibited by a Code of Advertising Practice, under the aegis of the Advertising Standards Authority, as well as by the Independent Television Commission's scrutiny. There are also various codes of practice in other European countries. The British Code of Advertising Practice (CAP) is based on the following general rules, modelled on the International Code of Advertising practice:

1. All advertisements should be legal, decent, honest, and truthful.

2. All advertisements should be prepared with a sense of responsibility both to the consumer and to society.
3. All advertisements should conform to the principles of fair competition as generally accepted in business.
4. The Code is applied in the spirit as well as in the letter.

The Advertising Standards Authority enforces the British CAP, and deals with complaints from individuals about advertisements, whereas the CAP handles complaints from businesses. Although financed by a levy on advertising revenues, the ASA's constitution has been carefully drawn up to ensure independence of action. If an advertisement is found to be in breach of the CAP, it has to be either withdrawn or amended; if this action is not taken, the media, who support the ASA, will refuse to accept the advertisement.

The International Chamber of Commerce (ICC) originated an International Code of Advertising in 1937; and in 1982 it adopted specific guidelines on advertising to children: advertisements should not contain any statement or visual presentation likely to harm them mentally, physically, or morally.

In the USA the Federal Trade Commission (FTC) was founded in 1914, and regulates marketing and advertising practices. The FTC has formidable powers: if an advertisement is judged to be misleading, it can impose severe penalties, including requiring the defaulting company to run 'corrective' advertising. In addition to investigating explicit advertising appeals that may be considered misleading, the FTC has also evaluated the impact of subjective product claims, and has demanded, for example, statistical and other data to substantiate some copywriting appeals. The activities of the FTC have also been subjected to scrutiny; one critic has argued that 'it is not clear that the FTC, or anyone else, has an adequate understanding of deceptive advertising that is based on a sound conceptual model and backed with good research studies'.[28] From their interventions, a body of law has resulted which is the product of case-by-case rulings: 'it is *prescriptive* rather than *proscriptive*. The result is that no overall definition or classification of deception in advertising exists'. One of the problems is an acceptable legal definition of what constitutes deception:

> most evidence used in deceptive advertising complaints comes from 'experts' who testify based on their special training and expertise. These experts testify as to their expectations of what consumers are likely to believe. Likewise, other experts testify on the technical aspects of the product. It is not hard to imagine that 'qualified' experts can be found to support each side of a case.[28]

Some early attempts to define deception in advertising have largely focused on the advertisers' intentions and practices, and have tended to overlook the impact on consumers of such advertising. Consumers' perceptions of deception have been found to differ from those of FTC attorneys when the same products have been involved. Buying behaviour is complex and entails the perceptual processes, of which subjectivity is an important determinant.

To facilitate research, three categories of deception in advertising have been proposed:

1. *Unconscionable lie* would refer to an advertisement that made a claim which was patently false, perhaps connected with the powerful rejuvenating effects of certain kinds of 'health foods'.
2. *Claim–fact discrepancy* might refer to an advertisement featuring a product whose claimed benefits could be enjoyed only by consumers who used it in a certain recommended way, or where the product claims can be appreciated fully only if there is access to the supporting evidence, as might happen where two out of three horticulturists find X brand of a weedkiller to be the best; it would probably be helpful to know where and how the tests took place which enabled this dramatic claim to be advertised.
3. *Claim–belief interaction* occurs when an advertisement or advertising campaign interacts

with the accumulated beliefs and attitudes of consumers in ways that are highly suggestive, but being careful to avoid making either explicit or implicit product claims which could be regarded as deceptive; for example, what has been termed 'surrogate indicators' of the qualities of some household cleaning products by the addition of blue or green colourings to give the impression of greater effectiveness.[28]

Research approaches in connection with the second and third categories of deceptive advertising practices have been proposed, based on the assumption that consumer attitudes are involved, and that an attitude towards a product is a function of beliefs about the product and the evaluation of such beliefs (see Chapter 5 and Fishbein's attitude model). It is suggested that a multi-attribute attitude model could, therefore, be used effectively in the study of deception in advertising.

Inevitably, there are critics of the various organizations engaged in the monitoring of advertisements; however, together with fairly extensive legislation, advertising excesses are largely held in check. Not surprisingly, the advertising profession defends itself with enthusiasm; the European Association of Advertising Agencies (EAAA) skilfully argues that 'because advertising is so visible, it attracts great attention, not least from those who are dedicated to the ideals of a free market economy'.[29] They declare that the role of advertising today is to help in building up the European economy, and also ensure that individual advertisments 'respect the plurality and the humane values of our European culture'. Advertisements are essentially persuasive mass communication; this is well recognized by consumers who are 'well able to take a balanced view of advertising claims'. This view appears to coincide with some of the theoretical explanations of advertising influence, although critics may feel a degree of discomfort in encountering such generalizations.

Two US reports dealing with agencies' evaluations of advertising measurement found that believability measures received only moderate support.[15,16] Of nine measures taken, believability ranked sixth place in the USA and tied with recall for fourth place in Europe. Nearly half US agency directors felt that disbelief or intrigue could sometimes be a highly valuable reaction to advertisements, but only a few European directors shared this opinion. In both surveys, many directors opposed believability measures because they felt that no clear relationship existed between belief and advertising effectiveness. Present methods of testing believability were considered to be unreliable.

In fact, there appears to be some doubt about the contribution that believability makes to the effectiveness of an advertisement. Maloney investigated this phenomenon with a total sample of 600 housewives (drawn from 6 US cities) who were divided into groups of 100.[30] Their responses to a food advertisement, differently designed for each group, were studied. During the interview respondents were asked if there was anything in the experimental advertisement which they found hard to believe. If the answer was in the affirmative, they were asked to give reasons. In all, 485 respondents found the advertisements they viewed presented them with no problems about believability, while the remaining 115 reported that they found something in the advertisements hard to believe. However, analyses revealed that exactly equal proportions (34 per cent) of these two broad classes of respondents were willing to try the product advertised. Maloney referred to the value of 'curious non-belief', which may lead consumers to try the advertised product. People tend to have different 'toleration levels'; what is believable to some may not be accepted by others, because advertisements are viewed against the background of personal beliefs, experiences, and general attitudes towards advertising. It has been noted that advertising messages are subject to 'levelling' and 'sharpening': what people believe from viewing particular advertisements is not easily discovered. There is a distinct difference between emphatic disbelief and non-belief which may contain a strong element of willingness to risk, for example, trial purchase of the product advertised. Maloney's research was restricted to food advertisements, so it would be unwise to generalize his findings although they certainly offer marketing men an interesting aspect of persuasive communications.

In Chapter 5, the effects of source credibility on attitudinal change were examined; in advertising this concept is applied when celebrities are used to promote the sale of products and services. Of course, while some of these personalities may be acceptable to specific audiences, such as teenagers, they would probably be rejected as irrelevant by older consumers on account of perceived differences in age and also social and cultural behaviour. Presumably, advertisers select celebrities to suit their products and types of consumers, particularly if they wish to appeal to specific social or cultural groups. Peer group influence should be borne in mind (see Chapter 8).

13.8 TWO-STEP FLOW OF ADVERTISING EFFECT

Communication between marketer and customer/consumer may not always be dependent solely on direct messages through, for example, advertising. Frequently, a two-step flow of communications is influential in acting as a screening and disseminating process between communicators and target audiences. The effects of opinion leadership related to marketing studies undertaken by Katz and Lazarsfeld were noted in Chapter 8.[31] Opinion leadership has also been observed to have influence in the adoption of innovatory products (see Chapter 11).

Cox has commented that advertising is not in itself a cause of audience effects; it works instead with and through various mediating factors such as audience predispositions and personal influence (e.g., word-of-mouth advertising).[18] Klapper directed attention to the influence of group membership and opinion leadership in advertising effectiveness.[32] Day reported research into the acceptance of a new branded convenience food product covering two matched diary panels of 1100 households in the USA; one panel acted as a control.[33] Data were recorded on awareness, preference, intentions and usage, recall of advertising, and word-of-mouth exposure. 'The basic question is whether observed differences in rates of attitude change between exposure groups are due to the effects of marketing stimuli or to other, possibly irrelevant differences between the groups'. Day concluded from this exhaustive research that 'ultimate success, in terms of creating reinforcing favourable attitudes, largely rested with the ability of the brand to generate favourable word-of-mouth communications and to provide a satisfactory usage experience'. He commented that these findings were 'completely surprise-free, having been articulated in various forms for some years'.

Maloney has suggested that it may sometimes be advantageous for advertisers to ignore potential 'opinion leaders' and to short-circuit the 'two-step flow' of communication in cases where products 'can be accepted with a minimum of financial or social risk'.[34] But even then, presumably, the subtle influence of word-of-mouth communication will still operate, perhaps to the advantage of an advertised product. The identification of these leaders presents marketing management with a difficult task; in Chapter 8 some methods of analysing consumer behaviour in an attempt to identify opinion leaders were examined.

13.9 FEAR APPEALS IN ADVERTISING

Contemporary industrial communities appear to be anxiety-ridden. From many sources, anxieties press hard on individuals: the general shortage of raw materials, the 'energy crisis', inflation, prospects of unemployment, the endemic threat to authority of all types, the growing crime rate, the possibility of nuclear war, etc. In this direful environment, marketing communications are transmitted with the objective of influencing peoples' behaviour favourably.

Motivation influences may lead to either 'approach' behaviour or to 'avoidance' behaviour; they may attract or repel an individual's behaviour with relation to some specific object (see Chapter 3). Maslow ranked 'safety needs' as second in his hierarchical sequence,[35] and there would seem to be a dominant motivation for people in general to seek security and to avoid situations of high risk. It would appear to be logical, therefore, for marketers to become better acquainted with the influence of fear appeals in their communications with target audiences. How far appeals based on producing anxieties can be effective in motivating action favourable to marketers is not well explored, though some general research findings are available.

Appeals based on fear have tended to be used in societies of all kinds for many years; the fear of retribution—the primitive approach to influencing behaviour—has had some effect, although not always leading to desirable forms of behaviour. It may build up strong antipathy towards those who crudely administer such 'negative' types of appeal. Stuteville has referred to the 'deterrence-by-horrible-example' theory which has inspired many road safety campaigns and anti-smoking crusades.[36] But the success of these types of campaigns is open to considerable doubt.

In studying anxiety and fear, problems of definition inevitably occur. Regrettably, the position is far from clear as to what psychologists actually mean when they talk about these phenomena. Kay felt that particular caution was needed when referring to 'anxiety':

> Anxiety is one of the most complicated and confusing personality factors one could choose to measure. Even a cursory survey of the literature reveals that psychologists have not even agreed upon its definition, let alone what is a valid way to measure whatever factor is represented by the definition which is adopted. Some contrast anxiety with fear, whereas others regard the terms as synonymous.[37]

To assist discussion, it is proposed to view anxiety as a reduced state of fear.

A landmark study of fear-based communications reported by Janis and Feshbach concerned dental hygiene lectures given to three matched groups of high school students in Connecticut.[38] Individual groups were exposed to messages containing either strong fear appeal, moderate fear appeal, or mild fear appeal. Their findings, which have attracted considerable controversy, were that a strong fear appeal was less effective than the other types of appeal in effecting any significant changes in dental hygiene practices. It was suggested that the ineffectiveness of the intense fear appeal may have been due to the high anxiety it raised among the audience. This 'boomeranged' by building up hostility towards the communicators, whose message was therefore rejected.

High fear appeals were found to be more effective than low fear appeals in presenting to seventh-grade students in Honolulu the dangers of smoking.[39] It should be noted that the students perceived these communications as originating from authoritative sources; fear-arousing messages from a different source may not have resulted in the same reactions.

In reconciling the results from the Janis and Feshbach experiment and the Insko, Arkoff, and Insko study just noted, Ray and Wilkie pointed out that even the mild appeal message from Janis and Feshbach contained as many as 18 references to the unpleasant results of not caring for teeth.[40] In the other study, 'although the messages contained references to smoking and lung cancer', they could not 'be extremely threatening to seventh graders who did not smoke and who probably considered themselves to be far from a disease state'. The two findings, although superficially contradictory, were considered by Ray and Wilkie to be acceptable. They suggested that high fear appeals were more effective with individuals who showed low anxiety, high self-esteem, high ability to face problems, and who regarded the topic investigated to be of low personal significance.

Stuteville has listed three psychodynamic techniques of dealing with extreme fear, based on 'observations of what people actually do or refrain from doing'.[36]

1. 'unwelcome information is denied or is attenuated' (see theory of cognitive dissonance discussed in Chapter 2).
2. The 'I am the exception to the rule' syndrome.
3. The 'magical defusing process'.

The first technique consists of challenging the validity of the dissonant information. 'To make an issue controversial enormously weakens it. . . . Significantly, the tobacco industry has always referred to the cancer data as the *cigarette controversy*'.

The second approach is a popular method of reassurance. The tobacco addict argues that not all heavy smokers develop lung cancer or heart disease; not all those who drive fast are killed. Danger is dismissed on the ground: 'It can't happen to me: I'm different'.

The last technique, the defusing of danger, is another favourite ploy. In smoking filter-tip cigarettes, people believe that they have 'defused' the inherent dangers. 'Often people in great but unavoidable subjective danger, joke and make light of their predicament. Fighter pilots facing dangerous missions characterise this almost flippant disdain of the perils ahead'.

To rely solely on high fear as an effective appeal may be inadequate; it should be augmented 'with other approaches aimed at the highly addicted'.[36] For example, social norms may be appealed to: smoking is an anti-social habit because it pollutes the atmosphere which colleagues or members of the family have to share; or life assurance cover protects loved ones; or bad driving habits are putting other people—perhaps very young or infirm people—at risk. Hence, the advertising appeal not only aims to intimidate particular kinds of individuals, but also uses the far more subtle approach of appealing to their social sensitivity and personal conscience. By adopting this strategy, communicators are far more likely to succeed in their objectives.

The ethical implications of using fear as a mass media appeal require thoughful deliberation. Sophisticated audiences may well find such messages distasteful, apart from lacking credibility. Advertisements for some cosmetics appear to capitalize on the fear of growing old and losing physical attraction: 'the ad for dish soap which implies that mother's hands will be as soft as her daughter's, and therefore mother will "appear" as young as her daughter, is a play on the fear of looking and growing old'. 'The typical mouthwash or deodorant ad first suggests the possibility of social disapproval and then strongly suggests that some odour is the cause of this feared condition. The sponsor's product is then offered as the *explicit* solution to the *cause* of the feared condition while the *implicit* claim is made that the feared condition will thus be avoided'.[41] While 'bad health and body odour *are* causes of social disapproval', advertisers have certainly not failed to emphasize the possible social effects of these personal problems. Marketers contribute substantially to the general sensitivity of these phenomena, but they need to handle their advertising appeals with care and responsibility. Failure to attain social acceptability despite the regular use of some branded deodorant, for example, may cause a strong reaction by individual consumers against the marketer, which may also affect other ranges of products.

Ray and Wilkie have suggested that 'fear appeals' could be useful in segmentation of markets.[40] Related to this concept is Bauer's theory of perceived risk[42] (see Sec. 9.6). Moderate fear arousal appears to be the most effective strategy, but this should be used with care and associated with other appeals. Positive arguments offering benefits from using a certain product or service seem to be generally acceptable.

The effect of anxiety-arousing appeals applied to specific product markets should be objectively studied. Crude attempts to frighten people into adopting (or discarding) certain types of behaviour have met with limited success. Far more information is needed about the whole subject of anxiety-arousing communications; this should be sought within the framework of other variables which affect buying behaviour.

An example of resistance to advertising which was considered to be offensive concerned television commercials for Schlitz beer in the USA, during which a football star proclaimed the slogan 'Drink Schlitz or I'll kill you!' Although research showed that viewers remembered the commercial, they were irritated and sales were affected adversely. The company dropped the campaign soon after it had appeared; viewers clearly rejected a threatening message.[43] It is as well to remember that advertising is *persuasive* communication and that viewers decide whether particular advertisements will be favourably perceived. Crude attempts to frighten or insult them are likely to have a 'boomerang' effect, as this example showed.

Research on fear appeals related to a health insurance plan was undertaken among assistants of a medium-sized mid-western city in the USA.[44] Of a random sample of 1600, 161 effectively responded to a postal survey. Each respondent received a brochure giving information on the group insurance plan, a coupon for obtaining extra information, and a section with copy on medical cost trends. This latter part of the communication was in four 'editions', selected from statements likely to represent either a low, a medium, a high, or a no-fear condition. These statements were carefully checked by 40 judges selected from the target community.

As noted, 161 effective responses were received; these were roughly equally distributed over the four 'treatments' in the brochures, and the slight variation in numbers was tested and found to be not significant. Survey responses were analysed by demographic, socio-psychological, and attitudinal variables. From this study, it became evident that a response to fear is probably specific to a situation, topic, and person. Different reactions occurred over different target segments. Higher level fear messages, for example, tended to motivate 'older liberals' and 'older blue-collar blacks', but did not affect the other demographic and socio-psychological groups. It would therefore have been unproductive for the health insurance plan operators to project a high fear appeal to the total market; separate strategies would be advisable for different groups of customers.

It would seem, perhaps, that like risk bearing, the ability to handle fear-inducing communications is not generalized. If fear is to be used as a motivator, then research is advisable to identify specific clusters of people; it should not be employed in a general haphazard manner. This coincides also with Ray and Wilkie's observations noted earlier.[40]

13.10 COMPARATIVE ADVERTISING

In 1967, the Advertising Association published a study,[45] *The Economics of Advertising*, which authoritatively reviewed the nature, functions, and effects of advertising and, among a wealth of information and opinion, stated

> Whether due to the laws of libel, of copyright or whatever, it is a fact that in the field of advertising there is very little scope for one manufacturer or retailer to draw attention to the defects in the products of others or to make direct and open comparisons.

Times change and so do business practices. Knocking copy—disparaging references to competitive products in a company's advertisements—was once frowned on; it has been transmuted into a more subtle approach in the form of comparative advertising, as typified in a fairly aggressive and challenging campaign run in the early 1990s by UK lawnmower manufacturers. The CAP tolerates a degree of this kind of advertising in the interests of vigorous competition and so that consumers' information needs may be fully met, but stipulates

1. The comparison must be fair and not mislead.

2. The basis of comparison must be unambiguous.
3. Arguments must be substantiated, and unfavourable generalizations about competitive brands should not be contrasted with specific advantages of the brand being promoted.
4. Price comparisons are allowable, but not when the alleged economies of the promoted brand have been 'manipulated'.

Comparative advertising has certainly swung into prominence since the early 1980s; its adherents argue forcibly that it is in the spirit of free enterprise and open markets, while its critics are equally emphatic about the dangers inherent in using it, such as causing confusion or irritation to consumers. Whatever its virtues or vices, comparative advertising has been adopted by leading car manufacturers like Ford and Volkswagen, cola drinks, and shampoos. Its diffusion may have been aided by the growing strengths of the consumer protection movement which, in its own publications, has regularly presented comparative tests on competing brands of many products and services.

How actually effective comparative advertising strategies are, is difficult to assess objectively. In the USA, Gorn and Weinberg[46] reviewed in 1984 relevant research: in terms of believability or credibility of both specific and general claims, attitudes towards the brand, purchase intentions, and actual behaviour, it was no more effective than traditional advertising. They suggested that one reason why comparative advertising research reports the latter finding is that 'it is less credible and even evokes more counter-arguing'. It may certainly lead to misconceptions of the promoted product, partly because competitive evaluations tend to become tedious after a while, and some consumers may resent having to plough through fairly long lists of product attributes, not all of which may seem relevant to their particular needs. As a result, they may develop negative feelings towards the promoted product.

One-sided versus two-sided presentations

The issue of one-sided versus two-sided presentation was first investigated by Hovland, Lumsdaine, and Sheffield[47] in research connected with the training and indoctrination films used by the US armed forces in the Second World War. It was found that the degree and direction of change differed according to the *original opinions* held: a two-sided presentation was more effective in producing *incongruent* change, and a one-sided presentation was more effective in resulting in *congruent* change. In addition, it was discovered that there was an *educational factor* involved; better educated individuals were less influenced by the one-sided than by the two-sided presentations, whereas the less-educated people were more influenced by the one-sided arguments. It may be that the former have greater self-esteem and perceive themselves as well able to judge for themselves when presented with the 'facts', and, indeed, relish the intellectual challenge involved. Less-well educated people may, on the other hand, feel at a distinct disadvantage in dealing with matters demanding comparative evaluations, and be content with a one-sided argument couched in terms that reinforce, i.e., are congruent with, their existing beliefs and attitudes. The same reaction may not, however, take place where the communicator attempts to persuade the audience to accept opinions that are contrary, i.e., are incongruent, with those are held at present by them.

Gorn and Weinberg[46] proposed that 'one possible approach to developing more effective comparative advertising' would be to design such an advertisement, which incorporates a two-sided (positive plus some 'negative' features) as opposed to the customary one-sided (positive features only) presentation. They stated that the latter 'would be expected to generate more counter-arguing than the former' because the two-sided approach would 'seem to be more honest'. However, available research on this aspect is limited and findings tend to be rather ambiguous. Etgar and Goodwin,[48] for example, undertook some limited research to evaluate the effectiveness of one-sided versus two-sided comparative advertisements, and reported that the latter 'yielded significantly higher attitudes toward a new-brand introduction than the more traditional, one-sided appeal'. Their research was influenced by what has been termed '*inoculation* or *immunization theory*', which is derived from medical practice when patients receive small doses of a vaccine (weakened disease cultures) in order to build up their resistance to specific diseases. In the case of the comparative advertising tests done by Etgar and Goodman, small amounts of 'negative' information were introduced into two-sided advertisements on the grounds that these limited 'doses' of unfavourable information would immunize the target audience against any future attacks by the competing brands, and also result in an immediate strengthening of attitude towards the promoted brand. The theory is ingenious and appealing, but extended research would be necessary to validate it. However, it appears to be consistent with research by Lumsdaine and Janis[49] who in the early 1950s studied the relative effectiveness of one-sided versus two-sided presentations in 'inoculating' an audience against the later impact of 'counter-propaganda'. From their research, they concluded that when a person 'has been given an advance basis for ignoring or discounting the opposing communication and, thus "inoculated", he will tend to retain the positive conclusion'.

The 'pro-and-con' approach applied to the promotion of products and services was also discussed in Chapter 5, when considering communication factors which influence attitudinal change. While there are obviously several psychosocial factors at work, and their interrelationships are subtle and complex, it would be well to bear in mind that existing and prospective customers seek products and services to solve their problems; they may well become irritated by communications that are more puzzling than helpful. Presentations incorporating a two-sided argument together with an 'inoculation' require skilful preparation and delivery if they are to achieve their desired objectives, otherwise they may easily 'backfire'.

13.11 WOMEN AND ADVERTISING

The role of women in economic, social, and cultural life was discussed in Chapter 6, when it was noted that significant changes in attitudes and behaviour had occurred since the 1950s. Female employment in Britain is projected to rise to 45 per cent of the total civilian labour force by the year 2000. Many of these jobs will be in middle and senior management, consistent with the better educational and social opportunities now available to girls and women. Dual income families are increasingly evident; in some cases, the major income earner is the female partner of the household. This was recognized by the National Readership Survey which in July 1992 amended their questions related to 'head of household' to that of 'chief income earner' (see Chapter 7): a pilot survey in 1991 had revealed that about 15 per cent of women could be classified as the latter. Self-employment has increased significantly in Britain since the late 1970s (see Chapter 8) and includes a growing number of women entrepreneurs, particularly in the service industries.

Women are playing a more prominent role in public life, as government ministers, Members of Parliament, senior civil servants, and in the legal, health, and education professions. Nevertheless, as the *Economist Guide: Britain* notes: 'The senior female executive is still rare in Britain, and only in certain sectors are a high proportion of middle managers female. For this and other reasons, women (and this applies equally to foreign women) may still find male counterparts condescending'.[50]

Apart from those energetically pursuing challenging careers, women in general have acquired new skills in dealing with the complexities of modern life. They are influential in buying a widening range of goods and services for their families and for personal consumption. Through the mass media, particularly television, many have gained new insights into the problems and practices of business and industry, including advertising. Women are, moreover, often prominent in crusading movements to improve what is popularly known as the 'quality of life': advertising is among the targets on which they focus. According to Rena Bartos, Senior Vice-President and Director of Communications Development at the J. Walter Thompson Company (JWT) in the USA, the most vocal critics of advertising are the better-educated, more sophisticated consumers who are, in fact, the best customers for many products and services.[51] Women consumers particularly resent condescension and sex-object imagery. The Commission on the Status of Women at the United Nations examined the ways in which women are depicted in the media and in advertising, and concluded that they are given two basic roles: the beautiful but passive glamour girl; and the housewife caring for the home and children. In both roles, women are shown as dependent on men, being identified socially through men and not in themselves.

Following the UN report in 1974, the National Advertising Review Board (NARB) investigated this matter and their conclusions closely paralleled those of the UN Commission. They reported that changing the stereotypes of women in advertising would result in greater equity in the treatment of women, and more intelligent marketing decisions (see Chapter 4 for a discussion on stereotypes). Bartos admits that stereotypes are outdated, particularly in view of the 'dramatic changes' in American women's aspirations since the early 1970s. While some advertising has kept pace with these changes, there is still some that perpetuates the stereotyped images of women. On the other hand, it is not easy to eradicate stereotypes 'because they usually reflect a commonly-held set of beliefs and assumptions that are often unexamined and totally unconscious'.[51]

Since strong, if somewhat differing, opinions about advertising are held by social critics and by advertisers, JWT decided to ask *consumers* how they felt about the way women are depicted in advertising, and so a cross-section of women were surveyed. The 'most striking' finding of this study was that women—irrespective of whether they were primarily home-makers or worked outside the home—had been affected by the changes that had taken place in society. They all responded 'most positively to contemporary commercials and contemporary imagery and most negatively to traditional ones'.[52] However, the portrayal of them as sex objects is 'particularly abhorrent' to women. 'While they do not reject sensuality per se, there is a very fine line that needs to be drawn between showing that women want to be attractive to the men in their lives and the suggestion of sex-object exploitation'.[51]

Career women, who are 'the more vocal critics of advertising as "sexist"', were reported by NARB to be younger, better educated, more articulate, and likely to be opinion leaders. They have high discretionary income and, as their numbers increase, will present a formidable challenge to some advertisers. Bartos notes, however, that it is 'conventional wisdom' that consumers like to complain that advertising insults their intelligence, but they still buy advertised products. 'Well, for one thing, they have no choice. They may be buying the products in spite of the advertising'. (This view is also taken by Lannon and Cooper, as discussed earlier.) A NARB report in 1980 tended to reinforce this viewpoint: 'We believe that people buy products *despite* being offended by their advertising *not because* it offends them'.[51]

Bartos comments that it is commonly agreed that 'a certain amount of irritation is necessary for advertising to be effective'; if advertisements are 'too soft' they may not attract attention. But it would be unwise to discuss consumer criticism of advertising because there is a lack of empirical evidence on 'the effects of consumer dislike on the credibility of individual company images and brand names'. He proposes that until advertisers have evidence proving that advertising which consumers say insults their intelligences has no harmful effect on brand image and credibility, they should 'proceed with caution'.

Among many interesting findings related to consumer changes in the 1970s in Britain, a JWT study indicated that women's horizons had broadened: 'While women still want children and will no doubt continue to till the end of time, the stereotyped notions of Career Mother and Professional Housewife are less rigidly adhered to',[52] women increasingly think of their lives in terms of phases, anticipating a return to work after the early years of child-rearing are over. An important fact to accept is that women work because a job gives them 'freedom, independence and a role of their own'. Such women are likely to buy a much wider range of products and services (as shown in Chapter 8); dual income households may well set new patterns of consumption in which the role of women will become more evident. Only in recent years have car manufacturers, for example, recognized that women are valuable customers both in their own right and as influencers in buying the family car.

Research findings from an analysis of 317 separate television commercials screened in the UK in 1981 and 1982 revealed that men and women are portrayed differently in accordance with traditional sex roles; men are projected as having more expertise and authority, and as being independent; women are shown as consumers of products and in dependent roles to men.[53] These findings were reported broadly to confirm those of previous monitoring studies. Stereotyping appears to be as evident in British television commercials as in American ones. The question is raised whether it is the function of television commercials to shape the cultural values of society, or, more simply, to sell goods. How far advertising should mirror life is debated by leading advertising agencies. A female advertising chief declares that what is happening is not role reversal but role extension. 'Women are taking on more jobs, not giving up the traditional ones, although domestic tasks are not the focus of their world any more. Our responsibility is to sell our clients' products and to do that we must take notice of social change further. We shouldn't be trying to change women; we should be trying to support them'.[54]

Some advertising professionals consider that women prefer commercials not to reflect real life: they want some degree of escapism, but not too far out. Generally, advertisers seem to accept that women may have broader horizons but insist that they still fulfil a traditional role.

The European Association of Advertising Agencies (EAAA), whose defence of advertising practices was mentioned in Sec. 13.7, reported[29] that most complaints about the ways in which women are portrayed in advertisements tended to fall under two headings: that they are generally shown in a traditional and therefore primarily household role, and that they are featured simply decoratively or to attract attention rather than because they are relevant to the product, hence 'the advertisement must have a salacious intent'. The EAAA says that the first complaint fails to recognize that most women still fulfil a household role, often in addition to other roles, and that a high proportion of products advertised are used by women in their housekeeping role. 'That is why father is often presented as the breadwinner and mother is the dishwasher, even though there are now plenty of women who are the key breadwinners and many husbands who do the washing-up'.

The other complaint is dealt with rather more circumspectly: the EAAA's view is that it enters the 'realms of what is and what is not decent'. It does not follow that any representation of an attractive woman in an advertisement is tantamount to offering a promise of sexual gratification—any more than does the portrayal of an attractive man'.[29] The EAAA admits that the issue is clearly sensitive, and because of changes in public attitudes, the whole question is being carefully studied, although it is believed that the present self-regulatory professional codes deal satisfactorily with this and other problems. Public opinion will doubtless influence the development of the EAAA's policies.

There is little doubt that women's tastes, both in terms of product and service characteristics and also promotional strategies, should be given more attention by marketers. A vast volume of consumer advertising is directly related to weekly shopping for groceries and other fast-moving consumer goods. Some industries, such as cosmetics and fashion, are almost totally dependent on women's patronage. But there are others where women's interest might be attracted by skilful advertising, e.g., life assurance. The socially emancipated women of the latter decades of the twentieth century expect to be treated with respect for their intelligence, economic independence, and cultural significance. Strident feminism will not be attractive to these sophisticated consumers who are well able to establish their own distinctive roles in modern society.

13.12 CHILDREN AND ADVERTISING

There is continuing uneasiness among some people about the ways in which advertising exploits children's desires. Television commercials, in particular, have been sharply criticized, especially in the USA, for stimulating the desires of young children. In some cases, it is alleged that the objective of commercials has been for children to put pressure on their parents to buy the advertised goods. It could well be argued that subjective perception on the part of critics has led them to believe that television commercials are far more influential with children than is in fact the case. On the other hand, marketers should not dismiss these criticisms as of small concern; it would be well to remember that the consumerist movement started in a comparatively insignificant way. In 1972 an article in the *Harvard Business Review* referred to marketing practices that affect children as 'perhaps the hottest issue involving consumer activists and marketers' and centred in particular around television advertising.[55] In 1971, one of the chief areas of discussion at the Federal Trade Commission's inquiries into modern advertising practices was concerned with the influence of television advertising on children.

Among the controversial issues related to advertising included in the EAAA's commentary[29] was the impact of advertising on children. To the oft-quoted criticism that advertising encourages materialism and produces demands on parents that they either cannot or are unwilling to meet, the EAAA respond that children are dependent on their parents for their needs and, inevitably, try to influence them, but these attempts are by no means limited to products advertised on television—peer groups, for instance, are influential. The belief that advertising exploits the natural credulity and sense of loyalty of children is challenged; research has shown that children are not naive about advertising, and that children over the age of 8 'know an advertisement when they see it and are quite clear-sighted about its motives'; this perception is said to increase with age. The EAAA invoke views from a 1984 conference on this subject, which declared that television advertising's effects are 'strongly mediated' by the child's environment, especially the home. The third major criticism—that advertising encourages bad eating habits which harm children's health, particularly in connection with campaigns encouraging consumption of confectionery, sugared cereals, crisps, and biscuits, which may result in tooth decay and obesity—draws a rather less impressive response from the EAAA. They contend that such foods, taken in moderation, are part of a balanced diet, and harmful only when eaten to excess or if dental hygiene is neglected. Responsibility is placed on the parents of these child-consumers to check such bad habits, which is doubtless morally laudable but, at the same time, tends to avoid the responsibilities attached to widespread advertising of these products to children. Of course, parents should care dutifully for their children, including, presumably, monitoring their exposure to the mass media. Patterns of consumption are influenced by family norms: these may be instrumental in fostering the development of discrimination in viewing television programmes and their surrounding advertisements (see Chapter 8). But the invasive nature of this medium renders this task unusually difficult.

Despite the apparent sophistication of children in today's electronic age of push-button entertainment, their minds are susceptible and they may well suffer psychological harm from the mixed emotions stimulated by some forms of advertising. Critics are particularly concerned about advertising directed at children under the age of 12, since these are thought to be far more vulnerable to commercial pressure. It is said that advertising targeted at children encourages materialism, suppresses creativity, and may give rise to conflict in families. Young children are limited in their abilities to cope with the persistent flow of persuasive messages about the desirability of owning or using particular branded products. Their cognitive processes are not fully developed and their powers of discrimination are relatively immature.

In general, there is comparatively restricted research aimed to discover the precise extent of the influence of advertising on young children. Some of it has resulted from small samples of US children, often 50 or fewer, and the validity of some methodologies used may be doubtful. One US researcher has suggested that 'children develop somewhat cynical attitudes towards commercials at an early age'.[55] However, the US Federal Trade Commission (FTC) was lobbied in the late 1970s to remove television advertising aimed at children. After long deliberations, the FTC reported that although it recognized that children aged 6 and under were unduly influenced by such advertising, it could identify no practical way of isolating that specific segment in order to enforce an advertising ban. As a result, no regulatory action was recommended; lobbying continues, however.

A counter-argument that has been strongly made in the USA supporting advertising to children is that restrictions would impede advertisers' freedom of speech to their specific audiences, and be in violation of the US constitution.

Hite and Eck[56] made a comparative study of the attitudes of manufacturers and those of consumers related to advertising directed at children. A stratified sample of 88 firms producing children's products, such as toys, confectionery and cereals, and also 178 consumers randomly drawn from a nationwide mailing list, were surveyed by postal questionnaire. It was found that the consumers 'had more negative attitudes regarding advertising directed toward children, and for that matter, of advertising in general, than did respondents from the business firms' who had 'more passive attitudes concerning advertising's usefulness in providing information on new products'.

Gorn and Goldberg[57] of McGill University conducted an experimental study of the effects of television commercials for snack foods on children at a summer camp in 1982. Over a period of two weeks, 5–8 year olds watched a half-hour video-taped TV cartoon each day, which included just under five minutes of advertising. One group was exposed to commercials for orange juice and various fruits; the other to commercials for Kool-aid and various highly sugared snacks like confectionary bars. After the daily television exposures, childrn were offered a selection of these products: 'their snack and drink choices reflected their TV viewing experience'.

Another US study[58] investigated the conditions under which children are likely to màke attitude-consistent choices when selecting from products advertised on television, and also whether age differences were significant factors. A total of 56 children (10 girls and 14 boys aged 9, and 15 girls and 17 boys aged 13) participated in this experiment, which included viewing commercials advertising a fictitious product; one commercial was intended to foster favourable attitudes towards the advertised product, the other to induce unfavourable attitudes. Subsequently, the children responded to a series of scale-rating questions to measure their attitudes. The researchers reported that 'even young children can be effective decision-makers' and are 'capable of forming attitudes on the basis of information presented in TV commercials. . . . However, it is equally evident . . . that there is a limit to children's comparison skills. . . . Younger children's comparison skills may be overtaxed'.[58] These findings, although based on relatively limited data, tend to endorse some of the concerns about young children's exposure to television advertising that were discussed earlier.

Gorn and Florsheim[59] studied the effects on US children of exposure to television commercials for adult products in the early 1980s. Their sample of 70 10-year-old local girl guides was studied in relation to commercials for lipsticks and diet drinks targeted at adult consumers. Results showed that television advertisements for lipsticks can influence young girls' perceptions of the products and brands which are associated with being an adult, and may, perhaps, affect their future consumption habits; the effects of the commercials for diet drinks were far less pronounced. Even though children may not, at present, be consumers of such products, it is suggested by the researchers—not altogether surprisingly—that advertisements aimed at adults may also affect the brand choices that children make later in their lives.

In the early 1970s research into children's reactions to television commercials in the USA involved 67 children, from 5 to 12 years of age, in the Boston area.[60] The sample was admitted to be skewed towards the upper-middle class. It was found that younger children showed 'low awareness of the concept of commercials, frequently explaining them as part of the show or identifying them simply by naming a category of products'. Older children, however, were more aware of the nature and purpose of commercials, and were able to differentiate more easily between programmes and advertisements. They were more able to organize the impressions received and to recall them in 'a coherent, unified sequence'. Children of all ages liked advertisements that amused them; among children in the age group 5–7 years, 43 per cent said they liked a commercial because the product was liked or possessed.

Nearly half the children surveyed felt that television commercials do not always tell the truth. This reaction was strongest with the older age groups, where 70 per cent of 11–12 year olds expressed this view. Only 18 per cent of the sample thought that advertising was always truthful, but of these 30 per cent were 5–7 year olds, and only 5 per cent at the upper limit (11–12) of the age range. Children appeared to judge whether commercials were truthful in several ways: younger children, in particular, felt that commercials could not be true if they did not match their 'literal perception of reality'; exaggerated messages or commercials featuring 'unreal people, objects, or actions' were dismissed as not being credible. A few children said that they disbelieved commercials because they had heard from others that advertisements were not truthful. Of the 9–12-year-old children, 73 per cent were suspicious about the motives of advertising. 'They seem to reason that since commercials are trying to sell, they do not tell the truth'.[60]

The study quoted does not, as the researcher admitted, permit generalizations to be drawn because of the size and nature of the sample. It suggests, however, that marketers should accept the ethical responsibilities implied in communicating with young children. If young audiences develop mistrust of the advertising of certain firms, the success of advertising programmes in the long term will be affected. Apart from ethics, it would be bad business policy to sow the seeds of disbelief and antipathy at an impressionable age. In addition, there is a risk of alienating the mothers of young children who may find exaggerated advertising aimed at their families to be personally distasteful. Advertisers cannot shrug off their responsibilities and say it is up to parents to take care of their children's viewing habits; this is, as Scott Ward remarked, a defensive tactic that is not likely to be effective.[60] In the USA, sponsored programmes present problems of quality which are not in the main, experienced in Britain, where more rigorous control of transmissions for children is exercised.

A limited survey among Canadian households indicated that television commercials for certain kinds of toys were influential on young children (5–8 year olds), who subsequently persuaded their parents to buy the advertised products.[61] A two-step flow of information also appeared to be active: of those children classed as 'low' viewers, nearly 40 per cent claimed that they 'first saw or heard of the toy through their friends'. Television advertising sets a trend which is swiftly disseminated through informal communication. Hence, there are two aspects of television commercials: direct influence and indirect influence through social contacts. The survey data showed that immediate purchase by parents at the child's request was limited to low-priced toys, while toys costing $5 or more were 'most often' bought at a later time because of children's desires. It was significant that one random sample of toys that had been advertised recently on television was found to have an average price of $5.12.

Rossiter studied the general effects of television advertising on children in the USA related to cumulative exposure (over age) and heavy viewing (within age groups). He found that cognitive effects were that children's understanding of 'the nature and purpose of television commercials increases dramatically with age and thus with heavy exposure: within age groups, heavy viewers were no less perceptive than light viewers.[62]

Attitudes towards television advertisements 'decrease dramatically with age and thus with cumulative exposure': within age groups, heavy viewers hold more favourable attitudes than light viewers. Age and therefore cumulative exposure have little effect on children's desires for advertised products, and their requests to parents to buy these goods. From these findings, Rossiter concluded that the developing child is able to handle television advertising in a more rational way than the critics believe. Television advertising is perceived quite critically by children themselves, who accept it as a 'social institution'.

As far as British children's attitudes may be judged, there appears to be developed at quite an early age a degree of bias in viewing advertisements. Advertising jingles are frequently subject to ingenious amendments, and are chanted as playtime tunes in place of some of the traditional nursery rhymes.

In 1980, the Advertising Standards Authority (ASA) in Britain monitored children's responses to 13 advertisements selected to include those aimed at as well as those featuring children.[63] This study was extended to over 300 children, of whom 100 were in the 8–11 age-group (55 girls and 45 boys) and 200 in the 12–14 age-group (122 girls and 78 boys). Only when it was established that children understood all the copy and the purpose of an advertisement, were they questioned further and their spontaneous reactions monitored. Their responses reflected strongly their sense of values: children are perceptive and criticize messages which conflict with their outlook on life.

An experienced British researcher has noted that there is a school of thought that views children as 'little sponges' waiting to absorb the latest advertising messages and then determined to buy the product at all costs. 'Our own research experience shows that this is emphatically *not* the case'. At a very early age, children are aware of the purpose of advertising and 'apply their own quite stringent criteria when evaluating advertisements'.[64]

Children think of advertising primarily in terms of television commercials, but as early as 4 years of age they are able to discriminate between programmes and commercials; the latter are expected to inform as well as to entertain—they are more likely to be successful if they fulfil both expectations. However, everyday experiences, family and friends, and shop window displays 'are of greater relevance and importance to the child' than television commercials. In particular, peer group influence becomes more pronounced with older children (see Chapters 6, 8, and 13).

Value for money is very important to children, particularly when spending pocket money. Of course, children employ various tactics to persuade their parents to buy desired products; most parents believe that the more persistent requests are for products owned by peer groups. Often, these goods have not been heavily promoted but have diffused by word of mouth and personal trial of friends' products (see Chapters 8, 11, and 13).

The research study, based on interviews with 4000 childrn every year in the UK, concludes that children, as other surveys have found, seek information, filter messages, and effectively 'block out what they do not consider to be of value to them'; they are far from helpless when exposed to advertisements.[64]

In 1988, the Advertising Association published results of a three-year investigation into the effects of advertising on children in the 7–14 age-group, based on research carried out by Tony Twyman of Research Bureau Ltd of London. Products of specific interest to children, such as sweets and toys, were covered, and also products like alcoholic drinks and tobacco which critics have suggested that advertisers, intentionally or otherwise, influence young people to consume. Some of the findings were, first, children have a high awareness and interest in advertising, particularly that seen on television; second, children's awareness of advertising is primarily determined by style and content rather than by the product advertised; third, the general high levels of awareness and interest shown by children do not establish that persuasion also took place; fourth, children notice and like television commercials for many reasons, for example, humour or cartoons, irrespective of the product promoted, hence, recall and popularity are insufficient evidence of advertising effectiveness or of unintentional advertising influence. The researchers emphasized the importance of this particular conclusion, 'since critics of advertising repeatedly use advertising recall and popularity tests as evidence of advertising effectiveness'.[65]

Upbringing and parental attitudes were suggested to be the main influences on sweet-eating habits; the amount of pocket money available also affects levels of consumption; higher rates of consumption tended to be associated with lower social class membership, but it is *not* associated with heavy ITV television viewing; also, there was no clear link between brand choice and advertising awareness. Awareness of cigarette advertising tends to be rather general and not very salient for most children. Beer advertising seemed to be very popular with children, largely on account of its entertainment value.

The survey gives 'many reasons for rejecting the hypothesis that advertising to children unfairly manipulates the young'. Social and situational factors are far more likely to lead them to consume alcoholic drinks or smoke cigarettes than advertising itself. It is unlikely that advertising recall and popularity are by themselves indicators of advertising effectiveness; 'children themselves do not believe that advertising exerts a significant influence on their level of consumption of the various product groups'.[65]

Children, it would appear from the research evidence available, are not unlike adults in dealing with advertising messages, which are liable to dilution and distortion. People, small and large, are not just *subject* to advertising: they take an *active* role in discriminating, and also rejecting, advertising messages. They are unlikely to buy simply because a product is advertised; there is the expectation of benefits and if these are not experienced to the degree anticipated, repeat buying is virtually certain not to occur. Obviously, children lack the experience of buying that adults have, but they very soon acquire a sense of value for money and, generally speaking, are not so vulnerable to advertising as some critics aver; in addition, parental influence is likely to be an important factor in establishing patterns of consumption (see Chapter 8).

Some of the research findings quoted are not entirely unexpected, while others appear to challenge the strongly held opinions of advertising's critics. Clearly, the interests of children must always be of paramount importance, so vigilance should continue to be exercised to ensure that those who profit from mass media advertising fully accept their responsibilities in this matter. In Chapter 15, trend data about the public's attitudes to advertising in Britain are presented, and developments in mass media are discussed.

13.13 SUMMARY

Hierarchical or linear sequential models of advertising, such as Starch, Colley, AIDA, and Lavidge and Steiner, have been sharply criticized as inadequate and simplistic. The viewer of the advertisements is not just a passive receiver; information is subject to distortion. Recall is a complex process involving perception, suppression, and verbalization. Apart from environmental influences, messages are seldom, if ever, received as planned by communicators: selective attention, subjective perception, selective retention, and fallible recall all affect advertising influence.

Repetitive advertising is largely defensive, and is vital in maintaining brand share in competitive markets.

How far advertisements need to be believable is not definitely established; disbelief or 'curious non-belief' may stimulate interest, but believability seems subject to personal experiences and beliefs. Advertising messages are 'sharpened' and 'levelled', so what people gather from advertising is not easily discovered.

Two-step flow of advertising effect is likely to be influential; opinion leadership and personal influence are mediating factors.

Fear appeals in advertising need sensitive handling. Some evidence suggests that a segmented target audience approach is advisable. Crude, anxiety-producing appeals may well 'boomerang' to the disadvantage of communicators.

The model of consumer buying influences given in Chapter 1 was extended to include the process of advertising to indicate that communication is subject to many influences.

Advertising and its effects on women were observed to pose problems; new horizons of female expectations have caused advertisers to rethink their approach to women consumers. Social and economic power is now more evenly distributed so that old stereotypes of women as sex objects or just housewives dependent for their social significance on men are now challenged. Advertisers should proceed with caution and not assume that distasteful advertising will not matter.

Because of its saliency, advertising's influence on children has attracted a variety of research investigations. The general findings tend to be reassuring, but some disquiet exists as well; constant monitoring by official and also trade organizations is important.

REFERENCES

1. Starch, Daniel, *Principles of Advertising*, A. W. Shaw, Chicago, 1923.
2. Starch, Daniel, *Measuring Advertising Readership and Results*, McGraw-Hill, New York, 1966.
3. Colley, Russell H., *Defining Advertising Goals for Measured Advertising Results*, Association of National Advertisers, New York, 1961.
4. Strong, E. K., *The Psychology of Selling*, McGraw-Hill, New York, 1925.
5. Rogers, Everett M., *Diffusion of Innovation*, Free Press, New York, 1962.
6. Lavidge, Robert J., and Gary A. Steiner, 'A model for predictive measurements of advertising effectiveness', *Journal of Marketing*, vol. 25, no. 6, October 1961.
7. Palda, Kristian S., 'The hypothesis of a hierarchy of effects: a partial evaluation', *Journal of Marketing Research*, vol. 3, no. 1, February 1966.
8. Haskins, Jack B., 'Factual recall as a measure of advertising effectiveness', *Journal of Advertising Research*, vol. 4, no. 1, March 1964.
9. McDonald, Colin, 'Myths, evidence and evaluation', *Admap*, November 1980.
10. Krugman, Herbert H., 'Point of view: limits of attention to advertising', *Journal of Advertising Research*, October/November 1988.
11. Burdus, Ann, 'Advertising research', in: *The Effective Use of Market Research*, Staples Press, 1971.
12. Lannon, Judie, and Peter Cooper, 'Humanistic advertising: a holistic cultural perspective', in: *Effective Advertising: Can Research Help?* ESOMAR, Monte Carlo, 26/28 January 1983.
13. McDonald, Colin, *How Advertising Works: A Review of Current Thinking*, Advertising Association in association with NTC, Henley-on-Thames, 1992.
14. Adler, Lee, Allan Greenberg, and Donald B. Lucas, 'What big agency men think of copy testing methods', *Journal of Marketing Research*, vol. 2, November 1965.
15. Boyd, Harper W., Jnr, and Michael L. Ray, 'What big agency men in Europe think of copy testing methods', *Journal of Marketing Research*, vol. 3, May 1971.
16. Boyd, Barper W., Jnr, Michael L. Ray, and Edward C. Strong, 'An attitudinal framework for advertising strategy', *Journal of Marketing*, vol. 36, April 1972.
17. Joyce, Timothy, 'What do we know about how advertising works?', *Advertising Age*, May/June 1967.

18. Cox, Donald F., 'Clues for advertising strategists', *Harvard Business Review*, vol. 39, November/December 1961.

19. Bauer, R. A., 'The initiative of the audience', *Journal of Advertising Research*, vol. 3, no. 2, June 1963.

20. Watson, David Lowe, 'Advertising and the buyer/seller relationship', *Admap*, August 1968.

21. Watson, John B., *Behaviourism*, People's Institute, New York, 1925.

22. Carrick, Paul M., Jnr, 'Why continued advertising is necessary', *Journal of Marketing*, vol. 23, no. 4, April 1959.

23. Gabor, Andre, and C. W. J. Grainger, 'Price as an indicator of quality: report on an enquiry', *Economica*, February 1966.

24. Politz, Alfred, 'The dilemma of creative advertising', *Journal of Marketing*, vol. 25, no. 2, October 1960.

25. Kelvin, R. P., *Advertising and Human Memory*, Business Publications, Richard D. Irvin, Homewood, Ill., 1962.

26. Stewart, John B., *Repetitive Advertising in Newspapers: A Study of Two New Products*, Harvard University, Graduate School of Business Administration, Boston, Massachusetts, 1964.

27. Ehrenberg, Andrew S. C., 'Repetitive advertising and the consumer', *Journal of Advertising Research*, vol. 14, no. 2, 1974.

28. Gardner, David M., 'Deception in advertising: a conceptual approach', in: *Promotional Management: Issues and Perspectives*, Norman Govoni, Robert Eng, and Morton Galper (eds), Prentice-Hall, Englewood Cliffs, New Jersey, 1988.

29. *Advertising: Its Role in Our Society, in Our Economy*, European Association of Advertising Agencies, Brussels, and NTC, Henley-on-Thames, 1986.

30. Maloney, John C., 'Curiosity versus disbelief in advertising', *Journal of Advertising Research*, vol. 2, no. 2, June 1962.

31. Katz, Elihu, and P. F. Lazarsfeld, *Personal Influence*, Free Press, New York, 1955.

32. Klapper, Joseph F., 'What we know about the effects of mass communication: the brink of hope', *Public Opinion Quarterly*, winter 1957/58.

33. Day, George S., 'Attitude change, media and word of mouth', *Journal of Advertising Research*, vol. 11, no. 6, December 1971.

34. Maloney, John C., 'Is advertising believability really important?' *Journal of Marketing*, vol. 27, no. 4, October 1963.

35. Maslow, A. H., 'A theory of human motivation', *Psychological Review*, vol. 50, 1943.

36. Stuteville, John R., 'Psychic defenses against high fear appeals: a key marketing variable', *Journal of Marketing*, vol. 34, no. 2, April 1970.

37. Kay, Herbert, 'Do we really know the effects of using "fear" appeals?', *Journal of Marketing*, vol. 36, no. 2, April 1972.

38. Janis, Irving L., and Seymour Feshbach, 'Effects of fear arousing communications', *Journal of Abnormal and Social Psychology*, vol. 48, no. 1, 1953.

39. Insko, C. A., A. Arkoff, and V. M. Insko, 'Effects of high and low fear arousing communication upon opinions towards smoking', *Journal of Experimental and Social Psychology*, vol. 1, August 1965.

40. Ray, Michael L., and William L. Wilkie, 'Fear: the potential of an appeal neglected by marketing', *Journal of Marketing*, vol. 34, no. 1, January 1970.

41. Spence, Horner E., and Reza Moinpour, 'Fear appeals in marketing—a social perspective', *Journal of Marketing*, vol. 36, no. 3, July 1972.

42. Bauer, R. J., 'Consumer behaviour as risk taking', in: *Proceedings of the 43rd National Conference of the American Marketing Association*, R. S. Hancock (ed.), Chicago, 1960.

43. Hornix, Jacob, 'Mediating effects in the advertising process', *Advertising*, no. 60, summer 1979.

44. Burnett, John J., and Richard L. Oliver, 'Fear appeal effects in the field: a segmentation approach', *Journal of Marketing Research*, vol. 16, May 1979.

45. Lees, D. S., *The Economics of Advertising: A Study by the Economists Advisory Group*, Advertising Association, London, 1967.

46. Gorn, Gerald, J., and Charles B. Weinberg, 'The impact of comparative advertising on perception and attitude: some positive findings', *Journal of Consumer Research*, vol. 11, September 1984.

47. Hovland, C. I., A. A. Lumsdaine, and F. D. Sheffield, *Experiments on Mass Communication*, Princeton University Press, New Jersey, 1949.

48. Etgar, Michael, and Stephen A. Goodwin, 'One-sided versus two-sided comparative message appeals for new brand introductions', *Journal of Consumer Research*, vol. 8, March 1982.

49. Lumsdaine, A. A., and I. L. Janis. 'Resistance to "counter-propaganda" produced by one-sided and two-sided "propaganda" presentations', *Public Opinion Quarterly*, vol. 17, 1953.

50. *The Economist Guide: Britain*, Hutchinson, London, 1990.

51. Bartos, Rena, 'Women and advertising', *International Journal of Advertising*, vol. 2, 1983.

52. Lannon, Judie, 'The new freedom', in: *Consumer Change in the Mid 70s*, J. Walter Thompson, London, September 1976.

53. Chappel, Brian, 'How women are portrayed in television commercials', *Admap*, June 1983.

54. Nuttall, Gwen, 'Keeping an eye on roles', *Marketing*, 4 August, 1983.

55. Ward, Scott, 'Kids TV: marketers on hot seat', *Harvard Business Review*, July/August 1972.

56. Hite, Robert E., and Randy Eck, 'Advertising to children: attitudes of business vs. consumers', *Journal of Advertising Research*, October/November 1987.

57. Gorn, Gerald J., and Marvin E. Goldberg, 'Behavioral evidence of the effects of televised food messages on children', *Journal of Consumer Research*, vol. 9, no. 2, 1982.

58. Roedder, Deborah L., Brian Sternthal, and Bobby J. Calder, 'Attitude–behavior consistency in children's responses to television advertising', *Journal of Marketing Research*, vol. 20, November 1983.

59. Gorn, Gerald, J., and Renée Florsheim, 'The effects of commercials for adult products on children', *Journal of Consumer Research*, vol. 11, March 1985.

60. Ward, Scott, 'Children's reactions to commercials', *Journal of Advertising Research*, vol. 12, no. 2, April 1972.

61. Frideres, James S., 'Advertising, buying patterns and children', *Journal of Advertising Research*, vol. 13, no. 1, February 1973.

62. Rossiter, John R., 'Does TV advertising affect children?', *Journal of Advertising Research*, vol. 19, no. 1, 1979.

63. Gould, Patience, 'Children show up the ad men', *Marketing*, 17 December 1980.

64. Smith, Glen, 'Children as the target for advertising', *Advertising*, no. 6, spring 1981.

65. *Market Research Society Newsletter*, London, April 1988.

REVIEW AND DISCUSSION QUESTIONS

1. Evaluate the options available to marketers when deciding which source and message type to employ in order to change consumer attitudes.

2. What effects do television commercials aimed at younger children have on their socialization as consumers? Should government or the advertising profession exercise any special regulatory function in this matter? If so, what broad directions should be followed?

3. Do you consider that fear appeal would be an appropriate advertising strategy for an AIDS awareness campaign on television aimed at the 18–25 age-group? Are there any reservations you might have in using such a strategy?

4. Describe three television advertisements where you consider the portrayal of women to be unsatisfactory. Explain the reasons for your dissatisfaction.

5. The marketing manager for the second largest brand of tea bags in the UK market is designing a television advertising schedule for the coming year. Should repetitive advertising feature prominently in this schedule?

6. What are the main drawbacks in utilizing linear sequential models of advertising?

FOURTEEN

MARKET SEGMENTATION

14.1 INTRODUCTION

In Chapter 1 the marketing concept was seen to be about satisfying the identified needs of people by supplying them with acceptable goods and services. If people were satisfied with their purchases, they would be likely to buy again; if not, they went elsewhere. Responsive suppliers prospered because they focused on what their customers wanted and made sure that the products (and services) offered were designed and made with those customers in mind.

Virtually by its definition, the marketing concept, as Levitt observes, leads logically to dividing customers into several specific types or segments of a market.

> When the marketing concept operates at full throttle, it generates products, services and communications that target the specifically discovered needs and wants of specific narrow benefit consumer segments. Each segment, therefore, has a better chance of getting what it really wants or needs than in the bad old days when Henry Ford told people they could have any colour Model T they wanted so long as it was black.[1]

Experienced marketers are not content merely to measure macro or total market demand—few firms supply an *entire* market—instead, they identify total demand and then break it down into segments or sectors with distinctive demand characteristics. Corporate resources are limited and they are more productively used when focused on making and marketing goods that really appeal to particular kinds of customers. Practically every market is capable of refinement into significant submarkets. Frequently the trend in these specialized sectors of the global market may be different from the general trend; for example, the UK grocery market as a whole is largely static, but the demand for certain kinds of products, such as 'diet' and 'health' foods, is rising rapidly. In the carpet industry, two distinctive market trends are observable, related to woven woollen carpets and tufted synthetic yarn carpets respectively. Women's fashion clothing trends are far more dynamic than those experienced in the menswear market.

Different trends characterize the prestige and popular ends of markets: Harrods experience distinctly different trading trends from, say, Woolworths. Specialized market sectors may arise from perceptions of quality and exclusivity, or because of economy and value for money. With constantly rising prices, consumers may consider durability to be of greater importance than immediate cost, so they switch to stores selling better-quality products. Several large retail distributors have steadily followed a 'trading-up' policy since the early 1970s. Effective marketing depends on the success with which trends like this can be spotted and evaluated.

In specialized market segments, customers may react differently to product characteristics such as price, quality, product design (including colour), packaging, advertising, and methods of distribution. In other words, the 'marketing mix' has to be specific to achieve success in individual market segments.

The personal and environmental behavioural characteristics discussed in this book are not only abstract notions, but also impinge on buying behaviour which, after all, is a part of general human behaviour. People are *motivated* to buy for many reasons; they *perceive* products and advertisements differently; they have various ways of *learning* about products and services; they are influenced by the consumption patterns of their social and professional *groups*; they often take account of *word-of-mouth, informal communication*; and they may buy to express their *personalities*. Also, they will have *sets of attitudes*—favourable or otherwise—about firms, products, or places; they may experience *dissonance* after buying certain products or services; they may regard themselves as *opinion leaders* or *innovators* in buying. Finally, they will, of course, be of different *age-groups*, and have *cultural* interests of many kinds.

These are just a few examples of how much impact psychology and the other behavioural sciences have on buying behaviour. By first understanding something about the origin and nature of these influences, some of which will be subtle, and then applying this knowledge in developing segmentation strategies, companies can position themselves advantageously in competitive environments. Strategic planning is based on two concepts: the market and strategic fit, i.e., the way in which a firm organizes its resources in order to secure an effective relationship with identified groups of customers, existing and potential. Segmentation offers marketers opportunities of establishing mutually satisfactory relationships.

14.2 NATURE AND PURPOSE OF MARKET SEGMENTATION

The term 'market segmentation' appears to have been first used in an article by Wendell R. Smith published in 1956:[2]

> Segmentation is based upon developments on the demand side of the market and represents a rational and more precise adjustment of product and marketing effort to consumer or user requirements. In the language of the economist, segmentation is disaggregative in its effects and tends to bring about recognition of several demand schedules where only one was recognised before.

Howard and Sheth noted that the concept of market segmentation seemed to rest on the idea that 'a company should segment or divide the market in such a way as to achieve sets of buyers'; these would lie in segments of the market and would be targets for the company's marketing plans.[3] Management has to face the problem of devising marketing mixes which are likely to be effective in these identified sub-markets. Research is needed to validate potential methods of subdividing total market demand.

Segmentation analysis assists marketing management by dividing total market demand into relatively homogeneous sectors that are identified by certain characteristics. Market strategy can then be devised which will be related to the needs of these markets segments. There may be changes in styling of products (a *de luxe* version for more demanding consumers), or in advertising appeals (emotive appeals related to prestige; 'economy' appeals for price-conscious buyers), or in methods of distribution (exclusive high-class stores; popular chain stores).

Segmentation encourages the development of specialist firms which can supply relatively small markets profitably. Big manufacturers with heavy investment in volume-production equipment are necessarily restricted in the type and variety of products they can offer. Their profitability depends on mass-market demand of sufficient size to warrant large-scale production and widespread distribution. To a considerable degree, the mass marketer has to cater for that mythical person, the average consumer. But people seek variety; they buy products for many reasons, which may include the satisfaction of owning something of unusual beauty or exclusivity. Through the medium of products, people frequently attempt to express their personalities; they may wish to present an idealized version of themselves to their friends. With mass-produced goods, personal satisfactions tend to be different; the influence of group affiliation may, in fact, be expressed in the ownership of the same type of washing machine, car, or even house.

The strategy of market segmentation recognizes that people differ in their tastes, needs, attitudes, motivations, life-styles, family size and composition, and so on. Market segmentation, as Sheth says, 'is considered to be the essence of marketing'.[4] It is a deliberate policy of maximizing market demand by directing marketing efforts at significant subgroups of customers or consumers. Before the days of mass production, small workshops and individual craft workers could cater for the needs of their customers, because there was intimate knowledge of those needs, and products could be supplied that had strong personal appeals. A strategy of market segmentation attempts to regain some of the benefits of this closer association with customers which was the strength of traditional business operations.

Mass markets may exist for some products, perhaps sugar or matches. But even in these product markets, specialist suppliers have established very profitable businesses. Milk is a generic product, but it also is differentiated, although the variety available is generally limited to the range carried on the delivery van or the supermarket shelves. Hence, even in generic markets there appears to be scope for supplying special versions of products. Soap, for example, is a highly segmented market ranging from industrial applications to luxury toilet soaps which have many of the characteristics of cosmetics. Even potatoes are a segmented market because of seasonal crops, and also by means of packaging. Substantial growth has taken place in the prepacked potato market in Britain. Further segmentation occurs when these ready-packed potatoes are graded for quality and size, and are sold under a brand name. Segmentation may be adopted, therefore, in practically all markets, although the bases of segmentation may differ, as will be discussed in Sec. 14.3.

14.3 FOUR DECISIVE FACTORS IN SEGMENTATION OF MARKETS

Four principal factors affect the feasibility of market segmentation: identification, measurability, accessibility, and appropriateness.

Identification of sub-markets is the responsibility of marketing research. This entails acquiring a thorough knowledge of the total market, evaluation of overall trends, and identification of sectors which appear to be of significant interest to a particular company and its resources, both present and planned. This stage should include both quantitative and qualitative data so that an understanding in depth is obtained of the market situation. It should be emphasized that this is not a once-off operation; markets are dynamic and demand continuous monitoring. There should be an appraisal of competitive marketing activities; these should be objectively compared with the company's products and proposed strategies. Market shares should be estimated, and brands should be evaluated for their product appeal. Media strategies would also require analysis and comparison; the copy platforms (i.e., basic advertising appeals) used by competitors would need identification.

The nature of demand in a specific product market should be examined. How far, for example, is it influenced by psychological variables? Do these tend to be more influential than economic factors like price (e.g., cosmetics)?

Measurability concerns the effective size of a sub-market as estimated by objective research. Hence, this information will largely depend on the availability of suitable data. Some types of data, e.g., psychological information, may not be readily available or may not be in a form suitable for use in a specific product market.

Accessibility refers to the ability with which a firm may be able to direct its marketing effort at particular sectors of a market. This requires careful analysis, planning, and control to ensure that marketing objectives are realized. Media should be examined for their cover of the specific sub-markets. The influence of behavioural factors would also need evaluation: reference should be made to group behaviour, opinion leadership, family life-styles, etc. Distribution facilities also require attention: what are the most effective methods of distributing products in specific market segments? What are the trends in distribution in those sub-markets? In overseas marketing, examination would need to include tariff barriers, quotas and other trading restrictions which may inhibit, if not prohibit, entry into a market.

Appropriateness relates to the needs of particular firms. Some companies will require far larger markets than others for satisfactory operation. Market opportunities should always be related to a company's resources and to its needs.

When Nestlé bought the Crosse and Blackwell Company it found that in most of the markets served by this subsidiary, Heinz was the dominant brand leader. They therefore produced new brands of soups that segmented markets where Heinz held 50 per cent or more of the share. Chef Box soups were marketed just at the time when shoppers were beginning to get price conscious, and market tests indicated that considerable infiltration could be made in this highly competitive market.

While acknowledging that Heinz have 'cornered the children's end' of the baked beans market, Crosse and Blackwell concentrated on the 'mature bean eater with Western, sold as a tastier barbecue-type bean'.[5] In pasta sales, they have successfully got through to children with Alphabetti Spaghetti, which is tempting these young eaters away from baked beans. Market segmentation has opened up new opportunities in a market which appeared to be practically impregnable.

Baxters of Speyside have built up an enviable niche with quality soups such as Royal Game and Cock-a-Leekie, Scotch Salmon Bisque, Cream of Smoked Trout, and Game Consommé.

The tea market in Britain is generally declining despite promotional campaigns to popularize tea drinking. However, Twinings are experiencing a rising demand for their specialist teas like Lapsang Souchong and Keemum, consumption of which is increasing by between 5 per cent and 10 per cent a year, mostly in the higher social groups. Their national advertising campaigns in the 'quality' journals have encouraged tea drinkers to become more venturesome in selecting their teas. So even in a depressed market, the general trend can be radically changed, provided that intelligent market analysis and planning have been undertaken. Saville Row tailors have no ambitions to serve mass markets; Cusson's Imperial Leather soap has a distinctive market appeal; and the Savoy Hotel is not just another catering establishment.

The motor industry in the UK is dominated by a few large organizations, of which Rover was, until its takeover by BMW in 1994, virtually the sole survivor of the British-owned manufacturers, the rest being members of multinational groups like Ford and General Motors, or the French car group Peugeot, or else are assembly plants for the large Japanese firms of Honda, Nissan, and Toyota. In 1995, the Japanese will be making up to 0.5 million cars in the UK. However, a few specialized car-makers have managed to retain their independence by folllowing highly selective production and marketing strategies. An outstanding example is the Morgan Motor Company of Malvern Link in Worcestershire. This family-owned, small but profitable firm, which prides itself on producing characteristically British-styled traditional sports cars, deliberately limits its weekly output to fewer than twenty cars. These are designed and made to high standards, and Morgan has carved out an enviable niche market of enthusiastic buyers, many of whom live overseas, particularly in Germany. Despite those who would advise it to grow larger, Morgan thrives at a time when many other companies experience practically every problem that can be imagined. Like the proverbial cobbler, Morgan sticks to its last, and its dedicated staff proudly produce high added-value cars, the demand for which is significantly influenced by such non-economic factors as aesthetics, nostalgia or personality (see Chapter 4).

An American marketing professor has suggested that 'astute U.S. marketing managers' would do well to look at European successes in segmentation of markets.[6] He considered that this success may be partly due to the fact that European home markets are smaller than the US market, so that 'European businessmen have been forced to develop skills' in differentiating their products in order to capture sales from different groups of people. One of the greatest strengths of European marketers, according to this commentator, lay in their highly developed talent for designing products of considerable aesthetic appeal, such as modern Scandinavian or Italian furniture, marimekko fabrics, Olivetti typewriters, or French *haute couture*.

This interesting viewpoint related to design appeal suggests that 'design sensitivity' might be a useful criterion for segmentation in some product markets (see Sec. 14.9). The growing influence of women in buying not only food and household goods but also an increasingly wide variety of other products was noted in Chapters 6 and 13. There are still plenty of opportunities in product and service markets for companies of all sizes. The small firm should not attempt to be a pale imitation of the larger organization which has substantial resources.

Since the early 1970s, according to Sampson, consumers and markets have changed substantially; the result is that many markets have 'de-massified'. 'A common scenario is not so much that of market segmentation but rather market fragmentation'.[7] Consumers can no longer be described in simple terms which will be valid for general application over a wide range of markets.

14.4 TYPES OF SEGMENTATION

Markets can be subdivided by several criteria. These will be affected by the type of product, the nature of demand, the method of distribution, the media available for market communication, and the motivation of buyers.

14.5 DEMOGRAPHIC ANALYSES

Basic methods of segmenting markets for consumer products have tended to rely heavily on demographic data—socio-economic grouping, age group, family size, and so on: the demographic analysis of market demand is seldom satisfactory (see Chapter 7).

Socio-economic groups' buying behaviour *is* significant in some product and service markets, such as the patronage of hotel restaurants, or the buying of antiques. However, socio-economic classification is readily understood and it has been widely used in media analyses for many years. In Chapter 7, detailed reference was made to the A–E socio-economic grading system popularized in Britain by readership surveys. The six main groups into which the British population are classified should also be related to the data given in Chapter 8 on group influences. Family life-cycle was seen to be a significant factor in the purchase of consumer durables: young couples are heavy spenders on household equipment.

Demographic segmentation tends to be a rather superficial method of grouping market opportunities. It may usefully serve as the first stage in market segmentation analysis, but to be content with socio-economic classification alone would be inadvisable. It was earlier pointed out that consumption habits are in many cases little influenced by socio-economic group membership. Social mobility is another factor which upsets simple demographic analyses. Workers classified in lower social groups may also, in fact, have greater free spending money than those higher up the social scale. The upgrading urge may lead to consumption habits above that of the general pattern of behaviour in a particular social group. Furthermore, consumers may not buy consistently 'all along the line'. Personal tastes and interests will influence buying behaviour; some women will be prepared to spend proportionately more on food for their families than others in their social group because of their concern for nutrition. Others may be willing to pay fees for private education for their children, because of social ambitions or family traditions. To enable this to be done, some parents may buy a smaller car or even do without one. The impact of dual incomes was also seen to be of considerable influence in buying behaviour. It often allows family patterns of living to rise substantially above that of the 'head of household' as characterized in the JICNARS definitions given in Chapter 7; however, the 'head of household' classification was replaced in the National Readership Survey by that of 'chief income earner'.

Other deficiencies of the popular socio-economic classification have resulted in more complex methods of consumer identification which will be discussed in Secs 14.10 and 14.11.

Geographic segmentation may be useful with some products. Markets could be analysed nationally, regionally, or locally. Communities could be studied for differences in buying behaviour attributable to locale, e.g., large cities and conurbations such as London, Birmingham, Manchester, or Glasgow; industrial towns such as Stoke-on-Trent, Wolverhampton, or Coventry; country market towns such as Ludlow. Food habits tend to have regional variations; soap preferences may be affected by the hardness of water in a district; colour preferences in textiles indicate certain regional tastes. Geographic segmentation could be extended, of course, to overseas marketing operations. Some large organizations 'zone' their trading areas. Socio-economic groupings could be considered within specific geographical areas, and analyses directed to identifying significant patterns of buying behaviour related to certain types of products. Also of particular interest to marketers of some products would be the age distribution within geographical areas of a market. Some seaside resorts tend to attract a relatively high proportion of retired people of middle-class status. Variations in the birth rate over regions may be of particular interest, for example, to makers of baby foods and other requisites for infants.

In *overseas marketing*, some basic geographic segmentation is often practised. Potential market opportunities could be based on gross national product *per capita*, and if this criterion is adopted, three main segments of world markets can be identified as follows: industrialized countries (ICs); developing countries (DCs); and less developed countries (LDCs). It has been noted that the second segment accounts for 19 per cent of the population and 32 per cent of the income of the world,[8] and since these countries are outpacing the IC segment, they offer very attractive business prospects.

Douglas and Craig warn against taking a country as a unit of analysis and assuming homogeneity of consumption tastes:

> Countries are often highly heterogeneous with regard to a variety of factors such as language diversity, socio-economic and technological development, social cohesion and wealth, and other factors affecting behaviour patterns. Consequently, it is often desirable to pay attention to sub-groupings within countries, such as cities, regions or communities; or cultural sub-groups, such as teenagers, or blue collar workers, when determining the appropriate unit(s) of analysis.[9]

The diversity of cultural and social behaviour in Europe has already been discussed at some length in Chapter 6, but it is timely to recall that within western Europe there are 17 states with 12 major languages and numerous sub-cultures. Parts of it are highly industrialized with large urban populations; others are still developing their economies and essential infrastructures, improving port facilities, road networks, and telecommunications systems. Considerable differences in cultural and economic behaviour exist, both between countries themselves, such as Portugal and Norway, and also within countries, like the north and south of Italy.

Unilever, the mammoth Anglo-Dutch organization marketing an extensive range of consumer products, were faced with the formidable task of reorganizing their European detergents business, which operates in 17 countries; Lever Europe was set up, on the board of which the 4 largest of the 17 national companies have seats. This new coordinating company has harmonized the sizes and design motifs on detergent packs, resulting in purchasing economies and also opportunities for unified pan-European promotional campaigns. Of particular concern was the need to speed up the development of new products which, largely because of the virtual autonomy which national companies once enjoyed, had taken up to 4 years to diffuse across Europe (see problems of innovation in Chapter 11). Under the new arrangements, almost the entire Lever Brothers' range will be common to the rest of Europe by the mid-1990s. Later activities are likely to include joint development of new products with the US company, leading to virtually simultaneous launches on both sides of the Atlantic. Established business practices impose certain constraints on this extensive rationalization scheme: 'While Procter and Gamble's leading laundry detergent is sold as Ariel almost everywhere in Europe, Unilever's sell variously as All, Omo, Persil, Presto, Skip and Via'.[10] Unilever does not propose to harmonize these, because they have 80 or 90 years' investment in these brands.

Education is a powerful influence on consumers' behaviour; the level of literacy in specific areas and regions may provide marketers with opportunities to sell sophisticated products and services. As noted in Chapter 7, social mobility characterizes contemporary society in Britain; this has been accelerated by educational facilities being more freely available, although there is still a social imbalance in further education students. Higher education gives entry to the professions; social aspirations and consumption levels are raised. In Japan, the significant educational reforms after the Second World War have resulted, according to a professor[11] at Tokyo University, in fundamental changes to the social class structure: 'One sociologist has labelled post-war Japan a "new middle mass" society; the vast majority of Japanese people today consider themselves to be members of the middle class'. It is important to realize that Japan has a 'very equality-oriented education system that provides virtually everyone with a common, homogeneous education through to the age of eighteen'.

The degree of westernization may also be a contributory factor in the consumption of products with distinctive cultural connotations such as Scotch whisky or some kinds of fashions.

Geographic segmentation is inevitably linked closely with *cultural* and *sub-cultural* factors (see Chapter 6). In the UK, immigrant populations tend to be clustered around the big cities; these sub-cultural groups may assimilate the consumption habits of the community at large and yet retain some of their characteristic buying preferences in certain foods or styles of clothing. Some cross-fertilization of tastes may occur, and new kinds of foods, dress, music, etc., become shared to some degree.

Geographical segmentation in exporting strategies should be related to economic development; it should also be evaluated against the closely linked factor of political stability. The overall politico-economic situation in a particular country should be rated for *risk*—yet another aspect of market segmentation. Risks in overseas markets could be assessed against several criteria,[9] such as the number of expropriations, rates of inflation, foreign exchange trends, etc. (As a factor in organizational buying behaviour, risk has been discussed in Chapter 10, and in innovation strategies in Chapter 11.) A portfolio approach to product and market development is advisable. Companies rarely make and market just one product to one market; complexity tends to be more characteristic of both product ranges and markets served. Hence, firms have to decide on a portfolio of products and markets that will be likely to generate an acceptable level of profit consistent with the risks inherent in specific trading ventures.

In 1991, the Swedish multinational, Electrolux—the world's largest white goods manufacturers—relaunched its ranges across Europe. These are targeted as 'upper mass market' branded products, which will be supported by 'common European-wide advertising and promotion',[12] with the Single Market clearly in focus. Electrolux believe that there is a gap in the market, below that occupied by the luxury labels of AEG or Miele, which will respond favourably to high-quality products incorporating many new features not to be found on the usual middle-market products. In line with this creative approach, Electrolux developed a 'two-plus-two' strategy involving two local or regional brands in each major market, like Tricity and Bendix in the UK alongside Electrolux and Zanussi models, which are regarded as pan-European. The range of new products available in specific countries will vary according to market conditions, and the current performance of the group's products. Skilful coordination of marketing efforts at both central and regional levels will be necessary so that this sophisticated product portfolio achieves its ambitions.

Colgate-Palmolive is another powerful multinational group, with sales spread across Europe and accounting for about one-third of its global turnover. In common with other leading companies, Colgate realized that there are significant differences in consumers across and within countries. Toothpaste, for instance, is regarded more as a cosmetic in Greece and Spain but as a family health product in the Netherlands and the UK. Different advertising appeals are designed to attract these distinct types of consumers. In northern Europe, Ajax cleaner was mostly used straight from the bottle to clean small areas; consumers attached importance to its ease of application and the shiny results it gave. But in southern Europe, Ajax was diluted by users to clean much bigger surfaces, often tiles or wood instead of plastic; this application left a cloudy film that had to be rinsed away. The product was reformulated to avoid the rinsing process. As with their toothpaste products, Colgate's advertising featured the distinctive attributes which make Ajax acceptable in both regions of Europe.[13]

Brand rationalization has also occurred in other consumer product markets: Mars renamed Marathon, one of their leading lines, Snickers, while Treets are now marketed as M&Ms.

Personality variables may be influential in some product markets. In Chapter 4 some of the principal theories of personality were examined in relation to certain types of products. It was observed that although personality variables appeared to influence buying behaviour, there was no reason to believe that there existed a generalized pattern of influence: individual products should be carefully analysed for the potential or actual personality factors influencing their sales. Chapter 11 on innovation indicated that the diffusion of new products appeared to be significantly affected by personality variables; some people and firms appear to be more ready than others to try new products and services, while others are content to wait and see.

For many years, Guinness stout has been promoted widely; its advertisements have ingeniously used many different appeals, ranging from humour to abstract themes like the 'Pure Genius' commercials, which resulted from psychological research into the mental images evoked by the dark brew. The 'man with the Guinness' concept projected the stylishness and individualism of the younger generation of beer drinkers. This brand repositioning is also being developed in international markets; the success of this strategy depends on how, and to what degree, *perceptions* of the product can be changed (see Chapter 2). To take a product up-market and make it appeal to younger consumers is a challenging task and demands thorough understanding of the psychological and socio-cultural implications as well as the physical needs of the targeted market segment.

Usage rate may be a useful segmentation base. Volume and frequency of purchase may provide valuable data for marketing strategies. A systematic approach would involve broadly dividing a specific product market into users and non-users. Non-users could be further analysed into potential users and non-potential users (but even these may buy a certain product as a gift). Actual users could then be grouped according to the degree of usage—light, medium, or heavy. Heavy users of some products are a relatively small proportion of all users, but they contribute significantly to the overall sales success. Target Group Index (TGI) revealed in the 1970s, for example, that while nearly all housewives surveyed bought baked beans, about one-third were heavy users. Most housewives bought floor and furniture polish, and heavy users again accounted for nearly one-third of total household purchases. Usage rate and motivational influences should be researched so that a fuller understanding of buying behaviour is obtained. In this way, it may be possible to convert light and medium users to heavier usage of a particular product. Toilet tissue purchasers may be affected by attitudes towards hygiene and laundry problems; these or other reasons for purchase deserve analysis.

Two US researchers have directed special attention to the significance of large users.[14] 'Most consumer studies tabulate light, medium and heavy users on the basis of frequency of purchase. It may be incorrect, however, to infer that heavy buyers are those who buy frequently. The other criteria—size purchased and number of packages purchased at a time—can also be deceptive when used alone'. To arrive at meaningful criteria for segmentation, the total volume purchased, e.g., monthly, should be calculated by multiplying the frequency of purchase by the size of package bought, and also by the number of packages usually bought at a time. The following points for investigation were considered by these researchers to be particularly important:

1. Are consumers able to purchase a particular product in large volume?
2. What is the competitive activity related to heavy usage and large packs?
3. Is the distributive strategy right to attract heavy buyers?
4. How do these heavy users buy, e.g., what discounts do they expect?
5. What are the media habits of large users, and how do these relate to the specific promotional campaign of a brand it is planned to extend into volume markets?

Low prices and special incentives to purchase are 'obvious considerations in winning and holding the large-volume buyer'.[14]

Brand loyalty has attracted attention as a possibly useful criterion for market segmentation. An analysis of a frequently purchased product in the USA identified a number of market segments:[15]

1. Current users who are satisfied and are likely to continue usage of the brand.
2. Current and regular customers who may reduce consumption or switch brands (three sub-groups reflected different reasons for and strength of dissatisfaction).
3. Occasional buyers of the brand who may increase usage provided some change is effected, such as price or more available distribution.
4. Occasional users of brand who are likely to reduce buying because of more attractive competing brands.
5. Non-users who might buy the brand provided certain features were added.
6. Non-users with strong negative attitudes to brand and little likelihood of attitude change.

Each of these segments was measured by size, product usage, and demographic and attitudinal characteristics to provide valuable clues for design and other changes to the product and its marketing strategy.

To obtain information about the level of usage and frequency of buying, it is advisable to use trend data from panel research, which will also indicate the degree of brand loyalty among specific products. (Details of this type of continuous market research are given in a specialist text.)[16]

In the late 1960s, US researchers studied one category of food product and the pattern of brand loyalty that affected sales. They reported that their findings did not support the usefulness of brand loyalty as a guide for segmentation of markets:

> Brand-loyal customers almost completely lack identifiability in terms of either socio-economic or personality characteristics. With the exception of one study by Kuehn, brand-loyal customers do not appear to have different average demand levels than non-loyal ones. Loyal customers do not appear to have economically important differences in their sensitivity to either the short-run effects of pricing, dealing, and retail advertising, or to the introduction of new brands.[17]

However, since this particular research was limited to one type of food product, it was admitted that further research would be needed over a wide range of product categories.

A pioneer study on brand loyalty was undertaken some years ago with consumer purchase panel data obtained from the *Chicago Tribune*.[18] This research—which covered toilet soap, scouring cleanser, 'regular' coffee, tinned peas, margarine, frozen orange (concentrate), and headache tablets—showed 'quite conclusively that a significant amount of brand loyalty does exist *within individual product groups*'. It was also found that families who are highly brand loyal do not necessarily buy large quantities of the products studied. The study 'did not attempt to uncover the reasons underlying the different behaviour patterns'.

Charlton in reviewing shop loyalty noted the research study just mentioned. 'It seems to be a fairly well accepted finding that brand loyalty does not generalise over product fields, i.e. a housewife brand loyal in one product-field is not necessarily brand loyal in another'.[19] The literature available on shop loyalty, although limited, enabled Charlton to make some general conclusions:

1. Shop loyalty is similar in nature and degree to brand loyalty, but no single measure is adequate.
2. As with brand loyalty, shop loyalty is restricted to product groups.
3. Shop loyalty does not appear to have strong relationships with socio-economic groupings, psychological traits, or level of expenditure.
4. Positive relationships occur between shop loyalty and brand loyalty related to private label brands.
5. Convenience of shopping is a major factor, but there is an overall decrease in the degree of shop loyalty.

Kuehn has studied brand choice behaviour from the viewpoint of a probabilistic process of learning.[20] He was concerned to find out about the relationship between a consumer's repeat purchases of a particular brand and the likelihood of brand loyalty being established. The effect of purchasing frequency was a factor also researched. Kuehn undertook extensive and elaborate research on data from the *Chicago Tribune* Consumer Panel. He developed a model describing brand-shifting behaviour. Considerable work remained to be done, commented Kuehn, on the influence of merchandising factors such as price, promotional campaigns, etc., on the brand model he had projected.

Research into brand loyalty was also undertaken by another US researcher, W. J. Tucker, who conducted an 'exploratory experiment' involving consumer choices of brand from among 'four previously unknown brands'.[21] Forty-two women took part in this experiment which consisted of studying 12 successive choices of branded food. Exactly half of the respondents reached the criteria of brand loyalty by the end of the 12 trials. 'The probability of selecting a brand the third time given two consecutive selections throughout the experiment was 0.396, significantly above chance at the 0.05 level'. Of those women who had not selected any brand on three consecutive trials, there were suggestions that some of them had acquired some relative degree of loyalty to two of the brands. In general, Tucker reached the 'almost inescapable conclusion' that women shoppers display considerable variance in their susceptibility to brand loyalty. Even when there is no discernible difference between brands, some consumers seem to exhibit brand loyalty; this brand loyalty should not, however, be regarded as trivial. At times, it would appear that shoppers frequently select brands on a trial basis, largely to explore possible alternatives, so repeat purchases are problematical.

Fitzroy has also discussed models of brand choice involving brand-switching matrices covering two or more competitive brands of products.[22]

A remarkable brand rejuvenation programme was organized in the late 1980s by Smith and Nephew, the British multinational, which together with Beiersdorf, a Hamburg-based company, market the Nivea brand of toiletries, first launched in Germany in 1906. Nivea Creme, the most widely known of this range, is seen as the core product with ancillary products such as lotions, soaps, sun preparations and talc forming a satellite product strategy; all of these have a common theme—a caring approach. The relaunch, with a television advertising campaign featuring rock music, focused on the message: 'Nivea knows how to treat a lady'. The outcome was very rewarding: sales of skin care products doubled in the UK over the following five years, through attracting new, younger consumers as well as retaining older users.

The *significance of dissonance* to brand loyalty deserves repetition; the implications of this psychological phenomenon on repeat purchases was discussed in Chapter 2. The influence of reference group behaviour on individual brand loyalty should also be borne in mind. Group cohesiveness, for example, may influence brand behaviour. Family members may have distinct preferences for certain brands of products; the discussion related to family buying behaviour should be associated with the problem of identifying factors affecting brand loyalty.

Various attempts have been made to isolate the influence of brand loyalty in consumer buying behaviour. There appears to be little relationship between brand loyalty and economic or demographic variables. The research studies on a relatively small number of grocery products are not entirely conclusive.

Clearly, brand loyalty is a matter of very considerable importance to marketers. To build strong brand loyalty is the ambition of marketing management. Unfortunately, there is still a great deal of work to be done before general guidelines could be of practical value.

In Chapter 13, the role of repetitive advertising was seen largely to be defensive and designed to keep particular brand names continuously in the customer's mind. Reinforcement of favourable attitudes and perceptions is fostered by reminder advertising.

14.6 PSYCHOGRAPHIC SEGMENTATION

Motives and *attitudes* influence buying behaviour. In Chapter 3, detailed examination was made of the structure of needs and motives related to the purchase habits of people of various socio-economic groups and interests. Successful marketing is closely linked with an appreciation of motivational influences in specific product markets. Rarely does one motive alone influence human behaviour; motivations interact and modify the effects of single motives, for example, consumers may be motivated by economy to choose the lowest-priced brand of a product, but, at the same time, they will also be motivated by safety, security, or risk factors. So they tend to select well-known brands, even though lower-priced alternatives may be available. The complexity of motivational influences was fully discussed earlier and it would be useful to recall some of the general findings of motivational theories when considering buying motives as bases for market segmentation. Generalizations over products are not advisable; research should be centred on motivational influences connected with specific types of products and services.

Yankelovich researched the watch market in the USA in the early 1960s and found the following:[23]

1. 'Approximately 23% of the buyers bought for lowest price'.
2. 'Another 46% bought for durability and general product quality'.
3. '31% bought watches as symbols of some important occasion'.

The manufacturers of Timex watches marketed a low-price watch which appealed to the first and second market segments. Timex noted that their competitors in the third segment tended to concentrate their advertising in November and December. 'But since buying by the other two segments went on all the time, Timex advertised all year round, getting exclusive attention ten months of the year'.

Stone analysed the motives and attitudes of a group of women shoppers in Chicago in the early 1950s.[24] Respondents were asked about the reasons why they shopped at particular kinds of stores, e.g., local shops or large chain stores. From his research, Stone was able to identify four types of shopper:

1. *Economic shopper* (33 per cent of total): extremely price-sensitive; aware of quality and variety of merchandise available; concerned with efficiency of sales staff
2. *Personalizing shopper* (28 per cent): tended to establish strong personal relationships with stores personnel; shopping provided substantial emotional satisfaction
3. *Ethical shopper* (18 per cent): felt strongly about the plight of the small shopkeeper; was willing to pay slightly higher prices or to put up with less variety to support the little man struggling against the retail giants
4. *Apathetic shopper* (17 per cent): shopping was a necessary but irksome task; convenience of location and ease of shopping were of paramount importance

Economic and personalizing orientations were more often adopted by women shoppers who had recently moved into an area, and ethical and apathetic orientations characterized those who had lived in an area for a relatively long period of time.

Leo Burnett, the Chicago advertising agency, engaged the help of IRI, a leading market research company specializing in data derived from electronic scanners at supermarket check-out desks, to find out more about shoppers' buying habits and the influences of different kinds of advertising and promotion.[25] The resultant findings directly challenged the simplistic notion that consumers fall into one of two groups: buyers or non-buyers. Instead, four different behavioural groups, each having its distinctive buying behaviour, can be identified:

1. *Long loyals*: committed to one brand irrespective of price or competition.
2. *Rotators*: regularly switch among a few favoured brands; price is not important but variety is.
3. *Deal sensitives*: mostly buy the brand on special offer from their favoured few.
4. *Price sensitives*: buy the cheapest product irrespective of brand.

These types of consumers varied across product categories and, to further complicate the picture, consumers generally lacked consistency in their motivations to buy different kinds of products, such as breakfast cereals, pet foods, and toilet tissues.

Leo Burnett stressed the importance to companies of recognizing that building up sales of their established branded products will depend on knowing more about their specific appeals to the types of consumers identified by their research. The first and second categories—long loyals and rotators—are, apparently, not price-conscious, so while price cuts may win the favour of the other two categories, the end result could be counter-productive and lead to an overall loss of market share. Extended research is advisable in order to evaluate these consumer categories in relation to demographic profiles, life-cycle stages, and so on.

In Britain, the original Attwood's Consumer Panel characterized housewives under five main psychological groupings:

1. Conscientiousness, related to housework.
2. Economy consciousness.
3. Conservatism in brand (a housewife who tends to buy better-known brands rather than experiment with a new brand or product).
4. Traditionalism in housework, related to the use of convenience or labour-saving products.
5. Willingness to experiment in shopping.

Panel members were classified on a scale basis from one to five on each of these psychological characteristics, e.g., one = extreme conservatism, five = no conservatism in choice of brands or products.

This psychological classification enables a study to be made of the effect of attitudes on consumers' buying behaviour. The technique is still being developed. The old demographic analysis by age, social class, size of family, etc., lacks the refinement of this more sophisticated approach, which can, of course, be cross-classified so that the traditional breakdowns of socio-economic/age groups are given more significance by attitudinal measurement.[16]

Attwood's research findings concerning traditional wax polish and the newer aerosol spray polishes were analysed by the normal socio-economic groupings and then classified also by the 'attitude to housework' scale. Aerosol spray polishes are associated with modern-minded orientation towards housework, and there is significantly higher usage in the upper social groups.

Ruth Zith's reported research in 1971 involved a cross-section of US housewives on the basis of which six groups were selected as being 'most meaningful' classifications:[26]

1. *Outgoing optimists* (32 per cent of total): these women are 'outgoing, innovative, community-oriented, positive toward grooming, not bothered by delicate health or digestive problems or especially concerned about germs or cleanliness'.
2. *Conscientious vigilants* (28 per cent): 'are conscientious, rigid, meticulous, germ-fighting with a high cleanliness orientation and sensible attitudes about food. They have high cooking pride, a careful shopping orientation, tend not to be convenience-oriented'.
3. *Apathetic indifferents* (14 per cent): 'are not outgoing, are involved with family, irritable, have a negative grooming orientation, are lazy, especially in terms of cooking pride'.
4. *Self-indulgents* (13 per cent): 'are relaxed, permissive, unconcerned with health problems, interested in convenience items but with relatively high cooking pride, self-indulgent towards themselves and their families'.
5. *Contented cows* (8 per cent): 'are relaxed, not worried, relatively unconcerned about germs and cleanliness, not innovative or outgoing, strongly economy oriented, not self-indulgent'.
6. *Worriers* (5 per cent): 'are irritable, concerned about health, germs and cleanliness, negative about grooming and breakfast, but self-indulgent with low economy and high convenience orientation'.

Zith's analysis also covered specific product categories, such as drugs, 'personal items', foods, and household. Those who bought chemists' products were classified as: 'realistics', who wanted something that worked and did not entail a visit to the doctor; 'authority seekers', who preferred to have a doctor-prescribed remedy; 'sceptics', who viewed all medicines as highly doubtful; 'hypochondriacs', who believed they were likely to catch any infection going around, and tended to seek immediate reassurance by taking some kind of medicine, although it need not be particularly effective.

Stone's research findings and Zith's analyses may usefully be compared with Attwood's five main groupings of housewives. It would also be advantageous to refer to Chapter 4 on personality traits, attitudes, and motivation, so that an overall appreciation may be obtained of what has been termed psychographic segmentation.

Lunn has given the following data on the market for fish fingers in Britain in 1972.[27] The heaviest buyers were mostly housewives who were very conservative in food habits, very concerned about nutrition, and tended to be 'down-market'. However, another large group of buyers was similar in many ways to the first mentioned, but these housewives were much more willing to experiment and much less concerned about food value: 'tastiness was all important'. To appeal to the second group of housewives, a product Crispy Cod Fries was launched.

Lunn also mentioned the research study of the confectionery market which revealed eight important characteristics of buyers: sweet-toothedness; weight consciousness; conservatism; extravagance and compulsive eating; compulsive eating; activity; self-organization; and self-consciousness.

A survey of radio and television audiences in the USA, based on a random sample of 754 respondents in a large city in the south-west, examined psychographic differences between users and non-users.[28] From factor analysis of the responses to 29 questions related to activities, interests, and opinions, it was established that users differed from non-users along the following psychographic dimensions: old-fashioned factor (e.g., 'I have some old-fashioned tastes and habits'); outgoing/individualist factor (e.g., 'I'd rather try to fix something myself before taking it to an expert'); service-quality-conscious factor (e.g., 'Banking is so important to me that I would go out of my way to find a bank with good personal service'); fashion-conscious factor (e.g., 'If my clothes aren't in fashion, it really bothers me'); and other-directed factor (e.g., 'I usually ask for help from other people in deciding what to do'). Differences were also observable within time periods of viewing and listening: e.g., the late fringe TV audience was less old-fashioned, more outgoing and individualistic, more concerned with service-quality considerations, and more fashion conscious than non-late-night viewers.

Although the researchers conceded that the profiles presented were insufficient as complete guides in the complex tasks of developing and coordinating creative and media advertising strategies, the psychographic dimensions identified would be useful in further exploratory research into these specific segments.

Factor analysis was also used in research on people's savings habits in the UK,[29] when the following four factors were found to represent generally the answers recorded: temperamental difficulty in saving (e.g., 'I have never been able to save'); sense of solidity (e.g., 'If you've got a bit of money saved you are not so likely to be pushed around'); concern with independence (e.g., 'I hate to feel I might have to ask someone for financial help'); and feeling of financial security (e.g., 'I feel it unlikely I shall have any financial emergencies in the near future').

A further example of segmentation based on a psychographic measurement was carried out by England, Grosse, and Associates for Esso Petroleum.[30] The following 'stable typology' emerged from three surveys based on a quota sample of 2000 motorists: 'the uninvolved', 'the enthusiast', 'the professional', 'the tinkerer', and 'the collector'. Each of these categories was described at some length; for example, 'the professionals' use their cars mainly for business, do high mileage, but virtually no servicing. They are likely to be male and white collar; their cars are relatively new, often company owned. Their cars must be kept on the road; they leave servicing to the garage, and tend to buy petrol companies' branded oils. This motorist typology was helpful in market planning.

A psychographic segmental approach to standardizing international advertising formed the basis of research by Alfred S. Boote of the Psychographics Research Corporation of Bedford, New York. He observed in 1982 'that during the past 15 years a growing number of international marketers have been confronted with the dilemma of whether to standardize across countries or tailor their marketing activities to specific countries'.[31] From surveys of international marketing and advertising managers over several industries, it seemed that standardization was not practised by the majority, often because of cultural and environmental factors. However, many marketers take a more favourable view and 'feel that the degree of standardization is dependent on the kind of product involved, the stage in its life-cycle, and the stages of economic development and concomitant social conditions of the respective countries'. Boote states that quantitative data collected on international markets has mostly been confined to environmental (including economic) and demographic factors, but there has been 'little or no published research concerning cross-cultural psychographic characteristics'.

Based on comparative values in three European countries—UK, Germany, and France—research was conducted in 1978 to obtain guidelines for an advertising campaign in these countries. The research design involved three stages: first, omnibus surveys were used to identify large samples of women owning several kinds of household appliances; second, 500 women were randomly sampled from those qualified as owners; and third, these were interviewed in their homes and asked to respond to 29 five-point scales, dealing with concepts such as 'Having a familiar routine'; 'Being able to plan all activities in advance'; 'Having something to keep me busy'. Some of these statements evoked significantly different responses between the countries. In three cases—'Having a familiar routine'; 'To be with people who have up-to-date ideas'; 'Having beautiful things in your home'—German women rated these value orientations as significantly more important to themselves than did the French or British respondents. French women said that 'Having beautiful things in your home' was important to them, and more so than was found with British women. Statements were subjected to ranking, and several striking differences between the three countries were observed; for example, 'Having something to keep me busy' was ranked in sixth place by the French and British, but attained only twenty-first ranking among the Germans.

Boote concluded that the values segmentation approach is useful in defining product expectations. 'For example, an appliance which is designed strictly for convenience and reliability in getting a household task done quickly (if not perfectly) but requiring no particular skill, is most appropriately positioned for consumers whose orientation is primarily away from home'.[31] Regarding the feasibility of a common advertising campaign, Boote conceded that there is, on balance, 'tenuous evidence' to support this strategy, but he warned that the findings of this research should not be generalized.

14.7 LIFE-STYLE SEGMENTATION

The concept of life-style relates to the distinctive or characteristic ways of living adopted by people and communities, and is expressed in the activities, interests, beliefs, opinions and demographics of individuals who consume a variety of products and brands; the major approach to life-style research is identified as AIO (Attitudes, Interests, Opinions) and, with related methods, became known as psychographics (see Chapter 6). Life-style research has resulted in useful segmentation variables, and specific examples have referred to the 'affluent middle-aged'.[32,33,34] Harold Lind drily observed that the reason why media reserch covers so inadequately the important middle-aged market is probably because 'the research is usually done by and for people under the age of 25 who have an implicit certainty that everyone above 35 is essentially, if not clinically, dead'.[34] In some media areas, there is a distinct bias towards the higher age groups as well as higher class levels.

In a state-of-the-art review of the literature about the elderly segment of the US market, Phillips and Sternthal have suggested that ageing should be 'viewed more adequately as a multidimensional process influenced by biological, psychological, and social forces, and one that is only partially related to chronological age. In sum, despite the fact that the elderly constitute a substantial segment of the population, it is not currently possible to identify a homogeneous elderly group of consumers'.[35]

Nearly 70 per cent of UK families with members in the 45–64 age group have no dependent children; often they have paid off their mortgages or the impact is greatly reduced; they may have recently inherited wealth; they have a period of relative affluence ahead and high disposable income. In leisure and consumer durable markets, these consumers, who can now indulge in sophisticated patterns of consumption, are a very profitable market segment. Trends in family patterns of consumption covering household durables, holidays, financial affairs, etc., indicate that many have adopted new life styles as they progress in their careers and family life-cycles (see Sec. 6.7).

Another significant example of life-style segmentation refers to the women's market (see discussion on the changing role of women in society in Chapter 6, and on advertising and women in Chapter 13). Bartos, writing in the *Harvard Business Review* in 1978, identified from self-concept research four 'distinctly different' segments of the women's market in the USA: '*career women*', with the strongest positive self-images, self-assured and very amicable; '*just a job working woman*', who are quite different from working women who perceive themselves as career-oriented; '*plan to work housewife*' has many of the perceptions of the career woman, and is far different from her stay-at-home neighbours; '*stay-at-home housewife*' sees herself as kind, refined, and reserved, much below the norm in feeling brave, stubborn, dominating, or egocentric.[36]

These groups have different shopping habits, brand preferences, and media habits. Also, they have different motivations and life-styles; the career woman is most likely to plan ahead, to be cautious, and brand loyal, while the stay-at-home housewife is the only one who is not an impulsive buyer. In the travel market, the career woman is from 50 per cent to 70 per cent above the general population norm, yet, Bartos notes, there is little evidence that her custom is specially cultivated by travel marketers. She is also far more likely to have shared in the family purchase decisions for a new car. Unmarried career women 'tower above the other groups' in making car purchases themselves.

Bartos pleads for more realistic assumptions about women's influence in buying a widening range of products and services. 'As traditional targets are re-defined, we also need to understand the context within which women use products and services. Do the traditional motivations of pleasing their husbands and competing with the neighbours still apply?'

Life-style research is supported by some leading research organisations, such as the Stanford Research Institute which developed VALS (values and lifestyles: see Chapter 6). The typologies that emerge from these analyses tend to be inventive generalizations, even stereotypes, which need to be interpreted with care. VALS admit that lifestyles may well change over time, but they are, nevertheless, useful in identifying trends in consumption. The rather fanciful descriptions applied to some life-style classifications should not, perhaps, be taken too literally.

14.8 BENEFIT SEGMENTATION

It is the essence of marketing that products and services should be designed to confer *benefits* on those who buy or use them. Approaching segmentation from an examination of the benefits that certain kinds of people (and organizations) seek, or, from a different but closely related angle, the *problems* for which solutions are sought, would seem to be logical. People have differing needs and expectations, influenced, perhaps, by their social class or cultural inclinations. Food, for example, fulfils several needs (as noted in Chapters 3 and 6).

Benefit segmentation is considered by some experienced Canadian researchers to be 'usually the most meaningful type to use from a marketing standpoint as it directly facilitates product planning, positioning, and advertising communications'.[37] In their view, although life-style, psychographic, or general attitudinal approaches 'work well statistically, they are *not* always helpful in marketing'.

A useful application of segmentation based on benefits concerned the Canadian Government Office of the US travel market to obtain a comprehensive picture of Americans who are potential holiday visitors to Canada. Following a pilot study, the major study was based on 1750 interviews from a national probability sample. Six segments of potential visitors were derived through multiple analysis techniques:[37]

1. Friends and relatives—non-active visitor (29 per cent).
2. Friends and relatives—active city visitor (12 per cent).
3. Family sightseers (6 per cent).
4. Outdoor vacationer (19 per cent).
5. Resort vacationer (19 per cent).
6. Foreign vacationer (26 per cent).

(The above segment readings were extended in qualitative terms.)

Segments 1 and 2 were considered to offer limited business potential; the other segments had holiday needs that could be met in various parts of Canada, and from the questionnaire data a profile was developed for each segment 'in terms of behaviour, psychographics, travel incentives, and image of a Canadian vacation'.

It was reported that, unlike a commercial firm, the Canadian tourist authority had 'special problems' in implementing the findings of the survey, and had to organize an extensive programme of meetings, seminars and publications so that the 'many elements of the travel industry' should know of this valuable information. As a result, improvements were made in advertising and media selection, which were designed to appeal to the personality traits and life-styles of target groups. Also, special promotional schemes and provincial tourist offices were organized to offer holidays related to the benefits sought by one or more target groups.

A benefit segmentation of the toothpaste market showed these principal benefits as related to people's value systems: product appearance, flavour; brightness of teeth; decay prevention; and price.[30] These desirable benefits were analysed with reference to demographic profiles, special behavioural characteristics (e.g., smokers), life-style, and brand preference. From this analysis, four distinctive market segments were identified: 'sensory', 'sociables', 'worrier', and 'independent'. For instance, the 'sociables' segment preferred a brand like Macleans Plus White which gave them brightness of teeth; these consumers were young, active, and smokers.

Nestlé have cleverly designed a range of beverages to appeal, for example, to those with specific tastes in coffee, and anticipated a demand for a fuller flavoured drink by introducing the first freeze-dried coffee, Gold Blend, in 1965. This premium-priced product was extensively promoted on television, projecting a hedonistic life-style. A notable benefit-based market segmentation has been developed with decaffeinated Nescafé; another profitable market niche is served by Nestlé with Alta Rica, made from arabica beans and promoted by advertisements in cinemas as well as television, featuring exotic journeys through Latin America. To ensure that these expensive products retain their appeals, Nestleé invests heavily in improving flavours, which are regularly subject to 'blind' tastings, as well as rigorously evaluating the effects of their advertising campaigns.

Fitzroy states that a potential problem is that of quantifying consumer preferences for different product attributes: 'an analysis of attitudinal responses typically ignored trade-off considerations, how changes in the level of one benefit affect another'.[22]

14.9 SEGMENTATION BY PRODUCT DESIGN

The sensitivity of individuals (and organizations) to aesthetic values and ergonomic benefits may offer a very useful segmentation approach. It has been successfully exploited by firms such as Heals, Wedgwood, Cartiers, Rolls-Royce, and Sandersons for several generations. Mary Quant, Terence Conran, and Laura Ashley also combined design skills with shrewd marketing strategies. Products can be 'positioned' by quality of design, and even in highly competitive markets new segments can be created. This was shown by ICI Paints Division, which in 1982 launched a range of 'natural white' emulsion paints: rose white, lily white, and apple white. The brilliant white sector of the market was moving to a commodity situation, where price cutting was becoming markedly apparent. 'I.C.I. had about 65% of this total market and were clearly exposed to competition with a virtually indifferentiated product. I.C.I.'s marketing team consulted all the previous market research, about both consumer attitudes to the use of colour and white paints', and discovered that 'many people lacked confidence in the use of stronger colours, but that they felt that brilliant white was too clinical and that it lacked individuality'.[38] From these findings, the whole Natural Whites concept was developed and proved to be a marked success: 'at long last, a significant way of further segmenting the market had been found'. Natural Whites attracted competition, of course, but ICI have a strong hold in this 'added-value' market segment.

The 'design approach' can also be used in marketing services, as shown by Holiday Inns which, because of its static market share, aimed to cater for the upper-middle sector in the USA. The increasing number of single people and couples without children, together with the rising divorce rate, has produced 'a new breed of business travellers with higher disposable incomes'.[39] Holiday Inns are introducing Crown Plaza hotels with extra facilities such as speciality restaurants and small seminar rooms with a boardroom. Higher tariffs will be charged but they will be up to 10 per cent less than their chief rivals. This new-style hotel has been tested successfully and is now operating in the USA, and franchises have been backed by extra marketing efforts. This 'upscale' chain is planned to extend to the Far East, South America, Africa, and Europe.

Tom Peters has stated: 'with a TV or two in every home, and a car or two in most driveways, the demand for these products is shifting from a desire for the product per se, almost regardless of quality, to a demand for customized alternatives with special features tailored for ever narrower market segments'.[40] Undoubtedly, as this leading US management writer has shrewdly observed, there is a growing expectation among consumers in the developed economies that products should be well designed in terms of functional efficiency and also aesthetic acceptability. This policy has been followed with evident success by Japanese manufacturers who benefited greatly from quality management training courses run by Dr J. M. Juran of the USA in the early 1950s. In his penetrating and radical text, *Juran on Leadership for Quality*,[41] he comments that product design is 'an essential part of product development (i.e., providing the product features required to meet customers' needs).' Not only in Japan but also across the world, Dr Juran has energetically propagated the theme of quality in manufacturing. In common with two other notable pioneers—W. Edwards Deming and Armand Feigenbaum—he has made a major contribution to improving efficiency in production by insisting that top management are fully committed to the concept of quality, and that they will pursue this policy throughout their organizations.

There is, after all, what has been termed by Thouless[42] a 'psychology of economic value'. To have economic value, an object should 'arouse desire, at least in some people, so that they are willing to give effort or to exchange other things they already possess for it. The behaviour they adopt towards such an object may be called a *positive* or *seeking* reaction'. This elegant phrasing may readily be translated into the pre-purchase activities which have been discussed in connection with buying behaviour; design confers added-value to products and increases motivation to buy.

14.10 'SAGACITY' SEGMENTATION

The general inadequacy of the traditional socio-economic groupings (A–E) has already been noted in Chapter 7 and earlier in this chapter. In an endeavour to improve the discriminating power of income and demographic classifications, Research Services Ltd developed in 1981 SAGACITY, which combines life-cycle, income, and socio-economic groups.[43]

Using data from JICNARS National Readership Survey 1980, Research Services grouped people into 12 easily described and identifiable groups which showed widely differing characteristics in terms of media behaviour and product usage.

The 'basic thesis' of SAGACITY is that people have different aspirations and patterns of behaviour as they pass through their life-cycle (see Chapter 8). Four separate stages are identified:

Dependent: Adults 15–34 who are *not* heads of household or housewives, unless they are childless students in full-time education.
Pre-family: Adults 15–34 who *are* heads of household or housewives but are childless.
Family: Adults under 65 who are heads of household or housewives in households with one or more children under 21 years of age.
Late: All other adults whose children have already left home or who are 35 or over and childless.

Cornish states that the cut-off point of 35 between the pre-family and late stage is arbitrary, and was chosen in preference to 45, which can be taken as the end of a woman's fertile period, on the grounds that the pre-family stage should include households only in the relatively early years of household formation.[44]

After life-cycle, SAGACITY then considers income and occupational characteristics of the individual or couple forming the household. Income is defined as 'the net income of the head of the household at constant prices on a 10-point exponential scale, adjusted by the working status of the spouse of the head of the household'.

Income breakdown is applied only to the Family and Late stages, and households are characterized as 'better off' or 'worse off'. For instance, a white-collar adult in the Family stage could be classified as 'better off' if the head of the household's claimed or estimated net income falls within the two highest of ten income brackets, provided that he or she has no working spouse. Adjustments are made to cut-off points where the spouse works full or part time. Dependent and Pre-family stages are not classified into 'better off/worse off' income groups on account of the relatively small sample sizes and also because differences in disposable income are considered to be less marked and therefore less important than in later stages.

Division by income rather than economic activity is stated to be particularly important at the Late stage, since there is a significant minority of retired people who qualify for the 'better off' income grouping, and who might well have consumption habits similar to those who are still working. (See pages 336–337 on the affluent middle-aged.)

The last element of the SAGACITY groupings refers to the occupation of the head of the household. Individuals are classified as non-manual (white-collar) occupations (ABC1's) and manual (blue-collar) occupations (C2DEs).

From combination of the three elements (life-cycle, income, and occupation) with stages in the family life-cycle, the following paradigm emerges (see Fig. 14.1).

To assist understanding of the SAGACITY system, descriptive notations have been given for each of the 12 groups, together with an indication of their size relative to the total adult population.[43]

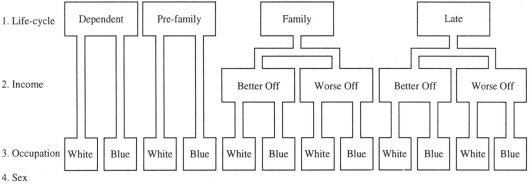

4. Sex
SAGACITY will often be applied to the male and female
populations separately as in the published tables.

Fig. 14.1 SAGACITY consumer segmentation model (*Source:* Research Services)[43]

Dependent, white (DW) 6 per cent: Mainly under 24s, living at home or full-time student, where
  head of household is an ABC1 occupation group.
Dependent, blue (DB) 9 per cent: Mainly under 24s, living at home or full-time student, where
  head of household is in a C2DE occupation group.
Pre-family, white (PFW) 4 per cent: Under 35s who have established their own household but
  have no children and where the head of household is in an ABC1 occupation group.
Pre-family, blue (PFB) 4 per cent: Under 35s who have established their own household but
  have no children and where the head of household is in a C2DE occupation group.
Family, better off, white (FW +) 6 per cent: Housewives and heads of household, under 65, with
  one or more children in the household, in the 'better off' income group and where the head
  of household is in an ABC1 occupation group (65 per cent are AB).
Family, better off, blue (FB +) 9 per cent: Housewives and heads of household, under 65, with
  one or more children in the household, in the 'better off' income group and where the head
  of household is in a C2DE occupation group (72 per cent are C2).
Family, worse off, white (FW −) 8 per cent: Housewives and heads of household, under 65, with
  one or more children in the household, in the 'worse off' income group and where the head
  of household is in an ABC1 occupation group (72 per cent are C1).
Family, worse off, blue (FB −) 14 per cent: Housewives and heads of household, under 65, with
  one or more children in the household, in the 'worse off' income group and where the head
  of household is in a C2DE occupation group (47 per cent are DE).
Late, better off, white (LW +) 5 per cent: Includes all adults whose children have left home or
  who are over 35 and childless, are in the 'better off' income group and where the head of
  household is in an ABC1 occupation group (60 per cent are AB).
Late, better off, blue (LB +) 7 per cent: Includes all adults whose children have left home or
  who are over 35 and childless, are in the 'better off' income group and where the head of
  household is in a C2DE occupation group (69 per cent are C2).
Late, worse off, white (LW −) 9 per cent: Includes all adults whose children have left home or
  who are over 35 and childless, are in the 'worse off' income group and where the head of
  household is in an ABC1 occupation group (71 per cent are C1).
Late, worse off, blue (LB −) 19 per cent: Includes all adults whose children have left home or
  who are over 35 and childless, are in the 'worse off' income group and where the head of
  household is in a C2DE occupation group (70 per cent are DE).

The power of SAGACITY to discriminate both in relation to markets and to media has been demonstrated by Research Services.[43,44] For example, package holidays abroad peak in the Pre-family and Late stages; even among the better off, demand is very much lower in the Family stage. The lower *per capita* disposable incomes of families with children and the problems associated with taking children abroad contribute to this trend. If NRS data showed that 20 per cent of all adults took a package holiday abroad, compared with 30 per cent in one SAGACITY group and 15 per cent in another, indices for these groups would be calculated thus:

$$\frac{30}{20} \times 100 = 150 \quad \text{and} \quad \frac{15}{20} \times 100 = 75 \quad \text{(The total population index will always be 100.)}$$

Clearly, the type of package holiday will influence the target market definition. Media can also be selected to cover the SAGACITY groups shown to be the most likely prospects.

Ownership of cheque books contrasts with the pattern of distribution of overseas package holidays in that it is a function of age and social grade rather than income. Joint-stock bank accounts are held by virtually all white-collar workers in the Pre-family and Family stages, but fall off in the Late stage. The index for holding a bank current account by blue-collar workers is below 100 for Dependent, Late, and 'worse off' groups. However, the Pre-family and 'better off' blue-collar groups have indices of 115 and 111 respectively. These figures may reflect a certain degree of success by the banks in attracting these groups of consumers who, as they enter succeeding life-cycle stages, may maintain usage and so change the blue-collar indices.

SAGACITY segmentation is clearly a creative and realistic approach which has generally been welcomed by marketing and advertising professionals, although the caveat has been expressed that since it 'does, however, presuppose the collection of class and income data . . . it would therefore benefit from any improvements to class and income classifications'.[45]

14.11 GEODEMOGRAPHIC SEGMENTATION

Geodemographics is a method of classifying households related to their geographical dispersion, as indicated in the Census of Population. Households are classified from multi-variate analyses of census data, and are organized into several clusters or groups with distinctive types of housing and family behaviour. Several geodemographic systems have been developed in the UK over the past few years: they have much in common, and have been applied in segmenting markets for direct mail and mail order campaigns, etc.

ACORN segmentation

The geodemographic analytical approach has existed as Census Tracking in the USA since the early 1970s; in the UK, the ACORN (A Classification of Residential Neighbourhoods) system was originated by Richard Webber at the Centre of Environmental Studies in Liverpool during 1977: this organization was wound up in 1979. It classifies people and households by the types of neighbourhoods in which they live; the central thesis is that areas with similar demographic and social characteristics will tend to share common life-styles and patterns of behaviour.

Webber's earlier research for Liverpool Council focused on the incidence of urban deprivation in different parts of the inner city. He discovered that provided sufficient census counts were taken, 25 significantly different kinds of neighbourhood could be identified. These were found to have distinctly different mixes of social problems. Later, Webber, with the cooperation of the Census Office, extended the methodology to classify each of the 17 000 wards and parishes in Britain. Based on the 1971 Census, 36 neighbourhood types were noted (extended to 38 in 1982), each having clearly defined characteristics of age, family structure, income, type of housing, etc.

Table 14.1   ACORN profile of Britain

ACORN Types		% of 1991 population		ACORN groups	
A 1	Agricultural villages	2.6			
A 2	Areas of farms and smallholdings	0.7	3.3	Agricultural areas	A
B 3	Post-war functional private housing	4.4			
B 4	Modern private housing, young families	3.7			
B 5	Established private family housing	6.0	17.6	Modern family housing, higher incomes	B
B 6	New detached houses, young families	2.9			
B 7	Military bases	0.7			
C 8	Mixed owner-occ'd & council estates	3.5			
C 9	Small town centres & flats above shops	4.1	17.9	Older housing of intermediate status	C
C10	Villages with non-farm employment	4.9			
C11	Older private housing, skilled workers	5.5			
D12	Unmodernized terraces, older people	2.4			
D13	Older terraces, lower income families	1.4	4.2	Older terraced housing	D
D14	Tenement flats lacking amenities	0.4			
E15	Council estates, well-off older workers	3.4			
E16	Recent council estates	2.8	13.2	Council estates – category I	E
E17	Better council estates, younger workers	5.0			
E18	Small council houses, often Scottish	1.9			
F19	Low rise estates in industrial towns	4.6			
F20	Inter-war council estates, older people	2.8	8.8	Council estates – category II	F
F21	Council housing, elderly people	1.4			
G22	New council estates in inner cities	2.0			
G23	Overspill estates, higher unemployment	3.0	7.0	Council estates – category III	G
G24	Council estates with some overcrowding	1.5			
G25	Council estates with greatest hardship	0.6			
H26	Multi-occupied older housing	0.4			
H27	Cosmopolitan owner-occupied terraces	1.0	3.8	Mixed inner metropolitan areas	H
H28	Multi-let housing in cosmopolitan areas	0.7			
H29	Better-off cosmopolitan areas	1.7			
I 30	High status non-family areas	2.1			
I 31	Multi-let big old houses and flats	1.5	4.1	High status non-family areas	I
I 32	Furnished flats, mostly single people	0.5			
J 33	Inter-war semis, white collar workers	5.7			
J 34	Spacious inter-war semis, big gardens	5.0	15.8	Affluent suburban housing	J
J 35	Villages with wealthy older commuters	2.9			
J 36	Detached houses, exclusive suburbs	2.3			
K37	Private houses, well-off older residents	2.3	3.8	Better-off retirement areas	K
K38	Private flats, older single people	1.5			
U39	Unclassified	0.5	0.5	Unclassified	U
		100.0			

Source: CACI.

British Market Research Bureau (BMRB) applied this 36-area classification to the 24 000 respondents in their Target Group Index (TGI) survey. It was found to be an efficient discriminator for market targeting for several products and services. CACI identified 40 variables from census data which are used to describe the different types of people living in each enumeration district. These variables are almost equally distributed over age and household type, housing, and social and employment status.

> ACORN was further developed by Webber on joining CAC Inc-International [CACI], and applied to the UK's 125 000 census enumeration districts, each of about 150 addresses which, because of their size, contain basically homogeneous households. The next stage was match the 1.25 million post codes against the census enumeration districts, and so enable a list of customers' addresses (with post codes) to be readily analysed by ACORN criteria.[16]

The British ACORN profile is shown in Table 14.1, from which it will be noted that there are 11 main groups, subdivided into 38 neighbourhood types, based on 1981 Census information and 1991 population projections by CACI. Group I, for instance, contains ACORN types 30 (high status non-family areas), D group contains 12 (unmodernized terraces, older people), 13 (older terraces, lower income families) and 14 (tenement flats lacking amenities).

Profiles of particular neighbourhoods related to the consumption of food, drink, car ownership, kitchen equipment, central heating, viewing and listening habits, occupation, newspaper readership, etc., can be supplied to guide marketing strategies.

Specific areas of high consumption can readily be identified from ACORN 'buying power' indices. For example, ACORN type J35 'villages with wealthy older commuters', which represent 2.9 per cent of the (1981) population and 2.8 per cent of the households in Britain, have 2.4 times the national average proportion of households with two cars, and 2.7 times the proportion of those living in seven or more rooms.

ACORN segmentation has been used successfully by leading building societies, car manufacturers, Next and Bejam in store location, catalogue and mailing shots, and advertising media selection. It clearly has particular relevance to direct marketing, leaflet distribution, and local media selection.

ACORN Life-styles

CACI has also developed ACORN Life-styles, which classify every UK household into one of 81 Life-style segments, and provide marketing management with specific targets for direct marketing operations. Analyses also extend to 24 Life-style groups and 81 Life-style types, which effectively integrate consumer demographic segments and geographic locations (shown in Table 14.2). As with ACORN, the Life-styles analysis is linked with TGI, and also the full demographic database at CACI. ACORN Life-style definitions are as follows:

> HOUSEHOLD COMPOSITION
> #### Singles
> Adults living on their own, usually without young children.
> #### Couples
> Two adults, almost certainly married, with or without young children.
> #### Family
> Two adults, almost certainly married. They have at least one other relation living with them: child or other adult
> #### Homesharers
> Multiple adults living together but not a couple or family.

AGE STRUCTURE
Younger
Youngest adults most often between 18 and
24 years of age.
Maturing adults most often between
25 and 44 years of age.
Older
Established adults most often between
45 and 64 years of age.
Retired adults most often over 65 years
of age

Table 14.2   ACORN 24 Life-style groups and 81 Life-style types

Rural areas and villages

LA	*Rural singles*	2.7%
LA01	Younger men	
LA02	Younger women	
LA03	Older single men	
LA04	Older single women	
LA05	Affluent singles in commuter villages	
LA06	Affluent singles in agricultural villages	

LB	*Younger rural couples and families*	2.2%
LB07	Young couples	
LB08	Young couples with elderly person	
LB09	Maturing couples	
LB10	Maturing families	

LC	*Older rural couples and families*	1.8%
LC11	Established couples	
LC12	Established couples, older children	
LC13	Retired couples	
LC14	Retired families	

LD	*Affluent rural couples and families*	2.4%
LD15	Affluent couples and families in commuter villages	
LD16	Affluent couples and families in agricultural villages	

Suburbia

LE	*Younger suburban singles*	3.7%
LE17	Younger single males	
LE18	Younger single females	

LF	*Older suburban singles*	4.0%
LF19	Older single males	
LF20	Older single females	

LG	*Younger traditional suburban couples and families*	9.7%
LG21	Youngest couples	
LG22	Youngest couples with elderly person	
LG23	Maturing couples	
LG24	Maturing families	

LH	*Older traditional suburban couples and families*	5.3%
LH25	Established couples	
LH26	Established families with older children	
LH27	Retired couples	
LH28	Retired families	

LI	*Younger very affluent suburban couples and families*	4.2%
LI29	Youngest couples	
LI30	Youngest couples with elderly person	
LI31	Maturing couples	
LI32	Maturing families	

LJ	*Older very affluent suburban couples and families*	2.3%
LJ33	Established couples	
LJ34	Established families with older children	
LJ35	Retired couples	
LJ36	Retired families	

Council areas

LK	*Younger singles in council areas*	5.1%
LK37	Single men	
LK38	Single women	

Table 14.2 (*cont.*)

Council areas (*cont.*)		
LL	*Older singles in council areas*	5.0%
LL39	Single men	
LL40	Single women	
LM	*Younger couples in council areas*	6.8%
LM41	Youngest couples	
LM42	Maturing couples	
LN	*Older couples in council areas*	5.0%
LN43	Established couples	
LN44	Retired couples	
LO	*Adult families in council areas*	6.2%
LO45	Youngest couples and families with elderly person	
LO46	Maturing families	
LO47	Established families with older children	
LO48	Retired families	

Metropolitan and cosmopolitan city

LP	*Affluent single metropolitan dwellers*	3.1%
LP49	Younger men	
LP50	Younger women	
LP51	Older men	
LP52	Older women	
LQ	*Affluent couples in metropolitan areas*	4.0%
LQ53	Younger couples	
LQ54	Younger families	
LQ55	Older couples	
LQ56	Older families	
LR	*Cosmopolitan inner city dwellers*	2.4%
LR57	Younger singles	
LR58	Younger couples and families	
LR59	Older singles	
LR60	Older couples and families	

Traditional urban households

LS	*Younger urban singles*	2.8%
LS61	Men	
LS62	Women	
LT	*Older urban singles*	3.5%
LT63	Men	
LT64	Women	
LU	*Younger traditional urban couples and families*	6.8%
LU65	Youngest couples	
LU66	Youngest couples with elderly person	
LU67	Maturing couples	
LU68	Maturing families	
LV	*Older traditional urban couples and families*	4.3%
LV69	Established couples	
LV70	Established families with older children	
LV71	Retired couples	
LV72	Retired families	

Homesharers

LW	*Homesharers in affluent areas*	3.4%
LW73	Male homesharers in very affluent areas	
LW74	Female homesharers in very affluent areas	
LW75	Mixed homesharers in very affluent areas	
LW76	Male homesharers in traditional suburban areas	
LW77	Female homesharers in traditional suburban areas	
LW78	Mixed homesharers in traditional suburban areas	
LX	*Homesharers in less affluent areas*	3.3%
LX79	Male homesharers	
LX80	Female homesharers	
LX81	Mixed homesharers	

Source: CACI.

One of ACORN's most interesting link-ups is with CCN Systems, a member of the Great Universal Stores Group. CCN has details of 18 million people in its computers, and with CACI has a joint service to sell these details, segregated by ACORN as well as geographically. Two major users are the AA and American Express.[46]

Other Census-based geodemographic analyses are operated by *Pinpoint Analysis* which, with the cooperation of the Ordnance Survey and using the Post Office's Post Code Address (PAF) has developed a database called Pinpoint Address Code (PAC) covering England, Wales and Scotland. Other specialized systems focus on people's financial characteristics, etc.

MOSAIC

Richard Webber, pioneer of ACORN for CACI from which he later resigned, has devised CCN Systems and the MOSAIC classification, particularly related to the needs of the large mail order firm, Great Universal Stores (owners of CCN). The MOSAIC database contains information at four geographic levels: 22 million residential addresses, 1.3 million full post codes, 170 000 post code groups, and 1000 postal sectors. Although like ACORN and Pinpoint analysis, it is based on the Census of Population for 1991, MOSAIC also classifies areas on the basis of data from CCN's annually updated databases, and the new version of MOSAIC uses the latest 1977/88 electoral roll information together with county court judgements and credit enquiry data to June 1990, to track changes in demographics.

PRIZM

PRIZM—Potential Rating Index by Zip Market—is rather like ACORN and based upon an analysis of postal districts in the USA.[49] The Zip code is a five-digit number that designates a particular post office in a particular city. There are 35 600 residential units with distinctive Zip codes. PRIZM identifies 34 key factors, such as education, race, affluence, social class, family life-cycle, mobility, etc., which collectively accounted for almost 90 per cent variation between these Zip code areas. Processing of these key factors resulted in 40 homogeneous categories or clusters of residential areas, which were given dramatic descriptions like 'God's Country', 'Bohemian Mix', 'Grain Belt', and 'Money and Brains'.

SRI VALS life-styles

Another life-style analysis has been developed by SRI International of the USA to describe three groups of people in terms of their value systems: 'outer directeds', 'money restricted', and 'inner directeds' (see Sec. 6.5). These have been further refined—for instance, 'outer directeds' are said to be of three main types: 'belongers', 'emulators', and 'achievers'. 'Belongers' want to conform and fit in with community norms (see Chapter 8); 'emulators' are socially ambitious and highly mobile; 'achievers' are aggressive, well educated, and hold senior posts in industry, business, and the professions. SRI has links with research organizations over five European countries through the Research Institute on Social Change (RISC).

Social-value groups

In the UK, Taylor Nelson's Monitor Survey (now operated by Applied Futures Ltd) identifies seven social-value groups which are based on shared values and beliefs:[48] self-explorers; social resisters; experimentalists; conspicuous consumers/achievers; belongers; survivors; and the unfortunate 'aimless'. Although these classifications have attracted critical comment, it should be borne in mind that they are derived from over ten years of intensive market and social research by Dr Elizabeth Nelson. Within these seven social-value groups, individuals will share specific patterns of attitudes and behaviour, which facilitate segmentation analyses, and cross-country comparative studies.

Overview

These competing geodemographic systems have much in common, and offer discriminating techniques for household analyses. The specialist research companies providing these services add new dimensions to the analyses from time to time, and offer clients consultancy advice related to their specific needs.

14.12 INDUSTRIAL MARKETS AND SEGMENTATION STRATEGIES

Segmentation bases in industrial products and services may include customer size, location, industrial classification, usage rate, and so on. The Standard Industrial Classification (SIC) may be useful as a framework for industrial market segmentation. The Census of Production analyses industrial undertakings on the basis of the SIC, which was first issued in 1948 to encourage uniformity in preparation of the UK official statistics related to industry. It was revised in 1958, 1968, and 1980. These revisions have tended to restrict comparative analyses over the years. The unit of analysis is the 'establishment', classified according to the main products manufactured. This could mean that the total production of some firms may be entered under one classification, whereas they may in fact produce considerable quantities of some other products which are important in those particular markets but which represent only a relatively small proportion of their total output.

Until the latest revision, SICs were subdivided into 'minimum list headings' (MLHs) which progressively narrowed industrial activities for the purposes of classification and measurement. To conform to European practice, the 1980 edition of the SIC has a decimal structure, resulting in rather more detailed classification of economic activities, since there are 334 'activity headings' compared with 181 MLHs. Full details of the revised SIC can be obtained from the Central Statistical Office (CSO).

The *International Standard Industrial Classification* (ISIC) was drawn up by the United Nations in 1948, and, like the SIC which it closely resembles, was revised subsequently. In export marketing strategies, the ISIC would prove a valuable source of data. In the USA the SIC system was developed by the federal government to facilitate the collection and analysis of industrial data. The basic reporting unit of the SIC system in the USA, like the British, is the establishment, which can result in some problems for analysts.

The Business Statistics Office (BSO) in the UK publishes registers of production firms which may be very useful for industrial marketing strategies. These classified lists of businesses are derived from the Census of Production and about 27 000 business addresses are covered. Special regional and alphabetical analyses are available from the BSO at reasonable cost.

The British Standard Regions could provide a useful framework for segmenting markets by location.

Some products are used by other consumers and in industry, e.g., soap, paper towels, lubricating oil, food (industrial caterers or domestic consumers). In such instances, the total market requires to be analysed by type of user, and then further refined by other forms of segmentation. The significance of derived demand in industrial markets was noted in Chapter 10; *segmentation by industrial end-use* may be an appropriate strategy. Another useful segmentation approach could be based on *buying power and industrial concentration*. This may relate to both the public and private sectors of the economy. Industries with high concentration characteristics are brewing, electronics engineering, computers, oil and petroleum, paint, etc.

A McKinsey director has referred to experiments by US industrial firms with *strategic market segmentation* (SMS).[49] This is a method of aggregating customer groups so as to maximize homogeneity of demand *within* segments and differentiation of demand *between* segments. Three constraints apply in pursuing this strategy:

1   Each segment should be of sufficient size to allow a niche strategy to result in profitable business.

2. Each segment should be measurable by such factors as customer size, growth, market shares, etc.
3. Each segment should be distinguished by buying factors such as price, after-sales service, etc.

SMS users have identified five different types of industrial market segments: end-use, product, geographic, common-buying factor, and customer size. They not only look at industry groups but also examine how customers *use* products. 'For example, one manufacturer of precision motors discovered that his customers differed by the speed of their applications, and that a new, cheaper machine introduced by his competitor wore out quickly when used in high- and medium-speed work'.[49] To the latter customer segment, he emphasized the significant life-cycle-cost advantage of his product and, at the same time, began developing a competitively priced product with an extra maintenance advantage.

Within some industries, it may be possible to develop attractive niches related to customer-size groups, for example, large, medium, and small. Specific marketing mixes could then be designed related to pricing policies, methods of distribution, and after-sales servicing arrangements.

It will be apparent from the many ways in which market segmentation can be approached that there is no shortage of new and often very creative ideas. But, as Wind has wisely observed, the most difficult aspect of any segmentation project is the application of it.[50] He perceives, and can offer, no rules that will assure successful translation from concepts to practice. Instead he suggests 'a few generalizable conclusions':

1. Involve all the relevant users (e.g., product managers, new product developers, advertising agency, etc.) in the problem definition, research design, and data interpretation stages.
2. View segmentation data as one input to the total marketing information and integrate them with sales and other relevant data.
3. Use segmentation data on a continuous basis.

It is of little value to management to produce sophisticated methods of market segmentation which, while academically admirable, cannot be put into practice in real market conditions.

14.13 SUMMARY

The marketing concept leads logically to market segmentation which focuses on disaggregative as opposed to aggregative demand.

Segmentation analyses divide macro market demand into relatively homogeneous micro markets; this strategy encourages the making and marketing of products and services which are more likely to be acceptable to certain types of people and organizations.

Four principal factors affect segmentation: identification, measurability, accessibility, and appropriateness. Markets can be divided by several criteria: demographic, usage, location, personality, brand loyalty, psychographic, benefit, life-style, design, etc.

Relatively new consumer segmentation approaches—SAGACITY and ACORN—provide more sophisticated analyses than the traditional socio-economic groupings.

Industrial segmentation may be used to great advantage in marketing to commerce and industry. Bases for segmentation may relate to customer size, industrial classification, location, usage rate, etc. A creative approach, such as strategic market segmentation (SMS) would encourage the development of effective niche positioning in competitive markets.

Market segmentation applies many of the behavioural concepts discussed in this book, and knowledge of these will give valuable guides to creative segmentation.

REFERENCES

1. Levitt, Theodore, *The Marketing Imagination*, Free Press, New York, 1983.
2. Smith, Wendell R., 'Product differentiation and market segmentation as alternative marketing strategies', *Journal of Marketing*, vol. 21, July 1956.
3. Howard, John A., and Jagdish N. Sheth, *The Theory of Buyer Behaviour*, John Wiley, New York, 1969.
4. Sheth, Jagdish N., 'A review of buyer behaviour', *Management Science*, vol. 13, no. 12, August 1967.
5. Thorncroft, Antony, 'The souped-up Mr Hamilton', *Financial Times*, 8 February 1973.
6. Sorenson, Ralph Z. II, 'US marketers can learn from European innovators', *Harvard Business Review*, September/October 1972.
7. Sampson, Peter, 'Consumer classification—the art of the state', *European Research*, vol. 10, no. 4, October 1982.
8. Weber, John G., 'Worldwide strategies for market segmentation', *Columbia Journal of World Business*, vol. 9, no. 4, winter 1974.
9. Douglas, Susan P., and C. Samuel Craig, *International Marketing Research*, Prentice-Hall, Englewood Cliffs, New Jersey, 1983.
10. Jonquières, Guy de, 'Unilever adopts clean sheet approach', *Financial Times*, 21 October 1991.
11. Amano, Ikuo, 'The bright and dark sides of Japanese education', *Royal Society of Arts Journal*, vol. CXL, no. 5425, January 1992.
12. Baxter, Andrew, 'A clean sweep through Europe for Electrolux', *Financial Times*, 3 October 1991.
13. Rawstorne, Philip, 'Focus on differences . . . and on similarities', *Financial Times*, 13 October 1988.
14. Barker, Stephen M., and John F. Trost, 'Cultivate the high-volume consumer', *Harvard Business Review*, March/April 1973.
15. Wind, Yoram J., *Product Policy and Concepts, Methods and Strategy*, Addison-Wesley, Reading, Massachusetts, 1982.
16. Chisnall, Peter M., *Marketing Research: Analysis and Measurement*, McGraw-Hill, Maidenhead, 1982.
17. Bass, Frank, Charles W. King, and Edgar A. Pessemier, *Applications of the Sciences in Marketing Management*, John Wiley, New York, 1968.
18. Cunningham, Ross M., 'Brand loyalty—what, where, how much?', *Harvard Business Review*, January/February 1956.
19. Charlton, P., 'A review of brand loyalty', *Journal of the Market Research Society*, vol. 15, no. 1, January 1973.
20. Kuehn, Alfred A., 'Consumer brand choice as a learning process', *Journal of Advertising Research*, vol. 2, December 1962.
21. Tucker, W. J., 'The development of brand loyalty', *Journal of Marketing Research*, vol. 3, August 1964.
22. Fitzroy, Peter T., *Analytical Methods for Marketing Management*, McGraw-Hill, Maidenhead, 1976.
23. Yankelovich, Daniel, 'New criteria for market segmentation', *Harvard Business Review*, vol. 42, March/April 1964.
24. Stone, Gregory P., 'City shoppers and urban identification: observations on the social psychology of city life', *American Journal of Sociology*, vol. 60, 1954.
25. 'Consumer behaviour: strategic shopping', *The Economist*, 26 September 1992.
26. Zith, Ruth, 'Psychographics for segmentation', *Journal of Advertising Research*, vol. 11, no. 2, April 1971.
27. Lunn, Tony, 'Segmenting and constructing markets', in: *Consumer Market Research Handbook*, Robert Worcester (ed.), McGraw-Hill, Maidenhead, 1972.
28. Teel, Jesse E., and William A. Bearden, 'Psychographics of radio and television audiences', *Journal of Advertising Research*, vol. 19, April 1979.
29. Morton-Williams, J., 'Research on the market for National Savings', in: *Leading Case Histories in Market Research*, M. K. Adler (ed.), Business Books, London, 1971.
30. Crimp, Margaret, *The Market Research Process*, Prentice-Hall, Englewood Cliffs, New Jersey, 1981.
31. Boote, Alfred S., 'Psychographic segmentation in Europe', *Journal of Advertising Research*, vol. 22, no. 6, 1982.

32. Gordon, Wendy, 'The lifestyle of the affluent middle-aged', *Admap*, February 1981.
33. Buck, S. F., 'The affluent middle-aged: spending and saving patterns', *Admap*, March 1981.
34. Lind, Harold, 'Media research and the affluent middle-aged', *Admap*, February 1981.
35. Phillips, Lynn W., and Brian Sternthal, 'Age differences in information processing: a perspective on the aged consumer', *Journal of Marketing Research*, vol. 14, November 1977.
36. Bartos, Rena, 'What every marketer should know about women', *Harvard Business Review*, May/June 1978.
37. Young, Shirley, Leland Ott, and Barbara Feigin, 'Some practical considerations in market segmentation', *Journal of Market Research*, vol. 15, no. 3, August 1978.
38. Hanscombe, Philip, 'ICI's "natural" paints story: in black and white', *Marketing*, 28 April 1982.
39. Upton, Gillian, 'New links in the chain', *Marketing*, 8 March 1984.
40. Peters, Tom, *Thriving on Chaos: Handbook for a Management Revolution*, Macmillan, Basingstoke, 1988.
41. Juran, J. M., *Juran on Leadership for Quality: An Executive Handbook*, Free Press, London, 1989.
42. Thouless, R. H., *General and Social Psychology*, University Tutorial Press, London, 1967.
43. Research Services Ltd, *Sagacity: A Special Analysis of JICNARS NRS 1980 Data*, 1981.
44. Cornish, Pym, 'Life cycle and income segmentation—SAGACITY', *Admap*, October 1981.
45. Twyman, Tony, 'Re-classifying people: the ADMAP Seminar', *Admap*, November 1981.
46. Clark, Eric, 'ACORN finds new friends', *Marketing*, 16 December 1982.
47. Lohmkuhl, David, 'PRIZM-ACORN-style lifestyle research', *Media World*, April 1982.
48. Bunting, C., E. Nelson, and S. Thomas, 'Social change analysis: a new area for the application of research', in: *MRS Conference Papers*, Market Research Society, London, 1982.
49. Garda, Robert A., 'A strategic approach to market segmentation', *McKinsey Quarterly*, autumn 1981.
50. Wind, Yoram, 'Issues and advances in segmentation research', *Journal of Marketing Research*, vol. 15, no. 3, August 1978.

REVIEW AND DISCUSSION QUESTIONS

1. Why do you think that some marketers prefer to base their market segmentation on psychographics rather than on personality?
2. Consumer behaviour is intended to provide marketers with a number of bases for segmenting customers. Which segmentation strategies would be most appropriate in the following product areas: (a) lawnmowers; (b) health spas; (c) personal computers; (d) car number plates; (e) skiing holidays?
3. Using the UK hair shampoo market as an example, suggest reasons why demographics and psychographics are both desirable types of consumer information for marketers to have concerning their target markets.
4. Discuss the view that demographic segmentation is too 'thin' and does not offer the marketer a sufficiently deep insight into markets.
5. From a marketing perspective, how would you compare the usefulness of the SAGACITY segmentation system with more traditional social classification systems?
6. Suggest possible benefit segments for the following products: (a) sun cream; (b) mouthwash; (c) a low-calorie canned fruit drink; (d) casual running shoes.

FIFTEEN

SIGNPOSTS FOR STRATEGY

15.1 INTRODUCTION

The core thesis of this book is that economics by itself cannot be expected to give complete and valid explanations of buying behaviour. Wider knowledge is needed before attempts are made to explain and predict patterns of consumption. Concepts from psychology, sociology, and cultural anthropology can provide valuable and highly relevant insights into the complex nature of demand for products and services for both personal and organizational consumption.

Just as business problems are made up of linked factors—involving for example, production, purchasing, finance, marketing, or personnel—consumption is also affected by many influences, some of which are often labelled 'rational' and others—generally less understood and therefore suspect—as 'irrational'. But it is the latter which, in many cases, are playing a bigger role in decisions to buy in several markets.

In Parts Two and Three, personal and environmental influences were identified and subsequently related to marketing strategies, specifically concerned with innovation, communication, and segmentation. This chapter will look at 'signs and portents'; at trends, some of which are well defined while others are emergent. Marketers must be alert to changes in perceptions, attitudes, and life-styles, and attempt to understand *why* these changes have occurred: their origins might well be located, for example, in psychological or cultural grounds.

15.2 SOCIAL AND CULTURAL FLUX

In addition to dire economic problems, such as industrial recession, structural unemployment, declining job opportunities, or severely restricted career prospects for school-leavers, there have been profound changes in cultural and social values and norms, several of which have been noted in Chapters 6, 7, and 8. The optimism which had infected public and private spending was shattered by the catastrophic rises in the costs of energy which resulted mainly from the setting up of OPEC in the early 1970s. These massive increases generated an almost interminable list of demands for more money from suppliers of raw materials, components, finished goods and, of course, from organized labour. The bandwagon of inflation careered on its headlong path to economic disaster, resulting, inevitably, in a high-cost, no-growth economy. From these depressive depths, Britain climbed back through the Thatcher years

(1979–90), when inflation was a prime target in political decision-making. At the same time, an extensive programme of privatization of the nationalized industries was vigorously pursued; British Telecom and British Gas became public limited companies, introducing millions of new investors to the stock exchange (other far-reaching changes were discussed in Chapter 10).

A survey of senior executives in ten western European countries published by *International Management* in 1980 indicated that they have 'a sense of foreboding over their inability to control external forces which will shape corporate destinies over the next decade'.[1] Their prime problem is perceived as inflation: other major problems are coping with shortages of adequately trained personnel; costs of labour and energy; keeping pace with new technologies; government intervention; and fluctuating exchange rates. A majority of executives felt that their jobs would be automated even further, particularly related to information access, financial management, and planning. Over half believed that their companies would 'have to enter into collective-bargaining type agreements with pressure groups, such as consumers and environmentalists, during the 1980s', in connection with pollution control, product safety, and plant location. It is of some interest to note that UK managers were generally the most optimistic about their abilities to control factors influencing their performance in the future. In retrospect, the findings of this survey seem strangely topical; a feeling of *déjà vu* pervades.

In the considered view of a highly experienced business consultant it is most unlikely that the western economies will regain the 'golden age economic growth rates of the 1960s' in the foreseeable future: they are experiencing not only economic and financial changes, but also a basic questioning of the traditional social structures and cultural norms that underpin western society.[2]. New production technologies, for example, will probably result in more highly automated, more capital-intensive mass production exploiting fully information technologies and the microprocessor. From these industrial changes, a four-sectoral economic structure may evolve:

1. Capital-intensive, highly automated and highly productive manufacturing and service activities, e.g., cars, airlines, telecommunications.
2. Labour-intensive, large-scale service sector, e.g., health, social welfare, and education.
3. Revived small-scale, entrepreneurial local sector, e.g., diverse industrial, commercial, and non-profit ventures.
4. Revived household and neighbourhood sector, e.g., DIY, informal or unpaid work, often indistinguishable from leisure.

Although it is not yet possible to discern how these sectors will interrelate, the last two sectors are thought to be the main sources of new work opportunities. Micro-technologies are capable of turning many homes into industrial workplaces. Work will be expected to fit in with people's lives: there will be a 'flexi-life' approach to earning a living, involving, perhaps, part-time working at more than one job, more concern with job interest, shorter working hours, earlier retirement, and longer holidays. Greater emphasis will be placed on participation in decision-making; business units may be run by small teams of equals whose expertise is shared to secure overall performance. Large companies are thought likely to become more like federations of small enterprises which, in turn, will draw on the services of outside specialist suppliers, many of whom will be self-employed, such as computer programmers and systems analysts.

In this projected new environment—which springs from 'wide-ranging societal and political changes'—management will have to become more entrepreneurial and also develop additional skills so that they can handle the uncertainty inherent in such complex conditions. Decision-making is a fundamental management responsibility; risk is an inherent factor in decision-making (see Chapters 10 and 11).

Like the European senior managers' survey quoted earlier, these sensitively perceptive views of the nature and direction of future economic activities are as relevant today as when they were given in the early 1980's.

Over a period of some years, *Harvard Business Review* (*HBR*) subscribers[3] have been asked for their views about the relationships that might exist between business and politics in the USA. It was felt that the gap was widening between business and social attitudes, and business was perceived to be on the defensive against organized consumer groups and unions. Industries and firms should be prepared to communicate more openly and intelligently on issues in which business and society were mutually concerned. *HBR* subscribers wanted to use the political process more effectively to improve overall perceptions and encourage cooperation. This greater emphasis on better corporate communications echoes some of the points made in Chapter 13, and the concept of rising expectations discussed in Chapters 3 and 4. It is confirmed in a survey by a group of McKinsey consultants[4] who recommended in 1980 that corporate leaders should not only be involved in business matters but also learn to cope with the increasing complexity of the external world. This will demand specialism in monitoring trends in social, economic, political, and international affairs (see Sec. 15.3 on social forecasting).

Christopher Lorenz[5] of the *Financial Times* has drawn attention to a stimulating study of the strategies and structures for the fast-moving markets of the 1990's. Lorenz believes that to succeed in the increasingly competitive environments of modern markets, companies must become two things above all; first, they must be *change-based and adaptive*—typified as *chameleons*—and second, they must be *alliance- rather than fortress-minded*, both externally towards other companies and internally between different departments and disciplines—typified as *collaborators*. Lorenz notes that the latter type relates closely to the Harvard concept of the 'boundary-less' company, while the former resembles 'living with ambiguity and paradox', or just 'reconciling opposites'.

Nevertheless, the chameleon company, in its avid pursuit of change should certainly not abandon all the well-tried management systems, otherwise they are likely to run into disaster. Lorenz critically comments that the report should have developed the theme of 'how to balance collaboration with the fashionable and important idea of "core competences"—to which they pay scant attention'. It is the core competence or leverage concept (which, incidentally, has been advocated for some years) that is seen to have a powerful effect on the performances of European and US companies. These sometimes use temporary alliances to achieve their corporate goals, but this type of collaboration is quite different from contracting-out or similar production strategies.

In Chapter 10 the skills of negotiation were discussed and cultural norms were noted to be a major influence in successful business deals. Negotiation clearly involves sensitive political skills, of which Antony Jay wrote perceptively:

> It is of course the increasing size of firms and corporations which makes it possible to study them in political terms. A small family firm can only be compared with a small feudal estate, and since both are entirely and personally run by the head of the family there is little revelation in the comparison. It is only as the commercial and industrial enterprises become as great and as complex as they are today that they begin to take on the apparatus of states and need to be studied as political institutions.[6]

Multinational corporations which feature so prominently in transworld trading with highly complex networks involving commercial, technological, and political commitments, have revenues comparable with some sovereign states. Their bargaining powers are formidable although perceptions of their corporate behaviour have varied considerably (see Chapter 13).

Dr Jerome B. Wiesner, president of the Massachusetts Institute of Technology, reflected on the role of technology in a changing world, and declared that all of the highly industrialized nations face similar problems. Of these, perhaps the most troublesome are 'those which are the consequences of success'.[7] Continued innovation is necessary to ensure economic progress, and as a result two groups of problems arise: the pragmatic and the conceptual. The first category covers identifiable factors such as economic, technical, and organizational matters, affecting innovation. The second category is less readily identifiable and relates to the general ideas that society holds about technology, economic and business behaviour, etc. Wiesner stated that a technologically based society must necessarily be in a continuing state of change and evolution; he regarded society as 'a learning machine'. The 'most serious problem is how to create a society which can learn more effectively to solve the growing numbers of problems calling for collective action'. Competitive enterprise by itself cannot cope adequately with the concomitants of economic progress—pollution, education, social welfare, and so on. These problems are common to all the mature industrialized economies. 'Healthy industrial societies can only exist in a state of dynamic equilibrium that involves continuing adaptation to the changing man-made world and to a natural world that is changing as the result of people's actions'.[7]

A highly useful method of examining and evaluating the options to decision-makers is the *scenario* which has been described as 'a prose description of future events and societal conditions that makes apparent the many interrelated aspects of society affected by potential change'.[8]

It has been contended[9] that traditional forecasting approaches are based on the assumption that tomorrow's world will be much the same as today's, but this ignores the probability of major changes that may arise from many influences, some of which, like the energy crises of 1973–4 and 1979, may have devastating effects. Scenario analysis provides managers with the opportunity to expand their professional horizons and project their minds creatively when planning for the future. Scenarios have been developed by the research group SRI International which developed the VALS life-styles typology (see Chapters 6 and 14), and also by large corporations such as Royal Dutch/Shell. In planning for the 1980s, for example, Shell used two alternative scenarios: The World of Internal Contractions (WIC) and Business Expansion (BE). The WIC scenario postulated slow growth in an environment of social stress. The BE scenario was more optimistic: although trade cycles would no longer be predictable, and there would be in general a perplexed, uneasy environment, healthy growth could be achieved in the long term, provided that strong political leadership, more adventurous industrial policies, and more closely integrated methods of international trading were pursued. How far these prognoses stood up to the test of time is open to discussion.

Traditionally, as a US oil market research executive has observed, people in corporations made decisions on the basis of information from specialized sectors of management: research and development, technical/financial, sales, and production.[10] These inputs seemed adequate at a time of more stable attitudes and behaviour. Today, such information is incomplete without data about the social and political environment in which those businesses operate:

> Understanding the changing nature of the corporate environment requires a variety of methods. These include monitoring the media and the literature for important signals of change. But much of environmental research is public opinion research. It is through the following of public attitudes that one can follow and perhaps anticipate changes in the corporations' social and political environment.[10]

Marked shifts in values have been identified by observers such as Gordon Rattray Taylor, who defined values as end-states, i.e., ways of life and patterns of behaviour, concepts such as security, honesty, freedom, piety, and justice.[11] Values are seen as determining attitudes; the former, Taylor asserts, have tended to be neglected on social research. There have been 'enormous shifts in values' and social equality and spontaneity are now favourably regarded in Britain.

As the business climate changes—and reflects in some measure shifts in societal expectations and values—organizations of all kinds need to be aware of the likely impact of these fundamental movements on their operations. Past patterns of consumer behaviour, for example, are being radically altered by the high incidence of divorce in the UK, the significant growth of one-parent families, the growing number of households without children, and the decline in size of households (see Chapter 8).

Apart from consumption changes triggered by demographic trends, deep-rooted attitudinal shifts have also affected people's expectations and preferences. Although seemingly more liberal in social norms and behaviour, people in their role as consumers are likely to be far less tolerant of corporate misdemeanours, particularly if they are affected personally. When business fails to come to grips with the complex problems of a radically changed global economy, the critics of the business ethic attract, with little trouble, eager recruits.

15.3 SOCIAL FORECASTING

Corporate performance in a complex, uncertain environment is affected by many variables, several of which are likely to be external to the company. Determinants of success were at one time more controllable, but the influence of governments, price control, national energy policies, as well as social and attitudinal changes have become far more intrusive. Hostile, and often well-informed, criticism of corporations in both the public and private sectors of the economy is now well established. Sometimes beliefs and attitudes are ambivalent; dependency often breeds dislike. Corporate decisions were usually made on the basis of information from specialized sectors of management: these inputs seemed adequate at a time of more stable attitudes and behaviour. But the volatile nature of many modern markets renders such information incomplete without data about the social and political environments in which businesses operate. Unless some systematic effort is made to include an appreciation of social trends when forecasts of demand are prepared, the resultant figures could be distinctly misleading.

It has been said that all one can hope for is an effective mixture of objective and subjective criteria that take advantage of the most appropriate scientific techniques together with the best available human judgement.[12] It is the quality of conceptual thought about the future and the factors which are likely to determine patterns of consumption that is of vital importance. In the USA, two major developments in the 1970s were identified: the relative growth of population in non-metropolitan areas ('the new ruralism') and the growth of the household economy relative to the market economy.[13] These same trends, overlooked by many observers, are reflected in the growth of DIY activity, and in the shrinking populations of large cities in the UK.

Nearly 30 years ago the *Wall Street Journal* warned against the dangers of economic forecasting models:

> Even the most learned economists, trying to take every probability into account, often find that there is one they've forgotten and that it alone is sufficient to throw their calculations off badly . . . there is a tendency for such often partially wishful projections to be taken up by an equally wishful public as having at least some reasonable accuracy. And there is also a tendency for the majority of the soothsayers themselves to bolster each other up into a belief that, since they agree so closely, there must be a good deal of truth in what they are telling each other.

Less than 20 years after these words were written, the developed economies were rocked to their foundations by the quadrupling of oil prices—an event that took the business world by total surprise. It was reported that in 1970 the US Cabinet Task Force on Oil commented: 'We do not predict a substantial price rise in world oil markets over the coming decade'.[11] With hindsight, this professional opinion appears quite incompetent.

Attempting to forecast social phenomena is indeed hazardous; so many interacting factors impinge on events. It has been suggested that human behaviour, variable though it is, could be placed along a continuum ranging between randomness and unpredictability to determinism and predictability.[12] Between these extremes of chaos and order lies a middle range which is the field of social forecasting.

Experienced US researchers have found that there are certain leading issues in areas such as employee benefits, consumerism, or equal opportunities which can be used when examining nations that have a similar culture to the United States. These, it is said, 'are very likely to accommodate to strains of various types in recognisably similar ways, and to develop similar or related conclusions'.[8] Of course, naive transference would not be acceptable; each event or trend should be evaluated within the USA for its validity and probability of occurrence.

Yankelovich and associates have developed social forecasting research in the USA, and in Europe, Taylor Nelson's Monitor Survey, now operated by Applied Futures Limited, is linked with RISC, the International Research Institute on Social Change (see Chapters 6 and 14). Another social forecasting service is offered by the Henley Centre, which has established professional expertise in identifying and evaluating trends and their likely strategic and tactical effects on British industry and commerce. Christine MacNulty of Applied Futures offers a scenario development projected 15 to 20 years ahead, which includes quantitative, technological, and qualitative data covering social and political trends. The *process* of scenario-building is regarded as more important than the actual scenarios; its intrinsic value derives significantly from the *approach* adopted when attempting to determine future patterns of consumption likely to affect particular industries and organizations. For instance, when considering the home of the future, Applied Futures state that they begin with the question: 'What is a home for?' The 'conclusion is that it is about human activity categorised as leisure, work and maintenance'.[14] So, the next step is to think about the sorts of home which would be needed to enable these activities to be followed in, say, the year 2010.

Social forecasting and life-style research have much in common, including rather colourful ways of describing consumers, their buying habits and social behaviour; social forecasting endeavours to highlight factors that may develop and affect patterns of consumption in the years ahead. There is the danger of generalizing too freely, and for social forecasting to degenerate into mere crystal ball gazing. Within the accepted limitations of qualitative or so-called soft data, social forecasting should be viewed, however, as having the potential to make unique contributions to the strategic planning of a wide variety of industries and public services. It should be accepted as a legitimate partner of economic forecasting in a market culture which is increasingly difficult to interpret in economic terms alone.

According to a survey published in 1978, social forecasting is largely neglected by UK firms.[15] Only about two-thirds of respondent companies either had a systematic method of keeping informed on social trends or intended to design such a system. It is significant that all the companies which had social forecasting arrangements intended to keep them. Among the report's conclusions is the observation that social forecasting has not yet come of age, but is identifiable along with economic and technological forecasting as an input into corporate planning.

15.4 SOCIAL RESPONSIBILITY OF BUSINESS

Business ethics

The fundamental shifts in attitudes and expectations that have just been discussed indicate that business activities are now viewed far more critically than a generation ago. The concept of social responsibility is being voiced in many circles: political, professional, academic, and trade unions, and also in the mass media. Industry and business practices are under close scrutiny; the essence of the business ethic is tirelessly debated; corporate behaviour is increasingly regarded with suspicion if not downright hostility. Partly because of the notorious City scandals of the 1980s and 1990s, ethical behaviour in business has become a hotly debated issue. Cynics may dismiss the concept of business ethics as a contradiction in terms: virtually an oxymoron. But the growing number of its proponents feel otherwise; businesses *can* be run efficiently and also practice ethical behaviour towards their customers and staff—a prime example is the John Lewis Partnership store group.

In the USA, courses on business ethics have been run in many colleges and universities for several years, and US business management has been active in drawing up a code of ethics.

Formal acknowledgement of the principles of business ethics in the UK was signified by the founding of the Institute of Business Ethics in October 1986 from an initiative by the Christian Association of Business Executives, supported by leaders of the Jewish and Islamic communities. The objectives of the Institute include the promotion of the 'positive aspects of wealth creation and the ethical principles which must underlie them', as well as research and publications. At Kings College, London, a Business Ethics Centre has been established, and leading business schools like Manchester and London have developed special courses on corporate ethics and business cultures.

A survey published by Edinburgh University in 1988 revealed that 42 per cent of the 74 respondents from the top 200 companies who were sampled said that they had a 'written code of ethics of some sort, setting down the company's approach towards employees, shareholders, consumers, the environment or society at large'.[16] However, although only four companies referred to the document as a 'Code of Ethics', and various other titles were used; they gave guidelines, some quite detailed, covering a range of issues such as share-dealing, hospitality, attitudes towards the environment, and so on.

Survey findings published by the Institute of Business Ethics in 1988[17] indicated that only 17 per cent of the general public rated the standards of honesty of top business people as 'high', 29 per cent rated them 'low' and 54 per cent had no opinion. These insights into public perceptions and attitudes are perturbing but, apparently, slightly more favourable than those held about national newspapers.

Earlier chapters have reflected on the complex nature of the perceptual processes, and on the ways in which people assimilate information and develop attitudes. In an age of mass communication, business malpractices are exposed rapidly to millions—a pragmatic argument in support of observing high standards of corporate behaviour, which reflect the fundamental if rather restricted motivation of self-interest. The counter-argument is based on acknowledging that ethics are at the heart of both personal lives and also corporate activities. Some of the early Victorian entrepreneurs, notably from Quaker families, combined astute business policies with committed humanitarianism.

Perceptions of marketing activities

Greyser suggested that three different models of the market-place are perceived by marketers and by consumers which may account for some of the conflicts that arise between marketers and public policy groups.[18] While no one can account for every situation, the following are *basic* views that tend to influence individual perceptions:

1. *Manipulative*: critics of marketing see it as 'persuading/seducing less-than-willing consumers to buy'. Advertising is perceived as an important and powerful one-sided weapon in this unequal battle.
2. *Service*: this pro-business model assumes that consumers are most intelligent, less

malleable, and use advertising as helpful information on available choice of products/ services. Businesses that meet the demands of these knowledgeable customers are likely to succeed.

3. *Transactional*: derived from communications research, this model projects a somewhat sophisticated consumer who takes an active role in the process of exchange, evaluating advertising, extracting useful information, and dealing with firms that will supply products which will provide attractive benefits, both functional and psychological.

Marketers should determine how they view their markets: are these projections based on objective information about how customers *actually* behave or do they derive from notions about how they *should* behave? (See Chapters 9 and 10 on buying models.) Greyser suspects that much of the criticism of advertising and marketing originates from a concept of how people *should* behave; such idealized concepts fail to recognize the mixed motivations that characterize behaviour, including buying behaviour (see Chapter 3).

The obsessive pursuit of maximum profit by highly organized entrepreneurs who prosper in a *laissez-faire* economic environment by exploiting gullible customers hardly fits with reality. Businesses satisfy rather than maximize performance; some have suggested that sub-optimal performance is probably nearer to the mark in many cases. Management of enterprises is of very variable quality; market information is often poor; the concept of *laissez faire* is clearly as outdated as the horse tram, in view of the vast expansion in government regulations of business in the areas of health and safety, employment rights, trading and advertising practices, etc. Moreover, the consumer or customer is by no means waiting to be 'taken for a ride' by the first slick merchant who comes along. Nowadays, the *transactional model* is closer to what is really happening in the market-place. This dynamic interaction between buyer and supplier characterizes behaviour in markets for many goods and services; the 'hammer-it-home' concept of advertising (as seen in Chapter 13) springs from a deficient understanding of the processes of communication.

Apart from exercising their rights as buyers—including the right to say 'No'—customers and people in general are becoming increasingly interested in the behaviour of industries and firms, and searching questions are being asked about their policies on a diverse range of issues, e.g., employment, pollution, use of energy, business practices, and community support. The feeling that business should accept some degree of social responsibility beyond those constraints imposed by legislation is growing in the UK; it has been a feature of the US economy since the late 1950s. Management decision-making should now take account of those issues in which the public at large has expressed interest and often alarm.

From the foregoing discussion, the 'rights' of industry to please itself have clearly been curtailed, and there is greater, if at times reluctant, willingness to accept that corporations are not answerable merely to their shareholders but to their work people and to society at large. As a result, costs may be increased and difficulties arise in dealing effectively with technological problems.

his cultural change has taken several years to diffuse through the boardrooms of the USA and Europe: the process of corporate readjustment is still going on. Much of the energy of this cultural challenge came from what has been popularly termed 'consumerism' which, when it first appeared in the early 1960s was 'mostly regarded by business executives as a transitory threat to be opposed at every turn by invoking ideology and denying the seriousness of the charges'.[19]

Consumerism

From virtually a one-man band in the 1960s to a sophisticated campaign organization in the 1980s, Ralph Nader has made consumerism a world-wide challenge to manufacturers of cars, domestic equipment, providers of services, etc. His sphere of interests now extends to political, economic, and social issues, although he admitted in 1980 that the consumer movement in the USA was on the defensive because of the corporate counter-attack.[20] 'The consumer–corporate relationship always goes through ups and downs'; environmental and consumer issues always slacken off whenever there is a recession or weakening of the economy. Then he was targeting multinational corporations and would examine them from 'a variety of perspectives'—worker, taxpayer, or consumer. Their role in developing countries would also be scrutinized, and while he confessed to being a 'long-time free trader', Nader thought it was objectionable on both economic and social grounds for production to be switched from the USA to low-cost centres in developing countries.

Clearly, Nader is painting on a much larger canvas than when he first achieved notoriety with his dramatic outburst against the car 'that wasn't safe at any speed'.

Consumerism, according to Bloom and Greyser, has moved through its life-cycle and has now entered the mature stage, but that does not mean it is declining or faltering.[21] Several public opinion surveys indicate that there is continuing, if latent, demand for consumer protection. Predictions of where the consumer movement is headed for differ widely; in contrast to earlier practice, consumerism will no longer be 'the exclusive domain of the traditional movement'. Many organizations are now involved in lobbying; large corporations have set up consumer affairs offices; chambers of commerce and local government have backed up federal legislation. This fragmentation is seen as 'something that will help the movement endure and overcome the failures of some of its individual organisations'.

A more restrained but still active consumer movement is predicted for the future: the public will change from their past role largely as 'cheering spectators to one of active participants'. In this new environment, businesses are seen to have three strategies open to them:

1. Accelerate the decline stage of consumerism by positive managerial action, such as improving quality of products and services, or toning down advertising claims.
2. Compete in the consumerism industry by either setting up an active consumer affairs department that really attends to complaints and offers consumer education, or by funding and/or coordinating activities 'designed to sell deregulation, reindustrialisation, and other pro-business causes'.
3. Cooperate with non-business competitors by assisting 'government agencies, non-profit organisations and coops in selling the latter groups' consumer offerings'.

Bloom and Greyser believe that the optimal approach for most businesses will contain elements of all the three strategies noted.[21]

A survey of consumer attitudes and practices in western Europe was conducted for a group of leading food-processing firms by a US market research organization in 1980.[22] It was reported that consumerism is expanding its coverage from consumer protection against faulty products and services to concern about, for example, scarce resources being used, in many cases, in the manufacture of products of perceived dubious value to society. *Consumption policy* questions whether existing patterns of production and consumption are tolerable in a society that has grown more conscious of the wastefulness of a lot of modern business practices. 'People are going to start questioning whether a detergent manufacturer really needs to produce five different brands of washing powder and then market them as apparent competitors'.

The UK Consumers' Association reacted to the findings of this survey by suggesting that emphasis on consumption policy—which is seen as a separate issue from consumer protection—may tend to simplify a complex situation. The US researchers agree that while consumer protection is a relatively straightforward concept, consumption policy has endless facets and can embrace virtually everything, from energy conservation, raw materials usage, the Third World, and ethics, to the behaviour of individual industries and firms.

This 'maturation' of consumerism appears to have become an accepted phenomenon in the 1980s and 1990s.

Environmental concerns and 'green' issues

The twin challenges of 'consumerism' and 'environmentalism' will need to be faced by industrialists, planners, and politicians in all the developed countries. Some are inherently reactive—waiting for regulations to be enforced or attitudes to harden before knowing how they will respond—while others are proactive—anticipating changes in public opinion or legislation and planning to influence these changes, so that the outcomes are favourable to them. But if proactivity is taken too far, the charge of manipulation may be made by perceptive critics. Instead of these diametrically opposed stances, an interactive approach is recommended by James E. Post of Boston University.[23] This recognizes that 'corporate goals and public goals are both changing, though not at the same rate nor even in the same direction'. Instead of waiting for new public goals to mature and then react to them or manipulate the political system to thwart any change, some firms have adopted a flexible approach that seeks to prevent public goals and emerging corporate goals from diverting too far. 'Sometimes action is taken to influence public opinion; at other times action is taken to change corporate behaviour'.

Firms should identify and evaluate the risks and opportunities in the markets in which they do business. The 'consumerist' and 'environmentalist' movements deserve as much attention today as the other market variables. In retail distribution, for instance, open dating of food products reassures customers and builds goodwill. Progressively minded store groups have now adopted this method and have found that sales have improved. The next move is towards unit pricing, which facilitates easy comparison of competitive brands of merchandise. Better sales-service arrangements are another positive way to meet the 'consumerist' challenge.

Asa Briggs speculated in 1972 on the trend in consumer psychology and the implications for marketers. There would, he declared, be a higher proportion of educated consumers, often displaying sophisticated tastes, who will have grown up in an atmosphere of modern communications. 'I take it for granted that the proportion of those who are critical of particular products and of the way that they are designed, advertised, marketed and used will increase. . . . I expect more tension, more confrontation and more counter-action'.[24] There will be a reaction in particular against wasteful use of resources and there will be a growing demand to recycle waste material. His projections are being confirmed by the research quoted earlier.

The chemical industry, for example, has attracted considerable and largely unfavourable attention in recent years. The president and chief operating officer of the Ciba-Geigy Corporation has referred to the phenomenon of 'chemophobia', which has been 'used to describe the almost spontaneous, negative response that occurs when people hear the words chemicals and chemical company'.[25] Chemophobia is perceived to have significantly affected the industry in the USA because of 'more burdensome regulations', higher costs and reduced productivity, shorter effective patent life, lower returns on investments, less research, and, ultimately, fewer new drugs and other 'chemical entities' introduced. Even if the pace of public regulations slackened, there are still many constraints to come through the pipeline of legislation; there is also 'the strong public sentiment against the chemical industry and against business in general'.

In 1983, *Fortune* magazine featured the dramatic accusations against the Dow Chemical Company made by local environmentalists.[26] It was alleged that this firm's predicament could be explained as much in cultural as in scientific terms. From its foundation in the late 1890s, Dow set a style that combined scientific integrity with crustiness and a disdain for amateurs'; this is echoed in the chairman's recent statement: 'We play our cards close, maybe because we have a high regard for the value of technical information. We don't back down easily or compromise. We are perceived as prickly, difficult, and arrogant'. This tough, uncompromising attitude was evident when, as the result of an accident in a Monsanto plant in 1949, a small amount of dioxin escaped and 121 workers were affected. These victims were monitored over the next 30 years and in 1980 the University of Cincinnati reported that the death rate among them was below average, and the rates of cancer and other chronic diseases were at or below normal. Dow's attempt to dismiss the dangers of dioxin by quoting results or soil samples and river pollution tests failed to appease critics, who accused it of trying to

> downplay the public health effects of dioxin. I don't understand why they think they can convince the public by having their corporate scientists say, 'This toxic chemical isn't so bad.' People just don't buy that kind of approach. Instead, why don't they say 'We recognise this is a serious problem and we're going to do everything possible to get to the bottom of it.'[27]

It is recognized that while Dow's 'policies are generally sensible and its technology is advanced, though far from perfect', its stubborn, strong-willed public posture has attracted hostile criticism, and its chairman acknowledged that there is need to improve their image. Perception, after all, is subjective, even in scientific and technical areas where few are really expert enough to provide objective assessment (see Chapters 1 and 6).

To counter the fear of synthetic chemicals and the compounds involved in their production and distribution, Ciba-Geigy propose:

1. Chemical companies should voluntarily do something about buried wastes and abandoned dumps. Nineteen companies, including Ciba-Geigy, have formed a task force to study a proposed site.
2. Attempts should be made to find common meeting ground with groups previously viewed as antagonists, e.g., the National Agricultural Chemicals Association has agreed with the Agricultural Chemicals Dialogue Group, which includes church leaders as well as environmentalists and industry representatives, on jointly developed guidelines for advertising pesticides in Third World countries. The Chemical Manufacturers Association also works closely with environmental groups on siting hazardous waste management facilities.

These new horizons of corporate responsibility are in line with those who view the modern corporation as a socio-economic institution rather than an economic entity with only incidental social responsibilities.[28] Businesses are more exposed to the public gaze and expectations of corporate behaviour have been sharpened over recent years. A survey of 260 'top managers' and 326 operating managers drawn from *Fortune*'s 500 Corporations list refuted suggestions by earlier studies that operating managers were likely to resist implementing corporate social responsibility policies.[29] There was 'little reason to suspect' that their behaviour would differ from the attitudes expressed in the survey, which coincided with those of top management. It is suggested by the researcher that managers in general seem to have come to terms with social responsibility as an element of corporate philosophy and are willing to take appropriate action to implement it.

In Britain, the Chemical Industries' Association undertakes regular surveys of public perceptions of the chemical industry. The 1987 poll found that less than one-third of people held favourable views of the chemical industry, and nearly half thought it did not care about the environment. More than 90 per cent were concerned or very concerned about chemical pollution, while over 75 per cent felt that the industry seriously damaged the environment, and more than 80 per cent of respondents worried about plant safety.[30] These concerns continued a trend that was observable in the 1980s and doubtless influenced by a number of calamitous events at chemical works, including a disastrous spillage of effluent into the Rhine from a warehouse operated by Sandoz, one of the leading Swiss chemical producers.

Tom Burke, director of the Green Alliance, has stated that three social forces interact to sharpen the difficulties facing industry as a whole: 'the growing strength of the pressure groups, the emergence of the green consumer, and the political maturing of the environment as an issue'.[30] In the early 1980s, it was estimated that membership of environmental organizations in the UK was about 3 million; these include the National Trust, World Wide Fund for Nature (formed from the World Wildlife Fund and the Friends of the Earth), and Greenpeace. Within the EU, the European Environmental Bureau includes 120 organizations from 12 countries.

Across the world, people, many of whom are organized into committed ecological groups, are alarmed about issues such as the destruction of the ozone layer and of the rain forests, acid rain, greenhouse gases, toxic waste, and river pollution. The Japanese newspaper *Asahi Shimbun* conducted a comparative survey[31] in 1990 in Japan, the USA and the former Soviet Union, in which respondents were asked which issues concerned them most. In Japan, 27 per cent of participants cited 'the environment'; in the USA, 18 per cent placed the environment in third place, after 'crime' and 'inflation'; in the former Soviet Union, 12 per cent ranked environmental issues as third, after 'inflation' and 'unemployment'. It was reported that about 80 per cent Japanese companies have already established sections to deal with environmental matters, and the government has formed a special department concerned with environmental issues.

In 1989, a survey of the British public's interest in 'green issues' identified that 42 per cent claimed 'to have consciously chosen one product over another for environmental reasons— specifically because of environmentally friendly packaging, formulation or advertising'.[32] The range of products investigated included those related to personal care, household duties, and food.

Pump-action hairspray products are increasingly demanded by consumers; enzyme and phosphate-free detergents like Ecover, which originated from Belgium, have experienced rapid sales and accounted for about 2 per cent of the UK market of £600 million in 1990. This success has attracted leading manufacturers like Procter and Gamble to this growing market segment, into which they have launched Ariel Ultra. Batteries that do not contain cadmium or mercury are now available; the demand for unleaded petrol is increasing every year, particularly because of its widespread adoption by the motor industry. In the distributive trades, major multiples like Safeway, Sainsbury, and Tesco have issued 'green' guides to their customers, and have ensured that their own-label products conform to these standards. B&Q, the large DIY chain, now sells biodegradable paint.

The apotheosis of 'greenery' is the Body Shop chain developed by Anita Roddick from a Brighton sidestreet shop in 1976. During her travels in Third World countries, she noticed that women retained smooth skins by applying raw cocoa butter; on returning to England, after a series of trials, she produced a limited range of toiletries and cosmetics made from natural ingredients, available in refillable bottles. From these humble origins, Anita Roddick's intimidating energy has driven the business forward to a multi-million pound turnover from over 1000 product lines sold in more than 600 shops across the world. Most of these are run by franchisees who have to adhere to strictly enforced standards of trading. Long before 'greenery' became espoused by the mass media, the Body Shop's philosophy of business anticipated events: from acorns mighty oaks do, indeed, grow.

Green buying policies are also evident in office supplies such as recycled photocopier paper, now marketed by Xerox and Hewlett Packard, as well as recyclable printer cartridges; both companies are reported to have introduced these products in response to pressure from their customers.[33] Among agriculturists, there has been support for organic farming methods, and for better management of effluents. But many more were also concerned about the economic consequences of abandoning pesticides and artificial fertilizers.

Anxieties have been expressed about some business activities which seem to be 'cashing-in' on the environmental crusade; for example, the Advertising Standards Authority's criticism of a large oil company which promoted its super-green petrol as causing 'no pollution of the environment', just because it was lead-free. Moreover, the lack of a legal definition of the term 'environmentally friendly' may have lead to misunderstandings about the intrinsic nature of certain products: 'recycled paper is not necessarily friendlier to the environment because much depends on where and how the paper is made'.[33]

Over 200 years ago, Adam Smith perceived that the interests of society followed naturally from the entrepreneur's concern with business success:

> generally, indeed, [he] neither intends to promote the public interest, nor knows how much he is promoting it . . . by directing that industry in such a manner as its product may be of the greatest value he intends only his own gain and he is in this, as in many other cases, led by an invisible hand to promote an end which was not part of his intention.[34]

Today, the famous 'hidden hand' is hardly likely to be strong enough to constrain the complex modern corporations which are so obviously different from Smith's classical entrepreneur.

15.5 ATTITUDES TO ADVERTISING IN BRITAIN

Since 1961, regular surveys of the public's attitudes to advertising and comparable issues in Britain have been commissioned by the Advertising Association (AA). A survey published in 1992 follows the general pattern of earlier surveys both in the methodologies used and the range of questions involved.[35] It was carried out by the British Market Research Bureau, as part of the Access Omnibus Survey, with a representative sample of the British population aged 15 years and over. A sampling technique known as GRID sampling was used; quota controls included housewives (working status); housewives (presence of children); other women; men 15–64; men 65-plus. Sampling stratification factors covered Standard Regions, commercial television areas within regions, and ACORN classification. (Fuller details of market research techniques are given elsewhere).[36]

Research questions related to three distinct aspects of advertising: its perceived importance in everyday life; basic approval or disapproval; and general reactions to different media. Respondents were asked what subjects people talked about most, subjects on which they held strong opinions, and the areas that they believed to be in need of major change.

Two lists of topics were involved; the 'old' list of twelve topics enabled direct comparisons to be made with earlier years; the 'new' list included topics that had come into prominence more recently.

'Old' list	'New' list
Advertising	Advertising
Big business	AIDS
Bringing up children	Clothing
Clothing and fashion	Drugs
Education	Education
Family life	Family life
Government	National Health Service
Professional sports	Politicians and political issues
Religion	Professional sports
Trade unions	Protecting the environment
Politicians	Trade unions
The Civil Service	Violent crime

Table 15.1   Attitude change 1972–92

	'Talked about most'						'Strongest opinions'						'Immediate attention and change'					
	72 %	76 %	80 %	84 %	88 %	92 %	72 %	76 %	80 %	84 %	88 %	92 %	72 %	76 %	80 %	84 %	88 %	92 %
Advertising	8	6	8	9	10	10	6	3	4	5	5	6	5	3	2	5	4	8
Big business	9	6	9	8	11	8	6	3	5	5	5	6	5	5	4	4	5	6
Bringing up children	45	43	41	40	43	35	29	25	25	30	27	29	11	8	9	8	12	11
Clothing and fashion	39	41	36	39	35	34	11	10	9	11	7	6	2	2	2	1	1	1
Education	44	54	53	34	40	40	32	28	30	31	35	34	24	24	23	26	32	42
Family life	57	54	53	53	57	53	31	26	26	32	26	30	6	6	5	7	8	7
Government	48	36	42	35	33	34	34	23	31	32	36	31	35	35	34	31	30	28
Professional sports	36	44	42	39	32	34	14	16	14	16	12	12	2	5	3	3	5	5
Religion	24	17	16	15	13	17	22	14	12	15	15	17	10	5	3	4	4	5
Trade unions	25	22	30	27	13	9	24	19	27	28	13	9	31	20	30	29	14	7
Politicians	n/a	22	23	25	23	30	n/a	14	13	24	19	21	n/a	15	11	17	10	18
The Civil Service	n/a	6	6	5	3	5	n/a	4	4	3	4	4	n/a	7	7	7	6	5
Other	n/a	n/a	n/a	n/a	10	14	n/a	n/a	n/a	n/a	3	8	n/a	n/a	n/a	n/a	3	6
None/don't know	3	3	3	2	2	3	8	8	8	9	8	8	13	12	10	11	12	14

Source: Advertising Association.[35]

Table 15.2   Trends in public opinion of advertising in general 1966–92

	1966	1969	1972	1976	1980	1984	1988	1992
Approve a lot	22	35	25	26	30	35	30	28
Approve a little	46	44	42	47	47	42	51	48
Disapprove a little	14	10	14	11	10	8	10	9
Disapprove a lot	11	6	10	8	6	7	3	5
Don't know	7	4	9	8	7	8*	6	10
	100	100	100	100	100	100	100	100
Approve	68	79	67	73	77	77	81	76
Disapprove	25	16	24	19	16	15	13	14
Don't know	7	4	9	8	7	8	6	10
	100	100	100	100	100	100	100	100

Source: Advertising Association.[35]

Table 15.3 Trends in opinions of types of advertising 1966–92

	1966	1972	1976	1980	1984	1988	1992
Newspapers & Magazines	%	%	%	%	%	%	%
Like	11	15	10	14	9	6	9
Quite like	30	35	29	33	28	25	27
Do not bother/don't know	44	38	49	44	51	59	55
Do not really like	9	7	6	7	8	5	6
Dislike	6	5	5	3	4	3	2
	100	100	100	100	100	100	100
TV commercials	%	%	%	%	%	%	%
Like	9	13	14	18	14	11	13
Quite like	24	30	34	32	39	41	40
Do not bother/don't know	39	33	36	34	33	33	30
Do not really like	14	12	8	9	8	9	12
Dislike	16	12	8	6	6	5	6
	100	100	100	100	100	100	100
Posters					%	%	%
Like					8	5	6
Quite like					24	21	27
Do not bother/don't know					55	62	56
Do not really like					6	6	8
Dislike					6	4	3
					100	100	100

Note: When figures do not add to 100% it is due to rounding error and/or due to the exclusion of the small proportion of 'Don't Knows'. No information on posters is available for years prior to 1984.

Source: Advertising Association.[35]

The AA report stated that 'the most striking' outcome of these inquiries was that advertising remained extremely low on people's list of concerns. Few people talked about it, fewer still held strong opinions on the subject, and only a small minority felt that any major change was needed in this area.[35] On the basis of the 'new' list, only 2 per cent of respondents in 1992 felt that advertising was in need of immediate attention and change, whereas on the 'old' list, the figure was 8 per cent—a doubling of the result for 1988 and the highest recorded figure since 1972. However, only 1 per cent of the sample felt strongly about advertising in 1992 on the basis of the more up-to-date list, but with the 'old' list of issues, 6 per cent of respondents held strong opinions about advertising—an increase of about one-sixth over 1988 but identical with feelings expressed in 1972.

Salient issues included education, family life, professional sports, clothing and fashions, and bringing up children. With the 'new' list, AIDS, drugs, education, the NHS, violent crime, and environmental protection featured strongly. It is clear that, compared with urgent issues such as AIDS, drugs, or violent crime, advertising is not a vital topic of general conversation, and does not inflame opinions in the way, for example, that political matters tend to (see Table 15.1).

Although advertising is, generally, of low salience, it is interesting to track trends in the public's opinion of advertising from 1966 to 1992. From Table 15.2 it will be seen that 76 per cent of respondents in 1992 approved of advertising in general compared with 68 per cent in 1966, although it is also evident that a slight decline in favourability has occurred since 1988. In 1966, 25 per cent of the British population disapproved of advertising, but thirty years later, this figure had declined drastically to 14 per cent. The AA report also indicated that these basic opinions do not vary greatly between sex, age, social grading, and other subsections of the sample. There was, however, a tendency for older people to have rather less favourable views of advertising than younger age-groups.

Respondents were also asked for their opinions of different types of advertising. Table 15.3 shows that TV commercials are liked by 53 per cent of those surveyed in 1992 compared with 33 per cent in 1966. Advertisements in newspapers and magazines are liked by 36 per cent in 1992 compared with 41 per cent in 1966. In common with TV advertisements, 'dislike' does not seem to reflect the opinions of many respondents. About one-third of respondents liked poster advertising but, in common with press advertising, over half were in the category of 'do not bother/don't know'.

An earlier comment[37] on people's liking for television and press advertising alluded to the fact that it was in part due to the very high standards of advertising in Britain, and also because of the efforts of the profession's Advertising Standards Authority and the other regulatory bodies, who endeavour to ensure that advertising practices are of a high standard.

Earlier studies have revealed that the strongest critics of advertising shared the following characteristics: more likely to be family centred; comparatively low exposure to advertising in terms of viewing and reading habits; politically non-radical; and concerned about materialistic values in society. Their main objection to advertising was that it tended to give a stereotyped image of life; also, family relationships were projected in unrealistic ways; and it made it seem all too easy for people to acquire products, even expensive ones.

An interesting insight into these advertising critics' perceptions was that none of them was worried about the effects of advertising on *themselves*—it was entirely focused on how *others* could be affected. It was conceded, however, that 'some advertising is necessary'. What people in general found objectionable in advertising was not easily determined because different people gave different reasons. Very few said that advertising was misleading; where it was regarded as offensive related to very specific cases; virtually no one saw it as harmful or wasteful; and intrusiveness did not appear to concern them.

15.6 EFFECTS OF GADGETRY ON VIEWING OF TV ADVERTISEMENTS

The viewing of television commercials is now subject to the use of remote control devices and video recorders. In November 1982 exploratory research was undertaken to assess how much these accessories influenced viewing habits, specifically the use of remote controls to switch channels in commercial breaks; the degree to which commercials were eliminated by using the video pause button when recording or through use of the fast-forward button in later viewing; and the extent to which Teletext is consulted during commercial breaks.[38]

Television was found to be the main, and sometimes the only, source of entertainment in most homes, with the set switched on almost continuously. Remote controls tend to be regarded as male gadgets to be operated during 'boring' programmes and in commercial breaks. In general, the pause button of video recorders was considered 'fiddly', but the fast-forward button was extensively used. Teletext is again viewed mostly as of male interest and is not often used during advertising time, but remote control and video recorder optional controls 'are used quite extensively to avoid seeing commercials'. The researchers emphasized that the study was necessarily confined to individuals who had these devices, and they were not at the time typical of the general population. Also, their present behaviour may not be maintained or, indeed, represent that of future users. Bearing these valid points in mind, this pilot investigation is useful in indicating that viewers are taking the initiative that these devices offer them, and choosing whether or not to view advertisements.

15.7 ADVERTISING UNDER CRITICISM

In view of its high visibility and intrusive nature, it is not surprising that advertising in particular has been the focus of harsh criticism both in the USA and in Europe. A survey of *Harvard Business Review* subscribers found that business people in general acknowledged the strong economic functions of advertising, but were now more inclined to question sharply the impact and role of advertising as a social force.[39]

Greyser has referred to the 'irritation factor' in advertising which seems to be related particularly to television commercials.[40] He observed that in both the UK and the USA, soap and detergent advertising was the most disliked class of product; others 'high scoring' in irritation in the USA were toothpaste, mouthwashes, deodorants, foundation garments, and proprietary medicines. Reactions to specific advertisements appeared to be influenced by product usage and brand preference:

> For example, U.S. consumers dislike only 21% of the advertisements for those products they *use*, whereas consumers dislike 37% of advertisements for products they *don't* use, only 7% of advertisements for one's favourite brand are disliked compared with no less than 76% for 'brands I wouldn't buy'. . . . These American data are supported, albeit less strongly, by U.S. findings'.[40]

Although brand preference is seen as 'a very important correlate of liking advertisements for that brand', Greyser pointed out that causality can be argued both ways: liking an advertisement may lead to purchase, or purchase may lead to greater attention to and liking for the advertisement featuring the purchased brand.

Another source of irritation was revealed to derive from the 'sheer frequency with which a given commercial is shown'.[40] This reaction was more marked when several brands in a product class used similar advertising themes. Mass media communications, such as television, inevitably expose many people to messages of 'perceived irrelevance'. Greyser outlined an 'irritation life-cycle' of an advertising campaign, and suggested that the sequence seemed 'plausible albeit with different consumers moving through some of all of its stages more or less quickly under different conditions'.

1. Exposure to the message on several occasions prior to serious attention (given some basic interest in the product).
2. Interest in the advertisement, on either substantive (informative) or stimulus (enjoyment) grounds.
3. Continued but declining attention on such grounds.
4. Mental 'timeout' on grounds of familiarity.
5. Increasing re-awareness of the advertisement, now as a negative stimulus, i.e. irritant.
6. Growing irritation.

Greyser proposed that companies might well consider including the degree of irritation, and its relation to the effectiveness of their advertising, in research programmes. An 'irritation index' may be a useful measure of audience reaction.

15.8 MASS MEDIA TRENDS

The mass media in Britain are highly organized, complex, and unrivalled in national coverage. Rapid change is occurring as new technological advance and electronic-based media diffuse; home viewers, at the touch of a button, will be able to summon up whatever takes their fancy: cookery, gardening, sport, news commentaries, religion, industrial and commercial knowledge, health information, children's entertainments, various kinds of music programmes, feature films, etc. Some of these programmes will be supported by advertising and offered free to viewers; some will be paid by subscription, while others will be on a 'pay-as-you-view' basis.

Traditionally, there has always been considerable choice *inside* a medium, such as the press, but of recent years options *across* media have widened significantly in Britain. With the advent of radio and, later, television, mass media started to move from being dominantly paper-based to their present dynamic state which is increasingly electronic-based. However, print continues to be an important element of the mass media; a glance at British Rate and Data Guide (BRAD) will confirm that amazing diversity of journals still available today, although not all are prospering.

The combined circulations of the popular and quality national daily newspapers in Britain was 16.2 million in 1984 and fell by about 7 per cent to 15.1 million in 1990. This negative trend was not, however, evenly distributed: 'qualities' actually increased 10 per cent over this period of time: from 2.4 million in 1984 to 2.6 million in 1990, whereas the sales of 'popular' dailies declined by 10 per cent from 13.8 million (1984) to 12.5 million (1990). Of the 'qualities', a new entrant was *The Independent* in 1987, whose circulation of 300 000 increased to 400 000 by 1990. The specialist journal, the *Financial Times*, achieved a remarkable 32 per cent growth over the period 1984 (218 000) to 1990 (289 000).

The overall performance of the popular Sunday newspapers fell by 7.4 per cent from 1984 to 1990, but some, such as the *Mail on Sunday* and the *News of the World*, actually increased their circulations, by approximately 18 per cent and 7 per cent respectively. The overall trend of the quality Sundays was marginally down (-2.0 per cent) over 1984 to 1990, but this decline would have been around 15 per cent had *The Independent* not launched a Sunday edition in 1990, which attained a circulation of 352 000. All the other Sunday newspapers incurred circulation losses, particularly the *Observer*, which lost over a quarter of its circulation.

In general, however, Britain remains dedicated to its newspapers, as evidenced by JICNARS statistics for July 1990 to June 1991 which indicate that 62 per cent of adults read a national newspaper and 71 per cent a national Sunday paper. Reading the national press tends to be done more by men than women, though there are distinct variations between the quality press and the popular papers, as well as different patterns of readership within these broad sectors. For example, in 1991, 55 per cent of *Mirror* readers were men, and 54 per cent of the *Sun*'s; the *Daily Mail*'s readership was 51 per cent male; *The Times* had 59 per cent male readership; both the *Daily Telegraph* and the *Guardian* had 55 per cent male readers. However, *The Independent*'s readership was 64 per cent male and the *Financial Times* readers were 76 per cent male.

The readership profiles of the national Sunday papers are less biased towards men; for example, 49 per cent of readers of the *News of the World*, 48 per cent of the *Sunday Mirror*, 49 per cent of the *People*, 49 per cent of the *Mail on Sunday*, 51 per cent of the *Sunday Express*, 48 per cent of the *Sunday Telegraph*, 45 per cent of the *Sunday Times*, and 46 per cent of the *Observer* are women. The readership profiles of the weekend colour supplements follow closely those of their respective newspapers, but there is a slight tendency for women to read these publications rather more than the papers themselves; for example, the *Sunday Times Magazine*'s readership is 46 per cent female compared with the paper's 45 per cent.

In January 1991, there were about 1330 regional newspapers, with a combined circulation of over 55 million, in the UK. Of these, approximately 40 per cent were paid-for newspapers, the rest being free newspapers. The latter journals were a significant innovation in the press media that occurred in the early 1970s; Target Group Index (TGI) reports that these are read by three out of four British adults. Critics have pointed out that one of the drawbacks of these free papers is that consumers do not regard them highly, because they come unpaid for and uninvited through their letterboxes; their level of editorial is also regarded as generally inferior to the paid-for journals; moreover, their distribution is not always reliable. However, this media innovation is now well established and, in many cases, offers the traditional press a distinct challenge in their overall design and journalistic standards. Some of the traditional press groups have, in fact, invested resources in the free newspapers, which confirms to some extent their now accepted role among the regional press.

The socio-economic profile of press readership varies, as might be expected, according to the nature of specific newspapers. ABC1 adults (see social class segmentation in Chapter 7) account for 17 per cent of the *Star*'s readers, 22 per cent of the *Sun*'s, 24 per cent of the *Mirror*'s, 42 per cent of the *Guardian*'s, 77 per cent of *The Times*'s, 82 per cent of the *Daily Telegraph*'s, and 87 per cent of both the *Financial Times*'s and *The Independent*'s readers.

The age profile of adult readers of the national press varies significantly: 43 per cent of readers of the *Daily Telegraph*, 38 per cent of the *Daily Mail*, and 34 per cent of the *Mirror* are 55 or over, contrasted with 17 per cent of *The Times*, and 16 per cent of the *Financial Times*. At the other extreme, the age-group 15–34 accounts for 2 per cent of readers of the *Daily Telegraph*, 50 per cent of the *Star*, 43 per cent of *The Times*, 49 per cent of the *Guardian*, 45 per cent of the *Sun*, 44 per cent of *The Independent*, and 38 per cent of the *Financial Times*.

The socio-economic and age profiles should be compared with the British adult population profile of 37 per cent (15–34) and 32 per cent (55-plus); and overall social class profile of 42 per cent (ABC1) and 58 per cent (C2DE). It will readily be seen, for instance, that the *Daily Telegraph* has an upmarket, ageing readership profile, whereas *The Independent* and *The Times* also have an upmarket readership but a much better balanced age-profile. The *Mirror* and the *Sun* have a similar overall readership profile: downmarket but fairly well balanced in terms of age.

The magazine market in Britain caters for an astonishing variety of interests and tastes, including romantic fiction, popular mass-circulation women's weeklies, home-interest monthly journals, special hobby and sports journals, trade, technical, business and professional publications, etc. Full details of these publications are given in British Rate and Data Guide (BRAD). Some of these publications have existed for generations, such as *Women's Weekly*, *The Lady*, *Vogue*, *Home and Gardens*, *The Economist*, or *Autocar* and *Motor*; others are relatively new, such as *Viewer Today*, or *Cycling Plus*. The mortality rate is fairly high; in 1991, 200 magazines ceased publication; these included that estimable journal, the *Listener*.

The upmarket publishers, Condé Nast, which own prestigious journals like *Vogue* and *Tatler*, and the National Magazine Company, publishers of *House Beautiful*, *Cosmopolitan*, *Good Housekeeping*, and other quality monthlies, have targeted their titles on clearly defined market segments or niches: this strategy has enabled them to survive, and even grow, in times of recession. The mass market women's weeklies, like *Woman* and *Woman's Own*, which have a more generalized appeal, have suffered circulation casualties, and appear to be more vulnerable than several of the upmarket monthlies. It should be noted that two statistics are generally quoted to indicate a publication's position: circulation and readership. The former is a certified figure issued by the Audit Bureau of Circulations (ABC) and is the result of objective, rigorous measurement; the latter is a factor of the former and is largely an estimate (see specialist text).[36]

Independent local radio (ILR), which relies for its revenue on advertising, commenced in the UK in 1973, with the opening of LBC and Capital Radio. Before that date, Radio Luxembourg was the principal commercial station broadcasting regularly to the UK. In 1991, 48 commercial radio stations were operating under licence from the Radio Authority, which took over from the Independent Broadcasting Authority in January of that year. A network of these stations now spans the principal cities and towns of the UK; listening figures are surveyed by JICRAR (Joint Industry Committee for Radio Audience Research), which estimated coverage in 1991 to be just over 43 million adults. The BBC also operates a local network of radio stations, but these are not financed from advertising; they make an appreciable contribution to the social and cultural life of the localities they serve.

Cable transmission

As a medium, cable television is not unique as a method of transmitting broadcasts. In the late 1920s in Britain, landlines were laid to provide better radio reception for homes in locations, such as behind hills, which had difficulty in receiving direct broadcasts. Later, these pioneer networks were modernized so that they could handle more radio programmes and, in time, television broadcasts.

Following the recommendations of the Pilkington Committee on the future of broadcasting, the first experiment in pay-TV was organized in Sheffield and south London. This scheme offered subscribers films and exclusive sporting events and was successful as a service. However, it was eventually closed down due to pressure from the BBC, the then ITA, and the Post Office. Further experiments were conducted in 1973 with 'community cable television' which provided a few hours of local interest programmes. No extra charge was levied but this scheme was also abandoned because of financial stringencies.

In 1982, the Hunt Committee Report of the Inquiry Into Cable Expansion and Broadcasting Policy opened the way for legislation to permit the expansion of the cable network, which was currently operating on a two-year experimental period. The Cable Bill was passed; the Cable Authority was set up in 1984 and awarded 11 operating franchises. The Cable Authority had responsibility for granting further franchises, and significant powers to regulate the cable industry and to maintain programme standards. In 1991, it was absorbed into the new Independent Television Commission, which is responsible for the allocation of all broadcasting licences in the UK.

The cable systems will typically serve about 100 000 homes; an installation charge is made and then basic cable subscribers pay a monthly subscription according to the number and type of channels accessible. Extra monthly fees would give access to 'premium' channels carrying feature films, etc.

The government is keen that cable television should develop in the UK, as it is seen to be a vital part of the information technology infrastructure as well as providing greater choice of entertainment, with the prospect of a range of interactive data services becoming available in time, e.g., tele-retailing and tele-banking, as well as home–office links. Also, the development of cable television is perceived in official circles as a stimulus to the equipment manufacturing industry in the UK.

Predictions on the future of cable television in the UK tend to be cautious. Much will depend, of course, on the attraction of programmes and the prices charged to subscribers. A report by J. Walter Thompson forecast that by the beginning of 1990 between 5 and 15 per cent of UK homes would be paying for extra services via cable; these services would include satellite relays, existing cable systems, and new wideband cable systems.[41] The most likely penetration for cable is considered to be around 10 per cent, but if 15 per cent is reached, then this would have a noticeable effect on commercial television audiences and inflate the cost per viewer of commercial air time. This view was also shared in 1983 in an assessment of cable and satellite television given in the *Financial Times*: 'Although many believe the contrary, it would be surprising if cable and satellite, taken together, left much of the 1983 structure of UK TV intact in, say, 15 years' time'.[42] Another projection was that by 1990, 65 per cent of UK homes would be passed by cable, and 30 per cent would buy cable services.[43,44]

However, some possible constraints have affected the rate of diffusion: for example, the high penetration of video recorders (estimated to be in 37 per cent of British homes in 1986 and 62 per cent in 1990—an increase of over 50 per cent), and the large number of rented sets. Such an apparently price-sensitive market as cable will doubtless be affected by other demands on disposable income. The actual progress of cabling UK homes has not lived up to the optimistic estimates quoted: in July 1991, only 1.9 per cent of homes were connected to any cable system (20 per cent of homes passed), which includes blocks of flats connected to an antenna, and old-fashioned television rental systems which have been upgraded to carry at least some of the new satellite channels. A year later, 2.45 per cent of UK homes were connected but, as the Independent Television Commission noted, the growth in cable connections slowed down in the first half of 1993, because of the effects of the recession on consumer spending.

Earlier, JICCAR (Joint Industry Committee for Cable Audience Research) had reported that the actual number subscribing to multi-channel or broadband networks had risen from 116 759 in October 1990 to 220 728 in October 1991—an impressive increase of 89 per cent. This upward trend was certainly in marked contrast to earlier market behaviour, and has been significantly influenced by the arrival in the UK of large North American telephone companies and cable operators, who were willing to invest heavily in order to develop demand. Southwestern Bell International, one of the four Baby Bell US telephone companies involved in the UK cable television industry, has franchises covering 1.25 million homes in the north-west and the west Midlands, was reported in 1991 as being optimistic about cable in the UK and expected their UK cable business to be profitable in four or five years.[45] But a more conservative view was taken by Aberdeen Cable, which has about 13 500 subscribers, a penetration rate of 14.5 per cent (penetration rate is the ratio between homes that have cable television available to them and those that actually subscribe). It is felt that it may take ten years to achieve penetration rates of 30–35 per cent in Britain: in the USA more than 50 per cent of homes have cable television.

Although the modern broadband or multi-channel systems achieved almost 1.5 per cent penetration rate of UK homes in 1992 (about 21 per cent of homes passed), of the 2 327 257 UK homes which could feasibly subscribe to broadband systems, only 473 415 opted to do so by July 1993—a disappointing adoption rate of 20.3 per cent.

Cable television advertisements are subject to the Code of Advertising Practice of the Independent Television Commission (see Chapter 14). Sponsored programmes are more evident on terrestial television—the 14 regional television companies in the UK.

A lucrative new market is being opened up by the TV cable companies—telephone services through cable television networks. Cable telephony is already operating in the USA and also in some regions of the UK.

In principle, the Hunt report favoured advertising on cable, but the industry was expected not to rely entirely on advertising revenues, which should be reducing its costs to the benefit of both programmers and operators. The IPA estimated that cable TV could attract, at 1980 prices, £120 million in advertising revenue by 1995, but this figure is viewed circumspectly by some, who point out that if a relatively high penetration rate is achieved by cable and advertising revenue as a whole does not increase significantly, then some degree of cannibalization of other advertising media will be likely.[43] The Advertising Association, in fact, were more guarded in their submission to the Hunt Committee: 'We have to point out that advertising money is finite and governed by a multiplicity of commercial factors. It cannot necessarily be expected to accommodate new media as they occur'.[46] JWT believe that cable will offer new opportunities for national and regional advertisers but the 1980s will be a time for experiment rather than substantial investment.[41]

A perceptive view of the need for expert marketing if cable is to be successful in the UK is given by a McKinsey consultant in *Marketing*.[47] He points out that 'the most sophisticated operators' in the US employ sales teams 'which move down the street as the cable is connected, selling packages of channels designed specifically to appeal to particular ethnic and demographic groups'. In the UK, the general practice appears to be that households are offered 'tiered' channels, made up of a 'basic' tier 'which contains inexpensive programming of dubious quality', plus 'premium' channels which are more expensive and can be selected by the subscribers. 'Tiering' achieved some success in the USA, but penetration rates fell as tiers became more complex. 'Most importantly, the cable operator loses the ability to provide a brand image for the service as a whole'. Packaging of attractive mixes of channels also reduces the complexity of decision making by prospective subscribers.

The diffusion rate of cable is observed to be likely to be considerably influenced by word-of-mouth advertising and social contacts: 'Children are . . . a major source of radiating reference' (see Secs 8.5, 11.7, and 13.8).

Adoption strategies need to be carefully planned; it is suggested that the 'entry ticket' to cable should be attractively priced and a free trial period offered. Through skilful marketing, cable television could become widely accepted, but innovation strategies must be expertly planned.

In 1960, there were 600 cable systems in the USA; in 1984, there were 6000. In 1970, 7 per cent homes had cable television; by 1984, 37 per cent subscribed, of which pay cable had the dominant share (54 per cent) and carried no advertising. The level of viewing in pay-cable households is higher at all times of the day than the basic-cable and non-cable households. Nielsen predicted that by 1990, about 75 per cent of homes in the USA would subscribe to cable services and the greatest increase would be in the pay-cable sector.[48] Nearly 25 per cent of the US homes now receive 12 or more stations; if cable, video games, and VCR are included, almost one-third of homes receive 12 or more channels.

Another sector which is 'just starting to evolve' is pay-per-view, which is said to be like buying a ticket for a specific event. Nielson believed that this system, which carries no advertising, could be yet another way of 'luring the viewer away from commercial-carrying fare'.[48] In the UK, the Hunt Committee recommended that pay-per-view should not be permitted at present.

The growth of cable in the USA was observed to be slow until 1975 when copyright problems were resolved, more capital was invested, and new networks were found to distribute programmes by satellites;[48] these satellite-delivered ('superstations') cable networks are likely to grow fast. Cable television in the USA is in a new stage of its life-cycle; many firms have left the scene, and a more professional approach is now focused on running profitable businesses.

Direct broadcast satellites (DBS)

This transmission system delivers television programmes direct to viewers within a satellite's 'footprint' who have their own 'dish' receiver (a parabolic shaped antenna). It is projected that this sytem will be the most important source of TV programmes by the end of the twentieth century. In November 1990, the two major competitors in the UK, Sky Television and British Satellite Broadcasting, merged to form BSkyB and thus significantly reduced the extremely heavy operational losses that had been incurred. Currently, there are three direct-to-home (DTH) satellites providing English language programmes; in addition, ethnic minorities are being offered specific programmes by satellite. In 1991, about 6 per cent of UK homes had adopted satellite television systems.

In the UK, a project called UNISAT is a joint venture between British Telecom, British Aerospace, and GEC Marconi to develop satellite broadcasting equipment, and the BBC is allying with the independent TV companies to operate two DBS channels in the late 1980s; one will offer first-run feature films to subscribers, while the other will go free to those having dish receivers.

The 1983 *Financial Times* review (quoted earlier) considered that DBS is 'in its infancy technically and operationally, but its basic simplicity and universality will probably make it an ideal means of national and international programme distribution'.[42] Together, cable and satellite transmissions challenge the status quo of traditional television operators. In the USA, Nielsen report that the cable operators and independent stations have gained audience at the expense of the broadcast networks.[48]

Undoubtedly, the design and costs of roof-top dishes on satellite subscribers' homes will be modified in time and encourage diffusion of the system. While at present DBS and other delivery systems using satellites and dishes are said to be unlikely to offer a serious threat to cable, the imminent introduction in the USA of new high-powered satellites could turn DBS into a real challenge to cable.[49]

Other electronic media

Video discs, video cassette recorders, Teletext, and videotext were in growing use and contributing to the sophisticated life-styles of the 1980s and 1990s. Modern communities, it is said, will have a 'wired-up' culture, with households possessing a home communication system that will receive transmissions from diverse sources, such as satellites providing local, national, and international coverage, and programmes via optical fibre cable. Home computers will be linked with these sophisticated systems so that programmes can be selected at will. Systems will be interactive, enabling viewers to respond instantly to programmes and commercials. Advertisers could learn quickly what effects their commercials were having on viewers. Specific product information may be requested by interested viewers, so that advertising becomes actively participative.

The future for mass media will be exciting, competitive, and complex. The laser, optical disc, fibre optics, and micro-technology will add new media opportunities and, inevitably, considerable risks. Diffusion and assimilation of these new media will not be easily determined; marketing strategies must take account of new life-styles which will be fashioned by these novel developments. People will have wider choice of television programmes—but how much more, if any, will they view? Although, as Nielsen observed, new technologies make change possible, they cannot bring it about themselves. 'Deep-seated socio-economic factors will, in the final analysis, be the major determinants'.[50] The micro-electronic revolution has already had a major impact on people's lives and led to new industries like the semi-conductor from which microprocessors, word processors, electronic computers, electronic measuring instruments, advanced telecommunications, photocopiers, and robotics have derived.

Traditional patterns of employment, product design, and product availability have been radically changed by these 'high-tech' industries. Electronics have simplified design and production; it has also reduced the demand for labour in many factories; digital watches, for example, had a disastrous effect on the Swiss watch-making industry, while microprocessors used in cameras, cash registers, and sewing machines have resulted in more reliable, compact products but also widespread labour redundancies. With amazing rapidity, electronics has transformed many industries; among these, the mass media businesses are now experiencing the dynamics of change.

15.9 TRENDS IN SHOPPING

The retail sector of the service industries of the UK is big business: it represents about one-quarter of GDP, and employs around one-tenth of the working population in stores of various types and sizes, of which there are about 340 000. Over the years 1985–90, the volume of weekly retail sales increased, in real terms, by just over 20 per cent; household goods experienced the largest increase in sales—37 per cent.

Concentration is a particularly marked feature of retail turnovers; of the 340 000 outlets, in 1988, 19 per cent were owned by large multiples, but they accounted for 61 per cent of total retail sales of around £115 000 million. This dominant position has been achieved through creative merchandising, heavy promotion, tight cost control, strategic locations, and aggressive buying power. In addition, the multiples have shrewdly moved upmarket, offering ranges of products likely to appeal to dual income families and the growing numbers of young professionals (see Chapter 8).

The abolition of resale price maintenance in 1964 accelerated the pace of competition in the retail trade as a whole, but was particularly effective in consumer durables, such as white goods (washing machines, refrigerators, etc.) and grocery products.

Membership of the European Union has also affected trends in retailing and in patterns of consumption. The hypermarket method of retailing, popular in France for several years, was introduced into Britain; car ownership has become widespread and has encouraged the development of out-of-town shopping centres which offer consumers easy car-parking, keen prices, and an increasing variety of goods, ranging from groceries, car accessories, electrical appliances, carpets, DIY products, and garden/leisure products. These mammoth-sized stores are almost all owned by a very small number of store groups, such as Tesco, B&Q, Asda and, more recently, Marks and Spencer. Many of these retail stores are located in specially planned environments incorporating recreational facilities, so that the shopping trip can become a family outing. The foundation and rapid growth of these out-of-town retail centres has been viewed by local authorities with mixed feelings, often fearing that high streets may become mere shadows of their former bustling activities. It would seem, however, that superstores tend to become accepted as part of a general retailing pattern, and in many instances encourage the development of small specialist shops selling ladies' fashions, gifts and greetings cards, and similar high-value goods.

Pedestrianized central shopping areas which are largely free of wheeled traffic, are now to be found in many cities and towns, and originated in the redevelopment of Coventry's city centre after the wartime Blitz. There is also a growing trend for large stores to divide selling space into shops-within-shops in an endeavour to 'personalize' business and cut costs. Often, space is rented or allocated to manufacturers who supply their own sales staff. This trend may develop to the stage where large retail organizations provide a building and services, and the responsibility of stocking and selling merchandise will be arranged by franchise. Manufacturers who wish to avail themselves of these prime selling sites are expected to contribute to the overall publicity campaigns for individual stores.

Large shopping malls on the North American model are also in many cities and towns in Britain; in Manchester, for example, the Arndale Centre occupies a prime site in the city centre, and has extensive shopping facilities. These include several small shops whose goods exemplify niche retailing.

Concentrated buying power is an established feature of some retail sectors, such as grocery where, in 1988, five major multiples accounted for over 60 per cent of total turnover in the UK. In 1950, 23 per cent of grocery sales were handled by the cooperatives, 57 per cent by independents, and 20 per cent by multiples (10 or more branches). From Table 15.4 it will be seen that, in 1988, multiples represented 8.5 per cent of shops but nearly three-quarters of total grocery turnover. Although comparatively fewer stores were operated by multiples in 1988 than in 1971, their share of total turnover increased by two-thirds, partly due to sales of higher-value products by many of these groups who are following a policy of strategic repositioning. But it is also evident that this trend, although significant, was less marked between 1982 and 1988.

The growth of large retail stores has generally resulted in less emphasis on personal

Table 15.4 Grocery sales in Britain, 1971, 1982, and 1988

	1971		1982		1988	
	Turnover %	Shops %	Turnover %	Shops %	Turnover %	Shops %
Cooperatives	13.2	7.4	13.1	7.3	10.9	5.4
Multiples	44.3	10.4	64.7	8.2	73.9	8.5
Independents	42.5	82.2	22.2	84.5	15.2	86.1

Source: Information for this table was supplied through correspondence of Peter M. Chisnall with A. C. Nielsen.

relationships with their customers and suppliers. Shoppers are unlikely to feel strong personal loyalties to the management of a large store whom they have probably never met, whereas the small shopkeeper was personally known to them and shopping had an element of social satisfaction. The traditional 'corner shop' has virtually disappeared under the barrage of price cutting from the highly organized supermarkets. But the retailing wheel appears to be turning and in many towns the small 'neighbourhood store' has reappeared, often run by industrious Asian families who are prepared to keep their shops open from early morning until late at night. Convenience is rated rather higher than price by their customers.

The independents, shown in Table 15.4 to have had 15 per cent of grocery sales in the UK in 1988, have seen this shrink to barely 12 per cent by November 1992—the lowest in western Europe—but they are determined to fight hard for their survival. Nisa Today's, the largest association of independent supermarkets and wholesalers, was founded in the late 1960s and negotiates bonuses and discounts with suppliers for its 718 members. It is now forming a central buying consortium in order to develop further their strong bargaining position with leading food manufacturers. Considerable buying economies are also planned by rationalization of own-label products bought by member companies. How far these initiatives will succeed in regaining the serious loss of market share suffered by independents over the past decades is problematical.

The growth of own-label, and own-brand goods has been significant, although it has long been the trading practice of stores like Marks and Spencer and Sainsbury; the latter introduced 1300 new private-label lines in 1990.[51] Multiples increasingly promote their own-label products in extensive advertising campaigns like Tesco's extra advertising expenditure of £13.5 million in 1990 supporting private-label merchandise. With the increased price sensitivity of consumers, own-label brands stocked by leading stores offer attractive economies, and are challenging the long-held dominance of the large manufacturers. How far own-label products will penetrate the packaged grocery market will depend on their matching or surpassing the qualities offered by the highly promoted brands and, at the same time, being able to maintain realistic price advantages to shoppers. The risk factor in buying has traditionally influenced brand awareness and loyalty (see Chapter 9); however, perceptions are likely to be favourably influenced by the reputation of leading store groups, like Safeways, who are confidently marketing a widening range of own-label products.

For retailers, own-label products help to establish store loyalty as distinct from loyalty to manufacturers' brands. Resistance to own-label growth is likely to be stiffest where there are very strong manufacturers, heavy advertising, and salient brand loyalty, as with detergents, pet foods, breakfast cereals, and confectionery.

'Generics' are basic food and grocery products (such as washing-up liquids, instant coffee, or tinned pet foods) which are offered without expensive packaging. The concept originated in the

1970s by Carrefour, the French hypermarket group, and appeared in the USA later in that decade. It was introduced in the UK by the International Stores group in 1979; they dropped this type of product in the early 1980s when it reported that generics had 'developed the image of being goods of adequate quality but certainly no match for own labels and brands'.[52] Generics, which are viewed by Simmons and Robertson as merely a variation of own labels account for about 1 per cent of all grocery turnover and about 2.5 per cent of all packaged groceries.[53]

In economy-conscious times, the attraction of generics and own-label products to shoppers is apparent from the fact that they accounted for about 24 per cent of Fine Fare's total turnover in 1983, and in conjunction with the 'pack your own' theme, penetration is projected to rise to around 45 per cent.[52] Trade attitudes towards the future for generics are distinctly different; supporters see generics as fulfilling a useful role along with own labels in providing extra benefits to consumers; antagonists view generics as more of a gimmick, of low quality, and inappropriate to their store image.

Retailers must obviously be careful in balancing the range and quality of products they offer for sale. Too far in one direction, e.g., own-label products, might well discourage product innovation by branded suppliers, lead to problems in obtaining adequate supplies of products both branded and unbranded, and possibly produce boredom among their customers, for whom price is not necessarily the prime factor in buying. Also, retailers who dedicate significant proportions of their stores to own-label merchandise must necessarily increase their marketing efforts to ensure that as the price differential between manufacturers' brands and their own store labels narrows, customers will continue to buy at their stores.

US firms like Avon Cosmetics have popularized 'home selling' of cosmetics and toiletries so that social contacts are turned to personal profit. This cultural import now seems to be an established feature of direct selling, and is principally focused on younger, lower-middle-class women. 'Party' selling is another American method that has been successfully practised in Britain for some years. 'Tupperware' is a well-known example of this mode of selling.

Traditional mail-order operations and target markets have changed radically; once largely patronized by lower-middle and working classes, catalogue selling has developed specialized merchandise aimed at the higher socio-economic groups; for example, the Swedish firm, IKEA's modern ranges of furniture and household goods are sold through their out-of-town stores and also by mail-order catalogue. The wider adoption of home telephones and credit cards has added to the impetus of mail-order selling in the 1980s and 1990s.

Direct selling 'off page' boomed for a few years in the upmarket Sunday colour magazines, but more recently the business is much reduced, and some over-trading appears to have taken place.

Rapid diversification has characterized the large retail chains; for example, W. H. Smith, Boots, and Tesco have developed widely from their original bases. DIY retailing has attracted investment by Woolworths, W. H. Smith, and other large groups. Discount stores like Comet have had a significant impact on radio, television, and household durables retailing.

Trading stamps, once strongly evident in retail distribution, are largely outmoded by fierce price cutting and extensive consumer advertising campaigns.

Retail and mail-order advertising expenditure increased, in real terms, by just over 50 per cent in 1990 compared with 1985; this excludes the very large sums spent on various other kinds of promotional activities. Of the top 100 UK advertisers listed by MEAL (Media Expenditure Analysis Ltd) in 1990, no fewer than 18 were retail organizations accounting for nearly £270 000 million, of which the Kingfisher Group (Woolworths, Comet, Superdrug, etc.) represented £47 264 million.

Because of their strategic buying power, many large retailers have been able to negotiate with their suppliers to transfer an agreed percentage of promotional budgets to boost the stores' advertising campaigns.[54] Manufacturers have not universally welcomed this initiative by the stores groups, although there is a trend towards giving 'advertising allowances' directly connected with exclusive featuring of certain branded products. Clearly, the opportunities for bargaining will be influenced by the market share and degree of brand loyalty of specific products.

Franchising as a retail activity was introduced to the UK by J. Lyons and Co., in 1955, when they founded the Wimpy hamburger chain, based on an original concept from the USA. Since the mid-1950s, many other franchisors have developed dynamic networks of franchisees: McDonalds, Kentucky Fried Chicken, Dyno-Rod, and Prontaprint. In 1984, less than £1 billion of turnover was attributable to franchise outlets; in 1990, this figure had multiplied almost fivefold, 'with consistent year on year increases of approximately 25%'.[55] Anita Roddick, founder of the Body Shop, has pursued a creative strategy of franchising on a worldwide basis. Others of the more than 1000 companies in the UK which have adopted a franchising strategy in order to develop further their businesses, include Clarks Shoes Ltd, Thorntons plc, Pronuptia Young Ltd, and the Swinton Group.

Computer-linked distribution systems

Computer-linked distribution systems involving centralized warehouses with tightly controlled stock levels, laser-operated check-out points, electronic funds transfer at point of purchase, in-store banks, flexible systems of payment, widespread acceptance of credit cards (including own-store cards), and higher levels of store design have all added to the dynamic of retail trading.

Teleshopping

'Teleshopping has been touted as being just around the corner for many years, but in Britain the development . . . has been extremely slow'.[56] It is essentially one of several new transaction services, such as telebanking, and often referred to as telematic services. The development of teleshopping was closely associated with Prestel, the computerized visual information system operated by British Telecom. For several reasons, this videotext system has not been widely accepted by consumers:

1. Product information available from the system is severely limited compared with physical shopping.
2. Selection may be restricted because only a few, generally large, retailers have adopted the system; further restrictions may arise from the narrowness of product/service listings.
3. If more than a few items are offered, viewers have to 'wade through a cumbersome series of menus' before eventually locating the desired product.
4. Following an extended search, frustration may arise because the desired products or services are unavailable.
5. Delivery of ordered goods may pose problems, including arranging suitable times, for some customers.
6. Some viewers may have difficulty reading videotext information, which is inevitably rather cramped on a small television or home computer screen.

Some successful trials of teleshopping have been conducted with housebound and disabled people in the UK, but it is reported that 'affluent and busy people, who spend enough money to provide a valuable basis for commercially-oriented teleshopping, are really most interested in using such a service to relieve themselves of routine, low-value shopping, and can somehow find time to shop for high-value items'.[56] However, in France, the 'Caditel' system on Minitel has indicated that there is a market for teleshopping for routine grocery products. But the French system has been promoted extensively, and terminals are provided free-of-charge.

In the USA, however, television shopping has been big business since the late 1970s; Home Shopping Network and QVC, the two largest US teleshopping companies, accounted for total sales of $2.7 billion (£1.5 million) in 1992. The former company's 7 days a week, 24-hour shopping presentations on US cable television network are viewed by around 60 million homes, while the latter, and younger, company reaches 47 million homes. In Britain, during October 1993, the first 24-hour television shopping channel was launched by BSkyB—the satellite broadcasting organization controlled by Rupert Murdoch's News Corporation—and QVC, the US television shopping specialists. This joint venture aims to introduce the well-established American television shopping habit, modified to attract the interests of British audiences, and available to subscribers of BSkyB's new multichannel package. QVC (Quality, Value and Convenience) targets higher spending shoppers in the UK, as distinct from US television shoppers, who tend to have below-average incomes. This retail shopping innovation is likely to draw other operators into offering similar services, although the heavy investment involved may discourage ready competition.

As far as Prestel is concerned, the rate of diffusion is distinctly slow and dependent on massive investment, the widespread availability of user-friendly domestic equipment, the negotiation of satisfactory pricing policies, and the extent to which public authorities may be willing and able to support videotext systems to aid disabled and elderly people and other special groups.

Another aspect of teleshopping that may impede its progress is inherent in the system, i.e., its impersonal nature. For many consumers, shopping is a socio-cultural as well as an economic activity. It provides them with opportunities for self-expression, for satisfying their curiosity (see Chapter 3), and for gathering new ideas and information, perhaps through meeting friends and others while shopping. Products can be assessed visually and also tactilely; the senses reinforce the impact of personal shopping; garments can be tried on; food may be sampled, and so on.

Although to some, shopping may be tedious and even resented, to others it is a welcome excursion, as the large shopping centre operators shrewdly recognize by including attractive cafés and play areas in landscaped environments. Families and friends may arrange to meet, and spend hours together, looking at new fashions, examining the latest types of gadgetry, or assessing the relative values of carpets and curtains. Shopping may become virtually a leisure activity and, to some degree, even a sport, in the sense that educated, sophisticated, and well-versed shoppers may enjoy searching for and evaluating competing products and services. Perhaps it is a modern-day version of the bargaining that brought life and laughter to the fairs and markets of medieval Britain.

Throughout this book, the complexity of buying behaviour has been discussed and illustrated; shopping is more than obtaining the 'necessities of life', or acquiring products and services which may be perceived by others as conspicuous. The concepts of life-style (Chapter 6), family life-cycle and group membership (Chapter 8), willingness to innovate and try new kinds of products and services (Chapter 11), and other factors impinge on shopping habits and affect the ways in which people of all socio-economic groupings seek to satisfy their many needs.

Household expenditure patterns have also changed over the years. As the standard of living has risen, relatively less is spent by consumers on food, while significantly greater amounts of money are devoted to leisure pursuits, communications, etc. Expenditure on food (in real terms) increases only marginally, whereas, for example, housing, alcoholic drink, entertainment, and motor vehicle running costs all showed very marked increases in expenditure. This significant trend has been reflected in retail distribution, where, for instance, traditional grocery businesses have extended their ranges of merchandise.

The large retail groups have been able to exert their very considerable buying power in attracting from manufacturers promotional allowances as well as bigger discounts. Retailers as a whole now spend far more than manufacturers on media; the gap is widening perceptibly each year.

With increased spending power and social mobility, the profile of customers of certain types of retail stores has changed. Some department stores have repositioned themselves in the market in order to attract a wider range of customers. Discerning store managers have noted the growing influence of women shoppers who now take a much more active role in selecting products of many kinds (see Chapters 7, 8, and 13).

15.10 HEALTHY, WEALTHY, AND WISE

The old nursery jingle has a new impact on the food trade: eating wisely and well means, to an increasing number of people, avoiding animal fats, sugar, salt, and various food additives, and deliberately choosing high-fibre foods, skimmed milk, polyunsaturated margarine, and so on. Health foods are no longer bought just by cranks and faddists. 'Eating for health' is catching on and its enthusiasts have made health foods a steadily growing sector of the food market. Nutrition and diet continue to be featured regularly in the mass media, and the dangers of saturated fats are now well known. Margarine, once poor people's substitute for butter, is now regarded as a wise way to health. People have moved up Maslow's hierarchy (see Chapter 3): food is no longer consumed to appease hunger, it is carefully chosen to ensure that vigour and health are maintained.

Vegetarian food is attracting much wider support than ever before, not only from professed vegetarians but also from increasing numbers of omnivores who have decided to vary their diets and reduce the intake of animal protein. It is estimated that around 10 per cent of the UK population have eliminated red meat from their diets, and about 9 million eat vegetarian meals three or more times per week.[57] More children than adults are vegetarian: the gradual disappearance of the 'family meal' because of changing life-styles, television viewing, and other factors such as the widespread adoption of microwave ovens (in over 50 per cent of British homes in 1990), have all encouraged the younger generation to develop their own eating preferences, which are often for non-meat dishes. The diffusion of vegetarianism will, therefore, be likely to be accelerated by the willingness of young consumers to adopt innovatory foods which are now being marketed by companies such as Heinz, Baxters, and Golden Wonder.

Healthy eating is becoming an attractive business proposition for some of the large food producers and distributors. In the breakfast cereals market, muesli and bran foods have become standard mass-demand products, supplied by companies like Kelloggs, Quaker, and Weetabix. Wholemeal products (bread, flour, pasta, spaghetti, and biscuits) are also appearing on grocery shelves after many years of quiet sales through specialist health food shops.

Sugar-free products are attracting the attention of consumers and also some large food manufacturers, such as Kelloggs, who have launched no-sugar muesli, and Del Monte, who market tinned fruit without syrup and a range of salt-free vegetables. Low-sodium salt is offered through grocery outlets; Kelloggs are marketing low-sodium cornflakes. Supermarkets routinely stock foods previous available only in specialist shops—pulses, lentils, sunflower oil, herbs, compost-grown cereals, etc. Decaffeinated tea and coffee have attracted sufficient consumer interest to ensure that they appear on supermarket shelves, supported by national brand advertising campaigns.

Chemists sell health foods on a wider scale; to some extent this new range of products compensates for the increasing competition they face from supermarkets and other multiples in the toiletries market. Boots has developed its own-label range of health foods, while Safeways, Waitrose, and ASDA have health-food sections in their supermarkets.

Leading store groups like Boots have become aware of growing public concern over the use of additives and E numbers in foods and drinks, and they have removed artificial colours and flavours from their own-branded products. Commonly used additives—including tartrazine, monosodium glutamate, the anti-oxidants BHA and BHT, and the colour caramel—have been eliminated from these product ranges.

Franchising is involved in retail distribution of health foods. Booker Health Foods, part of the Booker McConnell group, has a dominant influence at both wholesale and retail levels of the health-food market. In general, however, the manufacture and distribution of health foods is distinctly fragmented. Originally, health-food businesses seemed to be run by people with missionary zeal for whom profit was not the prime concern. More professional attitudes are now apparent, as health foods widen their appeal, and new outlets are located in better shopping areas.

The strong and growing interest in health, diet, and exercise reflects, perhaps, a hedonistic approach to living (see Chapter 6). It certainly appears to be a fundamental trend which can also be observed in the interest shown by consumers in low-calorie foods aimed at the weight conscious and slimmers. More and more people seem to be obsessed with their body weights, perhaps because the nature of work, in general, demands far less physical exertion. Workers in a service economy use less muscle power than their forebears. Food manufacturers have responded to the 'slimmers' by marketing special soups and other calorie-controlled products.

Drinking habits are changing radically in Britain: beer consumption by volume is down 10 per cent since 1980, particularly the 'heavier' brews such as 'bitter', which declined around 25 per cent. Lighter beers have, to some extent, offset the overall reduced demand; lager sales rose by over one-third during 1980–90, largely on account of the younger drinkers of both sexes. Consumption of wine, at least at popular price levels, is no longer class-related; its dramatic increase of over 50 per cent during 1980–90 has also been significantly influenced by its ready availability at supermarkets, which have extensively promoted their wine lists.

Consistent with the theme of 'healthy living', and doubtless accelerated by the introduction of severer drink-driving penalties, has been the emergence of the so-called alcohol-free and low-calorie beers. Sales of these types of drinks are relatively small, but are actually increasing in an overall declining market. A similar trend is observable in the USA where the large brewing groups are vigorously developing their own brands to challenge European imports which have had this market segment to themselves for some years.

Another revolutionary change in drinking habits has been the ready acceptability of branded mineral waters in restaurants, corporate dining-rooms, public houses, and private homes. Deliberate frugality is socially approved and, indeed, favoured by many who regard conspicuous consumption as outdated and even incongruous. Sales by volume of branded mineral waters have increased by a factor of 10 over the period 1985–90, and demand, which is still rising, is served by many national and regional brands.

Smoking is another consumption habit which, at last, has been reduced by the growing public awareness of its attendant health hazards. Official statistics (*General Household Survey* 1988) show that cigarette smoking is distinctly biased towards the lower socio-economic groups and that male smokers represent 33 per cent of the British male population of 16 years and over, compared with 46 per cent in 1976. Smoking is increasingly banned in workplaces and public transport, and only tolerated in some restaurants, which often have special areas for non-smokers.

In a series of voluntary agreements between the British government and the tobacco industry, certain restrictions were imposed on cigarette advertising. These included 'health warnings' on packs and in advertising, though these were somewhat diffidently displayed. Also, advertisements should not suggest that cigarette smoking contributes to business or social success, or to project it in terms of manliness or bravery; further, it should not imply sexual attractiveness. Young people and celebrities were also banned from appearing in such promotional campaigns. Intense lobbying, for and against, smoking has continued for some years, but it would seem that, at last, public opinion is hardening against cigarette smoking. Before long, the EU Council of Ministers may well ban all cigarette advertising except at the point-of-purchase.

In the developed countries of the world, consumers are now concerned not with eating enough but with eating what are perceived to be the right *kinds* of food. As the research by the Institute of Cey-Bert revealed (see Chapter 3), people are motivated to explore new tastes in food, while also pursuing the ideals of physical and mental health through a balanced diet and fresh natural products. Through holiday travel abroad, new gustatory pleasures may have resulted from more adventurous eating habits, and on returning home some of these products may be sought in the local stores. Consumption of yoghurt, for instance, doubled between 1983 and 1993, which is remarkable for a product that, at one time, would never be found on supermarket shelves.

15.11 PRODUCT LIABILITY

In line with the growing public interest in health and safety, standards of business behaviour, and the social and environmental responsibilities of industrial undertakings, consumers have increasingly demanded that products should be safe to use. As mentioned in Chapter 1, design can be an influential buying motive; in addition to the aesthetic and functional aspects of design, buying expectations have been expanded to include safety factors. Not only should products look well and work well, but also they should be safe to use. If product failure occurs, users will doubtless by annoyed and disappointed; in some cases, they may also suffer injury, even death.

'Safety lobbying' developed strongly in the USA and the principle of strict product liability became enshrined in legislation which has resulted in swingeing penalties. Manufacturers and distributors are held accountable for product-related injuries; 'a court or jury determines that a product's design, its construction, or its operating instructions and safety warnings make it unreasonably dangerous or hazardous to use'.[58]

Liability suits in the USA have escalated at an intimidating rate, and damages awarded have grown spectacularly, inflated to some extent by the contingency fee basis on which most plaintiffs' lawyers operate in these cases. US product liability legislation is also complicated in practice because of varying interpretations of strict liability in different states.

In Britain as long ago as 1893, the Sale of Goods Act conferred extensive new rights on buyers who were, in general terms, entitled to goods of merchantable quality fit for the purpose for which they were sold. But this protection was reduced in two ways: by privity of contract (by which contracts in English law are normally binding only on the parties who made them) and by exclusion clauses. The latter were rendered illegal by legislation passed in the 1970s; the former disappeared under strict product liability legislation. New product liability legislation in Europe has followed from the EC Directive on Liability for Defective Products of 25 July 1985, which required each member state to introduce legislation to comply with the Directive by July 1988.

Britain was the first country to implement the European Directive by the introduction of the Consumer Protection Act 1987, which came into force on 1 March 1988. Product liability forms Part 1 of the Act. The other members of the European Union have various methods of protecting consumers from the results of product failure. Under the Act, product liability means that people injured by defective products may have the right to sue for damages, and any person who supplies a defective product will be liable for any damage it causes.

Formerly, those injured had to prove a manufacturer negligent before being compensated;

this proof of negligence is no longer necessary in order to sue for damages. However, a producer may be able to reduce the impact of defective goods by pleading contributory negligence in the use of a certain product. Among several other defences which, according to the Act, producers could offer might be that the state of scientific and technical knowledge at the time that the products were under their control, was such that any such defects would not have been discovered. The degree of safety of a product is that which a person may generally be entitled to expect, after taking into account all circumstances. Product liability relates to manufacturers, processors, suppliers of raw materials and components, importers, and own-label branded goods.

While product liability legislation brings Europe closer to the US practice that has existed since the early 1960s, it has been drafted to avoid the draconian penalties that have imposed insufferable burdens on US companies. The product liability and safety provisions of the Consumer Protection Act 1987 provide for compensation for death, personal injury, and private property valued above £275. The plaintiff must be able to show that, on the balance of probabilities, the defect in the product caused the alleged damage. Claims can be made up to ten years after the product was supplied, but legal proceedings must start within three years of the alleged injury from a defective product. Businesses need to take out adequate insurance cover related to their responsibilities under the Act, install efficient product recall systems, check design and manufacturing standards both in their own factories and those of their suppliers, and ensure that records are maintained in view of their potential liability over the years. Risk can never be entirely eliminated: no product can be absolutely safe under all conditions of usage. This move towards higher safety standards and the improved legal protection of consumers follows the general trends in business and society; it can also be viewed as consistent with Maslow's second step in his hierarchy of needs (see Chapter 3).

Marketers will need to work more closely than ever with the other functional areas of management to ensure that products reach the market only after rigorous evaluation of their safety features. This responsibility includes checking advertising copy carefully so that it does not contain exaggerated claims about product features and applications.

15.12 HOME AND LEISURE

Trends in consumption have centred on products that make homes more comfortable and enjoyable: central heating, double-glazing, cavity insulation, solar panels, and security systems have all added to home comforts and safety. In 1951, 30 per cent of all homes were owner occupied; in 1990, this figure had grown to 66 per cent. Micro-electronics technology has provided automatic washing machines, automatic cookers, electronic entertainment, etc. The home of the future is likely to contain a sophisticated communications sytem with two-way linkages.

In many ways, living is less dangerous, unpleasant, and challenging (antibiotics, improved pollution control, better standards of safety at work, more extensive legislation, etc.), and almost as a reflex action, leisure pursuits have become more challenging. Adventure holidays, safaris, and other exotic locations reflect relative affluence and also, perhaps, the need for building in excitement and uncertainty to the 'soft, safe life' reviewed in Chapter 6.

15.13 SUMMARY

In this final chapter, some of the trends in society that affect patterns of consumption have been reviewed. Undoubtedly, there has been great change—and yet more is likely to come. The elctronic 'wired society' is still in its infancy, but new expectations will be forged as novel products and services are assimilated into everyday consumption. A rising generation takes for granted products that were revolutionary to their parents. Innovation is a continuous activity.

Economics cannot be expected to provide a full and valid explanation of complex buying behaviour. Psychology, sociology, and cultural anthropology have valuable insights to offer: an eclectic approach is recommended.

Lobbying and pressure groups have become expert in forcing change in industrial and commercial practices. 'Consumerism' is a permanent feature of markets and companies should respond positively.

Advertising continues to be the focus of considerable criticism, but an AA survey reveals generally favourable attitudes.[35]

Media trends show that while the British morning dailies combined circulation has fallen slightly, this negative trend was not evenly distributed: 'qualities' increased by 10 per cent over 1984–90; the Sunday nationals' combined circulation fell by about 6 per cent over 1984–90. However, the overall trend of the quality Sundays was only marginally down at -2.0 per cent.

'Free' local papers were a significant innovation of the early 1970s and continue, despite some casualties, to cover more than twice the numbers of homes reached by the paid-for local press.

Magazines have declined in three sectors: romantic fiction, downmarket weeklies, and the mass-market women's weeklies.

Independent local radio started in 1973; 48 commercial stations were operating in 1991, reaching just over 43 million adults.

Cable television is being extended through the UK by operating franchises. The take-up rate has not lived up to optimistic estimates: only 2.4 per cent of UK homes were connected in 1992.

Direct Broadcast Satellites (DBS) is the latest system of transmitting television programmes; it is projected to be the most important source of TV programmes by the end of the twentieth century.

Other electronic media such as video discs, video cassette recorders, Teletext, and videotext contribute to the sophisticated life-style of the 1990s.

Distributive systems in the UK, are still experiencing change, such as computer-linked warehouses, laser-operated check-out points, and widespread use of credit cards. Interactive home-based electronic shopping has been projected. Concentrated buying by large store groups has shifted the balance of power in negotiations with suppliers.

Health and diet, product liability legislation, increased home comforts, and more adventurous leisure pursuits are other significant trends noted.

The future for marketing management will, as always, be uncertain, but it will certainly not lack opportunities for those who are willing to find out what their customers want and then provide them with products and services which come up to their expectations.

REFERENCES

1. Arbose, Jules, 'How top managers see the 1980s', *International Management*, January 1980.
2. Latham-Koenig, Alfred L., 'Changing values in a post-industrial society', *McKinsey Quarterly*, autumn 1983.
3. Brenner, Steven N., 'Business and politics—an update', *Harvard Business Review*, November/December 1979.
4. Bales, Carter F., Donald J. Gogel, and James S. Henry, 'The environment for business in the 1980s', *McKinsey quarterly*, winter 1980.
5. Lorenz, Christopher, 'Chameleons in their true colours', *Financial Times*, 7 February 1992.
6. Jay, Antony, *Management and Machiavelli*, Penguin, London, 1970.

7. Wiesner, Jerome B., 'Technological innovation and social change', *Economic Impact*, vol. 16, no. 4, 1976.
8. Atron, M. J., and Audrey Clayton, 'Social forecasting: a practical approach', *Technological Forecasting and Social Change*, vol. 7, no. 4, 1975.
9. Wack, Pieere, 'Scenarios: shooting the rapids', *Harvard Business Review*, vol. 63, no. 6, 1985.
10. Zentner, Rene D., 'Application of survey research in corporate decision-making', in: *Attitude Research Enters the 80s*, Richard W. Olshavsky (ed.), American Marketing Association, Chicago, 1980.
11. Taylor, Gordon Rattray, 'Prediction and social change: the need for a basis in theory', *Futures*, vol. 9, no. 5, October 1977.
12. Arnopoulos, Paris, 'Towards a model procedure for social forecasting', *Technological Forecasting and Social Change*, vol. 13, no. 1, January 1979.
13. Marien, Michael, 'The two visions of post-industrial society', *Futures*, vol. 9, no. 5, October 1977.
14. Mazur, Laura, 'Back from the future', *Marketing Business*, December 1992/January 1993.
15. Romano, D. J., and J. C. Higgins, 'The role of social forecasting in business planning: a survey of current practice', University of Bradford Management Centre, Bradford, 1978.
16. Skapinker, Michael, 'Clarifying ground rules', *Financial Times*, 22 July 1988.
17. *Company Philosophies and Codes of Business Ethics*, Institute of Business Ethics, London 1988.
18. Greyser, Stephen A., 'Marketing and public policy: bridging the gap', *Advertising Quarterly*, no. 36, summer 1973.
19. Aaker, David A., and George S. Day, 'Corporate responses to consumerism pressures', *Harvard Business Review*, November/December 1972.
20. Hill, Roy, 'The consumer movement finds the going tougher', *International Management*, July 1980.
21. Bloom, Paul N., and Stephen A. Greyser, 'The maturing of consumerism', *Harvard Business Review*, November/December 1981.
22. Bickerstaffe, George, 'A new direction for consumerism', *International Management*, October 1980.
23. Post, James E., 'The cooperation in the public policy process—a view toward the 1980s', *Sloan Management Review*, fall 1979.
24. Briggs, Asa, 'What kind of Europe—old or new?', *Advertising Quarterly*, no. 33, autumn 1972.
25. Mackinnon, A. M., 'The chemical industry under attack', *Ciba-Geigy Journal*, no. 3, 1981.
26. Anderson, Jack, 'Dow vs the dioxin monster', *Fortune*, 30 May 1983.
27. Menzies, Hugh D., 'Union Carbide raises its voice', *Fortune*, 25 September 1978.
28. Macnaughton, Donald S., 'Managing social responsiveness', *Business Horizons*, December 1976.
29. Ostlund, Lyman E., 'Attitudes of managers toward corporate social responsibility', *Californian Management Review*, vol. 19, no. 4, 1977.
30. Burke, Tom, 'Is there a common agenda? Environment and industry: towards a common agenda', *Royal Society of Arts Journal*, vol. CXXXVII, no. 5394, May 1989.
31. Ishi, Hiroyuki, 'Basic environmental attitudes in east and west: why do the Japanese eat whales?' *Royal Society of Arts Journal*, vol. CXL, no. 5, January 1992.
32. McIntosh, Andrew, 'The impact of environmental issues on marketing and politics in the 1990s', *Journal of the Market Research Society*, vol. 33, no. 3, July 1991.
33. Knight, Peter, 'Green badge of courage', *Financial Times*, 20 November 1991.
34. Smith, Adam, *An Enquiry into the Causes of the Wealth of Nations* (Carman edn), Methuen, London, 1961.
35. Advertising Association, *Public Attitudes to Advertising 1992*, Advertising Association, London, 1992.
36. Chisnall, Peter M., *Marketing Research*, McGraw-Hill, Maidenhead, 1992.
37. Burdus, Ann, 'Advertising: the public view', *Advertising*, no. 69, autumn 1981.
38. Valladares, Daz, 'Why TV must adjust its set', *Marketing*, 24 March 1983.
39. Greyser, Stephen A., and Bonnie B. Reece, 'Businessmen look hard at advertising', *Harvard Business Review*, May/June 1971.
40. Greyser, Stephen, A., 'Irritation in advertising: the next battleground', *Advertising Quarterly*, no. 35, spring 1973.
41. Spandler, Richard, 'Cable penetration at 10% by 1990—JWT', *Marketing*, 5 January 1984.

42. *Financial Times*, 'Cable and satellite TV', 15 December 1983.

43. Spandler, Richard, 'Agencies reject cable's advances—for now', *Marketing*, 16 December 1982.

44. Townsin, M., 'What would cable do for advertising?', *Admap*, February 1983.

45. Snoddy, Raymond, 'A bigger choice for those who want it', *Financial Times*, 21 October 1991.

46. Advertising Association, 'Submission to Hunt Committee', Advertising Association, London, 1982.

47. Goodall, Christopher, 'Cable operators neglect marketing', *Marketing*, 23 February 1984.

48. Nielsen, A. C. Jnr, 'The outlook for electronic media', *Journal of Advertising Research*, vol. 22, no. 6, December 1982/January 1983.

49. Taylor, Paul, 'U.S. cable programmers battle for survival', *Financial Times*, 15 December 1983.

50. Nielsen, A. C. Jnr, 'The perspective of electronic media in the next five years', *Marketing Trends*, October 1984, A. C. Nielsen, Oxford.

51. Jonquières, Guy de, 'Brands left on the shelf', *Financial Times*, 31 October 1991.

52. Bond, Catherine, 'Own labels vs the brands', *Marketing*, 8 March 1984.

53. Simmons, Martin, and Bill Meredith, 'Own label profile and purpose', *Journal of Market Research Society*, vol. 26, no. 1, 1984.

54. Fulop, Christina, 'Retailer advertising and retail competiton in the UK', *International Journal of Advertising*, vol. 2, 1983.

55. Stern, Peter, 'Franchising in the 1990s', *Royal Society of Arts Journal*, vol. CXXXVIII, no. 5408, July 1990.

56. Miles, Ian, 'Just around the corner?', *Royal Society of Arts Journal*, vol. CXXXVIII, no. 5403, February 1990.

57. Harris, Clay, 'Carnivores lose ground', *Financial Times*, 10 May 1991.

58. Malott, Robert H., 'Let's restore balance to product liability law', *Harvard Business Review*, May/June, 1983.

REVIEW AND DISCUSSION QUESTIONS

1. Evaluate the relevance of social forecasting for marketing decision-makers.
2. Are businesses in general sufficiently motivated to educate consumers and provide adequate information for an informed choice?
3. Assuming that you were the consumer affairs director of a large fertilizer-producing company, what mechanisms would you establish to handle consumer complaints and to deal with consumer rights groups?
4. What are the principal lessons to be learned by advertisers from recent changes in society's attitudes towards advertising?
5. What advertising model, advertising schedule, and advertising appeals would you recommend for a television campaign to promote a new, premium-prices anti-perspirant spray to the 20–30-year-old female market?
6. Thinking of the supermarket where you shop most frequently, what are the three most significant retailing developments that you have witnessed there in the last five years or so?

Abrams, Mark, 110
Accessory equipment, 218
Achievement, need for, 220
ACORN market segmentation analysis, 342–6
Ad hoc situational factors, 237
Ad Weekly, 122
Added values, 222
Admass culture, 120
Advertisers' Annual, 127
Advertising:
  assessing effect of, 80
  attitudes, 298
  behaviour, 293
  believability of, 303–5
  children, effects on, 314–18
  communication role, 285
  comparative, 309–10
  consumer buying behaviour, 299–301
  deception in, 303–4
  diffusion in, 260
  effectiveness of, 288, 298
  fear appeals in, 306–7
  force of, 294
  free papers, 369
  hierarchical models of, 292–8
  humanistic view of, 297
  immunization theory, 311
  impact of consumerism, 277
  in developing trends in consumption, 298
  influence of attitudes on, 298
  influence on children, 314–18
  inoculation theory, 311
  irritation in, 368, 372
  levels of influence, 299
  linear models of, 292
  market feedback in, 287–8
  mechanics of, 292
  models, 292–5
  new products, 276
  one-sided vs two-sided presentations, 91, 310–11
  packaging design in, 289
  pro and con approach (*see* one-sided vs two-sided)
  professional aspects of, 292
  reassurance theory, 29
  repetitive, 300
  resistance to, 309
  retail, 377
  role of, 292, 293
  sales force support, 284
  S-R model of, 300
  stereotypes in, 72
  two-step flow, 306
  under criticism, 368
  women in, 311–14
  word-of-mouth, 306
  (*see also* Television)
Advertising agencies, 34
Advertising Association, 292, 309, 317, 364–6
Advertising campaigns, 66, 128
Advertising Standards Authority (ASA), 304, 317, 364
Advertising strategy, 35
Affluent society, 135
After-sales service, 29, 222
Aggressiveness, 59–60, 73
AIDA, 294
Alderson, Wroe, 35

Alexander, Milton, 126
Alexander, R. S., 225
Allen, David, 108
Allison, R. L., 26
Allport, Gordon W., 79, 80
Andreasan, A. R., 203
Andreasan model, 208–9
Ansoff, H. I., 106, 216, 251, 269, 276
Anxiety, 306–7
Applied Futures Ltd, 347
Argyle, Michael, 111, 214
Arkoff, A., 307
Arkwright, R., 250
Arms-length trading, 242
Arthur, H. B., 221
Asch, S. E., 35, 42, 81, 86, 87, 156
Asahi Shimbun, 363
Aspirations:
  and motivation, 55
  levels of, 56
Atkinson, R. C., 80
Attitudes, 79–97
  affect or feeling component, 81
  and behaviour, 92–7
  and marketing strategy, 80
  and needs, 87
  and social class, 137
  and traits, 61
  change in, 87–92, 157, 208
  characteristics of components, 81–2
  clusters, 82
  cognitive component, 81
  communication factors influencing, 90
  components of, 81
  conative component or action tendency, 81
  congruent change, 88
  constellation, 82
  definitions of, 79–80
  direction of change, 88
  effect of advertising campaigns, 128
  elements of, 294
  environmental influences, 86–7
  factors affecting change, 88
  family, 85
  formation, 83, 156, 208
  group, 85, 89–90, 156
  incongruent change, 88
  influence of public, 106
  interrelationships between, 82–3
  moods and attitudes, 97
  multiplex, 82
  negative, 81
  personal, 156
  personality factors affecting change 87–8
  positive, 82
  reinforcement, 88
  simplex, 82
  sources of, 84
  to advertising, 364–7
  to food items and food dishes, 119
  to housework scale, 334
  to stereotype female role, 72
  to work, 116
Attwoods Consumer Panel, 333–4
Augmented product or service concept, 14

Back-up service, 222
Bagozzi, Richard, 96
Baked bean market, 325
Bales, R. E., 176
Ballachey, E. L., 27, 44, 47, 52, 68, 82, 84, 87, 105
Bandwagon effects, 162, 252, 257
Banks and banking, 136, 184
Banton, M., 105
Bargaining, 216
Bartos, R., 312, 337
Bauer, R. A., 126, 162, 195, 220, 308
Bayton, J. A., 36, 40, 41, 120
BBC, 371
Bearden, W. O., 161
Becker Behavioural Engineering Corporation, 27
Becker's Black Box, 27
Beer, Stafford, 42
Beer drinkers, 26
Behaviour:
  and attitudes, 92–7
  and culture, 108
Behavioural influences:
  research into, 15–16
  systematic approach to study of, 16–17
Behavioural studies, 11–14
Bell Telephone Laboratories, 268
Bellizi, J. A., 234–5
Bennington College, 86
Berelson, B., 133, 162, 166
Berey, L. A., 182
Bird, M., 96
Birdwell, A. E., 69, 70
Birth control, 119
Black, J. S., 166
Blackwell, R. D., 196, 203, 204
Blois, K. J., 9
Bloom, P. N., 360
BMRB, 175, 364
Body Shop, 363, 378
Bonoma, T. V., 227, 230
Booker Health Foods, 381
Boote, A. S., 335–6
Booth, Charles, 142
Bott, E., 171
Boulding, Kenneth, 105
Bourne, F. S., 120, 160–1
Boyd, Harper W., Jnr., 299
BP, 279
Brand, G., 223
Brand choice, 36
Brand loyalty, 195, 261, 331
  dissonance and, 332

in consumer buying behaviour, 331
in market segmentation, 330
Brand names, 167
Brand preference, 70, 368
Brand rejuvenation, 332
Brand switching, 36
Branded products, 14, 70
Breach, R. W., 137
Brewery groups, 13
Briggs, Asa, 110, 361
British Crime Survey, 121
British Productivity Council, 229
British Rate and Data Guide, 369
Britt, S. H., 31, 61
Broadbent, S., 113
Brodbeck, M., 157
BSkyB, 373, 379
Buck, S. F., 114
Buckner, H., 223
Burdus, Ann, 278
Burke, T., 363
Burns, T., 250
Bursk, Edward C., 14
Bush, R., 36
Business behaviour, 89
Business enterprises, levels of activity, 12
Business ethics, 357–8
Business organizations, primary, secondary, and
        tertiary industries, 213
Business Statistics Office (BSO), 348
Buyclasses, 232
Buyphases, 232
Buyer-seller relationship, 301
    (*see also* Negotiation)
Buyers' market, 5
Buying behaviour:
    choice criteria, 198
    complexity of, 11
    consumer (*see* Consumer buying behaviour)
    factors influencing, 15
    importance of learning in, 30–1
    models of (*see* Models)
    organizational (*see* Organizational buying
        behaviour)
Buying decisions:
    children's influence on, 181–4
    (*see also* Decision-making)
Buying determinants, 225
Buying habits, 33
Buying responsibilities, 223
Buzzeli, R. D., 203

Cable television, 371–2
CACI, 343–6
CAD (Compliant/Aggressive/Detached) scale, 64
Calder, B. J., 315
California Psychological Inventory, 62–3
Campaign for Real Ale (CAMRA), 13
Cantril, H., 74, 80

Capital goods, 217
Capon, H., 90
Car market, 325–6
Car ownership, 69–70
Carman, J., 167
Carrick, P. M., 300–2
Carter, C. F., 251
Catholic culture, 45–6, 128
Cattell, R. B., 63
CCN Systems, 346
Centers, Richard, 67
Central Advisory Council for Science and
        Technology, 249, 263, 269
Central Office of Information, 80
Central Statistical Office, 148
Change concept, 208
Channon, D., 230
Charlton, P., 331
Chartered Institute of Marketing, 7, 8, 223, 292
Chemical Industries' Association, 362
Chemical industry, 361–2
Chemophobia phenomenon, 361
Cheskin, L., 54, 66
Chicago Tribune, 47, 126, 141, 331
Chicken Sara Lee, 303
Child-centredness, 182
Children:
    influence of advertising on, 314–18
    influence on buying decisions, 181–4
    (*see also* Family)
Chi-square analysis, 195
Christian Scientists, 128
Churchill, G. A., Jnr., 257
Ciba-Geigy Corporation, 361–2
Cigarette controversy, 308
Civic Societies, 157
Classical conditioning, 32
Clawson, Joseph, 36
Clothing:
    expenditures, 174–5
    trends in, 13
    (*see also* Fashion)
Code of Advertising Practice, 303–4, 372
Cognition, definition of, 23
Cognitive change, characteristics influencing, 27–8
Cognitive dissonance theory, 28, 332
Cognitive map, 23–4
Cognitive theories, 34–5
Cohen, J. B., 64
Coleman, J., 259
Coleman, R. P., 137, 166, 171
Coleman-Rainwater model, 142
Colgate-Palmolive, 329
Colley, R. M., 293–4
Communication: 274–291
    and diffusion processes, 256
    and suppliers, 276
    factors influencing attitude, 90–2
    informal, 256

innovation, 256, 263
interpersonal, 164
two-step flow of, 163, 306
verbal and nonverbal, 214
word-of-mouth, 258
Communications, Advertising and Marketing
     Foundation (CAM), 292
Communications strategy, 278
  stages in, 285–6
  (*see also* Advertising; Market communications;
    packaging)
Community antenna television system (CATV), 260
Comparative advertising, 309–10
Competition:
  protection against, 10
  surviving against, 10
Competitiveness, 62
Compliant individuals, 64
Compromise, 110
Compulsive eaters, 55
Computer programs, 16
Computers:
  adoption characteristics, 261
  'make or buy' approach, 269
Concentrated buying power, 230
Conditioned reflex, 32
Connectionist theories, 32
Consistency, 61
Consonance, 28, 89
Consumer behaviour, family influences on, 178–81
Consumer buying behaviour, 191–211
  and advertising influence, 299–301
  brand loyalty in, 195, 261, 331
  models of (*see* Models)
Consumer guidance magazines, 34
Consumer involvement theories, 74–5, 199
Consumer products, 5
Consumer spending habits, 170–2
Consumerism, 225, 359–60
Consumers' Association, 360
Consumption habits, 11, 85, 108, 136, 175
Consumption patterns, 136
Consumption policy, 360
Consumption trends, 15
Continental Can Company, 165
Cooper, P., 182, 296–7
Copeland, M. T., 50
Core product, 14
Corner shop, 376
Corporate image, 87, 274–7, 279–82
Cosmetics, 308, 377
Cost-benefit analysis, 288
Cotton industry, 5
Cox, D. F., 298, 306
Craig, C. S., 221, 327
Cranfield School of Management, 223
Credibility of communicators, 90
Credit culture, 118
Crespi, I., 82

Crompton, S., 250
Cross, J. S., 225
Cultural anthropology, 108
Cultural beliefs and values, 108–9
Cultural factors, 18
Cultural norms, 107
Cultural taboos, 108
Culture, 103–29
  concept of, 103–4
  definitions of, 103–4
  nature of, 106
  redefinition of products, 128
Cummings, W. H., 29
Cunningham, R. M., 225
Cunningham, S. M., 126
Curiosity, 48
Cyert, R. M., 225

DAGMAR (Defining Advertising Goals for
    Measured Advertising Results), 293
Darwin, Charles, 53
Data gathering, 16
Decision-making:
  in Japanese culture, 215
  industrial, 6, 220
  rational, 11
Decision-making unit (DMU) (*see* Organizational
    buying)
Decision rules, 294
Decoding communications, 286–7
De Haan, J. A. B., 134
Deming, W. E., 339
Demography, 168–70
  and buying behaviour, 168
  and market segmentation, 326
  and overseas marketing, 221
Denney, Reuel, 117
Derived demand, 218
Design aspects, 14, 49
Detached individuals, 64
Deterrence-by-horrible-example theory, 307
Deutsch, Karl W., 54
Developing countries, 327
Dichter, Ernest, 65, 178
Dinkies, 124
Direct broadcast satellites (DBS), 373
Dissonance, 29, 97, 332
Divorce, 169
Do-it-yourself activities, 118
Dolich, I. J., 70
Donne, John, 103
Dornbush, S. M., 67
Douglas, S., 107, 181, 221, 327
Dow Chemical Company, 361–2
Drive reduction theory, 52
Drucker, P. F., 5, 12, 215, 248
Dual incomes, 118, 175
  (*see also* Working wives)
Dun and Bradstreet, 223

Du Pont, 202–3, 287

Eassle, R., 184
Ebony, 127
Eck, R., 315
Eclectic approach, 193, 206
economic activity, 264
Economic analysis, 264
Economic and Social Research Council, 12
Economic developments, 248
Economic environment, 359
Economic factors, 18
Economic history, 5
Economic objectives, 11
Economic structure, 353
Ectomorphy, 60
Educational facilities, 328
Edwards's Personal Preference Schedule (EPPS), 62
Ego-involvement, 71
Ehrenberg, A. S. C., 96, 295, 303
Eisler, P., 254
Electrolux, 329
Electronic media, 374
Elicted responses, 33
Embourgeoisement of the working classes, 137
Emitted responses, 33
Emotional environment, 215
Emotional stability, 73
Encoding communications, 286–7
Endomorphs, 60
Engel, J. F., 196, 197, 203
Environmental concerns, 361
Engel-Kollat-Blackwell model, 196–7
England, Grosse, and Associates, 335
Environmental factors, 361
Environmentalism, 361–4
Erikson, R. A., 222
Estes, W. K., 36
Etgar, M., 311
Ethical implications, 357–8
Ethnic influences, 126
Etzel, M. J., 161
European Association of Advertising Agencies, 305, 313
European demographic scale, 153
European Society for Opinion and Marketing Research (ESOMAR), 152
European Union
   and consumption patterns, 375
   cultural factors, 110, 327–8
   product liability, 382–3
   socio-economic classification (EU), 151–2
Evans, Franklin B., 63, 73
Exchange concept, 4
Exchange terms, 4
Expected product, 14
Experimental psychology, 35
Expressive dispositions, 63
Extremeness and multiplexity, 88

Extroverts, 61
Eysenck, H. J., 62

Fabricating materials, 217
Factor analysis, 335
Familiarity principle, 121
Family, 167–77
   attitudes, 85
   buying organization, 178–9
   changes in structures, 168–70
   conflict and compromise, 179–80
   definition of, 168
   influences on consumer behaviour, 168–70
   life-cycle, 172–4
   marriage, influence of, 170–2
   roles and decision-making, 176–7
   types, 168–9
Family Expenditure Survey, 149
Faris, C. W., 232
Fashion clothing, 75
Fear appeals in advertising, 307–8
Federal Trade Commission, 304
Feedback, 207, 286–7, 300
Feigenbaum, A., 339
Female roles, 72, 121-3
Feshbach, S., 307
Festinger, L., 28, 30, 93, 200, 295
Field, J. G., 176–7
FIFO process (facts-in, facts-out), 295
Financial Times, 223, 354, 371, 373
Fish finger market, 335
Fishbein, M., 92, 94–5, 295
Fitzroy, P. F., 16, 36, 332, 338
Florsheim, R., 315
Flow charting, 207
Folkways, 107
Food buying:
   children's influence on, 183
   factors influencing, 12–13
Food needs, 41–2
Food products, 376–7
Food shortage effects, 44
Food tastes, exotic, 137
Food trade, 375
Food trends, 41–2
Ford cars, 29
Forecasting, social, 356–7
Formal product, 14
Fortune, 252, 361, 362
Franchising, 378
Free papers, 369
Freeman, Christopher, 12
Freud, Sigmund, 53–4
Freudian psychology, 54, 66
Frustration levels, 48

Galbraith, J. K., 47
Galvani, L., 250
Gatekeeper role, 224, 286

Gaudet, H., 162, 166
General Electric Company, 166
General Household Survey, 148
Generic product, 376
Geneva Disarmament Conference, 110
Geodemographic segmentation, 342–8
Gestalt psychology, 35
GNP per capita, 221
Goals, dual, 220
Goldberg, M. C., 315
Goodman, S., 311
Goodwill, 48
Goodyear, 251
Gordon, Wendy, 114
Gorn, G. J., 310, 315
Graham, S. L., 263
Granada Television 175
Green, P. E., 70
Green issues, 361–4
Greyser, S. A., 358–9, 361, 368
Grocery sales, 375
Groups, 156–85
    affiliations, 90
    attitudes, 157
    definition, 157
    formal, 157–8
    influences, 156–7
    informal, 157–8
    interaction, 156
    norms, 157
    pressure, 159
    primary, 157
    reference, 158
    secondary, 157
    types, 157–8
Grubb, E. L., 70
Guarantee cards, 29
Guardian, 72
Gubar, G., 173
Guinness promotion, 70–1, 329

Hague, Sir Douglas, 12, 191–2
Hakansson, H., 218, 220–1, 239–41
Hamilton, H., 255
Hanna, S., 91, 173
Hartwell, R. M., 137
Harvard Business Review, 16, 221, 314, 337, 354
Harvard Business School, 142, 171
Harvey-Jones, Sir John, 254
Haskios, J. B., 295
Health foods, 380–2
Health insurance plan, 309
Hedonistic orientation, 118–19
Heller, R., 9
Hickman, L. C., 67
Hilgard, E. R., 52, 80
Hill, R., 176
Hippocrates, 60
Hite, R. E., 315

Hobbes, T., 52, 118
Hobby pursuits, 118
Holiday-making patterns, 118
Hollingshead, A. B., 134, 141
Hollingshead social class system, 141–2
Holmberg, A. R., 44
Horne, A., 113
Horney, K., 64
Household expenditure patterns, 379
*Household Food Consumption and Expenditure
        Survey*, 148
Household typology, 177
Housewives:
    and household typology, 177–8
    and new products, 260–1
    and packaging, 334
    characteristics of, 172
    classification of, 114–15, 337
    cross-section of, 334
    food-buying by, 13
    influence of marriage, 170–1
    subjective verbal models, 196
    (*see also* Family)
Hovland, C. I., 80, 90, 91, 310
Howard, J. A., 30, 81, 104, 323
Howard-Ostlund model, 203–4
Howard-Sheth model, 203
Hulbert, J., 90
Hull, C. L., 33
Hulton Readership Surveys, 142
Hunt Committee Report, 371, 372
Hupp, G., 70
Hutton, Peter, 275, 277, 282
Hyman, H. H., 158, 162
Hypermarkets, 375

IBM, 269
ICI, 250, 254, 278, 279
Image development (*see* Corporate image)
IMP project group, 239–41
Impulse purchases, 54
Income:
    dual, 179
    in market segmentation, 340–2
Incorporated Society of British Advertisers, 143
Independence, 73
Independent local radio (ILR), 371
Independent Television Commission, 371
Industrial buying behaviour (*see* organizational)
Industrial clustering, 231–2
Industrial Market Research, 223
Industrial marketing, 5, 6, 10, 17, 219
Industrial Marketing Management, 105
Industrial Marketing Research Association
        (IMRA), 217, 223
Industrial markets and segmentation strategies,
        348–9
Industrial products, 49, 217
Industrial revolution, 134

Industrialized countries, 327
Influencers, 224
Information needs, 48
Information package, 286
Information processing, 203, 208
Information sources, 258
Inner-directed character, 66
Innovation, 247–270
    adoption process, 258–9
    bandwagon effects, 252
    basic groups, 253
    characteristics of, 262–3
    classification of, 253–4
    communicability, 263
    compatibility, 262
    complexity, 263
    continuous, 253
    defensive, 255
    delivery push, 255
    diffusion process, 255, 256, 259–60
    discontinuous, 253
    discovery push, 255
    divisibility, 263
    dynamically continuous, 253
    early industrial, 250
    empirical evidence of diffusion of, 259–60
    evolutionary, 254
    industrial, 250–1
    invention, 249–50
    laggard behaviour, 259
    lead time, 264
    'make or buy' approach, 269
    market research in, 270
    need for, 247
    need pull, 255
    offensive, 255
    opinion leadership, 261
    opportunities for, 247
    organizing, 267
    planning in, 263
    product champions, 268
    project teams, 267
    relative advantage, 262
    revolutionary, 254
    risk policies, 251–2
    success factors, 249–50
    technological, 249
    types of firms, 251
    use of term, 249
Innovation manager, 267
Insko, C. A., 307
Insko, V. M., 307
Installations, 218
Instinctive behaviour, 52
Institute Cey-Bert, 41
Institute of Practitioners in Advertising, 143, 372
Instruction manuals, 29
Integration role, 9
Intelligence tests, 59–60

Interaction model, 239–41
Interaction process, 239
Interconnectedness, 28, 88
Intermediate products, 217
International Chamber of Commerce, 304
International Management, 353
International Research Institute on Social Change, 116, 357
International Standard Classification of Occupations, 150–1
International Standard Industrial Classification (ISIC), 348
Interpretation role, 9
Introverts, 61
Investments, 221, 275, 278
Irrigation programme, 111

Jacobson, E., 70
Jahoda, M., 59
Janis, I. L., 307
Janis, J., 80
Japan, 214–15
Jay, Antony, 354
Jewkes, J., 250
Jews, 128
John Lewis Partnership, 183
Johnson, John, 127
Johnston, W. J., 227
Joint Industry Committee for Cable Audience Research (JICCAR), 372
Joint Industry Committee for National Readership Surveys (JICNARS), 327
Joint Industry Committee for Radio Audience Research (JICRAR), 370
Joint ventures, 269
Journal of the Market Research Society, 96, 121
Journal of Marketing, 126
Joyce, T., 97, 170, 179, 295
Jung, C. G., 61, 66
Juran, J. M., 339
Just-in-time (JIT) production, 231

Kamarck, A. M., 211
Kapferer, J. N., 74
Kassarjian, H. H., 34, 59, 68, 69, 73
Katona, G., 51, 55, 87, 89, 165, 166, 174
Katz, D., 80, 83, 89
Katz, E., 224, 255, 259, 306
Kay, H., 307
Kay, John, 12
Keech, Marion, 30
Kelley, H. H., 80
Kelman, H. C., 89
Kelvin, R. P., 302
Key informant method, 164
King, C. W., 166–7
Klapper, J. F., 306
Knowledge-based industries, 213
Kollat, D. J., 196–7, 204

Kossoff, J., 70
Kotler, P., 52, 109
Kretschmer, P., 60
Kroyer, K., 254
Krugman, H., 296
Kuehn, A. A., 36, 331

Ladies Home Journal, 67
Laissez-faire concept, 359
Langrish, J., 255
Lannon, J., 296–7
Lansing, J. B., 172
La Piere, R. T., 92
Laurent, G., 74
Lavidge, R. J., 294–5
Law of effect, 32
Lazarsfeld, P. F., 162, 166, 224, 306
Learning models, 36–7
Learning processes, 30–1, 84
Learning theories, 32–6
Lee, M. S., 74
Leisure, 116–17, 118, 383
Leisured classes, 168
Levi-Strauss, C., 106
Leo Burnett Agency, 333
Less developed countries, 327
Lestare bleach, 303
Levin, M. L., 255
Levitt, T., 17, 49, 221, 322
Levy, S. J., 137
Lewin, K., 36
Licensing agreements, 269
Life assurance, 44
Life cycle, 172–6
  family, 172–3
  in market segmentation, 340–2
  product, 265–6
Life-style, 336–7
  affluent middle-aged, 114
  concept of, 112
  cultural values, 115
  differences in, 122
  family, 168–9
  psychographics, 112
  research, 112
  segmentation, 340–2
  social values, 116
  of women, 121–2, 123
Lind, Harold, 336
Linton, A., 113
Linton, R., 104
Lippmann, Walter, 71
Lobbying, 360
Lorenz, C., 354
Lorenz, K. Z., 134
Lumsdaine, A. A., 310
Lunn, J. A., 79, 206, 335
Luxury goods, 13
Lydia Pinkham's Vegetable Compound, 201

McClelland, D. C., 45–6
McCracken, G., 104, 108, 111, 167, 203
McDonald, C., 295–6, 297
McGill University, 264
McGraw-Hill, 226, 264
McGregor, D. M., 53
Machine Tools Economic Development
    Committee, 5
McKinsey and Co., 6, 354, 373
MacNulty, C., 357
McVey, P., 234
Magazine market, 370
Maier, M. R. F., 43
Mail-order, 377
Maloney, J. C., 306
Management functions, 9
Mansfield, E., 249, 252, 256
Manzel, H., 259
March, J. G., 225
Marcus, A. S., 162
Market communication, objectives, 282–4
Market inertia, 252
Market leaders, 253
Market research, 8, 223, 270
Market segmentation, 322-50
  ACORN, 343–7
  analysis of, 323
  basic methods, 326
  benefit, 337–8
  brand loyalty in, 330
  by product design, 338–9
  concept of, 323
  decisive factors in, 324
  demographic, 326
  design sensitivity in, 338
  geodemographic, 342–8
  geographic, 327
  industrial, 348–9
  life-style, 336–7
  MOSAIC, 348
  nature and purpose of, 323
  personality variables in, 329
  PINPOINT, 346–7
  PRIZM, 347
  psychographic, 332-3
  risk assessment in, 330
  SAGACITY, 340–1
  socio-economic, 326–7
  strategy, 324
  types of, 326
  usage rate in, 329–30
  use of term, 323
Marketing, 372
Marketing:
  basic philosophy of, 41
  characteristics of, 7–8
  definition, 7
  development of, 4–5
  dynamic environment, 10

effectiveness, 7
essence of, 6
evolution of, 7
feedback, 285
industrial, 5–6, 10, 17, 219
opinion leadership in, 163
origins of, 3–4
overseas, 221
personality, 73–4
philosophy, 7
resistance to, 7
review of concept, 3–18
revolution in, 5
skills, 10
Marketing communications, 283–91
feedback, 286
measuring effectiveness, 288
methods of, 283
outline model, 286
phases of, 286
planning, 285
stages, 285
Marketing management, 7, 9–10, 51, 267, 289
Marketing research (*see* Market research)
Marketing Science Institute of America, 16
Marketing strategies:
and culture, 108–12
and product life-cycle, 265–7
attitude effects (*see* Attitudes)
Markin, R. J., 31, 35, 79, 82, 107
Markov processes, 16, 207
Marks and Spencer, 87, 107, 183
Marquis, D. G., 255
Marriage and consumer spending habits, 170
Marrian, J., 228
Marsh, C., 162
Marshall, Alfred, 52
Marshallien economic model, 50
Martilla, J. A., 226
Martineau, Pierre, 66, 138, 140–1, 171
Maslow, A. H., 42, 43, 47, 48, 52, 106, 125, 220, 307
Mass media trends, 369–74
Massachusetts Institute of Technology, 72, 142, 171, 247, 354
Materialism, 106
Mathias, P., 254
Mead, M., 109
Meritocracy, emergency of, 135
Merton, R. K., 163
Mesomorphs, 60
Micro chips, 248
Microelectronics, 248
micro-technology, 248
Midgley, D. F., 167
Mill, John Stuart, 12
Minnesota Multiphase Personality Inventory (MMPI), 63
Mitford, Nancy, 135

Mittal, B., 74
Mixed economy, 213
Mobility, upward, 136, 171
Models, 191–211
behavioural, 192
black box, 195
buygrid (MSI), 232
consumer buying behaviour, 191
decision-process (*see* Logical flow)
function of, 191
logical-flow, 196–7, 232
monadic, 193–4
multi-variable, 202–3
organizational buying behaviour, 213–43
perceived risk, 194
psycho-analytic, 194
qualities required, 192–3
subjective verbal, 196
types of, 193
Moods, attitudes and behaviour, 97
Moreno, J. L., 63
Mores, 107
Morgan, J. N., 172
Morgan Motor Company, 325–6
MORI Corporate Image Survey, 278
Mormons, 128
Morrill, J. E., 283
Mosteller, F., 36
Motivation, 40–56
and aspirations, 55–6
and behavioural theory, 225
and law of effect, 33
fundamental appreciation of, 51
instinctive theories, 52, 65
incentive theory, 52
overview of, 50–1
research, 65–6
study of, 52
theories of, 52–4
Motives, nature of, 54–5
Mueller, E., 165
Mullard, 280
Multi-national corporations, 354
Multiplexity, 28, 88
Mumford, Lewis, 111
Murphy, P. E., 174
Murray, Henry, 63
Muslims, 128
Myers, S., 255

n-achievement, 45
n-score, 45
Nabisco, RJR, 253
Nader, Ralph, 359–60
National Advertising Review Board (NARB), 312
National Readership Survey (NRS), 142–7
Needham, DDB, 112
Needs:
aesthetic, 48–9

affectional, 42
and attitudes, 87
belongingness, 43
biogenic, 41
categories of, 42–3
cognitive, 48–9
conflicting, 50
distinguishing clearly between motives and, 50
ego-bolstering, 42–3
ego-defensive, 42
emotional, 42
esteem, 43
food, 42
hierarchy of, 43
higher-level, 43
information, 48
lower-level, 43
nature of, 41
personal perception of, 54
physiological, 41-2
psychogenic, 42
psychological, 42
safety, 43
self-actualization, 43
sequential, 43
smaller hierarchy of, 48–9
Negative appeals, 91–2
Negotiation, 214–16
Negroes, marketing dilemma of, 126
Neighbourhood store, 376
Nepotism, 136
Nestlé, 338
New products, 261, 264, 276
Newcomb, T. M., 86
Newcomen, Thomas, 250
Newman, Joseph W., 16, 69
Newspaper and Periodical Contributors Committee, 143
Newspapers, 369–70
Nicosia, F. M., 206
Nicosia model, 206–7
Nielsen, A. C. Jnr., 374
Noise factors, 286
Non-rational factors, 13, 14
Nuffield Foundation, 228
Nystrom, P., 166

O'Brien, J., 162
Occupations:
    classification of, 142–53
    key, 149–50
Official Classification of Occupations, 147–8
Olins, W., 279–80
Opals, 125–6
Open University, 117
Operant conditioning, 33
Operating supplies, 218
Opinion leadership, 90, 162–7
    family influences, 167

and impersonal sources of imformation, 226
and innovativeness, 261
characteristics of, 165–6
classes of, 163
communication factors, 163
identification, 165
methods of measuring, 164–5
trickle-down theory, 163, 167, 182
Opinion Research Corporation (ORC), 259–60
Organizational buying behaviour, 213–43
    buying centre/DMU, 222–3
    complexity of, 219
    concentration of buying power, 214, 230–1
    dilemma in, 228
    models, 232–43
    multiple influences on, 222–3
    roles in, 223–4
    strategy research, 229–30
    time taken in buying, 228
    variable influencing, 238
    (see also Purchasing agents)
Organizational supplies:
    classification of, 217–18
    derived demand, 218
    nature of, 216–17
    types of, 217–18
Osgood's semantic differential scaling technique, 69
Ostlund, L., 203, 204
Other-directed character, 67
Out-of-town shopping centres, 375
Overseas marketing, 327
Own-label goods, 376
Ownership of products, 47
Ozanne, U. B., 257

Packaging, 289–90
    design, 289
    role of, 289
Packard, Vance, 47, 66, 140, 259
Palda, K. S., 202, 295
Palmer, J., 96
Park, C. W., 180
Party selling, 377
Pavlov's dogs, 32
P. E. Consulting Group, 5
PEP, 7, 228
Perception, 24–5
    factors affecting, 24–5
    fundamentals of, 24
    subliminal, 27
Perkin, M., 120, 128, 164
Personality, 59–74
    and marketing, 73
    characteristics and attitudinal change, 88–9
    definition of, 59
    psychoanalytic theories of, 65–6
    social learning theories of, 66–7
    theories of, 59–60
    variables in market segmentation, 329

Personality tests, 59–60
Personality traits, 60–1
Pessemier, E. A., 263, 264
Peters, T., 339
Phillips, I. W., 336
Physical groupings, 60
Pilkington Committee, 371
Pilkington float-glass process, 254, 268
Pill culture, 119
Pinpoint analysis, 346
Planning:
   innovation, 247–8, 263–4
   marketing communications, 284–5
   portfolio, 221
Plummer, J. T., 112
Polaroid, 252
Polavision, 252
Political economy, 11–12
Political involvement, 352–3
Politz, A., 121
Pollay, R. W., 182
Pop culture, 123, 167
Portfolio planning, 221
Positive appeals, 91
Post, James E., 361
Potential product, 14
Pressure groups (*see* Lobbying)
Prestel, 379
Price competition, 14
Price incentives, 284
Price reductions, 219
Priestley, J. B., 120
Primary or extractive sector, 213
Primary products, 217
Private sector, 213
PRIZM market segmentation system, 347
Procter and Gamble, 328
Product champions, 268
Product design, 14, 49, 338–40
   and market segmentation, 338–40
   industrial, 49–50
Product development (*see* New products)
Product failure, 251–2
Product hierarchy, 176
Product involvement, 75
Product levels, 14
Product liability, 382–3
Product life-cycle, 265–7
Product performance evaluation, 233
Product redefinition, 128
Product testing, 264
Promotional strategies, 167, 282–3, 288
Protestant ethic, 45, 46, 116, 128
Prudential Assurance, 279
Psychoanalytic theories, 65
Psychological factors, 18
'Psychological label', 66
Public opinion, changes in, 166
Public sector, 213

Purchasing agents (*see* Organizational buying)

Radio, independent, 370
Rank Xerox, 266–7
Rationality of consumers, 52
Raw materials, 217
Ray, M. L., 298, 307, 308
Reassurance theory (*see* Dissonance)
Reciprocal trading, 217
Recreation, 116–17
Reference groups, 158–62
   multiple, 161
   theory, 158
   two-way influence, 159
Regional concentration of industries, 230–1
Religious groups, 128
Research and development (R and D) programmes,
   264
Research Bureau Ltd, 114
Research Services Ltd, 146
Research techniques, 15
Retail advertising, 377
Retail trade, 374–7
Revson, Charles, 45
Riesman, David, 66–7, 112, 119
Risk:
   handling, 220
   innovations, 258
   models, 194–5
   policy, 251–2
   resistance to, 267
Rites of passage, 111
Robertson, T. S., 253, 260
Robinson, P. J., 232
Roddick, A., 363, 378
Roedder, D., 315
Roentgen, W. K. von, 250
Rogers, Carl, 68
Rogers, E. M., 162, 255–6, 258–9
Røhme, N., 153
Rokeach, M., 93
Role dispositions, 63–4
Roman Catholics, 128
Roseluis, T., 195
Rosenberg, M. J., 88
Ross, Alan, 135
Ross, I., 70
Rossiter, J. M., 316–17
Rowntree, B. S., 143

Safety lobbing, 382
Safety needs, 44, 120, 307
SAGACITY market segmentation system, 340–2
Sales force, 29
Samaritans charity, 280–1
Sampson, A., 136
Sampson, P., 96, 176–7, 178, 326
Samuelson, P. A., 4
Sappho Project, 249, 268

Satellite television, 373
Sawers, D., 250
Sayles, L., 232
Scenarios, 355, 357
Schjelderup-Ebbe, T., 134
Schlitz beer, 309
Schon, D. A., 268
Schmacher, E. F., 12, 104–5
Schumpeter, J. A., 249
Science Policy Research Unit, 249
Scientific American, 222
Secondary or manufacturing sector, 213
Security needs, 120
Selective attention, 25
Self-actualization, 68
Self-approval, 14
Self-concept, 68–71
    empirical evidence on, 69
    ideal, 68
    reinforcement, 88
    theories, 68
Self-confidence, 220
Self-esteem, 47
Self-fulfilment, 68
Self gifts, 71
Self-image, 47, 69, 70, 224
Self-improvement, 117, 220
Self-preservation, 220
Self-report method, 164
Self-sufficiency, 64
Sellers' market, 5
Selling effort, 6
Service economy, 8
Sevin, C. H., 267
Sex roles, 54, 72, 111, 119, 137
Sexual impulses, 66
Shanks, M., 219
Shapiro, B. P., 230
Sheffett, M. J., 59, 73
Sheffield, F. D., 310
Sheldon, W. H., 60
Shell, 267, 355
Sherif, M., 74, 85
Sheth, J. N., 81, 93, 104, 163, 203, 258, 323
Sheth's industrial buying model, 235–7
Shockley, William, 268
Shonfield, Andrew, 11
Shoppers, types of, 333
Shopping, trends in, 374–6
Shopping malls, 375
Simon, Herbert, 12
Singer sewing machines, 110
Single market, 110, 329
Single-parent households, 169, 170
Skinner, B. F., 33
Sleeper effect, 90–1
Sloanes, 124
Smith, Adam, 3, 10, 11, 364
Smith, Wendell R., 323

Smith and Nephew, 332
Smoking, dangers of, 307–8
Social class, 133–53
    and buying behaviour, 15–16, 47
    banking, 85
    different expectations, 235
    emergence of term, 134
    establishment, influence of, 135
    food consumption, 13
    household trends, 168–9
    in market segmentation, 143–7, 340–1
    measurement concepts, 138–9
    measurement criteria, 139
    measurement methods, 138–9
    (*see also* Socio-economic classifications)
Social conventions, 107
Social and cultural flux, 352
Social developments, 248
Social disapproval, 308
Social discrimination, 133
Social environment, 248
Social forecasting, 356–7
Social goals, 11
Social interaction, 156–7
Social learning theories, 66–7
Social mobility, 136, 171
Social norms, 308
Social orientation, 119
'Social register', 140
Social responsibility, 357–64
Social revolution, 136
Social science concepts, 11, 16
Social stratification, 133–8
Social Trends, 117, 121, 128
Social values, 116
Society and Community Planning Research
    (SCPR), 148
Socio-economic classifications, 142–50
    EC, 151–2
    harmonizing official and commercial, 152
    in UK, 142
    in US, 140–1
    JICNARS, 142–50
Sociological factors, 18
Sociometric analysis, 63–4, 164
S-O-R theory, 36, 299
Sony Corporation, 275
'Sources of Invention', 250
Southwestern Bell International, 372
Specialist markets, 228
Spiro, R. L., 181
Sport, 117
S-R model of advertising, 300
S-R theory, 32–3
SRI International, 112, 347, 355
    VALS life-styles, 112–13, 347
Stafford, J. E., 159, 162
Stalker, G. M., 250
Standard Industrial Classification (SIC), 348

Stanton, W. J., 217
Staples, W. A., 174
Starch, D., 29, 292–3
Steiner, G. A., 133, 294
Stereotypes, 71–2
Sternthal, B., 90, 194, 204, 336
Stewart, J. B., 302
Stillerman, R., 250
Stochastic learning models, 36
Stone, G. P., 333, 334
Stott, Catherine, 127
Strategic market segmentation (SMS), 348
Strauss, G., 229–30
Strength and number of wants, 89
Student population, 136
Stuteville, J. R., 308
Sub-cultures, 123–8
Subliminal stimuli, 27
Superculture, 106
Super-ego, 53
Supermarkets, 374–6
Superstores, 374
Systems selling, 222

Tarde, G., 255
Target audiences, 299
Target Group Index (TGI), 116, 330, 343
Task and non-task variables, 225
Taylor, G. R., 355
Taylor Nelson's Monitor survey, 347
Tea market, 325
Team effort, 8–9
Technological innovation, 249, 263
Technology, role of, 354–5
Teenage spending patterns, 184–5
Telephone, push-button, 260
Tele-shopping, 378–9
Television:
    and value orientations, 262
    audiences (US), 335
    cable, 371
    commercials, 72, 313, 366, 367, 368
    effects of gadgetry on viewing, 367–8
    satellite, 373
Television Consumer Audit, 147
Temperament types, 60
Tension role, 54
Tertiary or service and distributive sector, 213
Thompson, J. Walter, Company, 70, 170, 171, 173, 312, 371
Thorndike, E. L., 32, 53
Thouless, R. H., 41, 46, 61, 80, 97, 134, 156, 339
Thurstone's Temperament Schedule, 62
Tolman, E. C., 36
Toothpaste market, 338
Trade journals, 227
Trade unionism, 137, 157
Trading alliances, 242

Trading policies and practices, 225
Trading stamps, 377
Tradition-directed character, 67
Traditional markets, 10
Traits, 60–5
    and attitudes, 61
    catalogue of, 62
    characteristics, 61–2
    interaction of, 62
    theories, 60–1
Transactional model, 359
Transistors, 248, 268
Travel market, 338
Trevithick, R., 250
Trickle-down theory, 166, 182
Trust concept, 216
Tucker, W., J., 331
Turnkey operations, 217

U/non-U phraseology, 135
Uhl, K. P., 26
Uncertainty (*see* Risk)
Unconditioned response, 32
Unemployment, 184
Unilever, 328
UNISAT project, 373
Unisex marketing approach, 129
Unsolicited responses, 34
Urwick Orr and Partners, 287–8
US Cabinet Task Force on Oil, 356
Usage rate in market segmentation, 329
Users, role of, 224

Valentine, C. W., 54
VALS (values and life-styles), 112–13, 119, 347
Value for money, 317
Value orientations, 262
Veblen, T., 75, 168
Vegetarianism, 380
Veldman, T., 153
Venkatesan, M., 29, 158
Vicary, James, 27
Volkswagen, 29
Volvo, 44

Wagner, J., 173
Wall Street Journal, 356
Wankel, Felix, 253
War bonds, 51
Ward, Scott, 316
Warner, W. Lloyd, 140
Warner social class system, 140–1
Warren, N., 59
Watch market, 332–3
Watson, D. L., 300
Watson, J. B., 33, 300
Watt, James, 250
Webber, Richard, 342, 347
Weber, Max, 45, 46

Weber's law, 25
Webster, F. E., 226, 256
Webster-Wind model, 238–9
Weimann, G., 164
Weinberg, C. B., 310
Weiner, M. G., 15
Weiss, W., 90
Welfare society, 11
Wells, W., 93, 94, 172
Westfall, Ralph, 73
Which?, 34, 91
White, Irving, 128
Wicker, A. W., 92
Wiesner, Jerome B., 247
Wilkie, W. L., 307, 308
Williams, B. R., 251
Willmott, P., 171
Wilson, D. J., 220
Wind, Y., 107, 232
Women:
    and advertising, 311–14
    and society, 72, 121–3
    employment of, 72, 118, 122, 168, 180
    life-style differences, 122–3
    sexist views of, 312
    social status of, 141
    status in different cultures, 110
Woolworths Holdings, 279
Wootton, Barbara, 106
Work:
    attitudes towards, 116
    cultural reorientation towards, 116
Working wives, 118, 122, 168, 169, 175
Wortzel, L. H., 126

Yankelovich, D., 113, 332–3, 357
Young, M., 135, 171
Young, P. T., 24
Youth, sub-culture, 123–4
Yuppies, 124–5

Zajong, R. B., 89
Zip codes, 347
Zith, Ruth, 334